D0205971

Encyclopedia of Relationships Across the Lifespan

ENCYCLOPEDIA OF RELATIONSHIPS ACROSS THE LIFESPAN

Jeffrey S. Turner

Greenwood Press
Westport, Connecticut • London

Library of Congress Cataloging-in-Publication Data

Turner, Jeffrey S.
    Encyclopedia of relationships across the lifespan / Jeffrey S.
Turner.
       p. cm.
    Includes bibliographical references and index.
    ISBN 0–313–29576–X (alk. paper)
    1. Interpersonal relations—Encyclopedias.   2. Social interaction—
Encyclopedias.   3. Developmental psychology—Encyclopedias.
    I. Title.
    HM132.T83   1996
    302'.03—dc20   95–573

British Library Cataloguing in Publication Data is available.

Library of Congress Catalog Card Number: 95–573
ISBN: 0–313–29576–X

First published in 1996

Greenwood Press, 88 Post Road West, Westport, CT 06881
An imprint of Greenwood Publishing Group, Inc.

Printed in the United States of America

The paper used in this book complies with the
Permanent Paper Standard issued by the National
Information Standards Organization (Z39.48–1984).

10 9 8 7 6 5 4 3 2 1

To my brother and sister,
Gregg and Mindy
No finer siblings, no better friends.
What a lifespan treasure you are!

CONTENTS

PREFACE

The social relationships of a human being over the course of the lifespan are both complex and intriguing. From the early months of childhood through the years of late adulthood, social relationships shape the growth and development of a person in many ways. For the child, this journey begins with the parent-child relationship and spreads to siblings, the extended family, neighborhood friends and schoolmates, one's town or city, and ultimately one's state and country. Over the course of seven or eight decades, the developing person acquires a vast array of social skills and capacities, from learning how to speak a language and exchange meaningful communication with others to developing a social network of friends and understanding the culture into which one is born. As the lifespan unfolds, family, friends, school, religion, and the media transmit vast amounts of information about one's society, including how to participate in it.

This volume is designed as a reference manual for studying the developmental nature of such relationships. Exploring how social interactions change over time has become a popular field of study, and in recent years there has been an explosion of both research and theory. This encyclopedia carefully details the scope of such scientific activity, including accumulated knowledge as well as new research frontiers. The result is a book that is current, complete, and thorough in its coverage of the topic.

Containing hundreds of entries, *Encyclopedia of Relationships Across the Lifespan* explains a wide range of terms, concepts, themes, theories, and policies, as well as historical, international, and multicultural perspectives. The reader will discover that nothing more fully characterizes the study of relationships than the transitions that are encountered in moving from one life stage to another:

family relationships, childhood friendships, school relationships, adolescent peer groups, dating and courtship, marriage or alternative lifestyles, work relationships, adult friendships, grandparenthood, intergenerational care, widowhood, and the like. By studying such transitions, the reader will also come to realize that this field has not developed within a vacuum. Indeed, the study of lifespan relationships utilizes a multidisciplinary approach that combines behavioral and social science as well as a broad range of theoretical frameworks.

This reference volume makes available a rich and varied mixture of cross-disciplinary terminology and concepts. For example, themes related to developmental psychology allow one to understand the processes and life events that characterize relationships at particular stages in the human life cycle. Entries reflecting a psychological perspective shed light on the behavioral dynamics that occur within relationships, while sociological terms help the reader to see how human interactions operate against the backdrop of society. Social psychology concepts serve to expose how individuals think about and interact with others, while an assortment of research techniques is included to clarify important scientific methodology used within this discipline. Finally, this volume includes a representative body of terms and concepts from such varied fields as anthropology, history, religion, demography, ethnicity and race, and gender. All of these pursuits have application to the study of relationships across time and will prove useful in understanding the enormous diversity and complexity that characterize human interactions.

This volume is designed for a broad range of readers in college, university, institutional, and public library settings. The entries are of varying length and offer solid, comprehensive analyses of their respective topics. Each is a highly readable, succinct analysis that does not overwhelm the reader with detail. Rather, each topic is explained in a simple, lucid style, yet without sacrifice of intellectual depth. In addition to hundreds of entries, the volume also supplies over 1,000 sources for further reference. Representative sources conclude each entry and reflect the most relevant and up-to-date research available. For the reader desiring even more information, a selected bibliography containing over 220 research citations, all post-1993 publications, appears at the end of the volume. Also, an appendix lists the names and addresses of over 100 professional journals and over 65 organizations focusing on various aspects of relationships across the lifespan. Finally, a full index that includes detailed cross-referencing completes the volume.

A concerted effort has been made in this encyclopedia to highlight important international, racial, ethnic, and class differences to promote sensitivity to and tolerance of the beliefs and practices of others. To illustrate, the reader is exposed to the dynamics of lifespan relationships among African Americans, Asian Americans, Hispanic Americans, and Native Americans, as well as similarities and differences that occur in 14 representative nations around the world. It is strongly maintained that multicultural sensitivity enables readers to more fully appreciate the diversities and complexities of such topics as dyadic interaction, peer-group dynamics, family life patterns, and aging experiences. Thus, to understand relationships across the lifespan, it is important to be knowledgeable about how persons develop and interact in a cultural context.

In addition to its multicultural, worldwide, and historical focus, an important feature of this encyclopedia is its in-depth and scholarly coverage of those areas of relationships in the spotlight today. The 1990s bring a variety of important relationship issues to the forefront, including a number demanding our immediate and careful attention. For instance, while attitudes toward separation and divorce have become more tolerant in the 1990s, the reading public needs to better understand the consequences of marital dissolution for all concerned; the threat of AIDS and other sexually transmitted diseases has forced many people to alter their patterns of sexual activity, but we need to more fully understand the dynamics of sexual risk-taking behaviors; and the rising incidence of violence in families and among intimates—be it rape, child sexual abuse, or wife, husband, or elderly abuse—demands that we find more effective ways to prevent its occurrence, treat its survivors, and better understand its perpetrators. *Encyclopedia of Relationships Across the Lifespan* explains such issues and topics in a direct and sensitive fashion, carefully detailing their importance and significance.

It is recognized that the makeups of the persons reading this volume will be as diverse and fluctuating as the relationships being studied. As the need to understand love and commitment reaches new interest levels, as parent-child relations seemingly become more complex and demanding in these modern times, as caring for aging parents has become the norm rather than the exception, the population of our schools and libraries has changed to include individuals of all ages and from all walks of life. This reference encyclopedia speaks to the needs of all these readers, surveying and detailing the life stages they have faced, or will face, as daughters and sons, friends and confidants, wives and husbands, mothers and fathers, and even grandparents. Thus the lifespan perspective of this encyclopedia enables the reader to discover a diverse and rich assortment of research topics, from gender roles and interpersonal attraction to communication and sexual values.

The comprehensive and cross-disciplinary nature of this encyclopedia has appeal for many different kinds of readers. The writing style does not restrict itself to any one particular audience; rather, *Encyclopedia of Relationships Across the Lifespan* has appeal to undergraduate as well as graduate students, practitioners, and general adult readers. In the college environment, this volume represents an ideal reference manual for courses dealing with human development (child, adolescent, and adult), intimate relationships, marriage and family, communication studies, family studies, human sexuality, parenthood, social psychology, clinical psychology, general psychology, and general sociology.

In conclusion, this reference volume puts under one cover diverse information about lifespan relationships. In so doing, it provides a comprehensible source for reviewing and studying important themes and principles. Its inclusion of a variety of reference sources for further reading makes it an ideal stepping-stone for further research and investigation. Hopefully, the discovery and eventual utilization of information in this encyclopedia will prove to be an interesting and exciting venture for the reader. May the time spent with this volume be rewarded with new levels of awareness and understanding about this fascinating subject. Welcome to the study of relationships across the lifespan!

ACKNOWLEDGMENTS

Although an author bears the primary responsibility for the works he or she creates, many other individuals play a part in a book's development, preparation, and eventual publication. I would like to thank those who helped to make this reference encyclopedia a reality. More specifically, appreciation is extended to those at Greenwood Press who contributed their expertise to this project, especially Mildred Vasan, Senior Editor. Mim saw the early promise of this encyclopedia, convinced me of its research importance, and made many positive contributions toward its development and refinement. Thanks as well to the entire Greenwood team. I am also indebted to the Mitchell College and University of Connecticut libraries as well as numerous other libraries in the New England area for the provision of needed literary sources. The Population Reference Bureau of Washington, D.C., was particularly helpful in supplying important demographic information. My professional colleague and dear friend Donald B. Helms contributed his professional resources and offered constructive advice and support along the way. I am indebted to Laurna Rubinson and Virginia Otis Locke for sharpening my perceptions on all facets of lifespan relationships. A special note of thanks goes to Linda Brailey, who helped locate needed research studies and assisted in preparing the manuscript. Finally, to my wife and family goes my heartfelt gratitude. Their support and understanding of this project were sources of inspiration from beginning to end.

Encyclopedia of Relationships Across the Lifespan

A

**ABUSIVE FAMILY RELATIONSHIPS, CHILDREN AND ADO-
LESCENTS WITHIN.** Child and adolescent maltreatment are two of the
most widespread forms of family violence and abuse. Indeed, it has been estimated that over one million children and teenagers are victims of maltreatment
each year. Broken bones, lacerations, concussions, limb dislocations, and abrasions are commonplace. However, family abuse is not restricted just to physical
measures. Pain and suffering are inflicted on children and adolescents in a number of different ways—through neglect and abandonment as well as verbal,
emotional, and sexual abuse, to name but a few major forms.

Child abuse tends to be more common among children six years of age and
younger for several reasons. The child at this time is especially susceptible to
parental frustration as adults must adjust to the rather tedious chores of early
child care. Early economic hardships also cause tensions, and frustration on
the parent's part may develop because of the child's inability to interact with
the adult in a socially meaningful manner. Finally, abuse tends to be more
prevalent among those under six years of age because the child is most defenseless and unable to absorb the amounts of physical violence that an older
child can.

Other factors help explain why parents maltreat their offspring. Pressures from
work or the home, financial difficulties, a history of maltreatment in the parent's
background, and low levels of self-esteem are frequently cited as reasons behind
violence. Research indicates that many abusive parents were abused themselves
when they were children. For example, studies have shown that parents, particularly mothers, often abuse their children in much the same way that they had

been abused as children. Moreover, some research exists showing that husbands tend to abuse their wives much as they had been abused when young.

Many abusers are lonely, are frequently depressed, and have never learned how to contain their aggression. Physical illness, untimely childbearing, and a parent's poor ability to empathize with children can substantially increase the likelihood of child maltreatment. This is particularly true when social stress, social isolation, and family dysfunction exist. Evidence also exists that certain child and adolescent characteristics such as a difficult temperament or a health problem heighten the risk for maltreatment.

Many parents also abuse their children and teenagers in an effort to enforce discipline. Some have an overpowering need to impress other adults with a well-behaved child. Still other abusers identify with the child and consider every fault and mistake of their child to be their own. Also, there are those who perceive themselves as failures in life and feel that they are attaining superiority and command by exerting such forceful dominance.

A particularly bothersome feature of family abuse is the consequence of battering in later life. Many maltreated children and teenagers run a risk for aggressiveness, self-destructive behaviors, school failure, running away from home, and delinquency. Research shows that early harsh discipline is often associated with later aggressive behavior in both children and teenagers. Maltreated children and adolescents also tend to have more discipline referrals and school suspensions. One need not be the actual abuse victim to exhibit maladaptive behaviors, for a link often appears between aggressive behavior and witnessing parental violence. Finally, many abused children and teenagers are insecure, are mistrusting, foster poor self-concepts, and have low overall levels of self-confidence and self-reliance. (See CHILDHOOD, SEXUAL ABUSE DURING.)

Further Reading. Patton, Michael Q. (Ed.). (1991). *Family sexual abuse: Frontline research and evaluation.* Newbury Park, CA: Sage; Sabatino, David. (1991). *A fine line: When discipline becomes child abuse.* Blue Ridge Summit, PA: TAB Books; Salzinger, Suzanne. (1991). Risk for physical child abuse and the personal consequences for its victims. *Criminal Justice and Behavior, 18,* 64–81.

ABUSIVE FAMILY RELATIONSHIPS, ELDERLY WITHIN. Abuse of the elderly is a form of domestic violence directed toward aged family members. Elderly abuse has been gaining considerable attention in recent years. Many aged persons suffer maltreatment in their homes, often at the hands of their adult children or other caregivers. Most researchers regard the maltreatment associated with elderly abuse as similar to other forms of domestic violence. Some draw strong parallels to child abuse, since both children and the elderly are typically not as strong as their assailants and both are dependent on others for daily care.

To understand the dynamics of elderly abuse, one must recognize that the care of aging parents brings many adjustment challenges and demands. Today, the typical caregiver is middle-aged and often beset by competing role responsibilities and time demands. The rigors of providing regular care while maintaining one's own household are physically and psychologically exhausting. The loss of personal freedom, the lack of time for social and recreational activities, and other restrictions are often part of the sacrifices to be made.

Many middle-aged caregivers are women who start caring for an elderly parent at the time when their own children are beginning to leave home. Being placed back into a nurturing role just when it is expected that this responsibility is finished may prove overwhelming. However, researchers point out that various factors need to be examined when assessing the nature of elderly abuse, including precipitating elements. For example, the caregiver's age and the quality of the relationship between the caregiver and the elderly person, as well as the amount of assistance provided by other family members, are important factors to consider when examining the overall situation.

The literature invariably points out that over extended periods of time and without social support, caregivers experience mounting stress and the drainage of precious coping resources. In recent years, a number of publications have emerged on the topic of caregiving and its conflicting pressures. Also, support groups have been established to help adult children better handle the pressures of caring for aging parents, including abusive tendencies. One such group is Children of Aging Parents, which is based in Pennsylvania but has been branching out recently to other states. Other organizations, recognizing the need for providing support services for caregivers, offer a wide range of guidance and assistance. (See AGING PARENTS, CARING FOR.)

Further Reading. Cox, Carole. (1993). *The frail elderly: Problems, needs, and community responses.* Westport, CT: Auburn House; Harel, Zev, Phyllis Ehrlich, and Richard Hubbard. (Eds.). (1990). *The vulnerable aged: People, services, and policies.* New York: Springer; Romaine-Davis, Ada, Jennifer Boondas, and Ayeliffe Lenihan. (1995). *Encyclopedia of home care for the elderly.* Westport, CT: Greenwood Press.

ABUSIVE FAMILY RELATIONSHIPS, SIBLINGS WITHIN. See SIBLING RELATIONS.

ABUSIVE FAMILY RELATIONSHIPS, SPOUSES WITHIN. Spousal abuse, referring to maltreatment between husbands and wives, is quite prevalent in the United States today. Like other forms of domestic violence, husband-wife abuse may be one of our best-kept secrets because it happens behind closed doors. What is no longer a secret, though, are some sobering thoughts regarding spousal abuse: A person runs a greater chance of being killed by his/her spouse than by any other individual encountered throughout life. Also, the family looms as the most violent and assaultive group or institution in the country, with the exception of the police or the military at war.

Family violence experts note that spousal abuse is not confined to mentally disturbed or sick people. Batterers are not psychopathic personalities, nor are they violent in all of their relationships. Also, spousal abuse occurs among all socioeconomic classes, although its concentration is greater among the poor.

Additionally, abusers are at times loving, sensitive people. Surprisingly, the abused frequently love their batterers in spite of the pain they inflict.

Men who batter their wives share many of the characteristics of child abusers, including low levels of self-esteem and frequent depression. In addition, a wife batterer typically has a lower occupational status than that of his neighbors. Interestingly, his occupational and educational status is frequently lower than that of his wife. Abusive males also are likely to be jealous and insecure, and many lack direction in life. Many male batterers feel powerless and inadequate. They turn to violence as a way of trying to demonstrate power and adequacy.

It is difficult to fit battered women into any particular age classification, for wife abuse can occur at any age. It has been found, however, that pregnant women seem particularly susceptible to physical violence. Some research also indicates that battered women are more likely to be unassertive and to have low levels of self-esteem. Finally, abuse typically begins early in the marriage and increases as time goes on.

Abused women often remain in, rather than leave, the home that promotes violence. Why is this so? To begin, the woman may be ashamed. Because wife beating is so well secluded in our society, the victim often feels isolated and alone; she may feel that she is the only abused wife in the community. A second reason is fear. A battered wife may fear retaliation from the abuser. Third, many experience a sense of helplessness because they feel that little will come of their efforts to improve their situation. Finally, some battered women stay at the site of violence for practical reasons—some are 45 years old and have five children, no job skills, no place to go, and no money. They are literally trapped by the economics of their situation.

In recent years, husband abuse has received attention among family life researchers. Husband abuse may well be the most unreported crime in the nation today. This is because men, more so than women, are reluctant to admit the existence of the problem. This likely reflects, at least in part, traditional gender-role programming: men are taught to view themselves as the stronger, dominating sex, and reporting abuse is in violation of such teachings. It should be noted that injuries associated with husband abuse are usually less serious than those experienced by wives. Husband abuse typically occurs to certain categories of men—handicapped or sick men married to healthy women, older men married to younger and physically stronger wives, and small men married to big women. In each of these situations, note the physical superiority of the woman.

Further Reading. Gelles, Richard J., and Murray A. Straus. (1988). *Intimate violence.* New York: Simon and Schuster; Pagelow, Mildred Daley. (1992). Adult victims of domestic violence: Battered women. *Journal of Interpersonal Violence, 7,* 87–120; Stacey, William A., Lonnie R. Hazlewood, and Anson Shupe. (1994). *The violent couple.* Westport, CT: Praeger; Straus, Murray A., and Richard J. Gelles. (1990). *Physical violence in American families.* New Brunswick, NJ: Transaction.

ACTIVITY THEORY. See AGING, SUCCESSFUL.

ADOLESCENCE. The lifespan stage known as adolescence generally occurs between the ages of 13 and 19. As such, it encompasses the teenage years and serves as a bridge between childhood and adulthood. It is a period marked by numerous and complicated developmental tasks and physical, psychological, and emotional changes. Adapting to these changes places great demands on the teenager, in some instances causing anxiety, apprehension, doubt, and even guilt. Yet one cannot deny that adolescence is also a time of happiness, growing independence, new and exciting perceptions of the world, and satisfying social relationships.

While growth during the elementary-school years is relatively calm, during adolescence males and females experience pronounced physical developments that change them from children to sexually mature young adults. This point in development, during which biological changes begin to give the first indications of sexual maturity, is known as *puberty.* Adjusting to the many biological changes brought on by puberty is a formidable challenge, one that often heralds preoccupation with the changing physical self. How teenagers react to such biological changes will greatly affect the manner in which they ultimately perceive themselves.

Personality and social development acquire new dimensions during the adolescent years. Observers of this age group will discover that teenagers demonstrate heightened levels of self-awareness and intensified desires to be accepted by their peers. Establishing a personal sense of identity, examining one's values, beliefs, and attitudes, and developing personal and intimate social relationships are all important. The latter provide an outlet for new feelings and experiences, a source of support and security, and a mirror to one's own generation.

Personality developments in adolescence affect and are affected by social growth as they are in other stages of life. This means not only that the accuracy, stability, and acceptance of the self-concept affect the nature and degree of social relationships but also that feedback and reinforcement of others influence how adolescents ultimately perceive themselves. Other developmental forces also blend with personality and social growth. Heightened social cognitive skills, for example, give teenagers the mental prowess to examine themselves and others around them with greater understanding and awareness. Adolescents' acceptance of their changing physical selves and achievements in other developmental areas will affect sexual interests and social development, particularly if the teenager is an early or late maturer.

By the teenage years, the overall climate of the home environment may be affected not only by the method of control employed but also by the degree to which parents and teenagers seek to understand one another. Lack of understanding and empathy between parents and teenager is likely to disrupt family harmony and breed conflicts. Open discussions, democratic decision making, and parental explanations of the reasons for certain rules are sensible approaches to resolving domestic disputes. So too is seeking to understand and appreciate the position of the other party. The ability to take the perspective of another person into account is higher in homes fostering support, nurturance, and affection.

As the adolescent gropes for a sense of personal identity and fulfillment of the need to be accepted and recognized, the peer group becomes a critical agent of socialization. For many, security is found among friends who share the same feelings, attitudes, and doubts. Teenagers turn to their peers for approval of various activities and behaviors. This is not to say that a dichotomy suddenly develops between peer and parental influences. Indeed, most peers come from the same social class as the teenager's family and are thus likely to share the same values. Furthermore, while adolescents rely on peers for ordinary day-to-day decisions, they tend to lean toward parents in more critical matters. The perceived competence of parents and peers, though, is a critical element in determining the adolescent's eventual choice between the two.

Further Reading. Rice, F. Philip. (1993). *The adolescent: Development, relationships, and culture* (7th Ed.). Needham Heights, MA: Allyn and Bacon; Santrock, John W. (1995). *Adolescence: An introduction.* (6th Ed.). Madison, WI: Brown and Benchmark; Steinberg, Laurence. (1993). *Adolescence* (3rd Ed.). New York: McGraw-Hill.

ADOLESCENCE, CONTRACEPTIVE USE DURING. While rates of sexual intercourse have increased among today's adolescents, contraceptive usage is poor. Most sexually active teenagers do not consistently use reliable forms of birth control, and many do not exercise responsibility and rationality with respect to sexual decision making. Many adolescents do not have knowledge of those factors associated with sexual health and well-being, particularly those protective measures that reduce the risks of sexually transmitted diseases and unintended pregnancies.

There are a number of reasons why adolescents engage in poor forms of contraception or use none at all. To begin with, many are misinformed about available birth-control methods or how certain forms of contraception work. Many teenagers are also already sexually active before they use a contraceptive or visit a family-planning clinic. Some avoid the use of contraceptives because they want to get pregnant. While many say that they believe in responsible contraceptive use, few actually put this belief into practice.

This discrepancy between words and deeds is especially apparent when the male's involvement in birth control is considered. Most adolescent males are unwilling to assume the responsibility of contraception, although in recent years there has been an increase in condom usage. Younger adolescent males, especially, tend to abdicate their responsibility and view birth control as the female's "problem." Moreover, many adolescents have a prejudice against using condoms, even though this method can prevent pregnancy and control the spread of HIV infection.

Many adolescents also do not use contraceptives or practice safer sex because they think that they are invulnerable to the risks of pregnancy or contracting a sexually transmitted disease. This is the sort of magical thinking in which very young children often engage: "Nothing bad can happen to me." Many adolescents have difficulty understanding more specific sexual issues such as shared responsibility in contraception, birth-control alternatives, consequences of unsafe sexual practices, and perspective taking to envision pregnancy possibilities. The absence of mature thinking may also interfere with understanding the needs of one's sexual partner (including contraceptive needs), as well as grasping the notions of chance and probability attached to sexual risk taking.

Researchers have identified a number of factors associated with adolescent contraceptive usage. For instance, contraceptive use is greater among those who feel good about themselves, accept their sexuality, and have positive self-images. More effective contraceptive usage is also more likely in relationships that reflect good communication, mutuality, and reciprocity. Also, relationships characterized by nontraditional gender roles are often associated with greater contraceptive use.

As far as other factors are concerned, adolescent contraceptive use varies according to age. Those who have intercourse early (age 16 or younger) are less likely than those who have coitus later to use effective contraception. Programs designed to enhance contraceptive knowledge tend to promote more effective contraceptive use. Finally, a person's perception of the benefits (e.g., pregnancy prevention) and drawbacks (e.g., too difficult to obtain or use) of contraceptives affects overall usage. (See SEXUALLY TRANSMITTED DISEASES, SAFER SEX AND THE PREVENTION OF.)

Further Reading. Brown, Larry K., Ralph J. DiClemente, and Teron Park. (1992). Predictors of condom use in sexually active adolescents. *Journal of Adolescent Health, 13,* 651–657; Tanfer, Koray, Lisa A. Cubbins, and Karin L. Brewster. (1992). Determinants of contraceptive choice among single women in the United States. *Family Planning Perspectives, 24,* 155–161; Weisman, Carol, Stacey Plichta, Constance A. Nathanson, Margaret Ensminger, and J. Courtland Robinson. (1991). Consistency of condom use for disease prevention among adolescent users of oral contraceptives. *Family Planning Perspectives, 23,* 71–74.

ADOLESCENCE, DATING RELATIONSHIPS DURING. Adolescence typically marks the onset of dating relationships, or social engagements that enable two people to meet, interact, and pair off as a couple. As a form of socialization, dating serves a number of important functions. For example, it is a social means for individuals to learn more about themselves and how they are perceived by others, including strengths as well as weaknesses. Dating also teaches the importance of sensitivity, mutuality, and reciprocity and enables the individual to experience love and sexual activity within mutually acceptable limits. Finally, dating is the process through which one may ultimately select a marriage partner.

The complexion of dating has changed over the years for both adolescents and adults. In the past, dating was a structured and formal affair, profoundly affected by traditional gender-role stereotyping. The male usually took the initiative to ask the female out, provided transportation, and absorbed the expenses. Dating is more casual today, especially among the teenage population, and many couples share expenses and the transportation involved. Some females even take the initiative to ask the male out.

Other gender differences exist in adolescent dating patterns. For example, females usually start dating earlier than males. They also tend to have different attitudes about dating. Although females are anxious about dating during the early stages of adolescence, they tend to exhibit deep understanding, sensitivity, and emotional involvement toward their partners by late adolescence. Males tend to deemphasize the emotional and intimate features of the relationship. This is because of traditional gender-role learning that often teaches males to be emotionally reserved and guarded.

Adolescents look for certain qualities in a date. Physical attractiveness is equally important for both males and females, as are a likable personality and overall compatibility. How prestigious a date is appears to be more important for females. This latter consideration might be linked to the fact that females, more than males, view dating as a way to increase their popularity and status in the peer group. Finally, both males and females value honesty and the degree to which a partner can bring companionship and enjoyment to a relationship.

More serious dating may lead to going steady (also called "seeing" or "going with" someone). Although the meaning of this type of relationship varies from couple to couple, going steady generally implies a rather permanent relationship in which both parties refrain from dating others. In general, going steady is more common today than in the past and also begins earlier in the lives of teenagers. Many teenagers go steady as early as age 14 or 15.

Compared to random, casual dating, going steady has its share of advantages. One of the more practical benefits is that dates are assured, which promotes a sense of security for many adolescents. Going steady also encourages independence and practice with interpersonal communication skills. It can teach adolescents how to develop and handle intimacy with another human being. It can also teach the importance of openness, feedback, and conflict-resolution skills, all important prerequisites to marriage.

There are disadvantages to going steady, too. Exclusive dating arrangements reduce the adolescent's contacts with other peers, both male and female, which may restrict the person's overall social and personality development. Going steady also promotes the escalation of physical intimacy, which often leads to sexual intercourse before the partners are ready for it. This in turn increases the risk of teenage pregnancy and premature marriage.

Further Reading. Markstrom-Adams, Carol. (1991). Attitudes on dating, courtship, and marriage. *Family Relations, 40,* 91–96; Robinson, Edward, Ira Robinson, Ken Ziss, Bill Ganza, et al. (1991). Twenty years of the sexual revolution, 1965–1985: An update. *Journal of Marriage and the Family, 53,* 216–220; Thornton, Arland. (1990). The courtship process and adolescent sexuality. *Journal of Family Issues, 11,* 239–273.

ADOLESCENCE, EGOCENTRISM DURING. See ELKIND, DAVID.

ADOLESCENCE, FRIENDSHIPS DURING. From the adolescent years on, the behavioral dimensions of female and male friendships acquire unique characteristics. Intimacy and self-disclosure skills, in particular, increase at this time. Similarly, such prosocial skills as helping, sharing, cooperating, and comforting escalate. Such heightened interaction abilities are important ingredients for the formation and maintenance of intimate relationships.

As with all life stages, gender differences characterize the friendships of adolescents. For instance, females tend to have more intimate and exclusive friendships than males do. Moreover, the closer the female's friendships are, the more revealing her self-disclosure will be. This is often true regardless of whether females are interacting with the same or the opposite sex. Males, on the other hand, tend to downplay intimate self-disclosure and the emotional closeness of a relationship. Their emphasis, rather, is on such things as interest in the same activities. This prompts some to say that female friendships are face-to-face, while male friendships are side-by-side.

The notion that there are gender differences in adolescent friendships has received considerable research attention. To illustrate, it has been found that females' communication style centers around affiliation and reassurance, while that of males centers around dominance and competition. Such communication styles are thought to create gender differences in listening behavior. Males are often taught to listen for facts, and females are taught to listen for the mood of the communication. Males thus often have trouble listening for nonverbal cues, whereas females, who are listening for the mood of the communication, tend to pick them up much more readily.

It has also been discovered that females are more adept at social perspective taking; females also tend to learn how to communicate with close friends sooner. By the adolescent years, females are also likely to be more selective and exclusive in their friendships. This may be because once they have found a friend, females are more apt to invest their resources emotionally and offer a strong psychological commitment to their partner. The commitment from males is often not as great and is more objective and rational.

In regard to these gender differences in friendships, it is important to recognize that similarities also exist. The need to develop and maintain a friendship is a universal drive. Both males and females desire affiliation as well as companionship, and establishing friendships throughout life is humanity's way to alleviate loneliness. Moreover, most males desire emotional intimacy just as much as females do. Due to traditional gender-role socialization, though, it is difficult for males to fully express their emotions and disclose their sensitivities with partners. (See ADOLESCENCE, PEER-GROUP RELATIONSHIPS DURING.)

Further Reading. Brehm, Sharon S. (1992). *Intimate relationships.* (2nd Ed.). New York: McGraw-Hill; Duck, Steve. (1988). *Relating to others.* Chicago: Dorsey Press;

Eaton, Yvonne M., Mark L. Mitchell, and Janina M. Jolley. (1991). Gender differences in the development of relationships during late adolescence. *Adolescence, 26,* 565–568.

ADOLESCENCE, MARRIAGE DURING. Adolescent marriages are those legal unions formed during the teenage years. For a number of years, considerable concern has been generated over such marriages and the potential problems they pose not only to the partners, but to parents, educators, community welfare workers, and other social service agencies. Although the number of marriages in this age group has declined in recent years, adolescent marriages nevertheless represent a problem that needs continued attention and investigation.

Of the teenagers who marry, most are high-school juniors or seniors. Many of the couples are not well educated and are of low socioeconomic status. Furthermore, most early marriages are financially unstable. The husband's occupation is frequently limited to unskilled or semiskilled work. Those who marry young also have one of the highest divorce rates and an abundance of marital problems.

A number of factors contribute to the formation of adolescent marriages: among them, the wish to accelerate achievement of adult status, dissatisfaction with home life, loneliness, and the tendency to become involved in early and serious dating. Some teenagers feel that getting married is a way to salvage a doomed relationship, or that somehow it will promote heightened levels of intimacy and caring. Pregnancy, however, is the most important factor contributing to adolescent marriages.

Although some adolescent marriages are successful, most have difficulties for several important reasons. First, marriage for adolescents tends to reduce partners' independence and autonomy. Researchers point out that adolescence is a life stage that supplies teenagers with an opportunity to explore and experiment, behaviors that greatly influence identity formation and other important personality dynamics. Marriage at early ages tends to reduce this freedom to explore, in the process curtailing important psychological growth.

Financial problems also plague adolescent marriages and frequently contribute to domestic conflict and frustration. Unemployment rates are also higher among adolescents than other age segments, and unemployment poses additional domestic hardships and tension levels. In addition to disrupting family life, unemployment can have a negative effect on one's self-image and can lead to a loss of self-worth and perceived competencies. However, researchers have found that marital disharmony becomes moderate when adolescent husbands and wives have relatively high income levels.

Finally, the introduction of children usually creates problems for adolescent marriages. In addition to financial considerations and the further reduction of freedom, teenage mothers are more likely to give birth to premature and low-birth-weight babies. Mortality rates for both infants and mothers are higher during the teenage years. Also, teenage mothers often fail to provide proper prenatal and postnatal care. This all suggests that teenage mothers are particularly vulnerable and need special care, services, and support (see ADOLESCENCE, PREGNANCY DURING).

Further Reading. Balk, David E. (1995). *Adolescent development.* Pacific Grove, CA: Brooks/Cole; Phoenix, Ann. (1991). *Young mothers?* Cambridge, MA: Basil Blackwell; Santrock, John W. (1995). *Adolescence: An introduction* (6th Ed.). Madison, WI: Brown and Benchmark; Voydanoff, Patricia, and Brenda W. Donnelly. (1990). *Adolescent sexuality and pregnancy.* Newbury Park, CA: Sage.

ADOLESCENCE, PEER-GROUP RELATIONSHIPS DURING.

Peer-group relationships are an important facet of adolescent socialization. As the need to be recognized and accepted intensifies during this time, being in the company of others greatly impacts on developing interpersonal skills. With the teenagers' dependence on the family lessened, replacement security is found among peers who share similar feelings and attitudes. Adolescence thus becomes a critical time for developing friendships and becoming a member of a meaningful peer group. Such social networks supply important psychological benefits, including feelings of trust, self-worth, acceptance, and companionship.

Teenagers' interactions with peers are considerably influenced by developing social cognition abilities. More specifically, their advanced mental abilities enhance their awareness of themselves and others around them. Adolescence becomes a time when individuals can share, empathize, and understand the perspectives of others. As a result, teenagers become more sensitive to the needs of others. Adolescents are also able to develop expectations about friendships and make psychological inferences about people, cognitive capacities that eluded them earlier.

Adolescents typically do not want to be perceived as being different from one another. As a result, they tend to conform closely to established peer-group norms. Eager to attain social acceptance, adolescents pay close attention to current fads, such as length of hair, style of dress, and popular activities. They are also acutely aware of the types of behavior that will earn peer disapproval and rejection.

In addition to the nurturance of friendships (see ADOLESCENCE, FRIENDSHIPS DURING), adolescence becomes a time for the development of cliques and crowds. Such gatherings represent elite and exclusive socialization processes. Membership is frequently determined on the basis of similarity in such areas as social class, interest areas (such as style of dress), use of slang, athletics, and intellectual abilities.

Cliques usually consist of three or more persons who have common interests and a strong emotional attachment to one another. The clique is highly exclusive, usually consisting of adolescents of the same socioeconomic background who hold similar interests, attitudes, and beliefs. Usually, members of a clique come into contact daily, as in school or neighborhood cliques.

Although the *crowd* is more impersonal and lacks the strong bonds of attachment that cliques offer, it maintains rather rigid membership requirements. Being a member of a clique is often a prerequisite for crowd membership. The distinguishing features of crowds are heterosexual interaction, and emphasis is often on social events, such as athletic contests, concerts, and dances. However, crowds often have no planned activities. Many crowds congregate in a meeting place popular with all members, such as a parking lot, street corner, or neighborhood park.

Further Reading. Eaton, Yvonne M., Mark L. Mitchell, and Janina M. Jolley. (1991). Gender differences in the development of relationships during late adolescence. *Adolescence, 26,* 565–568; Gullotta, Thomas P., Gerald R. Adams, and Raymond Montemayor (Eds.). (1990). *Developing social competency in adolescence.* Newbury Park, CA: Sage; Sabatelli, Ronald M., and Stephen A. Anderson. (1991). Family system dynamics, peer relationships, and adolescents' psychological adjustment. *Family Relations, 40,* 363–369.

ADOLESCENCE, PREGNANCY DURING. Adolescent pregnancy is widespread in the United States today. There are more than one million pregnancies a year among adolescent females, and about 500,000 give birth to their babies. If present trends continue, approximately one out of every ten female teenagers will become a mother by her 19th birthday. Many adolescents become pregnant in their early or middle teens, about 30,000 of them each year under age 15. Currently, adolescents in the United States have one of the highest pregnancy rates in the Western world—twice as high as in England and France; three times as high as in Sweden; and seven times as high as in the Netherlands.

Pregnancy rates are higher for African-American than white adolescent females. Particularly disturbing is the fact that approximately one-half of all African-American adolescent females are estimated to become pregnant at least once before turning 20. Adolescent pregnancy rates are also high among Native Americans and Hispanic Americans.

Of the approximately one million adolescents who become pregnant annually, about 45 percent have abortions. Adolescents have about one-quarter of all abortions performed in the United States, and this overall rate more than doubles that of any other nation. Abortion rates are higher for African-American female adolescents than white female adolescents. The ratio of abortions to live births, however, is generally similar among African-American and white female adolescents. The higher rates of abortion among African-American women are attributable to higher pregnancy rates rather than to a greater likelihood of ending a pregnancy through abortion.

The overall rise in teenage abortion rates is due to many factors, including legalization of abortion and its overall accessibility. Unmarried adolescents who marry during pregnancy are less likely to seek an abortion, while teenagers receiving support for abortion from their boyfriends are more likely to elect abortion. Significant others beyond one's partner are also influential in the decision to abort. For instance, support for abortion from family members, especially the adolescent's own mother and sister, and from close friends is an important influence.

There are many health risks for the children of adolescent mothers. For example, the younger the mother is, the greater the chances of infant death. Adolescent mothers are more apt to have premature births than older mothers and are more likely to experience labor and delivery complications, including toxemia and anemia. The babies themselves often have low birth weights and frequently suffer from neurological problems and birth defects. Children of adolescent mothers also tend to have lower IQs and perform more poorly in school than children of older mothers.

Children also introduce drastic changes and disruptions into the lives of adolescents, their offspring, their parents, and the society as a whole. Many adolescent parents lack a supportive family as well as parenting skills. Adolescent mothers also cost the taxpayers huge sums of money each year and, in addition, often face social disapproval and financial hardships. Moreover, those adolescents who marry have an exceptionally high divorce rate (see ADOLESCENCE, MARRIAGE DURING).

Finally, developing as well as developed nations report lowered occupational status and reduced income as a direct result of curtailed education. In the United States and many European nations, women who are teenage mothers earn about 50 percent of the income of those who first gave birth in their 20s. Moreover, the cycle of poverty is influenced by this fertility pattern. That is, the children of teenage parents are more likely to become teenage parents themselves than those who were born when their parents were older.

Further Reading. McCullough, Mona, and Avraham Scherman. (1991). Adolescent pregnancy: Contributing factors and strategies for prevention. *Adolescence, 26,* 809–816; Voydanoff, Patricia, and Brenda W. Donnelly. (1990). *Adolescent sexuality and pregnancy.* Newbury Park, CA: Sage; Williams, Constance Willard. (1991). *Black teenage mothers: Pregnancy and child rearing from their perspective.* Lexington, MA: Lexington Books.

ADOLESCENCE, PREGNANCY DURING. INTERNATIONAL PERSPECTIVES. In addition to high proportions in the United States, rates of adolescent pregnancy are on the increase in other nations. Additionally, teenage mothers and their babies in other countries face just as many health risks. Adolescent mothers, as a group, suffer more pregnancy and delivery complications than women who bear children after the teenage years. Problems reported from diverse parts of the world include higher-than-average levels of toxemia, anemia, bleeding, cervical trauma, prolonged and difficult labor, and death. The risk of a teenage mother developing such problems, though, is greater in developing than in developed nations, and greater among those from lower socioeconomic brackets within countries.

Worldwide, pregnancy-related complications are the primary cause of death among adolescent females. In many parts of sub-Saharan Africa, teenage mothers account for almost one-half of pregnancy-related complications. Poor living conditions in these regions, as well as inadequate nutrition, prenatal care, and health education, aggravate the risks compared to developed nations. In most Latin American and Caribbean countries, childbearing and abortion are ranked in the top five causes of death for adolescent females, with the phenomenon most common in Jamaica. In Bangladesh, birth-related complications, including those developing from abortion, are the leading cause of death among teenage women.

Furthermore, pregnancy-related mortality rates are higher for teenagers than for older women in developed countries. In Canada, as an illustration, they are twice as high. Maternal mortality rates for adolescent females under 16 in England are four times the overall rate for older women. Additionally, many children born to teenage mothers suffer from reduced mental capability and psychological consequences. For example, many European babies born to teenage mothers suffer from slightly lower IQs compared to children born to older mothers, and many are also at a greater risk for abuse and health hazards.

It must be recognized, however, that many of the aforementioned consequences are not related directly to age but rather to inadequate prenatal care and nutrition. For example, European adolescents having first births and who participate in special prenatal programs tend to have no greater obstetrical risks than adult women. Among Swedish teenage mothers, complications are no more frequent than with older mothers if they experience proper prenatal attention. The same holds true for teenage mothers in Kenya.

However, one of the most dramatic and long-term consequences of teenage pregnancy is the curtailment of a woman's education and vocational aspirations. Throughout the world, many teenage mothers have not completed high school at the time of their child's birth. This does not mean that all will remain high-school dropouts. Many eventually receive a high-school diploma. But women who bear children in their teens are less likely to go on to (or complete) college than those who delay childbearing, and they are more likely to suffer long-term economic consequences because of their lower skill levels.

Further Reading. Donaldson, Peter J., and Amy Ong Tsui. (1990). *The international family planning movement.* Washington, DC: Population Reference Bureau; Freedman, Ronald. (1990). Family planning programs in the Third World. *Annals of the American Academy of Political and Social Science, 510,* 33–43; Senderowitz, Judith, and John M. Paxman. (1985). *Adolescent fertility: Worldwide concerns.* Washington, DC: Population Reference Bureau.

ADOLESCENCE, RUNAWAYS DURING. Adolescent runaways are persons under the legal age who leave home without parental permission. Each year, over one million adolescents choose this course of action. Most adolescent runaways are between the ages of 15 and 17, and there are slightly more male runaways than females. In recent years, there has been an increase in teenagers running away from home at earlier ages, many at the ages of 13 and 14.

Most runaways are from white suburbs, although adolescent runaways come from all ethnic and social levels. Though some travel only a short distance from home and return in less than a week, others stay away for longer periods. Older adolescents are more likely to stay away for longer periods of time and to travel to more distant locations. While some runaways never return home, most eventually do because of lack of money or a place to stay.

There are several explanations of why adolescents become runaways. Most leave home because of destructive family situations or because of a secret personal problem such as breaking the law or pregnancy. Some leave home to escape pressure and conflict. Others run away because of the freedom that awaits them. Some are drawn to drugs, sex, or an escape from routines in general. Finally, some runaways are throwaways. In the face of intolerable parent-adolescent relations, including those involving abuse and neglect, many teenagers are actually encouraged, and in some cases forced, to leave home.

In recent years, the care and treatment of runaways have increased significantly, although many runaways are never reported. Family therapy is frequently part of the overall treatment program. In cases of parental abuse or lack of parental cooperation, authorities may place the teenager in a foster home. An important step in combating this problem has been the establishment of hotlines that tell runaways the locations of temporary shelters and enable them to send messages to their parents if they desire.

Further Reading. Gavazzi, Stephen M., and David G. Blumenkrantz. (1991). Teenage runaways: Treatment in the context of the family and beyond. *Journal of Family Psychotherapy, 2,* 15–30; Kurtz, P. David, Gail L. Kurtz, and Sara V. Jarvis. (1991). Problems of maltreated runaway youth. *Adolescence, 26,* 543–555; Santrock, John W. (1995). *Adolescence: An introduction* (6th Ed.). Madison, WI: Brown and Benchmark.

ADOLESCENCE, SAME-SEX RELATIONSHIPS DURING. Sexual experiences in the company of same-sex peers are relatively common during adolescence. However, homosexuality at this time is much less common. Alfred Kinsey's classic human sexuality research conducted in the middle of this century (see KINSEY, ALFRED C.) revealed that more than half of all men and a third of all women had experienced some type of homosexual sex play as a child or young adolescent. More recent research tends to confirm Kinsey's prevalency data.

For both adolescent males and females, exhibition of genitalia is the most common form of homosexual play. For many, exhibitionism leads to each person stimulating the other's genitals. Some engage in oral or anal contacts with genitalia. Some males, more so than females, engage in masturbation to lone companions or to whole groups of males. Group masturbation among males also sometimes results.

But while homosexual sex play is fairly common during adolescence, it tends to have a short duration. Most adolescents confine their same-sex sexual encounters to a single year. Moreover, only a small number go on to establish a primarily gay orientation in adulthood.

Some adolescents do define themselves as lesbian or gay. These young people are faced with many problems stemming from society's disapproval of their sexual preference. These teenagers do not feel that they belong to any group and fin that they have no friends in whom they can confide. While some colleges and universities ahve organizations for assistance and support for lesbians and gays. these organizations do not extend to the high-school level because they could be accused of contributing to the deliquency of minors.

Contemporary researchers maintain that the problems encountered by gay or lesbian adolescents do not originate from secual orientation per se. Thather, the problems stem from society's stigmatization of gays and lesbians. Rejection from family and friends, social isolation, and aggression from heterosexuals are problems faced by gay and lesbian adolescents.

The threat of AIDS and other sexually transmitted diseases also represents a problem for the sexually active adolescent. AIDS is not exclusively a gay disease, nor is it a disease peculiar to the young. However, adolescence looms as an important time for AIDS prevention because many teenagers are sexually active and because it is during this time that adolescents learn many of the behaviors that will influence their social interactions.

In the wake of such problems, experts recommend that adolescent gays and lesbians receive supportive assistance and understanding. More specifically, programs emphasizing the physical, mental, emotiona, and social well-being of lesbian and gay youth need to be established. Staff-development programs for professionals working with gay and lesbian youth also need to be developed.

In our society, gay and lesbian teenagers do not have safe places in which to interact in other than sexual situations. Gay and lesbian adolescents need opportunities for simple socializing, like young people's groups or dances. Like most teenagers, gay and lesbian youth believe that they are immortal. They find it almost impossible to imagine getting a life-threatening disease like AIDS. As with heterosexual adolescents, any program of education or prevention must take this age-related type of thinking into consideration.

Further Reading. Coles, Robert, and Geoffrey Stokes. (1985). *Sex and the American teenager.* New York: Harper and Row; Hetrick, Emery, and A. Damien Martin. (1987). Developmental issues and their resolution for gay and lesbian adolescents. *Journal of Homosexuality, 14,* 25–44; Martin, A. Damien, and Emery Hetrick. (1988). The stigmatization of the gay and lesbian adolescent. *Journal of Homosexuality, 15,* 163–183.

ADOLESCENCE, SCHOOL RELATIONSHIPS DURING. Today's modern world is large and confusing, technically complex, and constantly changing. In order for adolescents to acquire that knowledge that will be of service to them in later life, the school remains more than ever a vital and essential institution. Through the efforts of educators, as well as continuing support from the home, adolescents are prepared and equipped to function effectively in society.

School relationships are important during adolescence not only because of the educational information that is acquired, but for other important reasons as well. For example, beyond the sheer amount of time spent in attendance, the school will come to represent the adolescent's society. It is a social setting where individuals from the same life stage can share common experiences and interests. The school greatly influences the course of social development, particularly interpersonal relationships. It offers a testing ground for ideas and discussions, along with an opportunity to engage in decision-making strategies. As such, the school has the potential to upgrade interpersonal sensitivity and communication skills.

One of the most prominent factors affecting academic performance is the teacher-student relationship. As in earlier school experiences, students respond most favorably to those teachers who are self-controlled, warm, and friendly in their classroom interactions. Democratic and integrative systems of classroom control tend to encourage cooperation, sensitivity toward others, and task-oriented student behaviors.

Teachers are in a prime position to enhance adolescents' capacities to face the many challenges that accompany the secondary-school experience. More specifically, teachers can help adolescents become academically successful, learn self-respect, and heighten individuality. Researchers have found that for both male and female adolescents, the strength of attachment to teachers is associated with young people's positive feelings about themselves.

It is especially important for teachers to help teenagers achieve a sense of identity because the educational process tends to manufacture high levels of conformity. This may explain why so many adolescents are without any commitment to self, morally parochial, and compliant. It may also explain, in part, why identity foreclosure is so common at this age.

A possible solution to this may be the development of a curriculum that is suited to each individual's capacity to absorb, rather than to follow prearranged outlines. Treating the adolescent in a mature fashion and teaching the importance of responsibility are also important. The school needs to represent an environment where the adolescent can develop each day. All too often, teachers forget how many times adolescents can be regarded as adults, treating them instead with childish protectiveness and circumscribing them with restrictions. Often, adolescents react to such measures with predictable behaviors: apathy, passive resignation, and rebellion.

Educational experts believe that the most favorable attitudes and greatest learning readiness evolve when students perceive that their teachers are interested in them as well as in the subject material being taught. In an ideal setting, the two can discuss not only academics, but also the student's career ambitions, interests, and goals. Should this result, the teacher looms as an instrumental force in shaping the adolescent's mental awareness and nurturing the development of dignity and self-respect.

Further Reading. Armstrong, David G., and Tom V. Savage. (1990). *Secondary education: An introduction.* New York; Macmillan; Balk, David E. (1995). *Adolescent development.* Pacific Grove, CA: Brooks/Cole; Slavin, Robert E. (1994). *Educational psychology: Theory and practice.* Boston: Allyn and Bacon.

ADOLESCENCE, SCIENTIFIC STUDY OF. Adolescence is the systematic field of study that examines the physical, cognitive, personality, and social dimensions of humans during the teenage years. Adolescent development, like child and adult development, is a subdivision of developmental psychology (see CHILDHOOD, SCIENTIFIC STUDY OF; ADULTHOOD, SCIENTIFIC STUDY OF). Researchers who specialize in this life stage are called adolescent psychologists or developmental psychologists. Adolescence is an active field of study and consists of numerous professional organizations, including the Society of Research on Adolescence. Research journals devoted to the study of adolescence include *Journal of Adolescent Research, Journal of Early Adolescence,* and *Adolescence.*

Adolescence, from the Latin word *adolescere,* meaning "to grow into maturity," is the life stage between childhood and adulthood. Like other phases of the life cycle, this period is marked by great change. Among the many challenges adolescents face are the need to adjust to pronounced physical changes, the search for their own identity, and the formation of new interpersonal relationships that include, for the first time, the expression of sexual feelings. Adolescent sexual development cannot be separated from other developmental forces. For example, how adolescents react to the physical changes that accompany sexual maturation, including whether they and others perceive these changes as attractive or unattractive, will affect how they ultimately perceive themselves.

Not long ago, researchers tended to focus on the inner turmoil and problems of adjustment faced by the typical adolescent and often borrowed the expression *Sturm und Drang* ("storm and stress") from the eighteenth-century movement in German literature to describe this period of life. Today, the problems faced by many teenagers—such as sexually transmitted diseases, pregnancy, and abortion—appear to many adults to far exceed the difficulties they themselves confronted in adolescence. Some contemporary researchers feel, however, that most modern teenagers meet the challenges of adolescence with considerable success.

Contemporary researchers believe that we should stop viewing adolescence as a time of disruptive and rebellious behavior because this myth distorts our perceptions of actual adolescents. Moreover, as in other life stages, wide individual differences shape the course and outcome of adolescence. Ethnic, cultural, and class differences must also be taken into account when exploring the total impact of adolescence.

Further Reading. Balk, David E. (1995). *Adolescent development.* Pacific Grove, CA: Brooks/Cole; Hurrelmann, Klaus. (Ed.). (1994). *International handbook of adolescence.* Westport, CT: Greenwood Press; Santrock, John W. (1995). *Adolescence: An introduction* (6th Ed.). Madison, WI: Brown and Benchmark.

ADOLESCENCE, SEPARATION-INDIVIDUATION PROCESS OF.

The separation-individuation process of adolescence refers to strivings for independence and autonomy that occur during the teenage years. More specifically, this becomes a time when the childhood ego separates from the egos of one's parents and seeks independence. The ego seeks to differentiate ''me'' from ''them'' by establishing an identity of its own, rather than merely reflecting the identities (egos) of parents. Prior to the separation-individuation process of adolescence, the sense of self was derived from the child's identification with parents, and esteem originated from parental approval. Now, the psychological chore entails developing a sense of self and learning to regulate self-esteem from internal sources.

Because of the adolescent's strivings for separation and individuation, parents are often faced with redefining past child-parent relations and gradually increasing the teenager's responsibilities. Parents may realize for the first time that their offspring are capable of making mature decisions for themselves and will soon be moving on and establishing their own independent lifestyle and living arrangements. How these forces blend, the adolescent's desire for an independent identity and greater autonomy, and the parents' reaction to such strivings, greatly influences the emotional climate of the home during this time.

Although many parents can meet the challenges of the separation-individuation process, there are some who do not fare as well. Part of the problem is that they resist granting to their children even a little individuation and adult status. Rather than promoting their uniqueness and encouraging independent and responsible behavior, such parents instead overprotect their children and encourage their dependence. Many do not let go of their teenagers because they dread the thought of the next phase of family life, the empty-nest stage. Although the empty nest has numerous positive consequences, some parents (and adolescent offspring) have difficulty adjusting to this transition. (See EMPTY NEST.)

Further Reading. Bartle, Suzanne E., and Stephen A. Anderson. (1991). Similarity between parents' and adolescents' levels of individuation. *Adolescence, 26,* 913–924; Rice, F. Philip. (1993). *The adolescent: Development, relationships, and culture* (7th Ed.). Needham Heights, MA: Allyn and Bacon; Stroufe, June W. (1991). Assessment of parent-adolescent relationships: Implications for adolescent development. *Journal of Family Psychology, 5,* 21–45.

ADOLESCENCE, SEXUAL BEHAVIOR DURING. Few topics about adolescent development arouse more general interest and curiosity than sexual behavior. This interest has led to a flurry of publications on the topic. The most consistent research finding is that the attitudes teenagers have toward sex have become more relaxed and tolerant. American society has moved from an antisex to a prosex orientation, the latter becoming quite obvious among contemporary adolescents.

As far as specific types of sexual activity are concerned, masturbation is widespread among adolescents. Masturbation is self-stimulation of the genitals or other parts of the body for sexual arousal and pleasure. Masturbation is usually the first sexual experience for both men and women, and it is the most common form of sexual expression other than heterosexual coitus. Once regarded as sinful and dangerous, masturbation today is widely recognized as a normal form of sexual expression. By age 21, masturbation is quite widespread, especially among male adolescents.

Another type of sexual activity that occurs at this time is petting. Petting is physical caressing that does not involve union of the genitalia but is a deliberate attempt to effect erotic arousal. Light petting is any sexual activity above the waist, such as fondling and/or oral stimulation of the breasts. Heavy petting includes sexual activity below the waist, such as manual or oral stimulation to the point of orgasm but without sexual intercourse. Petting is thus an alternative to intercourse and is one of the more common sexual activities during adolescence for both males and females.

As far as coital activity is concerned, research confirms that a greater percentage of today's adolescents are engaging in sexual intercourse than in the past. Indeed, a general theme in the literature is that most adolescents in the United States have become sexually active by age 19, although rates of coital activity are usually higher for men, especially among African Americans.

Research also shows that many adolescents have their first coital experience in their early teens, and few adolescents experience coital activity only once. Most adolescents in the United States experience sex again, often within six months of first intercourse. Moreover, sexually active adolescents often have more than one sexual partner, a trend that places them at a greater risk for unintended pregnancies as well as for acquiring a sexually transmitted disease.

Many factors are causing these high rates of adolescent coital activity. Among these are a desire for intimacy; feelings of trust, love, and caring; pressure from a desire to please one's partner; pressure from peers; and an attempt to improve a couple's relationship. Others include a physiological need for a sexual outlet or an experience to test the capacities, both sexual and physical, of two people seeking marital compatibility. Some view coital activity as a way to salvage a doomed relationship. Finally, sex may serve as a way to bolster an ego or as an activity to escape family pressures.

Finally, a number of reasons can be cited for not engaging in sexual intercourse. For females, two of the more common reasons are the fear of pregnancy and the guilt over loss of virginity. Others avoid premarital coitus because of religious reasons. Some couples also fear disapproval from family or friends. For many, another important reason for refraining is the fear of contracting a sexually transmitted disease. Given the widespread nature of sexually transmitted diseases among adolescents, including the risk for HIV infection, this reason has become increasingly popular today.

Further Reading. Cate, Rodney M., Edgar Long, Jeffrey J. Angera, and Kirsten K. Draper. (1993). Sexual intercourse and relationship development. *Family Relations, 42,* 158–164; Friedman, Herbert L. (1992). Changing patterns of adolescent sexual behavior: Consequences for health and development. *Journal of Adolescent Health, 13,* 345–350; Hatano, Yoshiro. (1993). Sexual activities of Japanese youth. *Journal of Sex Education and Therapy, 19,* 131–144.

ADOLESCENCE, SEXUALLY TRANSMITTED DISEASES DUR-

ING. The association between early age of coital activity and greater numbers of both recent and lifetime sex partners represents a connection to a high incidence rate of sexually transmitted diseases (STDs) among adolescents. Over 85 percent of all sexually transmitted diseases occur among persons aged 15–29 years. Males and females who have multiple partners over a specified period (e.g., several months) are at an increased risk for gonorrhea, syphilis, chlamydia, and chancroid. Increased numbers of sex partners over a lifetime are also associated with a greater cumulative risk for acquiring viral infections such as hepatitis B, genital herpes, and the human immunodeficiency virus.

A few statistics can be used to illustrate the foregoing. For instance, statistics on the prevalence of gonorrhea, syphilis, and chlamydia among sexually active females show that the highest rates of infection are among adolescents between 14 and 19 years of age. Genital warts, caused by the human papilloma virus (HPV) and one of the fastest-growing sexually transmitted diseases in the United States today, are particularly prevalent among sexually active adolescent females. All of this runs contrary to the impression that STDs are a problem endemic to the adult population. Moreover, epidemiologic data indicate that the rate of STDs declines exponentially past the age of 19 years.

Minority adolescents have higher rates for sexually transmitted diseases, with rates for gonorrhea, pelvic inflammatory disease (PID), and syphilis substantially higher among African-American adolescents than among their white counterparts. The average age-adjusted gonorrhea rate in African-American males aged 15 to 19 years is approximately 15 times greater than that of white males, and that of African-American females in the same age group is approximately tenfold that of white females. The rate of primary and secondary syphilis among African-American females is more than threefold greater than for white females, and the relative risk of death attributable to syphilis is more than three times greater for African-American than for white females. Rates for chlamydia are also substantially higher among African-American females than among white females.

Infections caused by HIV are obviously the sexually transmitted diseases of greatest importance. While relatively few persons develop AIDS as adolescents, this is a misleading picture. Approximately 20 percent of all AIDS cases have been diagnosed in the 20-to-29-year-old age group. Since the time between infection with HIV and the onset of AIDS symptoms is a median of 8 to 10 years, a large proportion of those aged 20 to 29 years diagnosed with AIDS were most likely infected with HIV as adolescents.

Particularly disturbing is the fact that during the early 1990s, the number of new cases of AIDS among 13-to-19-year-olds in the United States increased by 12 percent, compared to an 8 percent increase for adults of all ages. Rates of infection are highest among street and homeless teenagers who exchange sex for money or drugs. As with other sexually transmitted diseases, Hispanic-American and African-American teenagers are highly overrepresented among

persons with AIDS. More specifically, they comprise more than one-half of all
adolescents and three-quarters of all younger children (babies of infected parents)
known to have the disease. (See AIDS; SEXUALLY TRANSMITTED DIS-
EASES; SEXUALLY TRANSMITTED DISEASES, CATEGORIES OF.)

Further Reading. Cates, Willard, Jr. (1991). Teenagers and sexual risk taking: The
best of times and the worst of times. *Journal of Adolescent Health, 12,* 84–94; Di-
Clemente, Ralph J. (1990). The emergence of adolescents as a risk group for human
immunodeficiency virus infection. *Journal of Adolescent Research, 5,* 7–17; Ku, Leigh-
ton, Freya L. Sonenstein, and Joseph H. Pleck. (1992). Patterns of HIV risk and preventive behaviors among teenage men. *Public Health Reports, 107,* 131–138.

ADOPTION. Adoption is the act of legally becoming the parent of a child
not biologically one's own. Approximately one million children in the United
States live in adoptive families. Most adopted children are born in the United
States, although overseas adoptions have increased over the last 25 years. Most
couples adopt children who are under one year of age. Also, more white than
African-American or Hispanic-American couples choose to adopt a child.

Couples or individuals wishing to adopt a child can approach state-agency
adoption centers or private-agency adoption centers or consider direct adoption.
State-agency adoption centers are less expensive (often only legal fees are involved) but tend to have long waiting periods. On the other hand, private-agency
adoption centers are generally more expensive (sometimes as high as $25,000)
but usually offer expectant parents a shorter waiting period. Direct adoptions
often occur when a physician connects a couple who wants a baby with a pregnant woman who wants to give up her baby. In most instances, this mother is
a teenager who does not have the resources to take care of her baby.

Before 1970, state adoption agencies in particular often restricted adoption to
young, white, middle-class, affluent families. In the 1990s, however, laws have
been revised, making adoption more acceptable to more diverse social groups.
For example, adoption is possible for younger and older couples, single persons,
and dual-earner couples. However, adoption remains extremely difficult for
openly gay and lesbian couples. While society's tolerance for alternative lifestyles is growing, most agencies continue to believe that the best interests of a
child are rooted in the traditional heterosexual family. (See GAY AND LES-
BIAN RELATIONSHIPS, FAMILY LAW AND.)

Further Reading. Banish, Roslyn. (1992). *A forever family.* New York: Harper and
Row; Duprau, Jeanne. (1990). *Adoption: The facts, feelings, and issues of a double heritage.* Englewood Cliffs, NJ: Prentice Hall.

ADULTHOOD. See EARLY ADULTHOOD; MIDDLE ADULTHOOD;
LATE ADULTHOOD.

ADULTHOOD, AGEISM AND. Ageism, in its broadest sense, is discrimination and prejudice leveled against individuals on the basis of their age. Unfair

and demeaning stereotypes are often attached to the person being viewed. Adults, particularly the elderly, are usually vulnerable to ageist attitudes because they are frequently seen as being sick, senile, asexual, or useless.

Yet, while the elderly are usually the victims of ageist attitudes, it is possible that some ageism is leveled at all life stages. Consider some of the unfair, yet nonetheless frequently exercised generalities about certain age groups: Children do not respect their elders and are spoiled; teenagers are lazy and flighty; college students are irresponsible and too liberal; young adults have just too many idealistic plans; and the middle-aged are too busy to do anything except work on their midlife crises. Humorous as these sound, it is surprising how many people have come to accept them. A person who has reached a certain age is assumed to have acquired generalized qualities. In other words, it is guilt by age association.

Many ageist attitudes have deep historical roots, at least in the United States. Starting in the colonial period, a proportion of the elderly were categorized as superannuated, unnecessary, and a burden to others. With the growth of cities and the Industrial Revolution of the nineteenth century, these attitudes became applicable to greater numbers. By the early twentieth century, the aged became recognized as a wide-ranging social problem. Old age had become characterized as a time of dependence and disease.

Ageist attitudes, like other attitudes, are a product of socialization processes. As such, they can be transmitted by a number of social agents: parents, siblings, school, peers, books, and other forms of the media. In many instances, the elderly are portrayed by the media in such a way that the aforementioned stereotypes are reinforced. At other times, they are practically invisible to the general public; that is, the media prefer to capture the image of the younger adult.

More exposure to the elderly and increasing the younger public's knowledge of the elderly are needed to break ageist stereotyping. This will also enhance one's knowledge of adulthood and aging processes. Too many young people regard aging as a distant and remote event, something that cannot happen to them. It may also help to remove the overall negative qualities attached to the aging process itself, another belief held by many young people.

Further Reading. Gerike, Ann E. (1990). On gray hair and oppressed brains. *Journal of Women and Aging, 2,* 35–46; Palmore, Erdman B. (1990). *Ageism: Negative and positive.* New York: Springer; Vernon, JoEtta A. (1990). Media stereotyping: A comparison of the way elderly women and men are portrayed on prime-time television. *Journal of Women and Aging, 2,* 55–68.

ADULTHOOD, EXTRAMARITAL SEXUAL RELATIONSHIPS DURING.

An extramarital sexual relationship includes any sexual activity that occurs with someone other than one's spouse. Extramarital sexual relationships are quite common today, although different types exist. For example, there are different forms of involvement and escalation. Of these, the "isolated affair" is the most common. This relationship, commonly referred to as "the one-night stand," involves sexual activity with a partner but with no future involvement or emotional commitment. The less common "intense affair," on the other hand, is characterized not only by regular sexual activity between partners, but also by the emotional involvement of the two and the escalation of attachment.

The numbers vary as to how many men and women are thought to engage in extramarital relationships. However, there seems to be a fair amount of agreement that at least 50 percent of all married men and about 25 percent of all married women have affairs at one time or another. Such percentages, though, may be too low since some respondents may be reluctant to admit such behavior.

Many factors account for such high rates of extramarital sexual relationships. To begin with, some segments of our society have adopted a very permissive attitude toward sexual behavior. The resulting climate of freedom may encourage sexual expression that would otherwise be reined in. For example, some people have affairs because they are simply curious about "what it would be like" with someone else. Or boredom with their sexual relationship with their partner—quite possibly the result of their own inability or unwillingness to experiment with new ways to turn their partners on—may lead them to others. Many participants report sexual frustration as their underlying motivation. Others use these relationships for the companionship they offer or for a boost to their egos. The motivations of still others may be fueled by the constant visibility of the extramarital sex theme in the media. A faltering sense of masculinity or femininity within an existing relationship may prompt some to turn to an outsider for reinforcement or fulfillment.

There are other factors related to extramarital relationships. Those having affairs usually have lower degrees of sexual and marital satisfaction. However, there are some partners who have affairs who are very happy and satisfied with their spouses and their marriage. Those likely to have affairs have certain predictable qualities: they are usually liberated and have high needs for sexual intimacy and low levels of emotional dependency on their partners. Some couples engage in affairs as a form of rebellion or retaliation against their spouses. Some may launch into an affair to "get even" with a partner who had or is having an extramarital sexual relationship.

Many experts feel that opportunities for extramarital sexual relationships are greater in urban societies where people contact a variety of others each day. The workplace brings married men and women together, typically requiring them to spend considerable time together. In this vein, the growing incidence rate of extramarital sex among women may be explained, in part, by the greater number of women working outside of the home.

Dishonesty and deceit typically enter the extramarital sexual relationship. Participants find that excuses must be made to explain time away from home or work, as well as fluctuations in mood. The details of where and when to meet have to be carefully and secretly planned to avoid suspicion and discovery. Given these complexities, experts point out that extramarital relationships are usually doomed from the start.

Other problems accompany extramarital relationships. To illustrate, consequences of extramarital relationships include the violation of religious codes of behavior; the breaking of trust; guilt; anger; regret; lost respect and love; disruption of careers; loss of reputation; sexually transmitted diseases; sexual conflicts and dysfunctions; and even suicide or homicide. Such a list, which could easily be expanded, illustrates the many and serious consequences of extramarital relationships.

Further Reading. Humphrey, Frederick G. (1987). Treating extramarital sexual relationships in sex and couples therapy. In Gerald R. Weeks and Larry Hof (Eds.), *Integrating sex and marital therapy: A clinical guide.* New York: Brunner/Mazel; Pittman, Frank. (1989). *Private lies: Infidelity and the betrayal of intimacy.* New York: Norton; Seagraves, Kathleen B. (1989). Extramarital affairs. *Medical Aspects of Human Sexuality, 23,* 99–105.

ADULTHOOD, FRIENDSHIPS DURING. Friendships are important throughout the entire lifespan, but especially so during the adult years. Much like the benefits friendships offer in earlier life stages, adult friendships provide important sources of companionship and support. Also, friendships enable adults to gain insight into themselves, to assess their strengths as well as weaknesses. Friendships provide a sense of security and attachment, and they provide participants with reassurance of worth and competency. Additionally, a friendship provides a commitment between partners as well as a common purpose.

It has also been found that a connection exists between friendships and healthy adjustment during adult life. Indeed, most researchers feel that the establishment and maintenance of meaningful friendships represent life's most rewarding and important activities. Friendships also serve as a major source of comfort and defense in the presence of crises throughout the life cycle. Some investigators have found that the lack of a social support system may even trigger depression and feelings of alienation.

The friendships of adults offer a unique contrast to friendships of earlier years. Over time, social interaction and friendships have extended gradually so that they encompass multiple facets of their environment. The social sphere of the young child is limited primarily to the family, but gradually friendships emerge as involvement escalates with peer groups, athletics, or school activities. By adolescence, friendships have been forged with members of the opposite sex, work and school colleagues, and various members of the community. By adulthood, each new social avenue provides further opportunities to become deeply involved with meaningful others and to fulfill the need of sharing new feelings and experiences with others.

Compared to friendships of earlier years, adult friendships are characterized by greater levels of maturity and intimacy. Adulthood marks a time when individuals can express more compassion, understanding, acceptance, and empathy toward others. The capacity to be intimate also enables adults to overcome whatever interpersonal boundaries exist in potential friendships (see INTIMATE RE-

LATIONSHIP). The intimate adult also demonstrates a greater tolerance of the weaknesses and shortcomings of others. Moreover, adults are capable of seeing beyond limitations in others, perhaps because they have seen and accepted similar weaknesses in themselves.

Adult friendships can be differentiated by other characteristics. For example, adults are usually more apt to share all aspects of themselves and to feel understood and accepted. Because of more mature communication abilities and interpersonal skills, adult friends usually come to know one another in greater depth. Their friendships tend to have greater levels of mutuality and reciprocity. Adult friends usually come to know in what ways they can depend upon one another for support and understanding. Adult friends also build considerable trust in one another, including a sense of confidence in the integrity and honesty of the partner.

The need for human contact in general and friendships in particular remains important through all of adult life. Adults of all ages need a stimulating, caring network of family and friends to keep involved and interested in life. One's network of friends helps fill the need for affection, attachment, belonging, and a positive sense of well-being. All of these needs are psychological vitamins that better prepare individuals for dealing with the many challenges of adulthood. Without a network of meaningful friends, many adults experience loneliness, social detachment, and isolation.

The foregoing is particularly true during late adulthood. Many researchers feel that friendships are influential in maintaining positive self-regard and heightened levels of self-esteem during the later years. Elderly persons with a lifetime of positive social relations have typically come to realize, because of their interactions with others, that they are able to cope with aging experiences and generate a positive outlook on life. It has also been documented that supportive friendships provide individuals with an enhanced sense of personal control. Friendships also help older adults compensate for kin relationships lost through death. Although there is a predominance of family in the networks of aged persons, there is often a preference for friends as support providers. When family members are not available, friends often step in and offer important sources of companionship and understanding.

The experience of retirement during late adulthood often signifies the loss of job-related friends, although many compensate for this by realigning a friendship network or perhaps establishing a new one. Older adults who maintain a friendship network experience continued social and psychological benefits. Most believe that because of their interactions with others, they are better able to cope with aging processes and the demands of day-to-day living. Friendships are influential in determining how daily challenges are faced and how individuals feel about themselves as these challenges are met. Moreover, in the face of stress or crisis situations, friends are usually there to provide support, needed resources, and perhaps most of all, caring and love.

Further Reading. Blieszner, Rosemary, and Rebecca G. Adams. (1992). *Adult friendship*. Newbury Park, CA: Sage; Duck, Steve. (1992). *Human relationships* (2nd Ed.). Newbury Park, CA: Sage; Jacobs, Ruth H. (1990). Friendships among old women. *Journal of Women and Aging, 2*, 19–32; Turner, Jeffrey S., and Donald B. Helms. (1994). *Contemporary adulthood* (5th Ed.). Fort Worth, TX: Harcourt Brace.

ADULTHOOD, MATURITY DURING. Maturity is a state that promotes physical and psychological well-being. Adequately meeting the challenges of adulthood relies considerably on maturity. Researchers have identified a number of characteristics that are thought to be associated with this important life dimension. For example, the mature adult typically has an accurate self-concept, stable emotional behavior, a well-developed value system, and intellectual insight. Mature adults are also realistic in their assessment of future goals, appreciate and respect others, and possess effective problem-resolution skills.

It is important to note that maturity is achieved gradually; it is not a sudden and giant leap forward. Moreover, attaining maturity is not an all-or-nothing proposition: for example, a person may be intellectually mature but lack social maturity. Maturity does not come automatically with adulthood. People must work to achieve maturity, and the failure to do so can cause relationships with others to be superficial and shallow.

The formation and maintenance of intimate relationships are greatly influenced by adult maturity. Many investigators maintain that without adult maturity, relationships with others will always be superficial and shallow forms of interaction. It is adult maturity that allows a person to discover the innermost and subjective aspects of oneself and significant others, such as a partner, friend, relative, or teacher.

Within intimate relationships, maturity enables couples to sort out, accept, or change gender roles and responsibilities, understand the importance of commitment and intimacy, love and be loved, and communicate in honest and accurate ways. Maturity also has an important influence on sexual interactions. For example, maturity enables people to understand and appreciate the importance of responsible and safer sex and maintaining one's sexual health. The mature person is also knowledgeable or motivated to learn about contraceptive choices, the importance of avoiding unwanted pregnancies, and ways to avoid sexually transmitted diseases.

Further Reading. Derlega, Valerian J. (1984). Self-disclosure and intimate relationships. In Valerian J. Derlega (Ed.), *Communication, intimacy, and close relationships*. New York: Academic Press; Hendrick, Susan, and Clyde Hendrick. (1992). *Liking, loving, and relating* (2nd Ed.). Belmont, CA: Brooks/Cole; Weber, Ann L., and John H. Harvey. (Eds.). (1994). *Perspectives on close relationships*. Boston: Allyn and Bacon.

ADULTHOOD, SCHOOL RELATIONSHIPS DURING. Schooling opportunities are lifelong endeavors, and many adults enjoy and profit from a wide variety of educational experiences. A mere glance at the numbers of adult students furthering their education provides testimony to this fact. Today, approximately 65 million individuals are enrolled in over 100,000 schools and colleges in the United States. Educational specialists estimate that about 38 percent of the adult population aged 25 years or older is enrolled in higher education. In years to come, this figure is expected to increase.

There are a number of reasons why adults return to school. Most return to the classroom to upgrade their skills, establish financial security, and prepare for better jobs. Returning to school usually enables workers to make a significant upward movement in a particular profession or perhaps pursue a new career. Also, higher education usually enables people to make more money and decreases their chances of facing unemployment. Some adults return to school because of boredom or dissatisfaction with their old job. In this case, the classroom may be part of a plan for career revitalization or change. Finally, many adults involve themselves in educational programming because of the sheer enjoyment and challenge that learning offers.

Using the classroom to upgrade career skills is a reflection of today's vocational world and the vast number of jobs demanding higher education. Three out of the four fastest-growing occupational groups are executive, administrative, and managerial; professional specialty; and technicians and related support occupations. These occupations generally require the highest levels of education and skill and will make up an increasing proportion of new jobs. Office and factory automation, changes in consumer demand, and substitution of imports for domestic products are expected to cause employment to stagnate or decline in many occupations that require little formal education—apparel workers and textile machinery operators, for example. Opportunities for high-school dropouts will be increasingly limited, and workers who cannot read and follow directions may not even be considered for most jobs.

Researchers have found that returning to school has a number of important benefits beyond upgrading career skills. For example, the classroom offers intellectual challenges and opportunities to mentally engage in stimulating academic pursuits. The classroom environment also provides a setting for evaluation and feedback, which in turn affects levels of self-esteem and confidence. Many investigators have found that success in educational pursuits promotes improved states of psychological and physical well-being. The classroom also provides adults with unique socialization opportunities, including meeting and working with those who share similar interests and motivations. For adults returning to school, establishing a student support network often becomes a rewarding aspect of academic involvement.

Often, adults shy away from higher education because of anxiety. Many believe that they have been out of school too long and cannot compete with their younger counterparts. However, this is erroneous thinking on several counts. For example, adults may not be competing with younger students. Indeed, many colleges and universities have divisions of continuing education or evening programs that place adults alongside one another. Also, many institutions have made efforts in their overall programming to cater to the needs of adult students. Finally, many professors are aware of the adult students' concerns and will do all they can to help them get over the hurdle of initial anxieties.

It is also wrong to think that adults cannot compete intellectually with younger students. Researchers have shown consistently that aging processes do not bring an automatic reduction in thinking or reasoning capacities. Even elderly learners exhibit few losses in intellectual processes. This means that we cannot generalize about mental abilities and the adult population; each facet of intelligence needs to be scrutinized, particularly those applied to the classroom. Older learners prove continually that adulthood is a productive period of growth and development in terms of cognitive and creative output.

Many college and university settings are implementing innovative programming for older adult learners. For example, the Elderhostel, started in 1975, has become especially attractive to the elderly. The Elderhostel invites the elderly to reside for short periods on college campuses at low cost and attend a wide variety of classes, seminars, and workshops. In addition to the Elderhostel, specialized educational programs for the elderly are offered by government and industry as well as voluntary and religious organizations. Such programming will likely increase in years to come. Because of this, it is incumbent on adult educators, as both researchers and practitioners, to discover more about adult learners and the best ways to meet their needs.

Further Reading. Hart, Betty L. (1991). Never too young to learn, never too old to teach: Women, writing, and aging. *Educational Gerontology, 17,* 187–201; Sinnott, Jan D. (Ed.). (1994). *Interdisciplinary handbook of adult lifespan learning.* Westport, CT: Greenwood Press; Smith, Robert M. (1990). *Learning to learn across the life span.* San Francisco, CA: Jossey-Bass.

ADULTHOOD, SCIENTIFIC STUDY OF. The scientific study of adulthood examines the physical, cognitive, personal, and social characteristics of humans throughout the course of adult life. Adult development, like child and adolescent development, is a subdivision of developmental psychology. Those specializing in this portion of the lifespan are usually referred to as adult development psychologists, developmental psychologists, or gerontologists. Examples of professional journals focusing on adult development include *Gerontologist, Journal of Aging and Health,* and *Psychology and Aging.*

Compared to the study of child and adolescent development, the study of adults has only recently emerged as a scientific research pursuit. Several reasons account for this lag. Part of the problem appears to be that life expectancy was relatively short in the past, and few researchers directed their energies toward the adult population. Another reason is that infancy, childhood, and adolescence present the researcher with obvious and observable changes to study, especially physical, mental, and personality differences. While such changes do occur throughout the duration of adulthood, they are not as easily detectable, with the possible exception of old age. Thus a vast amount of literature focused on childhood and the adolescent years. This is bewildering to many, since adulthood represents the longest and perhaps the most significant portion of the entire life cycle.

A glance at demographics also reveals that there are more individuals in the life stage of adulthood than in any other stage. This may be surprising to those who think that the United States represents the land of the young. Over one-half of the population is between the ages of 18 and 64, and the median age is about 30 years. Another 12 percent are 65 years or older. This latter group represents one of the fastest-growing population segments in the country.

Today, however, developmental psychologists recognize the importance of the adulthood years and feel that it is a critical phase of the life cycle. Many view the latter stages of the life cycle as important periods for studying a diversity of scientific issues relative to their disciplines. By studying various dynamics of adult life, such as biological, personality, social, and vocational development, the entire life cycle is placed in a more balanced perspective. The study of adulthood, coupled with the already-accumulated research on the years preceding adulthood, enables us to view aging processes as lifelong processes.

The field of *gerontology,* the investigative pursuit that seeks to explore aging processes and the problems of the elderly, has been especially active in the field of adult development (see GERONTOLOGY). In the past decade, gerontologists have made important attempts to dispel myths about the elderly and about aging processes in general. They have also uncovered the enormous diversity in the experiences of growing old and have enabled us to take a more positive attitude toward aging and the aged population.

Thus, while the study of adulthood is a relatively new area of research, it is nonetheless an accepted area in the field of developmental psychology. The facts about life beyond adolescence are slowly being untangled and better understood. Publications, research centers, and college courses focusing on the entire spectrum of adult development attest to the fact that this area of study will mushroom in future years.

Further Reading. Bass, Scott A., Francis G. Caro, and Yung-Ping Chen. (Eds.). (1993). *Achieving a productive aging society.* Westport, CT: Auburn House; Hudson, Frederic M. (1991). *The adult years: Mastering the art of self-renewal.* San Francisco: Jossey-Bass; Merriam, Sharan B., and M. Carolyn Clark. (1991). *Lifelines: Patterns of work, love, and learning in adulthood.* San Francisco: Jossey-Bass.

ADULTHOOD, WORK RELATIONSHIPS DURING. See EARLY ADULTHOOD, WORK RELATIONSHIPS DURING; LATE ADULTHOOD, WORK RELATIONSHIPS DURING; MIDDLE ADULTHOOD, WORK RELATIONSHIPS DURING.

AFRICAN AMERICANS, AND LIFESPAN RELATIONSHIPS AMONG. African Americans are the largest racial minority in the United States, numbering almost 30 million. Overall, African Americans constitute about 12 percent of the total U.S. population. Over the course of the last 15 years, this population has grown by 13 percent, more than double the growth rate of the white population. There are approximately 10 million African-American households in the United States today. While African Americans are the most widely dispersed minority group, they are still highly concentrated in Southern states.

Any discussion of close relationships among African Americans must take into account the social status and living arrangements of blacks today. More specifically, there have been growing numbers of poor, female-headed African-American families. African-American families are three times as likely as white families to be poor, and the level of black unemployment is more than twice that among whites. While a significant majority of the 10 million African-American households are family households (that is, the household members are related by birth, marriage, or adoption), only one-half are headed by a married couple. More than one-fourth of all African-American children live with mothers who have never married.

Many experts believe that in the face of such stressors, African-American families have developed unique coping skills. In particular, a hallmark of African-American families is strong family ties. African Americans find strength and support within their own families and kin networks. To deal with day-to-day stressors, black families turn within, in the process providing gratification, help, and assistance. Older African-American females, particularly widows, are noted for taking into their homes grandchildren, nieces, nephews, and other relatives to combine the resources of the extended family and provide familial assistance and support. According to many contemporary scholars, the end result of such support is that African-American families tend to be stable and functional, not problematic and deviant. Indeed, most African Americans report a strong sense of family solidarity and cohesion.

Flexibility of family roles is another strength of African-American families. Because both African-American partners have almost always had to work outside the home to make ends meet, there are fewer rigidly defined gender roles. Instead, African-American families tend to be egalitarian, with both husband and wife sharing in the authority to make decisions and in other family responsibilities. Additionally, working mothers are not viewed as a threat to their husbands' egos; rather, their contributions to the household are regarded as a matter of economic necessity. Also, research does not support the stereotypic view that African-American fathers are invisible and uninvolved with their children. Rather, African-American fathers are more likely to share child care and domestic chores than Euro-American men. Research further shows that the greater the economic security of African-American fathers, the more active they become in child care.

African-American fertility rates are slightly higher than those of whites. The total number of lifetime births per African-American woman is about 2.4 children, compared to 1.8 for whites. About one-half of African-American children are born to single mothers, and four out of five will live in a female-headed household at some point in their childhood. However, as mentioned, many African-American single mothers are more apt to live in an extended family with their own mother or grandmother. In such domestic arrangements, child care becomes shared, thus enabling the mother to improve her situation through work or education. It is in this way that the extended family framework helps many African-American mothers to cope with adverse social conditions and economic impoverishment.

As far as parent-child relations are concerned, African-American parents view children as essential for family continuity. As a result, considerable emphasis is placed on their achievement and fulfillment. Spirituality and a strong religious orientation are dominant cultural values taught to children. The child-rearing practices of African-American parents are found to be similar to those of other groups in a number of respects. For example, compared to Hispanic Americans, blacks tend to encourage the early independence and autonomy of youngsters, practice authoritative modes of discipline, and encourage egalitarian family roles. The importance of educational achievement as a means to better one's quality of life is a frequent child-rearing theme. Like other minority parents, most African-American parents make active efforts to ensure that their children develop a positive ethnic-group identity.

Outside of the family, children and adolescents discover that peer relationships are an important facet of socialization. They also learn that in many schools, peer groups are often segregated according to ethnicity and social class. Much like other minority youths, the peer group provides African Americans with an important sense of brotherhood or sisterhood within the majority culture. In this sense, the peer group and other socialization agents within the wider community mirror parental socialization values. Additionally, the peer group helps forge a sense of identity and feelings of self-worth. Some researchers believe that African-American youths often rely on peer groups more than white adolescents.

With respect to dating and sexual relationships, African-American teenagers tend to initiate sex earlier and engage in premarital intercourse more frequently than white teenagers. However, while African-American adolescents have higher rates of coitus, the relative differences have been smaller over the last 20 years because the rates have been sharply increasing among whites. Also, such differences in sexual attitudes and behaviors may be due to variations within the African-American culture, such as ethnic or socioeconomic factors. Studies have shown that the sexual behavior of middle-class African Americans is more similar to that of middle-class whites than it is to that of lower-class blacks.

The socioeconomic status of African Americans also helps to explain the high birthrates among unmarried black teenagers. Rather than assuming that these high birthrates represent a cultural phenomenon, one needs to acknowledge economic circumstances. In support of this, teenage pregnancy rates among low-income whites are also quite high. In analyzing the connection between poverty and adolescent pregnancy, researchers have found that poor adolescents often receive less parental supervision than middle-class teenagers, which places them at risk for negative social situations. Also, some female teenagers perceive pregnancy as a way to share caring and affection in a love-starved world. Others view pregnancy as a way to receive modest government benefits and solve, at least partially, problems posed by unemployment.

African-American adolescents have higher rates for sexually transmitted diseases, including bacterial infections caused by syphilis, gonorrhea, and chlamydia. Moreover, the incidence rate for sexually transmitted diseases has significantly increased in recent years. Of greater magnitude, though, are the numbers of African-American males and females infected with the human immunodeficiency virus (HIV) and AIDS. As with other sexually transmitted diseases, African-American and Hispanic-American teenagers are highly overrepresented among persons with AIDS. Currently, they represent more than one-half of all adolescents infected by the viral disease (see ADOLESCENCE, SEXUALLY TRANSMITTED DISEASES DURING; AIDS, AFRICAN AMERICANS AND).

As one might surmise from the statistics mentioned earlier, marriage does not play a dominant role in the formation of African-American families. Compared to whites, far fewer African Americans marry, and divorce is more common. However, once again, many factors converge to affect such patterns. The increased employment opportunities for women make marriage less of an economic necessity. For that matter, the rules of the welfare system discourage marriage. The high unemployment rate among African-American males may also serve as a deterrent to marriage. Men may reason that they should not get married unless they are gainfully employed and can support a family. Finally, demographers point out that fewer African-American women are getting married in the 1990s because from a population standpoint, there are not enough eligible men available.

As indicated, the relationships of African-American families are marked by strong kinship bonds. African Americans are more willing than white families to take relatives into their households. Additionally, the family figures prominently in the social support of aging relatives. Both young and old family members interact frequently and nurture close affective bonds. Many researchers have found that having an adult child and relatives nearby tends to facilitate the emotional and social integration of older African Americans in family networks. Such intergenerational relations are particularly important in later life because they serve to reduce the negative effects of aging. A norm of reciprocity between generations is also evident in African-American families. Child-care services, transportation, household tasks, and care when someone is ill are often exchanged between grandparents, parents, and adult children. Finally, similar to trends observed with white caregivers, it is the adult daughter who typically provides the most support to aging parents. (See AFRICAN AMERICANS, INTERGENERATIONAL RELATIONS AMONG.)

Further Reading. O'Hare, William P., Kevin M. Pollard, Taynia L. Mann, and Mary M. Kent. (1991). *African Americans in the 1990's.* Washington, DC: Population Reference Bureau; Staples, Robert. (1994). *The black family: essays and studies* (5th Ed.). Belmont, CA: Wadsworth; Taylor, Robert Joseph, and Linda M. Chatters. (1991). Extended family networks of older black adults. *Journal of Gerontology: Social Sciences, 46,* S210–S217; Taylor, Ronald L. (1995). *African-American youth.* Westport, CT: Praeger.

AFRICAN AMERICANS, INTERGENERATIONAL RELATIONS AMONG. Young and old African-American family members are noted for their emotional connectedness as well as for the provision of many different types of assistance and support. For example, elderly adults are more likely to receive support from their children in times of need than from formal support networks. Adult daughters, in particular, are typically selected as the person to provide help when sickness or disability strikes. Childless black elderly, on the other hand, are more apt to rely upon brothers, sisters, and friends. It is important to point out that the parent-child bond is important across the entire life cycle of African Americans and reflects considerable mutuality and reciprocity. Younger adults tend to rely heavily on their parents, elderly adults are apt to rely on their adult children, and middle-aged African Americans tend to depend on both their parents and children.

Compared to whites, African-American grandparents also tend to take a more active role in grandparenting. This greater involvement may be traced to several reasons. For one, the greater probability of African Americans residing with grandchildren and in three-generational households offers increased opportunities for contact and involvement (see AFRICAN AMERICANS, LIFESPAN RELATIONSHIPS AMONG). Another possible reason is that higher incidences of divorce, unemployment, and mortality among African Americans have important consequences for both household arrangements and family child-care responsibilities. A third possible reason is that rather explicit cultural norms in support of extended family relations are in operation among African Americans.

It might be added that mothers of African-American teenage parents play a prominent role in the lives of their children and grandchildren. The support and assistance that teenage mothers receive from their extended family, particularly from their mothers, exert many positive influences. Among other benefits, such intergenerational support assists adolescent mothers with their educational and economic achievements, parenting skills, and their children's development. Also, such living arrangements tend to foster strong intergenerational bonds between young and old. Finally, regular contact with aged family members places the elderly in the mainstream of family activity. African-American elderly are neither isolated nor neglected; on the contrary, they are visible and active. Moreover, they are highly respected as important linkages to the past (see AGING ADULTS, KIN RELATIONS AND; AGING PARENTS, CARING FOR; AGING PARENTS, CARING FOR. RACIAL AND ETHNIC VARIATIONS).

Further Reading. Harel, Zev, Edward A. McKinney, and Michael Williams. (Eds.). (1990). *Black aged: Understanding diversity and service needs.* Newbury Park, CA: Sage;

Taylor, Robert Joseph, and Linda M. Chatters. (1991). Extended family networks of older black adults. *Journal of Gerontology: Social Sciences, 46,* S210–S217; Wilson, Melvin N. (1986). The black extended family: An analytical consideration. *Developmental Psychology, 22,* 246–259.

AFRICAN AMERICANS, LIFE EXPECTANCY OF. Life expectancy is an estimate of the average number of years a person can expect to live. Death rates vary according to a number of differentials, including race. According to recent statistics, life expectancy at birth for the white population (75.9 years) is about 4.2 years greater than for the African-American population (71.7 years). However, this racial gap is narrowing. Between 1950 and 1970, life expectancy increased among African-American persons by 3.4 years, compared to 2.6 years among white persons. Since 1970, the African-American population has experienced a rise in life expectancy of 6.4 years, compared to 4.2 years for the white population.

The decline in the racial disparity in life expectancy has been particularly pronounced among females. In 1950, white females could expect to live 9.5 years longer than African-American females. Today, though, the gap is about 3.4 years. Among males, the African-American/white gap has declined from 7.6 years in 1950 to about 5.1 years today (see LIFE EXPECTANCY, GENDER DIFFERENCES IN).

Up to about age 75, whites can expect to live longer than African Americans. Paradoxically, however, after this point African-American mortality rates are lower than white mortality rates. This life expectancy phenomenon is known as the *racial crossover,* and a number of theories have been proposed to explain it. For instance, African Americans at advanced ages may be a more biologically select group, particularly since they probably survived inadequate medical care when they were younger, or it may be that aging is in some way retarded among aged African Americans, a suggestion that there are racial differences in aging processes at the cellular level.

Why African Americans have higher mortality rates than whites prior to age 75 is also difficult to explain, although once again there is room for speculation. To begin with, there have been fairly predictable changes in causes of death among African Americans, with movement away from infectious diseases and toward degenerative diseases. Yet rates of death among African Americans for degenerative diseases exceed rates among whites. For instance, age-adjusted death rates for cardiovascular disease, cancer, and stroke are all higher for African Americans. The mortality trends for African Americans relative to whites thus present a somewhat anomalous picture. Given that African Americans have not progressed as far as whites in overall longevity, one might expect their rates of death due to degenerative diseases to be lower than those of whites. The fact that the reverse is true is an illustration of the disadvantaged position of African Americans in U.S. society relative to whites. (See LIFE EXPECTANCY; LIFE EXPECTANCY, GENDER DIFFERENCES IN.)

Further Reading. Gee, Ellen M. (1989). Living longer, dying differently. *Generations, 13,* 5–8; Gibson, Rose C. (1991). Age-by-race differences in the health and functioning of elderly persons. *Journal of Aging and Health, 3,* 335–351; Gibson, Rose C. (1991). Race and the self-reported health of elderly persons. *Journal of Gerontology: Social Sciences, 46,* S235–S242.

AGING, CHANGES IN SEXUAL FUNCTIONING DUE TO. Aging processes bring changes to sexual functioning in both females and males. As far as females are concerned, aging brings some alterations in the genitalia. Over time, the vagina shortens in both width and length, and its walls become thinner. Its expansive capacity is also reduced. The mons, labia majora, and labia minora lose fatty tissue, causing them to shrink and flatten. The folds of the labia majora and labia minora also become less pronounced. The clitoris, ovaries, and uterus also get slightly smaller. The loss of some fatty tissue leaves the clitoris less protected and more easily irritated. However, it still remains quite sensitive to sexual stimulation.

With increasing age, the glands that lubricate the vagina upon sexual stimulation respond more slowly and provide less lubrication. Consequently, many older women complain that they are never wet enough for comfortable penetration or that intercourse is scratchy and painful. The lack of vaginal lubrication and the less expansive nature of the vagina, referred to as the senile vagina syndrome, can also cause vaginal burning, pelvic aching, and urinary difficulties.

A woman's sexual responsiveness also changes with age (See SEXUAL RESPONSE CYCLE). For example, it usually takes longer for an older woman to become sexually aroused. Whereas a young woman's vagina will lubricate within 15 to 30 seconds after stimulation, an older woman's vagina may require 3 to 5 minutes to achieve lubrication. Even then, there is a reduced amount of vaginal lubricant. Orgasm is also shorter and less intense. Related to the latter, uterine contractions typically diminish from three to five per orgasm to one or two.

Aging processes also bring changes to the male sexual anatomy. For example, the scrotum hangs lower and the testes become smaller and less firm. Sperm production declines, but the aging male remains capable of manufacturing mature sperm cells. This means that, unlike women, men remain fertile and are able to conceive children throughout adulthood. Testosterone levels also decline with advancing age. By age 80, testosterone levels may be only one-sixth that of a younger male.

While the penis does not generally change in size or shape, it does become less sensitive to stimulation. Erections may not be as firm or full as those of younger males, and their angle tends to decline with advancing years. For many older men, there are changes in penile sensitivity and a decreased frequency of nocturnal erections. Pubic hair also tends to become sparse and finer. For most men, the prostate gland grows larger, a development that may cause medical problems.

Like older females, elderly males experience changes in sexual responsiveness. Although the capacity to respond to sexual stimuli remains, a man's drive to seek sexual release diminishes during late adulthood. It also takes longer for older men to achieve an erection and climax. Most experience a reduction in the amount and force of ejaculation, and the penis usually becomes flaccid immediately after ejaculation. Conversely, a younger adult's penis typically remains erect for minutes after ejaculation. Relatedly, the refractory period is longer, meaning that it takes an older adult longer than his younger counterpart to have a second erection and orgasm. While younger males may be able to experience several erections and orgasms in one day, most older males have only one orgasm or erection per day or per week.

Despite these changes in male and female sexual functioning, it is important to note that most elderly people are capable of enjoying sexual pleasure, and in some cases, the pleasure may actually increase. Sexual relations serve as a cohesive force in older marriages and other intimate relationships, and their continuation is considered desirable. Sex for many older persons offers a blend of understanding and appreciation that often transcends earlier developmental stages. (See AGING, IMPACT OF ON SEXUAL INTIMACY.)

Further Reading. Butler, Robert N., and Myrna I. Lewis. (1988). *Love and sex after 60.* New York: Harper and Row; Leiblum, Sandra R., and Gloria Bachmann. (1988). The sexuality of the climactic woman. In Bernard A. Eskin (Ed.), *The menopause: Comprehensive management.* New York: Yearbook Medical Publishers; Leiblum, Sandra R., and R. Taylor Segraves. (1989). Sex therapy and aging adults. In Sandra R. Leiblum and Raymond C. Rosen (Eds.), *Principles and practice of sex therapy* (2nd Ed.). New York: Guilford Press.

AGING, IMPACT OF ON SEXUAL INTIMACY. The manner in which aging impacts on sexual intimacy is a relatively new research pursuit. Researchers point out that sexual intimacy incorporates a broad range of activities and feelings, not just the act of sexual intercourse. The expression of love and tenderness has wide variation and, whether explicitly sexual or not, promotes psychological intimacy between adults of all ages. This includes such behaviors as holding, touching, and other forms of physical closeness. Indeed, when partners concentrate on enjoying each other and appreciate their own and the other's feelings and senses, they are likely to enjoy sexual intimacy in many different and rewarding ways.

Sexual functioning and desire are not immune to aging processes, and there is a decline in coital activity with age. There are also changes in sexual anatomy and physiology (see AGING, CHANGES IN SEXUAL FUNCTIONING DUE TO). However, when people understand the changes of aging and how to cope with these changes, they can share sexual intimacy for as long as they choose. Of course, ill health can create decreases in sexual activity, as can social and emotional problems and the side effects of certain medications.

Unfortunately, some members of our society regard older adults as asexual, while others have developed a number of cruel misconceptions concerning the sex lives of older people. Some maintain that sex is neither possible nor necessary during old age. Old men are often thought of as being either impotent or "dirty old men," and elderly women interested in sex are often seen as foolishly attempting to regain lost youth and vigor. Those elderly people who claim to be sexually active may be seen as either morally perverse or boastful and deceptive.

Along these lines, there are a number of false assumptions that society often makes about the sexuality of older adults. One, the elderly do not have sexual desires. Two, because the aged are physically fragile, sex is dangerous to their health. Three, the elderly are physically unattractive and consequently sexually undesirable. Four, the notion of sexual intimacy among elderly persons is shameful and even perverse. All of these assumptions are unwarranted, derogatory, and untrue. They represent blatant ageist attitudes that are upheld only by the uninformed and ignorant. These negative sanctions are particularly strong for older women and single elderly, as well as gays and lesbians.

Among both men and women, those who have enjoyed long and stable sex lives without lengthy interruptions are more likely to remain sexually active longer than those whose history is different. Sex among the elderly is thus likely to mirror sexual activities of earlier life. For partners who have experienced long-standing conflicts, age alone may be used as an excuse to give up sexual relations that were never satisfactory. Rewarding sexual relations will rely heavily on the physical vitality of couples and the mental commitment of each partner to want to share and sustain sexual intimacy. A marriage based on mutuality, understanding, and tenderness provides a vital basis for satisfying sexual relations throughout all of adulthood.

Further Reading. Adams, Catherine G., and Barbara F. Turner. (1985). Reported change in sexuality from young adulthood to old age. *Journal of Sex Research, 21,* 126–141; Turner, Jeffrey S., and Laurna Rubinson. (1993). *Contemporary human sexuality.* Englewood Cliffs, NJ: Prentice Hall; Weg, Ruth. (Ed.). (1983). *Sexuality in the later years.* Orlando, FL: Academic Press.

AGING, PROCESSES OF. Aging processes begin at birth and continue throughout the course of the lifespan. It is important to recognize that aging processes represent an interaction of forces and do not exist as a singular event. Three major aging processes have been identified: psychological, social, and biological.

Psychological aging is the individual's own perception of the aging process and consists of such elements as cognition, self-esteem, motivation, and feelings. In this regard, psychological aging can be defined as behavioral reactions that accompany the experience of growing old. A comment such as "I feel as old as the hills today" may serve as an example of a psychological reaction to a bodily state or change. Interestingly, a biologically young person may feel psychologically old, and the reverse is also true.

Social aging is the manner in which one's society intertwines with aging experiences. It is important to consider age-graded expectations when examining social aging, including those attached to roles, status, styles of dress, and verbal and nonverbal language. Some societies, for example, encourage youthful behavior and downplay the role of the elderly, while others regard maturity as a virtue. To go one step further, we generally expect an older couple at a rock music concert to react differently from adolescents attending the same event. Or some of us frown upon older adults when they wear clothing characteristic of their younger counterparts (and vice versa). Many expect such events as marriage and child rearing to take place at certain ages.

Biological aging is the manner in which the body functions over time. As we grow older, the body experiences changes in skeletal composition, sensory capacities, heart rate, and tissue structure, to name but a few areas. In general, the aging process in a biological sense causes the body to slowly degenerate and deteriorate.

It is important to reiterate that no one process of aging exists alone. Thus a 14-year-old adolescent female in the throes of puberty (biological aging) may feel that mentally she is a mature woman in the full sense of the word (psychological aging), but her parents may feel that she is too young to begin dating and thus may place restrictions on her social life (social aging). As another illustration, a 75-year-old man (biological aging) may be very pleased with his past life experiences and not regard advancing age as an obstacle to future success (psychological aging). However, he totally enjoys the retirement community in which he resides because it encourages an active lifestyle and places no age restrictions on activities or entertainment (social aging). These two examples illustrate the manner in which aging exists as a multifaceted experience.

Further Reading. Briggs, Roger. (1990). Biological aging. In John Bond and Peter Coleman (Eds.), *Ageing in society: An introduction to social gerontology.* Newbury Park, CA: Sage; Hendricks, Jon, and Cynthia A. Leedham. (1991). Theories of aging: Implications for human services. In Paul K. H. Kim (Ed.), *Serving the elderly: Skills for practice.* New York: Aldine de Gruyter; Turner, Jeffrey S., and Donald B. Helms. (1995). *Lifespan development* (5th Ed.). Fort Worth, TX: Harcourt Brace.

AGING, SUCCESSFUL. Successful aging refers to subjective well-being over the course of the lifespan, with particular emphasis on happiness and morale during late adulthood. Because of its subjective nature, the concept of successful aging is often difficult to explain, and frequently the description of it reflects the values and perspective of the person doing the defining. There is general agreement, though, on the importance of successful aging during the later years of life and its impact on personality and social functioning.

Experts agree that satisfaction with one's life is essential to successful aging. Those who feel that their life has been rewarding typically face their later years with few regrets and considerable personal satisfaction. Persons who have aged successfully also have a positive attitude about the past and the future. Consequently, life remains stimulating and interesting. Moreover, those who have met most of their personal, career, and financial goals will be able to relax during retirement and even go on to set new goals.

Many research investigations have centered on successful aging and the relative degree of involvement with one's surroundings. More specifically, researchers have sought to understand if successful aging is characterized by an active lifestyle and heightened involvement with others, or if elderly persons are more satisfied when their life space shrinks and their responsibilities and roles lessen. In the wake of such scientific inquiry, two theories of successful aging have emerged: the disengagement and activity theories.

The *disengagement theory* views aging as a mutual withdrawal process between aging persons and the social system to which they belong. Contrary to popular impression, such a gradual withdrawal from society is not a negative experience for the elderly. The aged frequently view disengagement in a positive light, since this is an age of increased reflection, preoccupation with the self, and decreased emotional investment in people and events. Because of this, disengagement is viewed as a natural rather than an imposed process.

The *activity theory* of successful aging suggests that retired individuals prefer to remain productive and active. In contrast to the theory of disengagement, this viewpoint maintains that the aged prefer to resist preoccupation with the self and psychological distance from society. Happiness and satisfaction originate from social involvement and the older person's ability to adjust to changing life events.

It is important to recognize that while both the disengagement and activity theories offer insight into the topic of successful aging, neither perspective fully explains the phenomenon of successful aging and overall adjustment. Both theories represent only a limited view of many possible patterns of aging. They cannot be applied to all aged persons, since not all disengagement or activity patterns influence the self-concept and life satisfaction in general. Indeed, researchers point out that one's activity can decline without affecting morale. For many, a more leisurely lifestyle is often regarded as one of the rewards of old age.

Other research investigations have explored how life satisfaction and successful aging are strongly related to various life conditions, including socioeconomic status, health, social support, and personal control. As far as socioeconomic status is concerned, not having enough money to meet the demands of day-to-day living can cause concerns throughout all of adulthood, not just the retirement years. However, the lack of financial security can intensify many of the problems associated with growing old. Good physical and mental health is critical to one's overall sense of well-being, as is a stimulating and caring social support system (see SOCIAL SUPPORT, ELDERLY). Finally, having personal control promotes independence and is vital to the maintenance of a positive self-concept and successful aging experiences.

Further Reading. Averyt, Ann C. (1987). *Successful aging.* New York: Ballantine; Baltes, Paul B., and Margret M. Baltes. (Eds.). (1990). *Successful aging: Perspectives* *from the behavioral sciences.* New York: Cambridge University Press; Elder, Glen H., Jr. (1991). Making the best of life: Perspectives on lives, times, and aging. *Generations, 15,* 12–17; George, Linda K., and Elizabeth C. Clipp. (1991). Subjective components of aging well. *Generations, 15,* 57–60.

AGING ADULTS, KIN RELATIONS AND. Kin relations are important throughout the entire lifespan, but especially during late adulthood. In general, aging adults keep in touch with whatever kin they have. For some, this means considerable contact with aging brothers and sisters, but for most, the focus of kin relations is on children and grandchildren. Upwards of 80 percent of the aged have living children, and interaction with them is considerable.

Some aged couples live with their children, especially when independent living in a separate location is no longer feasible. More elderly people are likely to live with an unmarried child than with a married one, and more with a daughter than with a son. The proportion of elderly living with their offspring is also higher for the widowed, divorced, and separated than for married persons.

In general, aging adults live near their children, although this is more true in urban environments than in rural settings. Females maintain closer relationships with other family members than do males. Couples tend to live nearer to the wife's parents and are likely to visit them more often. Also, working-class families are likely to have close family ties, and these ties are maintained by living near one another. Middle- and upper-class families have strong ties, too, but members are often geographically scattered because of career obligations.

Such patterns of closeness debunk the myth that the elderly are alienated from their children or rejected by their families. However, most research points out that the elderly often worry about their families no longer wanting or needing them. Further, when aged persons have no children, a principle of family substitution seems to operate, and brothers, sisters, nephews, and nieces often fill the roles and assume the obligations of children. The truly isolated old person, despite his or her prominence in the media, is a rarity in the United States. While retirees live apart from their children, they remain psychologically close. Another myth to be rejected is the notion that because of the existence of large human-service bureaucracies, families are no longer important as caretakers for the elderly. The family of the 1990s looms as an extremely important source of care and support, more so now, perhaps, than ever before.

As far as the dynamics of parent-child relations are concerned, research reveals that the psychological support given to the elderly is more important to their overall well-being than financial support. Moreover, it has been shown that many aging adults refuse to accept financial assistance from their offspring, largely because they want to be financially independent. In general, research shows that aging adults do not want to be dependent or impose on their children, but they also do not want to be neglected. (See AGING PARENTS, CARING FOR.)

Further Reading. Connidis, Ingrid Arnet. (1989). *Family ties and aging.* Toronto: Butterworths; Koch, Tom. (1990). *Mirrored lives: Aging children and elderly parents.*

New York: Praeger; Taylor, Robert Joseph, and Linda M. Chatters. (1991). Extended family networks of older black adults. *Journal of Gerontology: Social Sciences, 46,* S210–S217.

AGING PARENTS, CARING FOR. For elderly parents, advancing age often brings the need for assistance in day-to-day living. Moreover, incidences of chronic illness and disability steadily increase with age, further necessitating a more active caregiving role for adult children. Today, about one million adults provide direct physical and medical care to their parents every day, and many more tend to daily living needs, including financial support, household chores, shopping, and transportation.

This does not mean that elderly people needing care and attention are nursing-home candidates or residents. This is a myth that needs to be shattered. The fact of the matter is that only about 5 percent of the entire elderly population 65 years of age or older can be found within institutional settings. Most of today's aged reside instead in family settings: about 75 percent of men and 40 percent of women live with a spouse, while 8 percent of men and 18 percent of women live with relatives. The remaining numbers live alone or with nonrelatives.

Many adult daughters and sons tend to live within close proximity to their parents, a factor making them more available for assistance when it is needed (see AGING ADULTS, KIN RELATIONS AND). However, visitation and care tend to be more frequent along the female line. Such patterns of contact appear to reflect traditional gender-role programming; that is, females are taught to be more nurturant and responsive to the needs of the family, particularly when help is needed. Husbands are more likely to be in touch with the wives' parents than their own, unless the wife mediates contact with the husband's parents.

While women carry the brunt of caregiving responsibilities, experts believe that more male caregivers will be seen in the future. This is already occurring for caregiving spouses, but it is also likely that more sons will be helping caregiving daughters and daughters-in-law in the care of elderly parents. Also, the gender differences in caregiving for others, which have been pronounced in the child-raising years because of occupational and family structures, do not seem as prevalent in the later years with retirement. Researchers maintain that there are not large differences between male and female caregivers in the later years of adulthood.

The care of aging parents brings many adjustment challenges and demands. Today, the typical caregiver is middle-aged and often caught in a squeeze generation; that is, pressures often emerge from both aging parents and one's offspring. Couples at midlife are also typically confronted with competing role responsibilities and time demands. Juggling caregiving responsibilities with employment demands and household responsibilities is a formidable workload. While there are many caregiving rewards, many middle-aged adults experience considerable psychological stress and turmoil. Also, research indicates that the caregiving burden directly affects the caregiver's marital happiness. In recent years, a number of support groups and publications have emerged to better help caregiving couples handle such friction and turbulence.

It needs to be acknowledged, too, that caregiving involves important financial issues. Caring for and supporting an aging parent is an expensive venture, and many adult children are unprepared for its many financial implications. In recent years, medical costs at hospitals and nursing homes have increased dramatically, resulting in depletion of Medicare and Medicaid funds. Complicating matters is that many adult children wait until a parent is stricken with an illness or faces acute financial hardship before any real planning is done. Experts suggest that the time to work out financial considerations is before such situations occur, when parents are healthy and can make their plans and wishes known.

Further Reading. Blieszner, Rosemary, and Victoria H. Bedford. (Eds.). (1995). *Handbook of aging and the family.* Westport, CT: Greenwood Press; Gottlieb, Benjamin H. (1991). Social support and family care of the elderly. *Canadian Journal on Aging, 10,* 359–375; Kenny, Dennis E., and Elizabeth N. Oettinger (Eds.). (1991). *The family carebook: A comprehensive guide for families of older adults* (2nd Ed.). Seattle: Caresource Program Development; Levy, Michael T. (1991). *Parenting mom and dad: A guide for the grown-up children of aging parents.* Englewood Cliffs, NJ: Prentice Hall.

AGING PARENTS, CARING FOR. RACIAL AND ETHNIC VARIATIONS.

In the past, limited attention has been directed toward ethnic variations in caregiving, although we are seeing more interest today. Generally, elderly people of different ethnic and racial backgrounds in the United States are not isolated from their kinship networks and are the recipients of considerable intergenerational care and assistance. Caregivers typically live within visiting distance, interact by choice, and are connected to one another by means of mutual aid and social activities (see AGING ADULTS, KIN RELATIONS AND).

However, having family members nearby does not guarantee that sufficient help will be available to minority elders. For example, research indicates that some Hispanic-American elderly are less likely to turn to family members in times of need despite the fact that those who live alone have an average of four times more extended kin in the area than nonminority elders. Other researchers have found that some Mexican-American elders do not have full access to the necessary and culturally preferred caregiver patterns and social interactions.

Contrary to common belief, the minority family, with elderly people as a key component, represents a strong social force. Traditionally, the minority family has had to assume the role of caregiver. Minority families often rely on their own resources for the provision of social, economic, and physical needs of the aged. For example, both African Americans and Hispanic Americans have large and cohesive family systems that provide a great deal of help and emotional support to their kin. Rather than serving as an alternative support system, the role of the minority family is that of providing supplementary assistance to elderly members in need.

A wide range of multicultural investigations supports the foregoing conclusions. For instance, Hispanic-American elderly tend to have high levels of interaction with younger family members. Adult children are invariably the providers of care and assistance when the need arises. It has also been shown that elderly Korean-American parents maintain frequent contact with their adult children. While most want to live independently, most also rely on their children for assistance when it is needed. Mexican, Puerto Rican, and Cuban elderly families living in the United States reflect similar support systems. Among Asian-American caregivers, the family network, both immediate and extended, is the major means of assistance and support. Strong bonds of caregiving are also apparent among Native Americans. Among the Navajos, an ethnic minority long recognized for its enduring and reciprocal kin relationships, regular contact with and care of the elderly punctuate intergenerational relations.

African-American elderly are also active participants in family networks. Studies show that elderly respondents tend to have significant levels of interaction with family, relatively close residential proximity to immediate family, extensive familial affective bonds, and a high degree of satisfaction derived from family life. Such findings are consistent with existing literature on the kinship interaction patterns and support networks of older African Americans and the general African-American population (see AFRICAN AMERICANS, LIFE-SPAN RELATIONSHIPS AMONG).

It should be noted that some researchers have found that socioeconomic status rather than race or ethnicity is sometimes a better predictor of the structure and nature of a family's social support system. Indeed, it has been found that aging parents from low socioeconomic backgrounds have a greater likelihood than those from high socioeconomic levels to have more contact with their children. This is because working-class people are more likely to live near their relatives, while middle- and upper-middle-class persons have a greater tendency to move to another town or part of the country.

Further Reading. Gunter, Laurie M. (1991). Cultural diversity among older Americans. In Elizabeth Murrow Baines (Ed.), *Perspectives on gerontological nursing.* Newbury Park, CA: Sage; Padgett, Deborah K. (Ed.). (1995). *Handbook on ethnicity, aging, and mental health.* Westport, CT: Greenwood Press; Secundy, Marian Gray. (Ed.). (1992). *Trials, tribulations, and celebrations: African-American perspectives on health, illness, aging, and loss.* Yarmouth, ME: Intercultural Press.

AHRONS, CONSTANCE. See DIVORCE, PROCESSES AND TRANSITIONS OF.

AIDS. The acquired immunodeficiency syndrome (AIDS) looms as one of the most serious diseases to confront modern medicine. This condition is characterized by a breakdown of the body's immune system that makes people vulnerable to a variety of infections, certain forms of cancer, and various neurological disorders. AIDS is caused by a virus named the *human immunodeficiency virus*

(HIV) that is transmitted by blood and blood products (such as plasma), semen, vaginal secretions, and possibly breast milk. Thus, HIV is the causative agent while AIDS is the syndrome it causes. Because there is no cure, AIDS is a fatal condition, although patients are now surviving longer thanks to new medical treatments.

AIDS was first reported in the United States in the summer of 1981. At that time, doctors in New York and California began to see a surprising number of cases of Kaposi's sarcoma, a rare form of cancer that produces purple blotches on the skin, and of *Pneumocystis carinii* pneumonia, an equally rare form of respiratory infection. Both conditions are characterized by depressed immune systems, and both are often seen in cancer patients who are undergoing chemotherapy and in organ-transplant recipients. The cases observed, however, were in gay men. As the number of similar cases escalated, infectious-disease specialists began investigating this medical puzzle. In 1982, the disease was named the acquired immunodeficiency syndrome, and it became clear that a new peril had been unleashed in the world.

While AIDS was first considered to be primarily a disease of gay and bisexual men and injection drug users, HIV is also transmitted heterosexually, primarily through sexual relations with injection drug users, bisexual men, or prostitutes. In recent years, there has been an increase in the heterosexual transmission of HIV. Factors associated with an increased risk for heterosexual transmission include multiple sex partners and the presence of other sexually transmitted diseases. Men and women who have unprotected sexual contact, particularly with partners known to have risks for HIV infection, are at increased risk for HIV infection. A disproportionate number of AIDS cases continue to be reported among African Americans (see AIDS, AFRICAN AMERICANS AND).

As indicated, AIDS is characterized by a specific defect in the body's natural immunity against disease as the result of infection with HIV. Not everyone who has been infected with HIV will develop AIDS. Those who are infected, however, become susceptible to bacterial, viral, fungal, parasitic, and neoplastic (tumorous) disorders as the virus damages the body's immune system. These disorders remain dormant in or are fought off by people whose immune systems are normal. Such disorders are often labeled opportunistic infections because they take advantage of the body's crippled immune system. In a sense, nobody actually dies of AIDS. Rather, people die of disorders that are able to thrive in a body with a weakened immune system. Thus AIDS is a condition in which the body is susceptible to infection, and it is the specific diseases that result from such infection that kill people.

HIV, which lives and reproduces inside human cells, is extremely fragile. It cannot live in the air and can be killed by such agents as heat, ordinary soap and water, household bleach solutions, and the chlorine used in swimming pools. HIV has been found in blood, semen, vaginal secretions, breast milk, saliva, tears, spinal fluid, amniotic fluid, and urine. Of these, blood, semen, vaginal secretions, and possibly breast milk are most likely to transmit HIV from one person to another. Concentrations of HIV in urine, saliva, and tears have not been found to be sufficient for transmission.

HIV cannot pass through unbroken or undamaged skin, the lining of the respiratory tract, or the mucous membranes lining the digestive tract. However, if the skin's protective barrier is broken (by a wound, injury, needle puncture, or the like), fluid containing the virus can enter the body. HIV can enter the body through abrasions in the mucous membranes that line the vagina, endometrium, cervix, penile urethra, rectum, and mouth. For example, anal intercourse often damages the lining of the rectum, leaving an opening through which the virus can enter. For this reason, anal intercourse is especially risky for both males and females. Women also become infected through vaginal sex with a male carrier since penetration can cause tiny abrasions in the vagina. Men having vaginal sex with a female carrier are also at risk because they may have an abrasion and pick up infection from her vaginal secretions.

HIV is not spread by casual contact. In fact, HIV is fairly hard to catch and can be prevented. It cannot be spread by shaking hands, hugging, sneezing, coughing, or social kissing. Although HIV is sometimes present in the saliva of people with AIDS, there is little evidence to indicate that it is transmitted by kissing. To be safe, experts advise against deep, prolonged "French" kissing with someone who may be infected with HIV. This is especially true when one has open or bleeding sores in or around the mouth area. HIV also cannot be spread by casual contact in schools, swimming pools, stores, or the workplace. Objects touched or handled by persons infected with HIV are not contaminated and need not be feared, the only exception being objects (e.g., needles) that puncture the skin and contact internal body fluids (sharing razors and toothbrushes should also be avoided). HIV is not transmitted through food preparation or food handling. It also cannot be caught from toilet seats, bed linens, insects, or domestic animals.

Exposure to HIV occurs when blood, semen, vaginal secretions, and possibly breast milk that contain infected white blood cells get into an uninfected person's bloodstream. Antibodies usually develop in one to four months—on average, six weeks—after exposure. The average incubation period for AIDS, the time between infection with the virus and the onset of symptoms, is believed to be between three and five years. However, the incubation period can be as short as six months or as long as ten years or more. During the incubation period, a person is not said to have AIDS but rather is said to be HIV-positive. Although symptoms may not appear while HIV has not yet caused sufficient damage to the immune system, those carrying the virus are infectious to others. While they appear healthy, they can transmit HIV to a sexual partner or to someone with whom they share a contaminated needle or syringe for drug injection. A pregnant woman who carries HIV can pass it on to her baby even if she herself has not developed AIDS.

It is estimated that about 20 to 30 percent of those infected with HIV develop AIDS within ten years. Among those whose infection progresses to AIDS, 50 percent die within 18 months, and 80 percent within three years. Twenty percent of those infected with HIV will develop a condition called *symptomatic HIV infection,* once referred to as the *AIDS-related complex (ARC).* Symptomatic HIV infection has many of the symptoms of AIDS, but does not have the opportunistic infections or malignancies that characterize AIDS.

Individuals with AIDS almost uniformly have reduced numbers of lymphocytes, specialized white blood cells that are critical in combating infectious diseases such as tuberculosis and those caused by viruses. Lymphocytes may also be instrumental in destroying malignancies in their early stages. Two types of lymphocytes fight infection: the T-cell and the B-cell. A T-cell kills invaders directly, whereas a B-cell produces antibodies that fight the infection. In AIDS the numbers of T-cells are greatly reduced, and the so-called helper T-cell is the most profoundly decreased.

Just how cellular immune function is impaired by HIV is only partly understood. We know that gradually the virus eliminates the helper T-cells, which debilitates the cell-mediated immune response. However, some immune dysfunction is often present even before a decline of helper T-cells becomes evident, which means that the loss of helper T-cells is not the only cause of the impairment. We know that the development of particular opportunistic infections is related to the level of helper T-cells in the blood. Healthy individuals have about 1,000 such cells in every cubic millimeter of blood. However, in HIV-infected persons, the number declines by an average of about 40 to 80 every year.

When the helper T-cell count diminishes to between 400 and 200 per cubic millimeter, the first symptoms of AIDS usually appear: low-grade fever, swollen lymph glands (in the neck, armpits, and groin), unexplained weight loss, fatigue, night sweats, and recurrent diarrhea. There are also relatively benign but annoying infections of the skin and mucous membranes. Among these may be thrush (painful sores of the mouth), shingles (infection of the nerves and skin), unusually severe athlete's foot, and oral hairy leukoplakia (whitish patches on the tongue). Once such symptoms appear, a person is often said to have symptomatic HIV infection. The same is true for individuals who suffer from chronic, unexplained fevers, diarrhea, night sweats, or weight loss.

As immunity wanes still further, serious opportunistic infections usually develop. Many AIDS patients contract one or both of two rare diseases: Kaposi's sarcoma and *Pneumocystis carinii* pneumonia. *Kaposi's sarcoma* is a cancer of the tissues beneath the skin and the mucus-secreting surfaces of the digestive tract, the lymph nodes, and the lungs. The lesions characteristic of this disease are often first noticed as bluish to reddish discolorations or raised, firm, purple spots on arms, legs, or feet. These lesions can also appear in the mouth. The lesions neither itch nor are painful. *Pneumocystis carinii pneumonia* is a parasitic infection of the lungs. It is difficult to treat and may be life threatening. Some of the symptoms of this type of pneumonia may be fever (often very high, frequently worse in the afternoon and evening); cough (usually without significant sputum); shortness of breath (abnormal breathing sounds); and chest pain.

To date, there is no cure for AIDS. As of 1995, four drugs that directly attack HIV had been approved by the Food and Drug Administration: zidovudine (AZT), didanosine (ddI), zalcitabine (ddC), and stavudine (d4T). All of these drugs are in a class of AIDS drugs called nucleoside analogs. All have been shown to retard the spread of HIV by blocking the action of an enzyme essential to making new viral particles.

Of these antiviral drugs, zidovudine has been under the scrutiny of the medical community the longest. Zidovudine appears to delay the onset of AIDS in people who are HIV-positive but have no symptoms, but to date findings on the drug have been mixed. For example, white males treated with zidovudine developed such diseases as Kaposi's sarcoma or *Pneumocystis carinii* pneumonia more slowly, but among African-American and Hispanic-American men, early zido-vudine use proved no more effective than later treatment in staving off AIDS. Because zidovudine is highly toxic, about one-half of AIDS patients cannot tolerate its side effects, including various anemias.

Further Reading. Stine, Gerald J. (1993). *Acquired immune deficiency syndrome: Biological, medical, social, and legal issues.* Englewood Cliffs, NJ: Prentice Hall; *Surgeon General's Report to the American Public on HIV Infection and AIDS.* (1994). Washington, DC: U.S. Government Printing Office; United States Department of Health and Human Services. (1994). *Understanding HIV.* Rockville, MD: Public Health Service.

AIDS, AFRICAN AMERICANS AND. As with a number of other health problems, African Americans suffer disproportionately from HIV infection and AIDS. While there are more AIDS cases among white gay or bisexual men than among any other single group, HIV spread rapidly among African Americans during the early 1990s. During this time, the number of new AIDS cases among African Americans increased by almost 60 percent, while the number increased 38 percent among white gay or bisexual men. As a result, the African-American share of AIDS cases is growing.

It is estimated that about 50 percent of all AIDS cases among African Americans result directly or indirectly from injection drug use. High rates of injection drug use, lower educational levels, and reduced access to medical care all favor the continued transmission of HIV among poor African Americans. Education about AIDS remains the most effective way of stopping the spread of HIV. Indeed, a reduction in HIV transmission among gay and bisexual men has resulted from such educational strategies.

Research has demonstrated that Americans are becoming more knowledgeable about HIV infection. In addition, there have been efforts by the African-American community to respond to the challenge AIDS poses. Community organizations, government agencies, and private foundations have all joined forces in an effort to educate and inform. However, some population groups devastated by AIDS are difficult to reach through education alone. Injection drug users serve as a prime example. Many researchers feel that checking the spread of AIDS among African Americans must involve removal of the economic and social conditions that create drug abuse, namely crime, unemployment, homelessness, and school truancy. (See AIDS.)

Further Reading. Greaves, Wayne. (1994). AIDS and sexually transmitted diseases. In Ivor L. Livingston (Ed.), *Handbook of black American health.* Westport, CT: Greenwood Press; National Center for Health Statistics (1994). *Health: United States, 1994.* Rockville, MD: Public Health Service; O'Hare, William P., Kevin M. Pollard, Taynia L. Mann, and Mary M. Kent. (1991). *African Americans in the 1990's.* Washington, DC: Population Reference Bureau.

AIDS, CHILDREN AND. While the incidence of childhood AIDS is low—approximately 2 to 3 percent of all AIDS cases—it is growing swiftly. HIV can be transmitted from an infected mother to her fetus or infant before, during, or shortly after birth. (It should be noted, too, that children who receive transfusions of infected blood or blood products may also become infected.) As far as prenatal development is concerned, an infected mother may transmit HIV through the placenta to her unborn child. More rarely, infants have acquired the virus through ingestion of breast milk (HIV has been shown to be present in the breast milk of infected mothers).

Not all babies born to infected mothers will develop AIDS. For those who do, the prognosis is not favorable. Symptoms usually appear about four or five months after birth, and most succumb to infections that attack their weakened immune system before they are three years old. It is rare for these children to live as long as six years. To date, there is no cure for AIDS, although some drugs have been found to slow the progressive deterioration of the immune system.

Infants born with AIDS have certain distinguishing characteristics. Most have a small head, a prominent forehead, protruding lips, a flattened nose bridge, and wideset eyes. Many also have a bluish tinge to the whites of their eyes. Some infants do not seem sick at birth, but most will develop symptoms within eight or nine months. Infected infants often exhibit retarded motor and language growth and other developmental delays, cognitive deficits, and chronic diarrhea. Many have enlarged lymph nodes, liver, and spleen. Like adult victims of the disease, many children with AIDS are susceptible to bacterial infections such as pneumonia.

The spread of AIDS to children has given rise to a number of controversial issues. One, for example, is whether all women who are planning pregnancies should consider HIV-antibody testing. Many people believe that at least women who engage in high-risk sexual behaviors and those who use injection drugs should be tested when they become pregnant, and that those who test positive should be informed of the harmful effects of pregnancy on their own immunological status as well as on that of the fetus. Some researchers have found that the progress of clinical symptoms in HIV-positive, asymptomatic women may be accelerated by pregnancy, perhaps because of the immune alterations that naturally occur during any pregnancy. Other concerns focus on the actual delivery of an infant from an HIV-infected mother. The pediatrician and delivery-room attendants need to be informed ahead of time that the mother is infected because her body fluids and the placenta will contain HIV, and therefore infection-control precautions must be taken.

Further Reading. Rossi, Peter (1992). Early diagnosis of HIV infection in infants. *Journal of Acquired Immune Deficiency Syndromes, 5,* 1169–1178; Turner, Jeffrey S., and Laurna Rubinson. (1993). *Contemporary human sexuality.* Englewood Cliffs, NJ: Prentice Hall; Viscarello, Richard R. (1994). Human immunodeficiency virus infection in obstetrics and gynecology. In Joseph G. Pastorek II (Ed.), *Obstetric and gynecologic infectious disease.* New York: Raven Press.

AIDS, DIAGNOSTIC TESTS FOR. Considerable confusion and legal controversy surround ''AIDS testing'' and the diagnosis of the disease. AIDS cannot be diagnosed simply on the basis of a test. Rather, the diagnosis of AIDS is based on finding evidence of a weakened immune system.

What can be tested is the presence of antibodies produced by the body in response to HIV. This is done with an HIV-antibody test, referred to more specifically as the *ELISA (enzyme-linked immunosorbent assay) test.* While the ELISA test cannot isolate HIV, it can detect whether or not it has been present. Should a person test positive, a second ELISA test is typically given. Should this also be positive, a different test for confirmation is usually administered, called the *Western blot assay.* In 1994, an HIV-antibody test that uses fluid from the mouth instead of blood was approved by the Food and Drug Administration. This test, which measures the presence in the saliva of the antibodies to HIV, is considered useful for those people who would avoid blood tests. However, the blood tests are needed if a person tests positive with the saliva measure.

There are some limitations to HIV-antibody testing. Occasionally a person may have a positive test result even though he or she has never been infected with HIV. This is referred to as a ''false positive'' reaction, and successive testing should clarify this. Also, it is possible that a person who has been infected with HIV will not test positive. This usually happens when someone has not yet produced enough detectable antibodies. While detectable antibodies may develop within 2 months after infection, in some instances it can take up to 36 months for antibodies to appear. If antibody testing is related to a specific exposure, the test should be repeated to take such wide variations into account.

A confirmed, positive test result means that infection from HIV has occurred and that the virus can be transmitted to others. This is true even if no symptoms are present. It therefore becomes important to protect others from getting HIV. Those who test positive for HIV should get a complete medical examination and protect themselves from any further infection. It is possible to become infected with another strain of HIV, and infections of any type may accelerate the development of AIDS. Individuals must inform any previous sexual partners about the positive test result and urge them to seek medical advice and antibody testing from a doctor or health clinic. When medical assistance is sought, they should also inform all health-care practitioners providing care about the positive test result. This enables practitioners to protect both the patient and themselves. Women who test positive should avoid pregnancy until more is known about the risks of transmitting HIV to an unborn fetus. Because HIV has been found in breast milk, breastfeeding should also be avoided.

Further Reading. American Medical Association. (1988). *HIV blood test counseling: AMA physician guidelines.* Chicago: American Medical Association; Schonnesson, Lena N. (1992). *Sexual transmission of HIV infection.* New York: Haworth Press.

AIDS, PREVENTION OF. It is important for individuals to reduce their chances of exposure to HIV by not engaging in high-risk sexual behaviors. To do so, careful choices must be made about sexual activity, and safer sex practices must be followed. Along these lines, individuals should not have sex with multiple partners, or with persons who have had multiple partners (including prostitutes). The more partners one has, the greater the risk of contracting HIV. Also, one must not have sex with persons with AIDS, with people at risk for AIDS, or with persons who have had a positive result on the HIV-antibody test.

It is important for persons to know their sexual partners well before having sex. Prospective partners should be asked about their health and sexual history and what safety precautions they have used. If an individual or a partner is at high risk, oral contact with the vagina or penis should be avoided. Also, precautions should be taken to prevent contact with that person's body fluids.

Latex condoms must be used during sex from start to finish. Next to abstinence, a latex condom is the best way to reduce HIV risk during vaginal intercourse. Condoms made of natural materials such as lambs' intestines are not effective in preventing the transmission of HIV. Latex condoms must be used only with a water-soluble lubricant such as KY Jelly, or a contraceptive spermicide. Non-water-soluble lubricants such as petroleum jelly weaken condoms and increase the chances that they will tear during use.

All sexual activities (e.g., sadomasochistic acts designed to give and/or receive pain) that could cause cuts or tears in the linings of the rectum, vagina, or penis should be avoided. Other high-risk sexual activities include oral sex on a man without a latex condom; oral sex on a woman during her period or a vaginal infection with discharge without a rubber dam (a piece of latex, similar to that used in dental work, to cover the vulval and vaginal opening during oral sex); taking semen into the mouth; oral-anal contact; and sharing sex toys or douching equipment. Sharing needles in injection drug use is also a high-risk activity.

Finally, the mixing of alcohol or other drugs with sexual encounters is considered a potentially risky situation. Drugs tend to cloud rational thinking and can lead individuals to do things they would not do with a clearer head—such as having sex without using a condom. Moreover, there is some evidence that alcohol and drugs may suppress the immune system. (See SEXUALLY TRANSMITTED DISEASES, SAFER SEX AND THE PREVENTION OF.)

Further Reading. Core-Gebhart, Pennie, Susan J. Hart, and Michael Young. (1991). *Living smart: Understanding sexuality into adulthood.* Fayetteville: University of Arkansas Press; Hylton, Judith. (1990). *SAFE: Stopping AIDS through functional education.* Portland, OR: Portland Metropolitan Task Force on HIV/AIDS; Yarber, William L. (1993). *STDs and HIV.* Reston, VA: American Alliance for Health, Physical Education, Recreation, and Dance.

AIDS, WORLDWIDE RATES OF INFECTION. Worldwide, AIDS is widespread, having been reported in more than 125 nations. In the vast majority of cases, HIV has been transmitted through sexual intercourse. It is estimated that between 10 and 13 million persons worldwide may be infected with HIV, and this figure is expected to mushroom even more during this decade. Worldwide, there is one new HIV infection every 15–20 seconds.

Experts predict that worldwide, 40 million people will be infected with HIV by the year 2000. Two-thirds of the world's estimated AIDS cases are in central, eastern, and southern regions of Africa, where researchers believe that HIV may have originated. As many as 2 or 3 million Africans may be HIV carriers, and the number of women infected roughly equals the number of men. Already, 1.2 million Africans have died of AIDS. Because many of the infected women are in their prime, HIV transmission from mother to child is an increasing problem. In 1993, about 500,000 children carrying HIV were born in Africa.

The adult populations of some entire villages in Africa have already been destroyed by the disease. Moreover, in many African countries, AIDS is the leading cause of death among young adults. In Uganda, the number of AIDS cases is doubling every six months. In Rwanda, about 20 percent of the AIDS victims are children. The number of Africans infected is forecast to reach 20 million by the end of the century, by which time AIDS is expected to be killing 1 million Africans a year. (See SUB-SAHARAN AFRICA, LIFESPAN RELATIONSHIPS IN.)

In other parts of the world, rates of HIV infection and death from AIDS are on the rise. For example, in Latin America and the Caribbean, there have been about 1.5 million cumulative adult HIV infections, including AIDS cases and deaths. For South and Southeast Asia, the corresponding figure is 1.5 million, and for Western Europe, the figure approaches 500,000. In India, an estimated 1 million persons are infected with HIV. India faces the prospect of 15–20 million infections by the year 2000.

Further Reading. Feldman, Douglas A. (Ed.). (1994). *Global AIDS policy.* Westport, CT: Bergin and Garvey; Pollak, Michael. (1993). *The second plague of Europe.* New York: Harrington Park Press; Sabatier, Renee. (1988). *Blaming others: Prejudice, race, and worldwide AIDS.* Philadelphia, PA: New Society Publishers. Author.

ALIMONY. See DIVORCE, LEGAL ASPECTS OF.

ALLPORT, GORDON. Gordon Allport (1897–1967) was born in Montezuma, Indiana, and received his Ph.D. degree from Harvard University in 1922.

Although he was originally interested in philosophy and economics, he developed a strong interest in psychology, especially the study of personality. Following his graduation, Allport traveled abroad for two years and studied in a number of European cities, including Berlin, Hamburg, and Cambridge. During this time, Allport had the opportunity to meet and share ideas with a number of notable psychologists, including Sigmund Freud.

After serving as an assistant professor of psychology at Dartmouth College, Allport returned to Harvard University in 1930. In 1937, he was appointed chairman of the psychology department and earned the distinction of being appointed the first Richard Cabot Professor of Social Ethics. Remaining at Harvard until his death in 1967, Allport was also instrumental in developing the Department of Social Relations at the university.

Allport's contributions to the field of psychology are both numerous and diverse. His most significant involvement was in the areas of personality and social psychology, including an extensive investigation of adult maturity, values, and communication. His analysis of maturity, in particular, helps us to better understand how intimate relationships are forged and maintained throughout the course of adult life. He described how mature adults bring recognized skills and competencies to their relationships, including heightened levels of self-insight and understanding. Mature adults have learned to accept themselves as well as their partners, including shortcomings and weaknesses. In addition, their interactions are characterized by such important dimensions as empathy, confidence in self-expression, and a realistic appraisal of needs and purposes. From Allport's perspective, all of these factors contribute to the likelihood that a relationship will be guided by a common purpose and by shared goals and values.

Allport was president of the American Psychological Association in 1937 and served as editor of the *Journal of Abnormal and Social Psychology* from 1937 to 1949. During his professional career, he received numerous honors and awards, including the American Psychological Association Distinguished Scientific Contribution Award in 1959.

Further Reading. Allport, Gordon W. (1937). *Personality: A psychological interpretation.* New York: Holt, Rinehart and Winston; Allport, Gordon W. (1955). *Becoming: Basic considerations for a psychology of personality.* New Haven, CT: Yale University Press; Allport, Gordon W. (1961). *Pattern and growth in personality.* New York: Holt, Rinehart and Winston; Feist, Jess. (1994). *Theories of personality* (3rd Ed.). Fort Worth, TX: Harcourt Brace.

ANCIENT EGYPT, LIFESPAN RELATIONSHIPS IN. The Egyptian civilization rose to power over 5000 years ago and existed for nearly 2500 years. As with their Mesopotamian neighbors, farming was one of the chief Egyptian enterprises. Most Egyptians lived near the Nile for this purpose, an area rich with fertile soil.

The Egyptians divided themselves into four social classes: the royalty and nobles; artisans, craftsmen, and merchants; workers; and slaves. In time, Egypt's professional army almost became a separate class. At no point in their civilization did the Egyptians have a fixed caste system. This meant, among other things, that a person of the poorest class could rise to the highest class.

Egyptian men and women married early: the average age for men was 15 and for women, 13. A husband could take more than one wife, and if he was wealthy enough, he could keep a harem. While the husband was clearly the dominant figure in the marital arrangement, Egyptian women were held in high regard. They were the recipients of much affection from their husbands, and some of their social and legal privileges reflected the respect accorded to them. For example, Egyptian women could own property and level court suits.

Interestingly, while the husband ruled the family, Egyptians practiced *matrilineal* descent. That is, all property descended in the female line from mother to daughter. When a man married an heiress, he enjoyed her property only as long as his wife lived. On her death it passed to her daughter and her daughter's husband.

The practice of matrilineal descent helps to explain why Egyptians accepted marriage between brothers and sisters. Such marriages were very evident in royal families, with many pharaohs marrying their sisters or even their infant daughters. The marriages of Cleopatra serve as an excellent illustration of matrilineal descent. Cleopatra first married her eldest brother, whose right to the throne was thus established. When he died, Cleopatra married her younger brother, who ruled by right of this marriage. There were no children by either of these unions. When Caesar conquered Egypt, he in turn had to marry Cleopatra to make his accession legal in the eyes of the Egyptian people. Next came Marc Antony, who by marrying Cleopatra secured the throne. She had a son by Caesar and a son and a daughter by Antony. When Antony fell and Octavius arrived, he too was ready to espouse the much-married queen.

Children were very much a part of married life in Egypt, and large families were encouraged. The Egyptians held children in high esteem, and parents were very protective toward them. This is suggested by the numerous depictions of children that adorn the tomb walls at Memphis, Amarna, and Thebes. The young were viewed as essential parts of a growing civilization and were reared with care and concern. Supportive of this is the fact that as early as 1500 B.C., treatment for childhood diseases was prescribed, different from that given to adults.

The principal occupation of most Egyptian mothers was homemaking, a busy combination of activities. When children were reared, the infant was strapped to the mother virtually all of the time. Usually, babies were carried against the breast in a pouch suspended from the mother's neck. Children were raised to respect the devotion and dedication exhibited by Egyptian mothers. Egyptian youths were also advised to repay their parents for all the care that they received. Usually this meant caring for them as they became older and making certain that all of their needs were met.

Divorces were fairly easy to obtain in ancient Egypt, although they were not widespread. Witnesses were needed to make a divorce legal, and a man had to make financial provisions for his divorced wife. Should a wife want to divorce her husband, she too had to make arrangements for some form of compensation. **Further Reading.** Alfred, Cyril. (1961). *The Egyptians.* New York: Praeger; Champollion, Jacques. (1982). *The Egyptians.* Geneva: Minerva; Wilson, John A. (1963). *The culture of ancient Egypt.* Chicago: Phoenix Books.

ANCIENT FAR EAST, LIFESPAN RELATIONSHIPS IN THE.
The ancient Far East refers to a land region in the easternmost regions of Asia, particularly the countries of Japan, China, and Korea. Unlike its highly industrialized profile today, the ancient Far East was chiefly agricultural. Most of the people in these largely mountainous areas lived on coastal plains and tended to such crops as rice, tea, and spices.

Marriage was seen as a desirable arrangement and a legitimate way to bring children into the world. Parents arranged most marriages, and a patriarchal power structure characterized the household. It was customary for the wife to handle all aspects of the household, while the husband was in charge of the outside world. This meant that he was the principal decision maker and wage earner, while she assumed primary responsibility for domestic chores and child rearing.

At early ages, children were expected to make meaningful contributions to the household, and they were taught the importance of meaningful work, self-discipline, and dignity. Throughout the Far East, children were raised to be cooperative and obedient and to defer to their parents' wishes. Children were also taught to honor and revere the elderly, who were regarded as integral and valued members of society. Strong intergenerational relations, including supportive assistance between young and old, characterized the kin network in the ancient Far East.

The ancient Japanese and Chinese enjoyed very open and liberal forms of sexual expression. Sex was regarded as an important expression of human functioning, and men and women were encouraged to maximize its enjoyment. For many, sex was seen as a physical act capable of creating spirituality and perfect harmony. Such perceptions were particularly prevalent in ancient China under Confucian and Taoist influences.

The ancient Far East was noted for its depiction of sexual intimacy in rich erotic art. A wide range of artistic representations captured couples engaging in sexual intercourse, oral sex, and other forms of sexual intimacy. As in ancient India, Japanese and Chinese sex manuals offered readers glorified accounts of sexual pleasures. In ancient China, for example, "pillow books" provided newly married couples with narratives of sexual pleasuring techniques.
Further Reading. Frayser, Suzanne G. (1985). *Varieties of sexual experience: An anthropological perspective on human sexuality.* New Haven, CT: HRAF Press; Gregersen, Edgar. (1983). *Sexual practices.* New York: Franklin Watts: Schoonover-Smith, Linda. (1990). Human sexuality from a cultural perspective. In Catherine I. Fogel and Diane Lauver (Eds.). *Sexual health promotion.* Philadelphia: W. B. Saunders.

ANCIENT GREECE, LIFESPAN RELATIONSHIPS IN. The ancient
Greeks of 2,500 years ago called themselves Hellenes and their land Hellas.
While they never formed a national government, the Greeks were united by a
common culture, religion, and language. The classes in Greek society varied
from one city-state to another. Athens, for example, had three classes: citizens,
slaves, and metics, or resident aliens.

Marriage in ancient Greece was regarded as a means of producing legitimate
children and perpetuating the civilization. Many of the marriages were arranged
by families, often with little regard for the inclinations of the parties involved.
Greek brides were expected to be virgins, but this expectation was not leveled
against the bridegroom.

As far as structure was concerned, marriages were monogamous and, consistent with other civilizations, patriarchal. Greek women were often viewed as
inferior to men and were expected to be subservient. The perceived inferiority
of women was a persistent theme in Greek literature. Plato, for example, wrote
that there was not one branch of human industry in which the female sex was
not inferior to the male. While women possessed similar capacities and powers,
he felt that they were weaker and less competent overall. As far as intergenerational relations were concerned, the ancient Greeks respected the elderly for
the wisdom they possessed. The aged were cared for by younger family members
and were neither rejected nor ignored.

The ancient Greeks practiced *infanticide,* the killing off of children born weak,
deformed, or mutant (see CHILD REARING, HISTORICAL PRACTICES IN).
Good health and fitness were continually emphasized so that children could fill
the needs of this civilization. In Sparta, for example, an ancestral influence of
military preparation and a strict social code prevailed. Children were brought up
under rigid disciplinary measures and were viewed as a necessity for the continued existence of Spartan civilization in the Hellenic world. Upon birth it was
necessary for the parents to have the child's health status examined by a council
of elders. Babies pronounced in good health were automatically adopted by the
state, but were left in the home until seven years of age.

In most Spartan families, boys and girls grew up together under the supervision of the mother, but in wealthy families, an older house slave cared for the
young. Attempts to discipline the mind and body began shortly after birth. Swad-
dling was not permitted by the state, since it was thought that physical growth
might be hampered in the process. Children left alone in the dark were not
permitted to scream or cry out, the belief being that self-control should be taught
as early as possible. At the age of seven, Spartan boys were removed to the
state's barracks to begin their training in the military. Girls remained at home
and learned domestic responsibilities.

As in Sparta, the infant in Athens was examined at birth and exposed to die
at the mercy of the elements if judged unfit or deformed. The Athenians emphasized the importance of physical fitness during early childhood; however, it
took the form of gymnastics more than military skills. Unlike the Spartans,

however, the Athenians sought to educate the child's mind as well as the body. Greater responsibility and authority were given to the parents in regard to the child's upbringing. For example, the father, not the state, decided whether an infant should live or die, and Athenian parents were not required to send their boys away for military training.

Further Reading. Hooper, Finley. (1967). *Greek realities: Life and thought in ancient Greece.* London: Rupert Hart-Davis; Jaeger, Werner. (1945). *Paideia: The ideals of Greek culture.* (Vol. 3). New York: Oxford University Press; Milreaux, Emile. (1959). *Daily life in the time of Homer.* New York: Macmillan.

ANCIENT HEBREWS, LIFESPAN RELATIONSHIPS AMONG THE.

The ancient Hebrews were a nomadic desert people initially led by Abraham, his son Isaac, and his grandson Jacob around 1900 B.C. Jacob, who was also called Israel, had 12 sons. These 12 sons headed 12 tribes that came to characterize the Jewish people. This is why the Jews came to be known as the children of Israel or Israelites.

Many of the ancient Hebrews traveled to Canaan, an area later called Palestine. Here they lived for many years tending to their flocks of sheep or farming. The ancient Jews eventually became a nation with a king, a capital, and a temple at Jerusalem. This also heralded a social class system, with aristocracy and military dignitaries occupying the upper division and the working class, landless, and debtors on the lowest position.

Like the Egyptians, the ancient Hebrews married at young ages. The wedding was a simple affair, arranged by the fathers of the bride and groom. During early centuries, there was a purchase price for the wife, most often in the form of goods and services. In later centuries, a dowry was required (see MARITAL EXCHANGES). The wedding was a domestic ceremony that did not require the participation of a priest or magistrate.

The Hebrew marriage was patriarchal in scope. Polygyny was also recognized by Hebrew law, and its practice extended into the Middle Ages. The husband wielded considerable influence within the family, evidenced by the power of life and death that he could wield over his wife and children. He could sell his children or divorce his wife without much of a reason if he so desired. He could also have his wife put to death for adultery.

Obviously, this meant that the Hebrew wife played a subservient role, although she was respected by her husband. She was expected to obey her partner, bear his children, and perform the customary domestic chores. While the husband tended the flocks or tilled the soil, she typically saw to the cooking, weaving, and child-rearing obligations.

The Bible of the Hebrews was the Old Testament, and within it were directives for their existence. Those men most knowledgeable about the Hebraic laws were held in high esteem. Paramount among the laws was God's directive to "be fruitful and multiply." Procreation was extremely important so that family lineage could be maintained and the tribes of Israel could be perpetuated. Sons in particular were desired to carry on the family line. Nonreproductive sex was discouraged among the Hebrews since it was perceived as not fulfilling any useful purpose.

The Hebrew family produced as a unit and consumed as a unit. At an early age, children were expected to contribute to the household: boys typically helped their fathers tend the sheep, while girls assisted with the preparation of food. Strict discipline was employed by both parents in an effort to discourage irresponsibility and foolishness. Obedience was demanded, and the duty and obligation that children had to their father were second only to that to God. Also, the elderly were to be respected, consulted on family matters, and cared for during their later lives.

Further Reading. Daniel-Rops, Henri. (1964). *Israel and the ancient world.* Garden City, NY: Doubleday; Finkelstein, Louis. (1960). *The Jews: Their history, culture, and religion.* New York: Harper and Brothers; Meck, Theophile J. (1960). *Hebrew origins.* New York: Harper and Brothers.

ANCIENT INDIA, LIFESPAN RELATIONSHIPS IN. Many different races and religions characterized life in ancient India, one of the largest nations in the world. However, most of the people were followers of Hinduism, one of the oldest and largest major religions. Hinduism developed over thousands of years. Many cultures helped to shape Hinduism, and the religion itself includes beliefs about divinities, how followers should conduct their lives, and life after death. Hinduism has many sacred writings, including the Vedas, the Puranas, and the Manu Smriti.

As in many other civilizations, traditional gender roles characterized ancient Indian society. Women were subservient to men, and children were taught at early ages to conform to these societal expectations. Premarital sex was frowned upon, and most marriages were arranged by parents with careful attention to similarity of backgrounds. Adultery was condemned in ancient India, as were incest and rape.

Marital structure in ancient India was patriarchal in scope. The husband controlled household decision making and was the legal owner of the family belongings and property. A wife's primary responsibilities were to bear children and tend to the day-to-day operation of the household. The birth of male children, in particular, enhanced a woman's status, since sons were of greater economic value to the family. Elderly family members were respected and typically consulted on matters of importance to the family. Close ties usually existed between old and young Indian family members, and the elderly were given supportive care in times of need.

Hindu society regarded sexual expression as an important component of life. While a variety of different approaches to sexual behavior existed, many Hindus were taught that sex was an activity to be enjoyed and not repressed. This philosophy was evidenced in the *Kama Sutra,* a sex manual written for women and men in the fourth century. The *Kama Sutra* (meaning ''precepts of pleasure'') was considered to be a revelation of the gods and contained detailed descriptions of the male and female sexual organs as well as coital positions and pleasuring techniques. (See RELIGION, IMPACT OF ON INTIMATE RE-LATIONSHIPS.)

Further Reading. de Bary, William Theodore. (1958). *Sources of Indian tradition.* New York: Columbia University Press; Masson-Dunsel, Paul. (1967). *Ancient India and Indian civilization.* New York: Barnes and Noble; Sengupta, Padmini. (1950). *Everyday life in ancient India.* London: Oxford University Press.

ANCIENT ROME, LIFESPAN RELATIONSHIPS IN. At its height in A.D. 117, the Roman Empire included about a fourth of Europe, much of the Middle East, and the entire northern coastal area of Africa. While its millions of people spoke many languages and worshipped different gods, Romans were united by the empire's government and military power. The Roman Empire fell about 1,500 years ago. Roman society had two main divisions: citizens and noncitizens. Citizens included the ruling class of senatorial aristocracy; equites, a group of wealthy businessmen; and plebeians, or lower-class citizens. Noncitizens included aliens and slaves.

As in earlier civilizations, romance often had little to do with the Roman approach to marriage. Roman fathers chose wives for their sons, and the marriage itself was viewed as a private arrangement made between families. Betrothals were common in Rome, usually consisting of a number of presents from the bridegroom to the bride. A wedding ring was also given to the bride, which she immediately slipped onto her finger. The ring usually consisted of a circle of iron set in gold or a plain circle of gold. While there is some speculation that the ancient Egyptians made use of the wedding ring, it is known for certain that the Romans had this custom.

As far as the wedding ceremony itself was concerned, a sacrifice to the gods was first made: sometimes a ewe, but most often a pig. Ten witnesses and a selected official observed the exchange of vows and affixed their seals to the marriage contract, if one was desired. Following hours of festivities, a procession led by flute players and torchbearers brought the newly married couple to the husband's home.

The Roman family was patriarchal, and should unhappiness prevail, a divorce was relatively easy for the husband to obtain. The success of a marriage was often judged by the number of children brought into the world, preferably boys. Large families were continually stressed, particularly during the rule of Augustus Caesar, who offered material rewards to parents who could conceive three healthy male children. If this goal was attained, the mother was given full legal independence, while the father usually received some form of promotion in his career.

Like earlier civilizations, the Romans had no use for weak or deformed children since they could not be counted on for future civilian manpower or service in the army. When these unfortunate children were born, the parents generally decided upon infanticide, usually after consultation with five neighbors, who had to agree with the parent's sentence if it was to be carried out. Until the fourth century A.D., neither public opinion or law found infanticide to be morally wrong.

The children of Rome grew up chiefly under the mother's care. At six years, however, the boy was instructed by the father on how to become a respectful citizen, to till the ground, and to carry arms. Fathers also stressed physical fitness; they sought to teach their boys how to endure heat and cold and to survive other physical hardships. Girls, on the other hand, were instructed by the mother to learn how to prepare food, cook, and make clothes. As far as intergenerational relations were concerned, the elderly were valued members of the family unit. In times of need, younger family members—most often wives and daughters—supplied care and assistance to the elderly.

Further Reading. Frank, Tenney. (1932). *Aspects of social behavior in ancient Rome.* Cambridge, MA: Harvard University Press; Heichelheim, Fritz M. (1962). *A history of the Roman people.* Englewood Cliffs, NJ: Prentice-Hall; Starr, Chester. (1971). *The ancient Romans.* New York: Oxford University Press.

ANDROGYNY. Androgyny is a blending of typical male and female personality traits and behaviors in one person. According to this notion, both male and female characteristics are beneficial and important to possess. Androgynous persons view themselves as human beings, not as typecast males or females. Because they do not view personality traits as compartmentalized by sex, androgynous men and women feel free to be nurturant, assertive, sensitive, dominant, affectionate, and self-sufficient.

Being androgynous appears to have beneficial effects. Compared to people who exhibit traditional gender-role behaviors, androgynous individuals seem more competent and demonstrate higher levels of self-esteem. In addition, androgynous persons seem to be more successful in maintaining good interpersonal relationships, and they tend to deal more effectively with their surroundings, including situations involving stress. They also tend to be more secure with themselves, more flexible in their behavior, and less anxious.

Not everyone, though, agrees on the concept of androgyny or its perceived benefits. Some researchers feel that the concept of androgyny is too vague, trendy, and difficult to measure. Some argue that many gender-role behaviors such as male assertiveness and female nurturance have been in existence for years and will not budge to androgynous pressures. Other critics maintain that androgyny is a questionable model of psychological adaptation because it suggests that a person can be totally self-sufficient, completely feminine and masculine at the same time. Some maintain that focusing on androgyny draws attention away from women's real needs in society, including the power imbalance that exists between women and men.

However, proponents of androgyny maintain that the removal of gender-typed behavioral constraints would allow men and women to demonstrate the best qualities of both sexes. Proponents argue that children, especially, would benefit from a more tolerant acceptance of their total selves, rather than being continually told how society expects them to behave. Within the context of intimate relationships, androgynous couples seek to transcend traditional gender-role boundaries. Such boundaries often support the expectation that the female partner is to be directed by the male and that his wishes take priority. In androgynous relationships, there are no such boundaries; rather, the needs and wishes of both partners are always taken into consideration and discrepancies minimized.

Further Reading. Bem, Sandra L. (1974). The measurement of psychological androgyny. *Journal of Consulting and Clinical Psychology, 42,* 155–162; Hyde, Janet. (1991). *Half the human experience: The psychology of women* (4th Ed.). Lexington, MA: D. C. Health and Company; Matlin, Margaret W. (1993). *The psychology of women* (2nd Ed.). Fort Worth, TX: Harcourt Brace Jovanovich College Publishers.

ANNULMENT. Annulment is the invalidation of a marriage on the basis of some reason that existed at the beginning of that marriage. As a form of marital dissolution, annulment is less common than divorce. Some of the acceptable reasons for a legal annulment are insanity, fraud, and being underage. Other reasons pertain to marriages prohibited by law, such as incestuous and bigamous relationships.

Further Reading. Ruback, Barry. (1985). Family law. In Luciano L'Abate (Ed.), *The handbook of family psychology and therapy.* Homewood, IL: Dorsey Press; Turner, Jeffrey S., and Donald B. Helms. (1988). *Marriage and family: Traditions and transitions.* San Diego, CA: Harcourt Brace Jovanovich.

ANTINATALISM. See PRONATALISM.

ASIAN AMERICANS, LIFESPAN RELATIONSHIPS AMONG. Asian Americans, who include both Asians and Pacific Islanders, represent the fastest-growing minority group in the United States today. Asian Americans may be the most diverse of America's minority groups. They come from more than two dozen countries and do not share a common language, a common religion, or a common cultural background. Asian Americans number approximately 8 million persons, almost 3 percent of the total population. About 85 percent of all Asian Americans are in six groups: Chinese, Filipino, Japanese, Asian Indian, Korean, and Vietnamese. Of these, Chinese, Filipino, and Japanese represent the largest groups. Asian Americans tend to be concentrated in the western areas of the United States, particularly California.

Given the fact that Asian Americans come from many different countries and are such diverse people, many differences exist between groups. However, it is known that Asian Americans overall are as likely as non-Hispanic whites to have graduated from high school and are more likely to have graduated from college. Compared to other minority groups, they are more apt to work in professional and white-collar occupations. The median family income of Asian

Americans is slightly higher than that of non-Hispanic whites. However, a mixed picture of achievement often accompanies the socioeconomic status of Asian Americans. For example, many Asian immigrants earn low salaries and are hampered by their inability to speak English when they first arrive in the United States. This is especially true for recent refugees from Southeast Asia, many of whom are poor and uneducated.

As far as marital relationships are concerned, Asian Americans tend to marry later and experience less marital dissolution. Whites between the ages of 30 and 44 are almost twice as likely as Asian Americans to be divorced or separated. About 17 percent of all Asian-American marriages are of an interracial nature, with Japanese-American women and white men, and Filipino-American women and white men, being the most common marital arrangements. The interracial-marriage rate among Asian Americans is about the same as it is for Hispanic Americans.

Regarding family structure, more than three-quarters of Asian Americans live in married-couple families, and female-headed families account for about 7 percent of all Asian-American households. Asian Americans are also more than twice as likely as non-Hispanic white families to double up in households. The probability of a parent and a grown child living together is about five times higher among Asian Americans than it is in the total population. Also, the probability of an adult residing with a sibling is three times higher in the Asian-American community than in the non-Hispanic white population.

Asian Americans tend to have a lower fertility rate and consequently smaller families than other minorities. The average total number of children an Asian-American woman will have is about 2.3. Asian-American women tend to have their first child at later ages than do other minority groups, most during their 30s. This is a fertility trend that contributes not only to a smaller family size, but also to greater levels of economic well-being. Delayed parenthood increases opportunities for higher education and usually leads to better-paying jobs. Also, adolescent pregnancy is not widespread among Asian Americans.

Asian-American parenting styles tend to be authoritarian rather than permissive, and disciplinary strategies are more verbal than physical. Child rearing continually reflects the cultural emphasis placed on family loyalty and togetherness. Parents promote family honor as well as respect for elders. Children also learn that cooperation with others, pacifism, self-control, and self-discipline are desired character traits. These are all values linked to Confucianism, especially among Chinese, Koreans, Vietnamese, and Japanese. Within the home, children are also taught traditional gender roles, with the father being recognized as the undisputed head of the household. Such teachings are part of a social order in which there is a hierarchy of interpersonal relations; that is, parents are superior to children, and men are superior to women.

Other segments of the Asian-American population offer unique parallels to the foregoing parenting styles. For example, a strong patriarchal structure characterizes the households of most Asian Indians, and such Hindu values as honor and family loyalty are used to guide children's development. Most Asian-Indian boys and girls are taught traditional gender roles and learn at an early age to defer to their parents' wishes. While the importance of close sibling relationships is stressed in most Asian-American homes, this is particularly evident among Asian Indians, Pakistanis, and Cambodians. Finally, most Asian-American children, including Filipino and Vietnamese youngsters, are taught the importance of determination and dedication, particularly if one expects to succeed and get ahead in the world.

This early cultural emphasis placed on hard work, effort, and achievement shapes the schooling and educational experiences of Asian-American youth. Parents encourage their children to study hard, and proper attitudes toward school are continually emphasized. Education is seen as the key to a good job and a promising future. The earlier-mentioned educational accomplishments of Asian-American youth illustrate the emphasis placed on academic achievement. About 90 percent of Asian Americans graduate from high school, and they are more likely than whites to finish four or more years of college. Furthermore, Asian Americans are more likely to excel in graduate-school education. Almost one out of seven aged 25 or older (about 15 percent) hold a graduate or professional degree, almost twice the percentage for whites and almost four times the rates for other minority groups.

The strong emphasis placed on family relationships among Asian Americans is reflected in the care given to elders. Under the influence of Confucian ideology, which stresses children's moral obligation to care for and respect aged family, Asian-American elderly are the recipients of considerable social support. Because many Asian Americans live in close proximity to one another, contact and assistance are regular. Given such frequent contact, many Asian-American families are able to maintain the concept of "filial piety" and the values deemed influential to family life. Thus the family remains the focus of an elderly person's life, an instrumental source of support, companionship, and satisfaction.

Further Reading. Barringer, Herbert R., Robert W. Gardner, and Michael J. Levin. (1993). *Asians and Pacific Islanders in the United States.* New York: Russell Sage Foundation; Chan, Sucheng. (1991). *Asian Americans: An interpretive history.* Boston: Twayne; O'Brien, David J., and Stephen S. Fugita. (1991). *The Japanese-American experience.* Bloomington: Indiana University Press; O'Hare, William P., and Judy C. Felt. (1991). *Asian Americans: America's fastest growing minority group.* Washington, DC: Population Reference Bureau.

ATTACHMENT, EARLY PARENT-INFANT. Attachment, defined as the affectionate bond that exists between infant and caregiver, is a vital component of healthy personality and social functioning. Attachment serves as the first close relationship with another person and teaches the infant that others can be trusted. One's general tendency to be outgoing and friendly, as well as one's degree of social independence, temperament, and emotional investments in others, may be traced to the outcome of early attachment experiences. In this way, infant attachments help determine the type of social animal that we become, including the degree of comfort we feel in the presence of others.

There are several visible clues to developing attachment behaviors. One of these is the infant's smiling responses. During the first month, the infant may form a *reflex smile*. This smile is primarily physiological and may be the infant's response to a number of different stimuli, including internal stimulation (a bubble of gas in the stomach), being fed, or being stroked on the cheek. Reflexive smiles are not socially oriented.

The *social smile* appears during the second or third month of life. This is true smiling as we know it and can be evoked by the appearance of a caregiver, a voice, movement, or certain noises. Many infants smile, open their eyes wide, and make cooing noises at the same time, called a "greeting response." A caregiver's returning the greeting response often prompts the infant to continue this behavior.

The *selective social smile* occurs around five to six months of age. Instead of smiling in an undifferentiated way, as in the social smile, the infant now directs the smile only to familiar social stimuli, such as the mother or other familiar caregivers. Unfamiliar faces are readily detected at this age and cause the infant's withdrawal behavior.

The selective social smile is linked to another clue of developing attachment behavior called *stranger anxiety*. During the first six months of life, infants do not express distress toward unfamiliar faces. At about the age of six months, though, anxiety and wariness are apparent when strangers are introduced. The infant is evidently able to detect a noticeable difference in the stranger's face, as compared with the mental image of the caregiver's features stored in his or her developing mind. Growing levels of cognitive awareness are thus connected to stranger anxiety as well as to the development of the social smile.

Another indication of attachment is *separation anxiety,* which occurs by approximately the twelfth month. Separation from the caregiver is likely to result in the infant's considerable protest and distress. However, the infant's degree of protest and distress is affected by the situation in which he or she is left. For example, an infant's familiarity with the environment, including objects as well as people, as well as the possession of a transitional object (e.g., a huggable doll or stuffed animal) for some, tends to reduce anxious feelings and protest levels. (See INFANCY AND TODDLERHOOD, DEVELOPMENT OF TRUST DURING.)

Further Reading. Bowlby, John. (1988). *A secure base: Parent-child attachment and healthy human development.* New York: Basic Books; Brazelton, T. Berry. (1990). *The earliest relationship: Parents, infants, and the drama of early attachment.* Reading, MA: Addison-Wesley; Cortez, Jesus. (Ed.). (1992). *Infant-toddler caregiving.* Sacramento, CA: California State Department of Education; Lamb, Michael E., and Marc H. Bornstein. (1987). *Development in infancy.* New York: Random House.

ATTACHMENT, THEORIES OF. Theories of attachment are designed to explain how and why attachment behavior occurs, including what factors determine the strength of attachment bonds. Among the more important theories are the behavioral, cognitive-developmental, ethological, and psychoanalytic perspectives.

Behavioral theory stresses that attachment is a learned, rather than an innate, process. This viewpoint suggests that attachment is a series of stimulus-response mechanisms, much as many other childhood behaviors are. It is reasoned that the mother, or other caregiver, who is initially a neutral stimulus, acquires secondary reinforcing properties over time. Infants learn that the mother is the agent responsible for their primary reinforcers, such as tactile stimulation, milk, or warmth. Because she is continually associated with the dispensing of these primary reinforcers and with the satisfaction of the infant's basic needs, her continual physical presence becomes important to the infant.

Cognitive-developmental theory views the attachment process as a reflection of the infant's developing mental abilities. Attachment and proximity-seeking behavior ensue because the infant is cognitively aware of the perceptual differences between the mother and others in the environment. Attachment is further strengthened when the infant understands *person permanence,* the realization that the caregiver can exist even though she may not be physically present in the same room. The child's ability to construct a mental image of the mother's distinguishing characteristics will result in more proximity-seeking behavior.

Ethology theory proposes that an infant's social responsiveness develops largely through innate or inborn tendencies. A critical period during the early months of life is said to make the infant especially receptive to the caregiver (see CRITICAL PERIOD). During infancy, these innate systems are activated by the environment, and their expression elicits specific responses from the caregiver. Infant behaviors such as clinging and sucking promote close contact with the mother. Crying and distress capture the caregiver's attention, as do smiling and cooing. Later, infants call their mothers and follow them, further strengthening the bond between the two. Combined, these behaviors result in physical nearness and attachment to the caregiver. As history reveals, infants who can maintain this closeness have the best hope for survival.

Psychoanalytic theory, similar to the ethological approach, emphasizes instincts. Attachment is regarded as an emotional relationship shaped by the Freudian concept of instinctive energy (see PSYCHOANALYTIC THEORY; PSYCHOSEXUAL DEVELOPMENT). During the child's psychosexual stages of development, this energy is directed toward the mother because she is perceived as a source of pleasure and satisfaction. As the child's primitive needs are met during the oral and anal stages, bonds of attachment strengthen, and the mother is recognized as an object of both affection and security.

These theoretical perspectives offer contrasting views on the nature of attachment. Behavioral theory emphasizes how attachment is the result of environmental conditioning, particularly the notion of reinforcement. Cognitive-developmental theory chooses to stress the role of maturing mental abilities. While ethology theory underscores the importance of inborn tendencies, psychoanalytic theory relates attachment behaviors to instinctive energy shaping the developing personality.

Further Reading. Johnson, Daniel, and Edith Fein. (1991). The concept of attachment. *Children and Youth Services Review, 13,* 397–412; Kagan, Jerome. (1984). *The nature of the child.* New York: Basic Books; Krantz, Murray. (1994). *Child development: Risk and opportunity.* Belmont, CA: Wadsworth: Schneider, E. Lynn. (1991). Attachment theory and research: Review of the literature. *Clinical Social Work Journal, 19,* 251–266.

AUSTRALIA, LIFESPAN RELATIONSHIPS IN. Australia is the only continent in the world that is also a country. Australia is a member of the British Commonwealth of Nations and is composed of six states and two mainland territories. The states are New South Wales, Queensland, South Australia, Tasmania, Victoria, and Western Australia. The two mainland territories are the Northern Territory and the Australian Capital Territory. According to recent census figures, Australia has a population of about 17,000,000. A significant majority of the population lives in urban areas.

Most of Australia's population today is of British origin. As far as ethnic groupings are concerned, about 95 percent of the population is European, 4 percent is Asian, and about 1 percent is aboriginal. The aborigines were the original settlers of Australia, having arrived on the continent about 12,000 years ago from Southeast Asia. Almost all Australians are Christians, with the Church of England (Anglican church) being the largest religious group, followed by the Roman Catholic, Methodist, and Presbyterian churches.

The dating relationships of Australian adolescents tend to follow many of the patterns exhibited by U.S. teenagers. For example, dating typically begins by early or middle adolescence, and a substantial proportion of teenagers are sexually active. Adolescent males are more sexually active than females, and the percentage of adolescents who have premarital intercourse increases with age. Australian researchers have estimated that by age 20, about 60 percent of males and 50 percent of females have experienced coitus. Increased sexual activity among the young has prompted many Australian school systems to implement sexuality education programming.

Like adolescents in other nations, many Australian teenagers do not consistently use reliable forms of contraception at first intercourse. While contraceptive use improves with age, many do not initially use birth control for a variety of reasons: lack of knowledge, peer-group pressures, failure to plan ahead, and inaccessibility of family-planning services. In recent years, there has been an increase in oral contraceptive as well as latex condom usage, the latter reflecting, at least in part, a safer sex practice aimed at preventing sexually transmitted diseases.

Marriage is uncommon among Australian teenagers, although it remains a traditional lifestyle for adults. However, in recent years there has been an increase in cohabitation, particularly among younger couples. Cohabitation is popular among those wishing to establish financial independence, completing an education, or perhaps testing the feasibility or potential durability of a relationship. Much like cohabitants in the United States, many Australian couples regard this lifestyle as a precursor to marriage, not an alternative. However, there are some who choose to cohabit because they desire greater independence or question the traditional value placed on marriage.

Divorce has recently been on the increase in Australia. Researchers predict that if current divorce rates continue, 40 percent of all marriages will end in dissolution. Furthermore, the rates of divorce in Australia are about the same for people marrying for the first time as for those remarrying following divorce. Such divorce rates in Australia have created many single-parent households. In Sydney and Melbourne, for example, households headed by a woman have dramatically increased over the past ten years. Single parents face numerous problems, including financial hardship, child-care issues, loneliness, and an assortment of role realignments.

The fertility rate among Australian married couples is low, with the average total number of lifetime births per woman being about 1.9. Parent-child relations are marked by considerable warmth, care, and nurturance. Children are taught the importance of family honor and loyalty, and strong work and achievement orientations are evident in many households. While families are patriarchal in scope, recent shifts in traditional gender-role behaviors in Australia have created more egalitarian households. Many parents are transcending rigid and often unfair expectations accorded to individuals on the basis of their sex and are instead adopting more flexible gender-role standards. Such shifts are apparent in Australian homes as well as in the workplace.

Australia's strong kinship bonds are evident in the care given to aging family members. The role of families in the care of frail elderly has been increasingly recognized, and Australia has many support services to improve the quality of life for the caregiver as well as the aged family member. For example, the National Carers' Association provides supportive assistance to caregivers in the form of training programs, self-help groups, and consumer advocacy organizations. Caregivers of the elderly in Australia are also given opportunities to participate in policy making and in the development of services to improve and broaden outreach programming. The ultimate goal of all of these efforts is to strengthen the family, particularly the intergenerational ties between older and younger family members.

Further Reading. Amato, Paul R. (1987). Results of the Australian Institute of Family Studies. *Australian Institute of Family Studies Journal, 17,* 1–36; Costello, Brian R., and Janet Lee Taylor. (1991). Women in Australia. In Leonore L. Adler (Ed.), *Women in cross-cultural perspective.* Westport, CT: Praeger; Howe, Anna L. (1994). Commitment to carers: The Australian experience. *Ageing International, 21,* 54–59; Schultz, Noel C., Cynthia L. Schultz, and David H. Olson. (1991). Couple strengths and stressors in complex and simple stepfamilies in Australia. *Journal of Marriage and the Family, 53,* 555–564.

AUTHORITY, MARITAL. See MARRIAGE, VARIATIONS IN STRUCTURE.

BANDURA, ALBERT. Albert Bandura (1925–) graduated from the University of British Columbia in 1949 and received his Ph.D. from the State University of Iowa in 1952. Trained in clinical psychology, Bandura was the recipient of a Guggenheim Fellowship in 1973 and served as president of the American Psychological Association in 1974. He taught for many years as a professor of social science in the psychology department of Stanford University.

Bandura is best known for his contributions to the field of *social learning theory,* a school of thought suggesting that behavior is influenced by observing and copying others. He maintained that most learning theories are based on structured laboratory situations, which often have few similarities to real-world learning. Bandura argued that much of human behavior involves the simultaneous interaction of people and multiple stimuli. Bandura felt that to better understand these complex dynamics, psychologists should pay careful attention to the mechanism of modeling and imitation. Bandura's extensive research on these behaviors has helped to show how, and under what conditions, such observational forms of learning occur. (See SOCIAL LEARNING THEORY.)

Further Reading. Bandura, Albert. (1969). *Principles of behavior modification.* New York: Holt, Rinehart and Winston; Bandura, Albert. (1971). *Social learning theory.* New York: General Learning Press; Bandura, Albert. (1973). *Aggression: A social learning analysis.* Englewood Cliffs, NJ: Prentice-Hall; Thomas, R. Murray. (1992). *Comparing theories of child development* (3rd Ed.). Belmont, CA: Wadsworth.

BEHAVIORISM. Behaviorism is a major school of thought in psychology and is widely used in the field of lifespan development. Behaviorism maintains that environmental interaction and conditioning are largely responsible for the behavior we exhibit. Behaviorism was founded by John B. Watson in the early 1900s and has been shaped by a number of influential psychologists, including B. F. Skinner (see WATSON, JOHN B.; SKINNER, B. F.). The underpinning of behaviorism is that scientific psychology should study only observable behavior. Watson and others strongly believed that psychologists should abandon the study of consciousness, which was prevalent among psychologists at the turn of the century, and focus instead on what they could observe directly.

Behaviorism seeks to relate overt behaviors (responses) to observable events in the environment (stimuli). Particular attention is focused on *reinforcement,* an event following a response that strengthens the tendency to make that response. Many behaviorists such as Skinner place an emphasis on *positive reinforcement,* reinforcement that occurs when a response is strengthened because it is followed by the presentation of a rewarding stimulus. For example, a gold star attached to the homework paper of a young child may increase the probability of acceptable schoolwork in the future. *Negative reinforcement,* on the other hand, occurs when we behave in a way that reduces or eliminates an aversive stimulus. For instance, a mother gives in to her child's begging at the supermarket in order to halt a temper tantrum.

Primary and secondary reinforcers are two additional types of reinforcement in behaviorism. *Primary reinforcement* represents a satisfying stimulus related to primary, unlearned drives (food and drink are primary reinforcers related to the hunger and thirst drives). *Secondary reinforcement* is a stimulus that has acquired reinforcing qualities by being associated with primary reinforcement. Praise, approval, attention, or money all represent secondary reinforcement. Finally, *punishment* is viewed by behaviorists as an event that follows a response that weakens or suppresses the tendency to make that response. Spanking a child is an example of punishment.

Behaviorism has shed considerable light on how behavior is shaped by environmental determinants. With regard to growth throughout the lifespan, it shows how certain developmental changes do not depend on biological maturation. Rather, the course of development is continually shaped by one's surroundings. This means that when the nature-nurture issue in lifespan development is examined, behaviorists emphasize the importance of the environmental position. (See NATURE-NURTURE ISSUE.)

Further Reading. Bijou, Sidney W. (1979). Some clarifications on the meaning of a behavior analysis of child development. *Psychological Record, 29,* 3–13; Mahoney, Michael J. (1989). Scientific psychology and radical behaviorism. *American Psychologist, 44,* 1372–1377; Skinner, B. F. (1974). *About behaviorism.* New York: Knopf; Thomas, R. Murray. (1992). *Comparing theories of child development* (3rd Ed.). Belmont, CA: Wadsworth.

BEHAVIOR-MODIFICATION THEORY. See PARENTHOOD, CHILDREARING OPTIONS AND STRATEGIES.

BEREAVEMENT. Bereavement is the loss of a loved one by death. It is a statement of fact and does not embody one's reaction to loss. In this sense, bereavement is the objective event of a loss, rather than one's subjective reaction. (See GRIEF; GRIEF WORK; WIDOWHOOD.)

Further Reading. DeSpelder, Lynne A., and Albert L. Strickland. (1992). *The last dance: Encountering death and dying* (3rd Ed.). Mountain View, CA: Mayfield; Leming, Michael R., and George E. Dickinson. (1994). *Understanding dying, death, and bereavement.* Fort Worth, TX: Harcourt Brace.

BILATERAL DESCENT. See MARRIAGE, VARIATIONS IN STRUCTURE.

BIRTH CONTROL. See CONTRACEPTION.

BIRTHRATE. The birthrate, also called the *crude birthrate,* is the number of live births per 1,000 members of a population in a given year. Birthrates vary widely around the world. For example, in 1994 the birthrate in the United States was 16 births per 1,000 members of the population, while in Kenya it was 53 per 1,000, and in Denmark it was 10 per 1,000.

Further Reading. McFalls, Joseph A., Jr. (1991). *Population: A lively introduction.* Washington, DC: Population Reference Bureau; Shryock, Henry S., and Jacob S. Siegel. (1976). *The methods and materials of demography.* Orlando, FL: Academic Press.

BISEXUALITY. Bisexuality, a type of sexual orientation, is sexual attraction and emotional attachment to both females and males. The desire to have intimate relationships with both females and males is usually not in equal proportion. Rather, most bisexuals lean more toward one sex than the other. In this respect, "fifty-fifty" bisexuals are considered quite rare.

Like homosexuality, bisexuality is not well understood (see GAY AND LESBIAN RELATIONSHIPS; GAY AND LESBIAN RELATIONSHIPS, HISTORICAL AND LEGAL PERSPECTIVES). Many people see sexual orientation as exclusively heterosexual or homosexual, with no other possible variations. Adding to the confusion is the fact that many equate sexual orientation only with genital sexual activity, rather than considering the larger issues of loving and affection. An important point to remember is that genitality is not all of sexuality. Sexuality, including bisexuality, relates to affiliation and affection as well as to genital behavior. This simple distinction is critical to an understanding of all sexual orientations.

It is difficult to determine the prevalence of bisexuality. One estimate is that about 25 million Americans exhibit some combination of heterosexual and homosexual behavior, with more men than women having bisexual histories. Most bisexuals first eroticize the opposite sex and identify as heterosexuals. During their 20s or 30s, though, gay interests are often discovered. But there are instances where lifelong gays develop heterosexual interests and become bisexual.

It must be remembered, too, that bisexuals often prefer one sex over the other. However, they are attracted to both men and women and remain open to sexual involvement with both.

Bisexuality is not the chic sexual lifestyle—''the best of both worlds''—that many people tend to envision. On the contrary, bisexuals usually report feelings of isolation and alienation. To illustrate, a bisexual man or woman might be able to share his or her heterosexual desires with others, but must conceal affectionate feelings toward persons of the same sex. Difficulties also arise for many couples in which one person is bisexual and the other is either heterosexual or homosexual. If the bisexuality has not been previously acknowledged from the beginning of the relationship, issues of betrayal often surface and must be confronted. Finally, the lack of a bisexual subculture and social support network often adds to feelings of loneliness and alienation.

Further Reading. Klein, Fritz, and Timothy J. Wolf. (Eds.). (1985). *Two lives to lead: Bisexuality in men and women.* New York: Harrington Park Press; Paul, Jay P. (1984). The bisexual identity: An idea without social recognition. *Journal of Homosexuality, 9,* 45–63; Storms, Michael. (1980). Theories of sexual orientation. *Journal of Personality and Social Psychology, 38,* 783–792.

BLENDED FAMILY. See FAMILY COMPOSITION, TYPES OF.

BODY LANGUAGE. See COMMUNICATION, NONVERBAL.

BOHANNAN, PAUL. See DIVORCE, PROCESSES AND TRANSITIONS OF.

BRIDESERVICE. See MARITAL EXCHANGES.

BRIDEWEALTH. See MARITAL EXCHANGES.

BRONFENBRENNER, URIE. Urie Bronfenbrenner (1917–) was born in Moscow and is one of the leading figures in the field of ecological psychology, one of lifespan development's major theories. He spent many years of his professional life developing this conceptual framework, which is best seen as a progressive, mutual accommodation between an active, growing human and the changing properties of the settings in which the person lives. The manner in which relationships converge within these settings, as well as within the larger contexts in which the settings are embedded, is detailed in Bronfenbrenner's numerous articles and books.

Bronfenbrenner is also internationally known for his cross-cultural research in such locations as the Soviet Union, China, Israel, Nova Scotia, and Western Europe. His research in the Soviet Union during the 1960s earned critical acclaim among developmental researchers and child-care experts. This research focused on child rearing in the family and in collective settings, and how Soviet children compared with children from the United States. While in the Soviet Union, Bronfenbrenner also served as exchange scientist at the Institute of Psychology in Moscow.

In the United States, Bronfenbrenner is well known as a developmental and social psychologist who translates the results of social research into public policy. He is one of the founding fathers of Project Head Start (a federally funded early childhood education program established in 1965) and has served as a frequent advisor to the federal government on matters affecting national policy on children. Bronfenbrenner served for many years as professor of psychology and of child development and family studies in the College of Human Ecology at Cornell University. (See ECOLOGICAL THEORY.)

Further Reading. Bronfenbrenner, Urie. (1979). Contexts of child rearing: Problems and prospects. *American Psychologist, 34,* 844–850; Bronfenbrenner, Urie. (1986). Ecology of the family as a context for human development: Research perspectives. *Developmental Psychology, 22,* 723–742; Thomas, R. Murray. (1992). *Comparing theories of child development* (3rd Ed.). Belmont, CA: Wadsworth.

BRUNER, JEROME. Jerome Bruner (1915–) is a psychologist who has furthered our knowledge of child development, particularly the cognitive processes of children and adolescents. Bruner received an undergraduate degree from Duke University and a Ph.D. from Harvard University. His research on how we learn to perceive, remember, reason, and judge has important implications for many facets of lifespan development.

Bruner proposed that mental maturity is attained through three periods of cognitive activity: the enactive, iconic, and symbolic representation stages. During the *enactive stage,* which occurs roughly during the first two years of life, the child gains knowledge of the world through motor actions and responses. Although this is a fundamental period of cognitive development, Bruner stated that infants become increasingly able to refine their motor abilities and become more aware of environmental details. Reality is conferred upon objects in the environment only through the child's interaction with those objects.

During the *iconic stage* (roughly ages 2 through 7), thinking is characterized by the use of mental images. At this time, when children are asked to describe what a particular object looks like, they are able to generate a visual image of this object in their mind or even draw a picture of it on a piece of paper. In other words, objects can be conceptualized and represented even if they are not in the child's immediate surroundings.

Bruner's last phase of development is the *symbolic representation stage* (approximately ages 7–15). The most advanced form of cognitive functioning, this stage is characterized by the child's ability to transfer iconic images into language and to make logical derivations. For Bruner, language plays a critical role in the refinement and expression of mental maturity. The combined forces of mental maturity and language refinement promote cognitive mastery of the world. Additionally, the intellectual advancement of older children is marked by an increasing capacity to deal with several alternatives simultaneously, to tend to several sequences during the same period of time, and to allocate time and attention in a manner appropriate to these multiple demands.

Further Reading. Bruner, Jerome. (1960). *The process of education.* Cambridge, MA: Harvard University Press; Bruner, Jerome. (1966). *Toward a theory of instruction.* Cambridge, MA: Belknap Press; Bruner, Jerome. (1968) *On knowing.* New York: Atheneum; Thomas, R. Murray. (1992). *Comparing theories of child development* (3rd Ed.). Belmont, CA: Wadsworth.

BUDDHISM. See RELIGION, IMPACT OF ON INTIMATE RELATION-SHIPS.

BUNDLING, AS A DATING PRACTICE IN COLONIAL AMERICA. Bundling was a courtship ritual often practiced during colonial times in the United States. More specifically, it was a custom in which two unmarried persons of the opposite sex shared the same bed while remaining fully clothed. No one knows exactly where bundling originated, although the English and Dutch are often mentioned as the originators of this practice.

Bundling was practiced when nights were cold and stormy in colonial America. While lovers could walk off into the woods or other locations during warm months, cold nights forced them and everyone else inside to gather around the fireplace. Because there was no central heating, the fireplace became a crowded location in most colonial homes. Simple hospitality and often a parental desire to hasten the courtship process prompted an invitation for the suitor to stay and share the girl's bed.

A centerboard was kept in many colonial homes for nights when bundling was practiced. This was a board placed between the male and female to discourage any sexual intimacy. Whether or not the board remained in place was secondary to the fact that parents knew where their daughter was, and with whom.

Bundling was an accepted part of courtship in New England and the Middle Colonies by the late eighteenth century. It appears to have been most prevalent in Connecticut. By the early 1800s it was abandoned, although sporadic instances of it occurred as late as 1845.

Further Reading. Albin, Mel, and Dominick Cavallo (Eds.). (1981). *Family life in America, 1620–2000.* St. James, New York: Revisionary Press; Turner, Jeffrey S., and Donald B. Helms. (1988). *Marriage and family: Traditions and transitions.* San Diego, CA: Harcourt Brace Jovanovich.

BUTLER, ROBERT N. Robert N. Butler (1927–) is an internationally known gerontologist, author, and consultant. He was born in New York and received a medical degree from Columbia University's College of Physicians and Surgeons in 1953. He has been Brookdale Professor and chairman of the Gerald and May Ellen Ritter Department of Geriatrics and Adult Development of Mount Sinai Medical Center in New York City since 1982. As chairman of the first department of geriatrics in an American medical school, Butler is a leader in improving the quality of life for older people.

Before he came to Mount Sinai, Butler worked at the National Institutes of Health, where he created the National Institute on Aging in 1976 and served as its first director. Under his leadership, the need for federal funding for research in gerontology gained recognition. He was particularly outspoken about the few service-related research activities available to enhance the health of, and social service delivery to, the elderly in terms of efficiency, cost, and quality. Butler felt that future research on aging must be unusually inventive, taking advantage of a broad range of collaborative studies in seeking to telescope its natural development.

A prolific writer, Butler won the Pulitzer Prize in 1976 for his book *Why survive? Being old in America,* a penetrating social analysis of the elderly in the United States. He is a member of the Institute of Medicine of the National Academy of Sciences and is a founding fellow of the American Geriatrics Society. Butler has also served as a consultant to the U.S. Senate Special Committee on Aging, the National Institute of Mental Health, the Commonwealth Fund, and numerous other organizations.

Further Reading. Butler, Robert N. (1975). *Why survive? Being old in America.* New York: Harper and Row; Butler, Robert N. (1983). An overview of research on aging and the status of gerontology today. *Milbank Memorial Fund Quarterly: Health and Society, 61,* 351–361; Butler, Robert N., and Myrna I. Lewis. (1988). *Love and sex after 60.* New York: Harper and Row.

C

CALVIN, JOHN. See RENAISSANCE AND REFORMATION, LIFESPAN RELATIONSHIPS DURING THE.

CASE STUDY. The case study is a research technique employed in the field of lifespan development as well as in other branches of psychology. The case study's purpose is to accumulate developmental information on a single person rather than a group of people. Researchers maintain that studying a single subject over an extended time period yields a great deal of information on that one person. Usually, interviews are the primary source of data for a case study, and information is often gathered about significant life events, such as those pertaining to family, education, and vocation. While this method is excellent in such areas as clinical treatment of maladjusted individuals, one can never be certain that this knowledge will help in understanding others. Because the case study typically involves a single researcher and only a few cases, its reliability must be supported by testing the hypotheses generated by means of more systematic research techniques, such as a survey or an experimental study.

Further Reading. Breakwell, Glynis, Sean Hammond, and Chris Fife-Schaw. (1995). *Research methods in psychology.* Thousand Oaks, CA: Sage; Hessler, Richard M. (1992). *Social research methods.* St. Paul, MN: West; Yin, Robert K. (1984). *Case Study Research: Design and Methods.* Beverly Hills, CA: Sage.

CATHOLICISM. See RELIGION, IMPACT OF ON INTIMATE RELATIONSHIPS.

CELIBACY. See SEXUAL VALUES, IMPACT OF ON INTIMATE RE-
LATIONSHIPS.

CHASTITY BELT. A chastity belt was a device designed to ensure the
fidelity of wives as well as the virginity of young women. Chastity belts were
used during the Middle Ages, although they may have been introduced centuries
earlier in ancient Greece. The Greek poet Homer, for example, wrote about a
chastity belt in the *Odyssey* around 750 B.C. In the epic, Aphrodite, the goddess
of love, betrays her husband, Hephaistos, with his brother Ares. In an act of
revenge, Hephaistos creates a girdle (the ''girdle of Venus'') to prevent Aphrodite from further sexual betrayals.

The chastity belt was usually made out of metal and locked around the waist.
A connected and curved centerpiece covered the vaginal and anal areas, with
small openings left for body elimination processes. Sharp spikes often covered
the narrow vaginal opening. Velvet was sometimes used to cover the metal and
offer the wearer some degree of comfort. Wealthy men sometimes had their
wives' belts studded with diamonds or other precious stones, or inlaid with gold
or ivory.

The use of chastity belts provides an interesting commentary on the sexual
lives of those living during the Middle Ages. That is, women were regarded as
the sexual property of men, and extreme measures like this reflected this concept
of ownership. Interestingly, historians tell us that many women found ways to
rid themselves of the chastity belt while their husbands or lovers were elsewhere.
Spare keys were sometimes kept hidden by ingenious women.

How widespread the use of chastity belts was is not known, although it is
believed that they were used throughout Europe and particularly in Italy and
France. The fourteenth-century ruler of Padua, Francesco da Carrara, instructed
his wives to wear chastity belts. In the sixteenth century, King Henry II of France
had a chastity belt designed for Catherine de Medici. Not only the socially elite,
but the working classes as well used them. Merchants and soldiers, for example,
were especially likely to fit their wives with chastity belts. In Spain, the chastity
belt was used up to the nineteenth century.

Further Reading. Foucault, Michael. (1978). *The history of sexuality.* New York:
Pantheon Books; Gregersen, Edgar. (1983). *Sexual practices.* New York: Franklin Watts;
Tannahill, Reay. (1980). *Sex in history.* New York: Stein and Day.

CHILDBIRTH. Childbirth, or labor and delivery, is the climax of pregnancy
and encompasses three main stages: uterine contractions, delivery of the baby,
and expulsion of the placenta. During the first stage, uterine contractions begin
and increase in frequency as well as intensity. The precise physiological mechanisms that trigger uterine contractions are unknown, although it is speculated
that the fetus manufactures hormones that cause the placenta and the uterus to
increase the secretion of *prostaglandins* (human hormones). Prostaglandins, in
turn, stimulate the muscles of the uterus to contract and labor to begin.

Eventually, uterine contractions cause the amniotic sac to rupture, releasing the amniotic fluid (this is commonly referred to as "breaking of the waters"), although this may happen a few days before labor begins. Uterine contractions also create effacement and dilation of the cervix. Effacement is the shortening and thinning of the cervical canal. Dilation is the enlargement of the cervix so that the fetus can successfully pass through it.

During the second stage of labor, the fetus begins to descend down the vagina. Gradually, the vulva is stretched and eventually encircles the diameter of the baby's head (the head is normally the widest part of the fetus), a process referred to as crowning. When crowning occurs, the baby is usually ready to be expelled. Delivery generally takes place between contractions and as slowly as possible. Most babies present in a head-downward position for delivery, although some assume a breech position (the lower part of the fetus appears first). Once the head and shoulders are delivered, the baby's body is quickly expelled because of its smaller size. After the birth, the umbilical cord still connects the baby to the placenta. The cord is then clamped and cut.

The third and last stage of labor is the expulsion of the placenta (the placenta is an organ that allows nourishment to pass from the mother to the fetus and waste products to be channeled from the fetus to the mother). Once the baby has been delivered, the uterus begins to relax and contract, which reduces the area of placental attachment. This causes the placenta to detach itself and move toward the lower uterus. The actual expulsion of the placenta can generally be accomplished by the bearing-down efforts of the mother. If this is not possible, the clinician applies gentle traction to the cord while exerting pressure on the fundus (the upper, rounded portion of the uterus). (See NEWBORN.).

Further Reading. Eisenberg, Arlene, Heidi E. Murkoff, and Sandee E. Hathaway. (1991). *What to expect when you're expecting* (Rev. Ed.). New York: Workman; Madsen, Lynn. (1994). *Rebounding from childbirth.* Westport, CT: Bergin and Garvey; Nilsson, Lennart. (1990). *A child is born* (Rev. Ed.). Garden City, NY: Doubleday.

CHILDBIRTH, HISTORICAL PRACTICES. Throughout history, the birth of a baby has reflected unique observations, practices, and customs. For example, the ancient Egyptians held pregnant women in high esteem and paid special attention to their medical needs. Papyrus scrolls dating back to 2200 B.C. gave guidelines on how to relieve pain during labor, and scrolls from 1550 B.C. elaborated on health concerns during pregnancy.

Susrata, one of the most prolific of Hindu writers around 600 B.C. offered many thoughts on the subject of childbirth. Among other topics, he described the use of primitive forceps and the management of both normal and abnormal labor. In ancient Greece, the Athenians recognized the need for special attendants during the delivery process. In fact, Athenian law required that pregnant women be attended by midwives, usually women who had borne children and were past the childbearing age.

Superstition, charms, and rituals have also been apparent in many civilizations.

In medieval Europe, a fresh egg was often placed next to the newborn since it symbolized fruitfulness. Similarly, a gold coin was often given in an effort to ensure ample means in the baby's later life. Among many North American Indian tribes, ritual chanting was practiced when women went into labor in an effort to help lure the baby out of the womb.

Among the Arapesh in New Guinea, sanctions were directed at the father. He could not be present during the baby's birth, but following delivery he could lie with the newborn in bed. Both father and mother fasted for one day after delivery, then spent five days together in strict seclusion. For months afterward, a strict taboo against intercourse was observed.

Such practices were similar to those in Kurtachi, Solomon Islands. The father could not enter his home for three days after the birth of his child. Moreover, while labor was in progress, he had to abstain from food of any kind. He also could not carry anything heavy or touch a knife, axe, or any sharp instrument. To do so would reputedly injure the baby or cause it to die. On the fourth day, the father could see his child, and on the fifth day, he washed with his wife in the sea.

Modern perceptions of childbirth reflect our own unique attitudes, beliefs, and customs. Most apparent is the tendency to view childbirth as a normal, positive event rather than a traumatic, painful necessity. Moreover, childbirth for many today is an event to be shared by both parents. Growing numbers of couples not only share the birth experience but have the opportunity to choose among a variety of delivery alternatives. Modern-day parents thus represent an interesting contrast to their historical counterparts: they no longer have to accept either the pain and isolation in which women typically gave birth in past centuries or the regimented hospital rules and procedures that in more recent times have separated them during the birth of their child.

Today, our knowledge of childbirth has also become extensive and sophisticated. This is largely due to advancements in obstetrics, a branch of medicine that concerns itself with pregnancy, labor, and delivery. Modern obstetrics has helped to diminish many fears about childbirth. Rather than the painful trauma suffered by so many expectant mothers years ago, most women today experience safe, natural deliveries with less discomfort.

Further Reading. Foucault, Michael. (1978). *The history of sexuality.* New York: Pantheon Books; Gregersen, Edgar. (1983). *Sexual practices.* New York: Franklin Watts; Turner, Jeffrey S., and Laurna Rubinson. (1993). *Contemporary human sexuality.* Englewood Cliffs, NJ: Prentice Hall.

CHILDBIRTH, TECHNIQUES OF. Today, a variety of childbirth techniques are available to expectant parents. Although large percentages of mothers continue to deliver their babies in traditional medical and hospital settings, growing numbers are pursuing alternatives to hospital labor and delivery. Most are doing so because they object to the use of anesthesia during delivery and to other medical intrusions on the mother and the baby. Some also object to the deemphasized role of the father in the delivery of the baby. The following are some of the more popular childbirth techniques.

The Lamaze method. The Lamaze method (named after Fernand Lamaze, a French obstetrician) is one of the most popular alternative approaches. It represents an attempt to avoid the use of anesthesia and to allow both husband and wife to play an active role in the delivery of their baby. Expectant couples attend classes that stress special breathing exercises and relaxation responses. It is reasoned that fears during delivery cause women to tense their muscles, which delays the birth process and increases the mother's pain. Proponents of this approach feel that if women know what to expect and learn how to relax, their discomfort can be significantly reduced.

The Leboyer method. The Leboyer method emphasizes the importance of a gentle delivery and minimal trauma for the newborn. Developed by French obstetrician Frederick Leboyer, this delivery method offers a marked contrast to hospital childbirth procedures. The baby is born into a dimly lit delivery room that is kept relatively silent. Immediately after birth the infant is placed on the mother's stomach to be gently massaged, the belief being that tactile stimulation and contact soothe the baby and promote bonding. The infant is then further soothed by a warm bath. Only after this is the baby given a routine medical examination. Leboyer suggested that such steps are transitions that minimize the trauma of birth and the abrupt departure of the infant from the womb.

Home birth. A home birth, as the name implies, occurs in the home of the expectant parents. Such births have increased in recent years, often because many parents are rebelling against increased hospital costs and impersonal neonatal and postpartum care. Home births are often conducted by certified nurse-midwives, trained delivery specialists who provide qualified medical care to expectant mothers. Usually the midwife has earned a bachelor's degree in nurse-midwifery and works on a medical team consisting of a gynecologist and an obstetrician. The nurse-midwife spends considerably more time with the mother before, during, and after the delivery and offers close, personal attention in a relaxed and comfortable setting.

Rooming-in and birthing-room facilities. A rooming-in hospital facility allows the mother to care for the newborn in her own room. The infant is usually brought to the mother's room within the first few hours after birth and remains there (rather than in the nursery) during the duration of hospitalization. A birthing room offers a homelike and relaxed atmosphere within the hospital delivery unit. The mother goes through labor and delivery in this room rather than being rushed to the delivery room prior to birth. Many couples today combine the birthing room with natural childbirth approaches to labor and delivery.

Further Reading. Feinbloom, Richard I. (1993). *Pregnancy, birth, and the early months.* Reading, MA: Addison-Wesley; Stoppard, Miriam. (1993). *Conception, pregnancy, and birth.* New York: Dorling/Kindersely; Tuteur, Amy B. (1994). *How your baby is born.* CA: Ziff-Davis.

CHILD CARE, CROSS-NATIONAL VARIATIONS IN AVAIL-ABILITY OF. Around the globe, unique variations in child care exist. Surprisingly, the United States lags far behind almost all of the other major advanced industrial countries with regard to the supply, quality, and affordability of out-of-home child-care services for children under compulsory school age. Northern and Western European countries, in particular, are considered the leaders in child-care policies and programs. They have acknowledged the importance and value of early childhood education programs, whether or not mothers are working, for socialization and educational reasons as well as a wide variety of other developmental needs. Such programs are increasingly universal, free, and carefully monitored by child-care officials.

Compared to the United States, most European nations have also implemented extended maternity-leave policies. Leaves vary from one to three years, with complete job security for the mother and some pay for the entire duration. European maternity leaves do not exercise any negative impact on the situation of women in the labor market. Maternity leave in itself is not a threat to a woman's job identity: Hungarian women, for example, never doubt their role as full workers; Swedish women in the vast majority reenter the labor market and hold their jobs. If anything, maternity leaves of greater length contribute to a stable work identity: Women know when, where, and if they are going back, whereas in the United States women often drop out (or are forced to do so) and then have a problem finding another job afterward.

Many countries offer very attractive maternity-leave packages, including child-care payments and extensive medical coverage. For example, Hungary provides a child-care grant that equals about 40 percent of the mother's wages and lasts until the child is three. Countries such as France, Norway, and Sweden permit either parent to take an unpaid, job-protected leave, ranging from one to two years, when the paid leave ends. In Austria, a one-year paid leave is available for single mothers; married mothers can take the same time off, but without pay. In Sweden and Norway, the government also sponsors paid leave when care for a sick child is needed.

Such benefits to families are paid for in a unique fashion. These programs represent a type of "social insurance" and are similar in scope to Social Security and unemployment benefits in the United States. For example, in many nations (e.g., France, Finland, Hungary, Israel, Italy, and the United Kingdom), employers and employees each contribute a small percentage of their wages for such programming. In Sweden, employers and the government finance the benefits. In Austria and Norway, financing originates from employer, employee, and government contributions, while in Denmark, general tax revenues from national and local governments pay for it.

Further Reading. Kamerman, Sheila B. (1983). Time out for babies. *Working Mother, 4,* 80–82; Kamerman, Sheila B. (1991). Child care policies and programs: An international overview. *Journal of Social Issues, 47,* 179–196; Melhuish, Edward C., and

Peter Moss (Eds.). (1991). *Day care for young children: International perspectives.* New York: Routledge.

CHILD CARE, WORKING PARENTS AND. An important chore facing working parents is finding suitable child-care arrangements. In the United States today, child care or early childhood education facilities are often too expensive or insufficient in number. The demand for affordable child care is especially apparent among single parents, particularly when one considers that one-half of the households headed by single mothers aged 25 to 45 are poor. Those able to take advantage of early childhood education programming are usually well educated, work full-time, and have a comfortable family income. Because of financial restrictions, lower-income couples often find female relatives to care for their young, with grandparents an especially popular choice.

Among the early childhood education programs that do exist, the day-care center is the most convenient for working parents (see EARLY CHILDHOOD EDUCATION, IMPACT OF ON CHILD DEVELOPMENT). As the name implies, day care offers full child-care coverage, often beginning at 7 A.M. and lasting until 6 P.M. Some specialize in infant and toddler care and offer meals and learning sessions. For those offering a curriculum component, activities that encourage and facilitate learning are directed toward physical, cognitive, linguistic, personality, and social capacities.

However, day-care centers have aroused considerable controversy among child psychologists, educators, family studies experts, and parents. Though such facilities offer protective care to children and enable both parents to work, concern is frequently voiced about the effects of day care on children. Parental separation and the disruption of attachment bonds to caregivers are central issues for many. Some maintain that a full-time day-care center cannot provide this essential early social relationship, except under ideal conditions. Usually a child must share with other children the attention of a day-care worker, and in the typical ten-hour center day, work shifts change at least once. Add to this vacations and job turnovers, and a child may well have no one special person to be close to. Sometimes parents compound the problem of an unhappy child by blaming the center and switching the child to another. Finally, it has been noted that children in day care face considerable risk in the transmission of such diseases as respiratory and gastrointestinal illnesses.

Not everyone agrees on such potential negative effects of day care. Many feel that children are capable of adjusting well to day-care situations at an early age, and many also believe that these institutions offer rewarding learning experiences. Among proponents of day care, it is maintained that such arrangements promote socialization and stimulate important cognitive and linguistic competencies. Some feel that the developmental stimulation provided by effective day-care programming transcends levels available at home.

Thus for parents the issue becomes searching for a quality day-care center and not settling for a mediocre one. This can be a tedious chore, but one well worth the effort. Parents need to look for centers with such positive features as low adult-to-child ratios, good nutrition programs, excellent sanitation conditions, and adequate staff training. A successful day-care experience, however, goes beyond the center's qualifications. The parental warmth, acceptance, and care that the child receives in the home may greatly influence his or her response to the overall day-care experience.

In regard to this last point, it is maintained by most child-care and family studies experts that the critical variables in a child's adjustment are the parents' satisfaction with their lives and the quality, rather than quantity, of parent-child interactions. In this respect, paternal and maternal employment per se is not the major issue in either a child's adjustment to child care or smooth marital relations. Rather, the circumstances and stability of the family, the climate of togetherness that it offers, the attitudes and expectations held by the parents, and the distribution of the time available for meaningful interaction shape the course of domestic harmony and happiness for all concerned.

Further Reading. Frankel, Arthur J. (1991). The dynamics of day care. *Families in Society, 72,* 3–10; Sonenstein, Freya L., and Douglas A. Wolf. (1991). Satisfaction with child care: Perspectives of welfare mothers. *Journal of Social Issues, 47,* 15–31; Sugar, Martha H. (1994). *When mothers work, who pays?* Westport, CT: Bergin and Garvey; Zigler, Edward F., and Mary E. Lang. (1990). *Child care choices: Balancing the needs of children, families, and society.* New York: Free Press.

CHILDHOOD, COMPETITION DURING. The emergence of competition, the rivalry that occurs for some kind of reward or advantage, can be traced to the childhood years. Most children initially experience competition as they vie against one another to reach a goal or as they strive for victory, prestige, or accomplishment. For those children having a sibling, competition often begins at home, perhaps for the attention of parents (see SIBLING RELATIONS). Over time, competition will play an important role in shaping what aspirations the child will set for herself or himself.

Most experts believe that children learn to be competitive from environmental forces, most likely through the process of reinforcement or through modeling (see BEHAVIORISM; SOCIAL LEARNING THEORY). Thus a child who receives praise for winning a contest will be eager to compete again. It is conceivable that the child who does not receive praise for such behavior may learn other tactics (such as cooperation) to achieve the same goal.

Our society places a great deal of emphasis on competition. This is apparent in many facets of life, from sports to business. The emphasis on competition is especially obvious when schoolchildren compete for grades or class prizes. Even away from school, children are thrust into competitive situations, such as the merit-badge system in Boy or Girl Scouts. While constructive competition is healthy, some child psychologists believe that our society often places children in unfair competitive situations. Moreover, they maintain that many goals in life can be reached with emphasis placed on cooperation, not competition.

During middle childhood, many children are introduced to organized sports and more formal levels of competition. Being a member of a team, whether in baseball, basketball, football, wrestling, or soccer, helps a child learn to make contributions as a member of a group with a common goal. However, organized sports can cause frustration in some children, particularly when they become overeager to prove themselves on the playing field.

Experts point out that adults must pay special attention to the varied needs of the child competing at the organized level. For example, there are many children who fear failure and humiliation within the framework of team sports. Unfortunately, many parents dismiss these apprehensions and fears and force children to participate in organized sports. As a result, many children feel anger, resentment, anxiety, or even a loss of self-confidence when they participate in competitive sports.

In addition to appreciating psychological needs, adults must work closely with children to help develop skills needed for competitive play. Good instruction usually embodies the elaboration of a skill for a specific age, not the acceleration of a child through many different skills. Careful attention must also be given to the fact that success in one facet of the game does not automatically ensure success in all other phases. It is important to realize, too, that behind healthy competition must lie a framework of such mental qualities as dedication, concentration, and good sportsmanship.

Further Reading. Harris, John C. (1984). Interpreting youth baseball: Players' understanding of fun and excitement, danger, and boredom. *Research Quarterly for Exercise and Sport, 55,* 379–382; Murphy, Claire. (1983). *Teaching kids to play.* New York: Leisure Press; Wankel, Lois M., and Paul S. Kreisel. (1985). Factors underlying enjoyment of youth sports: Sports and age group comparisons. *Journal of Sport Psychology, 7,* 51–64.

CHILDHOOD, FRIENDSHIPS DURING. During childhood, finding a friend and sharing his or her experiences is a valuable social experience. However, in order to develop and maintain friendships, children must learn a variety of important interpersonal skills. For example, children will discover that certain behaviors facilitate friendship formation while others impede its progress. In particular, not sharing, constant quarreling, or intentionally hurting others do not allow interaction to proceed in a connected fashion. In time, though, most children will learn to respect the rights and privileges of others, in the process developing an understanding of how to make and keep friends.

During the early years of childhood, egocentrism has a tendency to interfere with learning such important relational skills as mutuality and reciprocity. *Egocentrism* is a style of thinking that inhibits a person from seeing another person's point of view. In other words, it is a person's tendency to think that others see the world from the same perspective. How preschoolers communicate or play with friends reveals their egocentrism. Because children are so involved in their own thoughts and often engage in their own playworlds, they cannot consistently engage in reciprocal interactions.

But while egocentrism hampers early friendships, those that form during the school years become closer and more meaningful. Friends discover unique ways of supporting and stimulating each other. It is from childhood friendships that individuals learn how to create and sustain friendships throughout life. A foundation of friendship behaviors is constructed so that one will always have friends, in good times as well as bad.

The fact that their egocentrism has weakened during the school years enables children to forgo some of their own personal desires and to adopt the viewpoints of others. Greater sensitivity and emotional responsiveness to others, the growing ability to engage in reciprocal exchanges, and better conflict-resolution skills permit close ties among friends to blossom. Also, research indicates that there are parent-child antecedents of children's friendships. More specifically, positive and secure parent-child relationships tend to be associated with more positive friendships and more negative family relationships with more negative friendships.

By late childhood, friendships become more reciprocal, although arguments and disagreements still exist and can even disrupt a relationship. Friendships typically contain more expressions of mutuality and supportive understanding, and children slowly learn how to successfully manage conflicts. As children's social horizons expand, a network of friends usually becomes apparent. Within this network, some friendships become stronger than others, and "best friends" become obvious. Stronger friendships are typically characterized by communication clarity, the sharing of common interests and activities, effective conflict-resolution skills, and self-disclosure.

School-age children usually form same-sex friendships, a pattern evident in early childhood as well. Same-sex friendships reflect unique gender differences. For instance, although both sexes focus their friendships on shared interests and activities, boys are typically more competitive and girls more cooperative. Boys tend to de-emphasize the intimacy or closeness of their friendships. They are also more oriented to groups, whereas girls are drawn to one-to-one friendships. Moreover, girls are usually more expressive to one another than boys are. Also, research indicates that girls expect and receive more kindness, loyalty, commitment, and empathic understanding from their best friendships. Finally, girls' appreciation of the emotional bond that friendships offer spills over into the adolescent years. (See CHILDHOOD, PEER-GROUP DEVELOPMENT DURING.)

Further Reading. Ladd, Gary W. (1988). Friendship patterns and peer status during early and middle childhood. *Journal of Developmental and Behavioral Pediatrics, 9,* 229–238; Ladd, Gary W. (1990). Having friends, keeping friends, making friends, and being liked by peers in the classroom: Predictors of children's early school adjustment? *Child Development, 61,* 1081–1100; Selman, Robert. (1980). *The growth of interpersonal understanding.* New York: Academic Press.

CHILDHOOD, GENDER-ROLE DEVELOPMENT DURING. Gender-role development, the learning of expectations regarding how males and

females should behave, begins early in life. For many, this socialization process begins at birth when the infant is swaddled in a pink or blue hospital blanket. As time goes on, children receive different gender-typed behaviors from their mothers and fathers. In homes having traditional gender roles, mothers are typically nurturant and affectionate and indulge in cuddling, kissing, and stroking their children. Fathers display their affection through outdoor activities, roughhousing, and sharing hobbies and sports. Many parents show their concern that their boys be "masculine" and their girls "feminine." Because of such messages, children have established at an early age a fairly clear picture of what society thinks is appropriate gender-role behavior.

Reinforcement of gender roles persists in many other ways throughout infancy and toddlerhood. Toys and games provide clues to the sex of the child, as do different sets of parental expectations for male and female children. For example, parents are more likely to play vigorously with their sons and demonstrate more apprehension about physical danger to their daughters. Other cues are related to the child's general patterns of behavior. For instance, girls typically stay closer to their mothers while shopping or while playing outside. By the end of the first year, boys have usually ventured further out into their environment and attained greater degrees of social independence than girls.

Throughout all of childhood, gender-role development plays a critical role in shaping the child's overall personality, including sexuality. By the early years, a child becomes aware of which sex he or she belongs to, the roles that the identification brings with it, and some of the gender expressions of that role. Young children begin to show a preference for same-sex playmates as well as sex-stereotyped toys, such as trucks for boys and dolls for girls. During middle childhood, children continue to exhibit a strong preference for sexually separate groups, in the process assuming gender-appropriate mannerisms, recreational patterns, attitudes, and values from the surrounding adult culture. By the middle years, most children also have a rather extensive knowledge of gender-role stereotypes, and these standards become even more deeply rooted over time.

School-age children generally perceive gender roles in much the same fashion as adults. In addition, they have developed an understanding of which stereotyped occupations go with which sex. Children's growing cognitive awareness and expanding social horizons contribute to gender-role development, providing a good illustration of the link between developmental spheres. Cognitive skills enable them to understand and sort out those behaviors appropriate to their sex. Exposure to a growing number of role models and to television and other media, including advertisements, also transmits gender-role behaviors to the child.

The gender-typed play that began earlier also becomes more evident during the school years. Elementary-school youngsters readily identify and state a preference for play activities that are appropriate to, and characteristic of, their sex. Boys typically involve themselves in physical and independent types of play, while girls are less physically oriented. Many toys for boys continue to require more physical types of expressions, while toys intended for girls do not. (See

ANDROGYNY; GENDER ROLE; GENDER-ROLE DEVELOPMENT, IN-
FLUENCES ON; GENDER-ROLE DEVELOPMENT, THEORIES OF.)
Further Reading. Lytton, Hugh, and David M. Romney. (1991). Parents' differential
socialization of boys and girls: A meta-analysis. *Psychological Bulletin, 109,* 267–296;
Paludi, Michele A., and Dominic F. Gullo. (1987). The effect of sex labels on adults'
knowledge of infant development. *Sex Roles, 16,* 19–30; Paradise, Louis V., and Shavaun
M. Wall. (1986). Children's perceptions of male and female principals and teachers. *Sex
Roles, 14,* 1–7; Richardson, Laurel. (1988). *The dynamics of sex and gender* (3rd Ed.).
New York: Harper and Row.

CHILDHOOD, OPPOSITIONAL BEHAVIOR DURING. Oppositional
behavior is the active and often negative assertion of independence and autonomy. Oppositional behavior can take many forms, such as refusing to comply
to a request, being angry and belligerent, or making demands at inappropriate
times. This type of resistance begins to surface during the early years of childhood and, although disruptive, is considered a normal expression of the socialization process.

To fully understand children's oppositional behavior, one must appreciate how
the quest for individuality and autonomy unfolds. By the second year of life,
children are driven to explore and experiment with their expanding surroundings.
Children are also in the midst of adjusting to new demands and routines. Experts
maintain that adults need to be sensitive to these developmental challenges. They
must realize that young children need to test the validity of adult standards in
order to develop an understanding of what will and will not be allowed. In the
midst of such strivings, overbearing adults run the risk of crushing the child's
emerging self-awareness and independence. Healthy autonomy will be the outcome if children encounter a reasonable balance between parental freedom and
control.

Oppositional behavior typically surfaces in the wake of demands placed on
the child. Adjustment is particularly difficult for the infant and toddler when
personal care and social training are involved. Oppositional behavior is frequently the result of rigid demands in toilet training, dressing, and eating; interruptions or restrictions in playtime activities; and being forced to go to bed.
Frequent irritability in the child may have other causes, including bed-wetting,
fatigue, or illness.

Temper tantrums are perhaps the best illustration of oppositional behavior.
Temper tantrums are expressed in many ways, from crying and screaming to
head banging and kicking. No matter how they are channeled, tantrums seem to
express the same message: anger and frustration in having to adjust to the rituals
and demands of grown-up life.

Temper tantrums are a normal phase of childhood development, yet they represent the ultimate in oppositional behavior. While handling temper tantrums is
an individual affair, most experts agree that giving in to the child's demands
only reinforces this type of behavior and increases the likelihood of its future

appearance. Getting angry and upset also serves as a reinforcer, since children can see that their behavior is taking its toll. Most experts suggest that ignoring the tantrum until it has extinguished itself and then talking to the child at a less emotional moment is an effective technique. In social situations, some parents prefer to remove the child firmly to a less public location to avoid social discomfort. Whatever course of action they choose, adults must use an approach with which they are comfortable and exercise consistency.

Finally, the manner in which oppositional behavior is expressed changes with age. After the second year, angry outbursts of an undirected physical nature, such as kicking and hitting, begin to decline. Temper tantrums, which started during toddlerhood, persist into the preschool years. The use of threats and insults tends to increase. Thus, while the amount of oppositional behavior appears to remain stable, the child's manner of expressing it changes.

Further Reading. Bukatko, Danuta, and Marvin W. Daehler. (1995). *Child development* (2nd Ed.). Boston: Houghton Mifflin; Kagan, Jerome. (1981). *The second year: The emergence of self-awareness.* Cambridge, MA: Harvard University Press; Wenar, Charles (1982). On negativism. *Human Development, 25,* 1–23.

CHILDHOOD, PEER-GROUP DEVELOPMENT DURING. Peer-group development refers to the social interactions that take place with an individual's associates, usually of the same age and status. Such interaction blossoms during childhood and provides opportunities for children to better understand themselves and how their behavior impacts on others. Furthermore, peer-group relationships give children the opportunity to increase their independence, competence, and interpersonal skills. Peer relations also offer new models for identification, influence self-concept development, and shape the character of children's play.

Peer-group interaction during the early years of childhood creates interesting behaviors. Indeed, rarely do two young children behave in the same way when placed in the company of others. Some may eagerly seek to join the company of others; others may scream to be taken away; and still others may become passive and watch the activity from a safe distance. When a certain degree of group comfort has been acquired, attempts at making further social contacts are often awkward. Conflicts are common among young children, but are usually short-lived and occur as frequently among friends as among nonfriends.

Time and experience teach children that certain peer-group behaviors are socially acceptable and others are not. For example, hitting a playmate may release an inner impulse, but it may also cause friends and playmates to cry, strike back, or run away. Gradually, children realize that how they relate to their peers greatly influences the treatment that they in turn receive. Because of such gains in interpersonal awareness, social competence increases during this time.

By the school years, children's peer groups are usually quite selective, usually consisting of individuals of approximately the same age who share a common play interest. Group members tend to keep an air of exclusiveness about them, and many factors determine peer acceptance and rejection. For example, children's ability to gain acceptance into an established group often depends not only on their ability to comply with the members' routines, but also on the degree to which they initiate group contact and the friendliness that they exhibit in the process.

Peer groups also discriminate on the basis of gender. At an early age, same-sex playmates are preferred. This trend persists and intensifies as children get older, although it is more pronounced in males than in females. It will be from these segregated play groups that gender differences emerge and become entrenched (see GENDER-ROLE DEVELOPMENT, INFLUENCES ON).

Children's peer groups also contain dominance hierarchies. Shortly after the group forms, internal group processes select one or a few as its leaders. Others become followers. Often, the group leaders are above average in intelligence, assertive, and well liked by the others. Being respected and accepted has also been found to be related to leadership and overall sociability.

Popular and unpopular group members also emerge over time. Popularity is usually linked to friendliness, extroversion, and the ability to get along with others. As far as unpopularity is concerned, peer-rejected children tend to be aggressive, impulsive, and disruptive. Some unpopular children, though, may be socially shy or perceive themselves to be negatively regarded by their peers.

As children get older, the activities of the peer group become more diverse. For example, by early childhood, a cooperative attitude of more sharing takes place (see PROSOCIAL BEHAVIOR, CHILD). Problem-solving skills within the peer group also begin to appear, although this tends to take place more among friends than among acquaintances. The peer group is also capable of devising more activities for all members. Goal-directed behaviors are also present. However, such developments do not imply that all signs of emotional and social immaturity have evaporated. On the contrary, selfishness, impatience, and disagreement punctuate many childhood peer groups.

Further Reading. Asher, Steven R., and John D. Coie. (Eds.). (1990). *Peer rejection in childhood.* New York: Cambridge University Press; Capland, Marlene, et al., (1991). Conflict and its resolution in small groups of one- and two-year-olds. *Child Development, 62,* 1513–1524; Howes, Carollee. (1988). Peer interaction of young children. *Monographs of the Society for Research in Child Development, 53,* 94–104.

CHILDHOOD, SCHOOL RELATIONSHIPS DURING. Entrance into school brings children into a new and complex social environment. Most children eagerly anticipate attending elementary school and each year look forward to the classroom's developmental challenges. Not only will the cognitive domains of the child be influenced, but numerous other parameters will be affected as well. For example, children will have to adjust to many new routines and demands: task-oriented behavior, conformity to authority, and impulse control, to name but a few areas.

School relationships will also shape the course of social development. Interaction both inside and outside of the classroom enables children to learn more about themselves and others. School relationships will serve to teach, among other social lessons, following rules and how to participate in group decision making. Moreover, school experiences will give children the opportunity to increase their independence, competence, and competitive skills.

Because children are still very dependent on adults, many become attached to or are awed by their teacher. This is not only because the teacher acts in many respects as a substitute parent but because the teacher conveys to the child the assurance that adult authority is trustworthy and that the school environment is safe, stimulating, and satisfying. In fulfilling these and other needs, teachers begin to exert strong influences on the child's behavior. In the process of instruction and the manner in which it is delivered, teachers transmit their personal attitudes and beliefs to their pupils.

Teacher behaviors affect child performance in many ways. On the whole, teachers are effective when they demonstrate warmth, understanding, support, and compassion toward children. Ineffective teachers frequently operate overly restrictive classrooms, are dependent, foster feelings of limited self-worth, and exhibit lack of self-control. Compared to effective teachers, ineffective instructors do not feel accepting of themselves and others. As a result, children often feel insecure and devalued in the classroom. Additionally, children's creativity and spontaneity are often curtailed.

Successful elementary-school teachers have a tendency to exhibit generosity in their appraisals of behavior and are warm, empathetic, and friendly in their social relationships with children. Teachers who exhibit genuineness, warmth, and friendliness in their dealings with children, rather than punitive and authoritarian techniques, also encourage favorable behavior, particularly constructive attitudes, conscientious attitudes toward schoolwork, and less aggressive behavior. Children in such classrooms tend to be accepting of themselves and their peers, cooperative, and motivated.

Although the main task and responsibility are to teach academic subjects, the teacher is also responsible, to an extent, for the psychological well-being of children. So it is that teacher behavior directly relates to the student's self-concept and peer acceptance. Teachers appear to be in a prime position to serve as a role model, as well as a reinforcer, of children's social interaction. The examples they set, the tone they establish for peer relations, and the feedback they give to children are important influences. Moreover, such important instruction sets the stage for later learning and instruction. (See EARLY CHILDHOOD EDUCATION, IMPACT OF ON CHILD DEVELOPMENT.)

Further Reading. Hamachek, Donald. (1990). *Learning in teaching, learning in growth* (4th Ed.). Boston, MA: Allyn and Bacon; Jarolimek, John. (1993). *Teaching and learning in the elementary school* (5th Ed.). New York: Macmillan; Woolfolk, Anita E. (1993). *Educational psychology* (5th Ed.). Boston, MA: Allyn and Bacon.

CHILDHOOD, SCIENTIFIC STUDY OF. Researchers exploring childhood systematically examine the physical, cognitive, personal, and social characteristics of humans during this early lifespan stage. The study of childhood, like that of adolescent and adult development, is a subdivision of developmental psychology. Researchers specializing in this portion of the lifespan are known as child psychologists or developmental psychologists. Examples of research journals devoted to the scientific study of children include *Child Development, Early Childhood Research Quarterly, Infant Behavior and Development,* and *Journal of Child Language.*

Child psychologists investigate such areas as cognition (thinking), psycholinguistics (development of language), physiology (growth), and socialization. Specialists in each of these subfields attempt to describe, understand, and explain the changes that occur in children, especially those that are universal. For example, child psychologists have determined that most children speak their first word when they are about a year old and begin to walk within a month or two thereafter, regardless of race, ethnicity, or culture. However, this does not mean that environmental influences do not help shape the course of human development. Indeed, a particularly intriguing issue among child psychologists is analyzing the developmental convergence of both genetic and environmental forces.

The discipline of child psychology also seeks to observe and measure behavioral alterations. While some child psychologists feel that behavior is best viewed in a discontinuous, stagelike sequence, others feel that changes are slow and continuous (see CONTINUITY-DISCONTINUITY ISSUE). Should a discontinuous perspective be taken, children's personality dynamics or social developments are seen as unfolding in a sequential fashion. Each stage usually results in more refined and adaptive behavior that makes the child more competent, efficient, and adaptable to life's many challenges and demands. A continuous perspective, on the other hand, regards change as subtle and slow and without distinctive spurts in development.

Child development is a rapidly growing field of study that produces immense quantities of research findings every year. Numerous other disciplines are child oriented and also attempt to explore behavioral development. Parents, cultural anthropologists, educators, nurses, pediatricians, and social workers all seek to understand children's behavior. These groups contribute to the vast and growing amount of research in the field of child psychology.

Further Reading. Berk, Laura. (1989). *Child development.* Boston: Allyn and Bacon; Krantz, Murray. (1994). *Child development: Risk and opportunity.* Belmont, CA: Wadsworth; Papalia, Diane E., and Sally W. Olds. (1993). *A child's world: Infancy through adolescence* (6th Ed.). New York: McGraw-Hill.

CHILDHOOD, SEXUAL ABUSE DURING. The sexual maltreatment of children can occur both within the family and outside of it. Within the family, *incest* means sexual contact between close blood relatives. *Child sexual abuse,* on the other hand, means sexual contact between an adult and a child who are in no way related. Both usually refer to interactions between a child and adult when the child is being used for the sexual stimulation of that adult or another person.

As far as incest is concerned, virtually every society prohibits intrafamilial sexual relationships. This prohibition is often called the *incest taboo.* In the United States, incest is a crime, and while laws in different states vary regarding the sexual relationship forbidden, close blood relatives always include father, mother, grandfather, grandmother, brother, sister, aunt, uncle, niece, and nephew, and sometimes first cousins. Many states include stepparent-stepchildren, step-sibling, and in-law relationships, although these individuals are not blood related.

It is difficult to assess the prevalence of incest because it happens behind closed doors and most victims live with secrecy and isolation. However, it is estimated that as many as 20 million Americans may be incest victims, meaning that about one in ten have been affected. The average age of a child encountering this kind of sexual assault is 11. Contrary to the belief that incest is a problem only among the poor, incestuous families are found in every socioeconomic and educational group.

Experts maintain that father-daughter and stepfather-daughter incest represents most of reported incest cases. Mother-son and mother-daughter incest constitutes most of the remaining reports. Sibling incest is also believed to be widespread, but it is rarely reported. The most prevalent sibling incest pattern appears to be the abuse of younger sisters and brothers by an older male sibling.

When the incestuous activity begins, victims often believe that they are hold-ing the family together. They fear that the offending parent will go to jail if the incest is discovered. Some children acquiesce because they are desperate for any type of affection. In many situations, the child believes that there is no one to help her, even if she wanted help. Offenders often try to convince themselves that there is nothing wrong with what they are doing, but most use either subtle coercion or direct threats to keep their children silent.

In many father-daughter incestuous relationships, the mother is aware of the circumstances. A number of mothers choose to remain uninvolved, perhaps be-cause they were victims of incest, or they are so insecure and frightened of their husbands or significant others that they are immobilized. Given the mother's passive stance, the child often searches for an available and safe person with whom to communicate. However, in so doing the child runs the risk of not being believed or even being rejected.

Like incest, the sexual abuse of a young child by an adult is a punishable crime in the United States. However, the incidence of child sexual abuse is not much easier to assess than the incidence of incest. Most researchers agree that the problem is occurring at a significant rate and acknowledge that male children are abused less frequently than females. However, reported cases barely scratch the surface. Many reports of child sexual abuse are never even passed on to protective agencies. Furthermore, many sexual abuse cases are investigated, but do not stand up to the rigors of the court. There are unknown numbers of children who remain silent and never tell or seek therapeutic assistance.

The effects of all forms of child sexual abuse are multiple and diverse. For example, the survivor's suffering may be expressed in physical ailments such as chronic pelvic pain or the psychological disturbances of depression or acute anxiety. Many survivors are left with strong feelings of guilt, betrayal, and powerlessness. Because of the trauma of sexual abuse, later sexual behavior may be affected, such as with sexual preoccupations or compulsive masturbation and sex play. Many female survivors of sexual abuse are hostile and angry, are distrustful of men or intimate relationships in general, and have a history of failed relationships or marriages. Finally, many child sexual abuse victims often feel isolated and turn to self-destructive behaviors, such as drug abuse or delinquency. (See THERAPEUTIC RELATIONSHIP, FOR SURVIVORS OF CHILD SEXUAL ABUSE AND INCEST.)

Further Reading. Faller, Kathleen C. (1990). *Understanding child sexual maltreatment.* Newbury Park, CA: Sage; Finkelhor, David. (1986). *A sourcebook on child sexual abuse.* Newbury Park, CA: Sage; Kempe, Ruth S. and C. Henry Kempe. (1984). *The common secret: Sexual abuse of children and adolescents.* New York: Freeman; Patton, Michael Q. (Ed.). (1991). *Family sexual abuse: Frontline research and evaluation.* Newbury Park, CA: Sage.

CHILDLESSNESS, VOLUNTARY. Voluntary childlessness is a conscious decision by a couple not to have children. Because it is a deliberate effort to avoid childbearing, voluntary childlessness is not the same as infertility, defined as the inability to achieve a pregnancy after at least one year of regular unprotected intercourse (see INFERTILITY). Unlike couples wanting a family, voluntarily childless couples do not regard parenthood as a necessary ingredient for marital happiness or satisfaction. However, temporary childlessness or delayed childbearing is more likely than permanent childlessness (see PARENTHOOD, DELAYED.)

Those choosing permanent childlessness represent a unique population segment, particularly when one considers the high premium placed on having children during early historical periods. For example, in the Old Testament, God's directive to Noah was "Be fruitful and multiply." Often, parents faced certain consequences if they did not bear children and produce large families. In the classical age of Greece, barrenness was sufficient grounds for a man to divorce his wife. In colonial America, single men were viewed with suspicion and penalized with special taxes for not doing their share to increase the population. This is a far cry from the sentiment expressed today in certain countries, such as the People's Republic of China, where parents are required to limit family size to one child (see FERTILITY, INTERNATIONAL DIFFERENCES IN).

Childless couples tend to be well educated, financially well off, and from urban settings, although there are exceptions. Increased levels of education among modern women have created a greater proportion of females who never expect to have children. In addition, childless couples enjoy the company of one another and are very involved in their careers. Many childless couples believe that their parents were very limited by the chores of parenting. Many women who choose to remain childless view their own mothers as never having the careers they longed for or as having their careers cut short once they became mothers.

While voluntary childlessness represents a legitimate lifestyle option, the decision to remain childless may prove difficult. Today, organizations such as the National Alliance for Optional Parenthood help couples in their decision making and offer a wide range of supportive services. Their central theme is that parenthood is a life option for couples, not a duty. These organizations seek to ensure that in the pursuit of life satisfaction and happiness, it is perfectly acceptable not to have children.

Further Reading. Faux, Marian. (1984). *Childless by choice.* New York: Doubleday; Jacobsen, Cardell K., Timothy B. Heaton, and Karen M. Taylor. (1988). Childlessness among American women. *Social Biology, 35,* 186–197; Polenko, Karen A., John Scanzoni, and Jay D. Teachman. (1982). Childlessness and marital satisfaction. *Journal of Family Issues, 3,* 545–573.

CHILD REARING. See PARENTHOOD, CHILD-REARING OPTIONS AND STRATEGIES.

CHILD REARING, HISTORICAL PRACTICES IN. The treatment of children throughout history reflects interesting practices and trends. One of the more interesting of these is that certain child-rearing practices seem to be recurrent. This is important, since child rearing is, at least in part, a practical extension of society's beliefs and viewpoints regarding the nature and purpose of children. A glance backward through time reveals five recurrent child-rearing practices. They can be summarized as follows:

Training and indoctrination of young children into a designated skill. In past historical eras, the training of a child generally occurred between the ages of 6 and 9. Before the age of 6, children were viewed as infants and were left at home in their mother's care. An important facet of the child's household upbringing was learning the accepted mores, folkways, and basic rules of society. In many cultures, the stage of childhood, between infancy and adulthood, simply did not exist. A baby outgrew infancy and either directly joined the adult world as a laborer or entered adulthood after a relatively short vocational training period.

Perceiving the child as a miniature adult. Because of the early practical training that children received, they were frequently viewed (and portrayed in pictures) as miniature adults. In addition to working alongside grown-ups, children usually engaged in the same activities as adults, such as dancing, singing, or going to the market. Clothing was usually identical for adult and child.

Education as a luxury. With the advent of more formal schooling, the child-rearing practice of education as a luxury became increasingly evident. That is, children who came from wealthier families received schooling and consequently learned a skill or trade. In almost all cases, only boys received this formal education. For a long period, only wealthier families could afford formal and advanced educational experiences for their children. For those who did not benefit from formal schooling, educational experiences emerged from the home. For example, boys learned the routines of farming or hunting for food, and girls were taught cooking and weaving. At an early age, children of both sexes were expected to make meaningful and productive contributions to the household.

The practice of infanticide. One of the more tragic recurrent practices was *infanticide,* the murder of babies, especially those deemed weak or deformed. Infanticide, which was practiced by several cultures, including Oriental, Greek (particularly Spartan), and Roman civilizations, reveals how children were viewed as a practical commodity to the community. If a child could not serve the needs of the community, it was killed, either by the sword or by abandonment. Instances of infanticide still haunt us today. With alarming regularity, the media informs us of infants killed or abandoned by their parents.

The practice of child abuse. Finally, child abuse looms as a recurrent historical practice. Many civilizations believed in whipping and beating children, sometimes with instruments that we would associate with torture chambers. Beatings for children began as early as infancy, persisted throughout childhood, and were frequently severe enough to shed blood or cause bruising. Historians cite numerous reasons for child abuse, including the caregiver's burning desire to foster such qualities as submissiveness, obedience, and reverence for adult demands and wishes. Another factor, though, has often been labeled the key contributing cause. Prior to the eighteenth century, children were perceived as "inherently sinful," that is, born with original sin. Many parents believed that children were evil and that the devil had to be beaten out of them. Fortunately, such beliefs began to subside by the eighteenth century, and children began to receive more humane care and treatment as well as more love and affection (see LOCKE, JOHN. DOCTRINE ON CHILDREN AND CHILD-REARING).

Further Reading. Aries, Philippe. (1962). *Centuries of childhood.* New York: Knopf; deMause, Lloyd. (Ed.). (1975). *The history of childhood.* New York: Harper and Row; Helms, Donald B., and Jeffrey S. Turner. (1986). *Exploring child behavior* (3rd Ed.). Monterey, CA: Brooks/Cole.

CHILD RELINQUISHMENT. See MIDDLE AGES, LIFESPAN RELATIONSHIPS DURING THE.

CHINA. See PEOPLE'S REPUBLIC OF CHINA, LIFESPAN RELATIONSHIPS IN THE.

CHIVALRY. See MIDDLE AGES, LIFESPAN RELATIONSHIPS DURING THE.

CIVIL MARRIAGE CEREMONY. A civil marriage ceremony is one in which the marriage is performed by a justice of the peace or government official rather than a member of the clergy. For various reasons, some couples avoid large, formal wedding ceremonies and instead choose this kind of observance. This may be due to financial considerations, pregnancy, a health problem in the family, or other reasons. The ceremony itself is relatively simple in scope. The following fictionalized wedding of "John" and "Mary" illustrates the steps in the civil marriage ceremony:

"We are gathered here in the presence of these witnesses for the purpose of uniting in matrimony, John and Mary. The contract of marriage is most solemn and is not to be entered into lightly, but thoughtfully and seriously and with a deep realization of its obligations and responsibilities.

"John, do you take this woman, Mary, to be your lawful wedded wife?"

"I do."

"Mary, do you take this man, John, to be your lawful wedded husband?"

"I do."

"Do you each promise to love and comfort one another, to honor and keep one another, in sickness and in health, in prosperity and adversity, and forsaking all others, to be faithful to each other as long as you both shall live?"

"We do."

(*For ring ceremony*) "John, place the ring on the third finger of Mary's left hand and repeat after me, to her: Mary, with this ring I thee wed." (Repeat, Mary to John, for double-ring ceremony.)

(*For no ring ceremony*) "Join hands.

"John, repeat after me to Mary: I, John, take thee, Mary, to be my lawful wedded wife.

"Mary, repeat after me to John: I, Mary, take thee, John, to be my lawful wedded husband.

"By virtue of the authority vested in me, I now pronounce you husband and wife."

In addition to being performed by a certified justice of the peace, the civil marriage ceremony must be witnessed by two persons of legal age. Following the ceremony, the couple, the justice of the peace, and the witnesses sign the marriage license.

Further Reading. Ruback, Barry. (1985). Family law. In Luciano L'Abate (Ed.), *The handbook of family psychology and therapy.* Homewood, IL: Dorsey Press; Turner, Jeffrey S., and Donald B. Helms. (1988). *Marriage and family: Traditions and transitions.* San Diego, CA: Harcourt Brace Jovanovich.

CLIENT-CENTERED THERAPY. See ROGERS, CARL R.

CLOSE RELATIONSHIPS, SCIENTIFIC STUDY OF. The scientific study of close relationships is a relatively new addition to the social sciences. The study of close relationships encompasses many areas, including patterns of interaction, styles of communication, gender roles, interpersonal attraction and rejection, affiliation, friendship, and love. Of particular interest to investigators is the exploration of those behavioral dimensions involved in the creation of relationships, and the manner in which relationships unfold over the course of the lifespan. Researchers exploring close relationships draw from a number of different disciplines, among them psychology, sociology, family studies, social psychology, and communication studies. Examples of research journals devoted to the scientific study of close relationships are *Journal of Social and Personal Relationships* and *Journal of Personality and Social Psychology.*

Further Reading. Hendrick, Susan, and Clyde Hendrick. (1992). *Liking, loving, and relating* (2nd Ed.). Belmont, CA: Brooks/Cole; Weber, Ann L., and John H. Harvey. (Eds.). (1994). *Perspectives on close relationships.* Boston, MA: Allyn and Bacon.

COGNITIVE-DEVELOPMENTAL THEORY. Cognitive-developmental theory is a major school of thought in psychology, particularly within the realm of lifespan development. The basic foundation of this theory is that cognitive maturity unfolds through a series of developmental stages. Our understanding of this sequential progression has been considerably enhanced through the efforts of Swiss psychologist Jean Piaget.

In developing this theory, Piaget explored how knowledge developed in humans. His research revealed that intellectual development proceeds in an orderly sequence that is characterized by specific growth stages. He postulated that these growth stages enable the child to develop certain concepts necessary for intellectual maturity. Consequently, Piaget believed conceptual development to be sequential, a series of qualitative intellectual advancements that eventually produce systematic and mature levels of thinking and reasoning.

The Piagetian design for mental growth hinges on two important mental processes: assimilation and accommodation. *Assimilation,* the more primitive of the two, is the perception and interpretation of new information in terms of existing knowledge and understanding. Put another way, children attempt to explain new phenomena by referring to their current frame of reference. A child who has been exposed only to cars, for example, may call a truck or a bus a car, simply because this is the only vehicle name that is stored in the child's existing mental organization.

Accommodation, on the other hand, is the restructuring of mental organization in order that new information may be included. Whereas the process of assimilation molds the object or event to fit within the person's existing frame of reference, accommodation changes the mental structure so that new experiences may be added. Thus, if an incident takes place that does not correspond with an existing mental framework, individuals may revise their way of thinking in order to interpret that event. The child who effectively uses accommodation skills in the previous example will develop a new mental structure to categorize a truck after it is realized that trucks cannot be put in the category of cars.

In order to chart the course of mental growth, Piaget proposed four stages of development. The first stage is labeled *sensorimotor development* (ages 0 to 2). During this early phase of development, the infant exercises rudimentary sensory and motor awareness and functions almost exclusively by means of reflexive responses. In the beginning, limited cognitive activity takes place and little distinction is made between the self and the environment. By the end of the first year, however, meaningful interactions with one's surroundings have begun. For example, by the end of this period the infant may shake or strike a crib mobile if its movement proves to be interesting; and when objects disappear from sight, the infant knows that, instead of disappearing totally "out of sight, out of mind," they remain permanent in reality.

During *preoperational thought* (ages 2 to 7), the child demonstrates an increase in language abilities, and concepts become more elaborate. Children are largely *egocentric* (self-centered) and view the world from their own perspective. Thinking tends to be impulsive, and the discrimination of objects tends to be on the basis of obvious physical appearances. By the end of this stage, the world is increasingly represented by the use of mental images.

By the time the stage of *concrete operations* (ages 7 to 11) is reached, individuals grasp the concept of conservation. By this concept, it can be understood that an object can conserve its amount, weight, or mass when it is poured into a different-sized container, placed into a different position, or molded into a different shape. The ability to consider viewpoints of others, classify objects and order them in a series along a dimension (such as size), and understand relational concepts (A is larger than B) is evident. However, a significant limitation of this stage is the child's inability to solve problems of an abstract nature.

Formal operations (ages 11 to 15), sometimes called *formal thought,* is the final stage of Piaget's theory. Abstract thinking is now possible, and scientific problem-solving strategies emerge. When a problem is approached, the individual draws a hypothesis and develops several potential solutions. Advanced logic and reason accompany formal operations. Such thinking abilities herald the relinquishment of childhood mental operations and the emergence of mature adult thought. However, it is important to note that not everyone reaches formal operations and the maturity of mental operations.

Piaget's theory of cognitive development is unique and one of the most comprehensive within the field of developmental psychology. Although his work was not widely recognized by the psychology community in the United States until the 1950s, Piaget is regarded as a leading authority in the field of cognitive-developmental theory. His research has stimulated vast amounts of research in psychology, lifespan development, and education, and his theory has provided a springboard for many investigators to launch their own ideas. Examples of such avenues of exploration are *moral development,* the manner in which standards of right and wrong are learned, and *social cognition,* how individuals interpret and use information about the social world (see PIAGET, JEAN; MORAL DEVELOPMENT; SOCIAL COGNITION).

Further Reading. Piaget, Jean. (1954). *The construction of reality in the child.* New York: Basic Books; Piaget, Jean. (1965). *The child's conception of number.* New York: Norton; Piaget, Jean. (1969). *The child's conception of time.* London: Routledge and

Kegan Paul; Piaget, Jean. (1972). Intellectual evolution from adolescence to adulthood. *Human Development, 15,* 1–12.

COHABITATION. Cohabitation is the living together of an unmarried man and an unmarried woman. Cohabitation is an extremely popular lifestyle today. Indeed, over the course of the last 25 years, the number of unmarried couples living together has increased by at least 495 percent. Moreover, it is projected that during the 1990s, about 7 percent of all U.S. households will consist of unmarried couples living together.

There are many reasons behind a couple's decision to cohabit. Sexual values are changing—for example, the widespread acceptance of the sexual standard of relational orientation or permissiveness with affection. By this standard, sexual activity is seen as a natural extension of serious, intimate relationships (see SEXUAL VALUES, IMPACT OF ON INTIMATE RELATIONSHIPS). Additionally, the availability of contraceptives and the relative ease of obtaining an abortion have reduced the risk of pregnancy among sexually active cohabitants. Peer support for cohabitation represents an additional reason, and many cohabitants are today less concerned about the status of marriage. Adults who have witnessed their parents' marriage break down may also have less faith in formal marriage as an institution that can provide security and happiness.

Today, most cohabitants are under age 35. Often, one of the partners is likely to have been separated or divorced. Cohabitation is especially popular among college students, largely because of the availability of off-campus housing, coed dormitories, and liberal student attitudes. In recent years, there has been an increase in the number of older cohabitants as well. It is estimated that there are approximately 350,000 persons over age 55 living together.

There are many types of cohabitation arrangements. Some couples live together for purely economic reasons. Some cohabit without any desire to become involved in a personal intimate relationship. For others, the opposite is true: cohabitation offers the opportunity to establish a close relationship. The largest number of cohabitants, however, are those who believe that marriage is on the horizon. In this instance, cohabitation is a precursor to marriage, not an alternative. In support of this latter point, many researchers have found that more than one-half of recently married couples had cohabited first.

Premarital cohabitation can last for years. Some partners enjoy this opportunity to combine love, work, and sexual intimacy in a setting that is free of parental control yet lacking in the constraints posed by a legal bond. Also, for some it fills the need to test the ability to relate intimately with a partner, a necessary skill for the survival of legal marriage. Cohabitation allows some people to grow and change together without forcing them to make a permanent mutual commitment before they feel ready for this. It may also allow them to separate without the burden of failure and guilt associated with divorce.

But while cohabitation has positive features, it is not without its share of problems. Potential legal problems are an important consideration, such as when "rights" regarding property and earnings surface. Some partners report guilt over their living arrangements, and even more are fearful of their parents' reaction. Because of the latter, many refuse to disclose their living arrangements to their parents. Another problem is that many couples feel closed in and stunted by their lifestyle. Pregnancy often poses complications for those choosing cohabitation over marriage. For example, when cohabitants do have children, separating can be as difficult and distressing as any legal divorce.

Further Reading. Bumpass, Larry L., James A. Sweet, and Andrew Cherlin. (1991). The role of cohabitation in declining rates of marriage. *Journal of Marriage and the Family, 53,* 913–927; DeMaris, Alfred, and K. Vaninadha Rao. (1992). Premarital cohabitation and subsequent marital stability in the United States: A reassessment. *Journal of Marriage and the Family, 54,* 178–190; Szlezak, Andrzej. (1991). Cohabitation without marriage in Poland. *International Journal of Law and the Family, 5,* 1–12.

COHORT. A cohort is a group of people sharing a common demographic experience whom researchers observe through time. The most commonly used cohort is the birth cohort, or individuals born in the same year. Examples of other cohorts include marriage cohorts or school graduation-class cohorts. When examining a particular type of cohort, researchers are able to explore those situations and events unique to a particular group. Whenever a research design is put into operation and data are collected, one must go a step further and examine cohort differences, often referred to as cohort analysis. This is especially true in cross-sectional studies, since subjects of varying ages are examined at the same time (see CROSS-SECTIONAL RESEARCH DESIGN). For example, suppose it is discovered that 60-year-olds are more financially cautious than 25-year-olds. Could that have been influenced by the 60-year-olds living through the stock-market crash and the Great Depression? Or was it because the 25-year-olds were reared in a world of charge cards, layaways, and instant credit? By exploring the experiences common to each age cohort, researchers might discover the answers to such questions.

Further Reading. Haupt, Arthur, and Thomas T. Kane. (1985). *The population reference bureau's population handbook.* Washington, DC: Population Reference Bureau; Shryock, Henry S., and Jacob S. Siegel. (1976). *The methods and materials of demography.* Orlando, FL: Academic Press.

COLONIAL AMERICA, LIFESPAN RELATIONSHIPS IN. The colonists who voyaged to America were in search of a better life in the New World. The colonial period began with the settlement of Jamestown in 1607 and ended with the start of the Revolutionary War in 1775. During this relatively short time, a wilderness was conquered and a new nation was established.

The colonists brought a number of European customs and beliefs to the New World that impacted on various lifespan relationships. For example, early marriages were encouraged. Delaying marriage was viewed as impractical since it resulted in a loss of harvest and a failure to cultivate important farmland. Remaining single was also not popular. Throughout colonial history, bachelors were viewed with suspicion and, in some instances, mistrust. In several colonies, such as Plymouth, single men had to pay special taxes that were levied against them because of their unmarried status.

The struggle that existed between church and state for the control of marriage also found its way to colonial America, although it was more evident in northern colonies than in southern ones. Divorces were also recognized in the New World, but divorce laws varied throughout the colonies, and, in general, divorces were not widespread. For example, there were only 40 divorces granted in the entire state of Massachusetts between 1639 and 1692.

Unlike customs in the Old World, most marriages in colonial America were not prearranged. However, it was expected that the prospective bridegroom would secure the father's permission for the bride's hand in marriage. In general, the courtship period was short. Also, families of the bride and groom tended to know one another.

While marriages were created early, the physical hardships that abounded created many widows and widowers. Females, usually assuming the responsibilities of motherhood at immature ages, typically suffered ill health and often succumbed to an early death. The fatality rate of males was also high for a host of reasons, including disease, famine, and the lack of proper sanitation. But while marriages were often short-lived, widows and widowers alike remarried, and for the most part, this was done rather quickly. Because of the cited reasons, three marriages by the same person were not at all uncommon during colonial times.

The colonial family was patriarchal, and the husband decided important matters affecting the household. His wife and children were expected to obey him without question. For children, respect for both parents was mandatory. This was very much in evidence in Puritan New England, where children had to stand up when addressing their parents, usually calling them "honored sir" or "honored madam." The physical abuse of children was no stranger to colonial America.

As in the Old World, children were viewed as economic commodities and needed hands on the farm. They were taught how to make contributions to the household at an early age and over time became vital components to the family enterprise. Boys were usually taught how to hoe, weed, plant, mend fences, and perform other farm-related chores. Girls, as has been the case throughout history, were given domestic chores such as milking, tending the garden, or candlemaking. As far as intergenerational relations were concerned, many scholars believe that the elderly during colonial times began to receive less-than-adequate care and treatment, a historical trend that helped to shape current ageist attitudes toward older adults. Many saw the elderly as weak, dependent, and a burden to others (see ADULTHOOD, AGEISM AND).

Further Reading. Albin, Mel, and Dominick Cavallo. (Eds.). (1981). *Family life in America, 1620–2000*. St. James, New York: Revisionary Press; Hareven, Thomas K.

(1984). Themes in the historical development of the family. In Ross D. Parke (Ed.), *The family*. Chicago: University of Chicago Press; Henretta, James A., W. Elliot Brownlee, David Brody, and Susan Ware. (1987). *America's history*. Chicago: Dorsey Press.

COMING OUT. Coming out occurs when gays or lesbians acknowledge, accept, and disclose their same-sex preferences to others. Some gays deny to themselves and others that they are attracted to members of their own sex. Others admit same-sex preferences to themselves, but not to heterosexuals around them. Such people typically lead double lives, enjoying same-sex contacts in secret and behaving heterosexually in public. But some gays and lesbians choose to fully disclose their homosexual orientation, a process sometimes called "coming out of the closet."

Disclosure of one's sexual orientation is a difficult decision. Indeed, to decide to come out may be one of the most painful yet important decisions a gay or lesbian may make. Most communities in which we live and work are conservative in their attitudes toward gays, thus making the coming-out decision even more uncomfortable for fear of repercussions.

In recent years, a type of forced coming out known as outing has attracted attention. *Outing* refers to the public disclosure, by someone else and without the individual's permission, of a public figure's homosexuality. Outing has created a rift in the gay/lesbian community. Some gay rights groups, believing that public figures lead public private lives, reveal the sexual orientation of a gay or lesbian person to the public. This procedure might have severe consequences in that the gay person's family might not be aware of the circumstances, jobs might be in jeopardy, or a host of other negative consequences may occur. Those who believe that outing is positive for the gay/lesbian community argue that the public has accepted this person and should now be aware that gays and lesbians are indeed role models for society.

Further Reading. Blumenfeld, Warren J., and Diane Raymond. (1988). *Looking at gay and lesbian life*. Boston: Beacon Press; Cass, Vivienne C. (1979). Homosexual identity formation: A theoretical model. *Journal of Homosexuality, 4,* 219–235; Coleman, Eli. (1985). Developmental stages of the coming out process. In John C. Gonsiorek (Ed.), *A guide to psychotherapy with gay and lesbian clients*. New York: Harrington Park Press.

COMMON-LAW MARRIAGE. A common-law marriage generally is one based not upon ceremony or compliance with legal formalities but upon the mutual agreement of two persons, legally competent to marry, to live together as husband and wife. Today, there are only 13 states and the District of Columbia—each with its own provisions—wherein common-law marriage is held to be legal. The states are Alabama, Colorado, Georgia, Idaho, Iowa, Kansas, Montana, Ohio, Oklahoma, Pennsylvania, Rhode Island, South Carolina, and Texas.

At times in the past, common-law marriages have been particularly useful, such as during the settlement of the American frontier. At that time, individuals who could marry two people were few and far between. Contrary to the thoughts of many, there is usually no minimum time interval required for a common-law marriage, even today. Interestingly, the effect of a common-law marriage parallels that of a ceremonial marriage in those states recognizing such arrangements. That is, the marriage is regarded as valid and requires a legal divorce to dissolve it.

Further Reading. Ruback, Barry. (1985). Family law. In Luciano L'Abate (Ed.), *The handbook of family psychology and therapy.* Homewood, IL: Dorsey Press; Turner, Jeffrey S., and Donald B. Helms. (1988). *Marriage and family: Traditions and transitions.* San Diego, CA: Harcourt Brace Jovanovich.

COMMUNE. A commune is a self-supporting community in which residents dedicate themselves to cooperative living. The concept of communal living is not a recent development. Rather, communes are rooted in antiquity, with some dating back to 103 B.C. The Oneida Community of New York State was founded as far back as 1848 by religious leader John Noyes. Other communes, also based on religious philosophies, have been around for some time, such as the Amish of Pennsylvania or the Hutterites of Canada. Some communes, though, are of more recent origin, such as the many ideological communes that sprang up during the 1960s and 1970s. Today, it is estimated that several thousand rural and urban communes are scattered throughout the United States, with about one million persons living within them.

As indicated, many communes are formed because of philosophical or religious beliefs. The commune often exists as a society whose life is governed by idealistic goals and a spiritual rebirth. This is attractive to those who join communes in an effort to escape alienation and isolation. Other communes are formed for other reasons, such as economic purposes.

Some communes, in an effort to encourage intimacy among their members, minimize the importance of marriage. Married couples are asked to share allegiance to the group as a whole. Frequently, communes use only first names, encourage emotional relationships among group members, and take away property belonging to the couple as a means of spreading the love bond between husband and wife to the commune as a whole. Some also encourage sexual relationships among group members.

Many communes are characterized by equality, whether in the form of shared domestic tasks or in the provision of emotional support. Child rearing, for instance, is considered a community task. Work assignments are also equally dispersed. Men and women frequently work side by side and typically earn the same amount of money, which is channeled to the collective.

While some communes succeed and meet their goals, many fail. Relinquishing all of one's resources to the group becomes a stumbling block for some. Others rebel at the loss of privacy. Many communes fail because the business enterprises undertaken, such as farming, are poorly planned and executed. Many communes also have a loose overall organization, which often leads to a general lack of leadership and needed direction. These factors, coupled with frequent membership instability, often create internal disharmony and unsteadiness.

Further Reading. Aidala, Angela A., and Benjamin D. Zablocki. (1991). The communes of the 1970s: Who joined and why? *Marriage and Family Review, 17,* 87–116; Eiduson, Bernice T., and Irla Lee Zimmerman. (1985). Nontraditional families. In Luciano L'Abate (Ed.), *The handbook of family psychology and therapy.* Homewood, IL: Dorsey Press.

COMMUNICATION, INTERPERSONAL. Interpersonal communication involves the exchange of information and messages between people. As such, it represents a complex and multifaceted process that occurs at both the verbal and nonverbal levels. It is shaped by the motivations and feelings of the communicators, and the exchange of messages tends to follow a stagelike progression (see COMMUNICATION, STAGES OF).

How humans learn how to speak and share meaningful forms of communication is a fascinating area of study. At a fundamental level, we know that the process of communication consists of both speech and language. At the outset, it should be realized that speech and language are related to, though also different from, each other. *Speech* is the concrete, physical act of forming and sequencing the sounds of oral language. *Language* is the system of grammatical rules and semantics that makes speech meaningful. Understanding the dynamics of communication also requires an awareness of *phonology,* the speech sounds relevant to a language.

Not everyone in our society communicates in the same fashion. Instead, there are many variations in language and communication styles, referred to as *dialects.* Dialects have at their roots the same general language but differ in their expressions and verbal details. Geography is an example of a factor creating dialectical differences in communication. Certain words may be difficult to understand when listening to geographical dialect differences. Often, different words are used to refer to the same object in different geographical locations. Age and social class may also contribute to dialect differences.

Another communication variation results because of gender differences. Researchers have found that traditional men tend to do more verbal interrupting and employ more hostile words and expletives. Men also employ fewer intensifying modifiers (adverbs such as "quite" or "so") than women. Women, on the other hand, appear better at initiating and maintaining conversations. Women also seem to be more verbally supportive of their conversational partners and tend to be more expressive, particularly with their feelings and emotions.

When people communicate, it is possible to identify different types and styles of expressions. For example, while people communicate using speech and language, they also establish personal space and territoriality when they talk. (Researchers interested in this aspect of communication refer to it as *proxemics.*) *Kinesics,* the study of bodily movements when we speak, is another dimension of communication. Kinesics pays special attention to body language, such as eye contact, posturing, gestures, and facial expression (see COMMUNICATION, NONVERBAL).

Paralanguage is another facet of communication. Paralanguage includes all of the vocal components that individuals use to communicate, such as volume (voice loudness or softness), pitch (voice highness or lowness), inflection (the change or lack of change in pitch when words are spoken), and enunciation (pronunciation and articulation). While the process of communication consists of speech and language, paralanguage serves to convey moods and attitudes while we speak. Put another way, the focus of paralanguage is on how we communicate.

Finally, metamessages are an important facet of communication. *Metamessages* represent intentional alterations of speech rhythm or pitch for emphasis, or the use of special verbal modifiers. Metamessages add another level of meaning to a sentence, often an incongruent one. For example, the language component of communication may seem simple or straightforward, but the metamessage may communicate sarcasm or hostility. We commonly refer to such contradictory styles of communication as "mixed messages," "double messages," or "double-talk."

Paralanguage and metamessages illustrate how many of the sentences we use often have two levels of meaning. One level is basic speech and language; the second is paralanguage and metamessages. While the interaction between the two need not be negative, it often creates problems. Experts contend that we can be better communicators if we expand our awareness of paralanguage and metamessages. By paying more attention to how we communicate, we can discover whether our voice reflects what we want to say, if the voice is congruent with the words spoken, or if there is something about the voice that is irritating and needs to be changed. (See LISTENING, ACTIVE AND PASSIVE STYLES OF; LISTENING, AND COMMUNICATION EFFECTIVENESS.)

Further Reading. Birtchnell, John. (1993). *How humans relate.* Westport, CT: Praeger; Knapp, Mark. (1972). *Nonverbal communication in human interaction.* New York: Holt, Rinehart and Winston; McKay, Matthew, Martha Davis, and Patrick Fanning. (1983). *Messages: The communication skills book.* Oakland, CA: New Harbinger Publications; Tannen, Deborah. (1990). *You just don't understand: Women and men in conversation.* New York: William Morrow.

COMMUNICATION, NONVERBAL. Nonverbal communication, also known as *kinesics,* is communication without the use of words. Such forms of communication include body posture and movement, gestures, eye contact, and the like. Because we continually convey messages with body language, it is important to analyze the impact of such communications on relationships.

Nonverbal communication can be especially effective at communicating feelings and attitudes, but it is not necessarily superior or better adapted to the expression of feelings than verbal communication. The two are better viewed as components of the total communication process, and their effectiveness or ineffectiveness rests with the individual speaker.

Nonverbal communication transmits a unique flow of steady messages. Our movements and actions as well as our facial expressions and silences all have something to say. To illustrate, consider the multiple meanings conveyed by eye contact. Extended eye contact may mean watchful attention, intense or careful scrutiny, interest in a potential partner, or even an attempt to establish dominance or superiority. On the other hand, the lack of eye contact may mean nervousness, disinterest, timidity, or even insecurity. Suffice it to say that eye contact may be used for a variety of different purposes.

It must be recognized that nonverbal communication can sometimes be vague and unclear. While nonverbal communication is revealing, multiple interpretations are possible, particularly when one considers racial, ethnic, and religious variations. Also, verbal and nonverbal modes of communication may be contradictory. We may say one thing in our words ("Yes, I enjoyed it") and another in our actions (bored expression). This is double-talk or a double message, and it creates confusion ("Did she really enjoy it?"). (See COMMUNICATION, INTERPERSONAL.)

Researchers have also discovered interesting gender differences in regard to nonverbal communication. To begin with, women tend to use more eye contact than do men. More specifically, women engage in longer and steadier gazes when they are sitting close to a partner. Men tend to make eye contact only when their partners are farther away. Facial expression also varies between women and men: women tend to use far more facial expressions than do men and tend to smile more often. Men touch others more than women do, and women are the recipients of more touching than are men.

Nonverbal communication researchers have uncovered some interesting patterns of body language, particularly within the realm of interpersonal attraction. For example, the pupil of the eye tends to dilate when there is interest in a potential partner. Before speaking to a person of interest, many people lean forward and align the upper body, as if to show that their conversation is imminent. Eye contact, a slight nod, and a friendly smile typically signal the beginning of a conversation. Conversely, the turning away of the upper body (the "cold shoulder"), tensed lips, and arm crossing represent negative nonverbal signals. The lack of any nonverbal communication whatsoever, such as expressionless eyes or a blank state, is usually a sign of indifference.

Further Reading. Buck, Ross. (1974). Communication of affect through facial expressions in humans. In Shirley Weitz (Ed.), *Nonverbal communication.* New York: Oxford University Press; Givens, David. (1983). *Love signals.* New York: Pinnacle Books; Hall, Judith A. (1984). *Nonverbal sex differences: Communication accuracy and expressive style.* Baltimore: Johns Hopkins University Press.

COMMUNICATION, SEXUAL. Sexual communication involves the exchange of messages that are related to the expression of human sexuality. While we are growing up, sexual communication is used to learn about many different aspects of our personal lives, from gender roles to human reproduction.

Later in life, we learn new aspects of sexual communication to help establish and maintain intimate relationships. Sexual communication comes to serve a number of important functions, including ways to express our motivations, thoughts, and feelings.

There are many advantages to establishing good communication about sexual matters. For example, it has been shown that talking about sex enhances a couple's acquisition of sexual knowledge and promotes overall sexual satisfaction. Researchers consistently find that people whose relationships are deep and meaningful are more satisfied than others with their sexual communication. Usually, the frequency of good sexual communication is positively related to a couple's adjustment and satisfaction. Effective sexual communication is also linked to optimum sexual health and well-being. Indeed, those couples who employ effective communication are usually more apt to minimize sexual risk taking and to engage in proper contraceptive usage.

Yet, in spite of such advantages, many people find it difficult to talk about sex with their partners. Many find it difficult to reveal their personal reactions, sensitivities, or sexual preferences. Indeed, most couples are poorly prepared to share their sexual selves in an open and frank manner. Many have inhibitions about speaking out, do not know how or where to begin, or are uneasy about hurting their partner's feelings when the topic arises.

Perhaps the most obvious reason that people are inhibited from talking about sex with their partners is that it makes them vulnerable. This is especially true for traditional males, who have been taught to hide their feelings and sensitivities. Revealing sexual needs or desires, as well as knowledge and attitudes, represents personal self-disclosure. Individuals often feel at risk in exposing private aspects of their identity. Moreover, a person may fear that talking about sex with his or her partner may result in embarrassment or shame.

There are other barriers to sex talk. Partners may feel that they do not need to discuss the sexual aspect of their relationship, or the topic may be perceived as a threat to the relationship. Talking about sex may be perceived as risky; that is, it may reveal discrepant preferences in a domain that is central to the relationship and integral to the identities of the partners. Because of this, many partners feel that it is easier to mask a sexual problem, rather than rock the boat.

Differences between men and women in the manner in which they think about and talk about sexual interaction also represent obstacles to couples talking about sex. Men and women often have different vocabularies for referring to male and female genitalia and the act of copulation, even when communicating with their intimate sexual partners. The use of different terminology is not inherently problematic, but it has the potential of creating communication difficulties. In this respect, more significant than a misunderstanding are the feelings that may be affected by how one's partner refers to body parts and sexual activities.

The fact that men and women communicate in different ways about their sexual relationships reflects the fact that men and women think differently about sex and its relational implications. Research suggests that sexual fulfillment and overall relationship intimacy are closely connected for women, and women are generally more ready to talk about their feelings. Men, conversely, tend to view their sexual relationships in primarily physical terms and often seem inclined to segment or distinguish sexual intimacy from other aspects of relational intimacy. Because of this, men and women may have difficulty in discussing sex in their relationship because of the way they have been socially programmed.

Further Reading. Crooks, Robert, and Karla Baur. (1993). *Our sexuality* (5th Ed.). Redwood City, CA: Benjamin/Cummings; Metts, Sandra, and William R. Cupach. (1989). The role of communication in human sexuality. In Kathleen McKinney and Susan Sprecher (Eds.), *Human sexuality: The societal and interpersonal context.* Norwood, NJ: Ablex; Turner, Jeffrey S., and Laurna Rubinson. (1993). *Contemporary human sexuality.* Englewood Cliffs, NJ: Prentice Hall.

COMMUNICATION, STAGES OF. The communication that evolves between two people is complex and multifaceted and must be understood if effective, meaningful interaction is to occur. This is as true for parent-child communication as it is for sexual communication between intimates or for the diversity of other ways that people communicate. The communication process can best be understood if it is broken down into four basic stages. These stages are sequential, but at times they overlap.

The first stage of the communication process is known as *encoding.* Here, a decision is made to communicate, and the sender translates the message to be conveyed into a set of symbols. Words represent the most obvious symbols, and this step is characterized by the sender selecting the appropriate words to convey the message. Encoding is thus a mental operation; it is not oral speech.

The second stage, *channeling,* entails the actual transmission of the message as encoded. Messages can be transmitted in a number of different forms. For example, they may be conveyed verbally, nonverbally, or in written form. Nonverbal messages may be communicated through body movements such as gestures, facial expressions, and posture.

Decoding is the third stage of the communication process. During this stage, the receiver interprets the message. The receiver perceives certain words or sees certain actions and interprets them as having a particular meaning. Depending on the skills of the sender in encoding and transmitting, and the skills of the receiver in receiving and decoding, the perceived meaning may match the intended meaning.

The final stage is called *understanding and feedback.* Should an accurate message be conveyed and successfully decoded, comprehension should take place at this time. However, some messages may be contradictory or unclear and thus distort comprehension and understanding. Feedback at this time from the receiver to the sender enables the participants to determine if the intended message has been accurately received. Should miscommunication result, feedback is the vehicle for repeating the progression of these four stages. (See LISTENING, ACTIVE AND PASSIVE STYLES OF; LISTENING, AND COMMUNICATION EFFECTIVENESS.)

Further Reading. Epstein, Laura. (1985). *Talking and listening.* St. Louis: Times Mirror/Mosby; McKay, Matthew, Martha Davis, and Patrick Fanning. (1983). *Messages: The communication skills book.* Oakland, CA: New Harbinger Publications; Smith, Neil, and Deirdre Wilson. (1979). *Modern linguistics.* New York: Penguin Books.

COMPLEMENTARY STYLES OF INTERACTION. See INTERACTION, STYLES OF WITHIN RELATIONSHIPS.

CONFIRMATION AND DISCONFIRMATION. Confirmation and disconfirmation are interpersonal processes that shape a person's definition of the self. *Confirmation* can be thought of as whatever actions cause another person to feel recognized or acknowledged. *Disconfirmation,* on the other hand, embodies the denial of another person's self-attributions or sense of being.

Confirmation and disconfirmation greatly impact on one's self-perception, including self-esteem and worth. Confirmation is viewed as the pivotal feature of all human interaction, a process that shapes a person's identity and causes one to feel accepted and endorsed. Put another way, confirmation implies recognition of another person as a unique being. It means acceptance of another person's individuality and a validation of one's significance or worth. Many researchers feel that confirmation of an individual's self-image is perhaps the most significant factor ensuring mental development and stability.

Confirmation begins early in life, such as when infant needs are met. Over time, a budding positive self-concept thrives on confirmation from others, particularly those from one's immediate surroundings. With age, one's self-perception is fueled by a host of other socialization agents, including friends, neighbors, teachers, and coaches. Should confirmation be encountered, self-worth and esteem usually escalate. But some relationship systems will emerge as more important than others, thus affecting the overall impact of confirmation.

Disconfirmation, on the other hand, negates the reality of a person, including his or her self-image. Because disconfirmation embraces unawareness of another person's point of view, it goes beyond accepting or rejecting the content of what the other person communicates. In essence, it discounts another person's right to exist. Like confirmation, disconfirmation is a lifelong process, and the negative appraisal of a person can begin early. Should disconfirmation be the case, negative self-worth usually compounds over time.

Learning how to interpret acts of confirmation and disconfirmation is also embedded in the life course. Persons tend to differ widely in the way they interpret the same acts toward them. However, individuals usually define and evaluate themselves by observing others' reactions. Both verbal and nonverbal behaviors serve to convey feelings of acceptance or rejection, or whether a person is valued or scorned.

Further Reading. Minuchin, Salvador (1974). *Families and family therapy.* Cambridge, MA: Harvard University Press; Nichols, Michael P. (1984). *Family therapy: Con-*

cepts and methods. New York: Gardner Press; Sieburg, Evelyn. (1985). *Family communication: An integrated systems approach.* New York: Gardner Press.

CONFLICT, PARENT-ADOLESCENT. Parent-adolescent conflicts are not uncommon occurrences. Indeed, disharmony and disagreement often accompany the strivings for separation and independence that teenagers often exhibit (see ADOLESCENCE, SEPARATION-INDIVIDUATION PROCESS OF). Also, the home environment may be affected by the parents' method of discipline as well as how well parents and teenagers understand each other. A lack of understanding and empathy between parents and teenagers is likely to disrupt family harmony and lead to conflicts.

The disagreements and conflicts between parents and teenagers can be numerous and diverse. Some of the common reasons cited for parent-adolescent conflicts are sexual behavior, money, dress, drugs, school performance, friendships in general, and the use of the family car. It is generally acknowledged that early adolescence is more stressful than late adolescence because parents are establishing new guidelines and parameters regarding acceptable and unacceptable behavior.

Disagreements between adolescents and parents also center on values. In the midst of the separation-individuation process, many adolescents reject the values and viewpoints of their parents. Disharmony concerning values tends to escalate when both teenagers and parents will not tolerate or accept the other's position. Obviously, good communication between young and old can do much to promote understanding and sensitivity. Parents and teenagers who are willing to listen and keep the lines of communication open are likely to minimize the psychological collisions in the home.

As far as gender differences within traditional homes are concerned, male and female adolescents tend to disagree more with their mothers than with their fathers, probably because the mother is more involved in the day-to-day operation of the household. Some researchers have found that conflict engagement with parents is more frequent shortly after a female experiences menarche, particularly conflicts between mother and daughter. This is a good example of how interpersonal processes occur in the family around a biological event such as puberty. Gender differences may also exist in parents' reactions to domestic disharmony. Fathers tend to report higher levels of stress if their offspring do not follow prescribed advice or if they become involved in deviant activities. For mothers, greater levels of stress are often reported when children desire more autonomy and independence.

Many teenagers try to escape adult authority when they experience the separation-individuation process. However, whether teenagers actually remove themselves from authority and gain freedom is open to question, especially if they seek the exclusive shelter of their peer group. Sometimes the pressure to conform to group expectations is just as great as, if not greater than, the pressure to conform at home. Adolescents may also find that their desire to be with others promotes a new type of dependence.

Teenagers' very desire to be independent may produce its own conflict. Teenagers can no longer be treated as children; on the other hand, they are not yet considered adults. In the United States, it is not clear when they pass from adolescent to adult status, since no rites of passage or formal initiation ceremonies exist that acknowledge an individual's entrance into adulthood. Complicating this issue is the fact that many adolescents have attained only token signs of independence. For example, adolescents may be given the privileges of dressing as they desire or going where they please, behaviors that on the surface seem to represent autonomy. Yet there is no guarantee that beneath the surface these same adolescents have attained psychological or emotional autonomy. Furthermore, some adolescents may have acquired privileges in exchange for their compliance with parental ideals and wishes. This type of trade-off causes many adolescents to settle for ritual signs of independence. Consequently, many forfeit true psychological growth.

Further Reading. Balk, David E. (1995). *Adolescent development.* Pacific Grove, CA: Brooks/Cole; Small, Stephen, Gay Eastman, and Steven Cornelius. (1988). Adolescent autonomy and parental stress. *Journal of Youth and Adolescence, 17,* 377–391; Whittaker, Shaun, and Brenna H. Bry. (1991). Overt and covert parental conflict and adolescent problems: Observed marital interaction in clinic and nonclinic families. *Adolescence, 26,* 865–876.

CONFLICT THEORY. Conflict theory is a major school of thought in human development, sociology, and family studies and is widely used in the study of close relationships. Conflict theory seeks to expose how disequilibrium, disharmony, and conflict are inevitable features of interpersonal experiences. Because of its inevitability, conflict is not viewed as an "evil" force; rather, it is an expected feature of social systems. Indeed, over the course of the lifespan, persons face the perpetual problem of coming to terms with themselves and the conflicting interests of those around them. Important concepts within this conceptual framework are power, competition, resources, negotiating, and bargaining.

In the study of relationships across the lifespan, conflict theorists emphasize the constant interplay of negotiation, problem solving, and conflict management. As an example, consider the potential for conflict when retirement occurs, including discontent or disagreement about household routines or responsibilities. The issue of power often weaves itself through such issues; that is, tension and conflict around domestic responsibilities are often fueled by the underlying issues of inequality or control. The potential for intergenerational friction exists when adult children provide care for aging parents, particularly when the latter are sick or disabled. For many, conflict often originates from such factors as conflicting interests or dwindling resources when coping with the multiple demands of caregiving.

Further Reading. Lips, Hilary M. (1991). *Women, men, and power.* Mountain View, CA: Mayfield; Sprey, Jessy. (1975). Family power and process: Toward a conceptual integration. In R. E. Cromwell and D. H. Olson (Eds.), *Power in families.* Beverly Hills, CA: Sage. Sprey, Jessy. (1979). Conflict theory and the study of marriage and the family. In Wesley R. Burr, Reuben Hill, and Ira Reiss (Eds.), *Contemporary theories about the family.* New York: Free Press.

CONFORMITY. Conformity is changing one's behavior in order to comply with expressed group opinions or norms. Conformity to others is a type of social influence that begins during childhood and continues throughout the lifespan. During childhood, conformity to others becomes apparent during peer-group interaction. While waging a battle to impress and be accepted by others, and at the same time striving to avoid rejection, children often conform to the norms established by the peer group. By the time adolescence is reached, conformity has expressed itself in a number of ways, from similar modes of dress, language, and hairstyles to similar activities and mannerisms. Adults, too, exhibit unique types of conformity, particularly when their judgments, actions, or conclusions are different from those reached by others.

Studies designed to measure conformity have repeatedly shown that individuals will go along with a group, even against their own better judgment. Exposed to group influences, many people will pattern their answers after others' responses to problem-solving situations. Many will conform even to obvious wrong answers, and the more uncertain people are in a problem-solving situation, the more likely they are to conform.

Psychologists have provided some explanations regarding conformity and why individuals tend to "go along" with the group. To begin with, strong pressures toward conformity exist in many social settings, such as learning to wait in line at a movie theater, wearing proper attire, or following traffic regulations. Thus we are programmed to a certain extent to obey, sometimes without even questioning the reasons. It is also known that people tend to conform when they like others and wish to gain their approval. Related to the wish for approval, the desire to be liked is a driving force behind the expression of conformity. Many people conform because they wish to avoid rejection or ridicule. Others do not want to be perceived as being different.

There are also explanations of why people choose not to conform. Many people resist conformity because they have a strong desire to maintain their own uniqueness or individuality. Some resist group pressure because they wish to maintain control over the events in their lives. Conformity in this sense is viewed as a restriction of personal freedom. Finally, research has revealed that certain factors tend to affect the expression of conformity. For example, conformity tends to increase with the number of individuals exerting conformity pressure and tends to decrease in the presence of social support, that is, one or more persons who depart from the majority's position.

Further Reading. Baron, Robert A., and Donn Byrne. (1994). *Social psychology: Understanding human interaction* (7th Ed.). Boston: Allyn and Bacon; Hendrick, Clyde.

(Ed.). (1987). *Group processes*. Newbury Park, CA: Sage; Smith, Peter B., and Michael H. Bond. (1994). *Social psychology across cultures: Analysis and perspectives*. Boston: Allyn and Bacon.

CONJUGAL FAMILY. See FAMILY COMPOSITION, TYPES OF.

CONSANGUINE FAMILY. See FAMILY COMPOSITION, TYPES OF.

CONTEXTUAL INFLUENCES ON LIFESPAN DEVELOPMENT.
Contextual influences on lifespan development are those influences that originate from the interrelationship between the changing person and the changing world. As such, contextual influences encompass such factors as culture, history, and life events. A wide array of contextual influences interact in complex ways, in the process affecting the life pattern of the individual. Lifespan development researchers have identified three major sets of factors that influence individual development: normative age-graded, normative history-graded, and nonnormative life events.

Normative age-graded influences are those normal or typical determinants that are closely related to one's age and are therefore rather predictable since they are similar for most people. Some of these are biological, such as the onset of menarche and menopause. Other normative age-graded influences involve socialization and cultural customs, such as marriage or retirement. These are sometimes referred to as developmental influences because their occurrence correlates highly with chronological age.

Normative history-graded influences are events that are widely experienced in a culture at a particular time. Such events can be biological (e.g., epidemics, malnutrition) or environmental (e.g., economic depression, war). However, biological and environmental events are often mutually influential. Normative history-graded influences often give a particular generation its unique identity, such as the Vietnam War or Great Depression generations.

Nonnormative influences refer to environmental and biological determinants that, while significant, do not occur in everyone, nor when they do occur, do they happen at a particular age. Thus nonnormative influences are unpredictable. Examples would include unemployment, winning a lottery, a birth defect, the onset of disease, or the unexpected death of a loved one.

These three sets of contextual influences interact with each other and appear to wax and wane at different times in an individual's life. Age-graded influences appear to dominate development from conception through childhood and puberty, but then are on the wane until they reemerge in late adulthood. History-graded and nonnormative influences become more common and powerful determinants during early and middle adulthood. For lifespan development researchers, particularly those exploring adult life, history-graded and nonnormative influences are especially important forces to examine. (See WORLD VIEWS OF LIFESPAN DEVELOPMENT.)

Further Reading. Baltes, Paul B. (1979). Life-span developmental psychology: Some converging observations on history and theory. In Paul B. Baltes and Orville G. Brim, Jr. (Eds.), *Life-span development and behavior.* New York: Academic Press; Baltes, Paul B. (1987). Theoretical propositions of lifespan developmental psychology: On the dynamics between growth and decline. *Developmental Psychology, 23,* 611–626; Elder, Glen H., Jr. (1977). Family history and the life course. *Journal of Family History, 2,* 279–304.

CONTINUITY-DISCONTINUITY ISSUE. The continuity-discontinuity issue is a philosophical issue debated primarily among developmental psychologists. Essentially, this issue concerns itself with whether growth and development from birth to death are gradual and continuous or adhere to age-prescribed stages. Those researchers who emphasize continuity see growth as being quantitatively acquired through interaction with the environment. The analogy of a seed being placed in the ground, sprouting, and gradually growing to maturity illustrates the concept of continuity. Similarly, those who see the life cycle as marked more by stability than by abrupt change see slow methodical change or gradation, with less relationship to the individual's age. A continuous developmental theory, then, emphasizes a subtle flow of maturation throughout the life cycle rather than distinct change. Within the field of lifespan development, this is referred to as a one-stage model of growth. Examples of theories reflecting this model are Skinner's theory of behaviorism and Bandura's social learning theory.

Discontinuity, on the other hand, is characterized by distinct spurts in growth and development. Researchers who emphasize discontinuous development tend to stress the role of heredity (nature) and maturation in the growth sequence. The analogy of a frog's life, beginning as an egg, hatching into a tadpole, and then experiencing distinct amphibious stages, illustrates the concept of discontinuity. Thus a discontinuous model of development emphasizes qualitative changes that make individuals fundamentally different from what they were before. For those perceiving the life cycle more as a time of constant change, significant and fundamental transformations would thus be stressed. Discontinuous development emphasizes stages of development, the assumption being that before one stage can occur, the person must have emerged from a previous stage. Stages of development are relatively sequential, with a definite order that allows no stage to be skipped, and are directly related to ages. Examples of discontinuous (or *age-stage*) theories emphasizing developmental change are Piaget's cognitive-developmental theory and Erikson's psychosocial theory. (See STABILITY-CHANGE ISSUE.)

Further Reading. Baltes, Paul B. (1987). Theoretical propositions of lifespan developmental psychology: On the dynamics between growth and decline. *Developmental Psychology, 23,* 611–626; Lerner, Richard M. (1986). *Concepts and theories of human development* (2nd Ed.). New York: McGraw-Hill; Thomas, R. Murray. (1992). *Comparing theories of child development* (3rd Ed.). Belmont, CA: Wadsworth.

CONTRACEPTION. Contraception is any natural, barrier, hormonal, or surgical method used to prevent conception. Related to contraception is *sterilization,* surgical intervention that permanently blocks reproductive capacity by preventing sperm or egg from being released. Some contraceptive methods (e.g., condoms, oral contraceptives) are reversible; that is, fertility is restored following the method's removal. Sterilization is considered irreversible because it permanently ends fertility in a man or a woman (although microsurgical techniques are having some success in reversing sterilization).

Some contraceptives are more effective than others, but all of them incur a certain number of failures. However, most unplanned pregnancies occur because of human factors. Choosing the contraceptive with the highest theoretical effectiveness, understanding that method, using it consistently, and being seriously motivated to prevent pregnancy are keys to successful birth control. The following are descriptions of the major forms of contraception available in the United States today.

Abstinence. Abstinence, the avoidance of intercourse, is clearly the surest method of birth control. When consistently used, it is 100 percent effective and has no cost factor. Some sex educators have advocated abstinence especially for young teenagers who are sexually active. Adolescent sexuality education programs encouraging abstinence emphasize reaching teenagers early with information on how and why to defer sexual activity, increasing their awareness of pressures to become sexually active, clarifying their values, reinforcing their ability to say no, and building assertiveness skills.

Sterilization. Sterilization is a surgical procedure that interrupts the reproductive tracts of either the male or the female so that fertilization is prevented. Sterilization has an excellent contraceptive effectiveness rating. For males, a *vasectomy* involves cutting the vas deferens to prevent the passage of sperm. The vasectomy does not interfere with ejaculation, since the sperm constitute only a very small portion of the semen. The sperm that are still produced by the testes degenerate and are reabsorbed by the body.

The most common form of female sterilization is a type of surgery called *tubal ligation* (often referred to as "tying the tubes"). In this surgical procedure, each fallopian tube is cut and tied (with rings or clips), thus preventing eggs from traveling through the tubes to the uterus. Menstruation continues, but the ovaries' eggs, when released, are trapped in the blocked-off tubes and reabsorbed by the body. As earlier mentioned, microsurgical techniques are having some success in reversing female and male sterilization. However, such procedures are surgically difficult and expensive.

Contraceptive implant. The contraceptive implant is a hormonal form of birth control that consists of six silicone rubber rods about an inch and one-third long. They are inserted in a fanlike arrangement under the skin of a woman's inner arm above the elbow. The minor surgical procedure is done with local anesthesia in a doctor's office or a clinic. The implants contain the hormone levonorgestrel, the synthetic progestin also used in oral contraceptives. The hormone is released slowly over five years. The implants can be removed anytime, and fertility is usually quickly restored. The contraceptive implant has an excellent effectiveness rating.

Depo-Provera. Depo-Provera is a hormonal contraceptive that is given as an intramuscular injection in the buttock or upper arm once every three months. To continue contraceptive protection, a woman must return for her next injection promptly at the end of three months. Depo-Provera contains a chemical similar to the natural hormone progesterone, which is produced by the ovaries during the second half of the menstrual cycle. Depo-Provera acts by preventing the egg from being released and also by changing the lining of the uterus so that implantation cannot take place. Depo-Provera has an excellent contraceptive effectiveness rating.

Oral contraceptives. Oral contraceptives, which are available by prescription only, fall into two broad categories: combination pills and minipills. *Combination pills* contain a synthetic estrogen combined with synthetic progesterone derivatives, called progestogens or progestins, which prevent ovulation (the release of an egg from the ovary). Because there is no egg, there can be no fertilization regardless of how many sperm enter the uterus during sexual intercourse. Combination pills also decrease the amount of mucus on the lining of the uterus, thus reducing the chances of a fertilized egg attaching itself to the uterine wall. The *minipill* contains progestin alone and does not always prevent ovulation. Rather, its major contraceptive function is to change the female's cervical mucus so that no sperm can enter. Both forms of oral contraceptives have excellent effectiveness ratings.

Intrauterine device (IUD). The intrauterine device is a small plastic device that is inserted in the uterine cavity by a physician. It prevents pregnancy by not allowing a fertilized egg to implant itself in the uterine lining and can remain in place for several years if no difficulties arise. Exactly how this happens is not known, although it is believed that the IUD acts as a foreign body, stimulating an inflammatory reaction in the endometrium. While this reaction creates no discomfort to the user, it creates an environment unfavorable to the implantation of the fertilized ovum. Despite its excellent contraceptive effectiveness rating, the IUD has posed a number of health problems to many users, and its popularity has waned in the United States. The IUD has been linked to a number of health problems, including pelvic inflammatory disease, miscarriages, infertility, and perforation of the uterus.

Condom. The condom is a thin sheath of latex rubber or processed tissue from lamb intestine that is placed over the erect penis before intercourse. The condom is categorized as a barrier method of contraception because it prevents sperm from entering the vagina when ejaculation occurs. The condom is the only temporary form of contraception directly under the male's control and is the major barrier method of birth control used around the world. The male condom has a very good contraceptive effectiveness rating. The latex condom offers good protection against sexually transmitted diseases.

Female condom. The female condom is made of two flexible rings that are connected to each other by a tube of thin polyurethane and one of which is also covered by a sheet of polyurethane. Thus this condom is designed to line the vagina. When it is inserted, the ring that is closed by polyurethane is placed over the cervix, just like a diaphragm; the other ring remains outside the vaginal opening. In addition to its contraceptive purpose, the female condom, like the male condom, can also afford protection from sexually transmitted diseases. The female condom has a very good contraceptive effectiveness rating.

Diaphragm. The diaphragm is also a barrier method of contraception. It is a thin sheet of latex stretched over a flexible spring rim that is coated with a jelly or cream spermicide and then inserted into the vagina so that it covers the cervix, the entrance to the uterus. The diaphragm needs to be carefully fitted by a doctor or a clinician during a pelvic examination. Different sizes are made to accommodate the variations in the size and shape of female internal genitalia. The diaphragm should remain in place until at least 6 hours after the last act of intercourse, but it should not be left in place for more than 24 hours. The diaphragm has a very good contraceptive effectiveness rating.

Cervical cap. The cervical cap, like the diaphragm, is a barrier contraceptive that blocks sperm from passing from the vagina into the uterus. The cervical cap measures about one and one-half inches in diameter and is made of soft rubber. It resembles a miniature diaphragm with a tall dome. Like the diaphragm, the cervical cap must be used with a spermicide and is available in different styles to fit the female's internal anatomy. The cervical cap has a good contraceptive effectiveness rating.

Vaginal spermicides. Vaginal spermicides are agents that have a sperm-killing effect. They are categorized as chemical methods and exist in a wide variety of forms, including aerosol foams, creams, jellies, tablets, and suppositories. Of these, aerosol foams are the most popular. Vaginal spermicides do not require a doctor's prescription, but should not be confused with lubricating gels and creams often found on the same pharmacy shelves. A vaginal spermicide must be used every time a couple has intercourse, and it must be in place before the penis enters or is near the vagina. Vaginal spermicides have a fair contraceptive effectiveness rating.

Vaginal sponge. The vaginal sponge is essentially a method of delivering a spermicide to the cervix and vagina. This disposable, spongelike device is slightly concave and round and is designed to feel like normal vaginal tissue. It is inserted deep into the vagina before intercourse takes place and will continuously release the spermicide for up to 24 hours. The sponge also provides a physical barrier between sperm and the cervix and traps sperm within itself. Unlike the diaphragm, additional applications of spermicide are not necessary even for multiple acts of intercourse. The sponge can be inserted several hours before lovemaking, but must be left in place for at least six hours following intercourse. The vaginal sponge has a fair contraceptive effectiveness rating.

Rhythm method. The rhythm method of birth control requires no mechanical or chemical means. Also called natural family planning, it means refraining from intercourse on days when conception is most likely, that is, during ovulation, which occurs once a month throughout a woman's life until she reaches menopause. The rhythm method thus depends on figuring out when ovulation will occur each month and refraining from intercourse during the days of greatest likelihood of conception (interestingly, the same techniques are used by couples who want to conceive). The rhythm method is the only method of birth control approved by the Roman Catholic church. Its contraceptive effectiveness rating is considered poor to fair.

Withdrawal. Withdrawal, also called *coitus interruptus,* is one of the world's oldest methods of birth control. It is also one of the riskiest. When the withdrawal technique is used, intercourse proceeds until ejaculation is about to occur, at which time the male withdraws his penis from the vagina. Many times, though, withdrawal is too late and semen enters the vagina. Also, preliminary ejaculatory liquid can escape before the penis is withdrawn. Withdrawal has a poor contraceptive effectiveness rating.

Further Reading. Committee on Contraceptive Development. (1990). *Developing new contraceptives: Obstacles and opportunities.* Washington, DC: National Academy Press; Harlap, Susan, Kathryn Kost, and Jacqueline D. Forrest. (1991). *Preventing pregnancy, protecting health: A new look at birth control choices in the United States.* New York: Alan Guttmacher Institute; Hatcher, Robert A., James Trussell, Felicia Stewart, and Gary K. Stewart. (1994). *Contraceptive technology* (16th Ed.). New York: Irvington Publishers.

CONTRACEPTION, HISTORICAL PRACTICES. Many mistakenly believe that contraception is an exclusive product of modern times. However, a glance backward through time reveals that birth control is hardly a recent phenomenon. Indeed, past birth-control practices reveal a number of unique customs. For example, primitive forms of diaphragms and cervical caps date back more than 2,500 years and have been made from materials as varied as gold and ivory. Cleopatra also reportedly experimented with using bits of hardened sea sponge and other materials as primitive intrauterine devices.

Among the Romans, a special charm was worn in an effort to prevent unwanted pregnancies. Often, such charms included the liver of a cat placed in a tube or a part of a lioness's womb sealed in ivory. The *Kama Sutra,* an ancient Indian sex manual written for women and men in the fourth century. suggested that the blossoms of the palash flower were effective as an oral contraceptive. In the seventeenth century, silk or linen condoms were used in the Orient and parts of Europe, primarily for the control of venereal disease. Among some Native American people, a ''snake girdle'' made of beaded leather and worn around the navel was a popular contraceptive symbol.

In remote corners of the world, some unique birth-control techniques are still practiced. For instance, many women of the Kavivordo people in Africa stand up after intercourse and shake their bodies in a quick jerky rhythm to remove semen from the vagina. Among the Sande of Africa, some women repeatedly slap the lower back and abdominal area to achieve the same result. In some primitive societies, plant and animal poisons are sometimes used to abort pregnancies. Unfortunately, such toxic substances run the risk of killing the mother, too. Sometimes, tight bands are also tied around a pregnant belly or sharp sticks are inserted into the vagina in an effort to extract the unwanted fetus.

But while many cultures have practiced contraception for thousands of years, only recently has birth control improved to the point where some methods are highly effective. In today's developed nations, effective birth control does not rely on magic or superstition. Rather, there are a number of sophisticated measures designed to prevent and space pregnancies, as well as techniques to abort unwanted pregnancies. Interestingly enough, though, even in these modern times, a number of folk ideas about contraception persist. For example, many people believe that douching immediately following intercourse prevents pregnancy, or that certain periods of the month are totally "safe" times to engage in unprotected intercourse. Thus, while ancient cultures used folk wisdom to guide their fertility, we still see unique variations of such thinking today. (See CONTRACEPTION.)

Further Reading. Foucault, Michael (1978). *The history of sexuality.* New York: Pantheon Books; Gregersen, Edgar. (1983). *Sexual practices.* New York: Franklin Watts; Turner, Jeffrey S., and Laurna Rubinson. (1993). *Contemporary human sexuality.* Englewood Cliffs, NJ: Prentice Hall.

COOLEY, CHARLES HORTON. Charles Horton Cooley (1864–1929) was a sociologist who studied the development of a person's sense of self as it emerged within social contexts. Cooley proposed that human development is a complex product of interaction with other humans in social groups. In his writings, he emphasized the importance of primary groups (e.g., families, play groups), small and intimate congregates whose members share complete concern and trust for each other. Cooley believed that membership in primary groups represented the vital connection between the individual and society. Moreover, he maintained that primary groups were basic and universal to all human societies. (See PRIMARY AND SECONDARY GROUPS.)

Cooley is also recognized for his concept of the "looking-glass self," a social process by which people develop their sense of self. Cooley maintained that individuals develop a sense of self through their impressions of others' attitudes about them. Using the analogy of a looking glass, Cooley felt that the sense of self represents a reflection of others' opinions. He saw three steps in the process of building the looking-glass self: our perception of how we look to others; our perception of their judgment of how we look; and our feelings about these judgments. Thus, as we use the looking glass to gain an estimation of our physical appearance, we also use the actions of others toward us to gain a social appraisal.

Further Reading. Cooley, Charles H. (1902). *Human nature and the social order.* New York: C. Scribner's Sons; Cooley, Charles H. (1908). A study of the early use of self words by a child. *Psychological Review, 15,* 339–357.

CORRELATIONAL RESEARCH. Correlational research is methodology designed to explore whatever relationship exists between variables. There are times when researchers exploring relationships across the lifespan might want to see if a connection exists between factors. As an example, we might want to discover if there is a relationship between marital conflict and spousal alcohol consumption. To explore the relationship between variables such as these, a technique called the *correlational method* might be employed. Although the statistics involved can sometimes get complicated, the idea behind the correlational method is simple: two variables are correlated when changes in one variable are associated with changes in the other variable. A *positive* or *direct* correlation exists when one variable tends to increase as the other increases. If one variable tends to decrease while the other increases, a *negative* or *inverse* correlation is said to exist. If there is no relationship between the variables, we say that they are *uncorrelated.* The correlational method can be used to assess data obtained from many different types of research techniques, including questionnaires, surveys, and experiments.

It is important to understand that correlational data do not establish cause-and-effect relationships. When one is interpreting correlations in lifespan development or any other discipline, it is important to remember that a high correlation does not necessarily indicate that a causal relationship exists between two variables. For example, a high positive correlation between marital conflict and spousal alcohol consumption does not ''prove'' that alcohol consumption causes marital friction. The correlation might be influenced by other factors— perhaps the disposition of partners, health factors, or a pileup of domestic demands. Even when correlations are very strong, they do not provide sufficient information to infer causality.

Further Reading. Creswell, John W. (1994). *Research design: Qualitative and quantitative approaches.* Thousand Oaks, CA: Sage; Heiman, Gary W. (1995). *Research methods in psychology.* Boston: Houghton Mifflin; Hinkle, Dennis E., William Wiersma, and Stephen G. Jurs. (1994). *Applied statistics for the behavioral sciences* (3rd Ed.). Boston: Houghton Mifflin.

COURTLY LOVE. See MIDDLE AGES, LIFESPAN RELATIONSHIPS DURING THE.

CRITICAL PERIOD. A critical period is a specific period of time when an environmental event exerts its greatest impact on the developing organism. *Ethologists,* researchers who explore human and animal behavior in natural settings, are particularly interested in exploring the dynamics of critical periods. They not only feel that organisms are especially sensitive to certain external stimuli, but maintain that some minimal sensory stimulation is needed during a specific time period if the organism is to develop normally (see ETHOLOGICAL THEORY).

Some researchers maintain that a *sensitive period* exists in humans, a highly significant time frame early in the lifespan that affects the course of certain developmental dynamics. To illustrate, in humans there seems to be a sensitive period between 6 and 16 months when the infant will usually attach itself to the primary caregiver. Prior to 6 months, babies may be handled by one and all, but it is during the critical period that attachment appears to develop. Those infants who, for one reason or another, are not left long in the care of one person may have difficulties in experiencing and expressing warm human relations. Research shows that institutionalized children deprived of stimulation tend to show maladaptive emotional and social behavior later in life (see FAILURE TO THRIVE). There is speculation that sensitive periods exist in other developmental arenas, such as language acquisition, cognitive development, and gender-role development.

Further Reading. Hinde, Robert A. (1983). Ethology and child development. In Paul H. Mussen (Ed.), *Handbook of child psychology* (4th Ed.). New York: Wiley; Hinde, Robert A. (1989). Ethnological and relationship approaches. In Ross Vasta (Ed.), *Six theories of child development: Revised formulations and current issues.* Greenwich, CT: JAI Press; Lorenz, Konrad. (1965). *Evolution and modification of behavior.* Chicago: University of Chicago Press.

CROSS-SECTIONAL RESEARCH DESIGN. A cross-sectional research design is a method of investigating developmental trends based on the comparison of groups that differ in age at a given time. In this design, researchers obtain comparative data from different groups of subjects more or less simultaneously. As an example, in a study exploring adult development, the analyst would select a number of groups of subjects aged (for example) 20, 30, 40, and 50 and record the differences among the various age groups. The differences would then be analyzed.

The cross-sectional research design differs from the *longitudinal design,* where the analyst collects data on the same group of individuals at intervals over a considerable period (see LONGITUDINAL RESEARCH DESIGN). Compared to the longitudinal research design, the cross-sectional approach is relatively inexpensive, easier to execute, and not overly time-consuming. However, it sometimes overlooks individual changes within the sample of subjects.

Further Reading. Breakwell, Glynis, Sean Hammond, and Chris Fife-Schaw. (1995). *Research methods in psychology.* Thousand Oaks, CA: Sage; Hessler, Richard M. (1992). *Social research methods.* St. Paul, MN: West; Hinkle, Dennis E., William Wiersma, and Stephen G. Jurs. (1994). *Applied statistics for the behavioral sciences* (3rd Ed.). Boston: Houghton Mifflin.

CULTURAL ANTHROPOLOGY. Cultural anthropology studies the social organization and patterns of behavior of people throughout the world. By undertaking such an exploration, cultural anthropologists seek to discover cross-cultural variations and similarities. Within the field of cultural anthropology are the two subfields of ethnography and ethnology. *Ethnography* is the description of the lives and culture of people in particular social groups. *Ethnology* is the study of the social patterns and cultural practices revealed by such description. Together these areas of study enable researchers to develop detailed and comparative cross-cultural analyses of human behavior.

Further Reading. Kottak, Conrad Phillip. (1994). *Cultural anthropology* (6th Ed.). New York: McGraw-Hill; Nanda, Serena. (1991). *Cultural anthropology* (4th Ed.). Belmont, CA: Wadsworth; Peoples, James, and Garrick Bailey. (1991). *Humanity: An introduction to cultural anthropology* (2nd Ed.). St. Paul, MN: West.

CULTURAL RELATIVISM. Cultural relativism is the belief that there is no universal standard of good or bad when evaluating cultures. Rather, this concept maintains that an aspect of any given culture can be judged only within the context of that culture. Thus any element of culture is deemed meaningful in relation to a particular location, time, and set of circumstances. Put another way, each culture is seen in its own terms. Cultural relativism encourages a sensitive and tolerant perspective of cultural ways and a closer analysis and appreciation of cultural variations. Cultural relativism seeks to combat *ethnocentrism,* the judging of behaviors and lifestyles of others as inferior or strange.

Further Reading. Adler, Leonore L., and Uwe P. Gielen. (Eds.). (1994). *Cross-cultural topics in psychology.* Westport, CT: Praeger; Calhoun, Craig, Donald Light, and Suzanne Keller. (1994). *Sociology* (6th Ed.). New York: McGraw-Hill; Ferrante, Joan. (1995). *Sociology: A global perspective* (2nd Ed.). Belmont, CA: Wadsworth.

CULTURAL ROLE SCRIPT. A cultural role script is a preconception of how one should behave in a social setting. It tells individuals what is expected of them in their roles as, say, dating partners or family members, as well as what expectations they should have for their partners. A cultural role script often reflects a scenario presented in the media or folklore, an image that instructs persons about appropriate goals, desirable qualities, and typical behaviors. Thus a cultural role script is a plan that individuals have in their heads.

Many cultural role scripts are aimed at sexual behavior and are deeply rooted in gender-role tradition. Often, these scripts define what sexual behaviors are right or wrong as well as the level of involvement each partner should have. For example, a traditional role script dictates male initiation of courtship behaviors as well as whatever sexual escalation is to take place. In another role script, men are often programmed to see themselves as the sexual experts, while women are portrayed as unknowledgeable participants. Other kinds of scripts portray when and where sex will take place, as well as what kinds of activity are appropriate or inappropriate.

Experts maintain that there is nothing wrong with following a cultural role script, provided it satisfies all of the individuals involved. Negotiation of a role script that individuals can be comfortable with is essential for relationship satisfaction and personal fulfillment. However, problems arise when one person chooses not to adhere to a traditional role script but fails to negotiate a new script.

Further Reading. Metts, Sandra, and William R. Cupach. (1989). The role of communication in human sexuality. In Kathleen McKinney and Susan Sprecher (Eds.), *Human sexuality: The societal and interpersonal context.* Norwood, NJ: Ablex; Simon, William, and John H. Gagnon. (1986). Sexual scripts: Permanence and change. *Archives of Sexual Behavior, 15,* 97–120.

CULTURE. Culture refers to everything individuals do or have as members of society. It represents the totality of humanity's existence and embraces such elements as knowledge, beliefs, customs, and morals. Culture is constantly communicated among people who share a common way of life, and it shapes perceptions and interpretations of life events. Moreover, culture is never static; rather, it is constantly changing. When studying relationships across the lifespan, researchers use the concept of culture to describe the wide variations that exist among groups of people in society.

Culture can be described as consisting of several major components: symbols, norms, and material and nonmaterial possessions. *Symbols* enable culture to be transmitted from one generation to the next. Language represents the most important symbol and enables humans to develop and interact in socially meaningful ways. *Norms* are expectations or guidelines for behavior within a society and can exist as folkways (norms shaping everyday habits and conventions), mores (norms related to a society's most cherished values), or laws (norms that are enforced through a society's legal system). *Material* and *nonmaterial possessions* represent the third component of culture. Material possessions represent all the physical objects that people make and attach meaning to, while nonmaterial possessions include such human creations as values, norms, or knowledge. (See ENCULTURATION; ETHNIC GROUP.)

Further Reading. Bryjak, George J., and Michael P. Soroka. (1994). *Sociology: Cultural diversity in a changing world.* (2nd Ed.). Boston: Allyn and Bacon; Buenker, John D., and Lorman A. Ratner. (Eds.). (1992). *Multiculturalism in the United States.* Westport, CT: Greenwood Press; Landis, Judson R. (1995). *Sociology: Concepts and characteristics* (9th Ed.). Belmont, CA: Wadsworth.

D

DATE RAPE. See RAPE, ACQUAINTANCE.

DEATH RATE. The death rate is the number of deaths per 1,000 members of a population in a given year. Like birthrates, death rates are affected by many population characteristics, particularly age structure, and vary markedly from nation to nation. For example, in 1994, the death rate in the United States was 8.5 per 1,000 members of the population, while in Guinea it was about 25 per 1,000 members of the population.

Further Reading. Haupt, Arthur, and Thomas T. Kane. (1985). *The population reference bureau's population handbook.* Washington, DC: Population Reference Bureau; Shryock, Henry S., and Jacob S. Siegel. (1976). *The methods and materials of demography.* Orlando, FL: Academic Press.

DEMOCRATIC APPROACH. See PARENTHOOD, CHILD-REARING OPTIONS AND STRATEGIES.

DEVELOPMENTAL CRISIS. See FAMILY CRISIS.

DEVELOPMENTAL-MATURATIONAL APPROACH. See PARENTHOOD, CHILD-REARING OPTIONS AND STRATEGIES.

DEVELOPMENTAL TASKS. See HAVIGHURST, ROBERT J.

DISABILITY AND CHRONIC ILLNESS, IMPACT OF ON LIFE-SPAN RELATIONSHIPS. A person with a disability or chronic illness has special needs, including those affecting the dynamics of lifespan relationships. Although most of us acknowledge that people with a physical disability such as cerebral palsy or a chronic illness such as arthritis face special bodily challenges, we do not often think about the various social adjustments such persons and those around them often have to make. This is as true for such social spheres as parent-child relations as it is for sibling interactions or the sharing of sexual intimacy.

Before exploring such social adjustments, the terms *physical disability* and *chronic illness* need to be clarified. A *physical disability,* such as cerebral palsy or a spinal-cord injury, is an impairment of body structure and function, including mobility impairments, amputations, skeletal deformities, and disfigurements. A *chronic illness,* such as diabetes or arthritis, is a progressive disorder caused by a nonreversible condition that often leaves the person with some type of disability.

It is important to point out that the needs of the disabled and the chronically ill are more like those of the healthy population than unlike them. Although being born with a lifelong disability such as cerebral palsy focuses a great deal of attention on other basic needs, the diagnosis of a disability or illness does not cancel out the need for intimate and meaningful social relationships. This applies to those relationships forged early in life as well as those created during the adult years. Should serious medical illness occur later in life, the need for intimacy often increases and serves to bring partners closer together.

Families of individuals with disabilities reflect unique dynamics. For example, parents usually express a variety of reactions when they learn that their child has a disability. Such reactions vary greatly and are influenced by a number of factors, including the severity of the disability or the supports available to the family. Most parents, though, report such feelings as shock, denial, sadness, fear, and anger. Many parents also believe that the child's disability was their fault. Some reason that the disability is punishment for a sin or wrongdoing.

The extra care and special accommodations required by some children with disabilities often alter how parents and siblings interact with the child, as well as with one another. The difficulty of living normally while relating to and caring for a disabled child often unleashes anxiety, confusion, and despair. Even the most competent and balanced family units can feel overwhelmed. Yet parents and siblings usually adjust to the reality of the disability in diverse and unique ways. Indeed, many families discover that having a child with a disability promotes family cohesion, adaptability, and solidarity. However, researchers have found that those families who were well adjusted before the birth of a disabled child are better at coping than those who were already having marital or family difficulties.

The adjustment of siblings to a person with a disability is also influenced by many factors, including parental attitudes and expectations, family size, and the severity of the disability. Many siblings experience the same emotions that parents do, including fear, guilt, or sadness. Some may be embarrassed or reluctant to bring friends home. For younger siblings, especially, limited understanding of the disability often creates misconceptions of the condition. For example, some may believe that a disability is contagious and can be spread through contact, especially of a tactile nature.

A wide variety of other sibling reactions have been documented by researchers. For example, many are jealous of the parental attention given to a disabled sibling, while others often resist their assigned caretaking responsibilities. With age, some siblings feel that being the brother or sister of an exceptional child singles them out as being different. Given such varied reactions, professionals stress the importance of including siblings during all forms of family intervention. While most children can successfully adapt to a sibling with a disability, it must also be recognized that they are in need of special attention, understanding, and support.

Other kinds of social adjustments are made during childhood and adolescence. For many parents, the entry of an exceptional child into school heralds the onset of a long ''letting-go'' process. This is the beginning of a transition in which parents must turn over some responsibility for their child to others. They are also in the process of giving more and more responsibilities to the child. Other social adjustments await children with disabilities as they make friends and become part of a wider social network. Still other challenges are posed by the many developmental tasks of adolescence, including rapid physical changes and the psychological adjustment to these changes.

Experimenting with newfound sexuality often proves to be troublesome for both the adolescent and the family. At least part of the problem can be traced to societal perceptions of the sexual needs of the disabled or chronically ill. Most people wrongly believe that the physically disabled and chronically ill are asexual throughout the lifespan. It is assumed that sexual activity is the domain of those who are in perfect physical health; sexual intimacy is not viewed as vital to the adjustment of the disabled or the maintenance of their everyday functioning. Such misconceptions have served to deny the sexuality of disabled and chronically ill persons. All people need validation that sexuality is a part of who we are; moreover, both the physical and psychological aspects of love promote psychological well-being. For many women and men alike, sex is part of love, and love needs expression no matter how ill or disabled one is.

Further Reading. Gartner, Alan, Dorothy K. Lipsky, and Ann P. Turnbull. (1991). *Supporting families with a child with a disability: An international outlook.* Baltimore: Paul H. Brookes Publishing; Hallahan, Daniel P., and James M. Kauffman. (1994). *Exceptional children* (6th Ed.). Boston: Allyn and Bacon; Powell, Thomas H., and Peggy A. Ogle. (1985). *Brothers and sisters: A special part of exceptional families.* Baltimore: Paul H. Brookes Publishing; Turnbull, Ann P., and H. Rutherford Turnbull. (1990). *Families, professionals, and exceptionality: A special partnership.* New York: Macmillan.

DISCIPLINE, CHILD. Child discipline is the parental teaching of limits in an effort to establish acceptable forms of child behavior and conduct. The goal of discipline is to make children responsible and to make them realize that they are accountable for the consequences of their behavior.

There are several styles of child discipline, although parents do not always fall into only one category. Rather, parents often mix approaches when dealing with their children. When an *authoritarian style* is employed, parents attempt to shape and control their children's behavior by enforcing a set standard of conduct. The emphasis is on obedience and the use of punitive, forceful measures to enforce proper behavior. An *authoritative style* is characterized by parents' attempts to direct their children's activities, but in a more rational fashion. Firm control is exerted, but verbal give-and-take is also stressed, and parents attempt to convey to the child the reasons for their discipline. Finally, a *permissive style* is usually nonpunitive, and parents usually behave in an accepting and affirmative manner toward the child. The child is consulted about policy decisions and given explanations for family rules.

As mentioned, parents do not always fall into only one category. Rather, the aforementioned styles of control are often mixed. As far as the overall effectiveness of each approach is concerned, the authoritarian and permissive styles appear to produce the least favorable results. Authoritarian parents generally allow little freedom of expression and dominate many aspects of the child's behavior. Frequently, this method of control breeds conformity and submissiveness. Among older children, it may breed rebellion and aggressiveness. Permissive parents, on the other hand, with their limited overall sanctions on behavior, have a tendency to nurture such child behaviors as selfishness, immaturity, and irresponsibility.

The authoritative method of control appears to produce the most favorable home climate. This democratic relationship has a tendency to foster such childhood behaviors as independence and self-confidence. Children reared in authoritative homes also have a tendency to be more cooperative and sensitive to the needs of others. Many researchers have found that when consistently applied, the authoritative method of control also creates responsibility, trustworthiness, and respect for authority.

Further Reading. Bigner, Jerry J. (1994). *Parent-child relations: An introduction to parenting* (4th Ed.). New York: Macmillan; Bluestein, Jane, and Lynn Collins. (1989). *Parents in a pressure cooker: A guide to responsible and loving parent/child relationships.* Rosemont, NJ: Modern Learning Press; Reynolds, Eleanor. (1990). *Guiding young children: A child-centered approach.* Mountain View, CA: Mayfield.

DISCIPLINE, CROSS-CULTURAL VARIATIONS IN CHILD. Similar to other facets of socialization, child discipline reflects unique cross-cultural variations. As is the case with any value, a culture transmits expectations or attitudes about proper child behavior, including approval and disapproval mechanisms. Parents have an awareness of these expectations and establish standards of behavior accordingly. They will decide how to treat children at various stages of their life and when to make them assume responsibility for their actions.

Cultural anthropologists tell us that there is mixed opinion among societies about the best way to raise and discipline children. For example, among the Yanomamo of the Amazon, children are regularly disciplined with physical beatings. Fathers encourage their sons to strike them by intense teasing, in the process praising the child for his fierceness. This practice sharply contrasts with the Semai of Malaysia, who seldom expose their children to physical punishment. The Semai refuse to hit their children, instead choosing to employ verbal forms of discipline. Semai children are brought up to control and even conceal their anger, rather than physically express it. Among the Rajput in North India, children are encouraged to be passive and even emotionally unresponsive. Parental interaction with their children is minimal and praise from adults virtually non-existent, the cultural notion being that such parental behaviors will ''spoil'' children and create disobedience and unruly behavior.

In other societies, children are disciplined with the threat of ghosts, spirit beings, and animals. For example, among the Hopi people of the American Southwest, children are sometimes threatened by ''kachinas,'' or masked dancers impersonating spiritual beings whom Hopi believe live in nearby mountains. When a Hopi child misbehaves, parents sometimes get a villager to put on a costume of an ''orge kachina,'' believed to eat children. When the ''orge kachina'' attempts to abduct the child for misbehaving, the parents come to the rescue. Children are supposedly so appreciative and grateful for being saved by their parents that they change their misbehavior.

The cooperative spirit typically demonstrated by Chinese children provides a unique reflection of yet another disciplinary style. Within the home, children learn to live a structured and orderly life. Good behavior seldom escapes notice, and when negative behavior occurs, firm disciplinary strategies are used rather than punitive approaches. Physical punishment does not have a place in Chinese homes, nor does harsh verbal rebuke. The dignity of the child is always acknowledged. Experts maintain that such an approach fosters an early mutual respect between young and old. (See PEOPLE'S REPUBLIC OF CHINA, LIFESPAN RELATIONSHIPS IN THE.)

In other countries, disciplinary strategies to some degree are shaped by the government. In Sweden, for example, parents are forbidden to spank, beat, or harm their children in any way. According to government officials, the physical punishment of children produces fear instead of love and respect. If parents choose to spank their children, they are breaking the law and can be arrested by local police. In addition, Swedish children have access to an emergency phone network and an ombudsman to protect children's rights.

The antispanking law, passed in 1979, informs parents that any act that, for the purpose of punishing, causes the child physical injury or pain is prohibited. This includes even pain that is mild and passing. The law is also meant to include psychological punishment, but Swedish legal experts feel that this aspect of the law is vague and much more difficult to enforce. Actually, the punishment for spanking does not parallel any consequences for breaking the law in the United States. Social pressure and the threat of social ostracism, though, are law enforcement enough in Sweden.

This Swedish law has produced mixed responses. Many social workers, doctors, and psychologists hail it as a tool to curb child abuse and maltreatment. Many parents, though, are annoyed with the legislation. Some firmly believe that spanking is a good disciplinary technique. Others report that while they would not spank their children under any circumstances, a parental right has been arbitrarily taken away.

Further Reading. Barnouw, Victor. (1985). *Culture and personality* (4th Ed.). Homewood, IL: Dorsey Press; Nanda, Serena. (1991). *Cultural anthropology* (4th Ed.). Belmont, CA: Wadsworth; Peoples, James, and Garrick Bailey. (1991). *Humanity: An introduction to cultural anthropology* (2nd Ed.). St. Paul, MN: West; Whiting, Beatrice B., and John W. M. Whiting. (1975). *Children of six cultures: A psycho-cultural analysis.* Cambridge, MA: Harvard University Press.

DISCIPLINE, QUALITIES OF EFFECTIVE CHILD. One of the more frequently expressed concerns among parents is how to effectively discipline children. While it is recognized that general theories exist (e.g., authoritarian, authoritative, and permissive styles), parents often search for practical and applied ways to teach acceptable forms of behavior. Child psychology experts tend to agree that effective child discipline encompasses the following:

A recognition that there are motivations for child misbehavior. Effective disciplinarians recognize that misbehavior does not just happen on its own. Rather, the child may be motivated in some way to engage in disruptive behavior. Some of the more common reasons for misbehavior include boredom or a desire for attention, revenge, power, and control.

A confident attitude. Parents who handle disciplinary situations effectively believe in themselves and their abilities to promote responsible behavior. They assume a take-charge attitude and handle themselves with self-assuredness and confidence.

An effort to relate discipline to the situation at hand. Good disciplinarians focus on the central issue and do not stray into unrelated problems. They tend to tell children that it is the misbehavior being rejected, not them as individuals. Furthermore, effective disciplinarians explain why they are upset with the misbehavior. (''You broke the vase and I'm angry because it was special to me.'') This helps to teach youngsters that misbehavior has implications for others.

Consistency. Research shows that erratic discipline confuses the child and seems unlikely to prevent similar problems in the future. If adults are going to discipline the child for one particular type of misbehavior, the reoccurrence of this misbehavior must also be disciplined. If there is more than one child at home, discipline should also be consistent among each of them as well.

A recognition that discipline is not a public spectacle. Effective parents recognize that discipline can be a sensitive affair, especially among older children. Talking with children alone, rather than in front of others, reduces embarrassment and other painful emotions. Also, effective disciplinarians respect children's feelings after discipline has been administered. Shame and guilt are fairly common reactions. Understanding adults do not attempt to increase the child's guilt after the situation has transpired, and they are open to whatever resolution the child wants to make.

An avoidance of angry emotional outbursts. There is no evidence that yelling, screaming, or other emotional tirades promote effective discipline. In fact, it is conceivable that children listen less when this sort of adult behavior occurs. Good disciplinarians avoid impulsivity and take time to carefully organize their thoughts. When this is done, their speech is deliberate and controlled, but firm. Experts note that children also seem to listen better when adults talk *with* them, not *to* them.

The establishment of limits in a clear and precise fashion. Children need to know what behavior is acceptable and what is not. Understanding adults spell this out so that there is no question regarding what misbehavior is or what it can encompass. Also, effective disciplinarians remember that many children, naturally, are going to test limits, which is all the more reason to be clear and consistent about behavioral expectations.

An effort to make discipline fit the misbehavior. Those adults who exercise sound judgment always examine the type and degree of disciplinary measure employed in relation to the misbehavior at hand. The discipline administered is compatible with the nature of the misconduct and not too lenient or too extreme.

A recognition that discipline needs to be as close in time as possible to the misbehavior. Good disciplinarians gather their thoughts after misbehavior occurs and then quickly administer consequences. Children have a tendency to better remember and more clearly associate those events occurring together in time and space. Misbehavior and discipline should thus be yoked together, the latter not being put off for hours or until day's end.

Follow-through. Effective disciplinarians discuss the misbehavior during a follow-up conversation to ensure that a lesson has been remembered. This does not mean dwelling on the misconduct nor accentuating the negative. Rather, it implies that both adult and child have the opportunity to reflect on the issue and the role that discipline plays in creating a more harmonious living arrangement.

Further Reading. Bigner, Jerry J. (1994). *Parent-child relations: An introduction to parenting* (4th Ed.). New York: Macmillan; Shure, Myrna B., and George Spivack. (1978). *Problem-solving techniques in childrearing.* San Francisco: Jossey-Bass; Turner, Jeffrey S. (1986). Ten steps to effective discipline. *Home Life, 8,* 8–12.

DISENGAGEMENT THEORY. See AGING, SUCCESSFUL.

DIVORCE. Divorce is the legal dissolution of a marriage. Divorce is widespread in the United States today; indeed, the United States has the rather dubious distinction of having a higher divorce rate than any other Western nation. Although death is the leading cause of family breakup in the United States, divorce rates are at an astronomically high level. In 1994, over 1,100,000 divorces were granted, a total involving nearly two and one-half million adults and over one million children.

It is often reported that almost 50 percent of all marriages end in divorce. This is a very misleading statement, and such a statistical analysis must be placed into a proper perspective. This percentage was arrived at by comparing all divorces granted in one year with the marriages performed in that same year. In 1992, for example, there were about half as many divorces as there were new marriages. But because divorces granted in any year are the result of marriages performed in earlier years, this statistic is misleading. It makes no sense to compare marriages contracted from one to fifty years ago with the number of the current year's weddings. A more accurate way of assessing the magnitude of divorce is to calculate what demographers call the *divorce rate* (see DIVORCE RATE).

Divorce does not affect all social groups equally. For example, divorce rates are higher among African Americans than among whites. However, because of a greater proportion of job instability, low income, and unemployment among African Americans, this is believed to represent an economic factor more than a racial one. Also, the higher the educational level, the lower the divorce rate will generally be. However, one interesting exception to this latter trend is women with graduate degrees. They have disproportionately high divorce rates, due perhaps to increased social independence and economic security. Another variation to consider in regard to divorce is its timing in the marriage cycle. Those who divorce tend to do so relatively early in their marriage. Divorce rates are at their highest two to five years after marriage, a statistic that has changed little over the years.

In the aftermath of divorce, persons need to critically examine themselves and what they want to do for the rest of their lives. The period immediately following divorce proceedings, however, may be a difficult time to think clearly and employ good judgment and logic. The legal battle may have been long, tiring, and expensive. If the divorce involved children, adjustments multiply and typically become more complex.

Following a divorce, it is not uncommon to experience many psychological states, including a sense of failure, loneliness, sadness, and fear. On the other hand, many often feel relieved to be starting over. As divorced individuals move from mutual identity toward autonomy, a redefinition of the self often evolves. This change in status is complete when an individual defines his or her status as "single" rather than "divorced." When one's new lifestyle attains stability and harmony, the redefinition process is complete. But experts point out that the completion of this process does not occur at the same moment for all. For either or both of the divorced parties, it may not happen until after the other has created a mutual identity with another person. With that step, the tentativeness is usually gone. Finally, the process for some may never be completed. One or both of the participants may never be able to fully construct a lifestyle of harmony.

Men, more than women, deny that they need help or support after a divorce. Such sentiments may reflect the image of independence that traditional men have been programmed to display by gender-role learning. However, divorced men, like divorced women, experience a wide range of feelings at this time: anger, guilt, shame, and fear, to name a few. Should children be involved, added concerns and anxieties mount for both men and women (see DIVORCE, CHILDREN AND). There is no discounting the fact that a man faces considerable change in his lifestyle. For example, there may be the issues of *alimony* (an allowance paid to a person by a spouse, granted by a court upon legal separation or a divorce) and child support. A man is also usually faced with the economic burden of finding a new place to live. Chores he might not have previously concerned himself with now become everyday realities: cooking, laundering, cleaning, and other domestic tasks.

A special set of adjustments and adaptations awaits women, too. This is particularly true if children are involved. Women have to make financial adjustments and usually carry the brunt of child-care responsibilities. Rebuilding a social life is especially hard when a woman has children needing continual care and attention. A divorced woman also often encounters difficulty establishing credit, a factor that hampers her financial independence. Frequently banks, credit card companies, and stores treat her differently than her male counterpart in similar economic situations.

In spite of the hurdles for both women and men, researchers see most divorced persons successfully adjusting to new routines. Of course, a new lifestyle brings costs, trade-offs, and sacrifices along the way. Success and happiness depend on a person's ability to turn problems into opportunities for new self-definitions, something most individuals are equipped to do. Thus divorce can be an opportunity for growth and the creation of new life opportunities. In the process of adapting and adjusting, many people discover strengths and emotional resources they never knew they possessed. They discover that they can survive loneliness and loss. They use the new freedom to gain fresh insights into themselves, change lifestyles, and find more fulfilling relationships.

Further Reading. Bumpass, Larry L., Teresa C. Martin, and James A. Sweet. (1991). The impact of family background and early marital factors on marital disruption. *Journal of Family Issues, 12,* 22–42; Gander, Anita M. (1991). After the divorce: Familial factors that predict well-being for older and younger persons. *Journal of Divorce and Remarriage, 15,* 175–192; Morgan, Leslie A. (1991). *After marriage ends: Economic consequences for midlife women.* Newbury Park, CA: Sage; White, Lynn K., and Alan Booth. (1991). Divorce over the life course: The role of marital happiness. *Journal of Family Issues, 12,* 5–21.

DIVORCE, CHILDREN AND. Each year, nearly one million children see their parents' marriage end in divorce. Should current rates hold, one of every three white children and two of three African-American children born within marriage will experience a parental marital dissolution by age 16. Most children of divorced parents live with their mother, and the majority will experience living in a fatherless home for at least five years. Moreover, the divorce experience is not necessarily over when the mother remarries. About one-third of white and one-half of African-American children whose mothers remarry will experience a second parental marital dissolution before they reach adulthood.

Divorce has the potential of creating numerous problems for children. Some children feel personally responsible for the divorce. Many are persuaded to take sides by their parents. Others may bear the brunt of displaced parental aggression. Coping with the divorce may also spill over to other aspects of the child's life and create additional problems, such as in schoolwork. Children may exhibit a wide range of emotional reactions: fear of abandonment, disturbed sleep patterns, anger, rejection, and sadness, to name but a few. It should be pointed out, though, that some of the problems that have been attributed to divorce may, in fact, be present prior to the parental separation. Nonetheless, given the potential for such turbulence, experts agree that children of divorce need love, understanding, and support to help them adjust.

Some children of divorce show remarkable resilience in the face of multiple life stressors. Despite a period of initial distress, some children may even be enhanced by coping with domestic instability. Individual characteristics, such as having an easy temperament, and familial factors, such as parental patience and affection, play an important role in buffering children from negative consequences associated with their parents' separation. Also important to the child is the presence of a meaningful support system, such as the presence and reassurance of other family members, friends, and teachers.

Custodial arrangements greatly influence a child's adjustment to divorce. Unfortunately, conclusive answers about the best arrangements remain elusive. Judicial decisions over time regarding child custody reflect the uncertainty that has plagued this issue. For example, until the middle of the nineteenth century, children automatically went to their fathers. But as economic conditions changed, the laws were modified to award custody to mothers as the natural nurturers of children during their ''tender years.'' Judges now make custody decisions on the basis of the child's best interests. Mothers still obtain custody in about nine out of ten cases, but fathers are more often seeking custody. Grandparents can also go to court to obtain the right to visit their grandchildren.

An alternative that brings flexibility to the courts is *joint custody*. Joint custody embodies the mutual sharing of parental rights and responsibilities after the divorce. Joint custody actually has two meanings. One is that both parents retain the rights they always have had as parents: for instance, the right to participate in decisions about schooling or health/medical considerations. The other meaning of joint custody is that every week, month, or year parents will alternate in providing the child's shelter. This is called *joint residential custody*.

Joint custody is becoming popular today. Among the reasons for its popularity are its similarities to the original marital household. Also, many believe that it requires children to make the fewest adjustments. Joint custody may also reduce the bitterness that often exists under sole-custody arrangements, particularly among fathers who pay child support but have only limited access to their children. Finally, joint custody often reduces the loss that a noncustodial parent sometimes experiences under the traditional sole-custody arrangements.

It needs to be pointed out, though, that joint custody may not be best for all families. For instance, children and adolescents often want a single home as a base and find alternating homes confusing. Moving from home to home can also disrupt a child's school education. Beyond this, joint custody does not ensure that each parent is capable of handling the responsibilities of child rearing. Current research suggests that children might be best served if their parents have joint custody in the legal sense, but are not required to alternate residences. At the same time, children should have easy access to the parent with whom they do not live. All of this points to the fact that while joint custody poses an alternative custodial arrangement, whether it is the final word has yet to be decided. (See REMARRIAGE.)

Further Reading. Healy, Joseph M., Janet E. Malley, and Abigail J. Stewart. (1990). Children and their fathers after parental separation. *American Journal of Orthopsychiatry, 60,* 531–543; Poertner, John, and Allan Press. (1990). Who best represents the interests of the child in court? *Child Welfare, 69,* 537–549; Wood, Joan I., and Gloria J. Lewis. (1990). The coparental relationship of divorced spouses: Its effect on children's school adjustment. *Journal of Divorce and Remarriage, 14,* 81–96.

DIVORCE, LEGAL ASPECTS OF. There are many legal sides to the dissolution of a marriage, and divorce laws have changed over the years. For centuries, divorce law centered around the concept of fault. In this concept, there was the requirement that one party had done something wrong while the other party was without fault. Thus traditional divorce law represented an adversary process. It should be noted, too, that once fault was determined, financial terms of the divorce were directed to the party at fault.

At one time, the notion of ''fault'' included only adultery and physical cruelty. Later, though, ''fault'' included such grounds as mental cruelty or desertion. Because divorce was an action in equity, it could be granted only if the party seeking the divorce was innocent of any wrongdoing. If both parties happened to be at fault, the doctrine of recrimination prohibited the granting of a divorce. Also, proof that parties colluded to obtain a divorce would bar a divorce.

In addition, traditional divorce law perpetuated the gender-typed division of roles and responsibilities apparent in traditional marriages. That is, in traditional marriage a woman presumably agrees to devote herself to being a wife, mother, and homemaker in return for her husband's promise of lifelong support. If the marriage did not endure, and if the wife were virtuous, she would be granted alimony. *Alimony* represents the husband's continued economic support, a perpetuation of this element of marriage. Traditional divorce laws also perpetuated the gender-typed division of roles as far as the children were concerned: The wife was typically responsible for their care, while the husband was responsible for their economic support.

In 1970, California passed legislation making it the first state to recognize the breakdown of a marriage as a ground for divorce. Called the Family Law Act, this legislation heralded the concept of *no-fault divorce*. This concept does not accuse either party of creating the marital breakdown, a factor that makes divorce proceedings simpler. No-fault divorce also helps to reduce the bitterness associated with adversarial proceedings, not to mention the complexities often arising with property settlements, alimony, and the like. Since its inception in 1970, nearly every state has instituted some variation of no-fault divorce proceedings.

The concept of no-fault divorce changes several basic elements of traditional divorce legislation. First, it eliminates the fault-based grounds for divorce. Second, it removes the adversary process. Third, financial settlements no longer originate in the concept of fault or gender-based role assignments. Finally, no-fault divorce redefines the traditional responsibilities of husbands and wives by implementing a new norm of gender equality. No-fault divorce attempts to institutionalize gender-neutral obligations between partners, including those related to economic support, division of property, and child support.

Whether no-fault divorce achieves all of the foregoing, however, remains to be seen. Some researchers have found that divorcing mothers are faring more poorly under the no-fault concept of divorce than they did under the former adversary system. Others have discovered that no-fault divorce reduces the bargaining power of spouses who did not want to divorce, which ultimately leads to significant declines in the financial settlements received by women. Furthermore, some maintain that the concept of no-fault divorce has led to a casual commitment to marriage among many segments of the population.

Further Reading. Dixon, Ruth B., and Lenore J. Weitzman. (1982). When husbands file for divorce. *Journal of Marriage and the Family, 44,* 103–114; Eshleman, J. Ross. (1994). *The family: An introduction* (7th Ed.). Boston: Allyn and Bacon; Parkman, Allen M. (1992). *No-fault divorce: What went wrong?* Boulder, CO: Westview Press; Wardle, Lynn D. (1991). No-fault divorce and the divorce conundrum. *Brigham Young University Law Review, 1,* 79–142.

DIVORCE, MEDIATION AND. Divorce mediation is a conflict-resolution process in which the disputants meet with a third-party mediator whose role is that of a facilitator and an impartial guide to negotiation. The mediator serves as an advisor who suggests options and can describe the range of decisions that courts are likely to make about a given issue.

Divorce mediation respects and supports the participants' ability to make decisions that affect their lives. In mediation, the separating partners control the results, taking responsibility for the final outcome instead of handing decisions over to the courts. Mediation provides a clearinghouse for cooperative solutions in which everyone can have his or her needs considered. This is especially important where children are involved and joint custody is anticipated.

Divorce mediation differs from the traditional adversary process, be it through the public judiciary or private arbitration, in several important ways. Most important, mediation is generally informal and less structured than either of the alternative procedures. Because it is private, it encourages an openness that is impossible in a public setting. The disputants retain control of the outcome rather than turning the decision-making power over to a judge or an arbitrator.

Divorce mediation offers several distinct advantages to couples. To begin with, it is often cheaper than a traditional divorce. Also, proponents maintain that disputes are settled faster when there is a mediation rather than an adversarial process. Third, participants are more likely to perceive a mediated settlement as fairer than a court resolution to the divorce.

There are different styles of divorce mediation, although each strives for the same goal: agreeing to a settlement and avoiding the cost of a court suit. In its simplest form, mediation can be performed by a single lawyer and a single mediator. However, other arrangements exist, such as with a lawyer-therapist interdisciplinary team. Court-sponsored public mediation programs are also available.

Further Reading. McKay, Matthew, Peter D. Rogers, Joan Blades, and Richard Gosse. (1984). *The divorce book.* Oakland, CA: New Harbinger Publications; Ruback, Barry. (1985). Family law. In Luciano L'Abate (Ed.), *The handbook of family psychology and therapy.* Homewood, IL: Dorsey Press; Teachman, Jay D., and Karen Polonko. (1990). Negotiating divorce outcomes: Can we identify patterns in divorce settlements? *Journal of Marriage and the Family, 52,* 129–139.

DIVORCE, PROCESSES AND TRANSITIONS OF. Divorce is a complex process and involves a number of transitions for couples as well as other family members. In an effort to better understand the complex dynamics of divorce, some researchers have identified certain processes or transitions. Two such theoretical models have been identified by researchers Paul Bohannan and Constance Ahrons. Bohannan has examined some of the divorce processes that confront couples, while Ahrons has focused her energies on the divorce transitions that affect the entire family unit. The following is a summary of each theoretical model.

Paul Bohannan's Theory

Paul Bohannan proposed that six components or processes of divorce exist. These components are not sequential and can overlap. Bohannan felt that it is important to understand these processes in order to find order and direction in the emotional chaos that frequently accompanies divorce.

Emotional divorce. The emotional divorce typically begins long before the actual break. It is centered around the deteriorating marriage and the initial motivations for considering a divorce. A wide range of negative feelings and behaviors characterize this component, including betrayals, accusations, and lack of affection and support. Partners usually feel misunderstood, rejected, and disillusioned. In many instances, one or both partners have psychologically departed long before the actual physical separation.

Legal divorce. During the legal divorce, couples go to court to sever the civil ties of marriage. The legal grounds for obtaining a divorce vary from state to state, so many couples find themselves lost in the shuffle of courtroom proceedings. Many partners never envisioned the many complexities of divorce proceedings or the amount of psychological energy needed. While couples typically experience relief once the legal separation is final, many exhibit varying levels of emotional sensitivity throughout this entire period.

Economic divorce. The economic divorce occurs when couples have to decide how they are going to divide their money and property. This is no simple task since complications arise due to tax laws. Legal assistance is usually needed, and couples frequently feel resentment, anger, and hostility concerning the redistribution of money and property. Bohannan also acknowledged that the economic divorce can be difficult for two reasons: first, there is never enough money or property to go around; second, people get attached to certain objects and may need them to support their image of themselves. As a result of these interacting forces, psychological turbulence is to be expected during this divorce component.

Co-parental divorce. The co-parental divorce focuses on the issue of child custody. The parental responsibility for child rearing and custody is determined by the court on the basis of the children's well-being. Visitation rights for the parent not getting custody must be determined. Worry and concern about the effects of the divorce on the children are frequently expressed during this stage. Bohannan pointed out that the issues of custody and economic settlement represent the two greatest difficulties divorcing couples face. Also, more divorces fail in the co-parental aspect than in any other way.

Community divorce. The community divorce implies that a divorced person's status in the surrounding neighborhood changes in certain ways. Divorce is viewed differently by people, and separated individuals must learn to adapt to these varying perceptions. Sometimes relationships with friends are altered. Many divorced persons report feelings of isolation and loneliness, while some also feel degrees of social disapproval. To ease such feelings, the social support of friends and family members is often stressed. Some divorced persons regret that divorcing one's spouse involves ''divorce'' from one's in-laws. Conversely, in-laws may become ''outlaws.'' However, many divorced persons keep in touch with those they now call ''the children's relatives.''

Divorce from dependency. The focus of the divorce from dependency is on the importance of divorced parties regaining psychological autonomy. The shift from being in a couple-oriented situation to being a single person requires role realignment and considerable psychological adjustment. Expectedly, those couples who maintained high levels of independence in their marriages are likely to regain autonomy more rapidly than are those marriage partners who were dependent on one another.

Constance Ahrons's Theory

At the foundation of Constance Ahrons's theory are the many family changes that accompany divorce. She maintained that divorce is an event that consists of five stages or transitions. These five stages represent a process during which family members acquire new roles and the family itself takes on a new definition.

Individual cognition stage. During the individual cognition stage, there is an awareness that something is wrong in the marital relationship. Individual reactions vary during the early phases of this stage: blaming one's partner, anger, depression, or even denial of the problem. Any resolution chosen at this stage depends on the couple's history of coping strategies. Some couples may decide to stay in the marriage until the children are grown. Others may decide to spend time and energy on interests outside the family while attempting to maintain the facade of an intact marriage. This process of emotional divorce, the withdrawal of emotional investment in the marital relationship, is self-protective and may have some positive benefits for the individual. However, this withdrawal will have implications for the entire family system. How long this stage lasts hinges on the coping behaviors used and other factors related to the family's vulnerability to stress.

Family metacognition stage. During the family metacognition stage, the entire family begins to realize that the marriage is deteriorating. Metacognition means that the family system begins to change in recognition of the problem. The problem is typically discussed by the family, and the dialogue often sums up each member's anxieties. It is also a time for potential solutions and consequences of the problem to be discussed. A key element of this stage is the family's adaptive ability. If the family has not demonstrated adequate and rational problem solving in past crisis situations, it is not apt to do so at this time.

Separation stage. During the separation stage, one parent moves out of the home and away from the family. The family at this time is in a state of flux, and family members often express more doubt in regard to family roles and boundaries. The family typically faces stress at this time, even if it has successfully coped with earlier stages. Also during this transition, the family typically shares its marital separation with extended family, friends, and the community as its members begin the tasks of the economic and legal divorce (note the connection to Bohannan's theory). Ahrons believed that these mediating factors can help and/or hinder the transitional process.

Family reorganization stage. The fourth transition is the family reorganization stage. During earlier stages, the lack of clear boundaries caused much of the confusion and stress. Now, the clarification of the boundaries themselves creates distress. As Bohannan suggested, and Ahrons reinforced, one of the most stressful chores confronting divorcing parents is that of redefining their co-parental relationship, the relationship that permits them to continue their child-rearing obligations and responsibilities after divorce. Ahrons took this a step further, though, by saying that adults must separate their spousal roles from their parental roles, terminating the former while redefining the latter. This complex process of ceasing to be husband and wife while still continuing to be mother and father creates the foundation for divorced-family reorganization. While divorce creates structural changes in the family, the relationship between former spouses is still the key to redefinition of relationships in the divorced family.

Family redefinition stage. The last stage identified by Ahrons is the family redefinition stage. The redefinition of relationships in the divorced family depends on the relationship between the parents. Although a continued and cooperative relationship between divorced parents reduces the crisis potential associated with divorce, its dynamics remain largely unexplored. The growing debate about custody rights reveals our lack of knowledge about the time-honored concept "best interests of the child" and brings the custom of sole custody into serious question. The trend toward shared custody and co-parenting represents an alternative and would thus play a role in the family redefinition stage (see DIVORCE, CHILDREN AND).

In summation, the theories of Bohannan and Ahrons shed considerable light on the individual and family factors involved in divorce. These theories show the many complexities of divorce as well as the interacting forces that operate before, during, and after marital dissolution. None of the identified processes or transitions exist in a vacuum, though, nor are these perspectives independent or mutually exclusive of one another. Also, since reactions to divorce are highly individualized, variations of the identified components are more than likely. They should not be taken as precise and rigid blueprints that everyone follows. Nonetheless, these theories are useful in helping us to understand the changes that people face when negotiating this painful process. They also succeed in capturing how divorce represents complex and multifaceted experiences.

Further Reading. Ahrons, Constance R. (1980). Divorce: A crisis of family transition and change. *Family Relations, 29,* 533–540; Ahrons, Constance R. (1983). Divorce: Before, during, and after. In Hamilton I. McCubbin and Charles R. Figley (Eds.), *Stress and the family.* New York: Brunner/Mazel; Bohannan, Paul. (Ed.). (1970). *Divorce and after.* Garden City, NY: Doubleday; Bohannan, Paul. (1985). The six stations of divorce. In Leonard Cargan (Ed.), *Marriage and family: Coping with change.* Belmont, CA: Wadsworth.

DIVORCE RATE. The divorce rate, also called the *crude divorce rate,* is the number of divorces each year per 1,000 members of the population. The divorce rate is calculated by using the number of divorces in a given year, not the number of people being divorced.

Further Reading. Haupt, Arthur, and Thomas T. Kane. (1985). *The population reference bureau's population handbook.* Washington, DC: Population Reference Bureau; Shryock, Henry S., and Jacob S. Siegel. (1976). *The methods and materials of demography.* Orlando, FL: Academic Press.

DOCTRINE OF INHERENT SIN. See LOCKE, JOHN. DOCTRINE ON CHILDREN AND CHILD-REARING.

DOUBLE STANDARD. The double standard is the use of one set of expectations and norms for males and a different set for females. Often, the double standard is directed toward the realm of sexual behavior. For example, the double standard asserts that men can have sexual relations prior to marriage, but women are expected to remain abstinent. While the double standard continues to exist, it does not have widespread appeal in today's society. It is viewed as demeaning to women, and the rejection of this standard may well be part of the social movement to remove all types of sexual inequality.

Further Reading. McCammon, Susan L., David Knox, and Caroline Schacht. (1993). *Choices in sexuality.* St. Paul, MN: West; Strong, Bryan, and Christine DeVault. (1994). *Human sexuality.* Mountain View, CA: Mayfield.

DOWRY. See MARITAL EXCHANGES.

DUAL-CAREER MARRIAGE. A dual-career marriage is one in which both partners pursue careers, as opposed to jobs. Careers refer to occupations requiring a high degree of commitment and having a continuous developmental nature. That is, positions are connected within an occupational cluster rather than unrelated.

Further Reading. Michelozzi, Betty N. (1992). *Coming alive from nine to five* (4th Ed.). Palo Alto, CA: Mayfield; Zunker, Vernon G. (1990). *Career counseling: Applied concepts of life planning* (3rd Ed.). Pacific Grove, CA: Brooks/Cole.

DUAL-EARNER MARRIAGE. A dual-earner marriage is one in which both partners are wage earners. Partners typically work at jobs, as opposed to careers. Such jobs are often unrelated and usually do not reflect a continuous developmental sequence.

Further Reading. Lock, Robert D. (1992). *Taking charge of your career direction* (2nd Ed.). Pacific Grove, CA: Brooks/Cole; Steers, Richard M., and Lyman W. Porter. (1991). *Motivation and work behavior* (5th Ed.). New York: McGraw-Hill.

DYAD. A dyad is a two-person group that represents the most basic and intimate of all possible relationships. Examples of dyads include dating partners, married couples, or two siblings. Through dyadic interaction, personal identities and emotional relations are maximized. Also, each member of the dyad is dependent upon the other. The behaviors expressed, such as roles, depend upon the behaviors expressed by the other within the relationship. Thus the roles of partners become intertwined and interdependent, which results in complementary interaction. Put another way, patterns of behavior emerge from the dyad that serve to mutually sustain and support both members. (See TRIAD.)

Further Reading. Bryjak, George J., and Michael P. Soroka. (1994). *Sociology: Cultural diversity in a changing world* (2nd Ed.). Boston: Allyn and Bacon; Landis, Judson R. (1995). *Sociology: Concepts and characteristics* (9th Ed.). Belmont, CA: Wadsworth; Levin, William C. (1994). *Sociological ideas: Concepts and applications* (4th Ed.). Belmont, CA: Wadsworth.

EARLY ADULTHOOD. The lifespan stage known as early adulthood generally occurs between the ages of 20 and 30. Most researchers recognize early adulthood as a unique and challenging stage of the lifespan. Individuals have traveled beyond the throes of adolescence and youth and now seek to attain the psychological maturity to face the challenges of adult life. The challenges to be met are perhaps more complex and diverse than any they have previously faced, but the rewards to be reaped from successfully meeting these challenges are boundless.

Early adulthood marks a time when individuals can embark on a chosen life course and find their niches in the outside world. Earlier, individuals could only chart their plans, thinking about what they would like to do with their lives. But now, having launched themselves from the family and completed formal schooling, at least for the most part, they can put plans into action. In the process, individuals will gain more confidence in their abilities, and their thinking will become more systematic and analytical. To actively shape a dream is no longer a remote thought, but a reality of everyday life.

Early adulthood provides a diverse landscape for learning about oneself and others and embarking on new and challenging life paths. Many dreams are shaped during this time, and while putting one's aspirations into effect is difficult, such lifework can be both exhilarating and rewarding. Indeed, such a quest enables young adults to realize their potential in life. In the midst of self-discovery, decision-making skills are learned, important values are nurtured, and responsibility blossoms.

During early adulthood, many developments take place within the spheres of personality and social functioning. Heightened levels of maturity bring relationships with others to new levels of satisfaction and enjoyment. This is particularly true when one enters the labor force (see EARLY ADULTHOOD, WORK RELATIONSHIPS DURING). Whether it involves launching a career, embarking on an independent lifestyle, sharing an intimate friendship, marrying, or becoming a parent, this represents a time when individuals can inquire, experiment, and explore. In the midst of self-discovery, a foothold in the world of grown-ups can be established.

Further Reading. DiGiovanna, Augustine G. (1994). *Human aging: Biological perspectives.* New York: McGraw-Hill; Hudson, Frederic M. (1991). *The adult years: Mastering the art of self-renewal.* San Francisco: Jossey-Bass; Keith, Patricia M., and Robert B. Schafer. (1991). *Relationships and well-being over the life stages.* New York: Praeger; Turner, Jeffrey S., and Donald B. Helms. (1994). *Contemporary adulthood* (5th Ed.). Fort Worth, TX: Harcourt Brace.

EARLY ADULTHOOD, MARRIAGE DURING. In the minds of many, there is an idealistic image attached to marriages during the early adult years. Some tend to picture the young adult couple as always engulfed in romantic bliss, perfectly tuned to each other's needs and responding favorably to every marital challenge. We have a tendency to look at young married couples and think "and they lived happily ever after"—further emphasis on the idealistic dream.

While the attainment of marital happiness is an admirable goal, the quest for a perfectly adjusted relationship is at best unrealistic. Sooner or later, most couples discover that the romance and happiness attached to the wedding and honeymoon do not last forever. Indeed, reality asserts itself and they see that the world is less than ideal. Ups and downs will begin to punctuate the relationship. The first misunderstanding or fight leads the couple to realize that each partner is only a human being, complete with weaknesses and differences. On a larger scale, they come to realize that their marriage does not fit into the "perfect" mold.

Of course, there are some couples, young and old, who will deny that problems exist in their marriage. Many researchers maintain that many individuals may remain in unsatisfactory marriages if barriers are strong or alternatives are lacking. In this respect, some may bury their problems in a shroud of silence because they are afraid that the underlying issues are too threatening or disruptive to bring up. Many feel that they are better off living with their problems, because any discussion of them will "rock the boat." Still others view the threat of divorce as a worse evil than existing difficulties. As a result of such thinking, many couples live in empty-shell marriages, the basic foundation of which is general unhappiness.

What factors promote marital happiness and satisfaction? Marital happiness and harmony are determined by the amount of effective interaction between the two partners. In this respect, stability is how two individual personalities blend and successfully meet one another's expectations for married life. Going a step further, marriages usually succeed when partners are trusting, share similar interests, demonstrate reciprocity, and perceive the presence of equity and agreement on important relationship issues. Almost invariably, the successful marriage is one in which there is good communication. Effective communication encompassing the clear and consistent expression of ideas, feelings, and wishes is the cornerstone of a healthy and satisfying relationship.

Satisfaction with roles within the marriage also determines happiness and satisfaction. Several different types of structures within marriages can be identified, each stressing different patterns of expectations and responsibilities for husband and wife (see MARRIAGE, VARIATIONS IN STRUCTURE). In the *patriarchal* marriage, the power structure is dominated by the husband, while the reverse is true in the *matriarchal* marriage, which is far less common. Many couples today opt for an *egalitarian* orientation to their relationship, emphasizing equality between partners, particularly within the realm of role sharing.

Establishing a power structure that is comfortable and acceptable to both partners is an important chore for newlyweds. Researchers note that couples who are attempting to achieve a role-sharing marriage often struggle to define and implement emerging values about themselves and the marital relationship. These values embrace equality of opportunity for career development and fairness in division of domestic responsibilities. Egalitarian values often run counter to long-held traditional gender-role stereotypes concerning marriage. Because of these stereotypes, a man and a woman may face difficulty forming a relationship based on egalitarian values. They enter it with expectations and attitudes molded by their earlier socialization and often face continuing pressure from society to maintain traditional conceptions of marital roles.

Many marriage and family experts believe that the benefits attached to egalitarianism are numerous. For both spouses, there is typically a greater opportunity to develop abilities and pursue personal interests without being limited by traditional gender-role expectations. Many partners also report relief from the stress and overwork that originate from having primary responsibility for a broad area of family life. Egalitarianism promotes greater levels of freedom and independence for both husband and wife.

Further Reading. Keith, Patricia M., and Robert B. Schafer. (1991). *Relationships and well-being over the life stages.* New York: Praeger; Merriam, Sharan B., and M. Carolyn Clark. (1991). *Lifelines: Patterns of work, love, and learning in adulthood.* San Francisco: Jossey-Bass; Smith, Audrey D., and William J. Reid. (1986). *Role-sharing marriage.* New York: Columbia University Press.

EARLY ADULTHOOD, WORK RELATIONSHIPS DURING. By early adulthood, individuals typically recognize that relationships forged in the workplace represent an important facet of adult life. These relationships and vocational development in general will blend with many developmental forces. Obviously, one's work serves a financial purpose, but it also represents an important part of one's identity. Work provides a social environment that stimulates interpersonal skills, such as engaging in goal-directed tasks with others and participating in decision making. One's vocation also contributes to feelings of self-worth, dignity, and ego fulfillment. In addition, work provides an activity through which creativity and originality can be channeled. In this respect, work is a form of self-expression. Finally, work represents status and a source of pride as well as satisfaction.

During early adulthood, individuals also discover that work and its consequent lifestyle are bound up tightly with one's ego and self-image. They discover that "what a person does" greatly affects one's perceptions of people, sometimes at the expense of appreciating someone's total identity. In the world of work, young adults learn new skills and change some behaviors to fit new roles. The implications extend far beyond the workplace as individuals discover new involvements and new ways of perceiving themselves.

Today there are thousands of different jobs to choose from, compared to only several hundred at the turn of the century. Finding one's vocational niche in the face of such overwhelming numbers can be, to say the least, a bit unsettling. Complicating matters is that new jobs are constantly evolving within the vocational arena, while some are being phased out. This heightens the need to choose jobs that offer stimulation, some promise of stability, and an outlet for creative talents.

Unfortunately, many young adults are unable to engage in efficient career-planning strategies. For instance, many hold romantic stereotypes of jobs that distort reality. Some approach a career decision with fear and anxiety, lest they make a mistake. Others shortchange themselves because they choose from among a very narrow group of occupations. Still others avoid the process altogether, certain that it will nail them down to a lifelong commitment they can never change. There are those who feel that even if they conducted a thorough career search, it would turn up absolutely nothing.

Many adults today are concerned with job satisfaction, the desire to find work that is meaningful, rewarding, and challenging. As evidence of the desire among adults to find rewarding work, consider the large numbers of workers switching jobs. While some workers are forced to change jobs, such as aging athletes, others change vocations because they discover that their job no longer serves personal goals and needs. In addition to meaningful and challenging work, certain factors constitute job satisfaction. Among these are pay, the ability to make meaningful contributions, the ability to express oneself and have others listen, job security, the chances for advancement, quality of working conditions, and the status or prestige of the job.

Career changes and the drive toward job satisfaction are more common among young adults than older adults, and greater among those having a college education. While meaningful and challenging work is desired by high-school graduates, they realistically do not expect to acquire such jobs because of their limited education. It is conceivable that young adults have stronger desires for job satisfaction because they have just launched themselves into the work force and are at the bottom of the career ladder. The jobs they hold often offer limited satisfaction.

Experts believe that seeking to obtain career satisfaction is an admirable goal, especially since it helps to create pride in vocational contributions and a commitment to one's employer. Furthermore, job satisfaction helps to promote sound mental and physical health as well as family stability. When workers are happy and satisfied, they tend to have a brighter outlook about themselves, feel more secure in their jobs, and get along better with their coworkers. Moreover, satisfied workers tend to report less job-related stress and work-related illness.

It should be acknowledged that in the face of growing levels of career dissatisfaction, many industries and companies are designing more stimulating work environments. More flexible schedules, the encouragement of employee input, and the implementation of job incentives are examples of this trend. Workplace wellness programs run by companies also reflect a desire to make the vocational environment healthier and more productive. All of these changes represent steps to enhance job satisfaction, encourage healthy behaviors among employees, and open new doors for creativity and learning. Moreover, such environments instill in workers the feeling that they are an important and worthwhile investment to the company.

Further Reading. Lock, Robert D. (1992). *Taking charge of your career direction* (2nd Ed.). Pacific Grove, CA: Brooks/Cole; Steers, Richard M., and Lyman W. Porter. (1991). *Motivation and work behavior* (5th Ed.). New York: McGraw-Hill; Zunker, Vernon G. (1990). *Career counseling: Applied concepts of life planning* (3rd Ed.). Pacific Grove, CA: Brooks/Cole.

EARLY CHILDHOOD. The lifespan stage known as early childhood generally occupies the fourth and sometimes the fifth year of life. During early childhood, children expand their social horizons and develop considerable independence and autonomy. Once socially restricted and dependent, preschoolers become more involved with their environment and venture into new and challenging social situations with peers and adults. These new experiences—originating from the neighborhood, school, or other socialization agents—are integrated into the child's total sense of being and contribute immensely to developing personality and social awareness.

Of paramount importance to the child during these years is entry into an early childhood education program. Beyond the obvious educational benefits, preschool programming offers a rich terrain for growth and development. From early schooling experiences, children will further develop their autonomy and ability to adjust to change. Moreover, they will deepen feelings of competency, trust, and initiative (see EARLY CHILDHOOD EDUCATION, IMPACT OF ON CHILD DEVELOPMENT).

While in the midst of others, children emerge as individuals, gaining insight into their own unique personalities. Socially, children can observe what effects their behavior has on others, a developing cognitive power that enables them to nurture concepts of right and wrong. Insight and observations also enable them to begin to realize the rights and privileges of others. Moreover, social experiences help children develop a self-concept—that is, the manner in which they perceive themselves.

The family continues not only to transmit appropriate behaviors, knowledge, and values to children but also to provide them with an emotional setting that makes them feel accepted and loved. It should be noted that the child must experience and learn to deal with negative emotions as well as the so-called positive emotions in order for psychological growth to occur. A favorable home environment and a positive emotional climate are critical influences in the child's personality and social development.

Certain factors in the child's interaction with the family are of particular importance during early childhood. For example, parental support, guidance, and fulfillment of the child's needs for security, trust, and understanding are extremely significant when one examines the quality of family relationships. Equally important are the methods of parental control in operation as well as relations with siblings. In general, sound personality and social growth are greatly affected by one's sense of identity and belonging to the family unit, not to mention the warmth and acceptance accorded by others.

Further Reading. Etaugh, Claire, and Spencer A. Rathus. (1995). *The world of children.* Fort Worth, TX: Harcourt Brace; Hetherington, E. Mavis, and Ross D. Parke. (1993). *Child psychology: A contemporary viewpoint* (4th Ed.) New York: McGraw-Hill; Turner, Pauline H., and Tommie J. Hammer. 91994). *Child development and early education: Infancy through preschool.* Boston, MA: Allyn and Bacon.

EARLY CHILDHOOD EDUCATION, IMPACT OF ON CHILD DEVELOPMENT. Early childhood education provides constructive learning experiences to young children and affects their development in an assortment of ways. Generally speaking, early childhood education seeks to stimulate all developmental spheres of the growing child through varied curriculum offerings. Such programming promotes social, self-help, and self-image skills. Equally important is the role of nurturing cognitive and linguistic abilities and, in general, learning readiness skills. Early childhood education programs also seek to establish and maintain a healthy learning environment and provide positive guidance and discipline. The establishment of a positive emotional climate that fosters trust and security is especially important.

The early childhood teacher is in a position to nurture the preschooler's growth and development and to promote positive learning experiences. Within the early childhood education setting, the teacher executes many functions, from guiding program activities to working cooperatively with parents. How the teacher interacts with the children is especially important, particularly with regard to her or his warmth, understanding, and support of the child's strengths and weaknesses. Indeed, most recognize that the success of early childhood education rests heavily on the teacher's commitment to children, the classroom climate that is established, and the type of role model that she or he represents.

The schedules and routines established by the preschool are the means through which goals and objectives are met. Although activities differ, the general thrust of programming is similar. Many schools offer a diverse mixture of free and structured play activities; creative play opportunities in art, music, and literature; and beginning subject-area exercises in cognitive skills, letter formation, language skills, and so forth. Other activities may focus on small and large muscle skills, listening abilities, recitation, or special programs, such as nutrition and safety awareness. The overall length of the early childhood education program (full- or half-day sessions) determines the extent of these activities.

Early childhood education programs vary in operating principles and philosophies, curriculum content, location, size, and an assortment of other details. To better understand their complexities, it is helpful to develop a classification system of some of the major types of early childhood programming available today. Such a classification system can serve to separate the basic differences that exist in structure and operating procedure.

Day care. As the name implies, this program offers full-day coverage to parents of preschool children. Such an operation is especially appealing to working parents. Although day care initially had no planned educational programs, most day-care centers have since been reorganized to meet the child's social, emotional, physical, and intellectual needs. The cost of day care varies considerably, and in some instances the centers charge fees on a sliding scale based on the family's ability to pay.

Industry-related day care. Industry-related day care is a response to the growing numbers of mothers in the labor force, as well as the multiple needs of dual-earner families. Employers use this kind of day care to attract workers and reduce turnover, as well as to decrease absenteeism and tardiness resulting from other child-care arrangements. Some of these facilities are located directly in a parent's workplace, while others may be located nearby in a separate facility. Some industries absorb all programming costs, some provide partial coverage, while others just reserve a place for employees' children.

Home day care. Like other forms of day care, home day care is attractive to working parents. It offers care and attention during the hours of the working day, but within a caregiver's residence. Like all early childhood facilities, a home day-care facility must be inspected and licensed by state officials, and the operator must be certified.

Compensatory programs. Compensatory programs are subsidized by the federal government. The best known of these is Project Head Start, which was introduced to help keep the blight of a deficient home environment from leaving a permanent impression on some of the country's children. Under the supervision of the Office of Economic Opportunity, federal grants were given to local community agencies capable of meeting basic outlined standards and implementing programs designed to improve the health of preschoolers and alleviate the prospect of school readiness deficiencies in disadvantaged children. Basically, Project Head Start consists of programs in education, medical and dental care, nutrition, social services, psychological services, parent education, and community volunteer programs.

Nursery school. A nursery school is usually private and tends to appeal to wealthier families. Because most offer half-day sessions, this type of educational setting often does not fit the needs of working parents. Nursery schools are generally more expensive than most other forms of early childhood education, and many place an emphasis on a learning readiness curriculum. The teacher-to-child ratio in these settings is usually small, which offers appeal to those parents desiring close individual attention to their child.

Parent cooperative program. A parent cooperative program is organized by parents who employ trained teachers to plan and teach the program. Parent cooperative programs can be found in private homes, but many programs operate in community centers, churches, or other buildings. (The more established and successful parent cooperative programs frequently have their own buildings.) Many times, parent cooperative programs are able to offer lower tuition fees than private facilities.

Laboratory school. College or university laboratory schools were among the earliest types of early childhood education programs in the country. The laboratory school focuses its energies on parent education, teacher learning, and research studies. Sometimes mobilizing the resources of an area to meet the needs of young children, the laboratory school is usually financed primarily by the academic institution.

Infant-toddler program. The infant-toddler program is one of the fastest-growing forms of early childhood education today. It has special appeal to dual-earner families and offers high-quality, individualized caregiving aimed at optimizing early growth and development. In addition to caregiving, programming typically focuses on infants' physical, emotional, and social needs, as well as sensory and exploratory play and peer interactions. Infant-toddler programs are expensive, particularly since individual care is required. Diapers, infant formula, and other financial considerations have the potential for further increasing center costs.

Special-needs programs. Some early childhood education programs employ qualified staff members who are capable of working with special-needs children. Many times, special-needs children are mainstreamed part-time or full-time into a regular early childhood education setting, such as when a hearing-impaired child is enrolled in a group of non-hearing-impaired children. Early childhood education centers are subject to legislation designed to secure and protect the rights of special-needs children, including making facilities and programs accessible. (See CHILDHOOD, SCHOOL RELATIONSHIPS DURING.)

Further Reading. Brewer, Jo Ann. (1992). *Introduction to early childhood education today.* Boston: Allyn and Bacon; Hildebrand, Verna. (1991). *Introduction to early childhood education* (5th Ed.). New York: Macmillan; Morrison, George. (1995). *Early child-*

hood education today (6th Ed.) Columbus, Ohio: Merrill; Spodek, Bernard, Olivia Saracho, and Michael Davis. (1991). *Foundations of early childhood education* (2nd Ed.). Boston: Allyn and Bacon.

EARLY CHRISTIANITY, IMPACT OF ON INTIMATE RELA-TIONSHIPS. When Christianity became the official religion of the Roman Empire in the late fourth century A.D., many aspects of intimate relationships were affected. For example, the church clearly made its presence known within the framework of the marriage structure. It ruled on the degree of kinship allowed between bride and groom, it decreed that a bride must be a virgin, and it even determined the only acceptable position for sexual intercourse (man above, woman below). Adultery, as one might expect, was a punishable offense. The church also condemned divorce, although it would fluctuate on this latter edict for some time.

The church's ban on divorce had numerous side effects. For example, it meant that couples could no longer separate if one spouse was sterile. As a result, more marriages were childless, and the natural population increase among the Christians was retarded. But the church's condemnation of divorce also helped to strengthen many marriages, increasing the solidarity between husband and wife and parents and children, and even intergenerational relations, including the care given to aging family members. It would be wrong to assume that unhappy marriages disappeared, but it is plausible that many partners reaffirmed their commitment to one another in the wake of the church's ban on divorce.

The church also came to affect many facets of sexual behavior. Sexual pleasure was not condoned, and marital sex was viewed as a necessary evil, tolerated only because of the procreative function that it served. Any nonprocreative sexual activity, including masturbation and homosexual acts, was condemned, and the church rejected any attempts at contraception. It forbade engaging in "suggestive" dances, wearing improper or revealing clothing, or singing "wanton" songs. Although kisses were often a form of salutation among early Christians, townspeople were warned that kissing more than once, for the purpose of pleasure, was sinful and should be avoided.

Numerous authorities served as architects for the church's position on sexual morality. St. Paul and St. Augustine were two of the more vocal proponents of sexual repression. Both firmly believed that men and women must learn to control their sexual impulses and achieve inner spiritual peace. As St. Paul stated (1 Corinthians 7:1–2, 7–9, 25, 28):

It is good for a man not to touch a woman. Nevertheless to avoid fornication, let every man have his own wife, and let every woman have her own husband. . . . For I would that all men were even as myself. But every man hath his proper gift of God. I say therefore to the unmarried and widows, it is good for them if they abide even as I. But if they cannot contain, let them marry: for it is better to marry than to burn. . . . Now concerning virgins I have no commandment of the Lord: yet I give my judgment. . . . If thou marry thou hast not sinned; and if a virgin marry she hath not sinned.

Along with many others, St. Paul and St. Augustine encouraged celibacy, the abstention from sexual activity. Sexual urges were viewed as the work of the devil, and inner fortitude was needed to protect the soul from evil forces. Celibacy was regarded as humanity's highest virtue and evidence that willpower can overcome lust and sin. Moreover, celibacy enabled men to execute their duties as Christians and missionaries of the faith.

Christianity did little to reduce the inequality between men and women that had persisted for centuries, not only in family life but in society as a whole. Women continued to be treated as second-class citizens in the Christian world. They could not hold public office, and they played a subservient role to men. Women were reared to be passive, tranquil, and silent. Their primary functions in life were related to the home and the family. Indeed, the Bible (1 Corinthians 11:8–9) actually says that women were created for the benefit of men. Such gender-role expectations were also evident in the upbringing of children.

Further Reading. Foucault, Michael. (1978). *The history of sexuality.* New York: Pantheon Books; Francoeur, Robert T. (1990). New dimensions in human sexuality: The theological challenge. In Robert H. Iles (Ed.), *The gospel imperative in the midst of AIDS: Towards a prophetic theology.* Wilton, CT: Morehouse-Barlow; Slowinski, Julian W., and William R. Stayton. (1991). Sexual values and moral development. In Robert T. Francoeur (Ed.), *Becoming a sexual person* (2nd Ed.). New York: Macmillan.

ECOLOGICAL THEORY. Ecological theory is a major school of thought in psychology, particularly within the field of lifespan development. Essentially, this perspective centers on the importance of culture or context in shaping the course of human development. Ecological theory maintains that to best understand behavior as it unfolds throughout the life cycle, close attention must be paid to the environmental context in which a person lives, including the other people involved.

One of the leading figures in ecological theory is Urie Bronfenbrenner. He has proposed a sociocultural view of development that enables us to better understand how ecological issues can be explored. His theory consists of four overlapping environmental systems that interact with the person and influence overall development. These four environmental systems are the microsystem, mesosystem, exosystem, and macrosystem.

The *microsystem* is the system closest to the individual and consists of the family, neighborhood, school, playground, place of work, and so forth. Since the microsystem represents firsthand experiences, of special importance are the behaviors of the people in these contexts. The microsystem changes as the child becomes an adolescent and as the adolescent becomes an adult.

The *mesosystem* reflects how microsystems influence each other. For example, parents' relationships with the child's friends or teachers, or how a church might affect child-rearing styles, reflect the influence of the mesosystem.

The *exosystem* is the wider context in which the individual might not participate directly, but is still nonetheless affected. Examples of the exosystem might be legal or welfare systems, school boards, or local governments.

The *macrosystem* represents the culture and subculture in which one lives. The macrosystem is important because it shapes one's values, beliefs, social roles, and lifestyle. It is best thought of as a societal blueprint, the totality of all other systems passed on from generation to generation.

These four environmental systems constantly interact with one another and mold human behavior. Researchers utilizing this approach carefully explore the ways in which these components directly or indirectly interact with one another. In so doing, an appreciation is gained of the numerous and diverse sociocultural influences that impact on a person's life. The person is regarded as an active participant in initiating and responding to developmental processes.

Ecological theory is one of the few perspectives offering insight into how the developing person is shaped by contextual influences, and such a conceptual framework is useful in studying lifespan development. People of all ages are affected by the systems proposed by Bronfenbrenner; consequently, his theory has the potential of shedding new light on lifespan experiences. One of the limitations of ecological theory, though, is that it downplays the importance of biological and cognitive forces. Other criticisms are leveled at the difficulty in pinpointing where one microsystem leaves off and another begins, and the difficulty in assessing the strength of the various system components. (See BRON-FENBRENNER, URIE.)

Further Reading. Bronfenbrenner, Urie. (1979). Contexts of child rearing: Problems and prospects. *American Psychologist, 34,* 844–850; Bronfenbrenner, Urie. (1986). Ecology of the family as a context for human development: Research perspectives. *Developmental Psychology, 22,* 723–742; Bronfenbrenner, Urie. (1989). Ecological systems theory. In Ross Vasta (Ed.). *Annals of child development* (Vol. 6). Greenwich, CT: JAI Press; Thomas, R. Murray. (1992). *Comparing theories of child development* (3rd Ed.). Belmont, CA: Wadsworth.

EGALITARIAN POWER STRUCTURE. See MARRIAGE, VARIATIONS IN STRUCTURE.

ELECTRA COMPLEX. See PSYCHOSEXUAL DEVELOPMENT.

ELKIND, DAVID. David Elkind (1931–) is an important researcher in the field of child and adolescent development. His specialty areas are cognitive, social, and personality developments of children, and the applied aspects of his research have helped guide child-rearing and educational strategies. Elkind received a Ph.D. in clinical psychology from the University of California at Los Angeles in 1955 and has held teaching positions at the University of Rochester and Tufts University. In 1964 he was a National Science Foundation Senior Postdoctoral Fellow at the Piaget Institute of Genetic Epistemology in Geneva.

One of Elkind's many research contributions has been within the area of adolescent cognitive development. Using Jean Piaget's cognitive-developmental theory as a foundation (see PIAGET, JEAN; COGNITIVE-DEVELOPMENTAL

THEORY), Elkind formulated a concept known as *adolescent egocentrism.* Elkind maintained that adolescent egocentrism is a unique form of self-centeredness that surfaces during the teenage years. He felt that the heightened introspection expressed at this time unfolds in two ways: the imaginary audience and personal fable. *Imaginary audience* behavior occurs when adolescents feel that they are always the focus of attention or on "center stage." *Personal fable* behavior emerges when teenagers feel that they lead a charmed existence and are protected from harm, risk, or even death. Perceived invulnerability—the attitude of "it can't happen to me"—is thought to originate from the spell of the personal fable and mirrors teenagers' conviction of personal uniqueness. Elkind felt that both behaviors reflect unique facets of adolescent cognitive development.

Elkind has authored hundreds of research studies, articles, and books exploring the growth and development of children. He is a member of many professional organizations and is a former president of the National Association of Young Children. He has served as a consultant to many state education departments, clinics, and mental health centers as well as to government agencies and private foundations.

Further Reading. Elkind, David. (1967). Egocentrism in adolescence. *Child Development, 38,* 1025–1034; Elkind, David. (1981). *Children and adolescents: Interpretive essays on Jean Piaget* (3rd Ed.). New York: Oxford University Press; Elkind, David. (1984). *All grown up and no place to go: Teenagers in crisis.* Reading, MA: Addison-Wesley; Elkind, David. (1994). *A sympathetic understanding of the child: Birth to sixteen* (3rd Ed.). Boston: Allyn and Bacon.

ELLIS, ALBERT. Albert Ellis (1913–) is the founding father of rational emotive therapy, a cognitively based form of psychotherapy aimed at correcting faulty or distorted styles of thinking. Ellis received a doctorate in clinical psychology from Columbia University and shortly thereafter began practicing in the areas of marriage, family, and sex therapy. In 1955, he combined elements of humanistic and behavioral therapy to create *rational emotive therapy,* which he successfully applied to individual clients as well as couples. In 1959 Ellis founded the Institute for Rational Emotive Therapy, a nonprofit and educational foundation to train professionals in this therapeutic approach.

Ellis maintained that thinking processes are the driving force behind how individuals feel and what they do. When thinking is logical and sensible, behavior is stable and harmonious. If thinking is contaminated by irrational thought processes, maladjustment is likely to occur. To correct dysfunctional behavior, individuals must change unrealistic and irrational perceptions and conditions. Ellis maintained that this can be done through systematic analysis and manipulation of thinking and reasoning processes.

Ellis proposed that many psychological disorders stem from a number of rather predictable irrational beliefs. These beliefs are usually self-defeating and reflect inaccurate assumptions about oneself and others. While irrational beliefs take a variety of forms, almost all reflect the notion that one must do something: "I must be a perfect person," "I must be in control." Such inflexible and unrealistic expectations create anxiety, frustration, and disappointment. Worse, these negative feelings tend to perpetuate the original irrational belief and create a vicious, self-defeating cycle.

Rational emotive therapy is very structured and time efficient, and it focuses directly on specific problems identified by the client or couple. The therapist plays an active role by pointing out illogical thinking and suggesting more realistic ways of handling problems. It is also important for clients to realize that their maladaptive behavior is largely self-inflicted. When all of this is accomplished, the client or couple have hopefully acquired more logical and responsible behavior.

Further Reading. Ellis, Albert. (1970). *The essence of rational psychotherapy: A comprehensive approach to treatment.* New York: Institute for Rational Living; Ellis, Albert. (1987). *The practice of rational-emotive therapy (RET).* New York: Springer.

ELLIS, HENRY HAVELOCK. Henry Havelock Ellis (1859–1939) was a British physician who made significant contributions to the study of human sexuality. Ellis was something of a rebel, for he persisted in studying human sexuality during the Victorian era when sexuality was taboo (see VICTORIAN ERA, LIFESPAN RELATIONSHIPS DURING THE). In his studies, Ellis sought to determine not only what sexual behavior fell within the normal range but how and to what extent individuals' sexual behavior might vary.

In 1896, Ellis published his now-classic *Studies in the psychology of sex,* a seven-volume work that presented the results of his findings over a period of 32 years. Because of the repressive nature of Victorian society, some of the books in this series were labeled obscene and, although they were made available to the medical profession, were kept from the public eye until 1935.

Ellis provided readers with an objective and systematic account of human sexual behavior. Throughout his books, he emphasized that sex was a natural instinct and a healthy form of expression, documenting his work with many case studies. In his research, Ellis established the interdisciplinary nature of this new area of study, drawing on many fields, including biology, psychology, sociology, history, and anthropology.

Ellis's emphasis on the naturalness of sexual expression differed considerably from the view offered by Richard von Krafft-Ebing (1840–1902), an Austrian psychiatrist and leading exponent of the Victorian approach to sexuality. Like Ellis, Krafft-Ebing analyzed sexual behavior in a systematic manner. Unlike Ellis, however, Krafft-Ebing focused his attention on sexual pathology, and his major work, *Psychopathia sexualis* (1886), included detailed and explicit case studies of very disturbed people. This emphasis on pathology set the tone for Krafft-Ebing's overall analysis of sexual variation. A recurrent theme in his book was that virtually all variations of sexual behavior—that is, anything other than male-female penile-vaginal intercourse—were atypical and practiced by the mentally unbalanced. He considered homosexuality, for example, a functional sign of degeneracy. Furthermore, he maintained that masturbation led people into such sexual deviations as sexual bondage and rape and ultimately caused insanity.

Ellis challenged the notion that sex was a pathological force. He denounced Krafft-Ebing's negative views of masturbation and homosexuality, as well as of other variations of sexual expression. For example, Ellis suggested that masturbation was a common sexual outlet not only for men but for women (the latter came as a real shock to Victorians). He also discussed male and female sexual arousal processes, including the importance of foreplay.

Ellis helped to transform people's thinking about human sexuality. He succeeded in establishing an objective body of knowledge about variations in sexual behavior, a collection of research that reflected tolerance and nonjudgmental observations and discussion. The concepts that he proposed set the stage for more modern views of sexuality.

Further Reading. Ellis, Henry Havelock. (1936). *Studies in the psychology of sex, 1896–1928.* New York: Modern Library; Ellis, Henry Havelock. (1939). *My life.* Boston: Houghton Mifflin.

EMILE. See ROUSSEAU, JEAN-JACQUES. DOCTRINE ON CHILDREN AND CHILD-REARING.

EMPTY NEST. The empty nest, or *postparental stage,* is the point in the family-circle life cycle where children have grown and departed from the home. For the middle-aged couple, this means a time when they are alone and living in a house that is filled with memories of their children. Both positive and negative experiences may accompany the empty-nest stage. For some parents, the empty-nest stage brings new levels of freedom, marital satisfaction, and fulfillment. For others, this stage becomes a period of reflection, restlessness, and even dissatisfaction.

Regarding the latter feelings, a number of factors may create psychological turbulence, particularly in traditional homes. For example, many parents, more often the mother, have focused a considerable amount of time and attention on their children. Those mothers who totally wrap themselves up in their offspring discover that when they reach the empty-nest stage of life, adjustment difficulties may begin. This often becomes a period of important self-evaluation, introspection, and reflection. Some even become depressed and lonely. The key issue appears to be ''Now what do I do?'' There is new freedom to fulfill some of one's own needs for a change, but some mothers are uncertain about what they want to do. It is important to note that such patterns will vary among those women who have been at home for years compared to those who have held down a job outside of the home during the stages of parenthood.

Positive reactions to the empty nest contrast with the aforementioned patterns. Although a period of adjustment is typical for parents, the empty nest heralds a time for high degrees of marital happiness, satisfaction, and shared activities. It may also create freedom from financial worries, freedom from extra housework, and freedom to travel. Furthermore, many postparental adults look back at their child-rearing years and report a high degree of pleasure, reward, and inner satisfaction in their roles as parents. Although some sadness is experienced, this emotion is outweighed by the joys and pleasures of past parenting.

It appears that the parents who best weather the empty-nest stage are those who do not try to foster dependency on the part of their children, but rather encourage autonomy and independence. Parents who believe that their children are mature enough for the work world, college, or marriage are more apt to let go than parents who still perceive their young adults as immature. Ideally, parents recognize their children as separate individuals in their own right and strive to show genuine care and concern, but not to the extent of overinvolvement. Such parents are usually not affected negatively when their children leave home. Indeed, a greater stressor may be the unexpected *return* of a young adult to the home.

Some parents may adjust to the empty-nest stage on a gradual basis. For instance, college, military service, or extended trips away from home may separate young adults from their parents for relatively short periods of time. This allows the parents to experience a household with one less child—or no children—without the feeling that they will never see the child again. Thus, even though the "nest" is "semi-empty," the experience is at least softened by the expectation that the child will return. Gradual adjustments to the empty-nest stage may also give parents time to evaluate themselves and their goals.

Once children have left the home, the husband and wife may discover that they have drifted apart over the years. With time together now, they may even be surprised at changes in one another that had gone unnoticed for some time. If couples find themselves dissatisfied with their marriage and discover that they no longer really "know" each other, it is difficult for them to offer mutual support and understanding during the middle and later years of adulthood. Some couples, assuming a pessimistic attitude, believe that their functions and responsibilities as parents are finished and thus view their lives as practically over. Some feel that there is little left to do with a life that has become devoid of meaning. In this case, the parental role has eclipsed the marital role. The outcome of this stage often becomes more positive when parents have other meaningful roles, such as work, school, or community involvement. The prospects for those seeking to revitalize or reconstruct a sagging marriage are considered favorable since the older couple now typically has more time, energy, and financial resources to invest in the relationship.

For many couples, the empty-nest stage is the most rewarding and happiest period of their life. When the children are gone from the home, mothers as well as fathers report an improvement in marital relations. Some feel that these years rival the happiness and satisfaction felt when the couple first met. Some even go so far as to label these years as a second honeymoon. Couples feeling this way usually have experienced much mutual understanding and support over the years. They are also likely to be optimistic about the future and have confidence in themselves and their abilities as a couple. They are further likely to have good communication skills, a strong sense of intimacy, and feelings of mutuality and reciprocity. (See FULL NEST; MIDDLE ADULTHOOD, MARRIAGE DURING.)

Further Reading. Kalish, Richard. (1989). *Midlife loss: Coping strategies.* Newbury Park, CA: Sage; Keith, Patricia M., and Robert B. Schafer. (1991). *Relationships and well-being over the life stages.* New York: Praeger; Mitchell, Valory, and Ravenna Helson. (1990). Women's prime of life: Is it the 50s? *Psychology of Women Quarterly, 14,* 451–470; Turner, Jeffrey S., and Donald B. Helms. (1994). *Contemporary adulthood* (5th Ed.). Fort Worth, TX: Harcourt Brace.

ENCULTURATION. Enculturation is the manner in which infants and children learn to be adult members of their society. In this sense, enculturation entails the transmission of cultural knowledge to the next generation. The process of enculturation involves observing, communicating, and interacting with others. Through enculturation, people become unified because they share common experiences. (See CULTURE.)

Further Reading. Landis, Judson R. (1995). *Sociology: Concepts and characteristics* (9th Ed.). Belmont, CA: Wadsworth; Levin, William C. (1994). *Sociological ideas: Concepts and applications* (4th Ed.). Belmont, CA: Wadsworth.

ENGAGEMENT. The engagement is a social transition designed to provide a clear indication that marriage between two people is about to occur. Variations of the engagement have existed in almost every society in the world. In the United States, the engagement is usually characterized by the presentation of an engagement ring to the fiancée, a shower for the bride, a party for the groom, and an announcement in the newspaper.

Much like wedding customs, the engagement is a practice rooted in the past (see MARRIAGE CEREMONY, RITUALS AND CUSTOMS). For example, the announcement is a remnant of colonial days and the posting of *banns,* a public notice of intent that was posted several weeks prior to the marriage at the church and other locations in the surrounding community. The engagement ring is a more recent engagement practice and enables the woman to display a symbol of commitment to the public. The bridal shower and a party for the groom represent extensions of familial and community assistance, including the opportunity to extend financial, material, and emotional support to the future bride and groom.

The engagement is an important transitional period between single and married status. It is the final opportunity prior to the legal union for each person to understand herself or himself in relation to the other. As such, it represents a time for the couple to discuss their expectations and ideas about marriage, their values, and their desired lifestyle. It is an important trial period to test each other's basic ideas about marriage in order to create a mutually satisfying relationship. The engagement period is also a time for couples to become aware of those factors that make marriages successful.

Further Reading. Cadogan, David. (1982). Questions to ask before you marry. *Marriage and Family Living, 64,* 12–13; Eshleman, J. Ross. (1994). *The family: An introduction* (7th Ed.). Boston: Allyn and Bacon; Murstein, Bernard I. (1986). *Paths to marriage.* Beverly Hills, CA: Sage.

ERIKSON, ERIK H. Erik H. Erikson (1902–1994) was born in Frankfurt, Germany, and was one of the world's foremost psychoanalytic scholars. After finishing high school, Erikson declared a "moratorium" and visited various parts of Europe to study art. During one of his journeys, he was given an opportunity to study child analysis at the Vienna Psychoanalytic Institute. It was at this institute, under the guidance of Anna Freud, among others, that Erikson launched a brilliant career in the field of developmental psychology.

Erikson left his native Europe when Hitler rose to power and served as a research associate in psychiatry, first in the Harvard Medical School and then at Yale University from 1936 to 1939. Following his stay at Yale, he accepted research and teaching posts at the University of California from 1939 to 1951. From 1951 through 1960, Erikson was senior consultant at the Austen-Riggs Center and a visiting professor at the University of Pittsburgh School of Medicine. He then became professor of human development and lecturer on psychiatry at Harvard University, from which he retired in 1970 as professor emeritus.

Erikson focused considerable energy on exploring the individual's personality development throughout the life cycle. Following Freud, who placed emphasis on psychosexual stages of development, Erikson stressed *psychosocial development* throughout life. At each stage of development, he theorized, from birth to old age, is a psychosocial crisis that must be resolved. Harmonious personality development is characterized by the successful resolution of these psychosocial crises. (See PSYCHOSOCIAL DEVELOPMENT.)

Further Reading. Erikson, Erik H. (Ed.). (1978). *Adulthood.* New York: Norton; Erikson, Erik H. (1980). *Identity and the life cycle.* New York: Norton; Erikson, Erik H. (1982). *The life cycle completed: A review.* New York: Norton; McAdams, Dan P. (1994). *The person: An introduction to personality psychology* (2nd Ed.). Fort Worth, TX: Harcourt Brace.

ETHNIC GROUP. An ethnic group is a category of people set apart from others on the basis of national origin, religion, race, or other distinctive cultural patterns. Ethnic groups usually share a sense of identity as well as similar values, beliefs, and ways of thinking. Examples of ethnic groups are Puerto Ricans, Jews, and Irish Americans. (See CULTURE.)

Further Reading. Gelles, Richard J., and Ann Levine. (1995). *Sociology* (5th Ed.). New York: McGraw-Hill; Gollnick, Donna M., and Philip C. Chinn. (1994). *Multicultural education in a pluralistic society* (4th Ed.). New York: Macmillan.

ETHNOCENTRISM. See CULTURAL RELATIVISM.

ETHNOMETHODOLOGY. Ethnomethodology is the study of both verbal and nonverbal methods that people use to communicate in everyday, routine activities. This type of observation technique focuses on the process rather than the outcome of an activity. For example, observers employing ethnomethodology might sit in on a college classroom while a particular topic is being discussed. The observers would pay more attention to the students' expressions of their feelings and attitudes and to the interaction among students and instructor than to any conclusions drawn from the discussions or to any consensus opinion reached.

Further Reading. Babbie, Earl. (1989). *The practice of social research* (5th Ed.). Belmont, CA: Wadsworth; Lofland, John. (1971). *Analyzing social settings: A guide to qualitative observation and analysis.* Belmont, CA: Wadsworth.

ETHOLOGICAL THEORY. Ethological theory is the study of human and animal behavior in natural settings. Initially influenced by the writings of Charles Darwin, this school of thought seeks to understand behavior in an evolutionary context and places considerable emphasis on the role of instinct in development. Notable contributors to ethology, besides Darwin, include Konrad Lorenz, John Bowlby, and Robert Hinde.

Observing an organism in its natural setting enables ethologists to learn how a species adapts to its environment. Ethologists maintain that we cannot understand why birds build nests unless we see how this behavior protects them from natural predators. Similarly, we cannot hope to understand the development of children's social groups or status hierarchies unless we observe free-play situations and appreciate how and why such socialization behavior emerges. Psychologists who restrict themselves to the laboratory study of animals and humans may miss critical aspects of behavior. Thus ethologists engage in naturalistic observation.

Ethologists maintain that in some species possessing instincts, there is a *critical period,* a specific time in which an environmental event will have its greatest impact on the developing organism (see CRITICAL PERIOD). Strong bonds of attachment develop between the caregiver and the young during the critical period, a social phenomenon known as *imprinting.* Whether or not a critical period exists in humans is unclear, although some ethologists such as Robert Hinde envision a less rigid concept of the critical period, called a sensitive period, being applied to the study of lifespan development. A *sensitive period* is a highly significant time frame early in life that affects the course of developmental dynamics. The sensitive period is a broader and more flexible time frame for behavior to emerge, often over a period of months or even years. Children may have sensitive periods for such behaviors as attachment, language, and gender-role development, to name but a few areas. Indeed, some ethologists are now suggesting that personality and social relationships have an ethological base; that is, they have an evolutionary/genetic heritage.

Further Reading. Bowlby, John. (1988). *A secure base: Parent-child attachment and healthy human development.* New York: Basic Books; Hinde, Robert A. (1989). Ethological and relationship approaches. In Ross Vasta (Ed.), *Six theories of child development: Revised formulations and current issues.* Greenwich, CT: JAI Press; Lorenz, Konrad. (1965). *Evolution and modification of behavior.* Chicago: University of Chicago Press.

EXHIBITIONISM. See SEXUAL BEHAVIORS, ATYPICAL.

EXPERIMENTAL METHOD. The experimental method is a series of steps by which a researcher tries to determine relationships between differing phenomena, either to discover principles underlying behavior or to find cause-and-effect relationships. The experimental method can be applied to the study of lifespan development or the behavior of individuals within relationships, just as it can to other disciplines.

Each experimental investigation must follow a procedure that is relevant to the phenomenon being investigated. Therefore, the scientific method used for one experiment may differ completely from the method used for an investigation of a completely different nature. For example, studying how children relate to authoritarian parents would involve methods totally different from those employed for investigating the behavioral reactions of middle-aged couples to stress. However, the basic principles of experimental methods remain the same. Regardless of specific experimental differences, certain common terms, definitions, and formats are universal to those using the experimental method.

The experimental method typically begins with a *hypothesis,* an educated guess made by researchers regarding what they think the results will be. Let us suppose that our hypothesis is that students will know more about relationships across the lifespan after a semester of college is over than they did before they enrolled. Before testing our hypothesis on a large group of people, say 1,000 undergraduate students, a *pilot study* is conducted, a small-scale research investigation designed to discover problems, errors, or other obstacles that might develop when the large-scale study is undertaken. Discovering procedural problems while testing 10 or 20 subjects will save much time and effort and many headaches before we begin testing 1,000 subjects.

In some types of research, two groups of subjects are chosen to prove or disprove the hypothesis. One group is called the *experimental group,* which is subjected to special conditions and is carefully observed by the experimenter. The special treatment given to the experimental group is called the *independent variable.* Concerning our hypothesis, the experimental group would comprise students enrolled in and receiving formal instruction (the independent variable) in relationships across the lifespan. The behavior affected by the independent variable, that is, the degree of knowledge acquired in class from the teacher, is termed the *dependent variable.*

Our other group of subjects, called the *control group,* is used primarily for comparison purposes. The control group would not receive the independent variable, the formal instruction in relationships across the lifespan, given to the experimental group.

To determine whether a hypothesis is correct, *pre-* and *post-tests* are usually administered to both experimental and control groups. In our case, the pre- and posttests would seek to measure the students' knowledge of relationships across the lifespan. Thus pre- and posttests are administrations of the dependent variable. Changes (if any) would appear in the experimental group, especially when contrasted with the control group.

In the last phase of the experimental method, investigators seek to draw conclusions and make interpretations. Unlike correlational studies, which simply attempt to establish correlations, or relationships, between or among two or more variables (see CORRELATIONAL RESEARCH), experimental methodology attempts to establish causality. That is, the experimental method tries to establish that one phenomenon, or variable, actually causes another. A well-executed experiment may provide insight into a hypothesis, but the results of an experiment may also raise many new questions and lead the researcher into other avenues of experimentation.

Finally, it needs to be pointed out that when conducting experimental research, especially, researchers must seek to control any extraneous variables possible. By seeking to control factors possibly affecting the outcome of experimental research, a researcher has greater confidence in making cause-and-effect statements. This is particularly important when one considers the enormous number of variables that developmental psychologists must take into account when seeking to pinpoint causal factors in development.

Further Reading. Creswell, John W. (1994). *Research design: Qualitative and quantitative approaches.* Thousand Oaks, CA: Sage; Heiman, Gary W. (1995). *Research methods in psychology.* Boston: Houghton Mifflin; Hinkle, Dennis E., William Wiersma, and Stephen G. Jurs. (1994). *Applied statistics for the behavioral sciences* (3rd Ed.). Boston: Houghton Mifflin.

EXTENDED FAMILY. See FAMILY COMPOSITION, TYPES OF.

F

FAILURE TO THRIVE. Failure to thrive is a condition often associated with the deprivation of early attachment between caregiver and infant as well as with social isolation from others. Due to these negative social conditions, failure-to-thrive children are often depressed, sad, withdrawn, and lethargic. Compared to children who are reared normally, failure-to-thrive children tend also to experience insomnia, loss of appetite, and developmental delays in such areas as speech and motor development. Researchers also note that failure-to-thrive children have difficulty with various aspects of social interaction, including the formation of meaningful relationships and the capacity to trust others, and they tend to have a greater susceptibility to infectious disease.

The length of time an individual is deprived of attachment and the degree of isolation from others are critical factors when examining the failure-to-thrive condition. In general, those who experience this condition for longer periods of time exhibit the most pronounced effects. Some investigators have found that the potentially harmful effects associated with failure to thrive do not necessarily persist in later life. More specifically, when failure-to-thrive children are removed from such negative social conditions and given special attention—such as physical, verbal, and mental stimulation—many exhibit marked improvement. Thus several factors must be examined when investigating the overall effects of the failure-to-thrive condition: the age of the child when deprivation occurs, the amount of time spent in the deprived condition, and the conditions of life preceding and following the experience.

Further Reading. Bowlby, John. (1988). *A secure base: Parent-child attachment and healthy human development*. New York: Basic Books; Dennis, Wayne. (1960). Causes of retardation among institutionalized infants. *Journal of Genetic Psychology, 96,* 47–59; Spitz, Rene A. (1949). Motherless infants. *Child Development, 20,* 145–155.

FAMILY BOUNDARIES. See FAMILY SYSTEMS, EXTERNAL BOUNDARY STRATEGIES.

FAMILY COMPOSITION, TYPES OF. Family composition refers to household structural variations. Several important types of family composition can be identified. The *nuclear family* consists of the mother, father, and children living in a home or residence of their own. Sometimes called the *conjugal family,* the nuclear family is two-generational; that is, it includes parents and offspring. Most individuals can expect to live in two nuclear families during their lives— the one into which they are born, called the *family of orientation,* and the one that is established through marriage and parenthood, known as the *family of procreation.*

The *extended family* consists of parents and offspring as well as other relatives such as grandparents, aunts, and uncles living in a single residence. Also called the *consanguine family* or the *family of kinship,* the extended family is thus multigenerational. *Modified extended families* are families that have a nuclear structure, but live in geographically dispersed locations. They are a modified version of the extended family because they maintain close ties and are united by an ongoing network of interaction.

A *blended family* results when a divorced parent with custody of children remarries (see REMARRIAGE). Also called the *compound* or *reconstituted family,* this household consists of parent, children, and stepparent. However, more complex arrangements are possible. For example, both parents may have children from previous marriages or may choose to conceive their own offspring. Finally, a *single-parent family* is one in which one parent assumes the responsibility for raising biological or adopted children (see SINGLE PARENTHOOD). The blended family and the single-parent family have become more common because of the increase in the divorce rate and the increase in adolescent pregnancy. (See DIVORCE; ADOLESCENCE, PREGNANCY DURING.) **Further Reading.** Bird, Gloria, and Keith Melville. (1994). *Families and intimate relationships.* New York: McGraw-Hill; Eshleman, J. Ross. (1994). *The family: An introduction* (7th Ed.). Boston: Allyn and Bacon; Gelles, Richard J. (1995). *Contemporary families: A sociological view.* Thousand Oaks, CA: Sage.

FAMILY CRISIS. A family crisis occurs when a situation creates disruption of normal family routines and appears insurmountable to problem-solving strategies. Since ordinary coping behaviors prove ineffective, the family usually restructures itself in some way. Often, a family crisis creates a period of disorganization and emotional upheaval during which the family members make various efforts to solve their problems. Eventually, some kind of family adaptation is achieved for better or worse. The outcome is frequently dictated by the way in which the family organizes itself during the crisis, including its application of resources and problem-solving strategies.

Two main types of family crises can be identified: developmental and situational. A *developmental* (or normative) *crisis* originates from predictable developmental changes over the course of the family life cycle (see FAMILY DEVELOPMENT THEORY). This type of crisis is related to the developmental tasks faced by the family at a given point in time, such as becoming a parent, raising adolescent children, adjusting to the empty nest, or becoming a grandparent. As the family faces developmental tasks, it needs to adapt to individual changes within the family unit (growth and development of family members) as well as family system changes (e.g., roles, rules, expectations). Developmental crises are regarded as normal and carry no stigma of deviancy. Domestic harmony and stability are measured by how effectively the family unit can deal with the developmental crises inherent throughout the family life cycle.

A *situational* (or nonnormative) *crisis* is not predictable or normal. Rather, this type of crisis is sudden and abrupt and can occur at any point in the family's development. Examples of situational crises include the death of a child, divorce, domestic abuse, or infidelity. Because of the unforeseen and unpredictable nature of situational crises, families often do not have the resources needed to successfully manage the situation. Situational crises, like those of a developmental nature, require family members to develop new styles of coping and adaptation. Should ineffective strategies result, the maladjustment of families can be long-lasting. Situational crises run the risk of never being resolved.

Further Reading. Alexander, James, and Bruce V. Parsons. (1982). *Functional family therapy.* Monterey, CA: Brooks/Cole; France, Kenneth. (1990). *Crisis intervention* (2nd Ed.). Springfield, IL: Charles C. Thomas; McCubbin, Hamilton I., A. Elizabeth Cauble, and Joan M. Patterson. (Eds.). (1982). *Family stress, coping, and social support.* Springfield, IL: Charles C. Thomas.

FAMILY DEVELOPMENT THEORY. Family development theory is a major school of thought in the discipline of family studies and is widely used in the study of close relationships. Family development theory proposes that marriage and family life represent a series of stages, or transitions, that present couples with a number of developmental tasks. These tasks are unique for each transition and must be adequately dealt with before the next stage can be entered. The successful resolution of developmental tasks depends on the resilience and flexibility of the family and its ability to apply adaptive resources.

Stages are usually characterized by the addition or subtraction of family members (through birth, death, or a family member leaving home), the developmental stages children experience, or the family's connection with other social systems, such as a family member's retirement from the labor force. In this fashion, a predictable chronology of family life stages can be charted: the unattached young adult, the newly married couple, the family with young children, the family with adolescents, launching of grown children, and the family in later life.

Since the family life cycle is viewed as an orderly sequence of events, the challenges inherent in each stage need to be addressed in a positive and healthy fashion. To illustrate the concept of stages, consider an aging couple being cared for by adult children. Such a unique family life stage poses an assortment of challenges for both generations and offers contrast to the demands posed at other points in the family life cycle. Generally, it is recognized that intergenerational caregiving brings the potential to initiate stress and requires the adaptive behavior of both adult children and aging parents. In this sense, a period of disorganization and emotional upheaval occurs during which adult children make various attempts to adapt to the needs of aging parents, and vice versa. The eventual outcome of this stage is frequently governed by the way in which all concerned perceive the event and how resourceful they are during the adjustment period.

Further Reading. Carter, Elizabeth A., and Monica McGoldrick. (1980). *The family life cycle: A framework for family therapy.* New York: Gardner Press; Rodgers, Roy H. (1973). *Family interaction and transaction: The developmental approach.* Englewood Cliffs, NJ: Prentice-Hall; White, James. (1991). *Dynamics of family development: A theoretical perspective.* New York: Guilford Press.

FAMILY LAW ACT. See DIVORCE, LEGAL ASPECTS OF.

FAMILY LIFE, HEALTHY CHARACTERISTICS OF. Family studies researchers have expended considerable energy exploring the complex dynamics of family life, including those processes and functions related to sound family health and well-being. Compared to unstable and ineffective family units, healthy families consistently demonstrate a number of unique qualities or dimensions. More specifically, effective families tend to share the following characteristics:

Intimate patterns of family interaction. Healthy families tend to seek intimacy, the mutual exchange of experiences in such a way that a further understanding of oneself and others is achieved. Effective families openly communicate, in the process sharing love, nurturance, and support, as well as mutuality and reciprocity. They employ nonthreatening techniques that enable them to get in touch with their own feelings and those around them. Family members share ideas, activities, and emotions without the feeling of being owned or judged. In this sense, healthy families tolerate the individuality of each family member and engage in active confirmation. That is, each family member is listened to, respected as an individual, and viewed as an integral facet of the total system. (See CONFIRMATION AND DISCONFIRMATION.)

An affectively responsive family unit. In healthy environments, family members are known for their warm, optimistic tone of feeling and for intensity. They have empathy for each other's feelings and interest in what each other has to say. The expectation of being understood prompts family members to respond to each other with concern and action. In short, their orientation is affiliative, with each person in the system expecting satisfaction and reward, which reinforces the involvement and investment in each other.

Meaningful patterns of communication. In addition to the exchange of intimacy and the desire to interact, effective families employ good communication strategies. Healthy families communicate in a clear and direct manner in both instrumental and effective areas. Positive communication embraces such areas as clear and congruent messages, supportive statements, and empathy. As previously mentioned, the effective family engages in confirmation rather than disconfirmation. Ineffective families tend to employ incongruent messages, lack of empathy, nonsupportive and negative statements, and double messages.

Skilled negotiation and problem-solving skills. Healthy families are effective in their ability to organize themselves, negotiate differences, accept directions, develop input from each other, and reach closure effectively and coherently. Effective families solve most problems efficiently and easily and therefore have few unresolved issues. The effective family usually has an assortment of conflict-resolution skills and creative coping skills. Also, self-esteem is an important dimension in healthy families, particularly between marital partners. In this respect, effectively communicating spouses rarely exhibit a "boss-employee" relationship that reflects a lopsided distribution of power. In addition, they employ compromise, as well as collaboration, exploring underlying issues, and arriving at solutions that best meet the needs of the family, in order to resolve conflict.

Effectiveness in handling change, including situational and developmental crises. Healthy families are flexible and adaptive when confronted with change: they can adapt their styles as the family and individual members need change. As they deal with situations that threaten domestic disruption, effective families are able to develop conflict-resolution skills and creative coping resources. Moreover, they are effective in meeting the assortment of developmental changes posed over the course of the family life cycle (see FAMILY CRISIS).

Ability to utilize support systems when needed. Effective families and ineffective families perceive support systems quite differently from one another. Effective families see relatives, friends, groups, and community as valuable supports in dealing with stresses and therefore turn to them when the need arises. On the other hand, ineffective families often view such support systems as evidence of their own inability to deal with challenges and stresses.

Encouragement of independence and autonomy. Effective families regard independence and autonomy as important to the development of all members, particularly children. Effective families do not try to foster dependence, nor are they overprotective. The individual uniqueness of each family member is accepted as well as respected, and a climate of mutual trust flourishes. There is also tolerance of uncertainty, ambivalence, and imperfection. In ineffective families, members are often expected to think and feel alike, with no comprehension of uniquely subjective human responses to the world.

Positive emotional and psychological climate. Healthy families are capable of expressing a wide spectrum of emotions, and family members are usually emotionally invested in one another. Ineffective families are often detached and devoid of feelings. Many ineffective families demonstrate a lack of involvement or, in some instances, overinvolvement. The effective family is also not a psychologically alienated unit; that is, it does not suffer from feelings of powerlessness, meaninglessness, normlessness, or isolation.

Further Reading. Boss, Pauline. (1988). *Family stress management.* Newbury Park, CA: Sage; Curran, Dolores. (1985). *Stress and the healthy family.* Minneapolis, MN: Winston Press; L'Abate, Luciano. (1990). *Building family competence: Primary and secondary prevention strategies.* Newbury Park, CA: Sage; McCubbin, Hamilton I., and Charles R. Figley. (1983). *Stress and the family.* New York: Brunner/Mazel.

FAMILY OF ORIENTATION. See FAMILY COMPOSITION, TYPES OF.

FAMILY OF PROCREATION. See FAMILY COMPOSITION, TYPES OF.

FAMILY PLANNING. Family planning is the conscious, voluntary decision making of couples about how many children they want and when, or if children are wanted at all. Family planning embraces contraception to space and prevent pregnancy, and efforts to induce pregnancy, including infertility therapy to help couples achieve wanted conceptions.

Further Reading. Haupt, Arthur, and Thomas T. Kane. (1985). *The population reference bureau's population handbook.* Washington, DC: Population Reference Bureau; Shryock, Henry S., and Jacob S. Siegel. (1976). *The methods and materials of demography.* Orlando, FL: Academic Press.

FAMILY POLICY. Family policy is government-sponsored legislation designed to assist the overall welfare and well-being of the family. Family policy proponents acknowledge that family life creates its share of stress and difficulties, and that many members need to turn to the outside for assistance with matters from elderly and child-care needs to parenting programs and domestic abuse intervention. An example of family policy was the 1993 Family Leave Bill, which made it illegal to fire employees who must take time off to care for babies or ill family members. It is generally agreed that the national government needs to have adequate, ongoing, profamily policy for these and countless other needs arising from the turbulence of contemporary times.

Further Reading. Aulette, Judy R. (1994). *Changing families.* Belmont, CA: Wadsworth; Jacobs, Francine H., and Margery W. Davies. (Eds.). (1994). *More than kissing babies? Current child and family policy in the United States.* Westport, CT: Auburn House; Popple, Philip, and Leslie Leighninger. (1993). *Social work, social welfare, and American society* (2nd Ed.). Boston: Allyn and Bacon.

FAMILY POWER. See POWER AND RELATIONSHIPS.

FAMILY SYSTEMS, EXTERNAL BOUNDARY STRATEGIES.
External boundary strategies of family systems are patterns of interaction between the family unit and the surrounding environment. Marriage and family therapists often observe and analyze such states when exploring the dynamics of family functioning. Any family system is subject to a succession of open and closed boundaries or states, often referred to as *family transformations.*

An *open family system* is chiefly characterized by its permeable boundaries. Members of the family have sustained outside relations with the surrounding community. The open family system maintains itself by a constant process of input and output, and it is regulated by both positive and negative feedback from others.

A *closed* or *rigid family system,* on the other hand, does not interact with the surrounding environment. It tends to turn inward and isolate itself from the larger community. Family members have few contacts outside the home, and usually a clear distinction is made between the family in-group and the outside community.

Thus, whereas the closed family system is cut off from its environment and requires a high level of commitment and cooperation from its members, the open family system is continually drawn into community activities. Family studies researchers note that both open and closed family systems have a tendency to "run down" and become disordered over time, largely because the family's energy flow becomes disorganized and unstructured. However, this tendency toward disorder tends to take place more rapidly in a closed family system because it is cut off from a healthy exchange of energy with its surroundings. An open system resists running down because it interacts with the environment, giving and receiving energy. Open systems are characterized by flexibility and adaptability. They do not operate within a confined range and have a constant influx of input and output from others.

Further Reading. Sieburg, Evelyn. (1985). *Family communication: An integrated systems approach.* New York: Gardner Press; Steinglass, Peter. (1987). A systems view of family interaction and psychopathology. In Theodore Jacob (Ed.), *Family interaction and psychopathology.* New York: Plenum Press.

FAMILY SYSTEMS, INTERNAL BOUNDARY STRATEGIES. Internal boundary strategies of family systems concern themselves with how distances are regulated between individual family members. Internal boundary strategies are a reflection of the degree to which individuality and autonomy are tolerated within the family unit. When family boundaries are *enmeshed,* there is a low tolerance for individuality. As a result, there is often dependency on other family members and an intrusion into privacy in everyone's personal life. When family boundaries are *disengaged,* there is a high tolerance for individuality. In such homes, autonomy is valued and expected. Family studies experts point out that in stable, functioning homes, there is a healthy balance of both enmeshment and disengagement. By this, boundaries are established that allow both for the expression of individuality and a secure connection to the family.

Further Reading. Anderson, Stephen A., and Ronald M. Sabatelli. (1995), *Family interaction: A multigenerational developmental perspective.* Needham Heights, MA: Allyn and Bacon; Nichols, Michael. P. (1984). *Family therapy: Concepts and methods.* New York: Gardner Press.

FAMILY SYSTEMS THEORY. See GENERAL SYSTEMS THEORY.

FATHERHOOD. See PARENTHOOD, THE ROLE OF THE FATHER.

FECUNDITY. Fecundity is the physiological ability of individuals or couples to have children. Some persons are *infecund,* or unable to bear children because of genetic dysfunction or disease, while others are *superfecund,* or able to have many children. The maximum fecundity of a population, which consists of persons with varying degrees of fecundity, is believed to be about 15 children per woman.

Further Reading. Haupt, Arthur, and Thomas T. Kane. (1985). *The population reference bureau's population handbook.* Washington, DC: Population Reference Bureau; McFalls, Joseph A., Jr. (1991). *Population: A lively introduction.* Washington, DC: Population Reference Bureau.

FEDERAL REPUBLIC OF GERMANY, LIFESPAN RELATIONSHIPS IN THE. Germany is a nation in central Europe, lying in the midst of the continent and sharing borders with nine other countries. Germany was once divided into the German Democratic Republic (East Germany) and the Federal Republic of Germany (West Germany). However, following economic and political collapse, East Germany reunified with the Federal Republic of Germany in 1990. About 80 million people live in Germany, the heaviest concentration being in West Germany.

In some respects, Germany represents a relatively homogeneous population. For example, German is the universal language, and the country contains no major minority groups (although it should be recognized that a large Jewish population that lived in Germany before World War II was systematically destroyed by the Nazi regime). However, Germany's diversity is reflected in its political factions: before its demise, East Germany was a socialist state, while West Germany exercises capitalism. Religion also divides Germany's contrasting population segments. A significant proportion of the population is Protestant, accounting for about 75 percent of the people in East Germany and almost one-half in West Germany. Roman Catholicism is the next most popular religion, representing almost one-half of the West German people.

Patterns of dating and courtship in Germany are similar to those in other European nations. However, unlike other nations, cohabitation is not widespread. Compared to countries such as Sweden and Denmark, where cohabitation has emerged as an extremely popular lifestyle, only a minority of Germans choose to live together. Singlehood, though, is also increasing in Germany and is becoming a common alternative to marriage. Germans cite numerous motivations for choosing the single lifestyle. For example, many remain single because of career and educational commitments, while others enjoy the freedom that this lifestyle offers. Still others are unwilling to make long-term commitments.

While most Germans choose to marry, changes have occurred in overall rates of marriage during the last 25 years. Once again, these changes draw attention to Germany's regional diversity. For example, the marriage rate has declined in West Germany but has remained about the same in East Germany. Also, East Germans are more likely to marry at earlier ages. The propensity to wed in East Germany may be due to special financial benefits available to those couples who married and had children. Such benefits included government stipends, maternity-leave programming, and the provision of low-cost child care. Such family-oriented social policies represented an effort among East Germans to increase the region's declining fertility levels.

Regarding the latter, Germany is characterized by small families. Today, the average German woman will give birth to 1.5 children. A number of reasons help to explain such low fertility rates: financial considerations, the earlier-mentioned upsurge in singlehood, more efficient contraceptives, an increase in women's liberation, and educational and vocational commitments. Germany is not alone in its declining fertility rates. Indeed, nations such as Austria, Denmark, and Hungary have reported steep fertility declines. Many European countries have dropped below 2.1 lifetime births per woman, about the replacement level needed to keep births and deaths in balance and thus retain population stability. As previously indicated, Germany, like a number of its European neighbors, has offered a variety of pronatalist incentives to its people.

In addition to declining marriage and fertility rates, Germany has recently experienced rising divorce rates. As a result of these increased divorce rates, coupled with other forms of marital breakdown (e.g., death of spouse, desertion), Germany now has more marriage dissolutions each year than weddings. Escalating divorce rates have in turn created a growing number of single-parent families. As in other nations, single-parent households in Germany are often beset with economic difficulties and other troubles.

Germany has a large proportion of elderly, which affects the nature of later life relationships. In 1990, about 15 percent of Germany's population was age 65 and over; by 2020, this figure is expected to mushroom to 25 percent. Increasing life expectancy has created a significant increase in single households, particularly among aged women. Because women live longer than men, and because women tend to marry men several years older than themselves, German women are much more likely to experience the death of a spouse. Studies show that only about 15 percent of German men live alone, whereas the corresponding figure for women is over 50 percent. It is estimated that about 80 percent of German women over age 75 live in single households.

As in the United States, German elderly prefer to live independently rather than move in with their children. However, this does not mean that the elderly are isolated or without social support from younger family members. On the contrary, strong intergenerational relations and family loyalty characterize the German kin network. While the nuclear family is the prevalent household structure, the extended family is equally important. This is especially true for aging family members, who are the recipients of regular contact and care. In recent years, the German government has expanded its services to aging persons and their families. Specialized seniors bureaus have been designed as part of the Federal Plan for the Aging and promote the health and well-being of older citizens and their families throughout the country.

Further Reading. Coale, Ansley J., and Susan Watkins. (Eds.). (1986). *The decline of fertility in Europe.* Princeton, NJ: Princeton University Press; Heilig, Gerhard, Thomas Buttner, and Wolfgang Lutz. (1990). *Germany's population: Turbulent past, uncertain future.* Washington, DC: Population Reference Bureau; Hohn, Charlotte, and Kurt Luscher. (1988). The changing family in the Federal Republic of Germany. *Journal of Family Issues, 9,* 317–335; Rueschemeyer, Marilyn. (1988). New family forms in a state socialist society: The German Democratic Republic. *Journal of Family Issues, 9,* 354–371.

FERTILITY, INTERNATIONAL DIFFERENCES IN. International differences in fertility refer to global variations that exist in the number of children that women have. The current emphasis placed on overpopulation and deliberate family planning has created a fertility decrease in many developed nations. In the United States, the average woman gives birth to about 2 children, down from an average of 3.2 in 1960. Should present trends continue, the United States will reach zero population growth by the year 2020. *Zero population growth* means that a given population does not decrease or increase; rather, it is in equilibrium, with a growth rate of zero.

Other developed nations such as Austria, Denmark, and Hungary have already reached zero population growth. In fact, the *fertility rate* (the number of children a woman will give birth to over the course of her reproductive years) in these nations is causing *negative population growth,* a decrease in overall population. Some countries, such as the Federal Republic of Germany, France, and Hungary, seek to avoid such a population downswing by implementing *pronatalist policies.* That is, couples receive government-sponsored incentives such as subsidized maternity leave, family allowances, and more accessible housing loans for families conceiving more than one child. Nations such as Ireland and the republics of the former Soviet Union have fertility rates of above 2.10 lifetime births per woman. This is about the fertility rate needed to balance a nation's births and deaths, thus maintaining a stable population.

As might be expected, the percentages of married women using contraception are highest in developed nations. For example, over 70 percent of married couples in the United States, Belgium, Denmark, Hungary, Portugal, and the United

Kingdom use some form of birth control. The lowest percentages can be found in Africa, where the concept of family planning, at least for limiting fertility, has yet to be fully accepted. For example, the percentages range from 3 percent in Cameroon to about 5 percent in Senegal and 7 percent in Kenya. In Asia, the figures range from about 7 percent in Nepal to 12 percent in Bangladesh and about 55 percent in Thailand. In Latin America, the percentages vary from 34 percent in El Salvador to 61 percent in Panama. In all of these nations, the percentages of teenagers using contraception are significantly lower.

Without adequate contraception, large families prevail in many parts of the world. For example, Kenyan women average eight children each, causing a population increase of 4.2 percent per year. Kenya's population was estimated to be 21 million in 1990, and if current fertility rates hold, it will quadruple to 83 million by 2025. In other nations, Haitian women give birth to about six children, a total that parallels the fertility rate of Pakistani women. In Tunisia, women average about five children.

Knowledge of family planning is an obvious prerequisite to lowering the birthrate in overpopulated countries. However, we must not lose sight of the fact that the number of children brought into the world is influenced by many factors. One of the most important is the economic role of children, particularly in developing nations. Larger families can typically be found in those agricultural areas where intensive labor is needed, such as Latin America. In India and Bangladesh, large families result from the desire for healthy male children. Boys represent economic security for the mother should she become widowed.

In some nations, certain customs and practices contribute to high rates of fertility. For example, in Rwanda (East Africa), contraceptive use has never been popular. Only about 11 percent of married women over age 15 use any form of family planning, and 80 percent of this figure rely on periodic abstinence. The average Rwandan woman is married before age 20 and bears eight children over the course of her adult years. In some African countries, a taboo on postpartum intercourse that can last as long as two years can reduce the fertility level.

No discussion of fertility differentials is complete without some reference to the People's Republic of China. Here, family planning is not a voluntary decision made by couples. Rather, it is the government that dictates family planning. In an effort to reduce overpopulation in a country whose population is expected to reach over 1.2 billion by the turn of the century, couples in this nation are allowed to have only one child. China is thus the first nation ever to restrict a couple's right to procreate. It has also raised the minimum age for marriage to 20 for women and 22 for men. Even later marriages are encouraged to reduce the couple's risk of having more than one child. (See PEOPLE'S REPUBLIC OF CHINA, LIFESPAN RELATIONSHIPS IN THE.)

The government imposes the one-child limit through incentives, peer pressure, and attempts to persuade newly married couples that their rational fertility decisions will mean a better future for their own families, their communities, and their nation. If the one-child limit is successful, it is estimated that the population will stabilize by the turn of the century. If it is unsuccessful and the population continues to grow, China's ability to feed its people is in jeopardy, among other consequences. China occupies only 7 percent of the globe's arable land but supports 25 percent of its population.

If Chinese couples follow government legislation, they are entitled to numerous benefits, including increased living space, pensions, free education, lower-cost health care, and better medical intervention. Eventually, the only child receives preferential treatment in the school system as well as in the labor force. Should couples give birth to a second child, the family forfeits all of these benefits.

Complicating this fertility plan is the fact that Chinese families have traditionally preferred male children. Should a firstborn be female, couples may try to conceive again in an effort to bring a male into the world. This places couples at odds with the government and incurs consequences. Indeed, in several Chinese provinces, couples expecting a second child will have their wages docked if the woman decides not to have an abortion.

In 1993, worldwide attention became riveted on China when its Family Planning Commission revealed figures on female-to-male birth ratios. These figures showed that for every 100 female infants born in China, 111.3 male infants were also born. According to demographic experts, these figures represent a highly unlikely ratio since the average global ratio is 106 males to 100 females. Interestingly, China matched that ratio before the government launched its one-child policy in 1979.

The mystery of what happened to China's female infants has become one of the deepest enigmas of a nation determined to curb its runaway population plight. If government figures are correct, about 750,000 female infants born in China are unaccounted for. What has happened to them? Demographic experts believe that one-half to three-quarters of them are simply not reported by parents, who hide them or send them to relatives in remote areas. By so doing, a woman can become pregnant a second time, hopefully with a male, without incurring any of the earlier-mentioned fines or loss of privileges.

The remainder of the missing girls, officials say, are aborted. About 10 million abortions are performed annually in China, and even rural towns now have ultrasound machines to determine the sex of the fetus. While doctors are legally barred from revealing the sex of a fetus, many can be bribed to do so. In remote areas of China, infanticide is performed by a midwife should a female baby be born. While many Western demographers support China's efforts to reduce its birthrate, they are concerned by such side effects of the one-child system.

China's one-child policy ran into trouble in 1991 when officials realized from birth registries that the policy was being increasingly flouted by peasants who either bribed local officials or had saved enough money to pay the fine for a second or third child. Chinese officials reported that one million ''unauthorized'' babies were born that year, thus creating serious consequences for the nation's family-planning movement. A crackdown on offenders was implemented in

1991, and since then, the birthrate has declined and the use of contraceptives has increased to 83 percent of married couples. In 1993, China introduced its version of the controversial French abortion pill RU 486. When taken over a three-day period, it induces a miscarriage.

Further Reading. Donaldson, Peter J., and Amy Ong Tsui. (1990). *The international family planning movement.* Washington, DC: Population Reference Bureau; Schmetzer, Ursalla. (1993). Where are China's female children? *New York Times.* May 15, B17–18; Van de Kaa, Dirk J. (1987). *Europe's second demographic transition.* Washington, DC: Population Reference Bureau; Wawer, Maria. (1991). Family planning operations research in Africa: Reviewing a decade of experience. *Studies in Family Planning, 22,* 279–293.

FERTILITY, PATTERNS OF IN THE UNITED STATES. Patterns of fertility, or the number of births a woman will have during her reproductive life, have changed considerably in the United States. Until the early decades of the nineteenth century, American women averaged about seven children each. But while large families were once the norm in the United States, this is not the case today. In the 1990s, the average woman in the United States gives birth to about two children.

This decline in fertility can be explained by a number of factors, including the postponement of marriage and the widespread use of contraception and abortion. Despite the fact that few American women believe that childless or one-child families are ideal, many women have delayed marriage and childbearing so long that they will have only one child or no children at all. There is also considerable variation in fertility rates among couples in the United States. A number of reasons can be cited to explain fertility differentials, the more obvious being age, race and ethnicity, and socioeconomic status.

As far as age is concerned, women are able to conceive a pregnancy beginning in their early teens and ending in their late 40s. The highest birthrates are for women between the ages of 25 and 29, followed by women between the ages of 20 and 24. In recent years, there has been an increase in fertility rates among women aged 30 to 44, a trend likely due to the growing numbers of women delaying parenthood.

In many countries, racial and ethnic minorities have higher fertility rates than majority groups. Often these differences arise from religious beliefs and cultural traditions, but they also are linked to the lower economic status of minority groups and the number of years they have lived in their adopted country. As immigrant groups assimilate socially and economically, they tend to adopt the fertility patterns of the majority. In the United States, for example, fertility differences among white ethnic groups (e.g., Irish, German, or Italian Americans) are becoming less distinguishable over time. Groups that have not fully assimilated may maintain their distinctive fertility patterns. In the United States, Hispanic Americans, African Americans, and Native Americans have higher fertility than the white, non-Hispanic majority.

Socioeconomic status also influences fertility rates. In nearly every contemporary society, the poor have more children than the rich. This is also true for the United States within all major racial and ethnic groups. In general, fertility goes down as the income and educational attainment of women increase.

In addition to these forces, other religious, social, and cultural factors can be cited to explain fertility differences. Most of these fertility differences can be explained by the age, income, or education differences among these groups. For example, in just about every culture, women who are employed outside the home have fewer children than those who are not, and rural women have more children than those from urban settings. People who actively practice a religion tend to have higher fertility than nonreligious people. There are differences between major religious groups in many countries, but these often converge with ethnic and socioeconomic differences.

Further Reading. Jones, Brian, Bernard J. Gallagher, and Joseph A. McFalls, Jr. (1988). *Social problems: Issues, opinions, and solutions.* New York: McGraw-Hill; McFalls, Joseph A., Jr. (1984). *Disease and fertility.* New York: Academic Press; McFalls, Joseph A., Jr. (1991). *Population: A lively introduction.* Washington, DC: Population Reference Bureau.

FERTILITY RATE. Fertility rate is the number of births that occur to a woman over the course of her lifetime. Fertility rate varies widely from country to country. For example, in 1994 the fertility rate in Rwanda was about 8 children per woman, while in the United States it was about 2. Also in 1994, the average worldwide fertility rate for all women was 3.5 children.

Further Reading. Haupt, Arthur, and Thomas T. Kane. (1985). *The population reference bureau's population handbook.* Washington, DC: Population Reference Bureau; Shryock, Henry S., and Jacob S. Siegel. (1976). *The methods and materials of demography.* Orlando, FL: Academic Press.

FETISHISM. See SEXUAL BEHAVIORS, ATYPICAL.

FILTERING AGENTS, IMPACT OF ON INTIMATE RELATIONSHIPS. Filtering agents are a sequence of decisions made by the couple about the quality of "fit" between their individual attributes. As two individuals acquaint themselves with each other, they acquire information about one another through a series of these filters. Over time, filtering agents test the compatibility of partners and serve to narrow down the field of eligibles.

In recent years, the manner in which filtering agents impact on intimate relationships has been studied fairly extensively. More specifically, researchers have identified various kinds of filtering agents and how they shape the course of relationship development. For example, interaction tends to be enhanced when individuals reside near one another, be it at home or at work. This nearness in place is referred to as *propinquity.* In its broadest sense, propinquity means that individuals need to have continual contact if the relationship is to endure.

Another filtering agent is *homogamy*. Homogamy means that we are attracted to and become involved with those with whom we have something in common, such as similar education, age, intelligence, or physical appearance. *Endogamy* is a filtering agent that encourages persons to marry within their own social group. In other words, a Catholic marries a Catholic, or an African American marries an African American. To marry outside of one's particular social group would be an *exogamous* choice. As an illustration, a Catholic marries a Protestant, or an African American marries a white.

The filtering agent of *complementary needs* assumes that individuals seek out mates to complement their own personalities. Thus a partner is chosen to fill the void of one's own personality. Complementary needs also implies that individuals tend to complement personality traits that they lack, but still hold in high regard.

The *parental image* filtering agent is Freudian in origin. It implies that during childhood, a person nurtured a deep affection for the parent of the opposite sex. When mate selection takes place, the individual sees the image of this childhood attachment. The expressions "She's looking for someone with her father's qualities" or "He wants someone like his mother" are applicable in this case. This filtering agent thus reflects unique variations of psychoanalytic theory (see PSYCHOANALYTIC THEORY; PSYCHOSEXUAL DEVELOPMENT).

Another filtering agent is *physical appearance*. In virtually all societies, physical appearance is an important factor in the selection of a mate. Indeed, individuals tend to select partners whose physical attractiveness roughly matches their own. However, men are usually more preoccupied with physical traits, while women tend to focus on psychological factors. Along these lines, men are more apt to emphasize good looks, while women have traditionally given emphasis to ambition, industriousness, education, and intelligence. When considering the importance of physical appearance, both men and women value cleanliness, neatness, and good grooming (see INTERPERSONAL ATTRACTION, PHYSICAL APPEARANCE AND).

Social exchange and role compatibility are two additional filtering agents. *Social exchange* means that persons are attracted to those who provide the greatest relational rewards and the fewest number of trade-offs or sacrifices. *Role compatibility* embodies the notion that between two persons there is stability and harmony in role "fit." That is, the set of roles one brings into a relationship and the role expectations one has for the partner are mutually agreeable.

Further Reading. Knox, David, and Caroline Schacht. (1994). *Choices in relationships.* (4th Ed.). St. Paul, MN: West; South, Scott. (1991). Sociodemographic differentials in mate selection preferences. *Journal of Marriage and the Family, 53,* 928–940; Surra, Catherine A. (1990). Research and theory on mate selection and premarital relationships in the 1980s. *Journal of Marriage and the Family, 52,* 844–865.

FRANCE, LIFESPAN RELATIONSHIPS IN. France is the largest country in Western Europe and one of the world's most important industrial and agricultural nations. The intellectual and cultural life of France has also impacted on other countries for centuries. France has a population of about 56 million people that is fairly evenly distributed throughout the country. The majority of the population is Roman Catholic, and French is the primary language. In some border regions, Breton, Basque, Flemish, and German are spoken.

As in other developed nations, French teenagers begin dating at early ages. Most are sexually active and have experienced premarital coitus by the end of adolescence. While birth control among French adolescents has increased in recent years, contraceptive behavior tends to be inconsistent and often ineffective. Many adolescent males and females use no contraception at first intercourse. Despite national efforts to educate the general public on the prevention of HIV and AIDS, many French teenagers engage in various types of sexual risk taking. For example, many do not limit the number of their sex partners or use latex condoms.

Marriage is a popular lifestyle in France, but overall marriage rates as well as remarriage rates have been declining over the past 25 years. French couples are also waiting longer to marry: recent studies show that the mean age of women at first marriage is about 23 years, while for men it is 25 years. As in other European nations, cohabitation and singlehood are emerging as alternative and acceptable lifestyle options. As far as patterns of cohabitation are concerned, the young are particularly drawn to this lifestyle, although there has recently been an increase in older French cohabitants. As in other nations, an important reason for the increase in singlehood in France is that more young adults are postponing marriage, usually because of educational or career pursuits. Many are in the midst of trying out different lifestyles and making provisional choices.

Family life has always been important to the French. The family unit is viewed as the basic component of society and the primary source of psychological and economic security. The nuclear family is the dominant household structure, and growing numbers of French homes are of the dual-earner variety. A patriarchal, or husband-dominated, power structure characterizes most homes, but many researchers have reported an increase in egalitarianism among many French couples. While the French are having fewer children in these modern times, the value of children remains significant in the lives of men and women. Parent-child relations tend to be characterized by considerable affection and understanding, and sibling relations are usually close-knit. Greater involvement of fathers in child care is increasingly apparent throughout many areas of France.

France's dwindling family size has not escaped the notice of demographers. France experienced a high birthrate from 1945 to 1965, but then a steady decline. Over the past 30 years, the level of births in France has continued to drop, although France's birthrate is still higher than that of almost all other Western European nations, except Ireland. Today, the average woman in France will give birth to 1.8 children. France's birthrate is thus below the replacement level (2.1 lifetime births per woman) needed to keep the nation's births and deaths in balance and thus ensure population stability. French women are also having their children later in life. The average woman has her first child at age 28.5, as compared to age 27 a decade ago.

In an effort to increase its fertility level, the French government has implemented a pronatalist policy under which incentives are offered to those couples having more than one child. While programming is not as extensive as in other European nations, such as the Federal Republic of Germany, government officials hope that such measures will promote a population upswing. Among the incentives offered are family allowances, a special grant for a couple's third child, maternity leave, and more accessible housing loans for those families with two or more children.

In France, the potential for long and satisfying relationships is enhanced by a two-and-one-half-year increase in life expectancy. Today, French women live an average of 81 years, while men live almost 73 years. Given these increases, France now leads all European nations in life expectancy. The combined demographic forces of low fertility rates and increased life expectancy have created a dramatic increase in France's elderly population. Those 65 years of age and older represent one of France's fastest-growing population segments, and France is currently one of nine countries having more than one million residents aged 80 years and over. Widows outnumber widowers in France five to one.

France has responded to its aging population with important health-care reforms, including assistance to elderly caregivers, more geriatric units within hospitals, and expanded residential-care facilities for the aged. The elderly in France are treated with considerable honor and dignity, and relationships between generations, including family caregiving, are invariably characterized by harmony and mutual respect. The French refer to the later years of life as *le troisième âge* (the third age). Following childhood and adulthood, the third age heralds a new developmental challenge, a time for discovery and renewed involvement with oneself and the world. While illness and death can occur, the French assert that there are also beauty and creativity to be sought and shared with others.

Further Reading. Davis, Kingsley, Mikhail S. Berstam, and Helen Sellers (Eds.). (1989). *Population and resources in a changing world.* Stanford, CA: Morrison Institute for Population and Resource Studies, Standford University; McIntosh, C. Alison. (1983). *Population policy in Western Europe: Responses to low fertility in France, Sweden, and West Germany.* Armonk, NY: M. E. Sharpe; Patriquin, Wendy. (1988). Spotlight: France. *Population Today, 16,* 12; Van de Kaa, Dirk J. (1987). *Europe's second demographic transition.* Washington, DC: Population Reference Bureau.

FREUD, SIGMUND. Sigmund Freud (1856–1939) was an Austrian physician who forged a revolutionary theory of personality in which sexual motivation played a dominant role. Born in Frieberg, Moravia, Freud received a medical degree from the University of Vienna in 1881. While practicing medicine in clinics, he became interested in neurophysiology, especially the functions of the brain. He spent considerable time seeking to understand abnormal brain functions and mental disorders, a pursuit that would eventually bring him to the fields of psychiatry and psychology.

Gradually, through treating neurotic patients with such techniques as hypnosis and free association (asking the patient to say spontaneously whatever comes into his head), Freud became convinced that sexual conflict was the cause of most neuroses. Freud traced such conflict to the forces of sexual and aggressive urges and the clashes of these forces with the codes of conduct required by society.

Eventually Freud developed *psychoanalytic theory,* which proposes, among other things, that our past plays an important role in determining our present behavior. Fundamental to Freud's theory are the notions that behavior is unconsciously motivated and that neuroses often have their origins in early childhood experiences that have subsequently become repressed. Freud also suggested that sexual urges were responsible for most human motivation. He held that because sexual thoughts and needs were often repressed, they were likely to provide unconscious motivation.

Although many of Freud's views are controversial, many researchers in the field of lifespan development have been influenced by such ideas as his theory of psychosexual development. According to this theory, the development and maturation of sexual and other body parts have great impact on early life experiences. Critics of psychoanalytic theory claim that many of Freud's concepts cannot be scientifically measured and are based on poor methodology. Some argue that his theories were bound to nineteenth-century Vienna and, furthermore, that he downplayed female sexuality.

Nevertheless, Freud's theory has lost none of its luster over the years. Proponents point out how Freud's ideas have extended into many disciplines, including history, literature, philosophy, and the arts. However we view Freud's specific theories, we cannot deny the power of his intellect and the strength of his motivation to discover new dimensions of human behavior. (See PSYCHO-ANALYTIC THEORY; PSYCHOANALYTIC THEORY, DEFENSE MECHANISMS AND; PSYCHOSEXUAL DEVELOPMENT.)

Further Reading. Feist, Jess. (1994). *Theories of personality* (3rd Ed.). Fort Worth, TX: Harcourt Brace; Freud, Sigmund. (1905). *Three essays on the theory of sexuality.* London: Hogarth Press; Freud, Sigmund. (1923). *The ego and the id.* London: Hogarth Press; Freud, Sigmund. (1938). *An outline of psychoanalysis.* London: Hogarth Press.

FRIENDSHIPS. See ADOLESCENCE, FRIENDSHIPS DURING; ADULT-HOOD, FRIENDSHIPS DURING; CHILDHOOD, FRIENDSHIPS DURING.

FROMM, ERICH. Erich Fromm (1900–1980) was a noted psychoanalytic scholar who explored the nature of productive and nonproductive facets of behavior within interpersonal relationships, including expressions of love. Fromm trained at the Berlin Psychoanalytic Institute and received his Ph.D. in psychology from the University of Heidelberg in 1922. He held teaching positions at Columbia University, Yale University, New York University, and Michigan State University.

Fromm maintained that men and women sometimes tend to alienate themselves and demonstrate hostile and aggressive forms of behavior. Fromm concentrated his energies on studying such negative behavior, particularly ways to overcome it. His works are directed toward the regulation of humanity, including the need for people to unite with others and to feel part of a group, such as within a family, church, or nation. Fromm saw control as a necessary way of life, including the setting of limits through boundaries, rules, and regulations.

In his writings, Fromm often stressed the importance of relating to others in a loving, caring fashion. He felt that in so doing, individuals nurtured their own integrity and self-worth. He stressed the importance of altruistic love, which embodies the unselfish concern for the well-being of another person. Fromm felt that loving should be an act of giving rather than receiving, and he believed that it should embrace such elements as respect, concern, and understanding.

Further Reading. Fromm, Erich. (1956). *The art of loving.* New York: Harper. Fromm, Erich. (1964). *The heart of man.* New York: Harper. Fromm, Erich. (1968). *The revolution of hope.* New York: Bantam Books.

FROTTEURISM. See SEXUAL BEHAVIORS, ATYPICAL.

FULL NEST. The full nest is the period of life when a couple's children have reached adult status, but residency within the home continues. By middle age, parents usually experience the empty-nest stage of family life. Their offspring will usually have grown up, set their sights on the future, and physically left the home. However, for a growing segment of the young adult population, moving out of the home right away is not the chosen lifestyle. Indeed, for many families of the 1990s, grown children continue to live at home. Today, about 20 million adults aged 18 to 34 are living in their parents' homes. For adults between the ages of 18 and 24, this breaks down to about 58 percent of all men and 47 percent of all women. Moreover, all indications are that this number will swell in years to come.

The full nest represents an interesting demographic trend, and some of the reasons given for remaining at home reflect lifestyle changes of these modern times. Financial explanations invariably find their way to the top of the list: young people often have trouble affording an independent lifestyle. Also, some remain at home to combat loneliness. There are also those who are still going to school, those who are postponing marriage, and those who have divorced (with or without children). Also, grown children may be using the home as a haven or retreat during times when they are out of work.

The full nest often brings its share of domestic happiness and satisfaction. However, it can also herald pressures and problems. For example, there is an attitude among some outsiders that effective parenthood includes launching children out of the home and into the mainstream of society. Other internal problems include conflicts over possessions and noise as well as disagreements about household space or territory. Finally, grown children may be disruptive to everyday household activity and thus create stress on the parental marriage bond.

Further Reading. O'Kane, Monica L. (1981). *Living with adult children.* St. Paul, MN: Diction Books; Turner, Jeffrey S., and Donald B. Helms. (1994). *Contemporary adulthood* (5th Ed.). Fort Worth, TX: Harcourt Brace; U.S. Bureau of the Census. (1994). *Statistical abstract of the United States: 1994* (114th Ed.). Washington, DC: U.S. Government Printing Office.

G

GALINSKY, ELLEN. Ellen Galinsky (1942–) is a professor of the Bank Street College of Education in New York and a specialist in human development and family relations. Galinsky was born in Pittsburgh, Pennsylvania, and received a graduate degree from the Bank Street College of Education in 1970. She is recognized for exploring the developmental dynamics of parenthood, particularly how it unfolds through a series of predictable stages.

In all, Galinsky maintained that the experience of parenthood consists of six stages. She felt that these stages bring a progressive transformation of parental self-images. Parents mentally picture the way they think things should be, especially in terms of their own personal behavior and that of their children. If such images are successfully achieved, satisfaction and happiness are experienced. If they are not attained, parents typically feel anger, resentment, and even depression. Consequently, parents' self-images—not to mention parental development—are shaped by interactions with their children. Put another way, a child's development leads the parent from one stage to the next. The following is a summary of Galinsky's stages of parenthood.

Parental-image stage. The parental-image stage occurs when the baby is born. During this time, parents seek to treat their children as they would have liked their parents to treat them. Images of parenthood are constructed around a desire for perfection, even though most adults are fully aware that child-rearing perfection is nearly impossible.

Nurturing stage. The nurturing stage is the second phase of parental development and lasts approximately through the second year of the child's life. Forming bonds of attachment to the baby is the major chore at this point, in addition to learning how much and when to give to oneself, one's spouse, job, and friends.

Authority stage. The authority stage, between two and four years, is a phase where adults critically question their effectiveness as parental figures. For the child, this is a time of newly discovered social independence, testing of new powers, and saying "no." Witnessing such developments may cause parents to discover flaws in their images of parental perfection. Parental growth at this time may well be measured by rejecting the images that are simply unrealistic.

Integrative stage. The integrative stage, encompassing the preschool years through middle childhood, is the fourth phase proposed by Galinsky. Further childhood gains in autonomy and initiative, as well as expanding social horizons, force parents to reexamine and then test their own implicit theories about the way things should be ideally and how they are in fact. Discrepancies between these two polarities are difficult for adults groping for effective parenting skills to accept.

Independent teenage years. During this stage, adolescents struggle for greater levels of freedom, responsibility, and, in some cases, emancipation from the home. In perhaps one of parenthood's most impactful stages, adults must learn to redefine authority regarding the teenager's growing independence, while lending support to the growing pains characteristic of adolescence.

Departure stage. The departure stage, after approximately age 18, occurs when adolescents leave the home. For the parents, this final stage becomes a period of assessment and evaluation of their overall past performances. Taking stock of the entire experience of parenthood reveals positive as well as negative features: the loose or crumbling pieces and the cracks, in addition to the cohesiveness, of their whole lives. Such an overview at this time in the family cycle, coupled with the assessments inherent in each of the previous stages, provides adults with a thought-provoking analysis and narrative of their performance as parents.

Further Reading. Galinsky, Ellen. (1981). *Between generations: The six stages of parenthood.* New York: Times Books; Galinsky, Ellen. (1986). Family life and corporate politics. In Michael W. Yogman and T. Berry Brazelton (Eds.), *In support of families.* Cambridge, MA: Harvard University Press.

GAY AND LESBIAN RELATIONSHIPS. Gay and lesbian, or homosexual, relationships are characterized by the sexual attraction and emotional attachment to persons of the same gender. To the best of our knowledge, virtually all past and present cultures have been predominantly heterosexual, and attitudes toward gays have varied. Some have condemned and punished gays, while others view homosexuality as an acceptable lifestyle. In the United States prior to 1973, homosexuality was labeled by the American Psychiatric Association as a disorder. Books on the topic treated homosexuality as a pathological problem to be solved, and those with same-sex orientations were viewed with a mixture of discomfort, fear, and disgust. Because homosexuality was seen as a sickness, the gay individual was usually regarded as perverted, unhappy, and desperately lonely.

In 1973, the American Psychiatric Association removed homosexuality from its classification of mental disorders. This classification change was largely the result of efforts by leaders in the gay liberation movement and their supporters, some of whom were prominent psychiatrists and clinical psychologists (see GAY AND LESBIAN RELATIONSHIPS, PREJUDICE AND DISCRIMINATION AGAINST). With society's liberalization of sexual attitudes, the general public's perceptions of homosexuality began to slowly change. Gays banded together to assert their human rights and demanded the respect and equality that had been denied. Many openly declared their homosexuality, and phrases such as "gay pride" were heard more and more. Meanwhile, researchers stepped up the pace of their scientific inquiries into the complexities of sexual orientation. As a result of this interest, homosexuality began to be better understood. (See SEXUAL ORIENTATION, THEORIES OF.)

Contrary to what was once thought, homosexuality is not a form of abnormal behavior or mental illness. Indeed, most gays and lesbians are well adjusted and emotionally stable. While some may exhibit anxiety or depression, so too do some heterosexuals. When maladaptive behavior does occur in lesbians and gays, some clinicians propose that it is often attributable to the social stigma attached to homosexuality instead of to something pathological in the nature of homosexuality itself. Additionally, gays and lesbians are not confused about their gender identity, the psychological awareness of being either male or female. Lesbian women are not different from heterosexual women in their sureness of being female, nor do gay men differ from heterosexual men on this dimension.

As far as the dynamics of gay and lesbian relationships are concerned, more similarities than differences can be drawn to heterosexual unions. Partners are sought so that a rewarding union may be formed, and the maintenance of a relationship hinges on mutual support, caring, love, and understanding. Both straight and gay relationships tend to flourish when partners possess maturity and authenticity, a stable sense of self, and a willingness to share intimacy on a regular basis. For all, the intimate relationship thrives on trust and commitment and offers such important social and psychological vitamins as security, affection, and comfort.

However, there are some differences among gay partners, including a tendency to maintain a more egalitarian relationship. For example, gay couples have been found to be free from a stereotypical form of role playing or mirroring of heterosexual roles sometimes associated with gay couples. There is usually one personality that is more prominent or outgoing, but this "dominance" does not necessarily indicate that one partner plays the masculine, sometimes called "butch," role while the other assumes the submissive, or "femme," role. Indeed, there is probably more of an equality between partners in gay and lesbian relationships than in heterosexual relationships because homosexuals are not forced into the types of roles to which many heterosexuals feel bound.

Researchers have found that most gays want to have steady relationships, although this is somewhat more important to women than to men. Heterosexuals, though, tend to value sexual exclusivity more strongly in a steady relationship. Both gays and lesbians, as well as heterosexual couples, desire certain elements in a close relationship: affection, companionship, and personal development. As far as qualities sought in partners, gays, lesbians, and heterosexuals all value such traits as honesty, affection, and warmth. Such findings shatter the myth that sex is the sole basis for gay and lesbian relationships.

All of this means that lesbian, gay, and heterosexual couples are more alike than dissimilar in terms of relationship dynamics. Thus, if we want to describe what goes on in a relationship between two gays or lesbians—what makes for the success of that relationship and what may create problems—we do not have to use a different language. We can use the same terms as we would in describing a relationship between two heterosexuals. In our intimate relationships, we are all much more similar than we are different.

Further Reading. Brehm, Sharon S. (1992). *Intimate relationships* (2nd Ed.). New York: McGraw-Hill; Clunis, D. Merilee, and G. Dorsey Green. (1988). *Lesbian couples.* Seattle, WA: Seal Press; De Cecco, John P. (Ed.). (1988). *Gay relationships.* New York: Harrington Park Press; Peplau, Letitia A., and Steven L. Gordon. (1983). The intimate relationships of lesbians and gay men. In Elizabeth R. Allgeier and Naomi B. McCormick (Eds.), *Changing boundaries: Gender roles and sexual behavior.* Palo Alto, CA: Mayfield.

GAY AND LESBIAN RELATIONSHIPS, FAMILY LAW AND. Family law in the United States affects gay and lesbian relationships in many ways. For example, gay and lesbian couples cannot legally marry. Moreover, no state statute expressly affirms the right of homosexual couples to marry. All courts faced with the gay/lesbian marriage issue have relied on the premise that a lawful marriage, by definition, can be entered into only by two persons of the opposite sex.

In Hawaii, interesting legal developments regarding the right of gay couples to marry have occurred. In 1994, the governor of Hawaii signed a bill banning gay marriages, a measure lawmakers approved after the state Supreme Court said existing prohibitions may be unconstitutional. The 1994 bill said the high court ruling encroached on the legislature's law-making function and infringed on the separation of powers of the respective branches of state government.

The Hawaiian state Supreme court ruled in 1993 the ban on gay marriages was unconstitutional because it involved sexual discrimination, unless the state could show a ''compelling interest'' for retaining it. The case, brought by three gays denied marriage licenses, was sent back to a lower court for further consideration. As this volume goes to press a rehearing is anticipated and the losing side is expected to appeal to the Supreme Court and a definitive ruling is expected by late 1996 at the earliest. To date, no other court has taken the stance that state prohibition of gay and lesbian marriage is unconstitutional.

Not being able to legally marry has many implications for gay and lesbian couples. For example, without the legal rights that are granted by a marriage license, no matter how many years a couple has been together, partners do not have the right to make medical or financial decisions for each other if one becomes incapacitated. A person may not even be allowed access to an intensive care unit in which his or her partner is being treated for a life-threatening or terminal illness. Partners cannot automatically inherit each other's property, and if they break up, they are not protected by divorce laws. In an effort to combat such discrimination, many gay and lesbian couples are drafting legal documents designed to approximate or duplicate many of the rights of a marriage license.

The rights of gay and lesbian parents are also legally limited. Many gay and lesbian parents who have children have brought them from a prior marriage or heterosexual relationship of one or both partners, and the issues emerging from such situations are enormously complicated. Child custody cases invariably focus on the sexual orientation of a parent.

Adoption is also extremely difficult for openly gay and lesbian couples. While society's tolerance for alternative lifestyles is growing, most courts continue to believe that the best interests of a child are rooted in the traditional heterosexual family. The courts do not deny parents their right to choose lifestyles, but they do seek to restrict childrens' exposure to alternative lifestyles. Some factors that the courts consider in determining custody and visitation rights are what peer pressures and social stigma would come to bear on the child or how the lack of a role model may affect the child during the formative years.

Gay and lesbian couples often face additional problems even if they successfully adopt. For one, just as in any custody case, a couple's custody of an adopted child can be challenged at any time. If couples keep their relationship a secret during the adoption process, this could mean having to spend much of their lives in fear of being discovered and losing the child. In another scenario, because only one partner can legally adopt the child, if a couple splits up, they could find themselves in untested legal waters and a precedent-setting custody battle. (See GAY AND LESBIAN RELATIONSHIPS, PREJUDICE AND DISCRIMINATION AGAINST; GAY AND LESBIAN RELATIONSHIPS, PARENTING AND.)

Further Reading. Ainslie, Julie, and Kathryn M. Feltey. (1991). Definitions and dynamics of motherhood and family in lesbian communities. *Marriage and Family Review, 17,* 63–85; Levy, Eileen F. (1992). Strengthening the coping resources of lesbian families. *Families in Society, 73,* 23–31; Ryder, Bruce. (1990). Equality rights and sexual orientation: Confronting heterosexual family privilege. *Canadian Journal of Family Law, 9,* 39–97.

GAY AND LESBIAN RELATIONSHIPS, HISTORICAL AND LEGAL PERSPECTIVES.

Homosexuality has existed since the beginning of time and was practiced and tacitly approved in a number of societies. For example, it was evident in ancient Greece as well as among the Tanalans of Madagascar, the Siwamis of Africa, and the Keraki of New Guinea. However, for just as long homosexuality has been viewed with mistrust and suspicion. Gays have represented a stigmatized minority group and have been the object of considerable fear, dread, and hostility.

In the Jewish faith, and later among the Christians, the wickedness of the ancient cities of Sodom and Gomorrah that caused God to destroy them was the practice of homosexuality (the word sodomy, or anal intercourse, originates from this). Homosexuality was viewed as sinful since sex other than that between a man and a woman was naturally wrong. The early Christian church believed that gays should be put to death by burning or hanging. The customary penalties were less severe, though, and ''offenders'' were usually exiled or administered forms of corporal punishment. During the Middle Ages in England, homosexuality was punishable by death and considered an offense as serious as heresy, blasphemy, and witchcraft. In 1861, the maximum penalty for homosexuality in England was changed to life imprisonment.

In the United States, laws against gays have been equally harsh. The Puritans denounced homosexuality, and many perceived it as a symptom of English moral corruption. Based on English common law, the early colonies implemented a number of sodomy statutes and condemned homosexuality as unnatural and a ''crime against nature.'' During the seventeenth and eighteenth centuries, punishment for gays varied in the colonies and included whipping, castration, and drowning. Some escaped with such lesser sentences as discharge from work, public ostracism, or imprisonment.

By the late nineteenth century, the medical and academic professions sought to understand homosexuality better, and a diverse body of researchers began to contribute their thoughts on the topic. However, gays remained a minority, and society continually sought to control homosexuality by upholding various sodomy laws. Most of these statutes were ill defined and nebulous. For example, North Carolina's original sodomy statute reads: ''Any person who shall commit the abominable and detestable crime against nature, not fit to be named among Christians . . . shall be adjudged guilty of a felony and shall suffer death without the benefit of clergy.'' Under such antiquated sex laws and social condemnation, homosexuals remained scorned and oppressed in American society.

Until the 1960s, homosexual behavior was prohibited throughout the United States through some type of sodomy statute. Then in 1961, Illinois became the first state to repeal existing statutes with the American Law Institute's Model Penal Code provision. In essence, the provision decriminalized homosexual acts between consenting adults in private. In supporting its position, the American Law Institute (ALI) noted that such nations as Great Britain, France, Italy, Denmark, and Sweden had repealed their sodomy statutes.

In 1969 at a gay bar called the Stonewall in Greenwich Village, New York, the gay liberation movement was born. Gay men were constantly being harassed by police, and in June of that year, they fought back. To simply be allowed to meet and drink in a bar, until June 28, 1969, was inconceivable to U.S. society.

Today, there are many gay/lesbian bars, restaurants, and hotels where lesbians and gays can congregate in safety.

The gay liberation movement has helped gays and lesbians to feel less guilty about their lifestyle and has even encouraged people to stop concealing their sexual orientation. The movement also provides a vehicle enabling important societal issues to be discussed. The political strength of the movement has brought about a change in the ways police deal with gays and lesbians. Gay liberation groups have been at the forefront of legal change, do public relations, and fight job and other forms of discrimination. The National Gay and Lesbian Task Force is a central clearinghouse in Washington, D.C., for many of the gay liberation groups.

As the gay rights movement emerged as a strong activist and lobbying force, the ALI proposal gained support in the 1970s when legislators in 20 additional states acted to decriminalize private, consensual homosexual conduct. To date, a total of 26 states have repealed their sodomy laws. Also as a result of gay and lesbian rights groups, many cities have passed gay/lesbian rights bills assuring lesbians and gays equal rights to housing and jobs. In some cities, gays and lesbians have been granted the same right as married people in regard to insurance and health benefits. (See GAY AND LESBIAN RELATIONSHIPS, PREJUDICE AND DISCRIMINATION AGAINST.)

Further Reading. Blumenfeld, Warren J., and Diane Raymond. (1988). *Looking at gay and lesbian life.* Boston: Beacon Press; Bullough, Vern. (1979). *Homosexuality: A history.* New York: New American Library; Mihalik, Gary J. (1991). Homosexuality, stigma, and biocultural evolution. *Journal of Gay and Lesbian Psychotherapy, 1,* 15–29.

GAY AND LESBIAN RELATIONSHIPS, PARENTING AND. While parenting among gays and lesbians is not widespread, growing numbers are choosing to form family units. Children may be adopted by the couple, or there may already be children from previous heterosexual relationships. Some lesbians utilize artificial insemination as a means to have children.

In almost all instances, seeking to become a gay or lesbian parent presents legal issues. For example, gays and lesbians often have to fight ex-spouses for custody of their biological children. Many placement agencies are reluctant to place children with known gay men or lesbians. Some organizations that provide artificial insemination services insist that eligible candidates show evidence of a long-term heterosexual relationship.

It is incorrectly assumed that homosexual parents create widespread adjustment problems for children, including those related to gender identity and gender-role development. For instance, many feel that exposure to gay parents will cause children to become gay or lesbian. Indeed, some people believe that homosexual parents try to persuade their children to be gay. Research indicates, however, that the incidence of homosexuality among children of gays is not above that in the general population. In fact, most children of gay parents turn out to be heterosexual. In addition, there is evidence to suggest that most homosexuals are brought up in exclusively heterosexual households.

There is also no support for the notion that gay parents serve as poor role models because they themselves were raised in unhappy, unstable homes. Most gay parents were brought up in intact heterosexual families and highly value secure and trusting relationships with their children. Research such as this shows that the aspirations of gay and lesbian parents do not differ from those of heterosexual parents. Indeed, when the two groups are compared, parenting behaviors, goals, and interests are usually the same.

Both gay parents and their children face special adjustments. In addition to legal complexities, gay parents often face problems similar to those of single heterosexual parents. For lesbians, who as women still earn significantly less than men, economic survival can be a major struggle. Children made the targets of ridicule by peers and others may become uncomfortable with their parents' sexual orientation. For this reason, many gay and lesbian parents inform their children as early as possible about their own sexual orientation. Most children can understand and come to accept their parents' homosexuality, and although they may have to defend their parents occasionally, they can usually expect their peers to get accustomed to their parents' lifestyles.

Further Reading. Blumenfeld, Warren J., and Diane Raymond. (1988). *Looking at gay and lesbian life.* Boston: Beacon Press; Bozett, Frederick W. (1987). *Gay and lesbian parents.* New York: Praeger; Schulenburg, Joy A. (1985). *Gay parenting.* Garden City, NY: Doubleday.

GAY AND LESBIAN RELATIONSHIPS, PREJUDICE AND DISCRIMINATION AGAINST. Gays and lesbians are an oppressed group, and prejudice and discrimination are aimed at them in many ways. Sometimes prejudice and discrimination are blatant and deliberate, while on other occasions they may be unintentional and unconscious. In the final analysis, though, they are harmful not only to those who are victims of them, but also to those who engage in them.

It is society that defines gays and lesbians as deviant and punishes them in a variety of ways. The visible sanctions are primarily financial and legal. However, more pervasive and more damaging are personal attacks, constant harassment, and a wide range of negative situations, such as mimicking, jokes, and the raiding of gay bars and meeting places. Furthermore, living without a support network is a difficult and alienating experience. Combined, all of these factors do little to foster equality.

Discriminatory treatment against gays and lesbians is still very much in evidence. For instance, marriages of lesbian and gay couples are legally prohibited. Many adoption agencies are reluctant to place children with gays and lesbians (see GAY AND LESBIAN RELATIONSHIPS, FAMILY LAW AND). The educational system has frequently denied gays and lesbians teaching positions due to a fear that children will be corrupted and recruited to the so-called homosexual way of life or be abused by them in some way. The media also tend to depict gays and lesbians in an unfair and unrealistic light.

Many gays and lesbians also face harassment and physical abuse simply because of their sexual orientation. Such antigay violence has risen dramatically in recent years. It has been found that many assailants tend to be white males in their teens and early twenties who are acting out society's prejudices against gays and lesbians. The purpose of the assaults is not theft, although this sometimes does happen. Instead, some choose to attack gays and lesbians simply because they do not like their lifestyles. Violence, intimidation, and humiliation are the means by which they make their beliefs known (see HOMOPHOBIA).

Many gays, lesbians, and other concerned persons actively seek to reduce hostility and the many types of prejudice and discrimination leveled against gays. By the 1950s, gays began organizing their own political groups. In 1951, the Mattachine Society was founded in Los Angeles, followed in 1955 by the Daughters of Bilitis in San Francisco. (The Mattachine Society was named after a secret fraternal order of unmarried men who dressed as women and performed in thirteenth-century France. The Daughters of Bilitis was named after the lesbian poet Bilitis who lived with Sappho on the island of Lesbos in ancient Greece.)

During the 1960s the gay liberation movement emerged as a political movement promoting the full civil rights of homosexuals and an end to discriminatory practices. The gay liberation movement embraced many subgroups, the best known being the Gay Liberation Front and the Gay Activists Alliance. In 1973, the National Gay and Lesbian Task Force was founded in New York City and now is located in Washington, D.C. The purpose of the NGLTF is to reeducate society, including its gay and lesbian members, to esteem gay men and women at their full human worth and to accord them places in society that will allow them to attain their full human and social potential and to contribute according to their potential. The organization was instrumental in getting the American Psychiatric Association to declassify homosexuality as an illness and has helped to launch legislation related to consensual sex and civil rights. At this writing, the NGLTF is the largest organization representing the gay liberation movement.

In addition, a number of organizations have been formed to combat antigay and lesbian violence and to assist victims. Among these are the Violence Project of the National Gay and Lesbian Task Force, the Committee on Lesbian and Gay Victims Concerns of the National Organization for Victims Assistance, and the Lesbian Caucus of the National Coalition against Sexual Assault. In addition to assisting victims, such organizations seek to implement crime-prevention programs, launch community education programs to dispel myths and fears about homosexuality, develop training sessions to sensitize police officers, and promote media education efforts for more accurate reporting.

Further Reading. De Cecco, John P. (Ed.). (1985). *Bashers, baiters, and bigots: Homophobia in American society.* New York: Harrington Park Press; Hunter, Joyce. (1990). Violence against lesbian and gay male youths. *Journal of Interpersonal Violence,*

5, 295–300; Katz, Jonathan. (1978). *Gay American history: Lesbians and gay men in the USA*. New York: Avon.

GAY LIBERATION MOVEMENT. See GAY AND LESBIAN RELATIONSHIPS, PREJUDICE AND DISCRIMINATION AGAINST.

GENDER. Gender refers to the social meanings attached to being a female or male. Gender can be thought of as encompassing the social dimensions of masculinity or femininity, while one's sex is the genetic and sexual anatomy with which one is born. Although we are born male or female, just knowing what sex we are does not necessarily establish how ''feminine'' or ''masculine'' we feel we are or how we conceptualize the roles we will play in society. The culture into which we are born teaches us about gender, including what attitudes and behaviors are appropriate to our sex. Gradually we develop an identity, a sense of self, that incorporates these teachings or, sometimes, rebels against them. This development of the way we see ourselves functioning as men or women in society has important implications not only for our individual growth but for the way we interact with others in intimate relationships throughout the course of the lifespan.

Further Reading. Jacklin, Carol N. (1989). Female and male: Issues of gender. *American Psychologist, 44,* 127–133; Kelly, Kathryn, and Donn Byrne. (1992). *Exploring human sexuality*. Englewood Cliffs, NJ: Prentice Hall; Turner, Lynn H., and Helen M. Sterk. (Eds.). (1994). *Differences that make a difference: Examining the assumptions in gender research*. Westport, CT: Bergin and Garvey.

GENDER IDENTITY. Gender identity is the psychological awareness or sense of being either a male or a female. It is generally accepted that gender identity occurs by age three. Gender identity is largely influenced by a person's developing cognitive awareness. Early in life, boys and girls become mentally aware of the fact that specific roles, activities, and behaviors are appropriate for their own sex. As cognitive development increases, children are better able to understand and sort out these roles and behaviors. Awareness of one's gender identity and comfort with it are considered important components of healthy personality and social functioning, including functioning within the realm of intimate relationships.

Further Reading. Hyde, Janet S. (1994). *Understanding human sexuality* (5th Ed.). New York: McGraw-Hill; Jacklin, Carol N. (1989). Female and male: Issues of gender. *American Psychologist, 44,* 127–133; Katchadourian, Herant A. (1989). *Fundamentals of human sexuality* (5th Ed.). New York: Holt, Rinehart and Winston.

GENDER IDENTITY DISORDER. A gender identity disorder is characterized by an incongruence between one's assigned sex and one's gender identity. Gender identity is primarily a psychological process, a type of self-awareness that enables individuals to realize that they are either a male or a female. The process of socialization helps to shape gender roles consistent with gender identity. Neither gender identity nor gender roles are mutually exclusive categories of one's overall sexuality. In this respect, while gender identity is the sense of knowing to which sex one belongs, gender roles represent the public expression of this psychological awareness.

In a gender identity disorder, something goes wrong in the formation of gender identity. In some cases, the disorder is mild, and the person simply feels some discomfort with his or her sexual identity. In more severe cases, the person not only feels uncomfortable but believes firmly that she or he belongs to the other sex. In such cases (once referred to as *transsexualism*), there is a persistent discomfort and a strong sense of inappropriateness about one's sexual identity. In general, the problem does not become acute until the person reaches puberty. Eventually the person becomes preoccupied with getting rid of primary and secondary sex characteristics and acquiring the sex characteristics of the other sex. Those with a gender identity disorder invariably want to live as a member of the other sex. They typically complain that they are uncomfortable wearing the clothes suited to their sexual identity and consequently dress in clothes of the other sex. This is referred to as *cross-dressing.*

Gender identity disorders are rare in both sexes. The causes of gender identity disorders are also obscure. Hormonal imbalances do not appear to play a role, and the impact of psychosocial influences remains uncertain. Many who develop this disorder report having a gender identity problem during childhood, but as indicated, the problem generally surfaces during puberty. Some researchers believe that extensive childhood femininity in a boy or masculinity in a girl seems to increase the likelihood of the disorder. The disorder may also develop within the context of a disturbed relationship with one or both parents. Males tend to seek treatment for this disorder more commonly than females. On the whole, efforts to alter gender identity through psychological means have not proven successful, and as a result, many persons with gender identity disorder have sought *sex-reassignment surgery,* that is, a physical change consonant with their cross-sexual identity.

Sex-reassignment surgery for males starts with removing the external genitals and creating an artificial vagina. Female hormones are administered to stimulate breast development, lessen beard growth, and provide a more feminine texture to the skin. Sex-reassignment surgery for women usually removes the breasts, uterus, and ovaries and seals the vagina off. Many female-to-male persons with gender identity disorders choose such surgical procedures, along with hormone therapy, but do not opt for an artificial penis. For those who do, a penis can be constructed from abdominal tissue or tissue from the perineum. Such a reconstruction functions normally in the process of urination, but is not capable of an erection. However, it may be possible to simulate an erection with an implant such as is used in the treatment of male erectile dysfunction.

Sex-reassignment surgery is a controversial area, and many physicians are opposed to it. To date, surgical results have been mixed. While some studies report satisfactory outcomes, many report such problems as dissatisfaction with the surgery, inability to perform sexually, or postoperative depression. For these reasons, clinicians stress the importance of carefully screening each candidate for surgery. Candidates must be emotionally stable and usually must undergo a trial period in which they receive hormone therapy, live in the new role, and acquire an understanding of the psychological adjustments they will need to make.

Further Reading. American Psychiatric Association. (1994). *Diagnostic and statistical manual of mental disorders* (4th Ed.). Washington, DC: Author; Dailey, Dennis M. (Ed.). (1988). *The sexually unusual.* New York: Harrington Park Press; Leiblum, Sandra R., and Raymond C. Rosen. (Eds.). (1989). *Principles and practice of sex therapy* (2nd Ed.). New York: Guilford Press.

GENDER ROLE. A gender role is a set of expectations that prescribes how females and males should behave. Such expectations are acquired in a developmental fashion over the course of the lifespan and reflect unique aspects of a given culture. Our culture is competitive, hierarchical, and achievement oriented and measures success in terms of power, prestige, and the accumulation of material wealth. Conventional masculinity embraces such qualities as independence, competitiveness, aggression, leadership, confidence, and self-control. Conventional femininity, on the other hand, emphasizes other qualities, such as dependency, passivity, nonaggression, sensitivity, nurturance, and noncompetitiveness. It is important to point out that what characterizes our culture may not characterize other societies.

Understanding the concept of gender roles is very important, for as the examples aforementioned of expected qualities indicate, gender roles determine hundreds of things males and females do every day. For example, they prescribe the way we sit, the way we stand, the kinds of jobs we take, and the kinds of people we choose as mates. They also account for a host of other expectations, ranging from who washes the dishes to who stays home with the children.

Further Reading. Adler, Leonore L. (Ed.). (1993). *International handbook on gender roles.* Westport, CT: Greenwood Press; Allgeier, Elizabeth Rice, and Albert Richard Allgeier. (1995). *Sexual interactions* (4th Ed.). Lexington, MA: D. C. Heath; Crooks, Robert, and Karla Baur. (1993). *Our sexuality* (5th Ed.). Redwood City, CA: Benjamin/Cummings.

GENDER-ROLE DEVELOPMENT, INFLUENCES ON. Gender-role development begins early in life and serves to establish an individual's sense of masculinity or femininity. A number of socialization agents are responsible for creating a person's gender-role development, the more influential sources being parents, play activities, peers, teachers and schools, and the media.

Parents affect a child's gender-role development in a number of ways. If they hold traditional or stereotyped views of gender roles, they will teach girls to be affectionate, gentle, and quiet and boys to be aggressive, independent, and active.

In time a boy will be taught that holding a job and supporting a wife and children will be his primary adult task. A girl, on the other hand, will be taught to handle most of the responsibilities associated with child rearing and maintaining a home for her husband and children. Today, however, many parents are attempting to ensure that both girls and boys have the same professional opportunities and that they learn to share the responsibilities of family life.

Children's play activities also shape the course of gender-role development. For instance, traditional girls are often given dolls and encouraged to play house. Traditional boys are given guns and trucks and are taught to play aggressive games and to avoid "sissy" play activities. Research has shown that by the preschool years, children prefer toys that are stereotypically appropriate for their gender. In general, girls' play behavior is more dependent (that is, girls tend to rely on playmates), quieter, and less exploratory. Boys often play with toys that require more gross motor activity, and they are more vigorous and independent. Parents frequently support and reinforce such sex-typed play behavior in both sexes, although this is more true for fathers than mothers.

Today, there is some evidence that the traditional view of "masculine" and "feminine" forms of play is changing. For example, although girls still engage in "feminine" activities, they now also enjoy types of play previously considered "masculine," such as track and field competition, basketball, baseball, and other organized sports activities. Schools are enlarging their athletic programs and encouraging females to participate more actively and more competitively. Success in sports and the accompanying social prestige no longer appear to be exclusively male. In fact, fewer activities are exclusively either female or male. (See ANDROGYNY.)

Peers are instrumental in shaping gender-role development. As children become more socialized, they learn more about gender-role standards and behaviors from their friends. By the preschool years, children start to prefer same-sex peer groups and choose same-sex "best friends." This tendency persists and intensifies throughout the years of middle childhood, although it is more pronounced in boys than in girls. Often, same-sex play groups openly torment one another, further solidifying gender boundaries. Although in adolescence the sexes begin to intermingle, again, gender differences persist, particularly in regard to friendships. The most striking of these is the emotional intimacy apparent in female friendships. (See CHILDHOOD, FRIENDSHIPS DURING; ADOLESCENCE, FRIENDSHIPS DURING.)

The school environment also contributes to gender-role learning. Unfortunately, some teachers deliberately, others unwittingly, contribute to gender-role stereotypes. For example, teachers may reward girls only when they are passive, well behaved, and well mannered but reinforce boys for being assertive and asking questions. Some teachers may perpetuate stereotypes by advising students that certain professions are appropriate for women and not for men, and vice versa. Sometimes a school's curriculum may stamp a course as masculine or feminine. For example, it may require girls to take a course in home economics and boys to take one in automobile mechanics. Fortunately, many U.S. schools are now recommending that all students enroll in a mixture of such courses.

Children's literature also transmits early gender-role behaviors. Stereotyping is quite evident within the pages of children's books. Girls are often portrayed as passive and domestic, boys as active and adventurous. Boys also outnumber girls in many stories. Careers are often cast in exclusively masculine or feminine terms. Today, active efforts are being made to eliminate gender stereotyping in children's books, including efforts to identify and revise books that have sexist themes.

Finally, television and the other media shape the course of gender-role development, including the promotion of gender-role stereotypes. Men on television are often portrayed as leaders, while women are cast as passive, submissive, and defenseless characters. Also, males usually outnumber female cast members. Moreover, many programs lack a regular female character. The same male-female imbalances are evident in television commercials. In recent years, though, television producers have made an attempt to change this picture and broadcast more programs featuring women, including a number with women protagonists.

Further Reading. King, Bruce M., Cameron J. Camp, and Ann M. Downey. (1991). *Human sexuality today.* Englewood Cliffs, NJ: Prentice Hall; McCammon, Susan L., David Knox, and Caroline Schacht. (1993), *Choices in sexuality.* St. Paul, MN: West; Morrow, France. (1991). *Unleashing our unknown selves: An inquiry into the future of femininity and masculinity.* New York; Praeger.

GENDER-ROLE DEVELOPMENT, THEORIES OF. The manner in which gender roles are acquired, including the forces that shape sex-appropriate behaviors, have attracted considerable research attention. Emerging from this body of research are a number of different theoretical approaches. Four theories of gender-role development are particularly important: cognitive-developmental, behavioral, social learning, and psychoanalytic theories.

Cognitive-developmental theory suggests that gender role emerges through the child's growing cognitive awareness of his/her sexual identity. Once children can consistently conceive of themselves as male or female, they organize their world on the basis of gender. Put another way, heightened levels of cognition enable children to realize that specific roles, activities, and behaviors are gender appropriate. In this fashion, a young boy decides, "I am a boy. I like to do the things boys do; the chance to do these things is rewarding." Cognitive-developmental theory emphasizes that the child is an active rather than a passive force in his or her gender-role formation. The reinforcement for imitating sex-typed behaviors originates from within the child, not from external socializers such as parents or siblings. Thus, rather than simply imitating behavior, the child reasons before he or she does so.

Behavioral theory proposes that gender-role behaviors are conditioned by the environment through the mechanisms of reinforcement and punishment (reinforcement would serve to strengthen a desired response, while punishment would serve to weaken an undesirable response). Children typically receive rewards and punishments from parents for behaviors consistent with the child's gender role. To illustrate, a young girl rewarded (e.g., given praise or approval) for her involvement in stereotypically female activities (washing the dishes; cleaning the house) is likely to repeat such behavior in the future. A young boy who is punished, ridiculed, or scolded for engaging in feminine activities ("that's a sissy game") or being overly sensitive ("big boys don't cry") will be unlikely to repeat such behaviors in the future. In contrast to cognitive-developmental theory, which emphasizes a person's active construction and regulation of gender development, behavioral theory views the individual as a passive participant, being shaped and molded by environmental influences.

The *social learning theory* of gender-role development, like behavioral theory, suggests that individuals are shaped by their environment. However, this approach emphasizes the way boys and girls specifically imitate the gender-typed behaviors they observe. Some of the models children use are parents, peers, teachers, and the people they see on television. Thus, when a boy sees on television or in real life that men usually handle mechanical repairs around the house, he learns that tending to such chores represents an activity that is appropriate for him to engage in.

Psychoanalytic theory proposes that a child develops gender roles by interacting closely with a parent and imitating the parent's behavior. Proposed by Sigmund Freud, this theory holds that a boy assumes his father's sex-typed behaviors because of the Oedipus complex, or the boy's romantic attachment to his mother (see PSYCHOSEXUAL DEVELOPMENT). The attributes of the father are perceived as being those that captured the love of the mother and are thus emulated by the boy. For girls, the Electra complex creates a similar situation, although in this case the daughter becomes romantically attached to her father and imitates her mother's behaviors. Beyond the Oedipus and Electra complexes, Freud did offer one other perspective on identification. That is, children develop strong emotional attachment and dependence on nurturant parents. The closeness offered by such parents leads to childhood identification and emulation.

Further Reading. Fausto-Sterling, Ann. (1985). *Myths of gender: Biological theories about women and men.* New York: Basic Books; Tavris, Carol. (1992). *The mismeasure of woman.* New York: Simon and Schuster; Turner, Jeffrey S., and Laurna Rubinson. (1993). *Contemporary human sexuality.* Englewood Cliffs, NJ: Prentice Hall.

GENDER-ROLE STEREOTYPE. A gender-role stereotype is a generalization that reflects a given society's beliefs about females and males. Gender-role stereotypes reflect expected characteristics or behaviors, attributes, or actions that men and women actually possess or exhibit or want to possess or exhibit. Stereotypes ascribe certain characteristics or behaviors to all representatives of a group whether individual members possess them or not. For example, a traditional gender-role stereotype is that girls are emotional and dependent, while boys are aggressive and competent. Such stereotypes abound in our society and impact on overall sexual and gender-specific behavior.

Further Reading. Basow, Susan A. (1992). *Gender: Stereotypes and roles* (3rd Ed.). Pacific Grove, CA: Brooks/Cole; McCammon, Susan L., David Knox, and Caroline Schacht. (1993), *Choices in sexuality.* St. Paul, MN: West; Williams, John E., and Deborah L. Best. (1990). *Measuring sex stereotypes.* Newbury Park, CA: Sage.

GENERALIZED OTHER. See MEAD, GEORGE H.

GENERAL SYSTEMS THEORY. General systems theory, also called *family systems theory,* is a conceptual framework often used in the study of intimate relationships. Essentially, this theory suggests that intimate relationships such as those found in marriage and the family exist as whole entities, not separate parts. In this respect, the whole is greater than the sum of its parts. Therefore, while the family consists of individual members, a full understanding of its dynamics will be elusive if its members are only examined one at a time. A general systems view takes into account all components of family functioning and how each contributes to the total operation of the family unit. This means that the behavior of the family is best understood as a product of its organizational characteristics.

A general systems perspective also encourages researchers to explore the tasks that accompany family life-cycle stages. All transitions require the modification of rules and strategies so that family tasks can be properly executed. For example, families face an assortment of challenges related to the modification of external boundaries (flexibility and individuality allowed between the family system and outsiders) as well as internal boundaries (flexibility and individuality allowed within the family system). General systems theorists emphasize that such modifications need to be examined as total patterns, not separate or isolated modes of interaction. In so doing, researchers can explore the family's complex interacting elements, including the relationships that organize them.

Further Reading. Sieburg, Evelyn. (1985). *Family communication: An integrated systems approach.* New York: Gardner Press; Steinglass, Peter. (1987). A systems view of family interaction and psychopathology. In Theodore Jacob (Ed.), *Family interaction and psychopathology.* New York: Plenum Press.

GENOGRAM. A genogram is a three-generational diagram or map of the people who make up one's family and is often used as a tool in marriage and family therapy. A genogram usually includes births, deaths, marriages, divorces, ages of family members, and so on. Some therapists ask clients to include the geographical location of various groups in the family system, cultural and religious affiliations, or educational and class levels. The purpose of the genogram is to explore multigenerational issues and themes in a rapid, effective way. The genogram is often used during the initial phases of the treatment process, primarily as a means to facilitate the exploration of family structure and to better understand how family systems originate and operate.

Further Reading. Bowen, Murray. (1978). *Family therapy in clinical practice.* New York: Jason Aronson; Hof, Larry, and Ellen M. Berman. (1986). The sexual genogram. *Journal of Marital and Family Therapy, 12,* 39–47; Nichols, Michael P. (1984). *Family therapy: Concepts and methods.* New York: Gardner Press.

GERMANY. See FEDERAL REPUBLIC OF GERMANY, LIFESPAN RELATIONSHIPS IN THE.

GERONTOLOGY. Gerontology is a branch of developmental psychology that involves the study of the aged as well as aging processes. The word *gerontology* is a term that originates from the Greek words *geras,* meaning old age, and *logos,* meaning the study of something. Closely allied with gerontology is a subfield known as *social gerontology.* Social gerontologists seek to meet the needs of the aged population by providing them with special services, programs, and policies. They are most concerned with the quality of life for the elderly. *Geriatrics,* a related field but differing in its emphasis, is the branch of medicine that provides the elderly with health care and health-related services. Each year, the allied fields of gerontology, social gerontology, and geriatrics have supplied fresh insights into the needs of the aged population, including interventions designed to upgrade the quality of life for older adults. Moreover, the combined efforts of these disciplines have helped us to better understand the dynamics of growing old, including the multifaceted and complex nature of physical, intellectual, psychological, and social processes of aging. (See ADULTHOOD, SCIENTIFIC STUDY OF.)

Further Reading. Ansello, Edward F. (1991). Aging issues in the year 2000. *Caring, 10,* 4–16; Atchley, Robert C. (1994). *Social forces and aging: An introduction to social gerontology.* Belmont, CA: Wadsworth; Bond, John, and Peter Coleman. (Eds.). (1990). *Ageing in society: An introduction to social gerontology.* Newbury Park, CA: Sage.

GESELL, ARNOLD L. Arnold L. Gesell (1880–1961) was a leading child development researcher and was influential in shaping child-rearing strategies in the early part of this century. Born in Alma, Wisconsin, Gesell obtained a Ph.D. degree from Clark University in 1906 and an M.D. degree from Yale University in 1915.

Among Gesell's more notable contributions to the field of child psychology was the establishment of the Clinic of Child Development at Yale during the 1930s. At the clinic, Gesell stressed the notion that growth and development take place in orderly stages and sequences. He expended considerable energy in exploring this principle, devising numerous norms of infant development and undertaking detailed investigations of specific behavior sequences such as walking and prehension.

Gesell also translated this developmental-maturational theme into applied

child-rearing formulations for parents (see PARENTHOOD, CHILD-REARING OPTIONS AND STRATEGIES). Because of this, Gesell was largely viewed as an authoritative figure in the child-rearing movement during the 1930s and 1940s, and his numerous books and publications were sought by parents as well as professionals. His popularity was likely due to his ability to translate the theoretical into the practical world of everyday parenting and child development.
Further Reading. Gesell, Arnold. (1928). *Infancy and human growth.* New York: Macmillan; Gesell, Arnold. (1940). *The first five years of life.* New York: Harper and Brothers; Gesell, Arnold. (1946). *The child from five to ten.* New York: Harper and Brothers.

GOODNESS-OF-FIT. See NEWBORN.

GOULD, ROGER. Roger Gould (1935–) is a psychoanalyst and a professor of psychiatry at the University of California at Los Angeles who created a theory of adult personality development. Gould was born in Milwaukee and received a medical degree from Northwestern University in 1959. His theory suggests that adulthood is not a plateau but rather a time for the continuous unfolding of the self. Gould's primary emphasis is on the importance of striving toward adult levels of consciousness and discarding irrational childhood notions about oneself and the world in general.

According to Gould, irrational childhood ideas have a tendency to restrict maturity and responsibility. These false assumptions frequently embody the concept of parental dependency. Ideally, as life experience builds, adults must abandon these unwarranted expectations, rigid rules, and inflexible roles, which hinder individual autonomy and independence. If this is accomplished, in time adults will come to be true owners of their selves with a more mature level of consciousness.

Gould maintained that young adulthood, in particular, is a critical period of development, since it is at this point that individuals realize how they can begin to take control of their lives. In particular, it is understood that four irrational childhood assumptions need to be questioned: Adults will always live with their parents; one's parents will always be there to help when things go wrong or not exactly as one wants; parents can always offer a simplified version (and solution) to complicated inner realities; and no evil or death exists in the world.

Gould proposed that by the time young adulthood is reached, individuals know intellectually that these assumptions are factually incorrect, but emotionally they retain hidden control of adult life until significant events unveil them as emotional as well as intellectual fantasies. The gradual shedding of these false assumptions, a process that lasts throughout adulthood, signifies an individual's shift from childhood consciousness to more mature levels of adult reasoning.
Further Reading. Gould, Roger L. (1978). *Transformations: Growth and change in adult life.* New York: Simon and Schuster; Gould, Roger L. (1980). Transformations

during early and middle adult years. In Neil J. Smelser and Erik Erikson (Eds.), *Themes of work and love in adulthood*. Cambridge, MA: Harvard University Press.

GRANDPARENTHOOD. Grandparenthood, a family life transition usually occurring during middle or late adulthood, is a status characterized by the presence of at least three generations. Definitively speaking, a grandparent is the parent of a parent, and there are at least two generations under this senior family member. Because men and women are living longer today, more children than ever before will get to know their grandparents. Over three-fourths of persons aged 65 and older have grandchildren, and three-quarters of these see their grandchildren on a regular basis. Grandparents can serve as sources of knowledge, wisdom, love, and understanding and can greatly affect the lives of their grandchildren.

The grandchild typically establishes a bond of common interest between the grandparents and the younger couple. Becoming a grandparent also adds a new dimension to the lives of retirees, and, in most instances, this dimension is a positive one. Many feel that the connection between grandparent and grandchild is a vital one, an experience that brings gratifying rewards to both old and young. Among grandparents, many idealize their roles and importance.

But becoming a grandparent does not always have positive features. For some, it represents a visible sign of aging. There may be disagreements between grandparents and adult offspring regarding child rearing. Many resist the stereotyped qualities and expectations attached to grandparenthood, such as the time, care, and services grandparents are supposed to render to their grandchildren. Along these lines, some feel exploited for baby-sitting services. Some researchers have found that not all grandparents are willing to involve themselves in the perceived expectations of grandparenthood, most notably child care.

It needs to be recognized that the roles attached to grandparenthood have changed over the years. As noted, many modern-day grandparents are middle-aged, which means that images of aging surrounding grandparenthood need to be adjusted. Additionally, many grandmothers today are apt to be working outside of the home. The dual-earner nature of a grandparents' home may reduce the availability of both grandmother and grandfather. The geographical mobility of families, the reduced number of children per family, high divorce rates, and the increased number of single-parent homes will likely affect the complexion of grandparenthood, particularly patterns of contact and interaction. With the rise of broken homes, especially, many researchers feel that grandparents are becoming increasingly important.

Many experts believe that adults of all ages need to define and better understand this important family role. For those who become grandparents, there is a need to be aware of status changes as well as familial expectations. Regarding intergenerational contact, grandparents have to be sensitive to the child-rearing principles that parents are employing. Indeed, it has been found that a lack of understanding about child-rearing principles, as well as the violation of them, poses distinct threats to family harmony. Clear communication and consistent expectations make it easier for grandparents to support and reinforce parents and act as parents with them.

Further Reading. Gee, Ellen M. (1991). The transition to grandmotherhood. *Canadian Journal on Aging, 10,* 254–270; Kivett, Vira R. (1991). Centrality of the grandfather role among older rural black and white men. *Journal of Gerontology: Social Sciences, 46,* S250–S258; Thomas, Jeanne L. (1990). The grandparent role: A double bind. *International Journal of Aging and Human Development, 31,* 169–177.

GRIEF. Grief is the deep and poignant distress caused by the loss of a loved one. It represents one's emotional reaction to another's death and can include a wide range of feelings and states, such as sadness, anger, depression, relief, or self-pity. Grief can also trigger a variety of physical expressions, including loss of sleep and appetite, restlessness, or tension. (See BEREAVEMENT; GRIEF WORK; WIDOWHOOD.)

Further Reading. DeSpelder, Lynne A., and Albert L. Strickland. (1992). *The last dance: Encountering death and dying* (3rd Ed.). Mountain View, CA: Mayfield; Leming, Michael R., and George E. Dickinson. (1994). *Understanding dying, death, and bereavement.* Fort Worth, TX: Harcourt Brace.

GRIEF WORK. Grief work means coming to terms with the physical and emotional demands brought on by another's death. Rather than denying or suppressing feelings, grief work acknowledges the importance of facing loss, dealing with the emotions that accompany it, and moving to resolution. (See BEREAVEMENT; GRIEF; WIDOWHOOD.)

Further Reading. Stern, E. Mark. (Ed.). (1990). *Psychotherapy and the widowed patient.* New York: Haworth Press; Wortman, Camille B., and Roxane C. Silver. (1990). Successful mastery of bereavement and widowhood: A life-course perspective. In Paul B. Baltes and Margret M. Baltes (Eds.), *Successful aging: Perspectives from the behavioral sciences.* New York: Cambridge University Press.

H

HALL, G. STANLEY. G. Stanley Hall (1844–1924) is recognized as one of the early pioneers of both child and lifespan development. Born in Ashfield, Massachusetts, Hall originally wanted to pursue a career in the ministry and received a B.D. degree from Union Theological Seminary. Hall developed an interest in philosophy and psychology, however, and eventually received a Ph.D. in psychology from Harvard in 1878. Hall seemed to be the first worker in many areas of psychology, although it should be recognized that he lived during the early infancy of this science.

Hall received the first American doctorate in psychology at Harvard and is generally credited with establishing the first psychological laboratory in the United States (1883 at Johns Hopkins University). He was the first American student in the first psychological laboratory (in its first year) in Leipzig of Wilhelm Wundt, considered to be the founding father of psychology. Hall was also the first president and the first professor of psychology at Clark University, an institution that would become famous for producing great psychologists.

Hall founded and initially financed a journal, the *Pedagogical Seminary* (since renamed the *Journal of Genetic Psychology*), in 1891. This periodical focused on the research being conducted on children. A considerable amount of research was being done at Clark University, where Hall and his students were developing the questionnaire, a technique that Hall believed would allow for a more systematic investigation of children and afford more opportunities to investigate larger samples of the population. In particular, he became interested in children's thinking and developed a questionnaire designed to elicit knowledge from children. While it lacked the sophistication of modern-day questionnaires, it nevertheless served its purpose well.

Hall's interest in genetics and evolutionary theory led him to study not only childhood but also adolescence and old age. His books on these life stages were among the first systematic efforts to carefully detail and explore the many complexities of aging processes. Hall's research made a lasting contribution to developmental psychology, and he succeeded in providing a solid foundation for other contributors to explore the lifespan.

Further Reading. Hall, G. Stanley. (1883). The contents of children's minds. *Princeton Review, 11,* 249–272; Hall, G. Stanley. (1891). The contents of children's minds on entering school. *Pedagogical Seminary, 1,* 139–173; Hall, G. Stanley. (1906). *Youth.* New York: D. Appleton and Company.

HARLOW, HARRY F. Harry F. Harlow (1905–1981) was a psychologist who conducted laboratory research on various aspects of infant attachment and the need for contact and comfort. Harlow was born in Fairfield, Iowa, and received his Ph.D. from Stanford University in 1930. He taught at the University of Wisconsin for many years and was president of the American Psychological Association in 1958. He also was editor of the *Journal of Comparative and Physiological Psychology* and was a member of the National Academy of Science.

Harlow's long-term research focused on the contact-comfort behaviors of rhesus monkeys and the manner in which they sought attachment and security. In Harlow's now-classic studies, two surrogate (substitute) mothers were built and placed in a cage; one was constructed of wire meshing and the other of the same material covered with a terry-cloth wrapping. Each "mother" was equipped with a nursing bottle (the nipple of which protruded through the "chest") and a light bulb behind the body, which provided heat for the infant.

The infant monkeys were then divided into two groups; Group A could receive nourishment only from the nursing bottle placed in the wire mother, whereas Group B could receive milk from the bottle of the cloth-covered mother. The monkeys in Group A fed from the wire mother, but they gradually spent less time with her. Eventually, these monkeys took nourishment from the wire mother and then spent the intervening time with the more comforting cloth mother. Several infants even clung to the cloth mother while reaching over to feed from the wire mother. On the other hand, the infants in Group B spent considerable time clinging to the soft covering of their cloth mother and almost never ventured over to the wire figure.

The cloth mother also played a central role in reducing an infant's fear and anxiety. This was apparent when a strange object (a mechanical teddy bear) was introduced into the cage with the infant, the cloth mother, and the wire mother. The infant invariably ran to the cloth mother and clung to her for security. After its fear was reduced by this form of contact and comfort, the infant would venture short distances from the mother and eventually attempt to explore the new object.

Harlow also studied the later behavior of those monkeys not benefiting from a real mother. It was learned that the mother's absence had severely hampered the monkey's normal development, particularly in the formation of attachment bonds as well as in other aspects of social behavior. Whereas the monkeys reared with cloth mothers showed no overt problems in infancy, some were retarded later in life when compared with monkeys brought up by real mothers. More specifically, the experimental monkeys became socially maladjusted, ignoring others and frequently passing time by biting and hugging themselves. Later, some of the females in the study group proved to be poor mothers, neglecting and abusing their young. However, when placed in the company of normal monkeys, the socially isolated monkeys began to recover from the effects of their experimental environment. This was largely because the normal monkeys encouraged social interaction and play behavior and discouraged solitary behavior.

All of Harlow's research provided much insight into the contact-comfort motive as well as attachment behaviors. His research showed that satisfaction of the hunger drive does not by itself promote and nurture the infant's attachment to the mother, a belief held for years by many. Rather, the attachment to the mother is encouraged by the need to establish contact with something that can offer comfort, softness, and warmth. Moreover, this need often manifests itself in the young child's selection of a cuddly or huggable doll or stuffed animal, called a *transitional object* by child psychologists. The use of a transitional object is considered a normal phase of child development, particularly when children encounter novel, irritating, or threatening situations. Transitional objects are typically outgrown as immature and dependent behavior is replaced with more independence and a more secure sense of self.

Further Reading. Harlow, Harry F. (1958). The nature of love. *American Psychologist, 13,* 637–685; Harlow, Harry F. (1962). The heterosexual affectional system in monkeys. *American Psychologist, 17,* 1–9; Harlow, Harry F. (1971). *Learning to love.* San Francisco: Albion.

HAVIGHURST, ROBERT J. Robert J. Havighurst (1900–1991) made many contributions to the field of lifespan development, most notably the concept of *developmental tasks.* He was born in Wisconsin and received a Ph.D. from the Ohio State University in 1924. Havighurst, who served as a professor of human development at the University of Chicago, stressed the importance of mastering developmental tasks appropriate to a given life stage. In his research, he used Erik Erikson's concepts of the interaction between the individual and society (see ERIKSON, ERIK H.; PSYCHOSOCIAL DEVELOPMENT) and noted that most societies appear to have a timetable for the accomplishment of various tasks.

According to Havighurst, a developmental task is unique to each major stage of the lifespan (e.g., infancy, adolescence) and may originate from physical maturation, from the pressure of the surrounding society on the person, and from the desires, aspirations, and values of the emerging personality. For example, children must learn to walk and talk, to distinguish right from wrong, and so forth. Adults, too, have developmental tasks appropriate to various stages of their personal and social growth. Embarking on a vocation and assuming civic responsibility are examples of adult developmental tasks. Successfully achieved developmental tasks are the building blocks for success with future tasks, all leading toward happiness. Failure to satisfactorily complete these tasks can lead to unhappiness, difficulty with accomplishing future tasks, and disapproval by society.

Further Reading. Havighurst, Robert J. (1972). *Developmental tasks and education* (3rd Ed.). New York: David McKay; Havighurst, Robert J. (1980). More thoughts on developmental tasks. *Personnel and Guidance Journal, 58,* 330–335.

HETEROSEXISM. See HOMOPHOBIA.

HETEROSEXUALITY. See SEXUAL ORIENTATION.

HIERARCHY OF NEEDS. See HUMANISTIC THEORY.

HINDUISM. See RELIGION, IMPACT OF ON INTIMATE RELATION-SHIPS.

HIRSCHFELD, MAGNUS. Magnus Hirschfeld (1868–1935), who founded the Institute of Sexual Science in Berlin, was a German physician best remembered for his progressive and outspoken views on human sexuality. Following his graduation from medical school in 1894, Hirschfeld devoted much of his attention to studying problems in sexual functioning and was particularly drawn to the study of sexual deviations and their etiology.

Homosexuality was of particular interest to Hirschfeld, and he wrote several books on the topic. In a departure from the thinking of the day, Hirschfeld maintained that homosexuality was biologically determined and not a disease or a crime. He felt strongly that homosexuals should be protected by law and not prosecuted. Furthermore, Hirschfeld argued that therapy should be aimed at helping clients accept themselves as members of what he called ''the third sex'' and at assisting them to be useful citizens.

During the 1920s, Hirschfeld was instrumental in organizing the World League for Sexual Reform. This organization brought professionals in the field of human sexuality together and promoted such causes as sexual equality, sex education, and the prevention of sexually transmitted diseases. Hirschfeld's many professional contributions and innovative ideas helped to construct a foundation for the infant field of human sexuality research.

Further Reading. Bullough, Vern. (Ed.). (1979). *The frontiers of sex research.* New York: Prometheus; Janda, Louis H., and Karin E. Klenke-Hamel. (1980). *Human sexuality.* New York: Van Nostrand.

HISPANIC AMERICANS, LIFESPAN RELATIONSHIPS AMONG.

Hispanic Americans (also called *Latinos*) are the nation's largest minority group, after African Americans. The Hispanic-American population includes people who trace their ancestry to Spanish-speaking countries throughout Latin America, as well as some with links to Spain, Africa, and southwestern regions of the United States. Cultures vary widely within Hispanic Americans, including population sizes. The major groups include Mexican Americans (about 14 million), Puerto Ricans (approximately 3 million), and Cuban Americans (about 1 million). Because of high birthrates and continuing immigration to the United States, the Hispanic-American population is currently increasing by almost 1 million persons a year. The Hispanic-American population is highly concentrated in southwestern regions of the United States.

Hispanic-American families, much like African-American families, tend to experience high levels of poverty. This is because Hispanic Americans are apt to have less education, lower incomes, and higher rates of unemployment than the general population. They have also faced discrimination in housing and schools and in obtaining jobs and promotions. Although the proportion of Hispanic Americans in white-collar occupations has grown in recent years, they still tend to work in low-paying, semiskilled jobs. Moreover, many are employed in economic sectors vulnerable to cyclical unemployment. Hispanic-American women, and Puerto Ricans in particular, are less likely to be working than other women. Within Hispanic-American groups, poverty rates tend to be higher for Puerto Rican families, followed by Mexican-American and Cuban-American families.

Hispanic-American families are more likely to be female headed than are white families. About 25 percent of Hispanic-American families are female headed, which is almost double the percentage for whites and Asian Americans, but about one-half the rate for African Americans. Female-headed households are a characteristic often associated with lower economic status and related problems. To illustrate, this kind of household reduces the potential earning power provided by two working parents. Of all Hispanic-American groups, Puerto Rican families have the highest concentration of female-headed households.

As indicated, there is a high birthrate in Hispanic-American families. The average Hispanic-American woman will have 2.7 children, about one child more per woman than the rate for non-Hispanic whites. Hispanic-American women will also have their first child at a younger age than non-Hispanic white women, and there is a greater likelihood that the mother will be unmarried. Teenagers account for about 17 percent of all births among Hispanic Americans.

Researchers studying close relationships among Hispanic Americans have long emphasized the importance of family life. Hispanic Americans are characterized by their strong sense of familism; indeed, most regard *la familia* (the family) as the center of their life. The family is a treasured entity, and close kinship ties are forged between the nuclear family, its relatives, and even entire neighborhoods. Loyalty to family members is especially important to Hispanic Americans, and kin relationships are marked by mutual support, assistance, and cooperation. It is also not uncommon for "fictive kin" to emerge and offer family support, particularly in the Puerto Rican community. "Fictive kin" are people who are not related to a family but who will informally adopt children during periods of family stress or crisis.

The parent-child relationship in Hispanic-American families is warm and nurturant. Children are regarded as important members of the overall family system, and at early ages they are taught the importance of loyalty, respect, and politeness. Important cultural values stressed by Hispanic-American parents are avoidance of interpersonal conflict, deference and respect for authority systems, and educational achievement. Within the family system, mutual support and attachment are apparent among siblings, particularly those who are close together in age. None of the foregoing family dynamics appears to be altered by social or economic status.

At one time, gender roles in the Hispanic-American family were portrayed as being traditional and rigid. The concept of *machismo* was used to explain family functioning, a type of traditional gender-role behavior apparent in many Latin American countries (see LATIN AMERICA, LIFESPAN RELATIONSHIPS IN). Machismo viewed the Hispanic-American male as a standoffish, swaggering authoritarian, the undisputed master of the household. The female, on the other hand, was seen as submissive and weak. Today, these gender-role behaviors are seen as inaccurate and misrepresentative of typical Hispanic-American families. Rather, most homes tend to reflect a decline in machismo and an upswing in egalitarianism, the latter being a sharing of gender roles and family decision making. While traditional masculine authority still exists today, it is characterized more by fairness and respect for others than machismo-like behavior. A number of explanations are given for this shift in gender-role behaviors, including increased urbanization and the feminist movement in both the United States and Latin America.

As far as intimate relationships among Hispanic Americans are concerned, Catholicism exerts a significant influence. For example, the church prohibits both contraception and abortion. For traditional Hispanic Americans, a high value is placed on female virginity. However, because each Hispanic-American group has its own unique background and set of cultural traditions, these factors impact on individuals and couples differently. For example, among traditional Hispanic-American adolescent males, sexual activity is encouraged, but it is frowned upon among females. While motherhood is valued, virginity until marriage is expected. To cite another variation, many acculturated Hispanic-American males and females (those who have adopted the attitudes and behaviors of a dominant group) are apt to regard abortion as a birth-control option.

As far as marital relationships are concerned, about 70 percent of all Hispanic-American family households consist of married couples. This compares to about 80 percent of non-Hispanic families. While the rate of intermarriage is several times higher than that of African Americans, intermarriages account for only about one-sixth of all Hispanic-American marriages. In interpreting these and other marital trends, differences in Hispanic-American groups must again be taken into account. For example, while marriage rates are lower among Puerto Ricans than Mexican Americans or Cuban Americans, this may be due to the popularity of nonmarital cohabitation within the Puerto Rican culture.

As mentioned earlier, in recent years there has been an upswing in the number of households maintained by women, a trend that has greatly increased the economic vulnerability of Hispanic Americans. Economic disadvantage among Hispanic Americans has been linked to a retreat from marriage, premarital child-bearing, and marital dissolution, each of which contributes to female family headship. Moreover, children who grow up in mother-only families are at an increased risk of poverty during childhood. This, in turn, heightens the risk of health problems, often delays intellectual development, and creates poor school performance. Hispanic-American children living in mother-only families are also less likely to complete high school and more likely to have low adult earnings than are children from intact families.

Finally, given the strong and extended kinship network among Hispanic-American families, aging family members are provided with considerable care and attention. The elderly are held in high esteem, and extending intergenerational support reflects the deep sense of family obligation characteristic of Hispanic Americans. Affective support, such as the provision of love and companionship, and instrumental support, such as transportation or the provision of food or housekeeping services, are commonplace. Many adult children live within close proximity to their parents, thus enabling frequent contact and interaction to take place. As in other racial and ethnic minorities, a high level of reciprocity exists between older and younger Hispanic-American generations. More often than not, females are more instrumental than males in the provision of intergenerational care.

Further Reading. Bean, Frank D., and Marta Tienda. (1987). *The Hispanic population of the United States.* New York: Russell Sage Foundation; Kivisto, Peter. (1995). *Americans all.* Belmont, CA: Wadsworth; Marden, Charles F., Gladys Meyer, and Madeline H. Engel. (1992). *Minorities in American society.* New York: HarperCollins; Marger, Martin N. (1991). *Race and ethnic relations* (2nd Ed.). Belmont, CA: Wadsworth.

HOMOPHOBIA. Homophobia, sometimes called "homosexual phobia," is a fear and dread of homosexuals as well as the fear of the possibility of homosexuality in oneself. Homophobia is closely allied with *heterosexism,* the belief that heterosexuality is the only acceptable and viable life option. Heterosexism forces gays, lesbians, and bisexuals to struggle constantly with their self-esteem and makes it much harder for them to integrate a positive sexual identity.

Homophobia and heterosexism are widespread in the United States. The presence of such attitudes along with the prejudice and discrimination that often accompany both is a constant theme in the research literature. Investigators have found that many people have negative impressions of homosexuality and cling to stereotypes about gays and lesbians. Additionally, many Americans feel that homosexuality should not be considered a socially acceptable lifestyle.

Certain variables appear to be associated with homophobic attitudes. For example, heterosexual men have more hostile feelings toward gays and lesbians than do women. Most of these men tend to be older and less well educated and to express traditional attitudes about gender roles. Those men and women who are more religious also tend to hold more negative attitudes than those who are less devout. This is likely because homosexuality is viewed as sinful and immoral according to religious teachings. Many perceive homosexuals as not fulfilling societal expectations, particularly those related to marriage and family life.

Homophobic attitudes can be changed, although this looms as a difficult chore since such feelings are usually deeply rooted and fueled by considerable fear and anxiety. Seeking to change such attitudes will require public education in sensitive, extensive, and diverse ways. Community outreach programming has been effective in educating the public about homosexuality, including dispelling myths and misconceptions about gays, lesbians, and bisexuals. Speakers' bureaus, newsletters, and support groups have been among the approaches utilized. At the college level, courses in human sexuality and gay lifestyles tend to alter students' attitudes toward same-sex preferences in a positive fashion.

Further Reading. De Cecco, John P. (Ed.). (1985). *Bashers, baiters, and bigots: Homophobia in American society.* New York: Harrington Park Press; Miller, Douglas J., and Robert E. Romanelli. (1991). From religion: Heterosexism and the Golden Rule. *Journal of Gay and Lesbian Psychotherapy, 1,* 45–64; Whitam, Frederick L. (1991). From sociology: Homophobia and heterosexism in sociology. *Journal of Gay and Lesbian Psychotherapy, 1,* 31–44.

HOMOSEXUALITY. See SEXUAL ORIENTATION.

HORNEY, KAREN. Karen Horney (1885–1952) was a noted psychoanalyst and personality theorist. A psychiatrist by training, she was born in Hamburg, Germany, and taught at the Berlin Psychoanalytic Institute for 14 years before moving to the United States to join the Chicago Psychoanalytic Institute. In 1941, she established the American Institute for Psychoanalysis, serving as dean. Horney was also one of the founders of the Association for the Advancement of Psychoanalysis and served as editor of the *American Journal of Psychoanalysis.*

In her research, Horney saw the importance of Freudian psychology and the sociocultural forces responsible for shaping personality. More specifically, she believed that during early parent-child interactions, infants experience *basic anxiety,* an outgrowth of a desire for safety. She maintained that basic anxiety originates from an infant's need to be secure and not isolated or helpless. Horney stressed that the need for early psychological safety leads to the creation of later defensive strategies within the interpersonal realm.

For example, in order to create security and satisfaction, children either move toward people (submission), against them (aggression), or away from them (detachment). When moving toward people, children accept their own insecurity and try to win the affection of others. When moving against people, children take for granted the hostility and lack of safety around them and decide to resist or fight. When moving away from people, children do not want to belong or resist, but rather choose simply to withdraw. According to Horney, each of these strategies creates a foundation for later personality and social functioning.

Further Reading. Horney, Karen. (1939). *New ways in psychoanalysis.* New York: Norton; Horney, Karen. (1945). *Our inner conflicts.* New York: Norton; Horney, Karen. (1950). *Neurosis and human growth.* New York: Norton.

HUMAN IMMUNODEFICIENCY VIRUS (HIV). See AIDS.

HUMANISTIC THEORY. Humanistic theory is a major school of thought in psychology that emphasizes an individual's uniqueness, personal potential, and inner drives. A person's self-concept and the maximization of human potential are paramount concerns of this school of thought. Humanistic psychology is often referred to as the *third force* in psychology because it challenges environmental learning theories and psychoanalytic stances. Humanists contend that individuals are not controlled exclusively by their external environment, nor is their behavior dominated by the irrational forces of the unconscious. Rather, people are free and creative and capable of growth and self-actualization.

Humanistic psychology has been shaped by numerous contributors, most notably Abraham Maslow and Carl Rogers. Maslow in particular developed a theory of motivation stating that individuals not only have the more obvious biological and psychological needs, but are driven to attain uniqueness and the full development of their potentialities, capacities, and talents. This uniqueness and pinnacle of success was referred to by Maslow as *self-actualization.* To reach this pinnacle of self-fulfillment, the basic needs must first be satisfied.

At the heart of Maslow's theory is the assumption that human needs (and consequently motivations) exist in a *hierarchy of needs,* from the most basic to the most advanced. The further one progresses up this motivational pyramid, the more distinctly human one becomes. Higher motives will develop only when the more basic ones have been satisfied.

The first set of needs in the hierarchy is physiological in nature, embracing adequate nourishment, rest, and the like. At the second level are safety needs, which motivate the person to achieve a sense of security. Next is the need for belongingness and love. Belongingness may be defined as the need to be part of a group and to experience sharing. Esteem is the fourth level of the hierarchic pyramid. By esteem, Maslow meant that individuals must receive feedback from others (in the form of respect and assurance) in order to realize that they are worthwhile and competent. The fifth need, self-actualization, means fulfilling one's individual nature in all its aspects. To reach the fulfillment of one's potential, all previous needs have to be met adequately. An essential component of self-actualization is freedom from cultural and self-imposed restraints.

The quest for self-actualization begins early in life. According to Maslow's hierarchy of needs, neither children nor adults can strive toward creativity unless fundamental needs have been met. The attainment of self-actualization also requires considerable ego strength, acceptance from peers, and self-respect. Self-actualization may not be attained until the middle years of adulthood. In the years prior to middle age, energy is frequently dissipated in diverse directions, including sexual relationships, educational advancement, career, marriage, and parenthood. The need to achieve financial stability during the young adult years consumes considerable psychic energy. By middle age, however, many people have managed to fulfill most of these needs and can spare the energy to strive toward ego maturity.

While the ideas of Maslow and other humanists have been mostly directed to adult development, humanistic theory also has application to children and adolescents. It has become increasingly recognized that emphasizing a person's uniqueness and potentials is important throughout the life cycle, but especially so during the formative years. Humanists stress the notion of helping both young and old to accept their total being and the strivings that characterize the process of "becoming." Thus the application of humanistic theory to early as well as later development, including how we can promote activities that create fulfillment and individuality, has important implications in the field of lifespan development. (See MASLOW, ABRAHAM H.; PARENTHOOD, CHILD-REARING OPTIONS AND STRATEGIES; ROGERS, CARL R.)

Further Reading. Maslow, Abraham H. (1968). *Toward a psychology of being* (2nd Ed.). New York: Van Nostrand Reinhold; Rogers, Carl R. (1961). *On becoming a person.* Boston: Houghton Mifflin; Thomas, R. Murray. (1992). *Comparing theories of child development* (3rd Ed.). Belmont, CA: Wadsworth.

HUMAN SEXUALITY, SCIENTIFIC STUDY OF. The scientific study of human sexuality is a broad discipline, embracing all aspects of human beings that affect their gender-specific and specifically sexual behavior. Not only human beings' anatomy and physiology but their thoughts, feelings, attitudes, and behaviors are of interest to the sexuality researcher, who may study such topics as sexual maturation and reproduction, sexual identities, sexual drives and response cycles, relationship dynamics, sexual lifestyles, sexual health and disease, and sexual dysfunctions. The scientific discipline of human sexuality is interdisciplinary in nature, with roots in psychology, sociology, education, anthropology, biology, medical science, health education, and counseling. Examples of research journals devoted to the scientific study of human sexuality are the *Journal of Sex Education and Therapy, Journal of Sex Research, Journal of Psychology and Human Sexuality,* and *Sex Roles.*

Further Reading. Hyde, Janet S. (1994). *Understanding human sexuality* (5th Ed.). New York: McGraw-Hill; Rathus, Spencer A., Jeffrey S. Nevid, and Lois Fichner-Rathus. (1993). *Human sexuality in a world of diversity.* Boston, MA: Allyn and Bacon; Strong, Bryan, and Christine DeVault. (1994). *Human sexuality.* Mountain View, CA: Mayfield.

IMPOTENCE. See SEXUAL DYSFUNCTIONS, CATEGORIES OF.

IMPRINTING. See ETHOLOGICAL THEORY.

INCEST. See CHILDHOOD, SEXUAL ABUSE DURING.

INDIA, LIFESPAN RELATIONSHIPS IN. India is the seventh-largest country in the world. It occupies a land region about one-third the size of the United States, stretching approximately 2,000 miles from north to south. India has more people than any other country in the world except the People's Republic of China. Despite government policies that foster family planning (India was the first country to adopt an official policy to slow population growth), India's population of about 853 million is expected to grow to 1 billion shortly after the year 2000. Today, about one of every seven persons in the world lives in India.

The people of India belong to many different races and religions. Most Indians are either Indo-Aryans, Caucasians who reside mostly in northern regions of India, or Dravidians, darker-skinned people who live mainly in the south. The vast majority of Indians are Hindus, but India has one of the world's largest Muslim communities. Other religious groups are Christians, Sikhs, Buddhists, and Jains. Fourteen major languages are spoken in India, which are further differentiated by hundreds of dialects. Of these many variations, Hindi is the official language of India.

Family relationships are an important facet of Indian society. According to traditional Indian custom, marriage is viewed more as a relationship between two families than between two persons. Rarely do couples date, and parents arrange most marriages. Parents often assess the worth of their offspring and look for a partner of equivalent value. However, it should be recognized that many young people have the right to reject any arrangement made by the parents. Generally speaking, the traditional wife is usually a number of years younger than her husband and probably has less education. Marriage is seen as a permanent relationship between husband and wife. Provisions for divorce do exist, but the proportion of divorces to marriages in modern-day India is very low.

In India, as in most Asian cultures, marital structure is patriarchal in scope. The husband or eldest son makes most household decisions, controls the family's finances, and is the legal owner of the land. Consequently, a woman's social position is severely limited. Her identity is constructed chiefly around her roles of wife and mother. Thus women administer the household, perform the cooking and cleaning, and see to it that the children are properly cared for. Motherhood, particularly the birth of sons, enhances a woman's prestige and status and gives her a greater degree of independence. Should the mother seek work beyond housekeeping, she usually gains employment as a farm laborer, street vendor, or maid. Thus, for most, work is often neither an emancipating experience nor a socially valued role.

As far as family planning is concerned, the average woman in India gives birth to 4.2 children. As indicated, there is a strong parental preference for male children. This is a deeply rooted tradition that dates back for centuries. Sons are especially preferred in remote areas of the country, where they help in the fields, add to the family income, and offer parents security in old age. While a son is a prize for an Indian family, a daughter is often viewed as a deficit, and female infanticide is still a problem in some tribal areas. Overall, infant girls receive less parental care and attention than boys. Where food is scarce, girls eat less than boys, a situation that often promotes malnourishment. Studies have also shown that parents tend to wait longer before seeking medical care for their girls than they do for their boys.

In recent years, India has experienced a significant increase in abortions. Abortion is not officially part of the country's family-planning policy, but it is legal and easily attainable. The increase in abortion parallels, at least in part, an increase in amniocentesis use among Indian women. Amniocentesis is the removal of fluid from the amniotic sac of a pregnant woman so that chromosomes of the fetus may be analyzed. Amniocentesis is chiefly used elsewhere in the world to determine the health of the fetus, but its recent use in India has been to determine the sex of the fetus. Growing numbers of pregnant women are visiting clinics specializing in amniocentesis, learning the gender of their unborn child, and then choosing abortion if the child is female.

Because of the emphasis placed on family life, many traditional Indian households include not only parents and children, but also sons' wives and their children. In such arrangements, the eldest male, whether father or grandfather,

makes all of the important family decisions. On his death, the authority is passed
to the next-oldest male. A wife's authority often rests on her husband's position.
If she is the wife of the oldest son, she might have household power or control
over an older sister-in-law. Child rearing clearly reflects the male position of
complete domination. While the mother tends to the day-to-day routines of child
care, the father represents the formal authority and is the disciplinarian. A father's power is extensive over his children during their formative years, and for
many this control extends well into adolescence. Reverence and respect for one's
parents represent important Indian child-rearing goals.

Close intergenerational relationships exist between old and young Indian family members, even when they do not share the same residence. Family members
exchange material support, live in close proximity to one another, and seek to
maintain generational solidarity. The notion of mutual support can be seen in
the types of care and assistance exchanged between generations. Adult children
typically support elderly parents if they become frail or ill, while aged parents
often provide financial and other forms of support to their adult offspring and
grandchildren. Widows are in particular need of intergenerational assistance
since over one-half of all Indian women over age 60 have lost their husbands.
Adult children loom as critical caregivers to elderly widows since the latter often
face economic deprivation and social isolation, particularly in rural areas. Many
elderly widows receive very little support from persons other than their own
family members.

Further Reading. Chen, Marty. (1992). *Widows and well-being in rural North India.*
London: London School of Economics; Kumar, Usha. (1991). Life stages in the development of the Hindu woman in India. In Leonore L. Adler (Ed.), *Women in cross-cultural
perspective.* Westport, CT: Praeger; Rodgers, Gerry. (Ed.). (1989). *Population growth
and poverty in rural South Asia.* New Delhi: Sage; Singhal, Uma, and Nihar R. Mrinal.
(1991). Tribal women in India: The Tharu women. In Leonore L. Adler (Ed.), *Women
in cross-cultural perspective.* Westport, CT: Praeger.

INDONESIA, LIFESPAN RELATIONSHIPS IN. Indonesia is a country in Southeast Asia consisting of over 13,500 islands. The islands, most of
which are small, extend across 3,000 miles of the Indian and Pacific oceans and
lie between Asia and Australia. The major islands of Indonesia are Java, Su-
matra, Kalimantan, Sulawesi, and Irian Jaya. Indonesia is the world's fifth most
populous nation, containing almost 177 million people, and this total is expected
to reach 216 million by the turn of the century. Almost two-thirds of the population live on Java, even though its land mass is less than one-tenth of the
country's total area.

The majority of Indonesia's population is Malay whose ancestors originated
from Southeast Asia. There are many different ethnic and cultural groups in
Indonesia, including some Arabs, Chinese, and Papuans. While Indonesian is
the official language, as many as 250 different languages are spoken. About 90
percent of Indonesians are Muslim; Hindus, Christians, and Buddhists comprise

most of the rest. Since Indonesia is an economically underdeveloped nation with little manufacturing, most Indonesians are farmers. Because of this, most of Indonesia's people live in rural areas, many in small villages.

Marriage is almost universal in Indonesia, with only a small percentage of individuals never marrying. While couples tend to marry early, many by ages 17 or 18, the age at first marriage has recently increased. Those residing in urban areas tend to marry later than those from rural settings, and those with higher levels of education tend to postpone marriage until later ages. The Indonesian marriage structure is patriarchal in scope, with the husband exercising dominance and control over his wife and children. The division of labor within the family unit, driven by its agrarian existence, reflects traditional gender roles as well. In most farming homes, men tend to the physically demanding agriculture chores and responsibilities, while women address their labors to the indoors, including cooking, child care, weaving, and sewing.

Regarding parent-child relationships, children are of great importance to Indonesians. They are regarded as economically valuable to the family and are the objects of considerable love and affectionate care. Most babies in rural areas are born at home and breast-fed by the mother. Following weaning, infants are typically placed in the care of an older sister. Also, because many Indonesian families reflect an extended structure, child care is often shared with other relatives. Such child-care arrangements not only serve to create a safe and secure environment for the baby, but they also tend to promote harmonious sibling relations and a strong kin network. In time, children are expected to assist with chores and household routines, the responsibilities mirroring the traditional gender roles of Indonesian society. By the school years, girls learn to assist in the preparation of food, while boys are taught to plant and harvest.

At one time, Indonesia's high fertility rates, coupled with densely populated areas such as Java, were of great concern to population experts. The Indonesian government even launched a "transmigration" program, a plan to relocate willing residents to more sparsely populated islands. Government-sponsored family planning, though, has proven more effective, and fertility has fallen by over one-third in only 15 years. In the late 1960s, the average woman gave birth to 5.6 children; today, the figure is 3.3. The fertility rate is higher for rural women than it is among urban women, and rural women are more apt to have children earlier in life than those from urban settings. Also, Indonesian women with a secondary or higher education have an average of one child less than those females with a primary education.

Heightened levels of contraceptive knowledge and use are largely responsible for the reduction of Indonesia's population growth rate. Studies have shown that educational efforts have been effective and that most Indonesian women are familiar with at least one method of family planning. Of the available methods, oral contraceptives are used the most frequently, followed by the intrauterine device, condoms, and sterilization. Women in the middle of their childbearing years are more apt to use birth control than are younger or older females. Like other trends, contraceptive use tends to be greater among urban married women than among those from rural areas.

Indonesia's declining levels of infant and child mortality, coupled with an increase in life expectancy, have created a large proportion of elderly persons. Currently, there are about 7 million residents aged 65 years or more, giving Indonesia the tenth-largest elderly population in the world. Demographers predict that Indonesia's aged population will double by the year 2000, at which point it will constitute 7.5 percent of the total population. As in other nations, females outnumber males within Indonesia's elderly population due to their greater life expectancy.

With advancing age, economic and social support are often needed for dependent family members. It is well documented in the literature that the Indonesian family looms as the most important source for such assistance, although recent fertility declines have the potential of undermining the availability of family members. Usually, though, the tightly woven nature of the family unit places considerable emphasis on caring for one's parents, and the burden of caregiving is typically shared among adult children and grandchildren. Elderly widows, in particular, are in need of such supportive assistance since they usually face increased levels of poverty, ill health, and loneliness. In recent years, Indonesia has begun to implement special services for its elderly population. Given Indonesia's aged-population projections, the need for more extensive and comprehensive programming is immense.

Further Reading. Althaus, Frances A. (1989). Indonesian fertility rate falls as age at marriage, modern birth control methods rise. *International Family Planning Perspectives, 15,* 153–155; Hugo, Graeme J. (1987). *The demographic dimension in Indonesian development.* New York: Oxford University Press; Hugo, Graeme J. (1991). Aging: A new challenge for Indonesia. *Ageing International, 18,* 3–23; World Bank Country Study. (1988). *Indonesia: The transmigration program in perspective.* Washington, DC: World Bank.

INDUSTRIAL REVOLUTION, LIFESPAN RELATIONSHIPS DURING THE. Those living in late nineteenth-century North America witnessed a nation beginning a transformation. The Industrial Revolution, as it came to be known, began to change the predominantly agrarian society of America into an urban and industrialized one. This change had many direct and indirect effects on lifespan relationships.

One of the most striking changes was a new alignment of the family in relation to work and the economic support of family members. Instead of functioning together as a productive agrarian unit, families now seldom worked together physically. In the growing number of nonfarm families, the husband and father went off to work in an industrial setting, while the wife and mother and the children remained at home.

The Industrial Revolution thus brought about an important shift in gender-role behaviors. Women, once partners in labor in farming families, were exclusively assigned to the home and the hearth. Caring for aging family members, a task usually shouldered by mothers and daughters throughout history, became a role even more entrenched during this time. Employment outside of the home and away from the family became the province of the man. It can be said, then, that as the Industrial Revolution brought about significant technological change, it also introduced a new dimension to gender-role behaviors and expectations.

Outside of the family, the need for female workers in the labor force became evident. However, along with this need came certain societal resistance. Due to gender-role stereotyping, women who worked outside of the home were often regarded as unfeminine or as negligent in their wifely and mothering responsibilities. However, the increased number of women joining the labor force has helped to change these attitudes and, in turn, to encourage more women to seek employment outside the home.

The frequent need to search for employment prospects during the Industrial Revolution also made the family unit more mobile, thus tending to isolate it from relatives. Previously, children had been regarded as needed hands on the farm and had been expected to make worthwhile and productive contributions. At least in the middle classes, they now became economic liabilities as parents had more mouths to feed in their daily struggles to carve out an existence in this new state of American history. Work and family life thus became separate enterprises; families still consumed as a unit but no longer produced as a unit.

The manner in which children were perceived also changed at this time. Children became the objects of a new type of sentimentality from their parents. Caring for children became a central concern, particularly for women. Many adults became committed to child rearing and the concept of parenting. As children grew older, school began to exert more of an impact on their lives. This latter point is part of a much larger theme that would have implications for children of the twentieth century: that is, parents saw fit to let other adults guide, instruct, nurture, stimulate, and protect their children. Whereas the family had once been the primary socialization agent, other institutions now played a role in the child's development. In addition to school, churches had youth groups, the concept of Sunday school emerged, and there were organized places away from the home in which youngsters learned, socialized, and developed a sense of self and of their group identity.

During the Industrial Revolution, smaller families became a desirable goal and birth control an important concern. During the 1920s and 1930s, Margaret Sanger led the birth-control movement in the United States. A nurse, Sanger wrote and distributed booklets on birth control and opened clinics to advise people on methods and techniques. Because it was illegal to distribute birth-control information, Sanger, who was responsible for founding the Planned Parenthood Federation of America, was arrested many times. (See SANGER, MARGARET.)

Abstinence, withdrawal, douching, and abortion were the most widely used methods of birth control at the turn of the century. However, other contraceptive

measures were under development. One of the goals of contraceptive development was to create methods that would be minimally intrusive in moments of
sexual intimacy. The oral contraceptive pill, introduced in 1960, was such a
method. The pill brought consumers a relatively inexpensive, reliable, and simple
form of birth control.

Fertility rates in North America declined significantly both during and after
the Industrial Revolution. The percentage of families with six or more members
was 51.8 in 1790, 32.8 in 1900, and 20.1 in 1930. Meanwhile, the percentage
of childless marriages increased. This trend provides an interesting contrast to
the high premium placed on having many children during early historical periods.

The path to marriage also changed, including new patterns of courtship. The
Roaring Twenties heralded new levels of autonomy and freedom as America
experienced a wave of prosperity and self-indulgence. Daring young flappers
shocked their elders with short skirts and the free use of cosmetics and cigarettes,
and many drank illegal liquor in clubs called speakeasies. The invention of the
automobile made it possible for young couples to be alone together and to engage in much more sexual activity than was possible within the home. The
sexual needs and sexual rights of women were being increasingly recognized.
The notion of the shy, passive female was being eroded.

Parental control over courtship lessened considerably, and arranged marriages
for the majority of couples became a thing of the past. Women experienced
much more freedom in selecting a mate, and for most partners of both sexes,
love and affection became pivotal features of the relationship. The concept of
romantic love was reborn and became increasingly popular.

Further Reading. D'Emilio, John, and Estelle B. Freedman. (1988). *Intimate matters:
A history of sexuality in America.* New York: Harper and Row; Mantoux, Paul. (1961).
The Industrial Revolution in the eighteenth century. New York: Macmillan; Moffit, Louis.
(1963). *England on the eve of the Industrial Revolution.* London: Cass and Company;
Peterson, Richard A. (1972). *The Industrial Order and social policy.* Englewood Cliffs,
NJ: Prentice-Hall.

INFANCY AND TODDLERHOOD. The lifespan stage known as infancy
and toddlerhood generally occupies the first three years of life. During this time,
numerous developmental challenges exist. For example, developing control in
physical expression, such as walking, and refining mental concepts to clarify
one's surroundings are important tasks. Personality and social demands are
equally significant, particularly interactions with one's parents and other family
members.

It is from early interactions within the family that children develop a better
understanding of themselves and their environment. Heightened cognitive powers blend with early personality and social forces to help young children realize
that they are separate, unique individuals. These processes also combine to foster
the development of such feelings as trust or mistrust, autonomy or self-doubt,
and a wide range of other behavioral expressions.

Socialization begins early in life. As infants begin to spend more hours of the day awake, they usually have more interactions with parents, from the rituals of feeding, diaper changing, and other custodial chores to recreational and playtime activities. These early interactions are the seeds of social development for the infant.

Parent-infant interaction is important because adults can provide critical stimulation to the infant's linguistic, cognitive, social, and physical capacities. Indeed, the lack of adult interaction and stimulation will retard growth in these areas (see FAILURE TO THRIVE). Through interactions with parents, infants also gradually develop a sense of the home's emotional climate. Interactions frequently reveal how parents feel about themselves and each other. Without question, the feelings parents have toward the child will also ultimately surface in direct or indirect ways.

Growing numbers of fathers share in child-rearing chores, and researchers point out that unique bonds of attachment form between fathers and their children. However, the mother is usually the dominant influence in the infant's life. From the earliest feedings and handlings to verbal exchanges and eye contact, the mother has an unremitting influence on the infant's personality and social growth. During the early months, the two will develop a bond of attachment that provides support and comfort to both. Numerous studies show that this special bond will strengthen over time. To observe this, one has only to watch the intense and unblinking gaze of the infant toward the mother, the clinging behavior of a two-year-old, or the upset face of a preschooler unexpectedly separated from mother. Witness, too, the intense reciprocal attachment behaviors from the mother to the infant as she tends to her child's needs.

Attachment is considered to be a vital component of healthy personality and social functioning. Attachment promotes such positive behaviors and feelings as satisfaction, trust, security, and happiness. Its absence or disruption, on the other hand, can result in anxiety, anger, inner turmoil, and other problems. For example, insecurely attached children seem to be less adept in overall social relations than securely attached children. For some, absence of attachment results in grief and depression.

Early as well as later social development appears to be affected by attachment experiences during the early years. Contemporary child psychologists feel that one's general outgoingness, social independence, and emotional investments in others may be traced to the outcome of these early social experiences. Also, it must be recognized that our need for security, reassurance, or nurturance, while most intense during infancy and toddlerhood, is never really left behind. These are important needs even in adult life (see ATTACHMENT, EARLY PARENT-INFANT).

Further Reading. Berk, Laura. (1993). *Infants, children, and adolescents*. Boston, MA: Allyn and Bacon; Field, Tiffany. (1990). *Infancy*. Cambridge, MA: Harvard University Press; Sroufe, L. Alan, Robert G. Cooper, and Ganie B. DeHart. (1992). *Child development: Its nature and course* (2nd Ed.). New York: McGraw-Hill.

INFANCY AND TODDLERHOOD, DEVELOPMENT OF TRUST DURING.

It is during the first few years of life that a child develops a sense of trust or mistrust in the world. Trust is an important facet of personality and social functioning, a basic interpersonal orientation that will extend throughout the lifespan. Essentially, trust is a feeling that various aspects of the environment are safe, secure, and dependable. A number of caregiving behaviors create trust, including feeding, attention, comfort, and affection.

The child's relationships with the mother or other caregiver are critical in the creation of early trust. Because the mother or other caregiver provides the infant with the first social relationship, the task is to create a warm environment conducive to the nurturance of positive feelings. Caregivers need to create a sense of trust by combining sensitive care of the infant's needs with quality interaction and feelings of love and tenderness.

It is important to understand that the development of trust represents a reciprocal, complementary form of interaction between parent and infant. The parent who meets the infant's physical and psychological needs will produce a child who is happier and more content, thus reciprocating the parents' enjoyment. Parents who have happy, trusting infants are apt to spend more time with them, which in turn results in the establishment of even more trust by the infant and stronger bonds of attachment. Such reciprocal bonds will increase during the early years.

Consider the consequences when a parent chooses to ignore the infant's needs, such as hunger pangs. Rather than cooing or gurgling in trusting contentment, a frustrated infant may express the need for food with irritability. The infant might whimper, cry, and finally scream as the hunger pangs increase. The unhappy infant may become an irritant to the parent, who may become cross and handle the screaming infant roughly, which produces further annoyance in the infant. This kind of parent-infant interaction eventually leads to an uncomfortable and insecure relationship with the environment, likely resulting in feelings of mistrust and insecurity.

Trust, over time, becomes an important element of sound personality and social functioning, and it also serves as a pivotal feature of quality interpersonal relationships. For example, trust tends to promote such behaviors as attachment, holding, touching, smiling, and making eye contact. Trust promotes more positive feelings toward oneself as well as those in one's surroundings. Those individuals who are trusting tend to be happier, more emotionally stable, and more secure in their intimate relationships. Moreover, they tend to be more relaxed, more tolerant, and less defensive toward others. (See ATTACHMENT, EARLY PARENT-INFANT; PSYCHOSOCIAL DEVELOPMENT.)

Further Reading. Allen, Bem. (1990). *Personality, social, and biological perspectives on personal adjustment.* Pacific Grove, CA: Brooks/Cole; Brazelton, T. Berry. (1990). *The earliest relationship: parents, infants, and the drama of early attachment.* New York: Delacorte; Lamb, Michael, E., and Marc H. Bornstein. (1987). *Development in infancy.* New York: Random House.

INFANCY AND TODDLERHOOD, EARLY SEXUAL AWARE-NESS DURING.

The early years are important for the development of healthy sexual attitudes and behavior. During infancy and toddlerhood, children explore their bodies, including their genitals, and learn that touching and stroking their bodies are pleasurable. Such early explorations are normal and help youngsters to become aware of themselves as sexual beings.

Sexual pleasure, though, is not confined to stimulation of the genitals, nor is all pleasant physical contact related to sex. This is true even of the youngest babies, who learn about the pleasures of physical contact through constant loving and fondling. Parents touch, kiss, and cuddle their babies, and the babies typically respond with affection. The quality of the physical intimacy given also reflects the feelings of the caregiver concerning intimacy itself.

Experts point out that children need to feel good about their bodies, and early sexual learning experiences shape later sexual feelings and attitudes. Some sources maintain that when infants discover their genital organs and engage in self-stimulation, they are initiating the active functioning of the sexual response cycle (see SEXUAL RESPONSE CYCLE). Years later this cycle will be physiologically ready for normal sexual functioning and will be accompanied by a sense of competence, fulfillment, and pleasure. Parents can help children accept sexuality as a good and important part of themselves. Parents thus loom as a child's first sex educators, both by their actions and by the verbal and nonverbal messages given to the child.

Further Reading. Calderone, Mary S., and Eric W. Johnson. (1989). *The family book about sexuality.* New York: Harper and Row; Gordon, Sol, and Judith Gordon. (1989). *Raising a child conservatively in a sexually permissive world* (Rev. Ed.). New York: Simon and Schuster; Heins, Marilyn, and Anne M. Seiden. (1987). *Child care, parent care.* Garden City, NY: Doubleday.

INFANCY AND TODDLERHOOD, SOCIAL PLAY DURING.

Play affects many aspects of the child's development, including those within the social sphere. During infancy and toddlerhood, play enables children to realize who they are and what effects their actions may have on the people around them. Furthermore, play gives children the opportunity to experience many of life's emotions and to view their position in life in relation to the rest of the world. Play brings children into contact with one another, thus enhancing peer relationships. In the process, the meaning and value of cooperation, rules, order, and structure become clearer.

During infancy and toddlerhood, children pay attention to the behavior of others and engage in primitive forms of social play. Research has shown that in some instances primitive games may even evolve, depending on the reciprocity that an adult can offer or the environmental effect a given action can cause. For example, an infant may laugh and elicit a smile from a nearby adult. This may encourage the infant to laugh again, with the hope of receiving another response. This type of exchange, with anticipated reactions from both young and old, may soon develop into a game and reflect active partnership. Interestingly, it appears that mother-child dyads having secure attachment relationships are more adept at these active partnerships than those in insecure relationships. The former demonstrate greater capacities for synchronous, well-timed, and mutually rewarding exchanges.

During toddlerhood, play serves as a vehicle for gradual socialization. Initially, toddlers do not extensively engage themselves in play activities; rather, they tend to observe whatever events happen to capture their interest. Most toddlers also choose to play independently with their own toys and make limited efforts to interact with other children. Behavior at this point is egocentric, expressive of a self-centered attitude toward one's own activities.

During the second and third years, a type of onlooker behavior emerges. Play behavior is characterized by the observation of others and a gradual interest in what other children are doing. Play is also parallel in structure; that is, children tend to play alongside rather than with other youngsters. By the end of the third year, most children can interact and show signs of cooperating and maintaining a play activity. There is also evidence of sharing, borrowing, and lending of play toys, although such behaviors are not consistently expressed (see PROSOCIAL BEHAVIOR, CHILD).

Further Reading. Field, Tiffany. (1990). *Infancy.* Cambridge, MA: Harvard University Press; Garvey, Catherine. (1990). *Play.* Cambridge, MA: Harvard University Press; Selman, Robert. (1980). *The growth of interpersonal understanding.* New York: Academic Press.

INFANTICIDE. See CHILD REARING, HISTORICAL PRACTICES IN.

INFANT-MOTHER RELATIONSHIP, BREASTFEEDING AND.
Choosing between breastfeeding or formula feeding is an important decision, one that impacts on the early relationship between infant and mother. Most new mothers will find that this issue has given rise to numerous opinions from a multitude of diverse sources, from watchful-eyed grandparents and in-laws to biologists, anthropologists, and psychologists. Infant feeding is almost always a focal chapter in every manual of child rearing. With such a barrage of advice, the issue often becomes a difficult one for the mother to resolve.

Until the 1930s, the approximate time when formula feeding was perfected, there was no really safe and reliable substitute for breast milk, although a woman might hire a wet nurse (a woman who breast-feeds and cares for an infant not her own) rather than nurse the baby herself. Since then, most mothers have had a choice—and a chance to weigh the supporting evidence for each alternative. The proponents of breastfeeding, supported by an international organization called La Leche League (*leche* is the Spanish word for milk), maintain that this approach promotes close physical and psychological bonding between mothers and infants. League members assert that nursing is the "natural" way to nourish an infant and that it prevents most feeding problems, as well as constipation and some allergic reactions. It is also argued that breast-fed babies have fewer serious illnesses, including respiratory and gastrointestinal illnesses. Also, breast milk may contain antibodies to many of the infectious organisms newborns are exposed to.

Many nursing mothers report a calm inner peace during feeding times. Some researchers believe that breastfeeding enhances attachment by providing the opportunity for frequent, direct skin contact between the newborn and the mother (see ATTACHMENT, EARLY PARENT-INFANT). It is also generally accepted that breastfeeding inhibits the mother's menstrual cycle, as well as the mood swings associated with menstruation. The apparent lack of irritability, tension, and restlessness, frequently related to the menstrual cycle, may enable nursing mothers to respond to the needs of the baby in a more relaxed and calm manner.

Bottle feeding is not without its share of support. For example, bottle feeding allows the mother greater mobility and freedom after birth. Most mothers cannot rejoin the labor force within a relatively short period of time unless they can rely on formula feedings for their babies. Bottle feeding also enables the father to feed his child and allows the mother to spend more time with her other children, who may resent the continual contact that the breastfed baby receives. In addition, some mothers find nursing physically annoying or painful, while others simply do not like the practice or are embarrassed by it, particularly in the presence of others. In recent years, some investigators have noted a steady decline in breastfeeding. Among the reasons cited for this decrease include breastfeeding no longer being considered "fashionable"; less emphasis on the promotion of breastfeeding in the popular media; and infant formula being marketed aggressively.

Obviously, the issue of the breast or the bottle is a controversial one, making the decision all the more difficult for the mother. However, there are merits attached to each, and this may relieve a sense of guilt for choosing one approach over the other. How to feed the infant is an individual affair that must be carefully weighed. What is probably more critical is the manner in which the mother interacts with the infant during feedings. Her warmth, care, and attention—as well as the trust that she conveys while meeting life's most basic need—may determine her success in this area, rather than the approach chosen. (See INFANCY AND TODDLERHOOD, DEVELOPMENT OF TRUST DURING; PSYCHOSOCIAL DEVELOPMENT.)

Further Reading. Bigner, Jerry J. (1994). *Parent-child relations: An introduction to parenting* (4th Ed.). New York: Macmillan; Grossman, Lindsey K., Christina Harter, and Carol Hasbrouck. (1990). Testing mothers' knowledge of breastfeeding: Instrument development and implementation and correlation with infant feeding decision. *Journal of Pediatric and Perinatal Nutrition, 2,* 43–64; Lamb, Michael E., and Marc H. Bornstein. (1987). *Development in infancy.* New York: Random House.

INFANT TEMPERAMENT. See NEWBORN.

INFATUATION. See LOVE, INFATUATION COMPARED TO.

INFERTILITY. Infertility is the inability to achieve a pregnancy after at least one year of regular, unprotected intercourse. It is estimated that about 15 percent of the population—approximately one in seven couples—is infertile at any given time. However, patience is sometimes the answer for many of these couples. Pregnancy statistics tell us that for normal women who are not using birth control and are sexually active, 25 percent will be pregnant in the first month, 63 percent will be in six months, and 80 percent will be in one year. An additional 5 to 10 percent will become pregnant the following year.

About 40 percent of infertility problems can be traced to the male, 40 percent to the female, and 20 percent of the time, couples share the problem of infertility and the reasons often go unknown. Among the more common causes of male infertility are poor sperm quality, low sperm count, and poor sperm motility, or movement. One of the causes of decreased sperm number and motility is varicocele, a condition that causes dilation of veins near the testicles. Other causes of decreased sperm number might include chronic fatigue and illness; poor nutrition; excessive use of caffeine, tobacco, or marijuana; too-frequent intercourse; hot spas or saunas; nervous stress; fear of impotence; certain medications and treatments such as radiation to the testes; and possibly tight underwear and pants.

The most common causes of female infertility are the blockage of fallopian tubes and the failure to ovulate. A number of causes may account for blockage, including tubal scarring from pelvic infections. Growing numbers of women develop pelvic inflammatory disease when sexually transmitted diseases such as chlamydia spread into the uterus and fallopian tubes, in the process affecting a woman's ability to conceive (see SEXUALLY TRANSMITTED DISEASES, CATEGORIES OF). Ovulatory defects include the inability of an ovary to develop or to release an egg or of the body to produce the proper amount or sequence of hormones. Another cause of infertility is the failure of the cervix at midcycle to secrete cervical mucus, a necessity for sperm survival. Or the cervix may produce abnormal amounts of mucus, which impedes the movement of sperm.

Infertility can be related to aging processes. Women under age 25 have about a 7 percent chance of being infertile, but by the age of 40, one out of every three females is unable to have a child. A woman in her thirties does not have many fertile years left. Male infertility is also partly determined by age; a man of 50 generally has a lower sperm count than a man of 20, although the natural decrease in his sperm count may not prevent him from having children if enough of his remaining sperm are healthy.

Other causes of infertility include sexual dysfunction, inappropriate timing of intercourse, and immunological factors. Also, stressful lifestyles, personal problems, vocational pressures, and general mental health may have physical effects on both male and female. Environmental conditions such as exposure to pollutants such as pesticides or work hazards are other considerations.

Infertile couples often face psychological pressures in their efforts to conceive. For example, depression, anxiety, anger, and guilt are common reactions. Because of this, the support of family and friends can be very beneficial to the infertile couple. In addition, other couples who have experienced infertility can provide beneficial support. One such self-help group is RESOLVE, a national organization offering counseling, referral, and support services to infertile couples. Through this group, infertile couples are able to meet and discuss their concerns with others who share their experience, including the traumatic physical, psychological, social, and relational effects of infertility.

Further Reading. Greil, Arthur L. (1991). *Not yet pregnant: Infertile couples in contemporary America.* New Brunswick, NJ: Rutgers University Press; Mahlstedt, Patricia P. (1987). The crisis of infertility: An opportunity for growth. In Gerald R. Weeks and Larry Hof (Eds.), *Integrating sex and marital therapy: A clinical guide.* New York: Brunner/Mazel; Pepe, Margaret, and T. Jean Byrne. (1991). Women's perceptions of immediate and long-term effects of failed infertility treatment on marital and sexual satisfaction. *Family Relations, 40,* 303–309.

INFERTILITY, INTERVENTION FOR. Many couples have problems conceiving and bearing a child, but today a number of medical interventions exist. The initial intervention for infertility usually includes a history and physical examination of both partners. The woman is often asked to chart her basal body temperature so that the physician can assess the regularity of her menstrual cycle, when she is ovulating, and the optimum time for the couple to have intercourse. The man may also be instructed to abstain from sexual activity for several days before the woman's fertile period is expected, in the hope that his sperm count will rise. Sometimes special drugs are administered to the woman to induce ovulation.

For men, fertility is tested with a semen analysis, which assesses the number, quality, and motility of sperm. Should infertility be traced to the male, surgery might be in order to repair blockage in the testicles, such as varicocele or blocked sperm ducts. Other forms of intervention might include the medical management of hormonal abnormalities or infections. Hormone therapy for men has not consistently demonstrated an increase in sperm production and is still considered largely experimental.

For women, blood and urine tests are given to determine estrogen, gonadotrophin, and progesterone levels, and cervical mucus tests are used to assess whether sperm can penetrate and survive within the cervix. A physician might use microsurgical techniques to assess the reproductive system and any disease or blockage. Microsurgery is sometimes employed to correct blocked fallopian tubes, and laser surgery has recently been used to treat endometriosis.

In about 75 percent of infertility cases, the aforementioned procedures prove successful. Should such measures be unsuccessful, hope lies in several sophisticated reproductive technologies: in-vitro fertilization, artificial insemination, surrogate motherhood, and embryo transfer. The following is a brief summary of these technologies.

In-vitro fertilization. In in-vitro fertilization, sometimes referred to as test-tube fertilization, one or more ova are surgically removed from the mother, combined with the father's sperm, and placed into the uterus. The procedure is usually employed when the woman's fallopian tubes are blocked or diseased. Women with normal menstrual cycles and men with normal sperm counts are considered good candidates for this procedure, which is one of the most common forms of reproductive technology.

Although the pioneer successes with in-vitro fertilization used the woman's natural menstrual cycle for the procedure, clinics today experience higher success rates by hormonally stimulating ovulation with fertility drugs and "harvesting" three to five eggs rather than just one naturally produced egg. When the eggs are mature, they are removed from the woman's body by a surgical technique called laparoscopy. In this technique, under general anesthesia, a small incision is made adjacent to the navel and a small tubelike scope is inserted, enabling the physician to see inside. The eggs are retrieved with a hollow needle and placed in a petri dish, where they are allowed to mature for several hours before they are fertilized with the father's sperm. The fertilized eggs are then placed in an incubator. About 48 hours later, when each egg has gone through the cell divisions necessary to produce a blastocyst, several are implanted in the woman's uterus.

Variations of in-vitro fertilization have been developed in recent years. For example, in *gamete intrafallopian transfer,* ova are gathered in much the same way as that just described and mixed with the father's sperm. Then, both ova and sperm are placed into one or both fallopian tubes, the normal site of fertilization. Should fertilization occur, the zygote then travels to the uterus, where prenatal development proceeds. Another technique is *zygote intrafallopian transfer.* Here, ova are retrieved and mixed with the father's sperm as in in-vitro fertilization. However, the zygote is transferred back to the woman's body at a much earlier stage of cell division and is placed in the fallopian tube.

Artificial insemination. Artificial insemination involves artificially injecting sperm (fresh or frozen) into a woman's vagina, either on or near the cervix, at the time of ovulation. There are three types of artificial insemination. One type uses sperm from the husband, often when his sperm count is low or the wife has one of the earlier-mentioned cervical mucus problems. When the husband's sperm count is too low, artificial insemination by donor is practiced, which utilizes sperm from an unrelated, usually anonymous donor. The donor is screened and matched as closely to the husband as possible for such characteristics as ethnic background, stature, complexion, and blood type. Special screening is also given to prevent genetic defects, sexually transmitted diseases, and other potential problems. A third type combines a mixture of sperm from a man who has a low sperm count and sperm from an unrelated donor. In this case, there can be some hope that the resulting child may be the husband's.

Surrogate motherhood. Surrogate motherhood occurs when the father is fertile but the mother is unable to carry the child to term. In the technique, which is a variation of artificial insemination, a chosen surrogate mother is artificially inseminated with the husband's sperm. The surrogate mother carries and bears the child, which is then given back to the couple. The surrogacy center handles the screening of candidates, arranges medical, legal, and psychological services, and offers a standard contract to govern the transaction.

Embryo transfer. Somewhat related to surrogate motherhood is embryo transfer, although it is much more experimental. Infertile women are usually the candidates for this technique, which involves impregnating another woman with the father's sperm. After several days, the fertilized ovum is removed from her uterus and placed within the wife's uterus, which has been hormonally prepared to accept it. This is done when the menstrual cycle of the wife indicates that she is prepared to accept a pregnancy. In some instances, the embryo is frozen and implanted at a later time.

Without question, these reproductive technologies represent important medical breakthroughs. However, it must be mentioned that along with critical acclaim has come considerable controversy, Many object to such technologies on the basis of religious, moral, or ethical principles. Compounding the problem is that clear-cut or comprehensive laws regarding reproductive technologies, particularly the surrogate motherhood arrangement, are lacking.

Experts believe that at a minimum, reproductive technologies have radically circumvented the traditional transition to parenthood. They create a wide range of options in fertility and reproduction that beg to be studied. For example, it is now technically possible for a child to have three mothers: a genetic mother, who provides the egg; a bearing mother, who carries the fetus and bears the child; and a rearing mother. How can we weigh genetic contributions, the experience of childbearing, and the years of child rearing? Is motherhood on the verge of being redefined? Obviously, we will not find the answers to such questions overnight. However, the complex issues raised by such questions must nonetheless be addressed.

Further Reading. Isaacs, Stephen, and Renee J. Holt. (1987). Redefining procreation: Facing the issues. *Population Bulletin, 42,* 1–37; Laursen, Niels H., and Colette Bouchez. (1991). *Getting pregnant: What couples need to know right now.* New York: Fawcett; Schwartz, Lita L. (1991). *Alternatives to infertility: Is surrogacy the answer?* New York: Brunner/Mazel.

INSTITUTIONAL CARE, ELDERLY. Institutional care for the elderly refers to a broad range of facilities and services designed to enhance the quality of life for older adults, including housing, personal care, and medical needs. Although only 5 percent of elderly people 65 years of age and older are institutionalized at any one time, the population of institutional care facilities is disproportionately old, in many cases over age 80. Gender differences in life expectancy also create variations in institutionalization. For example, more women than men enter institutional care facilities, and among them, more women than men have resided in one for five years or more.

It is incorrect to think that all institutional care facilities for elderly people are the same. On the contrary, several different categories of care exist, depending on the functional status and needs of the elderly person. These include the skilled-nursing, intermediate-care, residential-care, and adult day-care facilities.

In a *skilled-nursing facility,* medical care is available to residents on a full-time basis. Because of this, the skilled-nursing facility is suited for aged persons with chronic illnesses such as stroke, heart disease, or rheumatism. Aged persons who are bedridden or require frequent medications, catheterizations, or orthopedic care also tend to be skilled-nursing facility residents.

The emphasis of the *intermediate-care facility* is more on personal care and less on medical assistance. The typical resident does not have a serious illness nor is bedridden. Rather, she or he often needs assistance in daily routines and activities, such as eating, dressing, or walking. The intermediate-care and skilled-nursing facilities constitute most of the institutional care arrangements in the United States.

The *residential-care facility* is designed for independent elderly persons who require a safe and sheltered environment in which to live. The focus of this facility tends to be on professional services, such as housekeeping and laundering, as well as any other aspect of domestic life warranting intervention and assistance.

Finally, in the *adult day-care facility,* elderly persons maintain their own residences but receive medical support and assistance in a specially designated center. Beyond medical care, the adult day-care facility offers a wide range of programming, including meals, traveling, exercise, and social activities. Some of the centers offer day-care supervision to children as well, creating a unique blend of young and old. Many spokespersons feel that such a mixture of ages is a positive arrangement that enables the young to better understand the old, and vice versa.

There are many good institutional care facilities, and there are many benefits of such kinds of care, including the availability of immediate health care in time of crisis, companionship, regular nutritious meals, and organized activities. But for many elderly residents, adjusting to institutional care may pose problems. For example, many view institutional care in a very negative light. Such perceptions originate partly from a desire to remain in familiar surroundings and near relatives and friends. Most negative feelings toward institutionalization, however, are because of a perceived loss of independence and because of a belief that placement in an institutional care facility represents formal proof that death is near. Many of the aged also have a fear that once placed in institutional care, they will be rejected and forgotten by their children.

Many elderly residents react negatively to the frequent impersonalization of institutional care. Many are uncomfortable with the loss of privacy, and others resent the limited individual treatment accorded by staff members. Research also shows that perceived loss of control is an important concern among many elderly residents. Many researchers have found that the loss of perceived control promotes declines in physical and psychological status. For many, a sense of learned helplessness unfolds, a condition creating cognitive, affective, and functional deficits. There is also the risk of excess disability and possibly premature death.

In the midst of such impersonalization and uncertainty, many elderly residents develop what some researchers call *institutionalism*. Essentially, this is a psychological state brought about by a depersonalized environment. Persons afflicted with institutionalism often develop automatic behaviors, expressionless faces, and general apathy. They become disinterested in their personal appearance and suffer from a deterioration of morale. Social relationships for many become nonexistent. In those institutional care facilities where the identity, interests, and strengths of the resident are not assessed and developed, degrees of institutionalism are likely to surface.

Depersonalized institutional care environments have created a fair amount of criticism in recent years. Other criticism is leveled at programming in general, including limited intellectual stimulation of the residents. In short, many feel that elderly people simply have nothing to do in many institutions. There are also many institutional care facilities in the nation that are substandard, in some instances failing to provide minimal conditions for humane treatment.

Numerous recommendations have been made to upgrade institutional care facilities and particularly to improve the psychological and social climate. Attempts must be made to promote the growth of new relationships to take the place of those lost in the process of growing old or sick. Social integration of long-term-care residents is very important, particularly if social isolation and detachment are to be avoided. Residents should participate as much as possible in establishing the ground rules for their living situations. Achieving a sense of mastery and control is crucial to preserving a resident's self-concept and identity. Physical structuring of space should offer freedom and safety as well as privacy. Finally, regular interpersonal contacts with the residents are critical as the transition to the institutional care facility is made. This conveys to residents that they are not alone and isolated, are not discarded, and that they are still valued.

Further Reading. Forrest, Mary B., Christopher B. Forrest, and Richard Forrest. (1990). *Nursing homes: The complete guide.* New York: Facts on File; Savishinsky, Joel S. (1991). *The ends of time: Life and work in a nursing home.* New York: Bergin and Garvey; Schmidt, Mary G. (1990). *Negotiating a good old age: Challenges of residential living in late life.* San Francisco: Jossey-Bass.

INSTITUTIONALISM. See INSTITUTIONAL CARE, ELDERLY.

INTERACTION, STYLES OF WITHIN RELATIONSHIPS. The styles of interaction that exist within relationships are often identified as being symmetrical or complementary. Symmetrical and complementary styles of interaction result from the way partners behave with each other in a given context. Neither style is in and by itself "good" or "bad," or "normal" or "abnormal"; rather, these two styles simply refer to modes of communication interchanges.

Both styles have important functions, and both are usually present in the same relationship, although they do alternate and operate in different areas.

Symmetrical styles of interaction are characterized by equality and the minimization of difference, such as when two people share housekeeping chores. In symmetrical styles, partners usually create acceptance for one another, which in turn leads to the promotion of mutual respect and trust. Put another way, symmetrical relationships are characterized by similarity and balance.

Complementary styles of interaction, on the other hand, entail the maximization of difference, such as when one partner is dominant and the other is submissive. In complementary styles, two different positions exist, but in ways that fit together. One partner often occupies what can be described as the superior or primary position, while the other occupies a correspondingly inferior position. A complementary relationship may be established by the cultural or social context, or it may be the idiosyncratic relationship style of a couple. In either instance, it is important to stress the interlocking nature of the dyad, in which dissimilar but fitted behaviors complement each other.

Further Reading. Nichols, Michael P. (1984). *Family therapy: Concepts and methods.* New York: Gardner Press; Sieburg, Evelyn. (1985). *Family communication: An integrated systems approach.* New York: Gardner Press.

INTERFAITH MARRIAGE. An interfaith marriage exists when partners are of a different religion from one another. It is estimated that 15 to 20 percent of all marriages are of the interfaith variety. As far as intermarriages in general are concerned, interfaith marriages are more common than interracial marriages. This is probably because of a decline in religious prejudice over the years and more societal tolerance of ethnic and cultural differences. Also, interfaith marriages, unlike interracial marriages, present no visible signs of intermarriage, such as skin color.

Efforts to assess the stability of interfaith marriages have yielded mixed findings. Some researchers have found that couples of the same denominational affiliation are more apt to have stable marriages than those whose religions are different. However, other investigators have found minimal, if any, differences in the marital happiness of homogamous couples when compared to interfaith unions. There is also no support for the view that interfaith marriages have negative effects on children, including a secularization effect.

Interestingly, interfaith marriages have unique demographic variations. For instance, in New York, where there are large Catholic and Jewish populations, there is a high incidence of Catholic-Jewish marriages. In Iowa, Minnesota, and Pennsylvania, where the religious makeup is about fifty-fifty Catholic and Lutheran, a higher-than-average rate of intermarriage between these two faiths exists.

Although they do not encourage interfaith marriages, there is at present a greater acceptance of them by the clergy. In some states, such as Louisiana, Mississippi, New York, and California, an agreement exists between the Roman

Catholic and Episcopal churches dispensing with the requirement of obtaining written permission from a bishop before allowing an interfaith couple to be married in the church. The agreement also encourages the couple to continue worship in their respective faiths. A number of congregations have also devised activities and programs to reach out to intermarried couples. For example, many synagogues now offer workshops on Jewish holidays and the life cycle. The Roman Catholic church also offers a marriage-preparation course that includes special counseling for intermarried couples.

Further Reading. Glenn, Norval D. (1982). Interreligious marriage in the United States: Patterns and recent trends. *Journal of Marriage and the Family, 44,* 555–566; Ortega, Suzanne T., Hugh P. Whitt, and J. Allen William, Jr. (1988). Religious homogamy and marital happiness. *Journal of Family Issues, 9,* 224–239; Petersen, Larry R. (1986). Interfaith marriage and religious commitment among Catholics. *Journal of Marriage and the Family, 48,* 725–735.

INTERPERSONAL ATTRACTION, PHYSICAL APPEARANCE AND.

The manner in which we are attracted to others is usually influenced by the physical qualities of the person. Because physical attractiveness typically rests in the eyes of the beholder, variations will always exist in perceptions of beauty. Additionally, what one culture regards as physically attractive may not be considered attractive in another. For example, physical attractiveness may include extensive facial tatooing (Danakil), joined eyebrows (Syrians), absence of eyebrows and eyelashes (Mongo), large, pendulous breasts (Ganda), and crossed eyes (Mayans).

Many societies share certain similarities as far as physical attractiveness is concerned. For example, in virtually every society, some form of good grooming prevails, and the individual who does not follow the convention is considered unattractive. Poor complexion and excessive acne are almost always considered negative qualities. Good teeth, clear eyes, and a firm gait, on the other hand, appear to have cross-cultural appeal.

In many societies, men prefer women with a broad pelvis and wide hips. Mangaian men, for example, consider fat desirable, particularly in the breasts, hips, buttocks, and legs. A woman's slender waist, on the other hand, is a minority cross-cultural preference among males. The Dobuans and the Tongans, especially, consider obesity in either sex to be disgusting. For women the world over, male attractiveness is often associated with social status, skills, bravery, prowess, and similar qualities. Among the Toda of India, women reportedly find men especially attractive who are good at catching buffalo at funerals, a prestigious ritual act. Among women of ancient Oriental high cultures, a man's dignity and wealth were usually preferred over his strength and athletic ability.

Depending on the society consulted, the body has often been altered in a way to make it conform to aesthetic or erotic ideals. The piercing or perforation of ears, noses, and lips is quite common. Many women in the Oubangui-Chari region of Africa, particularly the Sara, once inserted large plates or discs inside the lower lip. Neck stretching has been practiced by Padaung women of Burma with the aid of coiled brass neck rings. In other cultures, teeth have been blackened, reddened, knocked out, dug out, filed, chipped, and drilled (and filled with decorative objects). Foot binding was practiced by upper-class Chinese women from the eleventh century A.D. until the twentieth century. Decorating the skin in some way also knows wide cross-cultural variation, including tattooing, painting, cutting, and, less frequently, burning. Modifications of male and female genitals have also been practiced for centuries.

Finally, it should be recognized that efforts to enhance physical attractiveness are rooted in antiquity. Archaeologists have found evidence of Egyptian perfumeries and beauty parlors dating to 4000 B.C. and makeup paraphernalia that dates to 6000 B.C. The ancient Egyptians preferred green eye shadow, which was topped with a glitter made from crushing the iridescent carapaces of certain beetles; kohl eyeliner and mascara; black lipstick; red rouge; and fingers and feet stained red with henna. Many Egyptian women shaved their eyebrows and drew in false ones.

Roman men liked cosmetics, and commanders often had their hair coiffed and perfumed and their nails lacquered before they went into battle. A second-century Roman physician invented cold cream, whose formula has changed little since then. It may also be remembered from the Old Testament that Queen Jezebel "painted her face" before embarking on her wicked ways, a fashion she learned from the upper class Phoenicians around 850 B.C. In the eighteenth century, some women were willing to eat "arsenic complexion wafers" to make their skin whiter, which worked by poisoning the hemoglobin in the blood so that they developed a fragile, lunar whiteness.

Further Reading. Ackerman, Diane. (1990). *A natural history of the senses.* New York: Random House; Gregersen, Edgar. (1983). *Sexual practices.* New York: Franklin Watts; Turner, Jeffrey S., and Laurna Rubinson. (1993). *Contemporary human sexuality.* Englewood Cliffs, NJ: Prentice Hall.

INTERRACIAL MARRIAGE. An interracial marriage exists when partners are of a different race from one another. *Miscegenation* is the technical name given to interracial marriages. As late as 1966, 17 states had formal prohibitions against one or more forms of interracial marriage. The U.S. Supreme Court overturned the 16 existing state antimiscegenation statutes (laws prohibiting mixed marriage) with a decision rendered June 12, 1967. At one point or another, 40 of the 50 states have had laws that prohibited blacks from intermarrying with whites. Pennsylvania, in 1780, was the first state to repeal its antimiscegenation law, while Indiana and Wyoming took this action as recently as 1965.

Interracial marriages are not widespread in the United States. They amounted to about 2 percent of all marriages in 1992. Contrary to popular belief, most interracial marriages do not occur between blacks and whites. Rather, intermarriages between Native American women and white men, Japanese-American women and white men, and Filipino-American women and white men are the most common. In 1992, marriages between blacks and whites represented only 0.5 percent of the total number of married couples.

Much like the research focusing on interfaith marriages, studies exploring the stability of interracial marriages and the adjustment of children have produced uneven findings. While some researchers have found a higher rate of divorce among interracial marriages, it should be recognized that other factors beyond race converge to create marital dissolution: age, educational level, and religious beliefs, to name but a few. Similarly, the adjustment of children transcends skin color and depends more on such factors as the quality of the parent-child relationship.

Further Reading. Schoen, Robert, and Barbara Thomas. (1990). Religious intermarriage in Switzerland, 1969–72 and 1979–82. *European Journal of Population, 6,* 359–376; Spickard, Paul R. (1989). *Mixed blood: Intermarriage and ethnic identity in twentieth-century America.* Madison: University of Wisconsin Press; Wilson, Barbara F. (1984). The marriage melting pot. *American Demographics, 12,* 34–37.

INTIMATE RELATIONSHIP. An intimate relationship is a reciprocal process in which two people become close with one another and discover the innermost, subjective aspects of each other's lives. An intimate relationship involves the mutual exchange of experiences in such a way that a further understanding of oneself and one's partner is achieved. Intimate relationships exist in a variety of contexts, such as a deep friendship or love relationship, and offer partners social support, a sense of belongingness, and security.

True intimacy requires *self-disclosure,* the process by which individuals let themselves be known by others. Self-disclosure involves decisions about whether to communicate one's thoughts, feelings, or past experiences to another person; at what level of intimacy to reveal personal information; and the appropriate time, place, and target person for disclosure. As a relationship progresses to more intimate levels, partners generally disclose more information about themselves and at a more personal level.

Individuals can disclose themselves through a number of different communication channels. Verbal self-disclosure uses words to let others know about oneself. Self-disclosure can also take place through body language or by one's tone of voice. The manner in which one gestures or chooses to emphasize words also says something about the person. Finally, persons disclose themselves through their actions.

It is generally recognized that for most, the capacity to be intimate with others matures during young adulthood. According to noted psychoanalyst Erik Erikson, the capacity to be intimate with others during young adulthood is an important milestone in psychosocial development. Prior to young adulthood, the individual was in the midst of an identity crisis, a struggle that reached its peak during adolescence. Erikson stressed the idea that now as a young adult, the individual is motivated to fuse this newly established identity with that of others.

In short, the young adult has developed the psychosocial capacities to give and receive intimacy. (See PSYCHOSOCIAL DEVELOPMENT.)

Although most young adults seek to gratify the need for intimacy through marriage, it is important to stress that intimate relationships other than sexual ones are possible. Individuals may develop strong bonds of intimacy in friendships that offer, among other features, mutuality, trust, empathy, and reciprocity. Intimate relationships may easily develop out of a capacity to share with and understand others. The psychologically and socially mature adult is capable of effectively communicating with others, being sensitive to another person's needs, and, in general, exhibiting tolerance toward humankind. The growth of friendship, love, and devotion is much more prominent among mature people than among the more immature. (See ADULTHOOD, FRIENDSHIPS DURING.)

Further Reading. Chelune, Gordon J., Joan T. Robison, and Martin J. Kommor. (1984). A cognitive interactional model of intimate relationships. In Valerian J. Derlega (Ed.), *Communication, intimacy, and close relationships.* New York: Academic Press; Derlega, Valerian J. (1984). Self-disclosure and intimate relationships. In Valerian J. Derlega (Ed.), *Communication, intimacy, and close relationships.* New York: Academic Press; Duck, Steve. (1992). *Human relationships* (2nd Ed.). Newbury Park, CA: Sage.

INTIMATE RELATIONSHIP, CONFLICT WITHIN. Intimate relationships, like other forms of human interaction, experience their share of conflict and disagreement. Broadly defined, a conflict is a situation that occurs whenever the actions of one person interfere with the actions of another. Communication participants can come into conflict over practically any kind of issue, although not all experience friction or turbulence in the same areas and at the same levels of intensity.

Within the realm of intimate relationships, such as spousal or parent-child relationships, conflict is inevitable for several reasons. For example, having more time together under the same roof allows for more opportunities for conflicts to take place. Also, most family members are intensely involved with one another and have diverse activities, which in turn offer more opportunities for conflicts. In addition, spouses as partners or parents assume a greater right to control or influence each other as well as other family members. Finally, roles may be assigned to family members on the basis of age or sex or other physical characteristics instead of interests or abilities. This in itself may lead to conflict.

It is a myth that most couples do not engage in conflict. Not having any conflict whatsoever is rare and even destructive, particularly since it can promote boredom and even depression. When couples deal with conflict in a constructive fashion, they can strengthen their relationship. In this sense, a couple can grow together more through adversity than through placidity.

Conflicts typically begin with some sort of precipitating event, such as stress, annoyance, or criticism. Once the conflict has surfaced, it can either be constructively negotiated and resolved, or it can escalate and intensify. Should the latter course of action be chosen, intensely angry fighting usually results. Power strategies such as the use of threat and coercion, along with such manipulation techniques as blame, often are employed when conflicts intensify. Before rational problem solving occurs, a conciliatory act (e.g., admitting at least partial ownership of the problem or pledging a willingness to work toward a remedy) is usually needed to reduce negative feelings. Conciliatory gestures from one partner are usually followed by reciprocity from the other.

The manner in which couples deal with conflict influences the overall stability of the relationship. The inability to deal with conflict constructively is a potent force in dampening relational satisfaction. Moreover, when conflict occurs, it often tends to be repeated. Experts stress that it is therefore important to learn how to handle conflict appropriately. It is important for couples to fight fair and constructively deal with conflict and anger. They need to demonstrate mutual respect and agree to cooperate when conflict surfaces. Moreover, couples need to engage in mutual decision making. That is, once the problem is confronted and the issues become clear, both partners support an atmosphere of give-and-take and compromise. When this is accomplished, power and responsibility are shared equally, and cooperation replaces resistance within the relationship.

Further Reading. Dinkmeyer, Donald, and Jon Carlson. (1984). *Time for a better marriage.* Circle Pines, MN: American Guidance Service; Peterson, Donald R. (1983). Conflict. In Harold H. Kelley (Ed.), *Close relationships.* New York: Freeman.

INTIMATE RELATIONSHIP, DEVELOPMENT OF. The manner in which intimate relationships begin, continue, intensify, or decline and terminate has long attracted the attention of researchers. One of the most extensive and comprehensive models of relationship development has been proposed by researcher George Levinger. The strength of Levinger's theory is that it embraces the relatively broad, often diffuse, changes over time in a relationship that emerge from personal, environmental, and relational factors. The following is an overview of the stages that he proposes.

Acquaintance stage. This stage begins when one person tries to meet another either directly or through mutual friends or others. Becoming acquainted with another person is influenced by physical, social, and psychological dimensions. The physical environment—for example, an urban or rural setting or the density and size of a community—may largely determine whom a person encounters and continues to see. Our social environment, or culture, shapes the mate-selection process with a wide range of values, beliefs, and norms. Our personalities and those of the people we meet affect the way we initiate and maintain relationships with others.

Initial impressions often govern subsequent interaction. A person's first impressions are based both on the potential partner's obvious characteristics, such as physical appearance or perceived competence, and on one's own values, goals, or moods. Deciding how to approach another person and what to say is usually challenging, particularly if shyness creates a barrier. Some researchers have found that as a general rule, the female covertly initiates the courtship sequence by sending nonverbal signals of availability and interest to the male; the male then opens dialogue in a presumably promising atmosphere. Certain research indicates that females employ a variety of nonverbal behaviors to show their interest in potential partners: smiling, short and long gazes, hair flipping, or downward glances. When her interest intensifies, the female tends to rely on such behaviors as leaning close, nodding, smiling, and laughing.

Initial interactions enable a couple to explore the possibilities for mutual enjoyment. If either person finds the time spent together unrewarding, he or she will probably break off the relationship, but if things go well, the couple will continue to see one another. As time goes on, their interactions will undergo transformations.

Buildup stage. During this stage, partners move from merely knowing each other to caring for each other. In this stage, both partners test their compatibility. Usually, each finds it easy to further the other's goals, and both look forward to rewarding future interactions. The couple's interdependence grows not only with the increased dating frequency but with the emotional connectedness that such dating brings.

It is during the buildup stage that *filtering agents* begin to exert their influence. Filtering agents shape the course of mate selection and serve to narrow down the field of eligibles. For example, individuals tend to select partners whose physical attractiveness roughly matches their own, and persons tend to associate with those having something in common, such as similar education or age. People also tend to be attracted to those who provide the greatest relational rewards and the fewest number of trade-offs or sacrifices. (See FILTERING AGENTS, IMPACT OF ON INTIMATE RELATIONSHIPS.)

Continuation stage. The continuation stage follows a mutual commitment to a long-term relationship. Partners have removed themselves from the interpersonal marketplace and have agreed to restrict their closest intimacies to the other. This stage is characterized by the consolidation of the relationship in a relatively durable midstage, marked by marriage in many couples.

During earlier stages, the relationship was characterized by the couple's experience of ambiguity, novelty, and arousal. Here the relationship reflects familiarity, predictability, and the reduction of emotional and cognitive tension. The more stable a relationship is, the less will be the partners' ambivalence or their self-consciousness.

Mutual trust is essential to the continuation of a healthy relationship. Trust embodies confidence in one's mate, including a realization that a partner will not hurt or manipulate within the relationship. Furthermore, it is characteristic of high levels of trust that there is no concern whatsoever about equality, about sharing material goods, services, or responsibilities. Partners simply take what they need spontaneously, knowing that they will not in any way be exploited by a greedy mate. It is characteristic of relationships of low trust that there is preoccupation with sharing equally. In fact, getting a "fair share" or equal share takes precedence over needs and desires.

An important feature of trust is openness. Openness mainly involves discussion of the emotionally laden "private" areas of a person's life. This may be very threatening indeed. Openness precludes pretense and the constrictive, censoring effects of affectation and lack of communication. Openness also involves nonjudgmental receiving and giving of information, opinions, and the like. Open giving and receiving are perhaps the most potent and important form of human giving. Giving is also a crucial part of receiving, since the privilege of giving is so therapeutic to the person doing the extending. Openness also means being in a condition to receive other people's messages and to respond to them. These messages convey ideas, thoughts, opinions, values, and, above all, moods and feelings without pride or prejudice of any kind. When this happens, there is no pretense between partners.

Deterioration stage. Of course, not all relationships deteriorate. However, of those that do, there are many signals and signs of impending collapse. For example, feelings of discontent and dissatisfaction begin to surface, and partners feel rejected and misunderstood. Usually, dissatisfied couples avoid self-disclosure of their feelings or problems. Partners no longer reinforce and support one another, but rather undermine each other's self-esteem through betrayals. A partner's actions, or even her or his mere presence, may interfere with the other's plans to carry out personal plans or activities. As the downward spiral continues, partners inevitably experience a loss of affection, openness, trust, enjoyment, and vitality in their relationship.

Termination stage. This stage is marked by the ending of the relationship. At this time, ties to one's partner are severed and wounds need to be healed. Also, new relationships need to replace old ones. The emotional impact of the termination stage varies widely among people. However, an important determinant is the degree to which a person's plans and behaviors involved the partner. The disruptiveness of the separation is often determined by the extent of such connections.

Further Reading. Levinger, George. (1977). Reviewing the close relationship. In George Levinger and Harold L. Raush (Eds.). *Close relationships.* Amherst: University of Massachusetts Press; Levinger, George. (1983). Development and change in close relationships. In Harold H. Kelley (Ed.), *Close relationships.* New York: Freeman.

IRELAND, LIFESPAN RELATIONSHIPS IN. Ireland is a small, independent nation in northwestern Europe. Officially called the Republic of Ireland, it occupies the southwestern five-sixths of the island of Ireland, one of the two main British Isles. The northeastern sixth of the island makes up Northern Ireland, which is part of the United Kingdom. Ireland is divided into 26 counties and has a population of about 3.5 million. Dublin, the capital of Ireland, and Cork, the second-largest city, account for about 25 percent of Ireland's total population.

Most of the Irish people are descendants of settlers from centuries ago, including Celts, Vikings, Normans, and Englishmen. About 95 percent of the population is Roman Catholic, unlike neighboring Northern Ireland, where only one-third of the population is Catholic. Most of the remainder in Ireland is Anglican or Protestant. English is the predominant language, although some residents speak Gaelic or Irish. About one-half of the population resides in cities and towns, while the rest live on farms and rural villages. In recent years, Ireland has experienced a drift of the population toward its cities.

Tradition and custom characterize Irish marriage and family life, and the influence of the church is apparent in many areas. Dating begins during adolescence, and marriage is a common lifestyle. In recent years, because more couples are delaying marriage, the average age of first marriage in Ireland has been rising and is now about 25 years for women and 26 for men. While the pursuit of educational and career goals is an important reason for the delay in first marriages, the living arrangements of young people prior to marriage are also influential factors. Ireland tends to have a high percentage of men and women between the ages of 20 and 24 who choose to live with their parents. While many young adults in other European nations choose more independent living arrangements, their Irish counterparts are less likely to leave home at this time.

A number of factors help explain such living arrangements. Financial considerations are particularly important: farmland and jobs are often scarce, and few young people can afford to marry and raise children. In some instances, living with one's parents is a way of maintaining the family estate. The limited availability of cheap rental housing looms as another influential factor. Also, some researchers maintain that compared to other European nations, the Irish place less of an emphasis on individualism, which might impact on the desire for more independent living arrangements. Regarding the latter, cohabitation is not widespread in Ireland. Compared to nations such as Sweden and Denmark, where cohabitation represents an extremely popular lifestyle, only a handful of Irish choose to live together outside of marriage.

Irish marriages are patriarchal in structure and function, and household activities reflect traditional gender roles. The husband's role is to be a good provider and the primary wage earner. He is also the final authority on household matters and the disciplinarian. The wife, on the other hand, tends to household duties and takes care of the children. She is usually the one who manages the budget, does the cooking and cleaning, and orchestrates all other household service activities. If she works outside of the home, she is expected to combine these responsibilities with her domestic chores. Given such a formidable workload, it is easy to see why the mother plays a strong and central role in the Irish family.

As far as family planning is concerned, the average woman gives birth to about 2.5 children over the course of her lifespan. This is slightly above the replacement fertility level necessary to keep births and deaths in balance and thus maintain population stability. Ireland joins Malta, Poland, and the republics of the former Soviet Union as the only European nations not dropping below the replacement fertility level. To help ensure Ireland's fertility level, the Irish government has implemented a pronatalist policy that includes child allowances, maternity grants, and maternity-leave packages. Contraceptives, including condoms, are prescribed only for married couples. Out-of-wedlock births are rare in Ireland, and abortion is only permitted to save a woman's life.

Parent-child relations are characterized by considerable warmth and affection. Children are raised to be respectful and well behaved, and child-rearing strategies tend to emphasize a structured and orderly existence. Discipline is typically firm and strict, and children are often taught to view things moralistically and to follow the rules of the church without question. The teachings of the church have a particularly strong bearing on childhood socialization, particularly the molding of attitudes, values, and standards of behavior expected within the community.

The extended family network in Ireland provides important sources of identity, stability, and security. However, in contrast to other European nations, the mutual exchange of goods and services is less evident among Irish extended families. This does not mean that cooperation and support along familial lines are lacking. On the contrary, family assistance is apparent in times of stress and crisis, such as times of sickness, financial need, and death. The Irish are also noted for providing care and support to aging family members. To neglect or abandon such intergenerational obligations brings considerable family shame and dishonor.

Further Reading. Davis, Kingsley, and Mikhail S. Berstam. (1989). *Population and resources in a changing world.* Stanford, CA: Stanford University Press; Humphreys, Alexander J. (1970). The new Dubliners. In Meyer Barash and Alice Scourby (Eds.), *Marriage and the family: A comparative analysis of contemporary problems.* New York: Random House; Patriquin, Wendy. (1987). Spotlight: Ireland. *Population Today, 15,* 12; Van de Kaa, Dirk. J. (1987). *Europe's second demographic transition.* Washington, DC: Population Reference Bureau.

ISLAM. See RELIGION, IMPACT OF ON INTIMATE RELATIONSHIPS.

ISRAEL, LIFESPAN RELATIONSHIPS IN. See MIDDLE EAST, LIFESPAN RELATIONSHIPS IN THE.

ITALY, LIFESPAN RELATIONSHIPS IN. Italy is a boot-shaped peninsula in southern Europe. Measuring about 750 miles in length and averaging about 125 miles in width, Italy extends into the Mediterranean Sea. The country also includes two large islands, Sardinia and Sicily, as well as a number of smaller islands. While northern Italy is predominantly industrial, southern portions of the country are agricultural. With a population of about 60,000,000, Italy has four cities boasting a million residents each: Rome, Milan, Naples, and Turin. Virtually all Italian people are Roman Catholic. Italian is the nearly universal language, although there are many regional dialects.

Family relationships are of utmost importance to Italians. The family unit is viewed as the cornerstone of love and affection as well as an important source of security and protection. The nuclear family represents the core of a close-knit and deeply embedded kin system. Family loyalty is extremely important to Italians, and relatives demonstrate strong commitment and familism. Italians learn to define themselves by their association with their family, and allegiance to the family surpasses all other loyalties. Providing an intense and wide network of support, the family looms as one's greatest resource and protection against stress and crisis.

While Italian marriage rates have declined in recent years, marriage remains a popular lifestyle. At one time, particularly in southern regions of Italy, marriages were arranged by parents. Today, though, Italian dating relationships are characterized by considerable free choice. Families of dating partners tend to know one another, and courtships and engagements are often long. Living together before marriage is not widespread in Italy. Because of such lengthy courtships, the average age at first marriage in Italy—approximately 24 for women and 25 for men—is higher than in other European nations. Relatedly, the average age at first birth for Italian women, about 25 years, is later than for Italy's European neighbors.

As far as power dynamics are concerned, the traditional Italian family is patriarchal. The husband represents the undisputed head of the household. He is usually a dominant figure, someone who is authoritarian and highly structured with his rule setting. His family role captures traditional gender-role qualities: assertiveness, independence, and control. The wife, on the other hand, tends to be nurturant and affective. Traditionally, she is most directly concerned with the raising of children and the maintenance of the domicile. Her life focuses on domestic activities and chores, and she receives her primary pleasure from servicing her family.

Italians are having fewer and fewer children. Thirty years ago, the average number of children born to an Italian woman over the course of her lifetime was over 2.5. This total was above the replacement fertility level necessary to keep births and deaths in balance and thus maintain population stability. Today, the fertility level has slipped to 1.4, below the population replacement level. As with other European nations, a variety of reasons can be cited to explain such low fertility, including the earlier-mentioned delayed marriages and first births, financial considerations, educational and vocational commitments, and a greater emphasis on individual self-fulfillment. In an effort to bolster its fertility rates, Italy has implemented several modified pronatalist incentives, such as family allowances, subsidized maternity leave, and more accessible housing loans for families with two or more children.

Regarding parent-child relations, the Italian mother plays a dominant and active child-care role. She represents a child's emotional sustenance, providing loving support as well as guidance, trust, and security. As far as child-rearing techniques are concerned, Italian youngsters are taught respect for authority as well as loyalty to all family members. Italian children are expected to always obey elders and minimize personal conflict. Following traditional gender-role lines, boys are brought up to be assertive, to demonstrate social independence at early ages, and to control themselves emotionally. Conversely speaking, traditional girls are expected to be passive and polite, are often restricted in their social boundaries, and are usually conditioned to be more emotionally expressive.

Supportive care and regular contact with aging family members are hallmarks of Italian families. Italians regard frequent contacts with the elderly not only as enjoyable, but also as a tradition capturing the closeness of the family network. Many family members tend to live in close proximity to one another, which makes regular contact and visitations easier. Most elderly parents are visited weekly by at least one of their children, with many reporting daily visits. Daughters and daughters-in-law provide most of the daily assistance, including housekeeping chores, tending to personal hygiene needs, and shopping. For elderly parents in Italy, like their counterparts throughout the world, the emotional support given by grown children is of far greater importance than material assistance.

Further Reading. Davis, Kingsley, and Mikhail S. Berstam. (1989). *Population and resources in a changing world.* Stanford, CA: Stanford University Press; Lopreato, Joseph. (1967). *Social class and social change in an undeveloped society.* San Francisco: Chandler; Rosengarten, Lucy, and Frank Rosengarten. (1990). Aspects of cooperative home care for the elderly in Bologna, Italy. *PRIDE Institute Journal of Long Term Home Health Care, 9,* 33–37; Van de Kaa, Dirk. J. (1987). *Europe's second demographic transition.* Washington, DC: Population Reference Bureau.

J

JAPAN, LIFESPAN RELATIONSHIPS IN. Japan is a country of over 3,000 mountainous islands in the Pacific Ocean, extending 2,000 miles from northeast to southwest. Japan lies along the northeastern coast of Asia and faces Russia, Korea, and China. Four major islands comprise most of Japan's territory: Honshu, Hokkaido, Kyushu, and Shikoku. Overall, Japan is a heavily populated country: about 125 million persons live crowded in a land area about 4 percent that of the United States. Despite limited natural resources, Japan is one of the world's most important industrial nations.

The Japanese are a Mongoloid people with a mixture of Malay and Caucasoid stocks. Many Japanese are descendants of people who originated from the mainland of Asia; other ancestors came from southern China, the Philippines, and the South Pacific. Koreans are the largest minority group in Japan, although there are groupings of Chinese and Europeans. The religion of Japan is Shinto, but four other religions have influenced the course of Japanese life: Buddhism, Confucianism, Taoism, and Christianity.

At one time, most marriages in Japan were arranged by parents. Today, however, only about 25 percent of marriages are structured this way. Instead, couples are free to choose their marriage partners. Overall, the average age at first marriage is about 28 years for males and 25 years for females. Studies comparing arranged marriages with "love matches" have found that the age of marriage is significantly lower among love matches. Also, the age difference between husband and wife is greater among arranged-marriage couples. As far as Japanese marital power relationships are concerned, it is customary that the wife controls all aspects of the household, including finance, while the husband is in charge of the outside world. Regarding living arrangements, many couples reside with their parents, although since World War II the proportion of Japanese multigenerational households has markedly declined. In recent years, the number of divorces in Japan has been increasing, but it is low by international standards.

The Japanese fertility level is about 1.8 children, down from 3.7 children in 1950. This figure places Japan below the replacement level, or the number of children needed just to replace a couple in the population. Japan's movement toward a small-family orientation can be explained by several factors. Prominent among these are the high costs of raising children, the increased employment of young people, later marriages and first births, and a high abortion rate. Couples who live in rural areas and who live with or near parents tend to have more children than others. Most Japanese couples have their first baby within five years of marriage.

Japanese parent-child relations are characterized by considerable love and affection. Children are taught at early ages to show respect to their elders and superiors, and a great premium is placed on civility and politeness. Obedience to the family and particularly the development of family loyalty and allegiance are important child-rearing goals. Additionally, children learn that self-discipline and self-control are valued character traits, as are diligence and hard work. Childhood group activities, such as those originating from neighborhood or child-care settings, are encouraged so that interpersonal skills such as cooperation with others, gentleness, conciliation, and order can be groomed. Traditional gender roles typically influence the course of childhood: boys are expected to be more physically active and aggressive, while girls are encouraged to be more nurturant and emotionally sensitive.

Japan has a rapidly growing proportion of elderly citizens within its population, more so than any other developed nation. Ten years ago, only 10 percent of its population was aged 65 or over; by the year 2025, nearly one-quarter of Japan's population is expected to be 65 years of age or older. Japan also has over one million residents aged 80 or over. Such population demographics are the result of the previously mentioned low fertility rate and the world's highest life expectancy. Today, the Japanese life expectancy is approximately 77 years for males and 82 years for females.

The graying of Japan creates unique implications for later life relationships. For example, with their increase in life expectancy, the Japanese face long periods of retirement as well as the possibility of long periods of disability. While family support of the elderly is traditionally strong, a decline in multigenerational households may reduce the available assistance. The increased employment of middle-aged women, the traditional caregivers of the elderly, and declining fertility rates also figure to impact on intergenerational support patterns. Since a majority of elderly women outlive their husbands, the provision of adequate support and assistance to widows becomes particularly important. Statistics show that almost 60 percent of Japanese females aged 65 years or older are widows, while a majority of males in this age bracket are married. This is because elderly Japanese men are much more likely to remarry than women.

Recognizing the manner in which familial support for the aged is changing, the Japanese government is taking steps to better care for its elderly. For example, Japan is revising its pension and medical treatment systems. Like the United States, Japan feared that its social security system would go bankrupt and in 1986 took measures to delay the age at which full pensions are received. Businesses have agreed to raise the retirement age from 55 to 60, and now the government wants to raise it to age 65. Policies have also been designed to unify public pension systems, reduce the tax burden of the working population, and ensure a balance between pension incomes of the elderly and living standards of workers. Additionally, government officials passed legislation to protect the economic welfare of women by giving them their own pension benefits.

Further Reading. Fukado, Naohiko. (1991). Women in Japan. In Leonore L. Adler (Ed.), *Women in cross-cultural perspective.* Westport, CT: Praeger; Martin, Linda G. (1989). *The graying of Japan.* Washington, DC: Population Reference Bureau; McConatha, Douglas, Jasmin T. McConatha, and Bethann Cinelli. (1991). Japan's aging crisis: Problems for the honorable elders. *Journal of Applied Gerontology, 10,* 224–235; Ogawa, Naohiro, and Robert D. Retherford. (1993). The resumption of fertility decline in Japan, 1973–92. *Population and Development Review, 19,* 703–741.

JOINT CUSTODY. See DIVORCE, CHILDREN AND.

JUDAISM. See RELIGION, IMPACT OF ON INTIMATE RELATIONSHIPS.

K

KIBBUTZ, ISRAELI. The Israeli kibbutz is a collective settlement in which work is shared and everyone works toward common goals. In the kibbutz, children are reared in group settings, from the nursery to high school. The group of children into which one is born remains the same, and as a result, close bonds of attachment usually develop. During infancy, a *metapalet* (a child-care worker of the kibbutz) tends to the baby's basic needs. Parents visit the infant daily, and the mother returns as often as necessary to feed the child. When the infant is weaned from the mother, the metapalet assumes full responsibility for feeding the child.

As the children grow older, they move to other living arrangements and come into contact with other metapalets and teachers. During adolescence, teenagers are part of the "youth movement" that exposes them to the kibbutz and communal sphere. They are encouraged to make group decisions and to develop such capacities as cooperation and sensitivity toward others. At the end of adolescence, members of the kibbutz work with the adults and contribute to the economy.

Initially, it was hoped that the kibbutz arrangement would revolutionize Jewish society and remove the division of social classes. Thus kibbutzim children represent the "children of the dream." The elimination of gender-role stereotyping and the patriarchal family structure was also envisioned. However, many feel that these goals have not yet been attained. For example, researchers have found that even though the kibbutz was founded on gender-egalitarian terms, most of the men are in agricultural and industrial roles and most of the women are in service or educational roles.

Research does show, however, that the children of the kibbutz grow up to be competent, emotionally stable, and well adjusted. For example, studies have shown that compared to Israeli family-reared youngsters, kibbutz children are more autonomous and self-reliant when faced with routine and daily tasks. Kibbutz children also tend to exhibit more effective stress-coping strategies, which may be related to the many attachments and adaptation abilities formed during the early years in the kibbutz. Some investigators have also discovered that kibbutzim children are better at sharing and cooperating than are nonkibbutzim youngsters, and that their moral reasoning is more directed to the humanness of needy others.

Further Reading. Eshleman, J. Ross. (1994). *The family: An introduction* (7th Ed.). Boston: Allyn and Bacon; Rosenthal, Miriam K. (1991). Daily experiences of toddlers in three child care settings in Israel. *Child and Youth Care Forum, 20,* 37–58; Spiro, Melford. (1979). *Gender and culture: Kibbutz women revisited.* Durham, NC: Duke University Press.

KINESICS. See COMMUNICATION, NONVERBAL.

KINSEY, ALFRED C. Alfred C. Kinsey (1894–1956) ranks as one of the most influential human sexuality researchers in the United States. He was born in Hoboken, New Jersey, and received his Ph.D. in biology from Harvard in 1920. He became an instructor in biology at Indiana University shortly thereafter and earned academic recognition for his work in the field of taxonomy (the science of identifying, naming, and classifying organisms). He remained on the faculty at Indiana University until his death in 1956.

Kinsey launched his detailed investigation of human sexual behavior in 1938. Over a span of ten years, Kinsey and his staff interviewed over 11,000 individuals (about 5,300 males and 5,900 females) using a sex history questionnaire that contained 521 items. The subjects represented a cross-section of geographical location, education, occupation, socioeconomic level, age, and religion in the United States. However, only white male and white female respondents were included in the published findings. This was because Kinsey deemed the population sample of black respondents insufficient in size for making analyses comparable to those made for whites.

In 1948, the research team of Kinsey and Indiana University associates Wardell Pomeroy and Clyde Martin published *Sexual Behavior in the Human Male.* In 1953, Kinsey joined with Pomeroy, Martin, and Paul Gebhard to publish *Sexual Behavior in the Human Female.* These four researchers were chiefly responsible for the thousands of interviews conducted, with Kinsey himself handling over 7,000. This is a staggering total when one realizes that the average interview required one and one-half to two hours of time.

Never before had a strictly scientific investigation like this aroused so much interest, not only among fellow researchers but among the general public as well. When the findings were released, prevailing conceptions of many facets of human sexuality were radically altered. Indeed, most readers of the Kinsey studies were astonished to discover how widespread certain sexual activities were in the United States. For example, most men and almost one-half of the women reported that they had engaged in premarital sex. Many couples also engaged in sexual practices considered objectionable by society at the time, such as oral sex. About 50 percent of married men and approximately 25 percent of married women also reported having had at least one extramarital affair.

Kinsey's research marked a major breakthrough in social science research. While critics pointed to several research flaws (e.g., using a disproportionate number of uneducated males and too many college-educated females; interviewing only those subjects who were willing to disclose their sex lives), Kinsey's research had many positive dimensions. In addition to its magnitude and scope, an outstanding feature of Kinsey's research was the unprecedented sophistication and expertise in employing the interview technique. Kinsey's staff provided scholarly objectivity and sophisticated interviewing techniques during the duration of the project. Thanks to Alfred Kinsey and his dedicated team of associates, human sexuality research began to emerge as a legitimate and respectable branch of social science inquiry.

Further Reading. Kinsey, Alfred C., Wardell B. Pomeroy, and Clyde E. Martin. (1948). *Sexual behavior in the human male.* Philadelphia: Saunders; Kinsey, Alfred C., Wardell B. Pomeroy, Clyde E. Martin, and Paul Gebhard. (1953). *Sexual behavior in the human female.* Philadelphia: Saunders.

KINSHIP. Kinship includes relationships established through blood ties as well as relationships formed through the institution of marriage. Kin are referred to as *relatives,* largely because many of our social roles are performed "relative" to them. A kinship system includes relationships based on blood or marriage and serves to provide continuity between generations. A kinship system identifies a group of people who can depend on one another for mutual aid (e.g., food, shelter, protection), although this is more true for preindustrial societies.

Further Reading. Macionis, John J. (1994). *Society: The basics* (2nd Ed.). Englewood Cliffs, NJ: Prentice Hall; Nanda, Serena. (1991). *Cultural anthropology* (4th Ed.). Belmont, CA: Wadsworth.

KISSING, CROSS-CULTURAL VARIATIONS IN. Kissing, which involves joining one's lips with those of another person, has long stood for an expression of friendliness, respect, or love in the Western world. However, not all peoples use this form of expression; in fact, some societies find the very thought of kissing disgusting. The Thonga of South Africa find all mouth-to-mouth contacts revolting because of the possibility of getting the other person's saliva into one's mouth. The Hindus of India are also not keen on kissing and very cautious when it is practiced, since they believe that contact with saliva renders the act ritually contaminating.

Kissing is not very widespread among some Japanese and Chinese, although generational differences in its practice exist. For example, older Okinawan men and women do not really care for kissing and tend to avoid it in public. However, younger couples are more apt to display their affection through kissing and include it in their sexual behaviors. Kissing is frowned upon by the Ainu of northern Japan and by the Miao of Asia.

An interesting type of erotic kiss has been labeled the "smell kiss" or "olfactory kiss." When it is practiced, the nose is placed near or against the partner's face and one inhales. The ancient Egyptians probably practiced this; their words for "kiss" and "smell" are the same. Some Samoans also express their affection by sniffing. Nose rubbing may be a variant of the smell kiss or simply an inaccurate label. Nose rubbing has been reported among the Eskimo, Tamil, Ulithi, and Trobriand Islanders. An interesting evolutionary interpretation of the smell and nose kiss has also been offered by anthropologists. Such behavior may be the long outcome of our first sniffing our prey, our food, or a potential mate before making too much of a commitment to move ahead.

Further Reading. Gregersen, Edgar. (1983). *Sexual practices.* New York: Franklin Watts; Turner, Jeffrey S., and Laurna Rubinson. (1993). *Contemporary human sexuality.* Englewood Cliffs, NJ: Prentice Hall.

KOHLBERG, LAWRENCE. Lawrence Kohlberg (1927–1987) was a psychologist and leading figure in the field of moral development. Kohlberg was born and raised in Bronxville, New York. After serving in the Merchant Marine following his high-school graduation, Kohlberg enrolled in college and received a B.A. in 1949 and a Ph.D. in 1958 from the University of Chicago. Kohlberg taught at the University of Chicago from 1962 to 1968 and then became a full professor at Harvard University, a post he held until his death. He wrote many books and research articles and was the recipient of many awards and citations.

Kohlberg is widely recognized for his contributions to the study of the development of morality. Inspired by Jean Piaget's thoughts on morality, Kohlberg provided more detailed structure in formulating a theory of children's moral development. Kohlberg felt that morality develops through a series of progressive, age-related stages. Like Piaget, Kohlberg viewed cognitive development as the foundation for moral thinking and reasoning.

Kohlberg believed that the successive moralities of children result from the cognitive restructuring of their experiences, not from a set of graded lessons taught by adults. Kohlberg also maintained that an interrelatedness exists between the various stages. Kohlberg suggested that moral development is characterized by increasing differentiation and that each stage includes everything that took place at previous stages. Kohlberg outlined moral distinctions that a child had been only dimly aware of at a previous stage and organized them into a more adequate and comprehensive structure. He suggested that principles learned during early stages are either permanently buried or are selectively utilized, depending on one's level of cognitive development. (See COGNITIVE-DEVELOPMENTAL THEORY; MORAL DEVELOPMENT; PIAGET, JEAN.)

Further Reading. Kohlberg, Lawrence. (1969). *Stages in the development of moral thought and action.* New York: Holt, Rinehart and Winston; Kohlberg, Lawrence. (1984). *The psychology of moral development.* New York: Harper and Row; Kurtines, William M., and Jacob L. Gewirtz. (1995). *Moral development: An introduction.* Boston, MA: Allyn and Bacon.

L

LATE ADULTHOOD. The lifespan stage known as late adulthood generally occurs between the age of 60 and the end of life. As such, late adulthood is the last developmental stage of the lifespan. It is a life stage that presents the potential for considerable happiness, satisfaction, and fulfillment. Unfortunately, societal images of the elderly capture them in an opposite light: unhappy, feeble, crippled, and sick. As with all stages of the life cycle, late adulthood has its share of difficulties, and numerous challenges require unique adjustment in terms of flexibility and adaptability. Such adjustments need not undermine satisfaction, though, and most elderly have demonstrated that late adulthood can be an emotionally fulfilling time of life, with a minimum of physical and mental impairment.

The retirement years pose their unique share of developmental tasks and challenges. In many respects, the tasks posed at this time—such as changes in financial status or social adjustments—are more of a challenge than those faced during any other stage of adulthood. Late adulthood is also a critical period of self-assessment, a time to reevaluate one's successes and failures. While evaluating the past and attempting to deal with the present, the older person is faced with preparing for the future. Maintaining self-acceptance and self-esteem is also important for the aged. As far as family life is concerned, most marriages are characterized by satisfaction during the retirement years. (See LATE ADULTHOOD, MARRIAGE DURING.)

Retirement presents older adults with special adjustments. Researchers have consistently found that leaving the world of work and relinquishing a significant part of one's identity are difficult chores. For many, such a transition brings about a major loss of self-esteem. The ability to deal with this stage of life depends to a considerable extent on past adjustment patterns. Those who adjust well to retirement are typically able to develop a lifestyle that provides continuity with the past and meets their long-term needs. Successful adjustment is also characterized by the harmonious resolution of demands and tasks throughout the course of one's life. Should the experience be negative, it is usually because the retirement event was perceived as being stressful or because of health and/or financial trouble. Some are unhappy because of inappropriate expectations for retirement or because they were overcommitted to the work role. (See LATE ADULTHOOD, WORK RELATIONSHIPS DURING.)

Further Reading. Baltes, Paul B., and Margret M. Baltes. (Eds.). (1990). *Successful aging: Perspectives from the behavioral sciences.* New York: Cambridge University Press; Marsh, DeLoss L. (1991). *Retirement careers: Combining the best of work and leisure.* Charlotte, VT: Williamson Publishing; Young, Rosalie F., and Elizabeth A. Olson. (Eds.). (1991). *Health, illness, and disability in later life.* Newbury Park, CA: Sage.

LATE ADULTHOOD, MARRIAGE DURING. Generally speaking, most marriages are characterized by satisfaction and not disenchantment during late adulthood. Indeed, the event of retirement may be responsible for bringing elderly couples closer together. For many, the relationship becomes the focal point of everyday life, and interests become increasingly directed toward one another. Shared interests typically provide a reflection of satisfaction, caring, mutuality, and reciprocity. These important relationship ingredients are particularly evident when partners care for one another in times of illness or disability.

It appears that marital harmony during late adulthood, as well as during earlier family transitions, arises from the level of regard and esteem that partners hold for one another. A number of researchers report that marital satisfaction tends to increase during the retirement years. Indeed, some investigators go so far as to label the retirement years a ''honeymoon'' transition because the couple now has greater opportunities for involvement with one another. For those who share marital intimacy and pursue mutual interests, retirement can mean years of relaxation and the enjoyment of one another's company.

However, many sources emphasize that the degree of marital harmony experienced hinges on the support that each spouse is able to give to the other after the retirement event occurs, as well as the importance of relationship durability and adaptation. Also, coping and eventual adaptation by the older couple are often facilitated when partners view the retirement transition as a challenge or an opportunity for growth. In this respect, attitudes toward retirement often determine patterns of adjustment.

Certain elements appear to characterize unsatisfactory marriages during the retirement years. For example, in traditional retirement patterns, wives may resent the intrusion of the husband into the household on a full-time, daily basis. This may be stressful and turbulent for the wife. In this respect, the husband's daily absence from the home except on weekends, because of work, was an acceptable pattern of life for the couple. The closer interpersonal contact now experienced is not.

It thus becomes important for the retired couple to adjust to new household routines during the final stage of the marriage cycle. When the husband retires and spends most of his time in the household, he frequently becomes aware of new responsibilities and expectations. For example, husband and wife often become coequals in domestic authority. However, this may not always be the case. The changing roles and relationships in retirement marriages may alter the relative power of some husbands and wives. It is possible that a husband's power declines when he loses the "leverage" provided by the breadwinner role. It seems that the same would hold true for women who are wage earners, although current literature on the topic is scant.

The sharing of certain domestic chores and tasks is evident among many retired couples, thus giving the relationship an egalitarian flavor. Certain research reports increased involvement in domestic chores among retired husbands. However, for traditional marriages, a continuation of division-of-labor patterns persists. This prompts some analysts to observe that for the most part, retired couples adhere to domestic responsibilities established earlier in their marriages, even though many expect to share more after retirement.

Changes in the health status of married couples may affect patterns of dyadic adjustment, including levels of satisfaction and happiness. When one partner needs assistance because of health reasons, the other is likely to become the caregiver. However, gender differences arise when caregiving situations develop. A steady stream of literature indicates that caregiving wives tend to experience more stress and feelings of burden than husbands, and husbands are more likely to receive help from other relatives when caring for their spouses.

Further Reading. Ekerdt, David J., and Barbara H. Vinick. (1991). Marital complaints in husband-working and husband-retired couples. *Research on Aging, 13,* 364–382; Lauer, Robert H., Jeanette C. Lauer, and Sarah T. Kerr. (1990). The long-term marriage: Perceptions of stability and satisfaction. *International Journal of Aging and Human Development, 31,* 189–195.

LATE ADULTHOOD, WORK RELATIONSHIPS DURING. As in other stages of adult life, the world of work greatly affects the psychological and social functioning of the older person. Like their younger counterparts, aged individuals need work that is satisfying and personally rewarding, including being with people whom one enjoys. When personal needs and vocational demands are well integrated, worker performance is typically satisfactory to the employer and rewarding to the employee.

Unfortunately, a number of myths exist about older workers. Such myths are a reflection of ageist attitudes, discrimination, and prejudice leveled against individuals on the basis of their age (see ADULTHOOD, AGEISM AND). For example, some falsely believe that older workers are difficult to train and therefore cannot be taught the production requirements of the company. Still other ageist attitudes are that all older workers are feeble, sickly, and incapable of and meeting the physical demands of the job. All of these myths are false and need to be debunked.

A vocational milestone during late adulthood is retirement. From a definitive point of view, *retirement* means the end of formal work and the beginning of a new role in life, one that involves behavioral expectations and a redefinition of self. Retirement is recognized as a normative transition, an experience that originates from a predictable developmental change over the life cycle. It involves moving from an economically productive role, which is clearly defined, to an economically unproductive role, which is often vague and ambiguous. This ambiguity in the retirement role is because of its relatively new and different social position, for which there is no precedent. In the past, people worked for nearly their entire lives. But today, people retire and live out their remaining years doing other things.

Retirement is a phenomenon of modern industrial society. In the United States, there are more than 27 million persons over the age of 65 who are classified as retired. Furthermore, the proportion of retirees in the general population will steadily increase. If present trends continue, it is estimated that there will be 33 million retirees in the year 2000. The retirement period for most people is also growing longer. On the average, the man who retires at age 65 will live for another 15 years. A woman who retires at age 65 will live for another 19 years. By the turn of the century, it is expected that, on the average, a person will live another 25 years after retirement.

In general, most are able to effectively adjust to the retirement role. Should the experience be negative, it is usually because the retirement event was perceived as being stressful or because of health and/or financial trouble. Some are unhappy because of inappropriate expectations for retirement or because they were overcommitted to the work role. Researchers have found that those women and men who are forced to retire unexpectedly for reasons of health or company layoffs, or who experience financial or health declines after retirement, tend to experience greater retirement stress than those whose retirement is voluntary, on schedule, and not financially burdensome.

Financial hardships, in particular, are common during retirement. Indeed, it is not uncommon for personal income to drop by one-third to one-half with retirement. This kind of financial reduction means that many persons encounter poverty for the first time in their lives. The chances of improving one's economic status during late adulthood are extremely limited. Minorities and female elderly are especially vulnerable to poverty during the retirement years.

Beyond financial adjustments, retirement signifies the loss of job-related social contacts. The retiree must adjust to the fact that a work-related reference group is now gone. The fact that feedback from employer and coworkers no longer exists has important implications for one's sense of identity. For many, this becomes a time to search elsewhere for a meaningful reference group and realign and reassess one's self-image. It appears that those who effectively adjust are the ones who manage to develop new interests and resist the shrinkage of one's social world.

A number of organizations developed in recent years have provided retirees with other types of social support, either by facilitating existing social ties or creating new ones. Examples include senior centers, clubs, or other forms of social organizations. Also, various agencies provide opportunities for retirees to help others. Among the more common are Foster Grandparents, Senior Companions, the Retired Senior Volunteer Program, and the Service Corps of Retired Executives.

Retirement also impacts on the quality of later-life marriages. It appears that marital harmony during retirement, as well as during earlier family transitions, arises from the level of regard and esteem that partners hold for one another. Those retirees who have vital, rewarding relationships will most generally experience continued positive interactions within the marriage, while partners with difficult, unsatisfying relationships will most likely face continued negative marital interactions. A number of researchers report that marital satisfaction tends to increase during the retirement years, and some go so far as to label these years as a "honeymoon" transition.

Further Reading. Bosse, Raymond, et al. (1991). How stressful is retirement? *Journal of Gerontology: Psychological Sciences, 46,* P9–P14; Mann, James. (1991). Retirement: What happens to husband-wife relationships? *Journal of Geriatric Psychiatry, 24,* 41–46; Perritt, Lea J. (1991). Adjusting to retirement: Vocational and avocational issues. *Topics in Geriatric Rehabilitation, 6,* 74–85.

LATIN AMERICA, LIFESPAN RELATIONSHIPS IN. Latin America is a region that includes Mexico and all of the countries south of it to the southern tip of South America. In addition to Mexico and South America, Latin America includes the nations of Guatemala, El Salvador, Honduras, Nicaragua, Costa Rica, Panama, Belize, and the islands of the Caribbean Sea (known collectively as the West Indies). Combined, this region consists of about 7.9 million square miles, approximately the same size as the United States and Canada. According to recent census figures, Latin America has a population of about 405 million people.

Most Latin Americans are of European ancestry, many of Portuguese and Spanish descent. Other main population groupings are Indians, who are descendants of the original inhabitants, and blacks, brought as slaves from Africa by the Portuguese centuries ago. Today, many from Latin America are *mestizo—* mixed European and Indian. Depending on the country, one will find considerable variation in these population groupings. For example, Costa Rica is predominantly European; Indians make up the largest population group in Ecuador; blacks comprise a majority of the population in the West Indies. As far as religion is concerned, most of the population in Latin America is Roman Catholic. About 5 percent of the population are Protestants, Jews, or members of other religious groups.

As far as close relationships are concerned, it must be kept in mind that multicultural differences exist among the countries of Latin America. However, it is possible to identify certain common themes that characterize close relationships in Latin America. For example, marriage is popular, and courtships tend to be of short duration. In addition to those who marry, there are many couples who live together in consensual and casual unions. This kind of arrangement is more common among lower-income, less educated, and rural couples. It also tends to be more popular among Latin America's indigenous and African-heritage peoples. In some Latin American locations, couples in consensual unions have higher fertility rates than married couples.

The nuclear family is the dominant marital structure in Latin America, and relationships with extended family members are considered an important part of the family network. Latin American households are patriarchal and ruled by the husband. Sibling relations tend to be very close. Female-headed households have become more common in Latin America over the last ten years, usually the result of divorce, abandonment, or death of the husband. Countries such as Mexico, Brazil, and El Salvador report high poverty rates for such single-parent households.

Traditional gender-role behaviors regulate most Latin American homes, often the result of the *machismo* concept. Machismo regards a man as authoritarian and superior, while a woman is viewed as dependent and secondary. While the husband is the principal breadwinner, the wife's primary responsibilities are usually raising a family and maintaining the home. In recent years, though, a growing number of Latin American women have entered the labor force, which correlates with a corresponding increase in higher levels of female education. However, even when the female works outside the home, she is usually expected to do the housework and child rearing as well. Thus, while social change has helped to erode certain aspects of machismo, it has not disappeared completely.

Most Latin American couples are having fewer children in these modern times. Twenty years ago, the average number of children Latin American women would have had was 6 or 7. Today, it is closer to 3 in nations such as Argentina, Uruguay, Chile, and Costa Rica. In the Caribbean, Cuban women now average about 2 children, the lowest fertility total in all of Latin America. Increased contraceptive use, higher levels of educational attainment, and the heightened social status of women are largely responsible for such fertility declines. As in other nations, contraceptive use tends to be higher in urban than in rural areas, and among more educated women. Among married couples, oral contraceptives and sterilization tend to be popular methods of birth control, while unmarried couples use the pill, condoms, or other forms of reversible birth control.

Latin American parents, particularly mothers, are warm and loving with their children. Mothers typically develop affectionate bonds with their children and are instrumental in providing emotional trust and security. Latin American parents place a great emphasis on their children becoming responsible and useful adults. Patterns of child rearing tend to be restrictive and structured, and traditional gender-role teaching is obvious. For example, girls are taught to assist with the housework and help with younger siblings, while boys are encouraged to engage in more vigorous, independent activities. Peer-group socialization in Latin America tends to reinforce similar gender-typed behavioral expectations.

For many children in Latin America, a dark side to childhood exists. Growing numbers of rejected, abandoned, and homeless children roam the streets, begging, stealing, and sometimes forming criminal gangs. Most live in poor, urban slums called "shantytowns," crowded makeshift shelters of cardboard and wood scraps. Cut off from the city's economic mainstream and many of its services, shantytowns are found everywhere, but are particularly widespread in Mexico City (Mexico), Bogota (Columbia), Rio de Janeiro (Brazil), and Caracas (Venezuela). Thousands of children have this lifestyle forced upon them, which exposes them to wretched living conditions, including disease, crime, and unemployment.

As far as intergenerational relations are concerned, Latin Americans are noted for their strong kinship ties. Elderly family members are accorded considerable respect and affection and are not abandoned or rejected by younger generations. Caring for aging parents is recognized both as a commitment and an expectation for grown children. In most cases, it is the family that provides elderly persons with both personal and nursing care. Caregiving in Latin America, as in other nations, is a woman's issue: the majority of elderly are women, as are the primary family caregivers. Primary caregivers in family settings are typically female spouses and daughters, followed by sisters and daughters-in-law.

Further Reading. Ardia, Ruben. (1991). Women in Latin America. In Leonore L. Adler (Ed.), *Women in cross-cultural perspective.* Westport, CT: Praeger; Kent, Mary. (1987). Survey report: Brazil. *Population Today, 15,* 8–9; Merrick, Thomas W. (1986). *Population pressures in Latin America.* Washington, DC: Population Reference Bureau; Ramos, Luiz R. (1992). Family support for elderly people in Sao Paulo, Brazil. *Ageing International, 19,* 34–36.

LEE, JOHN. See LOVE, CONCEPTUAL MODELS OF.

LEGAL SEPARATION. A legal separation exists when legally married couples maintain separate residences but have established legal responsibilities for such areas as support or rights of visitation. A legal separation often occurs before actual divorce proceedings and is distinguishable from informal separation, an arrangement between husband and wife where one or both decide to live separately. It should be recognized that not all couples who legally separate (or informally separate) eventually divorce. While many do divorce, others use separation as a time to work out a reconciliation. Still others remain married but choose to live in unresolved separations.

Further Reading. Eshleman, J. Ross. (1994). *The family: An introduction* (7th Ed.). Boston: Allyn and Bacon; Gelles, Richard J. (1995). *Contemporary families: A sociological view.* Thousand Oaks, CA: Sage; Ruback, Barry. (1985). Family law. In Luciano

L'Abate (Ed.), *The handbook of family psychology and therapy.* Homewood, IL: Dorsey Press.

LEVINGER, GEORGE. See INTIMATE RELATIONSHIP, DEVELOP-MENT OF.

LEVINSON, DANIEL. Daniel Levinson (1920–) is an important contributor to the study of adult personality development. He earned a Ph.D. at the University of California at Berkeley in social psychology and had a distinguished teaching and research career at Yale University from 1966 to 1992. Levinson maintained that adult personality development unfolds in a series of predictable stages. In his research, Levinson described what he called a "life structure," which is the underlying pattern of a person's behavior at a given time in life. There are three aspects to a person's life structure: the sociocultural world (e.g., ethnicity, occupation, class, status, religion), self-aspects (complex patterns of wishes, anxieties, conflicts, moral values, talents and skills, fantasies, and modes of feeling, thought, and action), and participation in the world (how a person uses and is used by the world).

Utilizing the concept of a life structure, Levinson suggested that adulthood is divided into *eras* of approximately 25 years each, and each era consists of unique developmental periods for personality dynamics. Between each era a major transition occurs (for example, the *early adult transition,* the *age 30 transition,* and the *midlife transition*). Individuals make psychological adjustments when entering an era during what Levinson called the *novice phase.* A reassessment of the developing life structure occurs during the middle of each era, labeled by Levinson as the *transition phase.* Finally, one enters the *culminating phase* of the era, where the life structure is reassessed and fine-tuned.

According to Levinson, the nature of adult personality dynamics can be best understood within this developmental framework. For example, the early adult transition enables us to see the developmental bridge that exists between preadulthood and early adulthood. We can study how becoming less dependent on one's family of origin requires launching a new life structure and making choices, defining goals, and establishing an occupation. During the midlife transition, Levinson's conceptual model is useful in studying how individuals assess previously established life goals and how they modify unsatisfactory aspects of their life structure. Finally, the late adult transition enables researchers to explore personality dynamics as middle adulthood's heavy responsibilities are reduced and individuals face living in a changed relationship with society and themselves.

Further Reading. Levinson, Daniel J. (1986). A conception of adult development. *American Psychologist, 41,* 3–13; Levinson, Daniel J., Charlotte N. Darrow, Edward B. Klein, Maria H. Levinson, and Braxton McKee. (1978). *The seasons of a man's life.* New York: Knopf.

LIFE EXPECTANCY. Life expectancy is an estimate of the average number of years a person can expect to live. At the turn of the century, the life expectancy in the United States was 47 years. Today this figure has risen to about 75 years, an increase of almost 28 years. The greatest gain in life expectancy (21 years) occurred during the first half of the century, largely because of dramatic reductions in infectious-disease mortality. However, significant improvements in life expectancy have also taken place since 1970. In fact, life expectancy has increased more since 1970 (about 4 years) than it did in the 20 years prior to 1970 (less than 3 years).

The chance of surviving to older ages has also increased in our society. U.S. citizens who reach their 65th birthday today can expect to live about another 17 years, compared to 12 years at the turn of the century. In the 50 years between 1900 and 1950, life expectancy at age 65 increased by 2 years; in the next 20 years, by 1.3 years; and since 1970, by 1.6 years. Furthermore, the proportion of individuals surviving from age 65 to age 85 was 23 percent in 1950, but close to 40 percent in the 1990s.

Today about three out of four deaths among aged persons are from heart disease, cancer, or stroke. Heart disease was the leading cause of death among the elderly in 1950 and remains so in the 1990s even though its occurrence has been dramatically reduced. The number of deaths due to strokes has also declined in the recent past. Death rates from cancer, on the other hand, have been increasing for several decades, especially the incidence rate of lung cancer. (See LIFE EXPECTANCY, CROSS-NATIONAL VARIATIONS IN; LIFE EXPECTANCY, GENDER DIFFERENCES IN).

Further Reading. National Center for Health Statistics. (1994). *Health, United States, 1993.* Washington, DC: U.S. Government Printing Office; National Center for Health Statistics. (1994). *Vital statistics of the United States.* Washington, DC: U.S. Government Printing Office.

LIFE EXPECTANCY, CROSS-NATIONAL VARIATIONS IN. Life expectancies vary greatly in the world. For example, in Liberia the life expectancy is about 45 years, while in Australia persons can expect to live 75 years. Greater life expectancies both in the United States and abroad can be attributed to such factors as low infant mortality rates, improved medical care, the control of infectious disease, proper sanitation, technological advances, better working conditions, and proper diets. Knowledge of aging processes and improved geriatric care are other important reasons behind increased longevity.

Exploring a few representative countries will reveal how life expectancy varies around the globe. Within the countries of the Middle East, great differences in life expectancy exist. For example, Israel, Cyprus, and Kuwait have life expectancies at birth of more than 70 years. Equally long lives are enjoyed by the peoples of Lebanon, Bahrain, Jordan, and the United Arab Emirates. However, life expectancy in the region's North African countries averages only 57 years, and in both North and South Yemen, it is only 48 years. In Afghanistan, the life expectancy of about 40 years is one of the lowest in the world.

The difference in life expectancy that separates the countries in the Middle East reflects the different levels of economic development within the region, high rates of infant and child deaths, limited health-care services for the elderly, and poor medical intervention in general. With regard to the last item, already-inadequate medical services in the poorer regions are being further taxed by rapid population growth. The increases in numbers of people combined with slow economic growth make it difficult to expand or improve health services. This is especially true for health-care services for the elderly, regarded by many as a neglected part of the population. Most countries in the Middle East have shortages of physicians, nurses, and paramedical workers. Finally, the impact of war in the Middle East on the region's life expectancy and on age distributions within the population needs to be recognized. In the war between Iran and Iraq, about 250,000 deaths and another 700,000 non-fatal casualties have been reported since the war began in 1980. In the Persian Gulf War in 1991, when Iraqi and allied forces collided, Iraqi casualties were said to number 50,000 to 75,000, although precise figures are unavailable.

Overall life expectancy at birth for the 42 countries of sub-Saharan Africa is up from 40 years in 1960, but is still estimated to be only between 50 and 55 years. While such infectious diseases as yellow fever and malaria have been controlled, tuberculosis still claims many lives. Malnutrition and poor sanitation are also widespread in many areas. Moreover, health care for peoples in sub-Saharan Africa is generally poor. Invariably, whatever medical intervention is available is directed toward the young (about 45 percent of the population is under age 15) and not the old. Even so, high rates of infant and child mortality abound. Deaths to infants under age one average more than 100 per 1,000 live births for all but 13 countries. Compare this to infant mortality rates in the United States and Western Europe of around 10 and lower. (See SUB-SAHARAN AFRICA, LIFESPAN RELATIONSHIPS IN.)

No discussion of life expectancy from a cross-cultural perspective would be complete without some reference to Abkhazia, a mountain village tucked between the Black Sea and the Caucasus Mountains in the former Soviet Union. Life expectancy in the former Soviet Union is about 71 years, but mountain villagers from Abkhazia are reported to live well beyond that. Indeed, Abkhazia claims to have five times as many centenarians as the United States. However, the reader should be cautioned that the recording of birth dates in developing countries can be haphazard and that old residents might be exaggerating their ages.

But while the exact number of centenarians may be suspect, it does appear that Abkhazians enjoy long lives. Certain factors appear to contribute to lengthier lifespans. Blood tests show that these mountain people are not strikingly different from their geographical neighbors, but they may have a genetic resistance to disease. Their diet is not unusual, although it is wholesome and includes little alcohol. Cancer is also rare among Abkhazians, probably because they live in the countryside. Gerontologists also believe that the Abkhazians' active lifestyle and their reverence for old age contribute to their longevity. Besides continuing to work during late adulthood, elder Abkhazians actively participate in a community council. They serve in a number of hospitality roles, an important element in their village culture, and are regularly sought out by the young for advice.

All of this contributes to a smooth aging transition that may help to avoid the shock of retirement. These cultural practices also help preserve the real power of the elders in the family and in the daily life of the rural village. Such conditions create psychological comfort among the aged and, coupled with their physical lifestyle, may help to explain why people live long lives in this remote land.

Further Reading. Lutz, Wolfgang. (1994). *The future of world population.* Washington, DC: Population Reference Bureau; McFalls, Joseph A., Jr. (1991). *Population: A lively introduction.* Washington, DC: Population Reference Bureau; Population Reference Bureau. (1985). *The Population Reference Bureau's population handbook.* Washington, DC: Author.

LIFE EXPECTANCY, GENDER DIFFERENCES IN. In the United States today, life expectancy is greater for women than it is for men. Moreover, women have made greater gains in life expectancy over the course of this century. Whereas female life expectancy was 48 years in 1900, today it is about 78 years. Males lived an average of 46 years at the turn of the century but can expect to live 71 years today. About three-quarters of American centenarians are women.

Some other interesting trends in life expectancy and gender differences can be noted. Between 1960 and 1970, life expectancy among females increased by 1.4 years, compared with 0.2 years for males. However, since 1970, average life expectancy has increased by 4.5 years for males and 3.7 years for females. Because of these trends, the difference in life expectancy between males and females increased between 1950 and 1975 from 5.5 to 7.8 years and subsequently has declined to about 6.8 years.

An analysis of mortality trends sheds light on why gender differences in life expectancy exist. To begin with, women were more susceptible to dying in the past from a number of infectious diseases, especially tuberculosis. Tuberculosis and other communicable diseases have been medically conquered, as has maternal mortality. As far as degenerative cardiovascular diseases are concerned, women have made greater gains in mortality reduction than men. In terms of cancer-related deaths, the sex mortality differential has been reversed in this century. In 1900, females were more apt to die from cancer, but now (age-adjusted) death rates for cancer are 30 percent higher for males than for females.

Thus elderly men are more likely than elderly women to die from heart disease and cancer, as well as from influenza and pneumonia, accidents, cirrhosis of the liver, bronchitis, emphysema, and asthma. Indeed, for all of the ten leading causes of death at ages 65 and over, mortality rates for males 65 to 84 years are well above those for females of the same ages, with the exception of diabetes. After age 85, the rates for males continue to be higher than those for females for all leading causes of death with the exception of cerebrovascular disease and diabetes.

Further Reading. Gee, Ellen M. (1989). Living longer, dying differently. *Generations, 13,* 5–8; McFalls, Joseph A., Jr. (1991). *Population: A lively introduction.* Washington, DC: Population Reference Bureau; National Center for Health Statistics. (1994). *Vital statistics of the United States.* Washington, DC: U.S. Government Printing Office.

LIFESPAN, CONCEPTUALIZATIONS OF THE. Conceptualizations of the lifespan are formulations about the course of human development, with particular emphasis on age-classification systems. These systems, which lifespan development researchers have arranged and rearranged, are constructed primarily to help clarify and organize data. Some researchers propose that the stages of human development may be interpreted in various ways. For instance, the same person might be classified as mature, old, or developing, depending on whether physiological, social, psychological, or anatomical criteria are being used. It should be recognized, however, that there is continuity in the life cycle of the human being. Only for scientific convenience do we identify stages of development. Life does not start or stop at the beginning or end of stages or age-classification systems.

Differences of opinion exist concerning conceptualizations of the life cycle. Age alone is not an adequate criterion for stage classification, as one can easily observe by examining cross-cultural life expectancies: one might be considered old in one culture but not in another. For example, in Burkina Faso in Africa, the average life expectancy hovers near 40 years. Indonesia's people live an average of 50 years, whereas in the Philippines, the average life expectancy is 60 years. In Japan, the average individual lives almost 80 years. Cross-culturally, then, it is possible at a given age to be a young adult in one country, middle-aged in another, and elderly in yet another. Thus it is impossible for developmental psychologists to devise a universal age-classification system.

The reasons for such differences in cross-cultural life expectancy are difficult to pinpoint. The greater life expectancy in developed nations, compared to underdeveloped countries, has been attributed to such factors as improved medical care, control of infectious diseases, technological advances, better working conditions, and nutritious diets. Such illustrations of the nature of aging processes underscore the need to carefully examine both the individual and the generalizations made in age-classification systems.

This discussion further implies that life expectancy at various historical periods must also be taken into consideration. More specifically, we would have difficulty in attempting to adapt present-day life expectancies to those of past eras. For example, at the turn of the century in the United States, the life expectancy was 47 years. Today this figure has risen to about 75 years, an increase of almost 28 years. Furthermore, the chance of surviving to older ages has also increased in our society. U.S. citizens who reach their 65th birthday today can expect to live about another 17 years, compared to 12 years at the turn of the century.

Compare today's figures in the United States to a life expectancy of about 25 years in Rome around A.D. 100 or 35 years in England during the 1200s! Moreover, consider the problems we face when attempting to understand the developmental period known as *childhood* as it existed in past centuries. In many cultures, right up through the medieval period, there was not one word to capture this critical developmental stage, largely because childhood, as we know it today, simply did not exist. In most cases, *infancy* was the term applied to the first six years of life. During this period, children were kept at home and attended to by their mothers to learn the folkways and mores of their culture.

Between the ages of six and nine, children, for all intents and purposes, entered *adulthood.* They either were sent directly into the workaday world or were given an apprenticeship to train for a particular vocation. Remarkably, the developmental period classified today as middle childhood was nonexistent, and most, if not all, of adolescence was omitted because the child began assuming adult responsibilities early in life.

Furthermore, the term *youth* generally signified *the prime of one's life.* Youth, during the Middle Ages, was followed immediately by the stage referred to as *old age!* Moreover, at 20, an age when most young adults in modern society are still preparing for a career, William the Conqueror had already been victorious in the Battle of Normandy. Charlemagne had recorded numerous victories in battle before he was crowned king of the Franks at age 26. There are young adults today who make significant and sometimes truly great contributions to society, but few, if any, are capable of shaping history as these individuals did. In contemporary Western societies, it is far more likely that such feats are accomplished by "older" adults.

As civilizations changed and technology progressed, the lives of humans changed also. With the advent of more complex divisions of labor, additional training and education were needed for job preparation, a factor that extended the developmental periods. As the lifespan lengthened, the periods of early, middle, and late adulthood emerged, lengthened in time, and began to assume their own unique identities within the life cycle. Compared with past centuries, our view of various life stages has changed considerably. Furthermore, it is expected that conceptualizations of the lifespan will continue to change in years to come.

Further Reading. Aries, Philippe. (1962). *Centuries of childhood.* New York: Knopf; deMause, Lloyd. (Ed.). (1975). *The history of childhood.* New York: Harper and Row; National Center for Health Statistics. (1994). *Health, United States, 1993;* Washington, DC: U.S. Government Printing Office; Turner, Jeffrey S., and Donald B. Helms. (1994). *Contemporary adulthood* (5th Ed.). Fort Worth, TX: Harcourt Brace.

LISTENING, ACTIVE AND PASSIVE STYLES OF. Active and passive listening styles refer to how verbal messages are attended to, particularly one's level of involvement with the speaker. An active listening style is one in which there is full participation, including the asking of questions and the giving of feedback to what is being said. Active listening may also embody clarifying what is being said and reciprocal turn taking in the overall conversation. A passive listening style, on the other hand, is characterized by the limited involvement of the receiver. Silence is often used by the receiver so that another person can explore his or her feelings or attitudes. Passive listening is not to be confused with disinterest; rather, this listening style allows others to explore their thoughts. Moreover, it gives others the chance to reflect and process what has been said without feeling pressured.

Further Reading. Epstein, Laura. (1985). *Talking and listening.* St. Louis: Times Mirror/Mosby; McKay, Matthew, Martha Davis, and Patrick Fanning. (1983). *Messages: The communication skills book.* Oakland, CA: New Harbinger Publications.

LISTENING, AND COMMUNICATION EFFECTIVENESS. The effectiveness of interpersonal communication relies considerably on good listening skills. Peak communication is a reciprocal process that requires both clear language and effective listening skills. Good listeners are able to decode messages and are skilled at attending, clarifying, confirming, and reflecting.

All too often, the words *hearing* and *listening* are used interchangeably. This is inaccurate. *Hearing* is the physiological process by which auditory impressions are received by the ears and transmitted to the brain. More specifically, the outer ear catches sound waves and guides them into the auditory canal. At the end of the canal, the waves vibrate the eardrum, sending vibrations across the three bones of the middle ear and moving the innermost bone in and out. Then a fluid translates sound waves into nerve impulses and stimulates nerves to send "messages" to the hearing center in the brain.

Listening is the psychological procedure involving the interpretation and understanding of sensory experience. Listening requires that we interpret what is heard around us and give it significance and meaning. Without this, messages are not understood and communication becomes fatally flawed. Using the previous definition of hearing, then, this means that it is possible to hear someone but not to listen.

Unfortunately, many individuals are poor listeners. Some lack the motivation to listen, others are inaccurate in what they translate, and still others have never been taught the importance of using this skill. Other reasons for poor listening range from the presence of distractions to tuning out what was said in self-defense. Another reason for poor listening is that people rely on selective listening; that is, they pick out bits and pieces of conversations that interest them and turn a deaf ear to the rest.

As far as traditional gender differences are concerned, women appear to be better listeners than men. Research shows that as boys and girls grow up, they are taught and reinforced in different styles of listening skills. For instance, traditional males are often taught to listen for facts, while females are often taught to listen for the mood of the communication. Males often have difficulty listening for nonverbal cues, whereas females, who are listening for the mood of the communication, tend to acquire them more readily.

It is important to acknowledge the role that silence plays in the listening process. Silence is an important element of conversations that is very often misinterpreted. For many people, it is the most difficult of all things to handle. It may seem unusual to consider silence important in a relationship, largely because our society places so much importance on "polite conversation" and discourages thoughtful silence. Most people have learned to feel uncomfortable with silences and to regard long pauses in conversation as being impolite or showing a lack of interest.

Silence can be a powerful form of communication. For example, socially we often use the "silent treatment" as a form of rejection, defiance, or condemnation. Fortunately, there are many ways that silence can be used as a positive force. For example, when silence is used constructively, a partner can be "drawn out" and made more communicative. Other times, silence offers a special form of nonverbal communication.

Silence may also help the less articulate partner to feel comfortable. By feeling accepted, a shy and quiet person may be able to accept himself. As a result, communication often becomes more confident and direct. Another value of silence in a relationship is that remaining silent after a partner's serious expression of feelings often allows that person to think and to come up with new insight into these feelings. One value of silence, then, is that it forces depth of thought about one's affective side.

Finally, silence can reduce the pace of the conversation. Many times, that pace is directly related to the amount of anxiety being felt by both people. Often silence can help to eliminate some of that tension. Above all, it is important to be sensitive to what another person is communicating through silence. Skilled listeners are adept at pinpointing the motives for silence and are aware of the many messages that this behavior can communicate.

Further Reading. Barker, Larry L. (1971). *Listening behavior.* Englewood Cliffs, NJ: Prentice-Hall; Swets, Paul W. (1983). *The art of talking so that people will listen.* Englewood Cliffs, NJ: Prentice-Hall; Walters, Howard. (1980). Don't just talk: Communicate! *Marriage and Family Living, 46,* 18–21.

LOCKE, JOHN. DOCTRINE ON CHILDREN AND CHILD-REARING. John Locke (1632–1704) was an English philosopher whose writings had great influence on a number of disciplines, including the budding science of psychology. Locke was born in Wrington, England, and attended Oxford University. He wrote on a number of subjects throughout his life, and he was influential in shaping new perceptions and images of children and their upbringing. Locke and Jean-Jacques Rousseau helped to change the thinking of the day regarding the nature of the child (see ROUSSEAU, JEAN-JACQUES. DOCTRINE ON CHILDREN AND CHILD-REARING).

Prior to Locke's contributions, a widespread belief was the *doctrine of inherent sin,* the notion that the child was born wicked and sinful. Because of such thinking, it was considered not only justifiable but also right and appropriate to punish children as often as possible. Adults believed that children who behaved badly were expressing the results of innate sin; consequently, the devil had to be literally driven from the body. Parents who neglected their duty to punish their children earned the disapproval of their more Christian neighbors who conscientiously beat the devil out of their children. Thus both children and adults were affected by the religious teachings of the day, and their alliance in the fear of Satan and the hope of salvation mirrored the social organization of the time.

By the eighteenth century, thanks largely to Locke's efforts, attitudes concerning the inherent qualities of children had begun to change. Locke viewed children in a new way, claiming that they were not inherently sinful but were products of societal influences that determined the qualities of goodness or evil. Concerning himself with the mind and mental attitudes, Locke emphasized that the most powerful shapers of childhood behavior were esteem and disgrace. By using these incentives, beating or chiding a child could be avoided. "Respect your child," Locke wrote, "reward him with praise and punish him with neglect or contempt and the child will behave accordingly."

Locke also theorized that infants have unformed minds that do not possess innate knowledge. The blank infant mind, termed *tabula rasa* by Locke, is a receptacle for sensory information. In this way, experiences are recorded and mental impressions are left behind. Locke further believed that the child was governed by strong passions or emotions. He maintained that it was the duty and obligation of rational members of society to create an environment capable of transmitting proper experiences to the child. He also felt that specific behaviors could be produced when parents and teachers supplied appropriate rewards. In addition, Locke stressed the importance of practice and drill in such learning tasks as math, the Scriptures, the alphabet, and even toilet training.

The ideas of Locke, as well as those of Rousseau, managed to gain support from some factions and to provoke opposition from others. Denunciations came from those firmly convinced that the child was inherently sinful, such as colonial America's religious leader Jonathan Edwards. Despite these criticisms, Locke's views came to be shared by other philosophers and educators. Thus began a movement that would place the child in a new and more favorable light. (See CHILD REARING, HISTORICAL PRACTICES IN.)

Further Reading. Aries, Philippe. (1962). *Centuries of childhood.* New York: Knopf; deMause, Lloyd. (Ed.). (1975). *The history of childhood.* New York: Harper and Row; Helms, Donald B., and Jeffrey S. Turner. (1986). *Exploring child behavior* (3rd Ed.). Monterey, CA: Brooks/Cole.

LONGITUDINAL RESEARCH DESIGN. A longitudinal research design is a method of investigating developmental trends by studying the same group of individuals over a considerable period (years and sometimes even decades). Suppose someone wanted to collect data concerning various facets of early adult development. The researcher employing the longitudinal design might begin by studying a particular group at age 20. Follow-up studies would be made at fairly regular intervals until the subjects reached age 40. At each follow-up session, relevant data would be recorded to be applied to the final research analysis.

Further Reading. Breakwell, Glynis, Sean Hammond, and Chris Fife-Schaw. (1995). *Research methods in psychology.* Thousand Oaks, CA: Sage; Heiman, Gary W. (1995). *Research methods in psychology.* Boston: Houghton Mifflin.

LOOKING-GLASS SELF. See COOLEY, CHARLES HORTON.

LOVE. Love is a complex and multifaceted human emotion that contributes to mutual sharing and support, As such, it typically rests at the heart of an intimate relationship. Because love is subjective and can be expressed and received in so many different ways, numerous definitions of it exist. Most researchers, though, regard love as a deep form of caring and giving that is instrumental in shaping the growth and development of the persons involved.

Loving relationships are usually reciprocal in nature; that is, the affection and support expressed by one partner are reciprocated by the other. Loving relationships are also characterized by mutual self-disclosure, the verbal and physical expression of affection and intimacy, sensitivity, and tolerance. Many researchers acknowledge how loving relationships also embrace mutual understanding and regard, as well as the giving and receiving of emotional support. A consistent theme in the literature is that love entails having high regard for a partner, as well as valuing the loved one in one's own life.

The romantic ideal attached to love abounds in society in many different forms. Love and romantic relationships are often the central theme of movies, plays, and popular songs. Descriptions, accounts, and narratives of it can be found in virtually all forms of the media, from movies and television to paperback books and supermarket tabloids. From childhood on, we are exposed to the romantic qualities of love and taught to expect that we will "fall" in love at some point in our lives.

Researchers acknowledge that gender differences exist in styles of love and loving. Within loving relationships, traditional females tend to openly express their feelings and become emotionally attached to their partners. Most traditional males tend to deemphasize love's emotional components and are cautious about falling in love. While men's first feelings on falling in love are usually as ecstatic as women's, many in time deemphasize these feelings and reduce levels of self-disclosure. Increased self-disclosure often depends upon the degree to which traditional males can accept themselves, their feelings, and their vulnerabilities.

Love offers the potential of bringing deeper involvement with another person and greater interpersonal rewards. More specifically, the capacity to reveal increasingly intimate details about oneself in a love relationship is enhanced by maturity, authenticity, comfort with one's identity, and the willingness to share oneself with an intimate partner. The security and trust offered by meaningful loving relationships help partners to fulfill such basic needs as belongingness, self-esteem, and strivings for self-actualization. (See LOVE, CHILDHOOD EXPRESSIONS OF; LOVE, CONCEPTUAL MODELS OF; LOVE, INFATUATION COMPARED TO.)

Further Reading. Branden, Nathaniel. (1981). *The psychology of romantic love.* New York: Bantam Books; Hendrick, Susan, and Clyde Hendrick. (1992). *Liking, loving, and relating* (2nd Ed.). Belmont, CA: Wadsworth; Kelley, Harold H. (1993). Love and commitment. In Harold H. Kelley and Ellen Berscheid (Eds.), *Close relationships* (3rd Ed.). New York: Freeman.

LOVE, CHILDHOOD EXPRESSIONS OF. Children are capable of giving and receiving love at early ages. However, because love has many dimensions and abstract qualities, they cannot fully comprehend it until their cognitive facilities are mature (see COGNITIVE-DEVELOPMENTAL THEORY). Usually, physical dimensions of loving (kissing, hugging, and so on) are understood before psychological (or mental and emotional) aspects (mutuality, reciprocity, and so on) are learned. Children learn about love early in life, particularly when bonds of attachment are formed with parents. It is usually from these attachments that children create early feelings of security and self-worth. Those children who receive their parents' love usually come to accept themselves as important objects of affection to others. In addition, those who have received love and affection are capable of giving them in return.

The expression of love changes during childhood, thus mirroring developmental advancements in cognition. Preschoolers usually express love physically, such as through kissing and hugging. This is also true of school-age children, but they have also learned that love can be expressed through other channels, such as sharing and talking. Leaving behind an egocentric point of view and developing sensitivity toward others help their expression of love gradually to mature. Thus growing levels of cognitive maturity enable the child to learn new ways of expressing and receiving love.

As with so many other forms of expression, gender roles often dictate how this behavior is expressed and received (see CHILDHOOD, GENDER-ROLE DEVELOPMENT DURING). If a culture deems it unmasculine for a male to exhibit sensitivity or tenderness, then such behaviors may not become part of a boy's expression of love. A child will learn such cultural endorsements of love and loving through a wide range of social vehicles, including one's family and friends, as well as educational experiences and the media. Such socialization experiences will teach children in both direct and subtle ways what love is and how it can be expressed.

Further Reading. Hendrick, Susan and Clyde Hendrick. (1992). *Liking, loving, and relating* (2nd Ed.). Belmont, CA: Wadsworth; Selman, Robert. (1980). *The growth of interpersonal understanding.* New York: Academic Press.

LOVE, CONCEPTUAL MODELS OF. Conceptual models of love are theoretical efforts to explain how love is expressed and received. Just as there are many different ways to experience love, so too are there a plethora of models to describe it. Three of the more noteworthy conceptual models of love have been developed by Ira Reiss, John Lee, and Robert Sternberg.

Ira Reiss's Theory

Ira Reiss developed a conceptual model of love called the *wheel theory*. He suggested that love consists of four components or quadrants within a wheel-like design. These four parts are rapport (feeling at ease with each other); self-revelation (disclosing personal details about each other's lives); mutual dependency (developing a reliance on one another and establishing interdependence); and personality and need fulfillment (satisfying each other's emotional needs). As each of these components fills, the wheel will begin to turn.

In a serious, long-lasting intimate relationship, the wheel will turn indefinitely; it may turn only a few times in a short-lived romance. Also, the weight of each component will cause the wheel to move forward or backward. To illustrate how the wheel can reverse itself, consider that the self-revelation component has been reduced because of some type of relationship disharmony. This reduction would affect the dependency and personality and need fulfillment processes, which would in turn weaken rapport, which would in turn lower the revelation level even further.

John Lee's Theory

John Lee developed a unique typology of love that consisted of three primary types, eros, ludus, and storge love, and three secondary types, mania, agape, and pragma love. Lee likened these six styles of loving to a color wheel: just as all colors are derived from the three primary colors (red, yellow, and blue), so do all styles of loving evolve from the three primary ones.

Eros love is characterized by the desire for sexual intimacy and a preoccupation with the physical aspects of the relationship. Erotic lovers usually report powerful attraction toward one another, as well as intense feelings of excitement and anticipation.

Ludus love is playful, flirtatious, and often self-centered. Ludic lovers do not want long-range attachments from their partners. Most also do not want their partners to be dependent on them. Ludus love has often been described as playful love, a style that regards love as a game.

Storge love is calm, affectionate love. Unlike eros love, storge love has no sudden, dramatic beginnings. Rather, it is characterized by quiet commitment.

It embodies companionship and the enjoyment of doing things together. Intense emotional involvement is usually avoided.

Manic love is intense and obsessive. Many manic lovers are overwhelmed by thoughts of their partners, so much so that they are always in a state of anxiety. They need continual affection and attention from their partners, as well as constant reassurance about the other's sincerity and commitment.

Agape love represents altruistic love. Agape lovers care deeply about their partners and seek to satisfy their well-being in a warm and kind fashion. This gentle style of loving also asks nothing in return.

Pragma love is characterized by sensibleness and logic. Pragma lovers are realistic when they approach a potential partner and seek to match themselves with someone whose background is compatible with their own.

Lee suggested that many combinations of love are possible. For example, by mixing the primary styles, one may have storgic-ludus love, ludic-eros love, or storgic-eros love. Although in one person a particular style usually dominates, we are all capable of experiencing each type. Different relationships, for example, may elicit different styles.

Research suggests that women tend to be more pragmatic, manic, and storgic with their styles of loving, whereas men often demonstrate erotic and ludic styles. It has also been suggested that individuals in love demonstrate higher levels of erotic and agape love than those not in love.

Robert Sternberg's Theory

Robert Sternberg maintained that love is based on three components: passion (an intense physical attraction and desire for someone); intimacy (feelings of closeness and concern for a partner's well-being); and decision/commitment (recognition of the fact that one is in love and a willingness to maintain the relationship). Sternberg conceptualized these components as a triangle.

Like Lee's model, Sternberg's love triangle enables us to see how the three components can exist in different patterns and different degrees. Based on different combinations of passion, intimacy, and decision/commitment, Sternberg identified seven forms of love: *liking* (intimacy, but no commitment or passion); *infatuation* (passion without commitment or intimacy); *empty love* (commitment without passion or intimacy); *romantic love* (intimacy and passion, but no commitment); *fatuous love* (commitment and passion but no intimacy); *companionate love* (commitment and intimacy, but no passion); and *consummate love* (commitment, intimacy, and passion).

Sternberg maintained that these combinations of love can help explain different interpersonal relationships. Liking, for example, is characteristic of friendships, and companionate love is common in long-term relationships. Empty love can probably be applied to those relationships that have become devoid of meaning. Sternberg felt that consummate love represents an ideal, complete form of love. It is the most rewarding of all love experiences and embraces all three components.

These three conceptualizations of love are useful in understanding the different experiences of love, including its many complexities. For example, Reiss's wheel theory sheds light on how a love relationship can be conceptualized as an ongoing cycle. The theories offered by Lee and Sternberg illustrate how love can reflect different feelings, thoughts, and actions. Better yet, they show how, in real life, a loving relationship rarely consists of a unitary style. Instead, love relationships are often characterized by the interaction of several styles.

Further Reading. Lee, John A. (1976). *The colors of love.* Englewood Cliffs, NJ: Prentice-Hall; Reiss, Ira L. (1960). Toward a sociology of the heterosexual love relationship. *Marriage and Family Living, 26,* 139–145; Sternberg, Robert J. (1986). A triangular theory of love. *Psychological Review, 93,* 119–135.

LOVE, INFATUATION COMPARED TO. Infatuation, often described as irrational or illogical love, is often confused with actual love. This is likely due to the fact that infatuation and love can feel identical in the early stages. For example, both initially produce strong feelings of pleasurable excitement as well as a strong desire to be with a particular person. However, there is one primary difference: with love, the feelings not only last but can deepen.

Probably the most significant difference between a "crush" and a loving relationship is the absence in the former of real caring for the other person. Crushes are based on images rather than on real people. People often develop crushes on those who reflect culturally accepted—and often rather superficial—qualities such as wealth, notoriety, and looks.

Researchers maintain that the more one is with someone else and gets to know that person, the better able one is to judge the difference between fantasy and reality. If infatuation is being experienced, time with the person will usually bring fantasies to an end and romance to a halt. But if such feelings do not weaken, a person may indeed be in love.

Further Reading. Bessell, Harold. (1984). *The love test.* New York: Warner Books; Rubin, Theodore I. (1983). *One to one.* New York: Viking; Turner, Jeffrey S., and Donald B. Helms. (1988). *Marriage and family: Traditions and transitions.* San Diego, CA: Harcourt Brace Jovanovich.

LUTHER, MARTIN. See RENAISSANCE AND REFORMATION, LIFE-SPAN RELATIONSHIPS DURING THE.

MARITAL EXCHANGES. Economic exchanges that accompany marriage are called marital exchanges. In most societies, marriage is recognized as a legal contract between the individuals involved or their respective families. In many societies, though, the marriage of a man and a woman is also typically accompanied by some kind of economic exchange. Marital exchanges illustrate the social, rather than the individual, importance placed on marriage. They represent symbolic efforts to preserve the goodwill between families and a way to facilitate the transfer of marital rights. In the United States, this usually takes the form of wedding showers and wedding gifts. In other parts of the world, more complex transfers of goods or services exist.

The most common form of marital exchange is bridewealth (also called brideprice). *Bridewealth* refers to payments of money or goods from the groom's parents or other kin to the bride's parents or other kin. Beyond money, bridewealth usually represents the most valuable symbols of wealth for a particular culture, such as livestock or jewelry. While the purpose of bridewealth is interpreted somewhat differently in various societies, it usually represents an effort to reimburse the woman's family for the loss of her services. Bridewealth also serves to legitimize marriage and entitles the husband to domestic and sexual rights over his wife. Bridewealth is practiced in many parts of the world, including sub-Saharan Africa, the Pacific Islands, and Southeast Asia.

Another form of marital exchange is brideservice. *Brideservice* is the custom whereby a husband is required to work for the family of the bride for a specified amount of time. Sometimes a brideservice is used as a substitute for bridewealth. It is less widespread than bridewealth and has been practiced among some Native

American and sub-Saharan cultures. It was more widespread in past historical eras, such as among the ancient Hebrews and Greeks. For most societies, the primary purpose of brideservice is to compensate the family of the bride.

One other variation of marital exchange is a dowry. A *dowry* is a payment to the groom and his family by the bride's family. The dowry, which represents a woman's share of parental property, is usually given to the bride on her wedding day. It is intended in most societies to be a share of the woman's inheritance that she is allowed to apply toward her new marriage. It is also not uncommon for the bride's parents or close relatives to periodically provide gifts throughout the marriage. Dowry transfers of any kind are considered rare forms of marital exchange, but can be found in parts of Europe and South Asia. Dowry transfers are especially popular in parts of India.

Further Reading. Kottak, Conrad Phillip. (1994). *Cultural anthropology* (6th Ed.). New York: McGraw-Hill; Nanda, Serena. (1991). *Cultural anthropology* (4th Ed.). Belmont, CA: Wadsworth; Peoples, James, and Garrick Bailey. (1991). *Humanity: An introduction to cultural anthropology* (2nd Ed.). St. Paul, MN: West.

MARRIAGE, LAWS GOVERNING. The institution of marriage is regulated and governed through laws. From a fundamental viewpoint, marriage exists as a contract between a man and a woman. Provisions of this contract are dictated by state, rather than federal, law, and a marriage declared legal in one state becomes valid in all states.

Before two people can marry, they must meet certain legal requirements. To begin with, both parties must be of a certain minimum age, which varies from state to state. In most states, the legal age is 18 for the male and 16 for the female with parental consent, and 21 for the male and 18 for the female without parental consent. Marriages between close blood relatives are forbidden. Another requirement prior to the marriage is that the couple must obtain a marriage license. Also, most states require a blood test to ensure that neither partner has a sexually transmitted disease. Most states have a three-day delay between the time of the blood test and the actual issuance of the marriage license. Presumably, this delay represents a "cooling-off" period, a time span that affords couples one last chance to change their minds.

The actual wedding ceremony must be performed by someone legally permitted to do so by the state. It must be witnessed by two persons of legal age. Following the ceremony, the couple, the witnesses, and the official performing the ceremony must sign the marriage license. Finally, the completed license is sent to the state capital, where it is recorded and filed.

Further Reading. Ruback, Barry. (1985). Family law. In Luciano L'Abate (Ed.), *The handbook of family psychology and therapy*. Homewood, IL: Dorsey Press; Turner, Jeffrey S., and Donald B. Helms. (1988). *Marriage and family: Traditions and transitions.* San Diego, CA: Harcourt Brace Jovanovich.

MARRIAGE, MOTIVES FOR. There are many reasons why individuals choose to marry, such as the need for some type of social approval or motivations reflecting personal reasons. While the motives for entering married life are numerous and diverse, it is possible to identify some of the more popular reasons. The following represent some of these motives.

Love. The love and commitment shared by partners are often the primary reasons for getting married. Couples desire to share themselves in an enduring and intimate relationship, one that they feel is best represented within the institution of marriage.

Companionship. The chance to spend one's life with someone in a permanent and visible institution is another important motive. The prospect of a regular companion also tends to generate emotional and psychological well-being, which in turn breeds feelings of security and comfort. Along similar lines, companionship provides couples with the opportunity to share, be it the routines attached to domestic life or leisure activities.

Conformity. For many couples, marriage represents the "thing to do" or the "natural progression" of relationship building. After courting and the engagement period, getting married is seen as the final stage of the mate-selection process. Contributing to this motive are the social pressures, both subtle and direct, from family, friends, and others prompting the couple to marry.

Legitimization of sex. Married status still provides social approval for many with respect to sexual behavior, even though a large proportion of men and women today engage in nonmarital intercourse. Also, many of today's Americans have adopted a more tolerant attitude toward premarital sexual relationships.

Legitimization of children. Children born into a marital relationship have a legitimate identity. Some segments of society strongly feel that a child born out of wedlock is immoral. It should be acknowledged, also, that many couples would never consider getting married unless they wanted to have a child.

Sense of readiness. Many couples report that a decision to marry occurred when they felt "ready." The couple had done the things they wanted to accomplish before marrying. This might have included finishing an education, launching a career, or tending to personal or family matters.

Legal benefits. This may not be one of the strongest motives for marriage, but it deserves to be acknowledged. Married status does have its share of tax advantages, and for couples concerned with the economic welfare of their relationship, this motive may receive more than cursory notice.

In addition to these reasons, it should be added that there are motives for not getting married. For example, some may feel that many of the goals just mentioned are possible through cohabitation, particularly the attainment of love, companionship, and sharing. Other motives against marriage might include a perceived reduction of freedom and a loss of independence.

There are also numerous questionable reasons for getting married. That is, some people may choose to marry for selfish reasons—for instance, to acquire a sexual partner or to obtain economic or emotional security. Some marry to escape the loneliness of a solitary existence or because they want to get away from an unhappy home situation. Some couples are also pressured into marrying by family and friends.

Further Reading. Gelles, Richard J. (1995). *Contemporary families: A sociological view.* Thousand Oaks, CA: Sage; Henslin, James M. (Ed.). (1985). *Marriage and family in a changing society* (2nd Ed.). New York: Free Press; Knox, David, and Caroline Schacht. (1994). *Choices in relationships* (4th Ed.). St. Paul, MN: West.

MARRIAGE, RECURRENT HISTORICAL TRENDS IN. One of the more interesting and obvious features about marriage and family life as it existed in the past is that certain trends appear to be recurrent. That is, certain practices have repeated themselves over the course of time. Such practices, which reflect unique societal beliefs, customs, and rules, can be summarized as follows:

Marriage was strongly encouraged. In many instances, marriages were also prearranged by the parents, more often than not by fathers. Remaining single earned disdain from many; indeed, unmarried adults were often viewed with suspicion and mistrust. In colonial America, for example, single men had to pay special taxes because of their unmarried status.

Individuals entered the institution of marriage at early ages. Throughout much of history, people married at surprisingly early ages. While an important reason for this was a shorter life expectancy, prompting for early marriages by one's parents also took place. For example, while in Rome the legal age for marriage was 14 for boys and 12 for girls, it was not uncommon for fathers to betroth their children at even younger ages.

Marriages were patriarchal in scope. The husband typically controlled the household, and the wife occupied a subordinate position. Husbands were responsible for family decision making and those factors affecting the family's welfare and operation. In some civilizations, such as ancient Greece, women were continually told of their lesser status. Plato, for instance, perceived women as being intellectually and biologically inferior to their male counterparts.

Household activities reflected gender-role stereotyping. Domestic chores usually mirrored clear-cut gender-role stereotyping; that is, chores were assigned on the basis of one's sex rather than on individual ability. While there were exceptions, household responsibilities followed a fairly predictable pattern. Husbands saw to the farming or other family enterprise, as well as to the physically taxing chores that had to be done. Wives handled such domestic chores as cooking, weaving, and child rearing. While women were relegated to a subordinate position in the home, it should be added that throughout much of history, they were respected for the work they did.

Families were self-sufficient economic units. The agrarian family of the past, complete with its gender-typed division of labor, was a unique self-sufficient economic unit. It produced as a unit and consumed as a unit. This was a trend that persisted from the earliest times to the Industrial Revolution (see INDUSTRIAL REVOLUTION, LIFESPAN RELATIONSHIPS DURING THE).

Children were regarded as economic commodities. Throughout history, children were expected to make meaningful contributions to the family enterprise. They were taught chores beginning at early ages, many by their seventh birthday. While children today are more or less economic liabilities, children of yesteryear loomed as valuable economic commodities.

Provisions for divorce have existed for centuries. Contrary to the beliefs of many, provisions for divorce have been around for some time. For example, a divorce could have been obtained in Mesopotamia and ancient Egypt as well as in most early civilizations. However, while provisions existed, the number of persons actually obtaining a divorce was relatively small. In many instances, those securing a divorce also met with social disapproval.

Further Reading. Aries, Philippe. (1962). *Centuries of childhood.* New York: Knopf; Henslin, James M. (Ed.). (1985). *Marriage and family in a changing society* (2nd Ed.). New York: Free Press; Turner, Jeffrey S., and Donald B. Helms. (1988). *Marriage and family: Traditions and transitions.* San Diego, CA: Harcourt Brace Jovanovich.

MARRIAGE, TRENDS IN. Over the years, marriage has reflected a variety of trends, most notably its ongoing popularity as a chosen lifestyle. Marriage in the United States is even more popular today than it was at the turn of the century. If current trends continue, about 93 percent of the population will exchange marriage vows at one time or another in their lifetime.

However, there have been some notable shifts in marriage trends among young Americans. In 1970, about 45 percent of males and 64 percent of females in their twenties had already married. By 1990, though, corresponding figures had dipped to 30 percent and 50 percent. Thus, while demographic trends indicate that most people marry, among modern Americans the decision is being postponed.

In 1994, the total number of marriages in the United States was over 2,400,000. Such large numbers existed even in the presence of a declining *marriage rate,* or the number of marriages each year per 1,000 members of the population (see MARRIAGE RATE). This is because the maturing of the large post–World War II baby-boom generation increased the number of people in the most common marriage ages.

Marriage rates peaked in the United States in 1946 in the surge of marriages that occurred following World War II. During that time, the marriage rate was 16.4 per 1,000 people. Marriage rates remained relatively high throughout the 1950s and then started to show a decline in the 1960s and 1970s. Today, the marriage rate per 1,000 persons is about 9.5.

The timing of marriage in the 1990s has changed from past eras. Because of the growing numbers who are postponing marriage, the *median age* at first marriage has increased (median age means that one-half of the people marrying for the first time in a given year get married before the given age, and one-half after). The following statistics help show how the median age at first marriage has changed over the years: In 1890, the median age was 26.1 for men and 22 for women. In 1976, it was 23.8 and 21.3 for men and women, respectively. In

1983, it was 24.4 for grooms and 22.5 for brides. In 1993, the median age increased once more: 25.9 for men and 23.6 for women. This represents the highest median age ever recorded for American women, and the highest for men since the median age of 25.9 in 1900.

A number of reasons account for the postponement of marriage. A strictly demographic factor during the last two decades has been the *marriage squeeze.* Given that women are usually two or three years younger than men at marriage, the marriage squeeze developed as a consequence of the upward trend of births during the baby boom. Because of this, a female born in 1947, when the birth rate had risen, was likely to marry a male born in 1944 or 1945, when the birth rate was still low. Consequently, about 20 years later, there was an excess of women in the primary ages for marriage, and this phenomenon continued for the length of time that the baby boom lasted. Therefore, by 1970, the number of men 20 to 26 years of age was only 93 percent of the number of women aged 18 to 24. The corresponding figure for African-American males was 82 percent.

This meant that by 1970, there was a shortage of men in the primary marriageable ages for women. This was true for young adults regardless of race. By 1980, this percentage had escalated somewhat, to 98 percent for all races. Today, the figure is close to 108 percent, as the declining birthrates of the 1960s and early 1970s create a reversal of the marriage-squeeze phenomenon.

There are other reasons for marriage postponement in the 1990s. More persons, especially women, are enrolling in college, graduate school, and professional schools. There are also expanding employment and career opportunities for women, and many men and women are placing their careers ahead of marriage plans. Finally, the high divorce rate in this country has prompted some to seriously question the traditional appeal of marriage and family life.

Further Reading. Glick, Paul C. (1990). American families: As they are and were. *Sociology and Social Research, 74,* 139–145; National Center for Health Statistics. (1994). *Vital statistics of the United States.* Washington, DC: U.S. Government Printing Office; U.S. Bureau of the Census. (1994). *Statistical abstract of the United States: 1994* (114th Ed.). Washington, DC: U.S. Government Printing Office.

MARRIAGE, VARIATIONS IN STRUCTURE. Because the institution of marriage is shaped and molded by culture, it varies enormously from people to people. Unique variations in marital structure exist, which in turn shape the forms that family life can take. Among the more notable variations are the number of spouses allowed by law, and patterns of residency, descent, and authority.

Monogamy versus polygamy. Monogamy is the marriage of one man to one woman. This is the characteristic form of marriage in the United States and the only type that is legal. However, because of escalating divorce rates, some observers feel that serial monogamy is the more accurate title for marriage in this country. *Serial monogamy* is a succession of partners through the process of marriage, divorce, remarriage, and so on.

It might seem that all societies would regard monogamy as the preferable marital arrangement, but this is not the case. Rather, a significant number of societies practice what is called *polygamy,* or plural marriage. The word *polygamy* comes from two Greek words meaning "many marriages." There are two basic forms of polygamy: polygyny and polyandry.

Polygyny is the marriage of one man to two or more women. Of the two forms of polygamy, polygyny is the more prevalent. Many societies have practiced polygyny at one time or another and many still do, particularly in regions of Asia and Africa. However, while a given society may permit polygyny, a monogamous relationship is usually the preferred arrangement. Often, polygyny is a sign that a man is successful, rich, and even powerful. Some kings and noblemen throughout history provide testimony to this, in some cases in extreme ways. For example, the Bible discloses that King Solomon had as many as 700 wives, while Lukengu, a legendary chief of the Bakuba tribe in Zaire, kept 800! In the United States, polygyny was also practiced among the Mormons (see MORMONS, POLYGYNY AMONG THE).

Polyandry is the marriage of one woman to two or more men. Polyandry has been an extremely rare occurrence throughout history. It is practiced, though, among some Buddhist Tibetans, some groups in Nigeria, and the Toda in southern India. In the Himalayas, some polyandrous households involve a number of brothers who share a wife, thus preventing the dissolution of family wealth or property.

Patterns of residency. Where a couple chooses to reside may also be influenced by social norms. *Patrilocal residency* means that the couple lives with or near the husband's relatives. *Matrilocal residency,* on the other hand, places the couple with or near the wife's relatives. While these two patterns of residency can apply to some couples in the United States, another is more apparent: neolocal residency. *Neolocal residency* occurs when the couple establishes its own separate living arrangement. The geographical location is not based on ties originating from either the husband's or the wife's family.

Patterns of descent. An important feature of marriage and family life is kinship, how family members are related to one another. Patterns of descent, important for the tracing of one's lineage as well as for inheritance and other purposes, can be traced in three separate ways. *Patrilineal descent* traces lineage on the husband's side of the family. *Matrilineal descent* places the importance on the wife's side. In the United States today, though, bilateral descent is the more prevalent pattern. *Bilateral descent* places equal importance on the families of both the husband and the wife. Power, property, and the like are transferred from both the husband's and the wife's side of the family to their offspring.

Patterns of authority. Variation also exists in the dyad's power structure, or who influences and dominates decision making within the household. A *patriarchal power structure* places the husband in this dominating position, while in a *matriarchal power structure* the wife is more influential. To date, there have been no truly matriarchal societies. An *egalitarian* (or equalitarian) *power structure* is emerging in the United States and other industrialized nations. The egalitarian system emphasizes the sharing of marital power between husband and wife. Spouses are regarded as equals, and decisions are reached mutually.

Further Reading. Bird, Gloria, and Keith Melville. (1994). *Families and intimate relationships.* New York: McGraw-Hill; Eshleman, J. Ross. (1994). *The family: An introduction* (7th Ed.). Boston: Allyn and Bacon; Gelles, Richard J. (1995). *Contemporary families: A sociological view.* Thousand Oaks, CA: Sage.

MARRIAGE AND FAMILY, DEFINITIONS AND DIMENSIONS OF.

Marriage and family are important concepts, and their clarification merits special attention. Marriage supplies the foundation for family life, and families are the basic building blocks of every society in the world. In fact, the family is the oldest human institution and, in many respects, the most important.

From a definitive point of view, *marriage* is an institutional act that unites a man and a woman. Marriage is intended to be a stable, enduring relationship and involves a legal agreement between husband and wife. This legal agreement exists in the form of a marriage contract, which stipulates reciprocal rights and obligations between spouses. These rights and obligations are expected to continue unless the marriage is dissolved by further legal action.

The social institution of marriage is the basis for the social institution of the family. A *family* is defined as a social arrangement consisting of two or more persons related by blood, marriage, or adoption. Typically, the family consists of parents and children. A family shares a common residence and represents a social system that operates with a set of norms and roles, although these vary from culture to culture.

What is universal in virtually all societies, though, are the functions the family performs. At least six such functions have been identified, all of which are essential in bringing order to society. One, the family regulates sexual behavior and reproduction. Two, the family meets the biological needs of a society's members (such as food, shelter, and protection). Three, the family provides status placement, bestowing status or rank on people by virtue of their birth and determining their relationship to one another. Four, the family offers emotional maintenance, including a sense of security and being wanted. Five, the family provides socialization by training children in appropriate skills and actions, as well as transmitting norms, values, and beliefs. Finally, the family represents a form of social control, demanding certain behaviors and restricting others, which lessens the need for overt control. (See MARRIAGE, VARIATIONS IN STRUCTURE.)

Further Reading. Boss, Pauline G., William Doherty, Ralph LaRossa, Walter R. Schumm, and Suzanne K. Steinmetz. (1993). *Sourcebook of family theories and methods: A contextual approach.* New York: Plenum Press; Copeland, Anne P., and Kathleen M. White. (1991). *Studying families.* Newbury Park, CA: Sage.

MARRIAGE AND FAMILY, SCIENTIFIC STUDY OF. The scientific study of marriage and family is a relatively recent research pursuit, but none-theless an active field of investigation. This discipline draws from many fields of study, including psychology, sociology, anthropology, history, human development, home economics, law, religion, education, and demography. Marriage and family researchers explore a wide range of topics, including dating and courtship, gender roles, interpersonal communication, alternative lifestyles, kinship systems, parenthood, intergenerational care, divorce, family policy, family stress and crises, and family therapy. From this broad array of research topics, marriage and family researchers seek to gain a better understanding of persons, relationships, and family structures. Examples of research journals devoted to the scientific study of marriage and family include the *Journal of Marriage and the Family, Family Relations,* and the *Journal of Sex and Marital Therapy.*
Further Reading. Copeland, Anne P., and Kathleen M. White. (1991). *Studying families.* Newbury Park, CA: Sage; Hawes, Joseph M., and Elizabeth I. Nybakken. (1991). *American families: A research guide and historical handbook.* Westport, CT: Greenwood Press.

MARRIAGE CEREMONY, RITUALS AND CUSTOMS. Marriage ceremonies have been practiced for centuries and are unique to each culture. When such ceremonies are studied, one discovers that a wide variety of rituals and customs exist, many of which initially appear to make little sense. However, experts inform us that most of them are remnants of earlier traditions, customs, and even superstitions.

The wedding ring, for example, is rooted in antiquity. The Romans used wedding rings, and rings have also been found in ancient Egyptian tombs. From the times of these early civilizations, the wedding ring has symbolized the highest form of trust and commitment. Wearing the ring on the third finger of the left hand is a custom dating back to Egyptian pharaohs. They believed that a vein in that finger ran directly to the heart.

The bridal veil is also a time-honored tradition. It has long been worn by Christian, Jewish, Moslem, and Hindu brides, to name but a few cultures. Over the centuries, the veil protected the bride against malicious spirits, from the "evil eye," and from the stares of curious outsiders to the ceremony. The veil also represented the bride's purity. Pulling the veil back after the vows were exchanged symbolized the bride's new status as a wife.

The color of the wedding gown has an interesting historical background. Throughout history, people have considered a marriage as a union of two families, not just a union of two individuals. The bride's family had to guarantee her virginity because it represented their honor. To do this, white wedding gowns were most often chosen, the purity of white symbolizing the bride's virginity. In support of this, as well as some other thoughts regarding wedding-gown colors, consider the following anonymous Victorian verse:

Married in white, you have chosen all right;
Married in gray, you will go far away;
Married in black, you will wish yourself back;
Married in red, you wish yourself dead;
Married in green, ashamed to be seen;
Married in blue, he will always be true;
Married in pearl, you will live in a whirl;
Married in yellow, ashamed of your fellow;
Married in brown, you will live out of town;
Married in pink, your fortune will sink.

The kiss at the altar is a wedding custom that has been with us for some time. For centuries, the purpose of the kiss was to seal or affirm the wedding vows. But the kiss is not required today to make the marriage legal. In earlier times, the priest gave the groom the "benediction kiss," the "kiss of peace," or the "holy kiss," as some called it, and the groom in turn kissed the bride. The priest's assistants then solemnly kissed each of the wedding guests. Today, the wedding participants and guests seem to prefer to do their own kissing.

Cutting the wedding cake is also a centuries-old tradition. Years ago, it was believed that the breaking or cutting of the wedding cake increased the wife's fertility and aided in the birth of the first child. Often, this was done by breaking or cutting the cake over the bride's head until the milder and less messy practice of sprinkling some of the crumbs on her seemed sufficient. There is speculation that this was where the practice of throwing rice on the couple developed.

Over the years, children have usually been a part of the wedding party. Children were often added to the wedding party to encourage fertility and to serve as a reminder of the purpose of marriage. In Roman wedding ceremonies, an offering was made in the form of a wheat cake to the god Jupiter. The couple also repeated prayers to Juno, the goddess of marriage. An altar boy participated in these rituals, and he seems to be the obvious predecessor of today's ring bearer in symbolizing the desired male child.

No one knows for sure how the honeymoon originated, but considerable speculation exists. For example, centuries ago, brides were often captured and carried off to locations where they could not be found by relatives. When the moon went through its 30-day phase, the couple drank a fermented honey brew called metheglin or mead. Honey has long been a symbol of life, health, and fertility; when it was combined with the lunar cycle, the word honeymoon thus evolved.

Further Reading. Chesser, Barbara Jo. (1980). Analysis of wedding rituals: An attempt to make weddings more meaningful. *Family Relations, 29,* 73–76; Tober, Barbara. (1984). *The bride: A celebration.* New York: Harry N. Abrams; Turner, Jeffrey S., and Donald B. Helms. (1988). *Marriage and family: Traditions and transitions.* San Diego, CA: Harcourt Brace Jovanovich.

MARRIAGE CEREMONY, RITUALS AND CUSTOMS. INTERNATIONAL PERSPECTIVES. From an international perspective, wedding ceremonies reflect a wide variety of rituals and customs. For example, before a Hindu wedding ceremony begins, a holy fire is lit to the fire god, Agni, who traditionally will bear witness to the wedding. Customs during the service are both religious and cultural. A tree is planted because of the ancient belief that plants and animals are representations of the gods, and this will ensure their presence. The bride's father gives her hand to the groom, then sprinkles her with holy water to indicate that his ties with her are washed away. A *thali,* a gold ornament threaded on a yellow string, is tied around the bride's neck. She will wear it for all her married life, its three knots reminding her of her duty to serve her parents, husband, and sons. The ceremony concludes when the couple circle the holy fire three times, throwing offerings of rice and flowers into the air.

In Japan, many wedding ceremonies take place before a Shinto shrine, even though a marriage is not regarded as a religious service. The ceremony brings the bride into the family of the bridegroom, and ancestors are honored in the ritual by bowing, ringing bells, and offering food before family shrines. Nine sips of sake are the essence of the ceremony, for there are no vows. Later, sips of sake are exchanged with the parents, both to honor them and to mark their formal acceptance of the marriage. A Shinto priest officiates.

Other examples illustrate the diversity that exists in wedding ceremonies. In India, the groom's brother sprinkles flower petals on the bridal couple at the conclusion of the ceremony to ward off evil. On the island of Fiji, the groom presents the bride's father with a *tabua*—a whale's tooth symbolizing status and wealth. In Bermuda, islanders top off their tiered wedding cake with a tiny tree sapling, which is planted by the newlyweds at the wedding reception. Finally, in Lithuania, the wedded couple are served a symbolic meal by their parents— wine for joy, salt for tears, and bread for hard work.

Further Reading. Chesser, Barbara Jo. (1980). Analysis of wedding rituals: An attempt to make weddings more meaningful. *Family Relations, 29,* 73–76; Tober, Barbara. (1984). *The bride: A celebration.* New York: Harry N. Abrams; Turner, Jeffrey S., and Donald B. Helms. (1988). *Marriage and family: Traditions and transitions.* San Diego, CA: Harcourt Brace Jovanovich.

MARRIAGE RATE. The marriage rate, also called the *crude marriage rate,* is the number of marriages each year per 1,000 members of the population. The marriage rate is calculated by using the number of marriages, not the number of people getting married, and includes both first marriages and remarriages. Today, the marriage rate in the United States is about 9.5.

Further Reading. Haupt, Arthur, and Thomas T. Kane. (1985). *The population reference bureau's population handbook.* Washington, DC: Population Reference Bureau; Shryock, Henry S., and Jacob S. Siegel. (1976). *The methods and materials of demography.* Orlando, FL: Academic Press.

MARRIAGE SQUEEZE. See MARRIAGE, TRENDS IN.

MASLOW, ABRAHAM H. Abraham H. Maslow (1908–1970) was instrumental in shaping humanistic theory, a school of thought in psychology that emphasizes an individual's uniqueness, personal potential, and inner drives. Born in Brooklyn, New York, Maslow earned his B.A., M.A., and Ph.D. degrees from the University of Wisconsin. From 1935 to 1937, Maslow taught at Columbia University on a Carnegie Fellowship, and he later taught at Brooklyn College. Following his stay at Brooklyn, Maslow went to Brandeis University, where he became chairman of the Department of Psychology. He remained at Brandeis until his death in 1970.

Among his accomplishments, Maslow served as president of the American Psychological Association in 1967. He was also president of the Massachusetts Psychological Association and chairman of the Personality and Social Psychology Division of the American Psychological Association. Maslow also was the founder of the *Journal of Humanistic Psychology.*

Maslow earned critical acclaim with his theory of *self-actualization,* which distinguished between an organism's basic needs, such as the needs for food, water, sex, security, and companionship, and what Maslow called *metaneeds.* The basic needs are often called deficiency needs because the organism is motivated toward fulfilling some deficiency. Only after these more basic needs are met can a person move on toward meeting metaneeds such as those for beauty, justice, and goodness. The ability to meet these higher needs can lead toward happiness, satisfaction, and, possibly, self-actualization.

Further Reading. Maslow, Abraham H. (1968). *Toward a psychology of being* (2nd Ed.). Princeton, NJ: Van Nostrand Reinhold; Maslow, Abraham H. (1970). *Motivation and personality* (2nd Ed.). New York: Harper and Row; McAdams, Dan P. (1994). *The person: An introduction to personality psychology* (2nd Ed.). Fort Worth, TX: Harcourt Brace.

MASTERS, WILLIAM H., AND JOHNSON, VIRGINIA E. William H. Masters (1915–) and Virginia E. Johnson (1925–) are perhaps the most famous team of investigators in the history of human sexuality research. Masters received his M.D. degree from the Rochester School of Medicine in 1943. At Washington University in St. Louis, Masters began exploring the physiology of sex, as well as the treatment of sexual dysfunction. Spurred on by the generally favorable response to Alfred Kinsey's human sexuality research (see KINSEY, ALFRED C.), Masters decided to launch a more detailed investigation on sexual functioning and enlisted the services of research associate Virginia Johnson, who had studied psychology and sociology at the University of Missouri. Masters and Johnson, who later married and then divorced, began a laboratory physiological study of human sexual response in 1957. The two founded and served as codirectors of the Masters and Johnson Institute in St. Louis.

Unlike Kinsey, Masters and Johnson directly and systematically observed (and filmed) sexual intercourse and self-stimulation, or masturbation. Whereas Kinsey's research represented a statistical analysis of sexual behavior, Masters and

Johnson broke new ground by using sophisticated instrumentation to measure the physiology of sexual response. They recruited a total of 694 female and male volunteers for laboratory study (all were paid for their services), including 276 married couples. The unmarried subjects participated primarily in noncoital research activities, such as studies of ejaculatory processes in males of the ways in which different contraceptive devices affected female sexual response. Although most subjects were between the ages of 18 and 40, Masters and Johnson included a group of subjects over the age of 50 in order to study the effects of aging on sexual response. A careful screening procedure was designed to weed out exhibitionists and people with emotional disturbances.

Following a tour of Masters and Johnson's laboratory facilities and inspection of the equipment to be used in the studies, each subject was invited to a private practice session. The purpose of this was to accustom people to engaging in sexual activity in a laboratory environment. When actual experimental sessions began, subjects performed acts of masturbation or sexual intercourse while being filmed or wearing devices that recorded physiological response to sexual stimulation. For example, a subject might wear electrode terminals connected to an electrocardiograph that would produce a record of her heart's activity during sexual intercourse. Or a subject might have a band placed around his penis to record size and speed of erection in response to manual stimulation.

In over 10,000 sessions, Masters and Johnson recorded subjects' responses to sexual stimulation and discovered striking similarities between the responses of men and women. From this research, Masters and Johnson developed a sexual model of response called the *sexual response cycle* (see SEXUAL RESPONSE CYCLE). The model consists of four stages of physiological response during which two basic physiological reactions occur: an increased concentration of blood in bodily tissues in the genitals and female breasts, and increased energy in the nerves and muscles throughout the body.

The Masters and Johnson research model was not without its critics. For example, many viewed the laboratory setting as dehumanizing and mechanizing sex. Many critics felt that the emphasis placed on the physiology of sex downplayed its interpersonal and emotional aspects. Some objected to the research design on ethical grounds, claiming that the project was an invasion of privacy. Finally, critics wondered if Masters and Johnson had selected a representative sample of the population. In fact, most of the subjects were well educated and more affluent than the average person. Moreover, their willingness to perform sexually under laboratory conditions suggested that they were not typical. Overall, though, the research of Masters and Johnson had enormous impact on the field of human sexuality. For the first time, scientific evidence on the physiology of the orgasmic response was systematically gathered. Because of these researchers' efforts, laboratory studies of sexual arousal achieved a new level of respectability among scientific researchers.

Further Reading. Masters, William H., and Virginia Johnson. (1966). *Human sexual response.* Boston: Little, Brown; Masters, William H., and Virginia Johnson. (1970).

Human sexual inadequacy. Boston: Little, Brown; Masters, William H., Virginia Johnson, and Robert C. Kolodny. (1988). *Sex and human loving.* Boston: Little, Brown.

MATE SWAPPING. See SWINGING.

MATRIARCHAL POWER STRUCTURE. See MARRIAGE, VARIATIONS IN STRUCTURE.

MATRILINEAL DESCENT. See MARRIAGE, VARIATIONS IN STRUCTURE.

MATRILOCAL RESIDENCY. See MARRIAGE, VARIATIONS IN STRUCTURE.

MEAD, GEORGE H. George Herbert Mead (1863–1931) was an early social psychologist and sociologist. Among his many contributions to both disciplines, Mead explored how one's personality is shaped and molded by society. He emphasized the importance of role taking and role playing, and how the learning of social expectations contributes to a person's developing sense of self. Role taking and role playing are social processes evident throughout life, from the play stage of childhood to the roles demanded throughout adulthood.

According to Mead, one's sense of self is greatly influenced by *significant others,* people of importance such as parents, siblings, and peers. Over the course of the lifespan, a person will internalize the values and attitudes of significant others and apply them to society as a whole, which Mead termed the *generalized other.* While significant others represent real persons, the generalized other consists of societal values and attitudes.

Mead also expounded upon an individual's *social self,* which he believed was composed of two related elements: the ''me'' and the ''I.'' The ''me'' represents the individual's objective involvement in social roles and role playing. The ''I'' is a person's subjective side and mirrors individual attributes. Compared to the predictable nature of the ''me,'' the ''I'' is spontaneous, unconforming, and creative. Mead argued that society needs both components of the social self in order to operate smoothly. If everyone behaved exclusively at the ''I'' level, there would be social chaos and disorganization. If the ''me'' level dominated, there would be no creativity, innovation, or social change. Finally, Mead argued that the social self undergoes change and modification throughout the lifespan, particularly as one's social statuses and relationships change.

Further Reading. Bryjak, George J., and Michael P. Soroka. (1994). *Sociology: Cultural diversity in a changing world,* (2nd Ed.). Boston: Allyn and Bacon; Mead, George H. (1934). *Mind, self, and society.* Chicago: University of Chicago Press.

MEAD, MARGARET. Margaret Mead (1901–1978) was a noted anthropologist who explored and carefully detailed cross-cultural differences in a wide range of topics, including gender, temperament, and rites of passage. In her most famous fieldwork, Mead set out for Samoa in 1925 in order to test the notion that puberty creates social and psychological stress for all adolescents. In her classic book *Coming of age in Samoa: A psychological study of primitive youth for Western civilization,* Mead concluded that puberty need not be a period of stress and turbulence. On the contrary, Mead observed that adolescence in Samoa was a smooth and tranquil period. For most, it was a time for happiness, self-indulgence, and a relatively carefree—and conflict-free—lifestyle. Such observations prompted Mead to discount the notion that a difficult adolescence was a universal experience, that it was always a period of conflict and turmoil. Rather, she maintained that the experience of adolescence varies according to cultural influences. Because of the role of culture, it is incorrect to assume that all adolescents share the same experiences.

In later research, Mead also analyzed three primitive societies (Arapesh, Mundugumor, and Tchambuli) on the island of New Guinea to see whether temperamental differences are universal. Her fieldwork disclosed that among the Arapesh, both men and women behaved in what our culture would call feminine fashions. In the Mundugumor tribe, both women and men possessed such "masculine" traits as assertiveness and competitiveness. Among the Tchambuli, women were independent, dominant, and managerial, whereas men were emotional, submissive, and dependent. Mead's research demonstrated that while individuals are born with a biological sexual identity, it is society and culture that truly impact on peoples' lives and leave an indelible imprint on the course of growth development.

Further Reading. Mead, Margaret. (1928). *Coming of age in Samoa: A psychological study of primitive youth for Western civilization.* New York: William Morrow; Mead, Margaret (Ed.) (1937). *Cooperation and competition among primitive peoples.* New York: McGraw-Hill.

MECHANISTIC MODEL OF LIFESPAN DEVELOPMENT. See WORLD VIEWS OF LIFESPAN DEVELOPMENT.

MEDIAN AGE. The median age is the age at which one-half of the population is older and one-half is younger. For example, the median age of the U.S. population in 1994 was 30.6. Utilization of the median age often occurs in the research of lifespan investigators, who seek to chart age differences in the population.

Further Reading. Haupt, Arthur, and Thomas T. Kane. (1985). *The population reference bureau's population handbook.* Washington, DC: Population Reference Bureau; Shryock, Henry S., and Jacob S. Siegel. (1976). *The methods and materials of demography.* Orlando, FL: Academic Press.

MESOPOTAMIA, LIFESPAN RELATIONSHIPS IN. The Mesopotamian civilization was founded before 3500 B.C. in the region now known as

Iraq. The people who migrated to the valley formed by the Tigris and Euphrates rivers probably came from the highlands of present-day Turkey or Iran. The culture they built included at one time or another the Sumerians, Persians, Assyrians, and Babylonians. Because Mesopotamia had great influence on the cultures of the ancient world—notably the Greek and Roman civilizations—which in turn influenced European culture and society, it is generally considered the cradle of Western civilization.

Like many other peoples, the Mesopotamians strongly encouraged marriage. This civilization accorded men a dominant cultural role, and public affairs were clearly in the hands of men. Women were expected to bear children, tend to the household, and minister to their husbands' needs. Children also subscribed to traditional gender-role socialization: boys were taught a wide range of farm-related chores, while girls learned various domestic responsibilities. The elderly were not isolated from the family unit. Rather, they were the recipients of considerable respect, love, and, when needed, supportive care.

Among the Sumerians, who ruled Mesopotamia around 3000 B.C., *monogamy* (the marriage of one man to one woman) rather than *polygamy* (having multiple marriage partners) was the law of the land, but interesting variations of the former were practiced. For instance, if a man's wife were sick or barren, he sometimes kept one or more concubines. A *concubine* was a woman who was not legally married to a man but could live with him and bear his children. Under certain conditions a husband could sell his wife, and he could also hand her over to someone else as a slave for years at a time in payment for a debt.

In most instances, promiscuous sexual relations were frowned upon in Mesopotamia. A young man who had seduced an innocent girl was legally required to ask her parents for her hand in marriage. To refuse to do so could cost him his life. The Sumerians also disapproved of *adultery,* sexual intercourse with a person other than one's spouse. However, the response to this offense was clearly stamped with sex discrimination. The unfaithful husband was not usually punished, although he was sometimes required to compensate his wife in some way. Adultery in a wife, however, was regarded as an extremely serious offense. During certain points in the Sumerian civilization, this offense was punishable with death by drowning. Sometimes both the wife and her lover were bound and thrown into the water to drown together. On other occasions, unfaithful wives had their nose or ears cut off, and their lovers were castrated.

Under the reign of Hammurabi (1792–1750 B.C.), sexual freedom increased, and premarital sexual relations were more widely tolerated. An effort was also made to improve the status of women, particularly within the institution of marriage. For example, once married, the wife assumed possession of the betrothal payment and added to it the *dowry,* or gifts given the couple by the bride's relatives (see MARITAL EXCHANGES). These two assets became the bride's inalienable property, which on her death she could bequeath to her children if she wished. If a woman's husband died, she inherited the same share of his property as did each of his children. A widow could marry again, taking with her her original dowry but relinquishing her share of her late husband's estate. Although it was difficult, she could divorce her husband, particularly if he neglected his conjugal duties.

Mesopotamia had the distinction of being one of the first civilizations to offer sacred sexual rituals in its temples. Religious rites and acts symbolizing fertility were encouraged by the priests in an effort to ensure the fertility of both the people and their fields. Religiously sanctioned prostitution, supervised by the temples, was also common in Mesopotamia. Again, the rationale for this activity was the assurance of fertility. The Sumerians established the first such temple in the sanctuary of Anu, their supreme deity, at Uruk. In some of the larger temples, such as those in Babylon, male prostitutes also occupied a special brothel, or house of prostitution. A senior priest was placed in charge of this facility and its occupants.

Further Reading. Ardehali, Paula E. (1991). Sexual customs in other cultures. In Robert T. Francoeur (Ed.). *Becoming a sexual person* (2nd Ed.). New York: Macmillan; Fellows, Ward J. (1979). *Religions east and west.* New York: Holt, Rinehart and Winston; Turner, Jeffrey S., and Laurna Rubinson. (1993). *Contemporary human sexuality.* Englewood Cliffs, NJ: Prentice Hall.

METAMESSAGES. See COMMUNICATION, INTERPERSONAL.

METANEEDS. See MASLOW, ABRAHAM H.

MIDDLE ADULTHOOD. The lifespan stage known as middle adulthood generally occurs between the ages of 30 and 60. While middle adulthood represents the longest stage of the life cycle, it is not the most widely researched. In fact, it has been only in recent years that researchers have concentrated their efforts and sought to better understand this life stage. The result of their labor is that we are getting a clearer picture of the special challenges facing middle-aged adults, the developmental forces in operation, and how such forces interact and affect the whole person.

The study of behavior during middle adulthood provides an excellent illustration of how developmental processes blend together. For example, how people react to the physical changes at midlife, including the perceived attractions or unattractiveness of aging processes, as well as the nature of treatment accorded by others, usually affects the manner in which middle-agers ultimately perceive themselves. Note the connection here between physical, cognitive, personality, and social forces. Along similar lines, career triumphs and reactions to failures have important implications for personality stability and the flavoring of social relationships, not to mention the body's stress levels. (See MIDDLE ADULTHOOD, WORK RELATIONSHIPS DURING.)

Affecting whatever personality dynamics exist during middle adulthood is the realization that one has reached an in-between stage of life, the middle of one's existence. One can look back and ahead, perhaps more so than at any other age.

For many, examining the past and anticipating the future often lead to an assessment of one's life: Where have I been, where am I now, and where do I want to go? Seeking to answer these questions honestly has important implications for personality growth (see MIDDLE ADULTHOOD, AND THE MIDLIFE TRANSITION).

Marriage and family life also acquire new dimensions during middle adulthood. Most marriages begin in early adulthood, with children being added to the primary family unit shortly thereafter. By the time these children are teenagers or young adults, and their numbers have stabilized, many of their parents have reached middle age. During this time, middle-aged parents find that they must face a number of developmental tasks. For example, many middle-aged parents discover that they represent the "squeeze" or "sandwich" generation. That is, they have their children on one end of the generational cycle, their aging parents on the other, and themselves in the middle. As a result of this squeeze, middle-aged persons frequently face growing pressures as they cope with the needs of their offspring and parents simultaneously.

Further Reading. Brody, Elaine M. (1990). *Women in the middle: Their parent-care years.* New York: Springer; Oldham, John M., and Robert S. Liebert. (Eds.). (1989). *The middle years: New psychoanalytic perspectives.* New Haven, CT: Yale University Press; Wolf, Mary Alice. (1991). The discovery of middle age. *Educational Gerontology, 17,* 559–571.

MIDDLE ADULTHOOD, AND THE MIDLIFE TRANSITION. The midlife transition, which occurs during middle adulthood, is a psychological period of review and assessment of one's life. Some writers prefer to view the midlife transition as a potentially negative and crisis-oriented period, a time of life filled with numerous conflicts. They emphasize the many changes that take place at this time, such as the permanent departure of children from the home, vocational adjustments, and the necessity of coping with the physiological and psychological consequences of aging.

Others regard the midlife transition as just another stage of the lifespan, having its equal and expected share of developmental challenges and responsibilities. These tasks are no more complex or intense than those at any other age. In fact, some go so far as to label middle adulthood and the midlife transition as euphoric stages of life. Emphasis is often placed on enthusiasm for one's career and the financial stability one is likely to now have, as well as the freedom from the responsibilities of parenthood.

Thus, depending on the interpretation taken, one is likely to read about the negative or positive aspects of midlife. One is also likely to run into some reference to the "inevitability" of a midlife "crisis" and the profound impact it has on the adult. According to some, heavy is the heart and overworked is the mind struggling with the midlife crisis and the problems of this age.

In weighing such research, one should recognize that a midlife "crisis" is not inevitable; indeed, there are many adults who go through life without any such experiences. Also, the word "crisis" tends to have a negative and disruptive ring to it. It needs to be pointed out that many midlife challenges and personal assessments are positive, productive, and rewarding. While there are some serious moments, midlife is not a time characterized by continual conflict.

Because of these considerations, experts tend to move away from the concept of a "crisis" and instead emphasize the notion of review and appraisal. Midlife is a time when there are new dimensions to one's family life, career, intimate relationships, community, and inner life. The midlife transition is characterized by a change in the way individuals see themselves and others around them. As persons move toward these new dimensions and experience changed perceptions, they may encounter uncertainty or strangeness. This is only natural, however, as one moves from one stable state to another.

During the transition, people often reflect on their life successes and failures. For some, this may be anxiety producing and even painful. There are some who just cannot bear to look at their inadequacies or shortcomings. As a result, they rob themselves of total growth and self-understanding. In its most productive form, the midlife transition enables individuals to examine their total selves, carefully exploring strengths as well as weaknesses.

The midlife transition acquires negative dimensions when anxiety, depression, and a sense of futility enter into the picture. Some become preoccupied with signs of aging and premature doom. Others dwell totally on the negative side of their lives and regard themselves as failures. Some report gloom and despair as they recall youthful dreams, current accomplishments, and the gap that exists between the two.

This last point is an important one, since the successful resolution of issues raised depends on one's ability to reassess and readjust. The optimism and dreams of early adulthood need to be put into perspective by the realities of midlife. It is possible that certain goals in life will not be met, and this requires acceptance and adaptation. This may be a painful procedure for many, but it is important to renounce some dreams, while critically evaluating modes of life that are possible and available. This type of reassessment may well lead to greater self-fulfillment in later adult life.

While the points made thus far can apply to both men and women, there appear to be gender differences in the midlife transition. These differences become clearer particularly when traditional family roles are taken into account. Consider the situation of the traditional male. His transition often places more emphasis on career assessment than upon family issues. This does not mean that his family is unimportant; indeed, research indicates that both job and family roles affect men's psychological well-being. It emphasizes, though, that in our competitive society, making it in the career world is a critical issue for males.

Women appear to confront the same issues and tasks at midlife as men, and they too create visions of future accomplishments. However, a noticeable difference between the sexes is that women's dreams tend to include both career and marriage. For large numbers of women, even among those working outside the home, the family is often the focus. A traditional woman's midlife transition is apt to revolve around her husband, the growing independence of her children, and ultimately their departure from the home. When her children do leave, she may feel no longer needed and perceive that a chapter in her life has ended. Also, along traditional lines, a woman spends years standing by her husband's side, often offering unfailing support as he gropes for his occupational niche in the world.

Many traditional women also define their life cycle in terms of their children's and husband's ages, or better yet, family stages. Whereas midlife for men may mean taking on new career challenges, such as becoming a mentor for younger workers, for women it may herald the beginnings of a career commitment. Once the major obligations of motherhood are met, many cease defining themselves exclusively in terms of mother or wife and instead see the vocational or career sides to their identity. Research also tells us that women at midlife become more self-confident, independent, decisive, and dominant. Interestingly, when launching career or educational plans at midlife, many women encounter some of the tasks, challenges, and problems faced by their husbands when they were younger.

Of course, there are variations on all of these traditional patterns, particularly when the mother has worked for most of her adult life. A growing number of women now do so, and the manner in which vocational and family life converges begs further scientific inquiry. Future research needs to explore such dynamics and discover how the abandonment of traditional domestic roles impacts on all facets of adult life, not just during the midlife transition. Along these lines, tomorrow's researchers need to continue their explorations of the quality of marriage in two-paycheck households, the division of household labor when both parents work, perceptions of family stages among working women, the impact of employed mothers on children of all ages, and the manner in which employment affects the formation and dissolution of marriage, to name but a few areas.

Beyond career and family life, other gender differences appear to exist in the midlife transition. For instance, the way aging processes are perceived deserves mention. Accepting one's changing physical self is an important facet of overall psychological adjustment. Often, though, there is a double standard attached to growing old that frequently places women on the losing end. Just consider how the same aging processes for men and women are often perceived differently. Older men get silver hair, women turn gray. Men get more distinguished-looking with age, women just grow old. Character lines crease men's faces, women own a collection of wrinkles. Unfortunately, many segments of society will not allow women to grow old gracefully.

Why is this so? Perhaps the biggest reason is that too much of what is valued about women is connected to their physical appearance. On the other hand, men at midlife appear to be perceived and measured more by what they have accomplished in life than by how they appear to others. Therefore, physical signs of aging are often perceived as part of the male's achievement of worldly success.

Further Reading. Hudson, Frederic M. (1991). *The adult years: Mastering the art of self-renewal.* San Francisco: Jossey-Bass; Turner, Jeffrey S., and Donald B. Helms. (1994). *Contemporary adulthood* (5th Ed.). Fort Worth, TX: Harcourt Brace; Wolf, Mary Alice. (1991). The discovery of middle age. *Educational Gerontology, 17,* 559–571.

MIDDLE ADULTHOOD, MARRIAGE DURING. For many, middle adulthood offers the potential for marital reassessment, a time for couples to critically evaluate their relationship. This becomes a point where couples can look back and ahead, perhaps more so than any other stage. While some couples discover that they have become even closer over the years, others find that their relationship has become less intimate and perhaps even devoid of meaning. Happily married couples usually report a shared and cherished history and the continual enjoyment of being in one another's company. Less enthusiastic couples now recognize that they must take active steps to improve and revitalize their relationship. For some, marital reconstruction is not the chosen path; consequently, divorce or separation lies on the not-too-distant horizon.

Such evaluations and assessments give marriage its unique quality and flavor at this time. Other unique challenges, too, await middle-aged couples, including those related to the care of aging parents and the upbringing of adolescent offspring. Caring for aging parents is a widespread form of intergenerational activity. Caregiving brings its share of rewards as well as demands. Particularly demanding are the competing role responsibilities and time constraints that adult children face. Moreover, caregiving arrangements pose numerous social, psychological, and financial implications. The pressures of caregiving are especially evident among daughters, who traditionally shoulder most of the work. (See AGING PARENTS, CARING FOR.)

Parenting adolescent offspring also creates unique adjustments for middle-aged parents. In particular, the creation of effective communication patterns between parent and teenager is especially important, including effective conflict-resolution skills. Parent-adolescent conflicts are not uncommon occurrences during this stage of the family life cycle. Indeed, disharmony often punctuates the strivings for independence and autonomy that teenagers exhibit, further necessitating constructive and effective conflict-resolution skills. (See ADOLESCENCE, SEPARATION-INDIVIDUATION PROCESS OF; CONFLICT, PARENT-ADOLESCENT.)

Parent-adolescent communication must, of course, work two ways. Teenagers as well as parents are responsible for developing meaningful communication skills, and this can be the most difficult of all the developmental challenges that face both parties. Good communication rests at the foundation of healthy family functioning and is the primary vehicle through which family members express warmth and affection, indicate their respect for one another, set limits, and make decisions. Effective communication also enables parents to convey their values and beliefs about the issues that are important to them, such as issues of safety and health, and to learn more about their adolescent's interests, values, and worries.

Another challenge facing middle-aged couples is satisfactory methods of control during the teenage years. A compelling body of research states that adolescents, given a choice, want a democratic relationship with their parents. They prefer households that are regulated on the basis of honesty, fairness, and mutuality. Consultations between parents and teenagers on issues of mutual concern and the provisions of opportunities to enhance teenage autonomy appear to foster the healthiest emotional climate. Not only are the parent-adolescent relations likely to prosper with such operating principles, but the personal growth of each party is likely to flourish.

Middle-aged couples face another developmental challenge when grown children have physically departed the home, a stage of family life known as the *empty nest*. The introspective nature of midlife is likely to trigger a myriad of reactions to the departure of grown children. From a positive perspective, the empty nest may result in feelings of satisfaction and contentment with parental performance and the independence of children. Moreover, the empty nest may herald freedom from financial pressures and an opportunity for partners to spend more time together. On the other hand, some middle-aged couples may dwell on the negative aspects of their parenting and family life in general. In addition, they may discover that they have not been communicating effectively or sharing their lives in meaningful ways over the years. (See EMPTY NEST.)

Further Reading. Koch, Tom. (1990). *Mirrored lives: Aging children and elderly parents.* New York: Praeger; Peterson, Candida C. (1990). Husbands' and wives' perceptions of marital fairness across the family life cycle. *International Journal of Aging and Human Development, 31,* 179–188; Pillemer, Karl, and Kathleen McCartney. (Eds.). (1991). *Parent-child relations throughout life.* Hillsdale, NJ: Erlbaum.

MIDDLE ADULTHOOD, WORK RELATIONSHIPS DURING. During middle adulthood, the work environment continues to exert significant influences on adult life. For many middle-aged workers, work is characterized by stability and maintenance. While there may be frustrations and difficulties, careers represent a plateau in the overall scheme of vocational development. Therefore, most middle-agers report that they enjoy their work and their work-related social contacts and are happy with their chosen professions. For others, though, the midlife experience is one of reestablishment rather than of maintenance. The processes of change in our culture contribute to a search by many for a new sense of establishment in life and work. People feel disestablished and look for certainty and confirmation, for ways to realign themselves comfortably and meaningfully within the same occupational milieu, if not the same job.

Middle adulthood often brings a reassessment of goals, aspirations, and life ambitions (see MIDDLE ADULTHOOD, AND THE MIDLIFE TRANSITION). For some it heralds a full-scale reorientation of major values, including those associated with one's work. The person who has spent a major portion of life searching for power or responsibility may now want inner meaning. Such an inner quest may produce tranquillity or, in some cases, turbulence. As far as the latter is concerned, an internal reassessment may raise havoc not only with one's work but also with one's lifestyle, interpersonal relationships, and family life.

Careers at midlife provide an interesting comparison to those launched during the young adult years. For those involved in an assessment of their lives, it is likely that some appraisal will be made of time, or better yet, the amount of time left. Many perceive that time is short in relation to the world of work. Unlike young adulthood, where idealistic assumptions are often made about career goals, many middle-agers assume that it is too late to launch new career plans or engage in another trial stage of work. Moreover, many adults at midlife feel that life is not as flexible as it once was.

Some researchers believe that an acute psychological awareness of time and the midlife career assessment converge to create unique behavioral dynamics. A middle-aged person may develop a subjective sense of being "on time" or "behind time" in relation to career development or accomplishments. Middle-aged individuals are often acutely aware of the number of years left before retirement and of the speed with which they are reaching their goals. If individuals are "behind time" or if their goals are unrealistic, reassessment and readjustment are necessary.

If this psychological preoccupation with time as it relates to vocational development holds true, then we would expect the young adult years to be a time for the development and implementation of a career path. If this is not done, it usually becomes evident later and may even accentuate the stresses of midlife. Of course, the process of career assessment and planning can still be done at midlife, but the realization that it was not accomplished earlier is often painful.

It should thus be evident that many middle-agers critically evaluate their past career accomplishments as well as their hopes and aspirations for the future. In a growing number of cases, especially among white-collar professionals, such an assessment may trigger a midlife career change. Such changes are not restricted to males, either. Both males and females are part of a throng of workers switching careers in an effort to seek new horizons and greater levels of personal fulfillment.

The quest for fulfillment in the workplace represents a motive virtually unheard of among our forebears. For that matter, the entire notion of changing careers at any point in the life cycle was practically nonexistent among our grandparents and previous generations. People were expected to stay at one job for the entire course of their work lives and not question whether they were happy or not, let alone make a job change. Job satisfaction was secondary to job subservience. In modern times, though, a new value has permeated many facets of society, including the workplace: the need to be satisfied and fulfilled in one's life. This value has prompted both young and old alike to question themselves and the work they do each day. Taking this value into account may help explain why so many workers today are vocationally packing it in and embarking on new and different career paths.

The motives for changing careers vary widely, from boredom to burnout. Some workers are dissatisfied because their jobs are tedious and offer little or no challenge. Others switch jobs in search of better pay and advancement. Some object to the excessive use of authority in the workplace, while others are restless from sticking with the same grinding routine for too long. Some feel drained, continually exhausted, and inadequate in their work. There are those who are bothered by the lower status accorded to their work, and many have been burdened by excessive employer demands and expectations. Others have encountered vocational inequality or sexual harassment. Any of these situations may prompt a person to change a vocation with the hope of discovering a job more important, satisfying, and enjoyable.

Dissatisfied employees contemplating a career change often fail to achieve a sense of accomplishment from their work contributions. Along these lines, many workers report unhappiness because of poor employer-employee relations, or because their ideas are constantly being sidetracked, devalued, or ignored. Research usually shows that the quality of supervisor relations is a critical determinant of job satisfaction. Also, many unhappy workers recognize that a gap exists between their perceived abilities and the utilization of these abilities on the job. Many report a lack of conformity between their own personal goals and the company's goals and policies.

Finally, some workers change jobs involuntarily. For instance, unemployment forces many into entirely new lines of work. The threat of unemployment may do the same thing. That is, employees may change vocations because they know that their company is failing and being laid off lies on the not-too-distant horizon. Others switch career fields because they know that their jobs are soon going to be phased out by automation. Given such scenarios, it is likely that blue-collar workers experience more involuntary midcareer changes, while those of white-collar workers are more voluntary.

Further Reading. Ackerman, Rosalie J. (1990). Career developments and transitions of middle-aged women. *Psychology of Women Quarterly, 14,* 513–530; Kimmel, Douglas C. (1990). *Adulthood and aging: An interdisciplinary developmental view* (3rd Ed.). New York: Wiley; Waskel, Shirley A. (1991). *Midlife issues and the workplace of the 90s.* New York: Quorum Books.

MIDDLE AGES, LIFESPAN RELATIONSHIPS DURING THE.

Historians chart the Middle Ages between the end of the Roman Empire in the West during the fifth century A.D. and the sixteenth century. Also known as the medieval period, the Middle Ages were characterized by the movement of Germanic tribes into the land in central Europe previously occupied by the Romans. Germanic and Roman lifestyles began to blend, but medieval civilization was also influenced by the Moslems in Spain and the Middle East, and by the Byzantine Empire in southeastern Europe.

Marriage remained important throughout the Middle Ages and was therefore strongly encouraged. In medieval England, marriages were arranged by the couple's parents, and in many instances the arrangements made between the two families resembled a shrewd business transaction. Concern was often expressed over the worth of the bridal partners' property ownership and the size of the dowry (see MARITAL EXCHANGES). Although monogamy was the preferred marital arrangement, polygamy was not uncommon during this period.

To function adequately as an economic unit and reap productive harvests, families were large in size. However, infant mortality rates were frighteningly high due to poor medical care, disease, and unsanitary conditions. As far as child-rearing techniques were concerned, two important developments transpired during the Middle Ages. The first was the belief that the child was born with *inherent sin.* Because the church felt that all children were born wicked and sinful, it was considered not only justifiable, but right and appropriate for parents to physically punish children as often as possible. Parents were often told that children who behaved badly were expressing the results of this innate sin; consequently, the devil had to be literally driven from the body (see CHILD REARING, HISTORICAL PRACTICES IN).

The second development at this time in history was *child relinquishment* or, in some cases, the actual abandonment of the child by many parents. Documentation reveals that many children were sold as slaves or abandoned to monasteries or nunneries. Child relinquishment in its most common form, though, was sending the infant or young child away to live with a wet nurse (a woman who breast-feeds other women's children) for two to four years. After this period of time, the child was returned to the family. Such practices were usually reserved for wealthier families and serve to illustrate the minimal amount of time many parents spent in raising their young. Education for all children was woefully lacking during the Middle Ages. In general, children were regarded as miniature adults and were expected to make meaningful contributions to the household at early ages.

During the eleventh and twelfth centuries, so-called *courtly love* came into prominence, and for many couples, relationship development acquired a new dimension. In courtly love, a man and a woman adored one another in a relationship that idealized both the woman's feminine qualities and the man's chivalrous behavior. *Chivalry* was a code of behavior applied to men of the upper classes—usually knights—in which the qualities of courageousness, honor, and the protection of the weak and of women were required. Courtly love prompted the lover to demonstrate his bravery and to compete for the hand of his beloved. Knights often displayed their courage and skill fighting with their rivals in the service of their ladies and typically wore their ladies' favors pinned to their clothing. Gloves, veils, flowers, and kerchiefs were used for this purpose. Courtly love also found its way into the poetry and songs of the minstrels who wandered throughout the countryside, making a living by entertaining others.

Whether married or single, women during the Middle Ages led controlled and restricted lives and were regarded as intellectually inferior to males. As in earlier societies, women were viewed as the property either of their fathers or of their husbands. Largely because of church teachings, women were often considered the source of sexual temptation and were thus to be avoided when possible. This was especially true among the Saxons, a Germanic people who, with the Angles and Jutes, conquered England in the fifth century A.D. The Saxons tended to view women as a necessary evil.

Women of the Middle Ages learned at early ages to subjugate themselves to male wishes and demands. Consider, for example, the situation faced by Frankish women. In the region known today as France, a woman could not hope ever to escape male domination. Even if her husband died, she had then to submit to the control of her eldest son. Some Frankish women were not allowed to inherit. Moreover, whatever property and possessions a woman brought into a marriage—including the dowry—became the husband's.

Christianity, which had become the official religion of the Roman Empire, remained dominant within the remnants of the empire during the Middle Ages. The church's efforts to overcome what it saw as sexual pollution continued to exert a forceful influence on sexual behavior (see EARLY CHRISTIANITY, IMPACT OF ON INTIMATE RELATIONSHIPS). It continued to advocate celibacy and banned all forms of sexual activity other than intercourse between married persons. In time, the church would make even procreative sexual activity illegal on Sundays, Wednesdays, and Fridays; for three days before attending communion, and for a period of forty days prior to Easter and forty days before Christmas. In addition, it was forbidden from the time of conception to forty days postpartum.

The repression of sexuality took many other forms. For example, church authorities like St. Thomas Aquinas (1225–1274) perceived masturbation as a greater sin than fornication and denounced its practice. Also, abortion was condemned by the church and laws were devised to prevent it, something that neither Jews, Greeks, or Romans had earlier implemented. Additionally, no Christian could marry a Jew or the follower of any other religion.

Prostitution was quite widespread during the Middle Ages. For some, prostitution was regarded as an inevitable evil. Aquinas remarked that it was a ''necessary condition of social morality, just as a cesspool is necessary to a palace, if the whole palace is not to smell.'' In many instances, rulers passed laws designed to regulate and control prostitution. In the French city of Avignon, Queen Joanna established a town brothel rather than have prostitution run rampant in the streets. In other cities, such as Paris, prostitutes were kept under the watchful eye of city officials and were prohibited from entering certain city districts. As time wore on, prostitutes were subjected to a wide range of rules and regulations. For instance, in various English cities and towns, prostitutes were required to dress in a certain way so that they could be distinguished from other women.

Public baths became popular during the Middle Ages and often served as centers for prostitution. Originally designed so that the poor could bathe more frequently, the bathhouses or "stews" were usually located on side streets. Thinly attired prostitutes often welcomed visitors to the establishment and led them to a tub that had enough room for five or six people. Following the bath, customers usually adjourned to separate rooms for more intimate sexual activity.

It has often been said that the Crusades brought about an increase in prostitution during the Middle Ages. The Crusades, which began about A.D. 1100 and ended about 1300, were military expeditions by the Christian powers of Western Europe to recapture the Holy Land from the Muslim forces that had taken over that area. The Crusaders not only suffered the hardships and dangers of battle but had to spend long periods of time away from their wives or lovers. Leaders of the Crusades acknowledged the frustrations of abstinence and often made prostitutes available to the men who served under them.

During the Middle Ages, sexual promiscuity and the absence of effective contraception produced many illegitimate births. Interestingly, though, illegitimacy often did not carry a social stigma, at least for males. Indeed, to be called a bastard during the Middle Ages was often a mark of distinction, particularly if one's natural father was a knight or nobleman. Many notable figures, including the emperor Charlemagne and the semilegendary King Arthur, are thought to have been bastards, and it is said that William the Conquerer did not resent the appellation "William the Bastard."

Further Reading. Delort, Robert. (1983). *Life in the Middle Ages*. New York: Greenwich House; Hoyt, Robert S. (1966). *Europe in the Middle Ages* (2nd Ed.) New York: Harcourt, Brace and World; Power, Eileen. (1950). *Medieval people* (9th Ed.) London: Methuen; Rowling, Marjorie. (1968). *Everyday life in medieval times*. New York: Putnam.

MIDDLE CHILDHOOD. The lifespan stage known as middle childhood generally occurs between ages 6 and 12. Middle childhood is an active period of growth and development. During this time, the interaction between child and society, which constitutes socialization, expands and becomes more complex. Observers of this age group will see that children wish to be with others and that social relations acquire many new dimensions, whether in peer-group relations, school activities, sports, or family activities.

As social horizons expand, children learn that they must adjust their behavior to meet the numerous expectations and demands of society. This is an ongoing process and requires adaptability. Socially acceptable or tolerable behavior in toddlers, such as clinging dependency, may not be acceptable in school-age children. Modification of behavior is necessary to meet the changing expectations of society.

Children gain insight into themselves and their developing personalities from the social relations of middle childhood. More specifically, the child's sense of personal awareness or self-knowledge grows through interactions with others and from inferences about personal experiences. While certain degrees of self-awareness were evident earlier in life, they were frequently based on the child's physical qualities or possessions. Children are now likely to include in their self-appraisals other facets of themselves, such as how they are perceived by others and their general competencies.

The fact that children now attend school full-time, have greater interaction with their peers, and display heightened levels of independence places the family in a new perspective. Children still need and rely very much on their parents, but their contacts with the outside world have expanded. As a result, their social relationships with other adults are considerably broader, including, for example, interactions with teachers, coaches, or summer-camp leaders.

The negotiation of new social boundaries and the parents' reactions to the child's strivings for independence make these years especially challenging. Many children want to spend more time away from the family. This threatens some parents, who need to be assured that this is a completely normal phase of child development and that they will remain special and unique in the wake of these social strivings. It is interesting to note that amidst these desires for social independence, many school-age children periodically tend to slip back into dependency, although usually in private and on their own terms. This age also marks the time when many want to spend more time alone doing private things or to keep secret what they do both within and away from the family.

Children's greater interactions with others enable them to bring back to the home an abundance of social experiences, whether these be tales about school or sports exploits or neighborhood news. Their increasing powers of social cognition also enable them to compare their home environment with those around them (see SOCIAL COGNITION). As a result, what other children have or do is weighed against what they have or are allowed to do, a comparison likely to breed a fair number of questions and possible disagreements with parents. Parents' values and standards are also tested when children bring home ideas, language, and attitudes different from those taught at home.

Further Reading. Edelstein, Sari F. (1995). *The healthy young child.* St. Paul, MN: West; Elkind, David. (1994). *A sympathetic understanding of the child: Birth to sixteen* (3rd Ed.). Boston: Allyn and Bacon; Hetherington, E. Mavis, and Ross D. Parke. (1993). *Child psychology: A contemporary viewpoint* (4th Ed.). New York: McGraw-Hill.

MIDDLE EAST, LIFESPAN RELATIONSHIPS IN THE. The Middle East is a land region covering parts of northeastern Africa, southwestern Asia, and southeastern Europe. There is considerable disagreement as to which countries make up the Middle East. The approach of this volume is to include the Arab states of Bahrain, Egypt, Iraq, Jordan, Kuwait, Lebanon, Oman, Qatar, Saudi Arabia, Syria, the United Arab Emirates, and Yemen; the territories of Gaza and the West Bank; and the non-Arab nations of Iran, Israel, and Turkey. According to recent estimates, the population of the Middle East is 265 million, and this figure is expected to increase to 575 million by the year 2025.

The Middle East is an extremely complex and diverse part of the world. Much of the Middle East is desert, and most of the people are poor farmers. Most of the people are Arab, but other population groups include Africans, Armenians, Copts, Greeks, Iranians, Jews, Kurds, and Turks. Most Middle Easterners are Moslems who practice Islam. Christians represent the second-largest religious group in the Middle East, including Coptic, Greek Orthodox, and Maronite branches. Most Israelis practice Judaism. Arabic is the major spoken language, while the Israelis speak Hebrew.

Given such vast diversities in the Middle East, any efforts to explore close relationships represent a simplification. The Middle East, much like other regions of the world, is not homogeneous, nor are its people and the relationships they forge. However, we can identify some general trends and themes. For example, marriage is customary in the Middle East, and premarital relations are frowned upon. Intermarriage within families (including among first cousins) is prevalent in the Middle East, and some communities practice polygyny (Islamic law, for example, allows men to have up to four wives if they can provide adequate justification and treat all wives equitably). At one time, early marriages prevailed, but the age at marriage has increased in many nations. Nations such as Egypt, Turkey, Iran, and Israel, to name but a few, have reported increases in the median age at marriage. Increased education, particularly among women, and financial restraints are among the forces creating this marriage pattern.

Marriages in the Middle East reflect a strong patriarchal structure. Men are recognized as undisputed heads of the household and exercise strong dominance over their wives and children. Women's rights and levels of participation within the family and Middle East society as a whole are considerably restricted. To illustrate, Middle East family law tends to favor men in matters of divorce, child custody, and inheritance. Moreover, activities that might bring women into contact with men outside of their families are discouraged. Because of this, some of the world's lowest rates of female labor-force participation can be found in the Middle East. With the exception of Lebanon and Israel, it is estimated that women constitute less than 20 percent of the entire labor force in the Middle East. Rather than be gainfully employed, women are instead expected to work in the home and bear children, preferably males. The failure to fulfill this latter goal can cause a husband to consider a new wife.

Fertility rates tend to be high in the Middle East, with the average woman giving birth to about 5 children. However, considerable variation in fertility rates exists among Middle East nations. For example, the fertility rate ranges from 2.9 children in Israel to about 7.9 in Gaza. Religion also figures prominently in a woman's fertility, since large families are encouraged in Islamic culture. To use Israel as an example, the average Muslim woman in this nation gives birth to about 4.7 children; this compares to 2.3 for Christian women and 2.6 for Jewish women. While family planning is permitted under Islamic law, contraceptive use tends to be low in the Middle East. Generally, educated women living in urban areas are more likely to practice birth control. Abortion is not allowed as a family-planning measure in the Middle East.

As indicated, a preference for male children is evident in the Middle East. This preference usually stems from several reasons, including needed farming assistance, economic security for parents when they reach old age, continuation of the husband's lineage, and heightened social status. As far as parent-child relations are concerned, children are brought up primarily in the mother's care and are the objects of considerable affection and attention. Respect for parental wishes is encouraged as well as expected, and cooperation is seen as a virtue. Close sibling relationships are usually the case in Middle East families, with brothers and sisters forming ties as both friends and companions. Traditional gender-role behaviors are also visible at early ages; female children are expected to assist with nurturing duties, such as baby care and housework, while male children receive an introduction to an assortment of activities involving more strenuous labor. For example, if farming is the family enterprise, young boys usually help with the planting, carrying crops to the market, tending to the livestock, or hauling firewood.

Middle East children soon discover that family life is of great importance, and both young and old hold it in high esteem. Loyalty to all family members throughout the lifespan is expected. The extended family tends to be the most prevalent structure, although there has been an upswing in nuclear families, particularly among educated, urban couples. Cohabitation is an unacceptable living arrangement in Islamic culture and is rare even among non-Muslims in the Middle East. Regarding the extended family, it is not uncommon for a number of different relatives to live under the same roof. For example, some couples might share a home with parents or grandparents; others might live with brothers, sisters, uncles, and aunts; and still other homes reflect a combination of the foregoing. Since domestic authority is a male province, such households are headed by the husband, grandfather, or an uncle.

The Middle East aged population is rapidly increasing, providing family members with lengthier periods of intergenerational contact. The elderly are integral components of family life and are highly valued and respected. Middle East cultures place considerable emphasis on maintaining contact with, and caring for, aging family members. To this end, the family is the major source of social support when the elderly are sick or disabled or when they face stress or misfortune. Given the close-knit, reciprocal nature of Middle East family interactions, children traditionally shoulder caregiving responsibilities as parents grow older. This is true for men and women living in urban as well as rural areas. However, women, more so than men, provide the bulk of personal care to aging family members. In recent years, there has been an increase in governmental health-care services to aged persons and their families.

Further Reading. Myers, George C., and Emily M. Agree. (1994). The world ages, the family changes: A demographic perspective. *Ageing International, 21,* 11–18; Omran, Abdel R. (1992). *Family planning in the legacy of Islam.* New York: Routledge; Omran, Abdel R., and Farzaneh Roudi. (1993). *The Middle East population puzzle.* Washington,

DC: Population Reference Bureau; Weeks, John R. (1988). *The demography of Islamic nations*. Washington, DC: Population Reference Bureau.

MISCEGENATION. See INTERRACIAL MARRIAGE.

MONOGAMY. See MARRIAGE, VARIATIONS IN STRUCTURE.

MORAL DEVELOPMENT. Moral development is the manner in which individuals learn standards of right and wrong. Although such codes of conduct differ from culture to culture, every society adheres to certain behavioral standards. Early in childhood, these standards are established when children learn that certain behaviors are labeled as good and others as bad. With age and experience, these standards of morality come to include empathy, as well as complex ideas, values, and beliefs. Moral development impacts on many aspects of relationships across the lifespan, including those behavioral standards and expectations connected to friendships, sibling relationships, and dating relationships. The perceived morality of sexual standards also illustrates how moral development can be applied to the study of relationships.

To appreciate the many dimensions of morality, including honesty, guilt, shame, and lying, insight must be gained into how morality develops throughout childhood and adolescence. One of the more influential developmental theories was proposed by Lawrence Kohlberg (see KOHLBERG, LAWRENCE). Inspired by cognitive development researcher Jean Piaget, Kohlberg developed an age-stage progression of morality. Kohlberg's theory consists of six stages divided into three levels: the preconventional level (ages 0 to 9), the conventional level (ages 9 to 15), and the postconventional moral reasoning level (age 16 and onward). At the *preconventional level,* children have little awareness of socially acceptable moral behavior, but after two stages, they start to show signs of moral behavior. In stage 1, *obedience and punishment orientation,* children start to follow rules in order to avoid punishment. True rule awareness has not yet been established; instead, their moral conduct is based largely on fear associated with rule violation. Kohlberg maintained that the seriousness of a violation at this time depends on the magnitude of the wrongdoing.

During the *naively egoistic orientation,* stage 2, children reason that a tangible reward usually follows their doing something right. A type of reciprocity starts to surface here; that is, children will do the right thing not only to satisfy their own needs but also to satisfy the needs of others. If the latter is the case, children reason that they will receive some sort of favor in return. (''You scratch my back and I'll scratch yours.'')

As children approach adolescence, they reach the *conventional level.* At this level, they learn the nature of authority, not only in the family, but also in society in general. During the third stage, called the *good-boy/nice-girl orientation,* there is a considerable degree of conformity. Children know that they must obey the rules in order to win praise or approval from others. During this phase, they also usually identify with emotionally important persons. Conforming behavior eventually leads to an internal awareness of rules and behavior, which in turn leads to a sense of respect. During the fourth stage, *authority-maintaining orientation,* children's identification shifts to institutions, such as church or school. Children seek to avoid the guilt and shame brought on by criticism from authoritarian figures.

The *postconventional level* is the last level of Kohlberg's theory. During this stage, individuals' morality reaches maturity. In the fifth stage, *contractual legalistic orientation,* individuals choose the moral principles to guide their behavior, being careful not to violate the rights and wills of others. In the sixth and final stage, *universal ethical principle orientation,* the emergence of a true conscience enables individuals to uphold behavior that respects the dignity of all humans. However, this last stage is difficult to distinguish from the preceding one. Even Kohlberg himself questioned whether stages 5 and 6 can be separated. Not everyone reaches the postconventional level of morality, just as not everyone attains Piaget's stage of formal operations (see COGNITIVE-DEVELOPMENTAL THEORY).

Kohlberg's theory of moral development has been influential among contemporary psychologists. It has attracted the attention of researchers and has stimulated much discussion of morality and how it is acquired. Most psychologists agree with Kohlberg's contention that cognitive developments underlie the progression of morality from level to level. However, there are some who feel that his developmental sequence is too restrictive. Other critics point out that there may be a weak relationship between what one says about morality and how one in fact behaves. Along these lines, many prefer moral reasoning that is more sophisticated than their own.

Kohlberg's theory has also been criticized because it does not appear to account for gender differences. Critics maintain that females use different reasoning than males do when confronted with moral issues. More specifically, females tend to be concerned with relationships and responsibilities, whereas males typically center their responses on rights and rules. Because Kohlberg's stages of moral development are primarily structured on the basis of rules, females often fail to reach the zenith of moral functioning.

Further Reading. Kohlberg, Lawrence. (1969). *Stages in the development of moral thought and action.* New York: Holt, Rinehart and Winston; Kohlberg, Lawrence. (1984). *The psychology of moral development.* New York: Harper and Row; Piaget, Jean. (1948). *The moral judgment of the child.* Glencoe, IL: Free Press.

MORMONS, POLYGYNY AMONG THE. The Mormons are members of the Church of Jesus Christ of Latter-day Saints, which was established during the early 1800s by Joseph Smith. The Mormons claim that the church as established by Christ did not survive in its original form and was restored in modern times by divine means. Consequently, the Mormons maintain that their church is the true church of Jesus Christ. Although their first church was founded in New York, many of the Mormons traveled west and settled in Salt Lake City, Utah.

Between 1844 and 1890, *polygyny* (the marriage of one man to two or more women) was considered the marriage ideal among the Mormons. While polygyny was condemned by most of the nation, Mormons defended the practice primarily on the grounds that God had chosen to introduce it in ancient Israel, and he had made his intentions known again to spokesmen on earth. Thus polygyny was often viewed in religious terms as a restoration of the Old Testament practice. However, the Mormons also cited other reasons for practicing polygyny: it was a way of introducing marriage and parenthood to women who might otherwise remain single, and it offered women an alternative to a variety of social evils and temptations.

But even though polygyny was considered the ideal, it was not widely practiced. In fact, only 5 percent of married Mormon men had more than one wife, and a significant majority of this figure had only two wives. The financial hardship of supporting additional wives and the fact that many of these women would not be legally recognized as wives in the United States were the primary reasons for the limited enthusiasm among the congregation. There were, however, exceptions to these low figures. Brigham Young, who led the Mormons' westward trek to Utah, was said to have had as many as 70 wives. He accepted his first plural wife in 1842 at the age of 41 and the last in the 1870s, shortly before his death.

In the wake of growing national disdain and condemnation toward this practice, the Mormon church prohibited polygyny in 1890. In 1895, the Utah state constitution promised that the practice would not be revived in the future. However, among some contemporary fundamentalist Mormon sects, polygyny still remains the ideal marital arrangement and is practiced despite its illegality.

Further Reading. Cassidy, Margaret L., and Gary R. Lee. (1989). The study of polyandry: A critique and synthesis. *Journal of Comparative Family Studies, 20,* 1–11; Kephart, William M. (1994). *Extraordinary groups: The sociology of unconventional lifestyles* (5th Ed.). New York: St. Martin's Press.

MOTHERESE. Motherese is a language style employed by adults, more often the mother, when speaking to infants. Often referred to as "baby talk," motherese typically consists of shortened sentences, easy words, the duplication of syllables, and an increase of voice frequency. Such caregiver speech is an attempt to simplify language for the infant and young child. When employing motherese, adults also use an abundance of concrete nouns, diminutives, and terms of endearment.

Researchers have found that motherese facilitates early language development, primarily because it draws the infant's attention to the adult's voice. As such, it is a valuable form of adult verbal stimulation. Its simplistic style is also beneficial because it takes into account the young child's limited information-processing skills.

However, most experts agree that benefits of motherese apply to younger children and not to their older counterparts. Children past the one-word stage still need adult input, but they respond more readily to language formulated in adult form than to language in simplified forms. What does appear important in talking to young children is the speed of what is being said, as well as the clearness and conciseness of the message.

Children need adults for accurate speech models; thus it is important that adults pronounce and use words correctly. This implies that adult use of motherese for children beyond the first year or so may well be a hindrance to language development, but so would speaking in an encyclopedic or diplomatic vein. There must be an optimum level of language complexity to challenge the child.

Further Reading. Helms, Donald B., and Jeffrey S. Turner. (1986). *Exploring child behavior* (3rd Ed.). Monterey, CA: Brooks/Cole; Kaye, Kenneth. (1980). Why we don't talk "baby talk" to babies. *Journal of child language, 7,* 489–507; Krantz, Murray. (1994). *Child development: Risk and opportunity.* Belmont, CA: Wadsworth.

MOTHERHOOD. See PARENTHOOD, THE ROLE OF THE MOTHER.

NATIONAL GAY AND LESBIAN TASK FORCE. See GAY AND LESBIAN RELATIONSHIPS, PREJUDICE AND DISCRIMINATION AGAINST.

NATIONAL ORGANIZATION FOR WOMEN. See SEXUAL REVOLUTION.

NATIVE AMERICANS, LIFESPAN RELATIONSHIPS AMONG.
The terms Native American, American Indian, and Native Alaskan refer to a diverse minority population in North America (Alaska and the continental United States) that reflects many different histories and cultures. Native Americans were the original inhabitants of the Americas and today live mostly in the northwest and western sectors of the United States. They are composed of at least 124 federally recognized tribes and bands, with approximately 450 or more subgroupings such as villages with distinct customs and traditions. The Cherokee, Navajo, Chippewa, and Sioux tribes are the largest Native American tribes. Combined, there are almost 2 million Native Americans living in the United States today. Approximately one-third of this total live on reservations or other Indian areas.

Like other minorities, Native Americans have historically experienced considerable hardship and discrimination, including government forced-relocation policies of the nineteenth century. Today, Native Americans are one of the most disadvantaged minority groups in the United States. They have the highest rate of unemployment, the highest rate of high-school dropouts, and the lowest median income of any racial or ethnic group. Over the past few years, all racial and ethnic groups have experienced an increase in median income with the exception of Native Americans. Compounding these economic problems is the fact that Native Americans live in some of the poorest rural areas in the United States. Among all minority groups, Native Americans also have the highest rates of substance abuse, particularly alcoholism. The general health status of Native Americans as a group is rated very poor, and their overall life expectancy is ten years below the national average.

Economic disadvantage resulting from poverty punctuates Native American family life. Native American families have high fertility rates, large numbers of illegitimate births, and a disproportionate number of female-headed households. Native American women tend to have their first child at a younger age than non-Hispanic white women, and teenagers account for about 20 percent of all Native American births. As in all cultures, teenage childbearing aggravates negative economic consequences for mother and child, in addition to creating such health risks as prematurity, infant mortality, and delivery complications.

Contrary to popular impression, interracial-marriage rates among Native Americans are the highest of any racial group (many mistakenly believe that marriages between African Americans and whites represent the largest percentage). The most frequent interracial-marriage composition is between a white husband and a Native American woman. Native Americans residing in metropolitan areas are more likely to intermarry than those living in nonmetropolitan areas or on or near a reservation.

Children are greatly valued by Native Americans. They are taught a number of cultural values at early ages, including the importance of group cooperation, honesty, and independence. Many Native American parents regard competitiveness as a lack of respect for and lack of loyalty to the group. Obedience is also seen as a virtue, and children are trained to exhibit patience, responsibility, and trustworthiness. A particular emphasis is also placed on a harmony with and reverence for nature. Family loyalty and traditions have long been important to Native American families, and children are brought up to respect and care for elderly family members.

The earlier-mentioned family difficulties place many Native American children and adolescents at risk. For example, high rates of alcoholism and homicide rates often create the loss of parents or siblings. Premature births by adolescent mothers often create developmental lags in children, such as neurological problems or lowered intelligence. Economic deprivation may trigger disruptive and aggressive behavior, both at home and at school. Running away from home is not an uncommon occurrence among Native American children. Given such problems, it should be fairly easy to see why Native American youth represent a particularly vulnerable population segment, one that needs considerable social service intervention.

The extended family is an important source of care and assistance for Native Americans. Kin form supportive bonds with each other and traditionally promote the welfare and safety of family members. Often, the extended family allows members to combine their economic resources, thus serving an important adaptive function. Given the extended family framework, children may also experience parenting from large numbers of relatives, especially in the face of domestic strain. Research has shown that relationships with supportive and caring kin are important modifiers of stress.

As noted, elderly family members are an integral feature of Native American families. Aged tribal members are respected for their wisdom and experience, and they serve as teachers and caregivers of the young. Research tells us that elderly Native American family members are more involved in child care than their white or Hispanic-American counterparts. Marital dissolution, whether through widowhood, divorce, or separation, does not isolate aged family members from their children or siblings. Finally, because intergenerational relationships are characterized by mutuality and reciprocity, younger family members provide regular care to aging family members. The bulk of care, though, does not fall equally on all family members. Rather, the primary caregiver is almost always a woman.

Further Reading. Foster, Morris W. (1991). *Being Comanche: A social history of an American Indian community.* Tucson: University of Arizona Press; Nabokov, Peter. (Ed.). (1991). *Native American testimony: A chronicle of Indian-white relations from prophecy to the present, 1492–1992.* New York: Viking; Nagel, Joane. (1994). *American Indian ethnic revival: Red power and resurgence of identity and culture.* New York: Oxford University Press.

NATURE-NURTURE ISSUE. The nature-nurture issue is the role of one's genetic or inherited endowment in relation to the role of the nurturing environment in shaping the course of growth and development. The nature-nurture issue is a fundamental issue in the field of lifespan development and stimulates thinking in many ways. Currently, researchers who are *nativists* (or hereditarians) believe that much behavior is dependent on genetic endowment. The opposite group, called *environmentalists,* asserts that environment is the major contributor to an individual's behavior. Since there are few definitive answers, the question of how much heredity and environment contribute to development is probably a futile one. To most, the critical issue is how these two forces *interact* with one another to affect development; those adopting this stance are sometimes referred to as *interactionists.*

Further Reading. Plomin, Robert. (1986). *Development, genetics, and psychology.* Hillsdale, NJ: Erlbaum; Turner, Jeffrey S., and Donald B. Helms. (1995). *Lifespan development* (5th Ed.). Fort Worth, TX: Harcourt Brace.

NEOLOCAL RESIDENCY. See MARRIAGE, VARIATIONS IN STRUCTURE.

NEONATE. See NEWBORN.

NEUGARTEN, BERNICE L. Bernice L. Neugarten (1916–) is a lifespan development researcher who has specialized in adult personality and social functioning. A psychologist and a sociologist by training, Neugarten was raised in Nebraska and served for many years as a professor of human development at the University of Chicago.

Neugarten received all of her undergraduate and graduate degrees from the University of Chicago, including a B.A. in humanities and an M.A. in education. She was the first person to receive a Ph.D. degree from Chicago's Interdisciplinary Committee on Human Development, a department that focuses on the psychological, sociological, anthropological, and biological forces that influence development throughout the life cycle. She was formerly chairperson of that committee.

Neugarten has distinguished herself in a number of diverse research pursuits. Her investigation of how society as a whole affects the aging process, referred to as the ''social age clock'' theory, is particularly well known. In this theory, she maintained that when certain ages are reached, society generates various behavioral expectations. Neugarten is also recognized for her detailed analysis of successful patterns of aging and life satisfaction. She has also studied various aspects of adult personality development, socialization processes, the American age-status system, menopause, and grandparenthood.

Her professional involvement has been very extensive. She was elected president of the Gerontological Society in 1969 and received from that society the Kleemier Award for her contributions to research in aging. She was also a consultant to the White House Conference on Aging; she is a member of the National Institute on Aging and the Federal Council on Aging and a fellow of the American Psychological Association.

Further Reading. Neugarten, Bernice L. (Ed.). (1964). *Personality in middle and late life.* New York: Atherton Press; Neugarten, Bernice L. (Ed.). (1968). *Middle age and aging.* Chicago: University of Chicago Press.

NEWBORN. The stage of life known as the newborn occurs during the first month or so of life. Lifespan development researchers technically refer to the newborn as the *neonate* and this life stage as the *neonatal period.* The newborn stage is an important transitional period from fetal to extrauterine life, the period in which the newborn adapts, adjusts, and stabilizes in the external world.

As the newborn is adjusting to extrauterine life, delivery attendants are taking measures to ensure its survival. Following the removal of mucus and fluids from the nose and mouth to assure normal respiration, the newborn receives an evaluation of basic life signs (called an *Apgar test*), including heart rate and respiration. Also, the newborn's footprints are taken, weight and length are recorded, and the baby's temperature is recorded with a rectal thermometer. Also, the baby is given an injection of vitamin K1 to prevent hemorrhaging, and eye drops of silver nitrate are administered to prevent contracting highly contagious gonorrhea in the eyes (the eyes are especially vulnerable if gonococci are present in the birth canal). For many male newborns, circumcision (the surgical removal of all or part of the prepuce, or foreskin of the penis) is another adjustment to extrauterine life.

Most people, especially parents of newborn infants, tend to view newborns as helpless creatures of miniature proportions who are incapable of anything except crying, feeding, burping, sleeping, and excreting. As a result, parents of newborns often perceive their function in these terms: feed, burp, and change the baby, and put the child in a crib to sleep most of the day. This view is incomplete because it overlooks a great deal of competent behavior exhibited by newborns, such as sensory abilities, making sounds, tracking objects, touching, and demonstrating early attachment behaviors (see ATTACHMENT, EARLY PARENT-INFANT; INFANCY AND TODDLERHOOD).

Behavioral differences exist among newborns from the moment they are born. Each child is born with a certain individuality, which influences caregivers from the very start. Some infants are very active, others are passive, and most are somewhere in between. Some are very responsive to environmental stimuli, showing an interest in the world about them; others respond irritably to environmental stimuli; still others are placid and smile frequently. Suffice it to say that no two babies are exactly alike in their overall dispositions.

But this does not mean that newborns cannot share certain general temperaments. On the contrary, researchers have found that beginning in the newborn period, certain types of temperament are established and remain fairly constant over the years. For example, the *easy child* is adaptable, mild, and cheerful. This youngster accepts schedules and routines and adjusts easily to changes in the environment. The *difficult child* is intense in mood, slow in adapting, and has a tendency to withdraw from people. The difficult child frequently has temper tantrums, shows irregular eating and sleeping patterns, and is generally hard to live with. The *slow-to-warm-up child* adapts slowly to environmental change and in general has a low activity level. This child demonstrates mild negative behavior, but positive behavior frequently evolves when parents are patient.

Research focusing on the enduring nature of temperament shows how we might inherit genetic behavioral predispositions, but how the environment affects personality development as well. Knowledge of temperament may also help parents develop a style of interaction that promotes the most effective infant-parent relationship. Indeed, child psychologists often refer to *goodness-of-fit,* the extent to which the temperaments of parents match the temperament of the infant. A word of caution, though, about the total predictive value of temperament: Because temperament is modified by experience, motivation, environmental events, and a number of other variables, there is no guarantee that a newborn or infant will retain the same temperamental qualities throughout the course of the lifespan.

Further Reading. Berk, Laura. (1994). *Infants and children: Prenatal through early childhood.* Boston, MA: Allyn and Bacon; Lamb, Michael E., and Marc H. Bornstein. (1987). *Development in infancy.* New York: Random House.

NONNORMATIVE CRISIS. See FAMILY CRISIS.

NORMATIVE CRISIS. See FAMILY CRISIS.

NUCLEAR FAMILY. See FAMILY COMPOSITION, TYPES OF.

NUPTIALITY. Nuptiality refers to the manner in which marriage occurs in a given society. Nuptiality includes many demographic characteristics, including the rate at which marriage occurs, the characteristics of those who marry, and the manner in which marital dissolution occurs (through divorce, separation, widowhood, and annulment).

Further Reading. Haupt, Arthur, and Thomas T. Kane. (1985). *The population reference bureau's population handbook.* Washington, DC: Population Reference Bureau; Shryock, Henry S., and Jacob S. Siegel. (1976). *The methods and materials of demography.* Orlando, FL: Academic Press.

NYMPHOMANIA. See SEXUAL ADDICTION.

O

OBSERVATION. Observation is a research technique employed in the field of lifespan development as well as in other branches of psychology. The collection of data begins when some type of observation is made, whether by somewhat unsophisticated means (watching children at play) or by very technical processes (recording brain waves on an electroencephalograph). Theories or, possibly, laws may be formulated from observations, provided, of course, that the data are supportive.

Several different types of observation exist in the social sciences. *Naturalistic observation* is the examination of behavior under unstructured (natural) conditions. *Structured observation* represents a slight extension of naturalistic observation, enabling the researcher to administer simple tests. *Participant observation* involves the researcher as a participant in the interaction being studied. When this is done, the researcher's direct involvement with the subjects provides observational data. All of these forms of observation differ markedly from controlled experiments, which employ situations that require subjects to be placed in contrived and perhaps unnatural environments.

Further Reading. Breakwell, Glynis, Sean Hammond, and Chris Fife-Schaw. (1995). *Research methods in psychology.* Thousand Oaks, CA: Sage; Hinkle, Dennis E., William Wiersma, and Stephen G. Jurs. (1994). *Applied statistics for the behavioral sciences* (3rd Ed.). Boston: Houghton Mifflin.

OBSERVATIONAL LEARNING. See SOCIAL LEARNING THEORY.

OEDIPUS COMPLEX. See PSYCHOSEXUAL DEVELOPMENT.

OPEN- AND CLOSED-ENDED QUESTIONS. Open- and closed-ended questions are ways to either facilitate or impede the flow of interpersonal communication. Open-ended questions require more than a yes or no answer; as such, they allow another person to share any feelings or information that she or he thinks is relevant. An example of an open-ended question is "How are you feeling about that?" Conversely, a closed-ended question is one that asks for a one-word answer (usually "yes" or "no") and provides little opportunity for further discussion. An example of a closed-ended question is "Did you feel sad?" Thus, while an open-ended question opens the door to a discussion of feelings, a closed-ended question elicits limited, factual information.

Further Reading. Epstein, Laura. (1985). *Talking and listening.* St. Louis: Times Mirror/Mosby; McKay, Matthew, Martha Davis, and Patrick Fanning. (1983). *Messages: The communication skills book.* Oakland, CA: New Harbinger Publications.

OPEN MARRIAGE. An open marriage is a nontraditional lifestyle that stresses freedom, openness, and the continual self-growth of both partners. Although we might expect this in any marriage, an open marriage and a traditional marriage make quite different assumptions. For example, an open marriage avoids creating a "couple image" or enforcing togetherness in the belief that only thus can the marriage be preserved. Proponents feel that an open marriage does not substitute new regulations for old ones; rather, it suggests ways in which couples can learn to communicate openly with one another in order to arrive at a fully understood and mutual consensus for living. An open marriage encourages trust, freedom, and open communication, both within and outside the boundaries of marriage. If so desired, partners are free to engage in other sex friendships and even in extramarital sex—although the latter is a controversial area. All points considered, this nontraditional lifestyle is not practical for most couples since it is likely to promote feelings of insecurity, resentment toward outside parties, and sexual jealousy.

Further Reading. Libby, Roger W., and Robert N. Whitehurst. (Eds.). (1977). *Marriage and alternatives: Exploring intimate relationships.* Glenview, IL: Scott, Foresman; Watson, Mary Ann, and Flint Whitlock. (1982). *Breaking the bonds: The realities of sexually open relationships.* Denver: Tudor House.

ORGANISMIC MODEL OF LIFESPAN DEVELOPMENT. See WORLD VIEWS OF LIFESPAN DEVELOPMENT.

OUTING. See COMING OUT.

P

PARALANGUAGE. See COMMUNICATION, INTERPERSONAL.

PARAPHILIA. See SEXUAL BEHAVIORS, ATYPICAL.

PARENT-EFFECTIVENESS TRAINING. See PARENTHOOD, CHILD-REARING OPTIONS AND STRATEGIES.

PARENTHOOD, ADJUSTMENTS OF. Becoming a parent is an important developmental challenge of adult life, one that poses numerous adjustments and adaptations. From the moment the infant enters the world to the time when maturity is reached, parents and children alike experience significant aspects of growth and development. Moments of joy and happiness directed toward one's offspring are interwoven with such feelings as sadness and frustration. Parents and children become partners in a myriad of life experiences.

The arrival of an infant changes parents' lives considerably. For example, mothers and fathers must learn to adjust to loss of sleep and frequent physical fatigue. Many express increased worry over financial matters and soon discover that the costs of rearing a child quickly escalate. Food, clothing, furniture, toys, and the like make parenthood an expensive venture. Most new parents also experience uneasiness about the unknown aspects of parenthood, particularly unfamiliar child-care routines and demands. Uncertainty often elevates parental anxiety and confusion, and many adults experience added pressure in the wake of mounting child-care chores.

In the midst of such adjustments, new parents often discover that it is difficult to enjoy each other's exclusive company. With the baby's arrival, patterns of intimacy and affection are changed and need to be redefined. Additionally, interactions and visits with friends become restricted. Parenthood may also mean that the child's needs compete with those of the spouse. Because of this, it is not uncommon for parents during stressful times to feel angry, jealous, and resentful.

There are many new mothers who report being overwhelmed by the constant flow of infant-oriented tasks to be carried out. Feeding and bathing the baby and laundering clothing, added to the regular household routines of cleaning, cooking, and shopping, are a full day's work. Countless other chores can be added to this list. A steady stream of research findings shows that new mothers and fathers experience stress originating from the multiple demands of child care, work, and marriage. Many have difficulty adapting to unfamiliar child-care demands, such as infant-soothing techniques, and marital conflict is common.

Many new mothers also report violated expectations of the father with respect to the sharing of child-care responsibilities. Many investigators have found that mothers do much more of the housework and child care than they had expected, and many mothers report less positive feelings about their husbands during the postpartum period than during pregnancy. Moreover, violated expectations concerning division of labor are related to negative feelings postpartum concerning the overall marital relationship. Also, postpartum adjustment is more difficult when mothers' expectations exceed experiences of support and assistance from extended family.

The foregoing does not mean that parenthood is a totally negative experience. Indeed, not all experts contend that parenthood looms as a turbulent and unstable period. Although it has its share of demands and strains, most parents are able to weather its difficulties. Even though some researchers find that the addition of children reduces marital happiness, most parents express overall satisfaction with their children and the parenting role in general. Such findings acknowledge the demands attached to parenthood, but also emphasize the bright side to raising children.

Experts believe that right from the very beginning, parents need to reject the idealistic myth of having the perfect family. Just like marriage, parenthood has its share of triumphs, but also its share of ups and downs, heartaches, and headaches. Too many new parents strive for perfection and in the process program themselves for failure. It is important for new parents to be flexible with their expectations and learn to take pride in their daily accomplishments. Fears and anxieties about child care tend to fade when parents learn that they do not have to do everything by the book. As a result of the experiences gained and lessons learned firsthand, parenthood begins to acquire a less tense and more realistic relaxed quality.

A critical component of effective parenting adjustment is the support partners give to one other, physical as well as psychological. For new parents, especially, openly discussing concerns and problems and working together as a team are instrumental in creating a favorable family climate. Research clearly shows that both informal and formal support beyond that offered by one another eases the transition to parenthood. Parents also need to periodically get away from the baby and enjoy their own private space. Husband and wife need to maintain a loving, harmonious relationship so that they can better fill the roles of mother and father.

Further Reading. Bigner, Jerry J. (1994). *Parent-child relations: An introduction to parenting* (4th Ed.). New York: Macmillan; Crnic, Keith A., and Cathryn L. Booth. (1991). Mothers' and fathers' perceptions of daily hassles of parenting across early childhood. *Journal of Marriage and the Family, 53,* 1042–1050; Rossi, Alice, and Peter Rossi. (1990). *Of human bonding: Parent-child relations across the life cycle.* New York: Aldine de Gruyter.

PARENTHOOD, CHILD-REARING OPTIONS AND STRATE-GIES. One of the major responsibilities of parenthood is adopting child-rearing standards suitable for healthy growth and development. Beginning around the turn of the century, the United States experienced an unprecedented interest in this topic. While child psychologists were scientifically exploring the foundations of behavior, child-care experts began to busily address themselves to the practical aspects of rearing children. In time, their guidance would find its way to books, magazines, professional journals, newspapers, and an assortment of parenting seminars and workshops.

The advice and guidance given by this country's child-care experts came in all shapes and sizes and focused on every conceivable aspect of child rearing, from toilet training to temper tantrums. In a general sense, though, these experts addressed themselves to parenthood's most persistent challenge: how best to raise children to become healthy, well-adjusted adults. In the light of such advice, it must be mentioned that a scientifically proven means of child rearing has yet to emerge. While suggestions are bountiful, clear-cut and precise answers are elusive. Because of this, it seems likely that parents will continue to be swept into a crossfire of opinion as they seek out the best way to raise their children.

Because of the numerous and diverse child-rearing strategies offered to past and present-day parents, it is helpful to categorize approaches according to their operating philosophy. This may promote a better understanding of the rationale behind a suggested guideline or opinion. While it is impossible to cover all approaches, the following are representative of some of the more popular child-rearing strategies to emerge.

Developmental-maturational approach. The developmental-maturational approach was developed by Arnold Gesell and is best known as an age-stage theory of child rearing. Gesell maintained that although individual variations exist, most children will pass through basic patterns of growth at fairly predictable ages. He expended considerable energy exploring this principle, devising numerous norms of infant and child development. Gesell stressed that parents should be aware of childhood's developmental sequences and should structure their expectations, demands, and child-rearing strategies accordingly. (See GESELL, ARNOLD L.)

Behavior-modification approach. Borrowing from B. F. Skinner and the theory of behaviorism, experts emphasizing the behavior-modification approach call attention to the child's surroundings. More specifically, it is maintained that the environment is capable of shaping a child's behavior. Practitioners advocate the use of *positive reinforcement,* or the rewarding of a desired behavior (a child is given a toy for good behavior), or *negative reinforcement,* giving children the opportunity to behave in a way that reduces or eliminates an aversive stimulus (children are sent to their rooms because of a temper tantrum, but can return when they calm down). Proponents claim that when consistently adhered to, these principles will enable parents to nurture desired behavioral patterns in their children. (See BEHAVIORISM; SKINNER, B. F.)

Humanistic approach. The focus of the humanistic approach, developed by Haim Ginott, is the development of parental empathy, sensitivity, and insight into the needs of children. Parents are urged to improve their communication abilities so that they can better appreciate children's feelings and motivations. Among other suggestions, Ginott advocated the practice of preceding statements of advice with statements of understanding, the resolution of conflicts without attacks on personalities, and the abolishment of all threats and sarcasm.

Parent-effectiveness training. Developed by Thomas Gordon, parent-effectiveness training (P.E.T.) seeks to teach parents how to enhance children's self-images as well as their potentials in life. Gordon's techniques include the practice of reflecting positive images back to the child, engaging in mutual negotiation when problems arise, and engaging in "active listening" or verbally feeding back to the child that which has been expressed. Gordon proposed that this latter communication technique enables children to better understand what they have said and assists them in solving their own problems. Gordon also advocated the use of "I" rather than "you" messages ("I get upset when you disturb me like that," as opposed to "You're a rude child to bother your father like this"). He felt that "I" messages are more likely to impart facts, while "you" messages tend to attach blame, promote rebellion, and reduce the child's self-concept.

Democratic approach. The democratic approach is popular in the writings of many child-rearing experts, the most notable being Rudolph Dreikurs. He believed that the family unit is the primary force in shaping children's behavior. Therefore, parents should seek to integrate children as fully as possible into the family network so that they can benefit from everyone's observations, feedback, and encouragement. Children are urged to take part in family decision-making processes, including the establishment of rules and expectations. By so doing, Dreikurs believed, they will learn "logical consequences" of their behavior, those expected behavioral standards that will ensure the fair treatment of all family members. The promotion of such a collective and cooperative atmosphere will promote security, trust, and a sense of belonging within the child.

Transactional-analysis approach. Popularized by Eric Berne, the transactional-analysis approach stresses the importance of three "ego states" and their relation to effective communication. The three ego states are the "child" (the source of spontaneity, but also the source of fear, helplessness, and intimidation); "adult" (the source of reason, but also the source of emotionless responses); and "parent" (the source of nurturance, but also the source of emotional response). Berne suggested that the adult psyche is capable of expressing these three unique ego dimensions when communicating with others. The analysis of communication patterns (called transactions), therefore, reveals interesting and complex dynamics.

In connection with child rearing, parents may inappropriately respond to a child's problem by activating helplessness within their own child state. Or both parents may be striving to solve the same child-rearing issue, but are unproductive because their ego states are incompatible (the father may be utilizing the nurturance facet of his parent state, while the mother's communication embodies the oppressive-adult ego state). In his approach, Berne stressed the importance of ego-state recognition and compatibility of exchange patterns, as well as the parental nurturance of the adult ego state in children.

All of these theories provide a great deal of insight into the nature of child rearing. However, these theoretical positions do not have to be examined or weighed in an either/or manner. Several of them could be operating at different times or under different conditions. For example, the fact that a child may be at a specific norm of Gesell's developmental-maturational theory does not mean that principles of reinforcement are not operating or that the child's interaction with the family unit becomes nonexistent. Thus, while each theory is an effort to explain child-rearing techniques, it is not uncommon for two or more of them to be operating simultaneously.

This is the primary reason why many parents today choose to be eclectic when viewing child-rearing theories. They select theories that they can accept and then develop their own strategies. Moreover, theories need to be adapted and modified to take each individual child into account. Generalized child-rearing theories without individual modification downplay the uniqueness of both child and parent.

It should be remembered, too, that a theory is really a perspective, one of several ways to view development. While each of these theories has broadened our understanding and offers us new areas of exploration, we have not yet been able to answer all our questions about child rearing. As indicated earlier, no theory has yet to explain the "best" way to rear children. This underscores the need to further investigate this field of study, as well as the need for reassessing the theories and viewpoints generated thus far.

Further Reading. Berne, Eric. (1964). *Games people play.* New York: Grove; Dreikurs, Rudolph. (1964). *Children: The challenge.* New York: Hawthorne; Gesell, Arnold. (1940). *The first five years of life.* New York: Harper and Brothers; Ginott, Haim. (1965). *Between parent and child.* New York: Avon; Gordon, Thomas. (1978). *P.E.T. in action.* New York: Bantam; Skinner, B. F. (1953). *Science and human behavior.* New York: Macmillan.

PARENTHOOD, DELAYED. Delayed parenthood represents a deliberate effort on the part of a couple to postpone having children. Not only are the numbers of couples choosing delayed parenthood increasing; the couples are also having fewer children. Delaying parenthood provides couples with the opportunity to develop their personal, career, and marital lives before they take on the responsibilities of parenthood.

Demographers have supplied information regarding those couples choosing to delay parenthood. For example, education appears to be an important determining factor. The more education a woman has, the greater the likelihood that a couple will wait longer to have children. In addition, the closer a wife's earnings parallel her husband's, the more likely she is to delay parenthood. Also, women who grew up in cities, Catholic women, and those whose parents are well educated and whose fathers have relatively high-status occupations tend to be older when they have their first child. However, when the women's education level is held constant, these associations lose their significance. Finally, the age at which a woman has her first child depends heavily on when she herself was born and when she married. Events such as wars and fluctuations in the business cycle caused by unemployment, inflation, and recession explain some variations in the timing of a woman's first child.

There are a number of advantages and disadvantages associated with delayed parenthood. On the plus side, older women who have developed competence in the world before bearing children often bring to the mothering experience strengths different from those of their younger counterparts. Older mothers with established careers are often more accepting and less conflicted in the parenting role than younger professional women. They have a tendency to reveal strengths concomitant with their level of maturity that are generally advantageous for their children's development. Research has indicated that levels of marital satisfaction are higher among women postponing parenthood and childless women than among mothers.

It must also be acknowledged that there are forces that may work against the couple delaying parenthood. Perhaps the biggest risk is that a woman's fertility will decrease with age and health risks will increase. Mortality rates associated with pregnancy and childbirth are substantially higher for women in their 30s and 40s than they are for women in their teens and 20s. The incidence of Down syndrome also rises sharply with the age of the mother. (Down syndrome is a chromosomal abnormality causing, among other characteristics, epicanthic eye folds, round heads, and usually mental retardation.) Another disadvantage associated with delayed parenthood is that older parents may not have the helping services of their aging parents. Finally, parents delaying parenthood may find the tasks associated with child care physically exhausting, maybe even more so than younger parents.

Further Reading. Bloom, David E. (1984). Putting off children. *American Demographics, 12,* 30–33; Cherlin, Andrew. (1990). Recent changes in American fertility, marriage, and divorce. *Annals of the American Academy of Political and Social Science,*

510, 145–154; Glick, Paul C. (1990). American families: As they are and were. *Sociology and Social Research, 74,* 139–145.

PARENTHOOD, MULTICULTURAL VARIATIONS IN. All racial, ethnic, and class groups may not have the same needs and value orientations nor share the same experiences related to parenthood. Moreover, the circumstances of a family's existence and background, to a large extent, shape patterns and processes of overall functioning during the parenting transition. An awareness of racial, ethnic, and class variations enables one to develop tolerance and sensitivity toward parenting differences and distinctions.

Unfortunately, limited information exists on parenting among different racial, ethnic, and class groups. However, interest is growing, as evidenced by the research attention given to Jewish, Irish-American, Italian-American, African-American, Hispanic-American, and other families. Such research is a welcome contribution to the literature since it moves one away from making generalizations about racial, ethnic, or class contexts. Racial, ethnic, and class images all too often contain stereotypes or simplified pictures of a culture. Our images of motherhood and fatherhood in Chicano-American and African-American families, especially, are greatly exaggerated. Chicano-American fathers, for example, are painted as standoffish, swaggering authoritarians. On the other hand, African-American mothers are portrayed as all-powerful matriarchs, and African-American fathers are, at best, aloof and, at worst, absent.

Perhaps a few illustrative studies will reveal how such stereotypes can be removed by sharpening our cultural perceptions. Since it is impossible to cover every culture within the confines of this volume, the aforementioned examples of Chicano-American and African-American families will be utilized. Many perceive the Chicano-American family as being male dominated and clinging to rigid gender-role expectations. In reality, though, such popular views of the Chicano-American family are fraught with misunderstanding. The dominant pattern of decision making, for instance, is egalitarian rather than patriarchal. The father and mother tend to share in child care and domestic chores. Indeed, sharp gender-role segregation is the exception rather than the norm in contemporary Chicano-American families.

As far as African-American family life is concerned, parents encounter many of the same characteristics and problems as white parents. For example, African-American parents experience the developmental changes in children and their own parents as they grow older as well as the problems attached to single parenthood. However, a racist environment often intensifies and changes the impact and meaning of life events. African-American families often do not have the same opportunities and experiences as white families; they thus face unique stressors and create unique patterns of coping.

Paramount among the stressors confronting African-American families is the denial of economic opportunities. African Americans often face job discrimination and experience inadequate education, higher unemployment rates, and inferior incomes. These stressful conditions are the result of a long, continuing history of inequities and have prevented African Americans from living without a high degree of stress. However, effective and functional coping strategies are emerging from this stress, including those related to family life. In particular, African Americans find strength and support within their own families and kin networks. To deal with day-to-day stressors, African-American families turn within, in the process providing gratification, help, and assistance. But African-American families also receive support from a network of friends as well as the broader African-American community.

Another coping strategy has emerged in African-American families: flexibility of family roles. In traditional white families, roles have been clearly and, until recently, rigidly defined: the husband is the wage earner and the wife handles the domestic chores, including child rearing. While there are more dual-employed white couples than ever before, both African-American partners have almost always had to work outside the home to make ends meet. African-American families also tend to be egalitarian, with both husband and wife sharing decision-making authority and other family responsibilities. (See AFRICAN AMERICANS, LIFESPAN RELATIONSHIPS AMONG.)

In regard to parenting and class differences, one must not make generalizations regarding socioeconomic status, nor should one automatically link culture and social class together. In relation to the latter, when an ethnic group is disproportionately poor (or wealthy), parenting differences due to ethnicity become confused with those originating from socioeconomic status. To illustrate, because African Americans have been disproportionately poor, many tend to think of the African-American family as one in which poverty-level mothers are invariably teenagers and fathers take little responsibility for their children. However, as rising numbers of African Americans move into the working class and middle class, it is wrong to assume that all African-American families are the same.

African-American parents' hopes, attitudes, and behaviors for their children are more like than dissimilar to those of other parents in their social class. As an illustration, consider the earlier-mentioned trend of greater father participation in child care. When economic sufficiency rises within African-American families, an increase in the active participation of the African-American father in the socialization of his children is observed. In research focusing on middle-income families, African-American fathers exhibit similarities to other middle-income fathers, including patterns of nurturance and love of their children. The notion that minority parents resemble other parents in their social class is supported in the parenting literature.

It is generally acknowledged that social class limits or expands parents' decisions and options in a variety of ways. To illustrate, birthrates tend to increase as socioeconomic status declines, and divorce rates are higher among families of lower-class status. Working-class parents also tend to maintain a more rigid division of household responsibilities, while middle-class parents tend to be more egalitarian. Socioeconomic status also impacts on parent-child relations. A body of research tends to indicate that lower- and working-class parent-child relationships are oriented more toward obedience, perhaps to assure family respectability. Middle-class parent-child relationships, on the other hand, tend to focus on internalized standards of conduct, leading to independent achievement and self-satisfaction.

Finally, besides fulfilling the health needs of their children and having access to quality medical care, upper-class parents typically create environments that nurture the talents and abilities of their children. Indeed, upper-class homes have the material and educational resources to develop the budding potential of their children. On the other hand, raising children in lower socioeconomic settings is qualitatively different. Health-care considerations, including access to quality medical care, are acute concerns. Moreover, access to child-oriented resources and educational support systems is elusive for most lower-class families.

Further Reading. McAdoo, Harriette P. (Ed.). (1993). *Family ethnicity: Strength in diversity.* Newbury Park, CA: Sage; McAdoo, John L. (1988). The role of black fathers in the socialization of black children. In Harriette P. McAdoo (Ed.), *Black families* (2nd Ed.). Newbury Park, CA: Sage; Taylor, Robert J., Linda M. Chatters, M. Belinda Tucker, and Edith Lewis. (1990). Developments in research on black families. *Journal of Marriage and the Family, 52,* 993–1014.

PARENTHOOD, THE ROLE OF THE FATHER. Until recently, the role and impact of the father in child care have been overlooked. While the importance of the father in the household is generally recognized, part of the problem is that American society has been "mother centered" in its philosophy of child care. With more dual-earner households, the father's influence on various aspects of child growth and development is now being increasingly recognized. Many researchers today actively explore the father's role and have succeeded in providing the field of family studies with a wealth of information.

Contemporary fathers represent an interesting comparison to their historical counterparts. In many ways, modern fathers want to avoid the mistakes that they feel their fathers made. They do not want to become overinvolved in their work or friends and neglect their children. The modern father tends to make a conscious effort to spend more time with his children, perhaps in an effort to be the father he never had. The modern father also does not wait until his children are older before he gets to know them; he starts early. As much as he might not like it, he devotes more time to child-care responsibilities. But the involvement of the new father still lags behind that of the mother. Research consistently shows that women still shoulder most of the responsibility for child care.

Adjusting to fatherhood may prove difficult for some men. Much of the problem is that many fathers are simply unprepared to assume an active parental role. This lack of preparation for fatherhood is often seen in such areas as developmentally appropriate parenting skills, knowledge of normal child development, and sensitivity to their children's needs. Poor preparation usually originates from limited contact with paternal role models, restricted institutional support for the paternal role, and few opportunities to prepare for parenthood. However, it should be recognized that uncertainty and confusion about parenting are normal for both fathers and mothers throughout the course of the family life cycle.

Many researchers maintain that the key element for new fathers is development of confidence—skills can usually be acquired later. Many fathers do not realize that most first-time mothers are just as incompetent and unsure of themselves as they are. It is conceivable that the difference is that women are expected to know ''how'' to parent and cannot just withdraw from the challenges involved. Along these lines, the role of mother embraces specific knowledge, ability, and motivation (see PARENTHOOD, THE ROLE OF THE MOTHER). Mothers who are uninformed often have to pretend that they know what they are doing and thus must learn the necessary child-care skills as soon as they can. Research shows that if a father has difficulty in dealing with an infant, he invariably turns to his wife for help. If the mother needs assistance, she is more likely to seek help from her mother or another female relative, friend, or pediatrician.

Other research indicates that paternal involvement is linked to a father's perceptions of competence as a parent. In other words, the father's appraisal of his parenting skills determines the level of his interaction. If this is true, a system of social exchange may be in operation. Perceptions of competency may prove quite rewarding and push the father toward heightened levels of involvement. Perceived incompetency, on the other hand, may prove discouraging and herald reduced involvement.

Whether or not the father's influence becomes positive is an important issue that hinges on a number of forces, including involvement in child care and family activities, his upbringing, the quality of his other relationships, personality characteristics (such as self-esteem and sensitivity), and the characteristics of his offspring. Researchers maintain that fathers influence their children by the way they behave toward their offspring and the manner in which they interact with their wives. Research on the latter issue shows that satisfying marital relationships as well as social support enhance both fathers' and mothers' sensitivity and responsivity to the needs of their children.

It must be noted that greater paternal involvement does not always create domestic harmony. Some investigators have found that paternal child-care involvement in dual-earner families is related to heightened marital conflict and lowered levels of marital satisfaction. When mothers are employed outside the home, some fathers may perceive their roles as being more restricted and their freedom reduced. Moreover, some experience depression in their parental role and see their children as being more moody and demanding. Many mothers have been subject to the stresses associated with the multiple role demands of being a parent and working outside the home. Most fathers, on the other hand, have not and may experience stress as they attempt to meet the changing expectations for paternal involvement in response to maternal employment.

Further Reading. Lamb, Michael E. (1986). The changing role of fathers. In Michael E. Lamb (Ed.), *The father's role: Applied perspectives.* New York: Wiley; Pillemer, Karl, and Kathleen McCartney. (Eds.). (1991). *Parent-child relations throughout life.* Hillsdale, NJ: Erlbaum; Yablonsky, Lewis. (1990). *Fathers and sons: The most challenging of all family relationships.* New York: Gardner Press.

PARENTHOOD, THE ROLE OF THE MOTHER. First-time mothers, like first-time fathers, discover that the parenting role needs to be defined, performed, and integrated with other role demands. In stable families, adjusting to the parenting role is accomplished with some degree of competency. However, in unstable homes, difficulty with role adaptation is often experienced, resulting in domestic disruption and disorganization. While minor roles can be performed indifferently without creating much domestic turmoil, the parenting role requires constant and at least adequate role performance.

Many first-time mothers often feel inadequate to the task of parenting, mainly because they have had limited contact with children prior to their own. However, some type of formal or informal support system during the early weeks is usually of great value. Should a supportive relative or friend assist with child care and domestic chores, the new mother is usually able to adjust to infant demands and develop confidence and competency in her new role.

Often, the mother discovers that an infant is more work than she ever imagined. Unfortunately, society tends to paint an unrealistic image of motherhood, in some instances idealizing it beyond recognition. The truth of the matter is that mothers find their lives significantly altered with an ever-increasing workload. Many feel overwhelmed in the face of physical demands, not only those attached to caregiving, but also those related to the father's needs. It may well be that one of the major problems facing the contemporary U.S. mother is overcommitment. She has more responsibilities than most can meet, and she is putting in more hours than her grandmother did running the household.

Not too long ago, mothers were expected to remain at home and care for their children, particularly during their offspring's early years of development. Many felt that this was the only way a mother could love and properly rear her children during this important life stage. To venture away from the family in search of a paycheck was viewed as uncaring and unwise. Today, however, increasing numbers of women are breaking this traditional stereotype of mothering and are working outside of the home. Moreover, there is growing acceptance that a woman can handle the multiple roles of breadwinner and mother.

Demographers tell us that the typical profile of the mother most likely to return to work before her child's first birthday conforms to the human-capital theories of labor-force behavior: the greater the investment of time and money in education, the more rapid the return to work after childbirth to minimize losses in earnings and depreciation of job skills. Beyond this, an investment in schooling may indicate a great personal commitment to a career. Any females who have spent many years in school may have delayed marriage and would, generally speaking, have fewer children than less educated women.

However, it is not only potential earning power that encourages females to seek employment, but potential wages in relation to the costs of working. For mothers of small children, child care is typically the greatest expense. The primary reason for the leveling off of labor-force activity among African-American females and high-school dropouts, who earn lower average salaries than other women, may well be a lack of affordable child care (see CHILD CARE, WORKING PARENTS AND).

While the dual-earner family reaps its share of benefits and personal satisfaction, certain sacrifices are common in homes with younger children. The responsibilities of child rearing and tending to domestic chores appear to be the biggest obstacles for women to hurdle in pursuing careers. In most instances, the woman still carries the brunt of the household tasks, which intensify when employment outside of the home occurs. Consequently, the problem is that a two-career marriage is really a three-career marriage, with the woman typically holding down two careers.

Often, a mother's employment status has minimal effect on what the husband does. Thus, while many husbands may say that they prefer an equitable domestic arrangement, in actual practice this is the exception rather than the rule. Should fathers offer child-care assistance, it is often qualitatively different than that provided by mothers. Often, paternal involvement falls under the category of "play," whereas mothers involve themselves in custodial activities such as feeding, diapering, and bathing.

There are other difficulties among working mothers. Many report some anxiety about their child's well-being and wonder if they have made the right choice. Many who are full-time mothers, however, often want to go back into the labor force. Thus a type of Catch-22 situation exists. In other instances, working mothers are happy and satisfied with their chosen profession, but feel inadequate in the mothering role. In this respect, many working mothers feel role conflict. (See WOMEN, EMPLOYED.)

Further Reading. LeMasters, E. E., and John DeFrain. (1989). *Parents in contemporary America* (5th Ed.). Belmont, CA: Wadsworth; Moen, Phyllis. (1992). *Women's two roles: A contemporary dilemma.* New York: Auburn House; Phoenix, Ann, Anne Woollett, and Eva Lloyd. (Eds.). (1991). *Motherhood: Meanings, practices, and ideologies.* Newbury Park, CA: Sage.

PARENTS ANONYMOUS. See THERAPEUTIC RELATIONSHIP, FOR SURVIVORS OF VIOLENCE AND ABUSE.

PATRIARCHAL POWER STRUCTURE. See MARRIAGE, VARIATIONS IN STRUCTURE.

PATRILINEAL DESCENT. See MARRIAGE, VARIATIONS IN STRUCTURE.

PATRILOCAL RESIDENCY. See MARRIAGE, VARIATIONS IN STRUCTURE.

PEDOPHILIA. See SEXUAL BEHAVIORS, ATYPICAL.

PEOPLE'S REPUBLIC OF CHINA, LIFESPAN RELATION-SHIPS IN THE. The People's Republic of China is the third-largest country in the world. Only the Russian Republic and Canada are larger in area. China also has the distinction of being the world's most populous country, containing approximately one-quarter of its people. China is an ancient civilization and predominantly a rural, low-income country. Despite recent advances in industrialization, much of the country is still relatively undeveloped. Most of the people live in the eastern third of the country, many in the great river valleys and coastal plains.

While the People's Republic of China contains more than 50 ethnic groups, most of the population is Han Chinese, commonly referred to as "Chinese." About 5 percent of the population are non-Han Chinese, the Zhuang and the Yi being two of the largest minority groups. The Beijing dialect, or Mandarin, is the national language of China. As far as religion is concerned, most Chinese follow a combination of the teachings of Buddhism, Confucianism, and Taoism. Among China's minority groups, Islam is widespread, particularly in western regions of the country.

As indicated, the People's Republic of China is an overpopulated nation. In an effort to curb its population, China implemented a one-child policy in 1979 (see FERTILITY, INTERNATIONAL DIFFERENCES IN). Couples pledging to have one child received a number of government benefits, including monetary bonuses, preferential treatment for housing, health care, education, and job opportunities. The one-child policy is considered controversial, and its implementation has provoked strong resistance over the years. Most critics question the government's right to intervene in a couple's reproductive decision making. However, there is no mistaking the fact that China's fertility rates have declined: Chinese women had an average of 5.8 children in 1970; today the figure has dropped to about 2.3. China's goal is to stabilize its population at 1.2 billion by the year 2000, the country's assumed population-carrying capacity.

Widespread access to contraception has been a vital part of China's population-planning program. Contraceptive use among women of reproductive age is currently about 85 percent, a significant increase from earlier years. Most Chinese use one of three birth-control methods: the intrauterine device (IUD), female sterilization, or male sterilization. Many Chinese women also use abortion as a birth-control method. Over the past 20 years, the number of IUD insertions, sterilizations, and abortions has nearly tripled, from 13 million to 35 million procedures. Approximately 10 million abortions are performed in China each year.

Raising the minimum age of marriage represents another effort to curb overpopulation. Marriage has always been early and universal in China, the legal age for years being 16 for women and 18 for men (the founding of the People's Republic brought legislation in 1950 that raised the age to 18 for women and 20 for men). Citing a link between later marriages and lower fertility rates, the government raised marriage ages to 25 and 27, respectively, for women and men in cities; and to ages 23 and 25 in rural areas. In 1980, the marriage law was amended, setting the minimum age at 20 for women and 22 for men.

Beyond the issue of overpopulation, Chinese marriages reflect interesting and unique dynamics. Prior to the Communist revolution, parents arranged all marriages. Today, though, only about 10 percent of marriages are prearranged. The earlier-mentioned 1980 marriage law promoted the importance of free choice in mate selection and equal rights for both sexes. However, China's traditional sexual morality still creates conservative patterns of dating and courtship. To illustrate, premarital sex and cohabitation are frowned upon, as are public displays of affection such as holding hands or kissing. While the government promotes the concept of egalitarianism within marriage, households have retained a traditional patriarchal structure that has endured for centuries. In most homes, the male is the unquestioned authority, while the female plays a supportive and often subservient role.

Family life is important in the daily lives of Chinese. The family is regarded as a strong, loyal unit, and respect for it is continually stressed. As far as parent-child relations are concerned, children are the objects of much love and affection. Mothers are the primary caregivers, although members of the extended family often provide assistance. Throughout their formative years, children are taught the virtues of self-discipline, dignity, control, and cooperation. Considerable emphasis is placed on a structured, orderly life. Parents have high standards for their children's achievement and stress the importance of inner drive and determination.

The elderly are an important component of Chinese family life. They are revered and respected for the knowledge and wisdom they possess. As such, they are neither ignored nor rejected by the young. Such intergenerational relations capture a wider theme about the life cycle among the Chinese: that late adulthood is recognized as a graceful and triumphant period of life, not a period of degeneration and deterioration. Elderly Chinese are appreciated as important individuals who still have much to contribute to the good of society.

If one keeps the foregoing in mind, it should come as no surprise that aging family members receive regular care and support from younger generations. However, China's one-child policy has created interesting implications for the care of aging parents. Demographic experts predict that 20 years from now, many middle-aged Chinese couples will be sandwiched between four elderly parents and one young offspring. In an effort to prepare for the future, government officials are seeking ways to assist with the care of the aged so that the burden on individual families will be lessened. In many Chinese cities and provinces, special committees have been established to address the needs of families and the aged, including the provision of care and needed social services. China is also planning to construct more institutional care facilities for the aged, recreational centers, and transportation centers.

Further Reading. Coale, Ansley J., Wang Feng, Nancy E. Riley, and Lin Fu De. (1991). Recent trends in fertility and nuptiality in China. *Science, 251,* 389–393; Poston, Dudley L., Jr., and David Yaukey. (1992). *The population of modern China.* New York: Plenum Press; Tien, H. Yuan, Zhang Tianlu, Ping Yu, Li Jingneng, and Liang Zhongtang. (1992). *China's demographic dilemmas.* Washington, DC: Population Reference Bureau.

PIAGET, JEAN. Jean Piaget (1896–1980) is considered to be the most important figure in the field of cognitive-developmental theory, a major school of thought in psychology. Educated at the University of Neuchâtel, Switzerland, Piaget at first had no intention of studying child psychology. As a child, he had always exhibited an interest in nature, and at age 11, he published an article in a natural history magazine on an albino sparrow he had observed in a park. He pursued this interest in nature while at college, but meanwhile began also to nurture an interest in the field of psychology, notably in the works of Sigmund Freud and Carl Jung. Upon graduation from Neuchâtel in 1916, he traveled to Zurich to investigate further the research undertaken by these two psychologists. His travels eventually brought him in contact with Dr. Theophile Simon, who offered him a position as an assistant in the Binet Institute, a children's clinic located in Paris.

Piaget's first assignment at the Binet Institute was to develop a standardized French version of the original IQ test, a task, he openly admitted, that was not challenging at first. However, his questioning nature soon opened new avenues for exploration and investigation. While he was devising the test, a major portion of his work consisted of directing test questions at the nursery-school children at the institute. At first, Piaget was concerned with finding standardized test items suitable for young children, but he soon became interested in the answers given to him rather than the questions he phrased. In particular, he was fascinated by the wrong answers given and the frequency with which they occurred. The Swiss psychologist was soon to discover not only that young children had profound misconceptions about the world in general, but also that for the most part, these misconceptions appeared to be universal for a given age level.

All of this led Piaget to believe that intellectual development proceeds in an orderly sequence that is characterized by specific growth stages. He further postulated that these growth stages enable the child to attain certain basic concepts necessary for intellectual maturity. Therefore, he believed conceptual development to be a building process, a series of qualitative intellectual advancements that could transport the child from a world of fantasy into a world of reality.

Piaget's numerous academic achievements included appointments to the University of Neuchâtel, the University of Lausanne, and the University of Geneva. At Geneva he established the International Center for Genetic Epistemology. He was also the author of a multitude of books and research studies on various facets of cognitive development. (See COGNITIVE-DEVELOPMENTAL THEORY.)

Further Reading. Flavell, John H. (1963). *The developmental psychology of Jean Piaget.* Princeton, NJ: Van Nostrand; Piaget, Jean. (1929). *The child's conception of the world.* New York: Harcourt Brace and Company; Piaget, Jean. (1932). *The moral judgment of the child.* Glencoe, IL: Free Press; Piaget, Jean. (1952). *The origins of intelligence in children.* New York: International Universities Press.

PLAY. Children's play refers to behavioral patterns that emerge when unstructured activities are engaged in solely for the pleasure that they offer. In a sense, play represents children's work, a meaningful set of activities that will help them better understand themselves and how to relate to their surroundings. Few activities reveal emerging character and resources for coping with the world more than the everyday play that the child engages in. As such, children's play serves to stimulate a number of developmental areas, including physical, cognitive, emotional, personality, and social domains.

At a fundamental level, play encourages exploration and manipulation of the environment. Early play behavior paves the way for more fully developed physical skills and levels of achievement and accomplishment. From a psychological point of view, a personal sense of identity is established through play. Play enables children to realize who they are and what effects their actions may have on the people around them. As a vital part of human functioning, children's play worlds unfold before their very eyes, eventually allowing them to interpret themselves and the environment in realistic terms.

Furthermore, play serves important personality and social functions. Individually, it gives children the opportunity to experience many of life's emotions and to view their position in life in relation to the rest of the world. Sociodramatic play, for example, provides children with the opportunity to transform themselves into the adult role or situation of their choosing. Play can also bring children into contact with one another and makes them consciously aware of the meaning of rules, structure, and cooperation. In so doing, play teaches and enriches important social skills and cognitive abilities.

Further Reading. Garvey, Catherine. (1990). *Play.* Cambridge, MA: Harvard University Press; McKee, Judy Spitler (Ed.). (1986). *Play: Working partner of growth.* Wheaton, MD: Association for Childhood Education International; Thorne, Barrie. (1993). *Gender play: Girls and boys in school.* New Brunswick, NJ: Rutgers University Press.

PLAY, AND CHILDHOOD SOCIALIZATION. Children's play is an important vehicle for early socialization. During the first few years of life, play enables children to discover who they are and what effects their actions have on their environment (see INFANCY AND TODDLERHOOD, SOCIAL PLAY DURING). For older children, play has new qualities that reflect growth and development, particularly their desire to participate and become involved in more socially oriented activities, increased use of higher-order mental processes, and imitation of and identification with adult behavioral patterns. Contacts with socialization agents other than the family, such as early childhood education settings or neighborhood peer groups, provide a myriad of new social activities and facilitate overall play development.

Play is an important social activity throughout childhood because it is a means by which children can better understand themselves and how they relate to others. For the young child, play groups enhance a sensitivity to the needs of others in addition to fostering a cooperative spirit. Play groups also help children to relinquish a self-centered frame of reference and to take the needs and feelings of others into account (see CHILDHOOD, PEER-GROUP DEVELOPMENT DURING).

The preschool play group is usually small, restrictive, and temporary (many groups dissolve after 10 or 15 minutes). This temporary quality is the result of a number of factors, including limited attending skills and impulsive desires to end activities prematurely in order to start something else. Because of the play group's temporary quality, preschoolers are faced with the chore of entering new social gatherings on a fairly regular basis. Some may be better at this than others, perhaps because they are more outgoing, gregarious, and secure in overall relationships. The quiet, timid, or shy child may have a more difficult time.

As a social vehicle, the play group teaches children that certain behaviors are expected and certain rules must be followed. Moreover, children will learn the importance of working toward group goals and sharing materials. Children learn these social processes best by interacting with one another (and with adults in situations that warrant grown-up intervention and guidance).

The extent to which adults should involve themselves in and structure playtime activities has received a fair amount of research attention. Many experts maintain that adults should provide guidance, support, and the environment for play but should be careful not to restrict children's freedom to play. Too often adults overinvolve themselves and overorganize play activities, which restricts children's spontaneity and free play spirit. While adult intervention has positive effects on the initiation and direction of play, it should be designed to minimize its obtrusive effects and to avoid controlling all the choices of the child.

Play during middle childhood continues to serve important social functions. While children often play alone at this age, they also continue to seek out the company of other children. Neighborhood and school interactions are the more popular play groups, and they further encourage cooperative forms of play endeavors. By learning how to share and be responsible to one another, to follow the directions of a leader, to develop self-confidence in a group setting, and to cope with success and failure, children come to understand what a group is, how it operates, and how they can interact with it. As a result of these developments, the play group is able to structure its own activities. Children within the group setting are also likely to demonstrate advances in sensitivity toward others, as well as increasing amounts of prosocial behavior. These social advancements typically increase as group experiences become more diverse (see PROSOCIAL BEHAVIOR, CHILD).

To suppose that the elementary-school play group is characterized by internal stability and smooth sailing is incorrect. Throughout all of childhood, group relations are fraught with the potential for disagreement or conflict. Middle childhood is no exception. While younger children are more likely to dispute the possession of a toy or object, elementary-school children are likely to experience disagreements over which activities to undertake, which children can play, and who has created group disharmony. It is the task of the group members to resolve group disharmony. Conflict resolution is an important phase of interpersonal development, and the play group affords children the opportunity to try out potential solutions, strategies, and decision-making skills.

By the time adolescence is reached, play interests change, owing primarily to a shift in values and a shortage of time. For the most part, play activities become less strenuous and physical, except for people who pursue competitive sports and other active interests throughout adolescence. There is also a marked increase in the intermingling of the sexes, which has been lacking throughout most of childhood. For many, the heterosexual friendships and recreational activities of adolescence are a valued counterpart to same-sex recreational pursuits.

Parents are much less involved in structuring, directing, or taking part in the recreational pursuits of their teenage offspring, who are increasingly independent and involved with peer-group interests. The peer group plays a significant role in determining the type and duration of activities to be undertaken. However, not all adolescents sever family ties and rely exclusively on the peer group for recreational purposes. Many adolescents, typically those from close-knit and nurturant homes, enjoy family-oriented recreational activities. Popular forms of family recreation include backyard sports, camping, boating, and indoor games.

Because of growing levels of physical, cognitive, and social maturity, adolescents typically enjoy a wide range of play activities. These activities also tend to be introspective, egoistic, and considerably more serious. Among adolescent activities are competitive and noncompetitive games and sports, video games, television viewing, dancing, and musical pursuits.

Further Reading. Casey, M. Beth, and Marjory Lippman. (1991). Learning to plan through play. *Young Children, 46,* 52–58; Garbey, Catherine. (1990). *Play.* Cambridge, MA: Harvard University Press; Smilansky, Sara, and Leah Shefatya. (1990). *Facilitating play: A medium for promoting cognitive, socio-emotional, and academic development in young children.* Gaithersburg, MD: Psychosocial and Educational Publications.

POLYANDRY. See MARRIAGE, VARIATIONS IN STRUCTURE.

POLYGAMY. See MARRIAGE, VARIATIONS IN STRUCTURE.

POLYGYNY. See MARRIAGE, VARIATIONS IN STRUCTURE.

POSTPARENTAL STAGE. See EMPTY NEST.

POWER AND RELATIONSHIPS. Power is the ability to direct another person's behavior in a way that he or she would not have done spontaneously. Within the context of relationships, power emerges when one partner perceives the other as being dominant. The study of power and how it influences relationships, including the related constructs of control, dominance, persuasion, and authority, has long intrigued social scientists.

Over the years, many researchers have sought to explain power, and a number of different definitions and perspectives on the topic have been offered. For example, power has been viewed as the production of intended effects, or the ability of a person to produce intended effects on the behavior of another individual. Others propose that power occurs when a person can get another individual to do something that he or she would not otherwise do. Still others suggest that power is an exercise of influence: it is the process of affecting others with the assistance of (actual or threatened) severe deprivations for nonconformity with the policies intended. It should be added that in most marriages, both spouses have a certain degree of power within their own particular areas of interest.

Power can be viewed as a punctuation of an interaction in which one person perceives the other as being controlling or dominating. Power conveys the health of the relationship since it reflects how partners confirm or disconfirm each other. Going a step further, tension and conflict around power and authority are what people fight about in relationships. Inequity, control, and dominance therefore have important implications for dyadic harmony and stability. In this respect, the issue is not really what people fight about, but instead why they fight.

Some researchers feel that power has both nonlegitimate and legitimate properties. More specifically, nonlegitimate power is neither earned nor consented to, and it can become domination. Nonlegitimate power often encompasses coercion, threats, and punishment. Legitimate power, on the other hand, is earned and consented to. It represents a process involving bargaining and negotiation and moves toward authority—an institutionalized state. Put another way, it is recognized that a person or group in a position of authority has the right to be in charge. Compared to nonlegitimate power, legitimate power typically relies on ''friendly persuasion'' and the provision of benefits.

It has also been discovered that power reflects gender differences, particularly within traditional relationships. Traditional males are taught to make decisions, direct others, and assume control. Traditional females, on the other hand, are programmed to be submissive, dependent, and reliant on others. Thus men and women receive different messages regarding power and its ultimate expression.

It also appears that traditional women are less competitive and aggressive in verbal interactions. Research tends to show that traditional women demonstrate greater needs for relational solidarity (the drive to be friendly or establish rapport) than relational power. Traditional men, on the other hand, are programmed to compete and win. They talk, interrupt, and overlap more frequently, while women often respond with silence. Males also control the topics of conversations in male-female dyads and may employ abrupt and direct methods to do so. In male-male dyads, men use less abrupt and direct strategies to change the subject.

Researchers have further found that many of the qualities that women exhibit in marital conversation and conflict originate from their subordinate position. Women often expect noncompliance during conflict and, like other subordinates, resort to such communication techniques as emotional appeals, moral persuasion, and harassment through coercion. Husbands, on the other hand, are able to be more calm, conciliatory, and chivalrous because of their greater power in marriage.

Finally, researchers have distinguished the nature of family power, which incorporates the behaviors of family members other than the marital dyad, from marital power, which focuses on behavior between spouses. Along these lines, different types of family power can be identified. For example, the resources of a particular family member may increase his or her ability to exercise control in a given situation. Family power often emerges in the face of problem-solving, decision-making, conflict-resolution, and crisis-management situations. Who makes the decisions and who wins are obvious cornerstones to family power structures. However, one must recognize that family power involves asymmetry of relations between members with regard to the ability to change the behavior of others. Family power exists because of one's relationship within the system, not just one's personal characteristics.

Further Reading. Kranichfeld, Marion L. (1987). Rethinking family power. *Journal of Family Issues, 8,* 42–56; Lips, Hilary M. (1991). *Women, men, and power.* Mountain View, CA: Mayfield; Scanzoni, Letha D., and John Scanzoni (1981). *Men, women, and change: A sociology of marriage and family* (2nd Ed.). New York: McGraw-Hill.

POWER AND RELATIONSHIPS, THEORETICAL PERSPEC-TIVES ON.
Different theoretical perspectives can be used to explore the manner in which power emerges within a relationship. Theoretical perspectives are important to acknowledge since they provide a conceptual framework and a guide for investigating power. A theory organizes and gives meanings to facts, and it serves as a foundation for further research. In the study of power, theories have been proposed focusing on individual behavioral dynamics as well as relationship interactions. The following represents an overview of such theories.

Freudian and neo-Freudian theories. Freudian or psychoanalytic theories often view power strivings as an outgrowth of narcissism. Some distinguish between healthy and neurotic drives for power. Healthy strivings for superiority are balanced against social interest, while neurotic power strivings are likely the result of an early inferiority complex. Freudian theorists might also argue that persons with neurotic needs for power have a desire to dominate others and seek to avoid situations in which they are relatively helpless.

Motivational theories. Motivational theorists choose to identify power as a motive underlying behavior. Power is often seen as embracing a variety of different needs, such as dominance or aggression. Some motivational theorists conceptualize the power incentive as a negative goal in which persons avoid feelings of powerlessness. Others maintain that individuals with a high need for influence enjoy influencing others for the purpose of perceiving themselves as being influential.

Authoritarian theories. Authoritarian theories maintain that individuals having heightened levels of authoritarianism not only display a greater concern for power in their relationships with others, but they also tend to admire individuals who are in positions of power. Additionally, individuals having high levels of authoritarianism expect persons with lower power to accept without question influence from those in power. These theorists believe that authoritarianism is also linked to such variables as prejudice, ethnocentrism, and political-economic conservatism.

Locus-of-control theories. Locus-of-control theories suggest that as we observe ourselves and others, we may infer that certain situations are caused by factors that reside within the person (e.g., motivation, ability), or factors that reside outside of the person (e.g., luck, task difficulty). Related to the former, "internal locus of control" means that persons believe that they can control their own lives. On the other hand, those with "external locus of control" perceive their lives as being controlled by people or things beyond their control. Going a step further, it is reasoned that individuals with internal locus of control have the potential to wield power. They are more likely to exercise control and influence, thus changing the behavior or attitudes of others.

Resource theories. Resource theorists argue that the balance of power in a system reflects the relative resources that each person has. Thus whoever has the most resources will wield the most power. For example, the power of a husband varies positively with his socioeconomic resources (income, education, occupational prestige, or a composite of these variables). But the employment of a wife increases her power and concomitantly seems to limit the power of her husband. When the wife's socioeconomic resources are compared to the husband's, the larger the discrepancy between them, the greater the power differential.

Social exchange theories. Social exchange theorists propose that individuals desire the maximum positive outcomes or rewards in relationships along with the least amount of costs or trade-offs. This bartering of rewards and costs determines the flow of the relationship, including power dynamics. For example, researchers have found that the partner who can supply services that others demand can exercise power over them. Similarly, should a partner become increasingly dependent on the other, power dynamics are affected. Investigators have found that the more dependent one partner is on the other, the less power this person has in the relationship.

Family development theories. Family development theories suggest that patterns of power and control ebb and flow at various points in the family life cycle. As a result, they converge with and affect generational patterns of relating and functioning. Different stages of the life cycle can be used for illustrative purposes. For instance, when aging parents turn to their grown children for support and assistance, generational roles are redefined and family power shifts. To cite another example, when a husband retires and spends increased amounts of time in the household, he frequently becomes aware of new responsibilities, expectations, and power distributions. Related to a point made earlier, it is possible that the husband's power declines when he loses the ''leverage'' provided by the breadwinner role. It seems that the same would hold true for women who are wage earners, although limited research has been conducted on this topic.

Further Reading. Berger, Charles R. (1985). Social power and interpersonal communication. In M. L. Knapp and G. R. Miller (Eds.), *Handbook of interpersonal communication.* Beverly Hills, CA: Sage; Falbo, Toni, and Letitia A. Peplau. (1980). Power strategies in intimate relationships. *Journal of Personality and Social Psychology, 38,* 618–628; Winter, David G. (1973). *The power motive.* New York: Free Press.

PRAGMATICS. Pragmatics is how language is used in a social context, including the use of a wide range of behaviors, such as gestures, facial expressions, pauses, pointing, or turn taking. Pragmatic rules exist in every language, and learning such rules begins at a very early age. During early verbal interactions, for example, children learn to establish eye contact and pay attention to their partners when communicating.

As children get older, other aspects of pragmatics are learned. Reciprocal turn taking and a greater range of expressions to convey messages now accompany communication. More complex styles of interaction between speaker and listener are also evident, such as initiating and terminating conversations. Children learn to tailor their speech, such as expanding or deleting their sentences depending on the listener's communication needs. Children also know that when listeners move away, they have to raise their voices in order to be heard.

Older children and adolescents demonstrate the greater use of gestures, pauses, and facial expressions. Children are now more skilled at taking turns during conversations. They also are better at adapting information to fit the listener's needs. Moreover, many can adopt the listener's point of view if the situation calls for it.

Other advances in pragmatics include a more meaningful exchange of questions and answers. Although younger children do ask questions, they often encounter problems in listening to the answers. Older children, on the other hand, use questions to acquire desired information. Fabricating a question, asking it, and listening for the answer are all important social exchanges that improve with age.

Further Reading. Gleason, Jean Berko. (Ed.). (1993). *The development of language* (3rd Ed.). New York: Macmillan; Hulit, Lloyd M., and Merle R. Howard. (1993). *Born to talk: An introduction to speech and language development.* New York: Macmillan.

PRENUPTIAL AGREEMENT. A prenuptial agreement, or personal marriage contract, is a document drafted by some couples before they marry. In its most common form, a prenuptial agreement spells out how assets will be divided if the marriage dissolves. Prenuptial agreements, however, may also include other items, including the expectations partners have for one another. Items might range from how household tasks are to be handled and role responsibilities assigned to how many children the couple desires.

Besides recognizing that divorce is a possibility in their lives, couples cite other reasons for drafting prenuptial agreements. Some feel that love is often blind during early stages of the relationship and want to clearly assess the union in writing. Others seek a written commitment to go along with the psychological commitment. Still others use prenuptial agreements as a way to periodically examine the health and growth of their relationship. Over time, the agreement is reviewed to see whether goals, ambitions, and related aspirations have been met.

Those prenuptial agreements that focus on financial divisions do have legal substance. However, for this document to be upheld by the law, it must be shown that it is fair, that it was executed voluntarily, and that it was entered into in good faith. To meet these criteria, the prospective bride and groom must each have a lawyer. Because this is a contract being negotiated, both parties must be represented by counsel, or the contract may later be ruled invalid. Both partners must also make a full financial disclosure, and negotiation must take place without coercion or threat.

From a legal standpoint, there is growing support for prenuptial agreements. Such agreements are seen as providing the parties some degree of certainty regarding their estates in the event of divorce or the death of one of the parties. Also, it is expected that making prenuptial agreements valid should reduce the amount of litigation and the acrimony that often follow a divorce. In addition, it has been suggested that such agreements may force parties who are about to marry to realize the seriousness of marriage and may actually reduce the number of divorces, since the parties know from the start of their marriage what will take place if a divorce occurs.

Further Reading. Ruback, Barry. (1985). Family law. In Luciano L'Abate (Ed.), *The handbook of family psychology and therapy.* Homewood, IL: Dorsey Press; Turner, Jeffrey S., and Donald B. Helms. (1988). *Marriage and family: Traditions and transitions.* San Diego, CA: Harcourt Brace Jovanovich.

PRIMARY AND SECONDARY GROUPS. Primary and secondary groups refer to interpersonal settings within which socialization takes place. A primary group is a close-knit group such as the family or an intimate friendship. It is characterized by continuous face-to-face interaction, strong ties of affection and attachment among its members, and an enduring quality. A secondary group offers less intimacy and personal interaction than the primary group and exists in such settings as the school or work arena. Compared to primary groups, secondary groups are characterized by less commitment of the self and weaker bonds of affection among the members. It is possible for primary groups to form within secondary groups, such as when two students in a classroom setting forge an intimate friendship.

Further Reading. Calhoun, Craig, Donald Light, and Suzanne Keller. (1994). *Sociology* (6th Ed.). New York: McGraw-Hill; Stark, Rodney. (1994). *Sociology* (5th Ed.). Belmont, CA: Wadsworth.

PRONATALISM. Pronatalism represents an effort to increase a nation's fertility level. Pronatalistic policies are often implemented by those nations experiencing declining fertility rates, most notably those countries with less than 2.1 lifetime births per woman. This total of children is about the number needed to keep births and deaths in balance and create population stability. Many European nations such as Austria, Denmark, and Hungary have dropped below this total, prompting the implementation of pronatalistic policies to help boost fertility back up to replacement level. To encourage couples to have more children, pronatalistic policies often include family allowances, subsidized maternity-leave packages, and more accessible housing loans for families with two or more children.

Pronatalism is in striking contrast to *antinatalism,* an effort to decrease a nation's fertility level. In overcrowded nations such as the People's Republic of China, the government sometimes takes active steps to discourage large family size. China's 'one-child policy' is illustrative of such government intervention. In this family-planning policy, Chinese couples honoring the nation's desired family size are provided with such incentives as monetary bonuses, preferential treatment for housing, health care, education, and job opportunities. (See FERTILITY, INTERNATIONAL DIFFERENCES IN; PEOPLE'S REPUBLIC OF CHINA, LIFESPAN RELATIONSHIPS IN THE.)

Further Reading. Davis, Kingsley, and Mikhail S. Berstam. (1989). *Population and resources in a changing world.* Stanford, CA: Stanford University Press; Van de Kaa, Dirk J. (1987). *Europe's second demographic transition.* Washington, DC: Population Reference Bureau.

PROSOCIAL BEHAVIOR, CHILD. Prosocial behavior is peer sensitivity and being responsive to the needs and feelings of others. It pertains to such areas as cooperation, comforting, sympathizing, altruism, sharing, and helping others. Prosocial behavior is often referred to as Good Samaritan behavior.

While children tend to be egocentric (self-centered) during early childhood, they are capable of demonstrating prosocial behaviors. Toddlers, for example, are able to share with others and exhibit some insight into the emotional state and needs of others. Prosocial behaviors in the form of sharing and the provision of comfort also begin to emerge during this time. By the preschool years, children can perform such prosocial acts as helping, cooperating with, and comforting others. However, it is important to stress that even though the ability to demonstrate prosocial behavior appears early in life, this does not mean that it is consistently expressed. Usually this does not transpire until later in childhood or adolescence.

Friendship is an important factor in facilitating children's prosocial behavior. More specifically, children tend to be more altruistic to someone they like than to someone they dislike. Also, early prosocial behavior seems to be greatly influenced by the child's exposure to positive adult role models and certain social situations. Children are apt to learn such behaviors as helping and cooperating by receiving adult guidance and positive reinforcement, by interacting with other children, and by observing adults and other children behaving in socially constructive ways. Youngsters exposed to altruistic adults are likely to imitate such behaviors, especially if the adult model is affectionate and nurturant. Other adult behaviors, such as handling disciplinary situations in a positive manner, have also been shown to increase children's levels of prosocial behavior.

Interesting cross-national differences appear to exist in the teaching, and ultimate expression of, prosocial behaviors. For example, in the republics of the former Soviet Union, Israel, and Mexico, a high premium is placed on cooperation and the teaching of altruistic behavior. As another illustration, Chinese parents tend to stress the avoidance of interpersonal conflict and, instead, encourage cooperative interaction. The results of such training are evident in the high levels of prosocial behavior demonstrated by children in these countries.

This does not imply that American children are not taught the same lessons or lack prosocial sensitivity. What it does imply is that compared with children from other nations, American children are not taught altruism as consistently. Rather than the other countries' everyday emphasis on helping others, American children often receive sporadic instruction in prosocial development and limited structured opportunities from adults to put this behavior into practice. But given such opportunities, prosocial behavior may develop more fully.

Further Reading. Dixon, James A., and Colleen F. Moore. (1990). The development of perspective taking. *Child Development, 61,* 1502–1513; Zahn-Waxler, Carolyn, et al., (1992). Development of concern for others. *Developmental Review, 28,* 126–136.

PROTESTANTISM. See RELIGION, IMPACT OF ON INTIMATE RELATIONSHIPS.

PROXEMICS. See COMMUNICATION, INTERPERSONAL.

PSYCHOANALYTIC THEORY. Psychoanalytic theory is a major school of thought in psychology and is widely used in the field of lifespan development. Essentially, this theory emphasizes the dynamics of the unconscious mind and one's past experiences as being the major determinants of future behavior. The psychoanalytic school of thought was devised by Sigmund Freud.

One of Freud's major beliefs was that individuals are generally not aware of the underlying reasons for their behavior. He assumed that mental activity must occur at three levels of consciousness. He called the first level the *conscious* level of awareness. Freud used this term to refer to what a person is thinking or experiencing at any given moment. The second level is called the *preconscious* and is all of a person's stored knowledge and memories that are capable of being brought up to the conscious level. The third and largest level of consciousness is the *unconscious,* a vast area of irrational wishes, shameful urges, socially unacceptable sexual desires, fears, and aggressive feelings, as well as anxiety-producing thoughts that have been *repressed* (pushed down to the unconscious to be forgotten).

Freud also reasoned that the personality consists of three components. The *id* is the original inherited system, the instinctive aspect of one's personality. The id contains the basic motivational drives for our physiologic needs such as food, water, sex, and warmth. Freud maintained that the id contains the driving life force of an organism. One such dynamic force is the *libido,* which supplies *libidinal energy.* (Libido means lust or desire in Latin.) When this energy builds up, there is an increase in tension and unhappiness, which must be released by the organism. When the tension level is lowered, feelings of contentment and pleasure arise.

The id also operates on the *hedonistic* or *pleasure principle,* which is, in many respects, an extension of homeostasis (the tendency of the body to maintain internal equilibrium). This hedonistic drive pushes the organism to seek that which produces a pleasurable state and to avoid that which causes any discomfiture. The id's forces, operating at the unconscious level, drive the organism toward instant gratification of its primary or biological needs. Freud also wrote of a *tension level.* Without tension, we have no motivation, but as a biological need arises, it increases the tension level, and the higher this level, the greater our motivation to satisfy this emerging need.

Freud believed that an infant operates solely at the id level for the first eight months of life until the ego commences its slow and gradual development. Until this time, the id is in total control of the child's behavior. Thus, when the internal tension level increases because of hunger pangs, soiled or wet diapers, gas bubbles, or other tension-producing stimuli, the infant will cry until the tension level is changed to an acceptable or pleasurable state.

The *ego* is the organism's contact with the external environment. Its purpose is to satisfy the desires or demands of the id and, later, the superego. As the ego develops, it learns to operate on the *reality principle;* that is, it learns to choose attainable goals before discharging tension or energy, which makes for a more efficient ego. However, Freud viewed the ego as a servant of the id, not as a separate or sovereign entity. According to Freud, the ego exists to further the aims of the id. Over a long time, socially acceptable behavior may prove to be more beneficial to the organism than behavior that produces instant gratification. However, until the former type of behavior is learned, infants, toddlers, or preschoolers operate at a primitive level, wanting everything for themselves immediately and exhibiting little tolerance for more acceptable behavior. Ego maturity is, in part, the process of restraining the id's demands until they can be met according to the mores, folkways, and values of one's culture.

The third component of the Freudian personality system is the *superego,* which appears when the child is approximately five years old. It operates on what might be called the perfection principle. The superego consists of the internalization of the morals taught by one's religion, society, and family. The superego is similar to the id in that it makes largely unconscious demands on the ego. However, the superego also resembles the ego by virtue of its intent to exercise control over the id's urges. The child who steals without compunction because it is allowable according to his or her principles will suffer no emotional consequences for such an act or, at best, might intellectualize the possibilities of getting caught. The child whose values say that theft is improper behavior and whose superego is sufficiently developed to operate on such a principle will be bothered by the conscience and will most likely experience emotions such as guilt or remorse. The opposite set of emotions originates from the ego ideal, the portion of the superego that makes one feel good for having behaved according to one's internalized principles.

Behavior, then, can be defined as the result of the interaction of these three personality components and their relationship to the outer world, each one seeking to attain a form of psychological satisfaction by directly influencing behavior. Thus, when the id signals the ego that the body is in need of fluids, the ego, evaluating reality, attempts to choose an appropriate form of behavior to satisfy the id. This would be accomplished by conforming to acceptable social behaviors (such as not drinking from a puddle) and by adhering to standards within the superego (not stealing soda water).

Finally, Freud believed that sex and aggression were two basic instinctive drives of the id. These drives cause no conflict in most of the animal kingdom, but in humans, they are often diametrically opposed to cultural values. The satisfaction of these basic drives leads to a struggle between the id, ego, and superego as to what behavior should be adopted. In the course of this struggle, the individual often becomes highly anxious, which produces an increase in the person's tension level. The ego must alleviate this tension; if relief cannot be accomplished by consciously coping (that is, finding a satisfactory solution), unconscious ego forces take over. These protective devices are called *defense mechanisms*—the unconscious means used by the ego to reduce conflict and tension. Many people believe the explanation of ego defense mechanisms to be among Freud's major contributions to psychology. (See FREUD, SIGMUND; PSYCHOANALYTIC THEORY, DEFENSE MECHANISMS AND; PSYCHOSEXUAL DEVELOPMENT.)

Further Reading. Freud, Sigmund. (1905). *Three essays on the theory of sexuality.* London: Hogarth Press; Freud, Sigmund. (1920). *A general introduction to psychoanalysis.* London: Boni and Liveright; Freud, Sigmund. (1923). *The ego and the id.* London: Hogarth Press.

PSYCHOANALYTIC THEORY, DEFENSE MECHANISMS AND.

According to psychoanalytic theorists, defense mechanisms are patterns of behavior that function to relieve anxiety. They attempt to deal with the pain and turmoil of such threatening situations as failure, mistakes, and accidents and in some cases succeed in freeing the individual from some anxiety. By middle childhood, defense mechanisms are used with surprising frequency. With age, these mechanisms become more elaborate and intertwined with one's overall personality. However, defense mechanisms are, at best, temporary and do not resolve underlying conflicts. In most cases, defense mechanisms produce automatic and rigid reactions that enable the individual to avoid, rather than deal with, struggles. Such patterns of behavior have a tendency to distort reality.

Although defense mechanisms are a normal behavioral expression and do have some beneficial value, they should not be used in excess. When they are used excessively, such as in the case of the perpetual excuse maker or cover-up artist, troubles begin. The very nature of their title—defense mechanisms—indicates their temporary quality. As we are assaulted with the problems of daily life, defensive behavior yields few, if any, long-lasting solutions. Consequently, for the person who persists in relying too frequently on defense mechanisms, life becomes a battle of offense versus defense, and although we hear that "the best offense is a good defense," defense alone may win a few battles, but never the war.

It has often been said that defense mechanisms deal with the symptoms rather than the causes of problems. Just as taking two aspirins for a headache or a sleeping pill for insomnia does not explain the root of the problem, continual use of a defense mechanism does not address the need or frustration that initially caused the anxiety. Thus, while defense mechanisms are considered useful, their adjustive or maladjustive quality depends on how often the child uses them.

Just as anxiety exists in all shapes and sizes, so too do defense mechanisms. It should be realized, however, that these behaviors are highly individualized and will differ from person to person and from situation to situation. In this sense, it is possible that no two people will use the same coping device in the same manner. The following are some of the more common defense mechanisms.

Repression is the pushing of anxiety-producing thoughts and experiences to the unconscious level. Mild repression, such as conveniently forgetting a dental appointment, may help lower the anxiety level for a while. More serious repression is called amnesia, forgetting who one is and all the life experiences that theoretically are causing much anxiety.

Displacement is the rechanneling of hostile feelings to objects less dangerous than those arousing the conflict. Displacement can be seen in the case of a teenager who, after insulting a friend, is hit by that friend. Obviously, she cannot hit the friend back unless she wants to deepen her predicament. Instead, she may seek other channels through which she can release her inner hostility, such as kicking a wall or throwing an object. Displacement may also explain why so many bedroom doors are slammed shut following family disagreements.

Projection is the blaming of one's failures on someone else in order to protect against unfavorable self-evaluations; motives that are personally unacceptable are attributed to others. For example, a person caught stealing may accuse others in the store of stealing or even blame the security guards for not taking adequate safeguards against stealing.

Rationalization is the attempt to justify and provide logical excuses for one's failures or shortcomings. A person unable to capture a role in a local theater company may rationalize that it is just as well because the rehearsals are long and boring anyway.

Denial of reality is the refusal to acknowledge the existence of hurtful situations. For this reason, people may deny that a beloved relative has died. Some may deny to others that they are performing poorly at work, despite knowing that their job is "on the line."

Compensation is finding a rewarding activity to substitute for a failure in another activity. For example, the unathletic middle-aged man may find satisfaction in pursuing a particular hobby, or an obese woman may try to excel in organizing her closet.

Regression is a retreat to an earlier developmental period so as to escape the anxiety of a situation. That is, an earlier developmental level may be perceived as having less stress and turmoil and greater security. For example, an adult facing frustration may resort to having a temper tantrum or engaging in other childish behaviors.

Reaction formation is the substitution of an opposing attitude for an unwanted and perhaps objectionable desire. People who are anxious and concerned about their passivity and dependence, for example, may use reaction formation in behaving aggressively and assertively when in the company of peers.

Further Reading. Freud, Anna. (1946). *The ego and the mechanisms of defense.* New York: International Universities Press; Freud, Sigmund. (1921). *Group psychology and the analysis of the ego.* London: Hogarth Press; Freud, Sigmund. (1923). *The ego and the id.* London: Hogarth Press.

PSYCHOSEXUAL DEVELOPMENT. Psychosexual development suggests that early sexual experiences are important to personality development throughout the course of the lifespan. According to psychoanalyst Sigmund Freud, psychosexual development unfolds in an age-stage framework. Freud maintained that the individual must successfully pass through five sequential stages in order to reach psychosexual maturity. These stages encompass the years from infancy through adolescence. The following is an overview of the stages of psychosexual development.

Oral stage. During the oral stage (ages 0 to 1½), the mouth is the primary source of pleasure. Enjoyment is derived from being fed or from sucking on a pacifier or one's thumb. Freud maintained that either the overgratification or undergratification of this need—and of others to follow—may lead to what he labeled a *fixation.* A fixation is a preoccupation with one particular aspect of psychosexual development (e.g., thumb sucking) that may interfere with or manifest itself in subsequent psychosexual stages. Thus the child fixated at the oral stage, perhaps deprived of thumb sucking, may seek to fulfill this need later in life. Such behaviors as smoking, gum chewing, or nail biting may be the individual's way of gratifying the previously deprived oral need.

Anal stage. During the anal stage (ages 1½ to 3), the anus and the buttocks become the source of sensual pleasure. Satisfaction is derived from expelling or withholding feces, but external conflicts are encountered when toilet training begins. Freud maintained that the manner in which parents conduct toilet training, particularly the use of rewards and punishments, may have consequences for the development of later personality traits.

Phallic stage. The phallic stage (ages 3 to 5) is characterized by interest in the genital organs. Pleasure is derived from manipulating one's genitals, and curiosity is directed toward the anatomical differences between the sexes. Children also have a tendency to develop romantic feelings toward parents of the opposite sex. The attraction of boys to their mothers is called the *Oedipus complex,* and the romantic feelings of girls toward their fathers are labeled the *Electra complex.*

Latency period. The latency period (ages 5 to 11) represents a rather tranquil period compared to the psychosexual turbulence of previous stages. However, there is an increased awareness of personal identity, surroundings, and the importance of social interaction. The latency period is also a time of ego refinement, for the child seeks to develop those character traits deemed socially acceptable. Defense mechanisms begin to develop as children attempt to avoid failure or rejection in the face of life's growing expectations and demands (see PSYCHOANALYTIC THEORY, DEFENSE MECHANISMS AND).

Genital stage. Freud's final psychosexual period is called the genital stage (the adolescent years). This stage chronicles the simultaneous reemergence of the first three stages as puberty introduces a time of biological upheaval. During this time, adolescents become interested in members of the opposite sex. Individuals may encounter their first experience with romantic love, although immature emotional interactions permeate the early phases of this stage. In time, however, people realize that they are capable of giving and receiving mature love.

Further Reading. Freud, Sigmund. (1923). *The ego and the id.* London: Hogarth Press; Freud, Sigmund. (1938). *An outline of psychoanalysis.* London: Hogarth Press.

PSYCHOSOCIAL DEVELOPMENT. Psychosocial development is the manner in which a child is socialized into a particular culture. Our understanding of psychosocial development has been greatly enhanced by the work of psychoanalyst Erik Erikson. Erikson contended that in order to attain psychosocial maturity, a person must pass through eight innately determined, sequential stages of development. These stages encompass the years from infancy through old age. For Erikson, the course of development is reversible, meaning that the events of later childhood can undo—for better or worse—personality foundations built earlier in life. Stages are related to ages in the sense that age leads to movement to a new stage, regardless of experience and regardless of reorganizations at previous stages.

Essential to Erikson's theory is the development of the person's ability to deal with a series of crises or potential crises throughout the individual's lifespan. Each stage of life has a crisis that is related in some way to an element in society. The development of personality begins with ego strengths that commence at birth; as the years pass, ego strength is accrued, one quality at a time. Each quality undergoes rapid growth at a critical period of development. The following is an overview of psychosocial development as theorized by Erikson.

Basic trust versus basic mistrust. The first of Erikson's eight psychosocial crises is called basic trust versus basic mistrust (ages 0 to 1). During this stage, the nature of parental interactions with the infant is critical. If infants are recipients of proper care, love, and affection, they develop a sense of trust. If these basic needs are not met, they become suspicious, fearful, and mistrusting of their surroundings. (See INFANCY AND TODDLERHOOD, DEVELOPMENT OF TRUST DURING.)

Autonomy versus doubt. During autonomy versus doubt (ages 1 to 3), developing motor and mental abilities gives the child the opportunity to experience independence. If this growing urge to explore the world is encouraged, children grow more confident in themselves and more autonomous in general. However, if their developing independence is met with parental disapproval or discouragement, children may question their own abilities and harbor doubts about their own adequacy.

Initiative versus guilt. During the third stage, children experience the psychosocial crisis known as initiative versus guilt (ages 3 to 5). Increasingly refined developmental capacities prompt the child to self-initiate environmental exploration and discovery. Parental reinforcement will encourage such initiative and promote purpose- and goal-directiveness. Parental restrictiveness, on the other hand, is likely to promote guilt whenever children seek to discover the world on their own.

Industry versus inferiority. Industry versus inferiority (ages 5 to 11) is characterized by the child's desire to manipulate objects and learn how things work. Such an industrious attitude typically leads to a sense of order, a system of rules, and an important understanding about the nature of one's surroundings. Inferiority may result, however, if adults perceive such behavior as silly, mischievous, or troublesome.

Identity versus role confusion. The fifth psychosocial crisis, perhaps Erikson's most famous concept, is identity versus role confusion (adolescence). The task is to develop an integrated sense of self, one that is personally acceptable and, it is hoped, distinct from others. Failure to nurture an accurate sense of personal identity may lead to the dilemma of role confusion. This frequently causes feelings of inadequacy, isolation, and indecisiveness.

Intimacy versus isolation. The task of intimacy versus isolation (young adulthood), stage six, is to develop close and meaningful relationships with others. Having attained a sense of personal identity in the previous stage, individuals are now able to share themselves with others on a moral, emotional, and sexual level. For many, intimacy means marriage; for others, it implies the establishment of warm and nurturant friendships (not that the former cannot encompass the latter). Those unable or unwilling to share themselves with others suffer a sense of loneliness or isolation.

Generativity versus self-absorption. Erikson's seventh stage is called generativity versus self-absorption (middle adulthood). The positive pole of this stage, generativity, means that adults are willing to look beyond themselves and to express concern about the future of the world in general. A caring attitude, for example, is directed toward the betterment of society and future generations. The self-absorbed person tends to be preoccupied with personal well-being and material gain.

Integrity versus despair. The final stage is integrity versus despair (late adulthood). Those persons nurturing a sense of integrity have typically resolved previous psychosocial crises and are able to look back at their lives with dignity, satisfaction, and personal fulfillment. The unsuccessful resolution of previous crises is likely to produce a sense of despair. For these individuals, past lives are usually viewed as a series of disappointments, failures, and misfortunes. (See ERIKSON, ERIK H.)

Further Reading. Erikson, Erik H. (1963). *Childhood and society* (2nd Ed.). New York: Norton; Thomas, R. Murray. (1992). *Comparing theories of child development* (3rd Ed.). Belmont, CA: Wadsworth.

Q

QUALITATIVE RESEARCH. Qualitative research is concerned with the nonnumerical examination and analysis of surveys, case studies, or observations. Social scientists employing qualitative research methodology often seek to discover the dynamics of human relationships, such as how people fall in love or why couples argue. The research emphasis is placed on getting to know the subjects by becoming actively involved in their lives and discovering their motivations, values, beliefs, and other important factors. (See CASE STUDY; OBSERVATION; SURVEY.)

Further Reading. Breakwell, Glynis, Sean Hammond, and Chris Fife-Schaw. (1995). *Research methods in psychology.* Thousand Oaks, CA: Sage; Creswell, John W. (1994). *Research design: Qualitative and quantitative approaches.* Thousand Oaks, CA: Sage.

QUANTITATIVE RESEARCH. Quantitative research is a methodology that stresses the compilation of information so that it can be quantified, or converted into numbers. Thus quantitative research seeks to present findings in statistical terms. Those investigators utilizing this methodology use a variety of statistical techniques and designs, often to establish relationships between variables and to examine causal connections. For example, researchers may seek to discover if parent education programming impacts on styles of child discipline, or if excessive alcohol consumption is related to domestic abuse. (See CORRELATIONAL RESEARCH; EXPERIMENTAL METHOD.)

Further Reading. Heiman, Gary W. (1995). *Research methods in psychology.* Boston: Houghton Mifflin; Hinkle, Dennis E., William Wiersma, and Stephen G. Jurs. (1994). *Applied statistics for the behavioral sciences* (3rd Ed.). Boston: Houghton Mifflin.

R

RACIAL GROUP. A racial group is a category of people who are set apart from others because of physical differences. Racial groups are commonly distinguished by physical traits such as skin color, hair texture, or facial features. Examples of racial groups are whites, Africans, Asians, and Native Americans. **Further Reading.** Levin, William C. (1994). *Sociological ideas: Concepts and applications* (4th Ed.). Belmont, CA: Wadsworth; Schaefer, Richard T., and Robert P. Lamm. (1995). *Sociology* (5th Ed.). New York: McGraw-Hill.

RAPE. Rape is an act of a sexual nature that is forced upon an unwilling victim or that an unwilling victim is forced to perform on someone else. Most commonly, rape is forced sexual intercourse, in which a man's penis penetrates a woman's vagina. However, other forms of forced sexual violation may occur: a man may have forcible anal intercourse with a woman; a man may have the same with another man; a woman or man may be forced to perform fellatio. It must also be realized that the primary motivation of rape is rarely sexual. Rather, it is an act of aggression and violence reflecting a desire to control, degrade, and humiliate another person.

Different types of rape can be distinguished. *Acquaintance rape,* or date rape, is forced sexual intercourse or other forms of sexual activity between people who know each other (see RAPE, ACQUAINTANCE). *Statutory rape* involves the sexual assault of a minor, where a man has intercourse with a female under the age of consent. The age of consent varies from state to state, but usually falls between the ages of 12 and 16. *Male rape* is the sexual violation of a man and usually involves anal intercourse and fellatio (see RAPE, MALE). Finally, *marital rape* is forced sexual intercourse or other forms of sexual activity between married partners (see RAPE, MARITAL).

Each year, it is estimated that over 90,000 rapes occur. *Forcible rape* involves the use or threat of force, compared to rape in which the survivor is impaired by the use of alcohol or other drugs, developmentally disabled, or otherwise unable to give consent. However, this figure is misleading because rape is one of the most underreported crimes. Only about 20 percent of all rapes are reported to authorities. This could put the number of rapes each year over 400,000.

The high-risk ages for rape are between 13 and 24. However, females as young as 5 months or as old as 91 years have been reported as rape survivors. African-American women are much more vulnerable to rape than are white women. The risk of rape is so elevated for African-American women that elderly African-American women (aged 65 to 85) are just as likely to be raped as young white women (aged 16 to 19). Also, married women are about one-quarter less likely to have been raped than never-married or divorced women, and widows are nearly ten times less likely to have experienced rape than never-marrieds.

Rape is essentially a young man's crime. Most men arrested for rape are between the ages of 20 and 24. The next-largest group are males between the ages of 15 and 19. Adolescent males between the ages of 12 and 19 represent almost one-quarter of the rapes and attempted rapes against all ages of survivors.

A number of myths about rape abound in society and serve to create confusion and uncertainty about what rape is, who gets raped, who the rapist is, and where such crimes occur. For example, many believe that rape is primarily a sexual crime. Rape is a violent assault that is acted out, in part, sexually. Another myth is that most rapes occur as a ''spur of the moment'' act in a dark alley by a stranger. In reality, rape often occurs in one's home, and, contrary to the thoughts of many, the perpetrator is often not a stranger. Very often the offender is a relative, friend, neighbor, or other acquaintance of the survivor. Also, many mistakenly believe that most rapes are interracial. The overwhelming majority of rapes (more than nine out of ten) involve persons of the same race or culture.

Another myth is that rape is a nonviolent crime. Rape is a violent crime, and most rapists either carry a weapon or threaten the survivor with violence or death. Often the rape is accompanied by a great deal of verbal abuse and other physical abuse. Finally, many believe that women are ''asking for it'' by their dress or actions. Research shows that rapists look for available targets they perceive as vulnerable, not women who dress in a particular way. No person asks to be hurt or degraded, just as no one asks to be robbed because he or she is carrying money in his or her pocket. Rape is the responsibility of the rapist, not the survivor.

According to some researchers, women have been socialized to become vulnerable to rape. They are seen as physically weak and needing men's assistance to carry heavy packages or open doors. Such a weak person could not possibly fend off a 200-pound attacker. Women are also socialized into specific traditional gender roles, such as nurturance. For example, females are the nurturing sex, in that they are seen as taking care of others' needs and being extremely gentle and caring individuals. This may help explain, at least in part, why survivors have difficulties really fighting off the offender by kicking or gouging. In this regard, some writers argue that the woman has been "socialized" into being the victim.

"Being ladylike," a characteristic that females are socialized to, can also contribute to having the crime go unpunished. When the first activity a raped woman does is take a shower so as to appear neat and clean, she has actually destroyed the evidence of her rape (hopefully, with more education, women survivors will refrain from washing away the evidence). Fear, a socialized reaction, also contributes to women being victims. Women and girls are taught to fear sexual crimes, and when they do occur, females often become immobilized with fear and cannot fight off their attacker.

On the other hand, as some writers point out, traditional male socialization has created a climate in which some men confuse sexuality and aggression. In such men, the characteristics traditionally associated with masculinity—dominance, power, aggressiveness, and physical strength—have become associated as well with traditional notions of male dominance in sexual activity and of feminine weakness, passivity, and subservience. Male socialization processes have often pressured men into "proving" their masculinity. For some men, such proof may take the form of raping a woman. Some may also feel that they establish their heterosexuality—another aspect of traditional manliness—by such an act.

Further Reading. Ledray, Linda. (1986). *Recovering from rape.* New York: Henry Holt; Matlin, Margaret W. (1993). *The psychology of women* (2nd Ed.). Fort Worth, TX: Harcourt Brace Jovanovich College Publishers; Turner, Jeffrey S., and Laurna Rubinson. (1993). *Contemporary human sexuality.* Englewood Cliffs, NJ: Prentice Hall.

RAPE, ACQUAINTANCE. Acquaintance rape is rape that occurs between people who know each other, at least casually. Often they have met through a common activity, mutual friend, as neighbors, as students in the same class, at work, or while traveling. Many have met at a party or on a blind date. Some may have a closer relationship—as steady dates or former sexual partners. While acquaintance rape is largely a hidden phenomenon because it is the least reported type of rape (and remember that rape, in general, is the most underreported crime against a person), many experts have shown that acquaintance rape is the most prevalent rape crime today.

Like other kinds of rape, acquaintance rape is an act of aggression and violence. Thus acquaintance rape is often an attempt to assert anger and power. Acquaintance rape occurs more frequently among college students, especially freshmen, than in any other age group. However, it can occur anytime, anywhere, and to anyone.

The relationship between alcohol use and acquaintance rape and sexual assault among college students has been well documented. Researchers have found that many victims said later that they drank too much or took too many drugs to realize what was going on; by the time they realized their predicament, it was too late. Thus use of alcohol as well as other drugs impairs judgment, which in turn contributes to the sexual assault.

Other researchers maintain that "mixed signals" are an important element in acquaintance rape. The female acts in a friendly manner, but the man interprets this as an invitation to have sex. "No" is interpreted as "maybe," and even a strong protest can be ignored under the delusion that women say "no" when they mean "yes." Sometimes a woman is not clear in her own mind about what she wants or may think that she will make up her mind as she goes along. If she changes her mind at some point and decides not to engage in sexual relations, the man may feel rejected and angry. Some men interpret a woman's nonverbal messages, such as her enjoyment of kissing and caressing, as meaning that she automatically wants to have intercourse. At this point a man may decide that he has been teased or misled and "deserves" sexual intimacy, regardless of the woman's wishes.

It should be acknowledged, too, that while acquaintance rape is usually a spontaneous act, many episodes are planned, some days in advance, others in the preceding hour(s). Sometimes men plan to have sex with a woman even if they have to force the issue. These men have usually forced sex before and gotten away with it. They typically look for victims who are unassertive, perhaps someone who is not very popular and would be flattered to go on a date. Such men usually do not see themselves as sexual offenders. On the contrary, many are just out to enjoy themselves and have a good time. Why these men consider rape "a good time" is not understood.

Like other forms of rape, acquaintance rape has devastating effects for survivors (see RAPE, EFFECTS OF). Researchers have found that survivors of acquaintance rape experience shame and guilt and are more likely to direct anger at themselves than they are to express hatred, disgust, or anger against the men who had violated them. Survivors also tend to fear and mistrust men and even people in general. Many indicate that they have learned a lesson the hard way and are smarter and more careful because of the incident. Many also have difficulties in subsequent romantic relationships with other men and tend to fear or be repelled by sex. Many try to block the event out from their minds and to forget what had happened.

The long-term consequences for women who have been sexually abused or assaulted as a result of acquaintance rape must be seriously considered. When negative attitudes about themselves persist, women may drop out of school, ruining a potentially rewarding career. Worse, they may face life in general with reduced self-esteem. It is clear that acquaintance rape has devastating effects on survivors. Experts agree that we must do everything we can to prevent this behavior, to deal with any incident appropriately and efficiently, and to provide support for those women who have been victimized.

Further Reading. Parrot, Andrea. (1988). *Coping with date and acquaintance rape.* New York: Rosen; Ward, Sally, et al. (1991). Acquaintance rape and the college social scene. *Family Relations, 40,* 65–71; Ward, Sally K., Jennifer Dziuba-Leatherman, Jane G. Stapleton, and Carrie L. Yodanis (1994). *Acquaintance and date rape: An annotated bibliography.* Westport, CT: Greenwood Press.

RAPE, EFFECTS OF. No two rapes are identical, nor do any two people respond to rape in exactly the same way. Most survivors report a mixture of fear, terror, panic, and confusion during the actual attack. Some women talk to their attackers during the rape, promising anything, bargaining for freedom, or just trying to make the attacker believe that they should be allowed to live. Some women attempt to focus on a past experience in an effort to mentally block out the trauma. Some women fight. Others attempt to flee. Some focus on their attacker, cataloging every detail that might be helpful to the police.

The more psychological effects of rape have been conceptualized as the *rape trauma syndrome.* This syndrome, which encompasses the many aspects of a survivor's life that are affected by the experience of rape—psychological, social, physical, and specifically sexual—is divided into two phases: the acute and the long-term reorganization phases. In examining each of these phases, parallels can be drawn also to the American Psychiatric Association's category of *post-traumatic stress disorder.* In this type of disorder, a person who has suffered a sudden, emotionally distressing and painful event is affected by a number of factors that are clearly present in the rape trauma syndrome.

The acute phase occurs after the attack and can last from days to weeks. It is characterized by such general response patterns as trembling, shaking, disbelief, and shock. The degree of trauma experienced during this phase is influenced by the circumstances surrounding the assault, especially such factors as the amount of violence, the length of time over which the assault took place, the type of activities, and the number of attackers. During the acute phase, rape survivors often complain of a decrease or loss of appetite, stomach pains, and nausea. Whether they are physically or psychologically harmed, survivors of sexual violence often react initially with feelings of fear followed by anger. Survivors of sexual violence may also feel embarrassment, shame, and guilt. Many survivors initially blame themselves for the rape.

In addition to these behaviors, certain features of the posttraumatic stress disorder can be identified: the experiencing of a stressful event of significant magnitude; intrusive imagery, or the continued reexperiencing of the event; numbness and diminished interest in normal activities; and an assortment of other symptoms, such as a lack of concentration or the inability to make simple decisions. Let us look at these factors in a little more depth.

Stressor of significant magnitude. Survivors have experienced an event that is markedly distressing and disruptive. As a stressor of significant magnitude, rape encompasses a wide range of stressful states, such as aggression, hatred, and degradation. A rape attack often heightens a woman's sense of helplessness, intensifies conflicts about dependence and independence, generates self-criticism and guilt that devalue her as an individual, and interferes with partner relationships. The stress that rape creates seriously erodes the survivor's adaptive resources.

Intrusive imagery. The survivor of trauma often reexperiences the event. That is, images of the event will intrude into the person's mind repeatedly and without warning, sometimes in waking hours, sometimes in dreams. Some women actually feel as if the traumatic event were recurring, and some report intense psychological distress at exposure to events that symbolize or resemble an aspect of the traumatic event.

Numbness. Many survivors of trauma develop a feeling of numbness or a reduced involvement with the environment. Many try to avoid thoughts or feelings associated with the trauma, or to avoid activities or situations that arouse recollections of the trauma. Others may demonstrate an inability to recall an important aspect of the trauma or feel detached or estranged from other people. Some people experience a diminished interest in significant activities, a restricted range of feelings, or a sense of a foreshortened future.

Symptoms. People experiencing posttraumatic stress disorders typically exhibit a range of symptoms not evident before the event. Common among rape survivors are difficulty falling or staying asleep, irritability or outbursts of anger, difficulty concentrating, hypervigilance, and an exaggerated response to any sudden stimulus. Many people react physiologically when exposed to events that resemble in some way the traumatic event. For example, a woman who was raped in an elevator might break out in a sweat when entering any elevator.

Now that some of the dynamics of the acute phase have been explored, let us examine the long-term reorganization phase. This phase is characterized by women restoring order to their lifestyles and reestablishing a sense of control in their world. This phase can last from months to years. Today's researchers are beginning to get a clearer picture of the long-term effects of rape. In general, studies have shown that stress-induced reactions gradually dissipate for many women. However, it is not uncommon for many survivors to remain fearful or display other adjustment difficulties up to one year after the assault. Indeed, some investigators have found that many survivors had not fully recovered for as long as four to six years after the attack. Other studies have compared patterns of adjustment among rape survivors to those of survivors of aggravated assault and other crimes. They discovered more mental health problems among the rape survivors, including greater levels of depression and suicidal tendencies.

Further Reading. American Psychiatric Association. (1994). *Diagnostic and statistical manual of mental disorders* (4th Ed.). Washington, DC: Author; Burgess, Ann W., and Lynda L. Holmstrom. (1985). Rape trauma syndrome and posttraumatic stress response. In Ann W. Burgess (Ed.). *Rape and sexual assault.* New York: Garland; Williams, Mary Beth, and John F. Sommer, Jr. (Eds.). (1994). *Handbook of post-traumatic therapy.* Westport, CT: Greenwood Press.

RAPE, MALE. Male rape is the sexual violation of a man and usually involves anal intercourse and fellatio. Contrary to what many believe, any man can be raped, regardless of his sexual orientation, and male rapists are not necessarily gay, nor are they raping out of lust. It must be remembered that a rapist's motivation is to humiliate and hurt, not to release a sexual drive.

Male rape is not a widespread form of sexual assault. Reported male assault survivors are usually young children or prison inmates. In most cases, the assailant is also a male. Males are unlikely to report having been sexually assaulted. Older adults are another group who are unlikely to report having been sexually assaulted, probably because of extreme embarrassment and shame. People with physical and mental disabilities make up yet another underreported group.

Many male rape victims are attacked by groups of men and tend to sustain more physical trauma than female victims. Those who come to the attention of the authorities may be a highly select group, however, since the physical trauma may be what precipitates their coming to a hospital. In many instances, these men initially come to the emergency room to get treatment for the nongenital trauma and do not report the sexual assault, which is usually discovered later. Male rape is more common in settings where women are absent, such as male prisons. As in female rape, men are often raped in an effort to punish or control.

While it is highly unusual, females can rape males. The notion that it is impossible for a male to respond sexually when he does not choose to is wrong. Male sexual responses can occur in a variety of emotional states, including fear and anger. In reported and corroborated cases, men have been forced by a single female or a group of females to participate in sexual activity, including intercourse under threat of physical violence. The men report being restrained physically, fearing not only for their safety but also for their lives. Despite their fear, anxiety, embarrassment, and terror, they report having had erections even though they felt no sexual desire.

Victims of male rape encounter many of the same problems that female survivors face. Researchers have found a wide range of physical, psychological, social, and sexual consequences. Physical consequences may include injury and disease infection. Psychological distress may be manifested in anxiety, depression, shame, and anger. The man may experience flashbacks to or preoccupation with memories of the assault, impaired ability to concentrate, and difficulty in attending to tasks. He may also feel vulnerable and inadequate, and his self-esteem may plummet. His relations with other people may be marked by distrust, withdrawal, isolation, or aggressiveness.

Some investigators feel that the trauma of sexual assault for a male victim may be even more psychologically devastating in some respects in regard to impact and recovery than it is for a female victim. Since both sexual power and strength and aggressiveness have traditionally characterized the male in our society, being physically overpowered and attacked sexually devalues a man. In addition, having been socialized to ''fight one's own battles,'' many men feel that seeking assistance in the form of rape crisis counseling is yet another disgrace. To ask for help is tantamount to an admission of helplessness or weakness.

Further Reading. Cotton, Donald, and A. Nicholas Groth. (1982). Inmate rape: Prevention and intervention. *Journal of Prison and Jail Health, 2,* 47–57; Ledray, Linda. (1986). *Recovering from rape.* New York: Henry Holt; Weinstein, Estelle, and Efrem Rosen. (1988). Counseling victims of sexual assault. In Estelle Weinstein and Efrem Rosen (Eds.), *Sexuality counseling: Issues and implications.* Monterey, CA: Brooks/Cole.

RAPE, MARITAL. Marital rape is a type of sexual assault in which a woman is forced by her husband to have sexual intercourse or other forms of sexual activity against her will. Many states do not recognize marital rape as a violation of the law, but a growing number of people believe that it should be a crime subject to prosecution. At present, in over half of the states, a husband can force his wife to have intercourse, and such an act is not legally considered a rape. In several states, marital rape is not even a crime when the husband and wife are separated.

There are several reasons why marital rape is not a crime in so many states. For one, implicit in the civil marriage contract is the belief that a married man has the right to have sex with his wife whenever he so desires. Within marriage, women who do not comply can be forced to do so. Participating in sexual intercourse and other sexual acts may be perceived by a man as a duty for the woman in the marriage with no right of refusal. Such acts may therefore not be viewed even by the wife as rape. What activities constitute marital rape, how to assess the degree of force or coercion, and how to categorize long-term live-in relationships are factors that have prevented marital rape from achieving uniform legal status.

Explanations regarding why men rape their wives are speculative. Indeed, there may be as many reasons why husbands rape their wives as there are men who do it. However, researchers offer certain motivations for consideration, many of which are intertwined. For example, it is believed that some men do not see their wives as people with a right to say no to sex. They hold the traditional idea that a wife belongs to her husband, and that sex can occur whenever a husband wants regardless of a woman's desires. Such men do not see women as their equals or as people who have as much choice over their sex life as they do. Whether their partners desire them as much as they desire their partners does not seem to matter.

As far as other motivations are concerned, some men make their wives into symbols of things they hate and want to get back at. Other men are threatened by their wives—their intelligence, perhaps, or their independence—and want to regain some superiority by dominating them. Still others believe that their wives deny them sex all the time and that they therefore have a right to take it by force. Finally, some men think that getting sex all the time is the only proof of their manhood, regardless of how they get it.

Researchers agree that marital rape is a vicious and brutal form of abuse. Victims of marital rape endure intimate violation and experience trauma, much as the survivors of other types of sexual assault, yet their suffering remains the most silenced, because the crime against them in many states is not legally regarded as a crime at all. Many investigators contend that as long as marital rape remains legal, it can only be concluded that society condones it, which must in turn be interpreted as a threat to all women. They propose that while criminalization of marital rape is by no means a complete solution, it must be regarded—if only in a symbolic sense—as an important first step to making this a safer society for women.

Further Reading. Benedict, Helen. (1985). *Recovery.* Garden City, NY: Doubleday; Weinstein, Estelle, and Efrem Rosen. (1988). Counseling victims of sexual assault. In Estelle Weinstein and Efrem Rosen (Eds.), *Sexuality counseling: Issues and implications.* Monterey, CA: Brooks/Cole.

RATIONAL EMOTIVE THERAPY. See ELLIS, ALBERT.

REAL SELF AND IDEAL SELF. See ROGERS, CARL R.

RECONSTITUTED FAMILY. See FAMILY COMPOSITION, TYPES OF.

REISS, IRA. See LOVE, CONCEPTUAL MODELS OF.

RELATIVES. See KINSHIP.

RELIGION, IMPACT OF ON INTIMATE RELATIONSHIPS. All human societies have some form of religion, which is broadly defined as beliefs and practices that concern themselves with the ultimate meaning of life. Religion serves to unite people into a moral community and instructs followers to perform certain actions and refrain from others. For our purposes, it is important to acknowledge that religion embraces morals and values, forces that are instrumental in shaping and guiding intimate relationships. For many, religion provides a foundation for moral commitment as well as a standard of right and wrong behavior. In this sense, religion has the potential of impacting on many relationship dynamics, including sexual decision making.

While all religions have certain beliefs, traditions, and philosophies, religious doctrines and practices vary, particularly as they apply to intimate relationships. Because of such variations, a brief overview of some of the world's major religions is in order: Judaism, Catholicism, Protestantism, Islam, Hinduism, and Buddhism. Given the confines of this volume, all world religions could not be included, and the descriptions that follow are not intended to be exhaustive reviews. For more in-depth coverage of specific religions as well as various religious issues, the reader is encouraged to consult the sources listed at the end of this entry.

Judaism

Judaism is the religion of Jewish people and one of the oldest religions known to humanity. While its followers are smaller in number than those of the other religions discussed in this entry, Judaism is nonetheless considered a major world religion. Today, there are millions of followers of Judaism spread over much of the world, the largest number living in the United States and Canada. In the United States, about 2 percent of the population defines itself as Jewish, which amounts to about 6 million persons. Other large groups of Jews live in Israel, the former Soviet Union, France, and the United Kingdom.

Providing the historical roots of both Catholicism and Protestantism, Judaism emphasizes *monotheism,* the belief in a single all-powerful God. The Hebrew Bible, which contains the sacred books of Judaism, holds that God acts through history to change events on earth. Many believe that Abraham, his son Isaac, and his grandson Jacob (also called Israel) were the first Jewish leaders. Jacob's 12 sons eventually headed 12 tribes that came to characterize the Jewish people. Many Jews traveled to Canaan, an area later called Palestine. Under the leadership of Moses in the 1200s B.C., Judaism began to take definite form (see ANCIENT HEBREWS, LIFESPAN RELATIONSHIPS AMONG THE).

Today, it should be recognized that there are three main branches of Judaism: Orthodox, Reform, and Conservative. Orthodox Judaism subscribes to the most traditional beliefs, while Reform Judaism embodies the most liberal views. The beliefs of Conservative Jews represent a middle ground between the two other branches. Conservative Judaism often modifies Orthodox Judaism less drastically than Reform Judaism.

Jewish views of intimate relationships, including human sexuality, originate from the Jewish Bible as well as from the Talmud, an interpretation of the Bible as it applies to everyday life. Judaism encourages marriage and regards sexuality interactions within the framework of marriage as both normal and healthy. While sex serves a procreative purpose, it is also a source of considerable enjoyment and pleasure. Sexual relations are viewed as expressions of love between husband and wife, and the Talmud urges married couples not to neglect or ignore this important relational dimension. As far as divorce is concerned, marriage is viewed as a serious commitment, and couples are advised to make every effort to preserve the union. However, if serious incompatibilities or irreconcilable differences exist between husband and wife, then divorce is permissible.

Judaism also condemns certain forms of sexual behavior. For example, premarital intercourse is frowned upon and adultery is forbidden. Also, incest is prohibited and same-sex relationships are viewed in a negative light. Regarding these and other sexual prohibitions, the three branches of Judaism are not always in agreement. To illustrate, while Orthodox Jews are strongly opposed to abortion and premarital sexual relations, a more liberal stance is evident among Reform Jews. While Orthodox Judaism often relegates females to inferior status, the teachings of the Reform and Conservative branches tend to convey more gender equality.

Catholicism

The Roman Catholic church represents the largest body of Christians in the world today. In the United States, about 25 percent of the population is Roman Catholic, or about 58 million persons. Roman Catholicism is the predominant religion in southern European nations as well as in Ireland, South America, and Central America. In addition to its popularity in the United States, Roman Catholicism is widespread in Canada, the United Kingdom, Germany, and many African locations.

Like Jews, Roman Catholics believe that there is only one God. They also believe that Jesus Christ was the Messiah who founded the Roman Catholic church. The church serves to bring salvation to its followers and, through God's protection, preserves Christ's teachings. Catholics believe that their church is guided by the Holy Spirit, who was sent by Christ to humanity. Today, the bishop of Rome, also called the pope or ''holy father,'' is regarded by Roman Catholics as their spiritual leader as well as the Church's supreme authority. He governs the church and its worldwide clergy from Vatican City, an independent state within the city of Rome.

As far as intimate relationships are concerned, the Catholic religion views marriage as a sacred union, a gift coming directly from God. Because of this, marriage is seen as a holy sacrament equal to communion or ordination. Catholicism condemns premarital sexual relationships; sexual intimacy can only be shared within the framework of marriage. Even then, the traditional Catholic interpretation of sex is that it serves a procreative function. Thus sexual activity in marriage is acceptable provided it has the potential for reproduction; all other forms of sexual behavior are condemned. While the Catholic church in recent years has acknowledged the significance of marital sexual intimacy, the importance of procreation continues to be taught.

The preservation of marriage and family life is of paramount importance to Roman Catholics. Because of this, the Catholic church takes a strong stand against any forces perceived to threaten the purpose of marriage or disrupt its stability. For example, divorce is considered a sin and is not permitted. Infidelity, like premarital sexual relationships, is condemned. While a gay sexual orientation is not in and of itself sinful, all homosexual acts are. Masturbation is also seen as sinful activity because it serves no procreative purpose. Regarding birth control, the use of all artificial contraceptive methods (e.g., condoms, oral contraceptives) is prohibited. Only abstinence and the rhythm method are approved by the Catholic church. Finally, abortion is considered sinful because it violates the Catholic church's respect for life.

Protestantism

Protestantism refers to all Christian denominations outside the Roman Catholic or Eastern Orthodox churches. There are several hundred such denominations, usually classified into conservative, moderate, and liberal religious perspectives. In the United States, about 56 percent of the population is Protestant.

As a separate branch of Christianity, Protestantism was begun in the sixteenth century when Martin Luther led a split from the Roman Catholic church. Protestantism was an outgrowth of the Reformation, a European political movement that resulted in sweeping political, religious, moral, and social changes (see RENAISSANCE AND REFORMATION, LIFESPAN RELATIONSHIPS DURING THE). As the name implies, Protestantism represented a protest against many of the teachings and practices of Catholicism. More specifically, followers rejected the authority of the pope and saw the Bible as the final rule of faith. A particular emphasis was also placed on individualism; that is, individuals should rely on their own judgment and conscience as far as religious matters are concerned.

Like Catholicism, Protestant religions regard marriage as a sacred union and agree that it is intended to be a lifelong commitment. However, unlike Catholics, Protestants differ in their interpretations of the functions of marriage. For most denominations, a greater emphasis is placed on the relational aspects of marriage rather than its procreative functions. Protestants stress the importance of loving interaction between marital partners, the provision of mutual support and comfort, and a commitment to the healthy growth and development of children. Moreover, most take a positive and accepting view of human sexuality. Most Protestant denominations favor responsible family planning by married couples.

Premarital sex and adultery are regarded as sinful. Many denominations view an extramarital relationship as a violation of trust by a spouse as well as a violation of a religious promise to God. Same-sex sexual practices are typically viewed as against the law of God, but many denominations believe that gays and lesbians have a right to Christian fellowship. As far as the breakdown of marriage is concerned, divorce is usually recognized as a tragedy, but not grounds for condemnation. Most feel that the continuation of a hurtful, destructive relationship is worse than the legal termination of marriage. Provisions for remarriage exist among most denominations.

Regarding all of the foregoing, it is important to remind the reader that Protestant denominations can usually be divided into conservative, moderate, and liberal perspectives. As a result, perceptions of intimate relationships can vary widely within denominations as well as between denominations. To illustrate, conservative Protestants are likely to totally condemn abortion as well as any form of homosexual behavior. Moderate Protestants are more apt to be open-minded about such topics as premarital sexual relationships and divorce. Liberal Protestants, as the name implies, are characterized by an even greater willingness to develop new insights and understandings, including those related to sexual intimacy.

Islam

Islam, the second-largest religion in the world after Christianity, is based on the teachings of the prophet Mohammed. The followers of Islam are called Moslems, who form the majority of populations in 40 nations. The largest numbers of Moslems are found in Asia and Africa, most notably in the Middle East, where Islam was born in the seventh century A.D. (See MIDDLE EAST, LIFESPAN RELATIONSHIPS IN THE.) In the United States, Islam has more than 2 million followers.

Like Jews and Christians, Moslems are monotheists, and all three groups share in common the prophets of the Old Testament. Moslems believe that Mohammed was the last major chosen prophet of God (Allah), through whom Allah revealed his Word. The Koran contains Allah's revelations to Mohammed. Essentially, Islam is based on five principles: faith that there is no God but Allah, and Mohammed is his Prophet; regular prayer; giving alms; fasting during the daylight hours of the Moslem month of Ramadan; and undertaking at least one pilgrimage to Mecca.

Regarding its impact on intimate relationships, Islam strongly endorses marriage. Polygamy is acceptable in Islam, although it is not as popular today as it once was. Under Islamic law, men are allowed to have up to four wives if they can provide adequate justification and treat all wives equitably. Moslems believe that marriage is a contract that gives partners the legitimate status of a family and establishes the legal and moral rights and duties of the couple and their children. Since Islamic society is patriarchal, the husband or the oldest male has full authority over the family. Divorce is seen as very undesirable in Islam, although not impossible. However, because of the subordinate status of women, it is far easier for a male to initiate a divorce than it is for his wife.

According to Islamic teachings, Mohammed also influenced his followers on matters of sexual intimacy. For example, because sexuality is seen as a gift from Allah, celibacy should be discouraged. Adultery has long been regarded as a very serious offense. Indeed, in countries such as Saudi Arabia and Iran, it is sometimes punishable by death. Moslems condemn homosexuality, and heterosexual anal intercourse is prohibited. Also, nakedness is to be avoided whenever possible. Today, contraception is regarded as permissible, provided the chosen method does not adversely affect the couple's health and is suitable to their economic circumstances. Moslem populations tend to disagree about abortion. To illustrate, most nations permit abortion for medical reasons, although some nations (e.g., Tunisia and Turkey) permit abortion on request. There are currently four Islamic nations (Burkina Faso, Côte d'Ivoire, Mauritania, and Niger) in which abortions are illegal and there are no exceptions.

Hinduism

Hinduism is the traditional religion of India and represents the third-largest religion in the world, after Christianity and Islam. It is also recognized as the oldest major religion in the world. While no one knows exactly how old Hinduism is, its followers believe that it has existed since humans were first created. Most Hindus live in India, although there are sizable numbers who live in Bangladesh, Sri Lanka, Indonesia, and Africa.

Hindus believe in a supreme and absolute power or spirit called Brahman. The primary goal of life is to be united with Brahman; when this occurs, humanity will take part in perfection. However, it is believed that a person's soul must be repeatedly reborn until it becomes pure enough to be united with Brahman. This is known in Hinduism as reincarnation. The law of karma determines what happens to a soul in reincarnation. Hindus maintain that whatever one's present condition is in life has been earned by past deeds in a previous life.

Hinduism places a high premium on marriage, and both priests and lay persons marry. Thus celibacy does not play a central role in Hinduism. Marriage is regarded as a permanent union, although provisions for divorce do exist. Family life is important to Hindus, and couples are encouraged to have children. As far as gender roles are concerned, women play an inferior and subservient role to men in Hindu society. Within the home, masculine dominance is readily apparent. The husband is the legal owner of the land, controls the finances, and makes the major family decisions. A Hindu woman's identity is primarily that of wife and mother. (See INDIA, LIFESPAN RELATIONSHIPS IN.)

Hindus regard sexual intimacy to be physical as well as a special form of spiritual energy. However, many different approaches to sexual expression exist in Hinduism. For example, those regarding sex as the pursuit of pleasure and enjoyment have an open and permissive attitude, as shown in the *Kama Sutra*. The *Kama Sutra* is a fourth century A.D. book describing erotic rituals, coital positions, and ways to heighten sexual pleasuring (see ANCIENT INDIA, LIFESPAN RELATIONSHIPS IN). Other Hindu documents, though, are not nearly as permissive as the *Kama Sutra* and obviously represent a different sexual philosophy. For example, some forbid oral sex and stipulate that sexual intercourse must only take place in private quarters. Various Hindu books of law prohibit a wide range of sexual behaviors, including homosexuality, rape, and incest.

Buddhism

Buddhism developed from Hinduism and was founded in India by Gautama Buddha, known as Buddha, in the fifth century B.C. But while Buddhism began in India, it gradually disappeared there by about A.D. 1000. It spread eastward to Tibet, China, Japan, and parts of Southeast Asia. Today, most Buddhists live in Asia.

Like Hinduism, Buddhism believes in reincarnation and karma. However, unlike Hindus, Buddhists place considerable emphasis on the way a person should live in order to escape repeated reincarnations. Suffering is seen as an important part of human existence and a way to achieve Nirvana, a state of enlightenment and complete peace. Buddhists are taught to follow an Eightfold Path of righteous living in order to escape repeated reincarnations and attain eventual Nirvana. The Eightfold Path emphasizes such virtues as demonstrating understanding and purpose in life, exhibiting proper behavior and conduct, engaging in meaningful work, and practicing constructive meditation.

Because self-purification is regarded as a means to liberate oneself from worldly suffering, Buddhists see celibacy as highly desirable. However, in actual practice, celibacy is demanded of priests and encouraged for monks and nuns, not laypersons. Instead, marriage represents a desirable arrangement and a legitimate way to bring children into the world. As in Hinduism, parents arrange most marriages, and a patriarchal power structure characterizes the household. There is little discussion of sex in the teachings of Buddha. However, in the contemporary Mahayana tradition of Buddhism, love of others is stressed, and among the Tantric Buddhists of Tibet, the release of sexual energy is seen as a way of transcending the limitations of human life.

Further Reading. Brusich, Judy. (1990). Religious influence and sexuality. In Catherine I. Fogel and Diane Lauver (Eds.), *Sexual health promotion.* Philadelphia: W. B. Saunders; Parrinder, Geoffrey. (1980). *Sex in the world's religions.* New York: Oxford University Press; Peter W. Williams. (1990). *America's religions: Traditions and cultures.* New York: Macmillan; Weeks, John R. (1988). *The demography of Islamic nations.* Washington, DC: Population Reference Bureau.

REMARRIAGE. Remarriage is marriage by anyone who has previously been married. The United States has the highest remarriage rate in the world. Statistics tell us that over 40 percent of marriages are remarriages for one or both partners. Each year, about 1.5 million people will remarry. This means that in the United States today, divorce tends to be a transitional rather than a terminal event for those committed to marriage. However, it is important to point out that the pathways to remarriage are varied. For example, partners can be single, divorced, or widowed with no children, divorced or widowed with custody of children, divorced or widowed without custody of children, or divorced or widowed with custody of some children but not others.

Those who choose to remarry do so within relatively short periods of time. The average interval between divorce and remarriage is approximately three years. Widowed men and women who do remarry tend to take longer to remarry than do divorced individuals, even when age is considered. A divorced person at any given age has a greater chance of marrying a second time than a never-married person has of marrying a first time.

Additionally, remarriage rates for women of all ages have diminished over the last 20 years. White women are more likely than African-American women to remarry, and for the most part, they remarry more quickly. Younger women are far more likely to remarry quickly following a divorce, especially when their first marriages were relatively brief. Rapid remarriage is also more likely among females who were married when they were young and who had less than a college education. In both first marriages and remarriages, the man is the same age as or older than the woman in approximately four in five marriages. However, the magnitude of the difference is significantly greater in remarriages than in first marriages.

There is also evidence that rates of remarriage among African Americans are only one-quarter those of white non-Hispanics and that remarriage rates have been declining disproportionately among African Americans over the last two decades. Because of lower marriage rates and higher rates of divorce and illegitimacy, the low rate for African-American remarriage reinforces a pattern in which a much smaller proportion of the life course is spent in conventional two-parent families among African Americans than among whites—with many more years spent in female-headed households both in childhood and for women as adults.

A large number of remarriages involve children, creating what is known as a *blended* (or *reconstituted*) family (see FAMILY COMPOSITION, TYPES OF). Today, there are over 11 million remarried families in the United States, including over 3 million stepfamilies. About one out of five of all married families are remarried families, and about 8 percent of all married-couple families are stepfamilies. Approximately 10 million children under age 18 are in remarried families, about 9 million are in stepfamilies, and almost 7 million are stepchildren. The reason for the differences in the numbers is that some children are born to remarried parents, while others are brought into the remarriage. The numbers mean that of all children in the United States under the age of 18, nearly one in six lives in a remarried family, and about one out of ten is a stepchild.

The approximately six million stepchildren at the present time constitute one of every seven children under 18 years of age who are living in a home with two parents. Furthermore, some children who are not now stepchildren will become stepchildren before age 18, and some children who were formerly stepchildren have seen their parent and stepparent divorce. It is thus reasonable to expect that one-third of the children now under 18 have already experienced being a stepchild in a two-parent family or will do so before they reach the age of 18 years.

Divorce rates among the remarried are high. Indeed, researchers point out that the divorce rate for remarriages is about 25 percent higher than it is for first marriages. However, the divorce rate varies by the type of remarriage. For example, when only one of the partners was previously married and the other was single, chances for divorce are no greater than they are for marriages in which both partners are in a first marriage. However, the chances for divorce escalate about 50 percent if both partners were previously married and have no children.

The chances for divorce are also 50 percent if both partners were previously married and one or both of them brought children into the remarriage.

Remarriage poses an assortment of adjustments and adaptations. For instance, remarriage entails the acquisition of a new set of kin relationships, including steprelations. Such new relationships often create role uncertainty as well as confusion regarding familial expectations. Furthermore, many in a remarriage have to contend with a partner's continuing relationship with an ex-spouse. For many, there are unresolved emotional issues from the first marriage that may spill over to the current relationship. Financial issues may also pose problems. For example, financial obligations to ex-spouses and children or how family finances are to be managed may present a unique set of problems and pressures.

Finally, special adjustment challenges often accompany such families. Family study researchers point out that remarriage with children is part of a unique process of family redefinition. Such relationships begin with a loss: a spouse or parent has died or there has been a divorce. A once-existing love relationship has disappeared. Children and parents have been separated either totally or partially, depending on the custody and visitation arrangements. In some situations, brothers and sisters have been separated. There may have been a severing of relationships with grandparents, or alienation from friends and a familiar community. Thus the parent's remarriage sometimes looms as a significant crisis—both a risk and an opportunity.

Many adults enter a remarriage expecting the impossible of themselves and the rest of the family. While most succeed in their new roles, some have difficulties. For instance, stepmothers often report excessive preoccupation with their position in the family, as well as feelings of rejection or ineffectiveness. Many stepfathers report similar difficulties, as well as problems related to household decision making such as the implementation of effective disciplinary strategies. In addition, researchers have found that many grandparents feel somewhat isolated and uncertain of their roles, while ex-spouses may compete for the love and loyalty of their children. The issue of ''turf,'' or who owns which possessions in the redesigned family network, is also difficult for many.

In general, research reveals that stepchildren are usually a well-adjusted lot. Compared to children from natural families, most are just as happy and emotionally stable. They tend to have no more behavior problems than do children from intact homes, and they usually have similar levels of self-esteem. Stepchildren also do as well in such areas as academic achievement and problem-solving resourcefulness. However, certain research indicates that stepchildren exhibit more internalizing behavior (e.g., anxiety, depression) than children from nuclear families.

Further Reading. Bumpass, Larry L., James Sweet, and Teresa Castro Martin. (1990). Changing patterns of remarriage. *Journal of Marriage and the Family, 52,* 747–756; Glick, Paul C. (1990). American families: As they are and were. *Sociology and Social Research, 74,* 139–145; Pasley, Kay, and Marilyn Ihinger-Tallman. (Eds.). (1994). *Stepparenting: Issues in theory, research, and practice.* Westport, CT: Greenwood Press;

Visher, Emily B., and John S. Visher. (1990). Dynamics of successful stepfamilies. *Journal of Divorce and Remarriage, 14,* 3–12.

REMARRIAGE RATE. The remarriage rate is the number of remarriages per 1,000 formerly married (e.g., divorced or widowed) men or women in a given year.

Further Reading. Haupt, Arthur, and Thomas T. Kane. (1985). *The population reference bureau's population handbook.* Washington, DC: Population Reference Bureau; Shryock, Henry S., and Jacob S. Siegel. (1976). *The methods and materials of demography.* Orlando, FL: Academic Press.

RENAISSANCE AND REFORMATION, LIFESPAN RELATIONSHIPS DURING THE. During the periods known as the Renaissance and the Reformation (the fourteenth to the seventeenth centuries), people and institutions underwent significant religious, moral, and social changes. Indeed, the Renaissance and Reformation swept away customs and institutions that had dominated European societies for almost a thousand years. Among the many important developments of this period of time, commerce and wealth vastly increased, intellectual advances were made, and the Protestant faith was established.

Marriage remained strongly encouraged during these historical periods. It was perceived by most as a desirable union. Protestant reformer Martin Luther (1483–1546) remarked that marriage was ''God's gift to man, a heavenly and spiritual state, a school of faith in love in which every menial task, every trouble and hardship, is a means of religious education.'' Luther, however, did not believe in the indissolubility of marriage and the prohibition placed on divorce by the Catholic church. He permitted divorce and conceded authority on such matters to the state.

Although there was an increase in clandestine, or secret, marriages, those of a prearranged nature continued to be much more common. For many, romance played little or no role in the overall path to marriage. Indeed, in some instances the bride and bridegroom had not even met prior to their wedding day. Women remained subordinate to men during the Renaissance and Reformation, particularly within the marriage relationship. They were expected to be virgins when they married, although this expectation was not as great among Protestants as it was among followers of the Catholic church. Once marriage vows were exchanged, the primary responsibilities of women were to bear children, tend to child-care responsibilities, and handle domestic chores.

The livelihood of most families during the Renaissance and the Reformation continued to be agricultural. Many hands were needed to cultivate the soil, and the institution of marriage remained an economic necessity.

The duration of married life revolved around a simple but rugged farming existence. Work began at sunup for both husband and wife and continued through the day into the sundown hours. Husband and wife made a formidable and impressive economic pair: he handled primarily the outside farming chores, while she executed the domestic tasks necessary for day-to-day survival. To say that each relied on the other would be an understatement.

As in other historical eras, children were needed to maintain maximum agricultural yield on the farm or to provide the necessary manpower to continue a family trade or business. With skilled merchants being in constant demand, many children were taught the practical aspects of a given trade. Many parents sent their children away to the home of a middle-class citizen willing to teach a particular trade. In obvious similarity to customs practiced in the Middle Ages, the boy would live in his new home as he became a skilled apprentice. Girls would remain at home and learn domestic chores from their mothers. Because many families tended to live within close proximity, the elderly were the recipients of regular contact and care from younger generations.

During the Reformation, sexual attitudes and behavior were shaped by the weakening of the Catholic church. The Church's efforts to regulate sexual behavior began to be questioned, as did its insistence that sexual pleasure was associated with evil. Gradually, the notion of individual freedom without the severe restraints imposed by the Church was promoted by Protestant leaders.

The issue of celibacy, in particular, was attacked by many, including Protestant reformers Luther and John Calvin (1509–1564). Both Luther and Calvin felt that celibacy was endangering Christianity and that it was contrary to the nature of humanity. In addition, Luther maintained that sex within the institution of marriage was an acceptable and necessary activity, although he saw the act of intercourse as unclean. Calvin, on the other hand, did not view intercourse as unclean but agreed that it must be practiced beneath the holy veil of marriage vows. Both Luther and Calvin felt that moderation was needed to control carnal desires. Neither man tolerated masturbation, fornication (sex between unmarried persons), or adultery.

Prostitution came under attack during the Renaissance and Reformation, and many brothels were closed. Public officials carefully scrutinized and supervised those that remained open. A decline in prostitution at this time was also caused by the arrival of syphilis, a highly infectious and potentially fatal sexually transmitted disease (see SEXUALLY TRANSMITTED DISEASES, CATEGORIES OF). The disease was believed to have been brought back from Haiti to Portugal by Columbus's sailors in 1494. Over the next few years, it spread throughout Europe, and by 1500, the "bad pox," as it was called, had reached such faraway locations as Russia and China.

Once thought to be transmitted exclusively by prostitutes and called a typical soldier's disease, syphilis took a heavy toll on the civilian population. Poor medical knowledge of the disease, questionable treatment approaches (treatment with mercury, a poison, was the standard medical regimen), and unsanitary living conditions no doubt hastened the spread of this disease. In an effort to alert and inform the general public about syphilis, numerous proclamations from government officials were issued. For example, in 1495 the German emperor Maximilian instructed men to avoid prostitutes, whom he held responsible for spreading the disease. Some protection against infection was afforded in 1560 when Fallopius invented the first condom, then a linen sheath to be worn under the prepuce. Interestingly, the condom was first used as a disease-prevention measure rather than a contraceptive device.

Further Reading. Hillerbrand, Hans J. (1973). *The world of the Reformation.* New York: Scribner; Martin, Alfred von. (1963). *Sociology of the Renaissance.* New York: Harper and Row; New, John F. (1969). *The Renaissance and Reformation.* New York: Wiley; Spitz, Lewis W. (1971). *The Renaissance and Reformation movements.* Chicago: Rand McNally.

RETIREMENT. See LATE ADULTHOOD, WORK RELATIONSHIPS DURING.

ROGERS, CARL R. Carl R. Rogers (1902–1987) was an internationally known therapist and an important contributor to humanistic theory, a major school of thought in psychology. Born in Oak Park, Illinois, Rogers is also recognized as the founding figure of *client-centered* or *person-centered therapy.* Rogers received his Ph.D. from Columbia University Teachers College and over the years taught at a number of universities, including Ohio State University, the University of Wisconsin, and the University of Chicago. He received many honors during his professional career, including the Distinguished Scientific Contribution Award, bestowed on him in 1956 by the American Psychological Association.

Rogers believed that people can become fully functioning human beings only when they are given the freedom and emotional support that enable them to grow psychologically. He maintained that each of us has a *real self,* which consists of our self-perceptions, and an *ideal self,* which represents the self we would like to become. When these two selves are congruent, we are probably living without conflict and are likely in the process of developing into fully functioning people. Thus healthy growth and development are seen as embracing congruency and movement toward such important personality dimensions as flexibility, autonomy, and self-acceptance.

However, when these two selves are incongruent, we likely suffer from such conditions as lack of self-esteem, rigidity, and feelings of inferiority, guilt, and other negative emotions, all of which serve to stifle positive self-development. The essence of Rogers's person-centered therapy is to overcome such negative states. This is an ''insight'' therapy (so called because it stresses self-knowledge and growth) that emphasizes providing a supportive climate for clients, who play a major role in determining the pace and direction of therapeutic intervention. (See HUMANISTIC THEORY.)

Further Reading. Feist, Jess. (1994). *Theories of personality* (3rd Ed.). Fort Worth, TX: Harcourt Brace; Rogers, Carl R. (1961). *On becoming a person.* Boston: Houghton

Mifflin; Rogers, Carl R. (1974). In retrospect: Forty-six years. *American Psychologist,*
29, 115–123; Rogers, Carl R. (1980). *A way of being.* Boston: Houghton Mifflin.

ROLES, DEFINITION AND DIMENSIONS OF. The study of roles
and how they affect patterns of interaction is an important research area, particularly when studying relationships across the lifespan. Broadly defined, a *role*
is a pattern of behavior associated with one's *status* or social position. A role
embodies expectations and attitudes that one is expected to demonstrate during
social interactions. While individuals occupy a status, they play a role.

Researchers have identified various aspects and dimensions of roles. For example, it must be understood that roles exist in relation to each other. The role
of a daughter can be understood only in relation to the role of a parent, and the
role of a spouse interfaces with the role of a parent. The theory known as
symbolic interactionism is particularly useful in understanding how roles and
other symbols shape human behavior (see SYMBOLIC INTERACTIONISM).
Symbolic interactionists are particularly interested in how persons nurture both
a concept of self and their identities through roles and the interactions of people.

To illustrate, consider how symbolic interactionists might examine how adult
children care for aging parents. Analyzing roles would be particularly useful,
most notably how adult children adjust to the caregiving role and how aging
parents adapt to being the recipients of assistance. In this way, the dynamics of
intergenerational caregiving might best be understood when they are examined
in the context of the social setting in which they occur. Symbolic interactionists
would also explore the redefinition of generational roles that often takes place
during caregiving situations. That is, elderly parents once gave assistance; now
they are receiving it. This shift requires the redefinition of role expectations as
well as the realignment of family power.

Other dimensions of roles are equally important to acknowledge. For example,
persons often play several roles at the same time, known as a *role set.* To
illustrate, a man may be a father, but he also plays the role of a husband and
company employee. In the foregoing example, he may also be a son as well as
a caregiver to his own parents. Also, it is not uncommon for an individual to
experience difficulty in meeting the responsibilities or obligations of a role,
termed *role strain.* For instance, the woman who successfully plays the roles of
wife and company executive but has trouble providing care to her newborn child
is experiencing a type of role strain, particularly as far as the mothering role is
concerned. *Role conflict* occurs when a person is faced with competing demands
in roles originating from two different social statuses. Role conflict can be seen
when a female business manager hires a close friend: the demands of being a
supervisor might clash with the role of being a good friend.

Finally, *role exit* is the process of disengaging from a role that was central to
one's identity. Many examples of role exit can be cited, such as those originating
from parenting, retirement, or divorce. In the earlier example of intergenerational
care, role exit also embraces how adult children restructure their lives after

disengaging from the caregiving role. Researchers might explore the feelings and emotions grown children experience when the caregiving role ends, including perceived successes, failures, and self-doubts. Attention might also focus on the kinds of new relationships grown children forge after exiting the caregiving role, or whether caregiving experiences influence their own expectations for assistance when it is needed. (See STATUS, DEFINITION AND DIMENSIONS OF.)

Further Reading. Calhoun, Craig, Donald Light, and Suzanne Keller. (1994). *Sociology* (6th Ed.). New York: McGraw-Hill; Landis, Judson R. (1995). *Sociology: Concepts and characteristics* (9th Ed.). Belmont, CA: Wadsworth; Stark, Rodney. (1994). *Sociology* (5th Ed.). Belmont, CA: Wadsworth.

ROUSSEAU, JEAN-JACQUES. DOCTRINE ON CHILDREN AND CHILD-REARING.

Jean-Jacques Rousseau (1712–1778) was born in Geneva, Switzerland, and was an influential writer of the Age of Reason, a cultural movement of the 1700s. His ideas had great impact in many areas, including political philosophy and education.

Rousseau's thoughts on children and their upbringing are particularly noteworthy. Like John Locke, Rousseau discounted the concept of *inherent sin* (a belief that the child is born sinful) and instead viewed childhood as a positive state. He emphasized the importance of adult empathy, understanding, and compassion in meeting children's needs. Rousseau viewed children as unformed adults, born with no knowledge and having very little mental life of their own.

In 1762, Rousseau wrote the classic *Emile,* in which he voiced his observations and concerns about the nature of childhood and the treatment and education accorded to youngsters. In his tale of Emile, a young boy representative of all the children he had tutored, Rousseau described life stages from the first year of life to adulthood. Thus in many respects Rousseau earned the distinction of being one of the first lifespan scholars.

Rousseau perceived the child as having no ideas, will, or habits during the first year of life. While adults generally attempted immediately to mold the unformed child, Rousseau believed that the child's own nature would guide him. During the second stage (ages 1–12), Rousseau believed that nature continued to provide the guidelines, and the role of a tutor was to prevent harmful influences, such as meddling adults, from influencing the child.

By the third state (ages 12–15), Rousseau said, the mind is filled with many years of experience. During the early periods of this stage, Emile operated at a practical level of reasoning, but he progressed to a higher mental level and periodically applied abstract reasoning to quantity, number, and spatial tasks. Rousseau was opposed to pure book learning at this time, but he encouraged Emile to read Defoe's *Robinson Crusoe,* which he used as a lifetime model and inspiration for young Emile.

In the fourth stage (age 15 through adulthood), Rousseau encouraged Emile to widen his social contacts, gave him books to read, and imparted more formal instruction, confronting him with religious, ethical, and political issues. Because his tutor had prevented him from listening to adult opinion on these issues, Emile was now free to develop his own ideas. During the final stage (the early twenties), Emile traveled in order to learn of other cultures, married, and raised his son as he had been raised.

Emile was Rousseau's attempt to show that children are different from adults and should be treated as unique individuals. He emphasized that we must respect their rights, thoughts, and feelings. When children are allowed to follow nature's path of development, maintained Rousseau, they will seek out experiences that are important and beneficial. Strong in his belief that children were corrupted by the nature of the civilization into which they were born, and firmly against the rote style of learning prevalent in his day, Rousseau argued that children can learn more effectively through a process of reasoning, self-realization, and insight. (See CHILD-REARING, HISTORICAL PRACTICES IN; LOCKE, JOHN. DOCTRINE ON CHILDREN AND CHILD-REARING.)

Further Reading. Aries, Philippe. (1962). *Centuries of childhood.* New York: Knopf; deMause, Lloyd. (Ed.). (1975). *The history of childhood.* New York: Harper and Row; Helms, Donald B., and Jeffrey S. Turner. (1986). *Exploring child behavior* (3rd Ed.). Monterey, CA: Brooks/Cole.

S

SAMPLE. A sample is a group of individuals from a defined population that a researcher wishes to investigate. The sample is assumed to be representative of a larger group of individuals from the defined population. Thus a sample represents a subset of the population being studied.

Further Reading. Heiman, Gary W. (1995). *Research methods in psychology.* Boston: Houghton Mifflin; Hinkle, Dennis E., William Wiersma, and Stephen G. Jurs. (1994). *Applied statistics for the behavioral sciences* (3rd Ed.). Boston: Houghton Mifflin.

SANGER, MARGARET. Margaret Sanger (1883–1966) initiated and led the movement to find safe and effective methods of birth control. She became interested in women's health issues through her experiences in nursing. Sanger worked with many poor women in New York for whom pregnancy was a "chronic condition" and who often induced their own abortions, frequently dying in the process.

Frustrated in her efforts to help these women within the medical context, Sanger left nursing and founded the National Birth Control League in 1914. Although the league's magazine *Woman Rebel* did not violate the Comstock Act of 1873, which made it illegal to send contraceptive information through the mail, Sanger barely escaped imprisonment by fleeing to Europe, where she visited the world's first birth-control clinics.

In 1916, Sanger opened a birth-control clinic in Brooklyn where women could obtain diaphragms and birth-control information, including the publication *Birth Control Review.* She was jailed for 30 days and the clinic was closed. But ultimately she won the right to keep the clinic open, and within two years doctors were legally allowed to dispense contraceptive information.

Sanger founded the American Birth Control League in 1921, and she promoted the concepts of women's health and reproductive rights both at home and abroad. Sanger also promoted birth-control research, fighting for a reliable birth-control method that could be controlled by women, but it was not until 1960 that birth-control pills became available in the United States.

Further Reading. Hyde, Janet, S. (1994). *Understanding human sexuality* (5th Ed.). New York: McGraw-Hill; Sanger, Margaret. (1938). *Margaret Sanger.* New York: Norton; Turner, Jeffrey S., and Laurna Rubinson. (1993). *Contemporary human sexuality.* Englewood Cliffs, NJ: Prentice Hall.

SATYRIASIS. See SEXUAL ADDICTION.

SCHOOL RELATIONSHIPS. See ADOLESCENCE, SCHOOL RELATIONSHIPS DURING; ADULTHOOD, SCHOOL RELATIONSHIPS DURING; CHILDHOOD, SCHOOL RELATIONSHIPS DURING.

SELF-ACTUALIZATION. See HUMANISTIC THEORY.

SELF-CONCEPT. A self-concept is a person's unique individuality. A self-concept consists of those characteristics that the individual perceives and toward which attitudes and opinions are formed, consciously or unconsciously. Put another way, a self-concept consists of self-attributes and the knowledge and feelings individuals form about themselves. The development of a self-concept is a social process that converges with other aspects of social awareness, such as role playing and the awareness of status.

Further Reading. Baron, Robert A., and Donn Byrne. (1994). *Social psychology* (7th Ed.). Boston, MA: Allyn and Bacon; Crano, William D., and Lawrence A. Messe. (1982). *Social psychology: Principles and themes of interpersonal behavior.* Homewood, IL: Dorsey Press.

SELF-DISCLOSURE. Self-disclosure is the process of revealing personal and intimate aspects of oneself to others. Self-disclosure is an integral feature of intimate relationships and involves sharing feelings, perceptions, and information. As intimate relationships become more intense, levels of self-disclosure usually escalate. Usually, a norm of reciprocity exists for self-disclosure; that is, when one partner reveals something personal, the other responds with a comparable revelation. (See INTIMATE RELATIONSHIP.)

Further Reading. Brehm, Sharon S. (1992). *Intimate relationships* (2nd Ed.). New York: McGraw-Hill; Duck, Steve. (1988). *Relating to others.* Chicago: Dorsey Press.

SELF-EFFICACY. Self-efficacy is a person's competence in dealing with the environment. One's perception of competence at a task influences the choice of, persistence toward, and affective feelings about the task. In this sense, self-efficacy embodies skills that are required for the successful performance of a task as well as the individual's beliefs about personal effectiveness. The most efficacious individuals are those who can most effectively handle a variety of situations even when these situations are stressful or ambiguous. Conversely, nonefficacious persons are largely ineffective with such tasks and tend to evaluate their behaviors negatively and to see themselves as being inadequate.

Further Reading. Sears, David O., Letitia Anne Peplau, Jonathan L. Freedman, and Shelley E. Taylor. (1988). *Social psychology* (6th Ed.). Englewood Cliffs, NJ: Prentice Hall; Triandis, Harry C. (1994). *Culture and social behavior.* New York: McGraw-Hill.

SELF-ESTEEM. Self-esteem is a personal judgment of worthiness that is expressed in the attitudes that individuals have toward themselves. Put another way, self-esteem consists of self-evaluations that affect the amount and quality of personal regard that persons possess. Perceptions of adequacy and competency are important components of self-esteem.

Researchers have found that levels of self-esteem impact on behavior in many ways. For example, low self-esteem is often associated with social isolation, a preoccupation with one's own problems, and an acute sensitivity to criticism. High self-esteem, on the other hand, is often linked to greater levels of autonomy, popularity, and positive interpersonal relationship skills. Also, the foundation for positive self-esteem appears to be rooted in childhood. Parents who supply unconditional love to their children and who are available for family discussions and activities tend to promote high levels of self-esteem in their children.

Further Reading. Ross, Lee, and Richard E. Nisbett. (1991). *The person and the situation: Perspectives of social psychology.* New York: McGraw-Hill; Sears, David O., Letitia Anne Peplau, Jonathan L. Freedman, and Shelley E. Taylor. (1988). *Social psychology* (6th Ed.). Englewood Cliffs, NJ: Prentice Hall.

SELF-MONITORING BEHAVIOR. Self-monitoring behavior is the degree to which persons regulate their behavior on the basis of feedback from others. Research has shown that individuals widely differ in the extent to which their behavior is shaped by others in their social environments. High self-monitors act in accordance with the reactions of others. They usually are quite conscious of the ways others react to them, and they tend to adjust their behavior accordingly. Conversely, low self-monitors downplay the feedback of others and instead use their own beliefs and attitudes to guide their behavior. Thus low self-monitors do not care much about what others think and usually act in line with their own attitudes or dispositions.

Further Reading. Baron, Robert A., and Donn Byrne. (1994). *Social psychology* (7th Ed.). Boston: Allyn and Bacon; Myers, David. (1993). *Social psychology* (4th Ed.). New York: McGraw-Hill.

SENSITIVE PERIOD. See CRITICAL PERIOD.

SERIAL MONOGAMY. See MARRIAGE, VARIATIONS IN STRUCTURE.

SEX RATIO. The sex ratio is the ratio of males to females in a given population. This ratio is usually expressed as the number of males for every 100 females. The sex ratio at birth in most countries is approximately 105 or 106 males per 100 females. After birth, gender ratios tend to vary because of different patterns of mortality and migration for males and females within a given population.

Further Reading. Haupt, Arthur, and Thomas T. Kane. (1985). *The population reference bureau's population handbook.* Washington, DC: Population Reference Bureau; Shryock, Henry S., and Jacob S. Siegel. (1976). *The methods and materials of demography.* Orlando, FL: Academic Press.

SEX REASSIGNMENT SURGERY. See GENDER IDENTITY DISORDER.

SEXUAL ADDICTION. Sexual addiction is an excessive or insatiable desire for sexual stimulation and gratification. Once referred to as *nymphomania* for females and *satyriasis* for males, sexual addiction tends to escape a precise operational definition. Clinicians are not in agreement regarding its symptoms or the criteria to be used in making a diagnosis. For example, some believe that symptoms of sexual addiction reflect symptoms of other addictive behaviors, such as a compulsive need, lack of control, increasing frequency over time, withdrawal symptoms when partners are not available, and interference with everyday functioning. Others feel that the concept of addiction applied to this form of sexual behavior is too vague and value-laden.

Sexual addiction is not widespread and is more prevalent among men than among women. It is not uncommon for sexual addiction to combine with other unusual forms of sexual expression, such as paraphilias (see SEXUAL BEHAVIORS, ATYPICAL). Sexual addicts often have sex with total strangers, and emotional intimacy is nonexistent. Many engage in such behavior as a means to cope with feelings of fear or sadness; others find it a way to escape life's problems or responsibilities. Reassurance of one's masculinity or femininity, physical attractiveness, or sexual prowess may be other motivating forces. Some sexual addicts are caught up in the sense of power that compulsive sexual behavior brings, while others enjoy the thrill or danger of having sex with strangers.

Having a healthy sexual appetite is not unusual and needs to be differentiated from sexual addiction. For instance, a man or woman who wants more coital frequency within a relationship sharply contrasts with the sexual addict who compulsively moves from partner to partner in an uncontrolled fashion. Sexual addicts often seek to reduce such tension or insecurity under the illusion of sexual power and intimacy, but their encounters are devoid of fulfillment, satisfaction, and pleasure.

Sexual addiction often reflects a compulsive and obsessive sexual state, not excessive sexual desire. Sexual addicts tend to be highly anxious people who seek to relieve their discomfort with sexual activity. In all compulsive states, anxiety tends to increase when the compulsive act is prevented. Indeed, sexual addicts typically experience a wave of anxiety when they are not engaging in physical stimulation or seduction.

Therapeutic intervention for sexual addiction is varied. Some treatment plans utilize variations of the Alcoholics Anonymous recovery program, including Sexaholics Anonymous (SA), Sex and Love Addicts Anonymous (SLAA), and Sex Addicts Anonymous (SAA). Among the tenets of such programs are admitting the existence of the sexual addiction, a recognition that the sexual addict is powerless over the control of the addiction and that one's life has become unmanageable, and developing alternative expressions and resources for dealing with anxiety and frustration.

Further Reading. Kaplan, Helen S. (1979). *Disorders of sexual desire and other new concepts and techniques in sex therapy.* New York: Simon and Schuster; Turner, Jeffrey S., and Laurna Rubinson. (1993). *Contemporary human sexuality.* Englewood Cliffs, NJ: Prentice Hall.

SEXUAL BEHAVIORS, ATYPICAL. Atypical sexual behaviors are those that differ from the sexual behaviors engaged in by most people in a given society. Many atypical sexual behaviors are known as paraphilias. The term *paraphilia* is derived from the Greek word *para,* meaning beyond the usual, and *philia,* meaning love. A paraphilia is a condition in which a person becomes sexually aroused by objects or situations that do not normally lead to arousal in other people. Important diagnostic criteria for the paraphilias include a six-month duration of the disorder, during which time the person has acted on these urges or is markedly distressed by them. In varying degrees, a paraphilia may interfere with the capacity for reciprocal, affectionate sexual activity.

The causes of atypical sexual behaviors remain obscure. However, we do know that they are rare among females. Also, many individuals exhibiting atypical sexuality have other disorders, such as substance-use disorders or personality disorders. It is important to note, too, that a distinction can be made between those individuals who occasionally act on an unusual urge and those who repeatedly do so. The person who occasionally departs from usual sexual behavior is quite different from the person who regularly expresses atypical sexual behavior. Finally, it needs to be acknowledged that unusual behaviors can be distinguished by the harm they inflict on the person or others. For example, some unusual expressions such as fetishes (the use of an inanimate object for sexual excitement) usually have no direct negative effect on others. However, incest and child sexual abuse reflect disregard of the child's developmental, emotional, and safety needs. What follows is a description of the major forms of atypical sexual behavior as distinguished by the American Psychiatric Association.

Exhibitionism. Exhibitionism involves the exposure of one's genitals to a stranger, usually a woman or a child. Exhibitionism is also sometimes referred to as "indecent exposure" or "flashing." Usually, there is no attempt to molest the involuntary viewer; consequently, individuals with this disorder are not considered dangerous. However, lewd gestures are often used in an effort to attract strangers. Some exhibitionists may masturbate while exposing themselves, while others masturbate later while thinking about the act. Embarrassment, fear, and shock on the part of the viewer are desired by the exhibitionist, prompting speculation that the display is an effort to prove one's masculinity or demonstrate power.

Fetishism. Fetishism involves the use of an inanimate object, or fetish, to produce sexual excitement or gratification. Sexual arousal is usually obtained by touching, fondling, or rubbing such objects. Kissing, tasting, or smelling the object are also common. Often, the person masturbates while touching the fetish, or he may ask his partner to wear the object during their sexual encounters. Shoes, lingerie and stockings, and furs or gloves are common objects in fetishism. When a fetish is an article of female clothing that is used in cross-dressing, the condition is called transvestic fetishism.

Frotteurism. Frotteurism (from the French verb meaning "to rub") is recurrent, intense, sexual urges to touch and rub against a nonconsenting individual. Usually it is a man who rubs against a woman. It is the touching rather than the coercive nature of the act that is sexually stimulating. The person with frotteurism usually rubs his genitals against the stranger's thighs and buttocks or attempts to fondle her breast or genitalia with his hand. In the process, he often fantasizes about an exclusive, caring relationship with his victim, but he also realizes that to avoid possible prosecution, he must escape detection after touching the victim. Often, victims do not protest the frottage because they cannot imagine that such a provocative sexual act would be committed in the public arena.

Pedophilia. Pedophilia involves sexual activity with a prepubescent child (generally age 13 years or younger). The sexual assault of a child can occur both within the family and outside of it. In the former case, incest means sexual contact between close blood relatives. Child sexual abuse, on the other hand, means sexual contact between an adult and a child who are in no way related. Both usually refer to interactions between a child and adult when the child is being used for the sexual stimulation of that adult or another person (see CHILDHOOD, SEXUAL ABUSE DURING).

Sexual masochism. Sexual masochism consists of intense sexual urges and fantasies involving the act of being humiliated or made to suffer. Sexual masochism can occur in both heterosexual and homosexual relationships. Also, there are different types or degrees of sexual masochism. For example, some masochistic urges may be invoked during masturbation or sexual intercourse but otherwise not acted upon. In such instances, the masochistic fantasies for women and men might involve being raped while being bound or held by others. Other persons, though, act on their masochistic tendencies by themselves, for example, sticking themselves with pins. Masochistic acts with a partner might include bondage (restraining parts of the body, such as with rope or chains), spanking, whipping, being urinated or defecated upon, or being beaten or cut. Masochistic acts with a partner may also include psychological pain, such as feelings of humiliation, degradation, powerlessness, or fear.

Sexual sadism. Sexual sadism is intense and recurrent sexual urges to inflict pain on a sexual partner. Like sexual masochism, sexual sadism occurs in both heterosexual and homosexual relationships, and degrees of this condition appear to exist. For instance, mildly aggressive behaviors typically serve to increase the emotional excitement of the moment, while at the opposite end of the continuum, pain is inflicted. It is from the act of injuring another person that sexual stimulation and gratification are derived. It is not uncommon for sexual sadism and sexual masochism to be present in the same person, a condition referred to as *sadomasochism.*

Transvestism. Transvestism is characterized by sexual urges and fantasies involving cross-dressing, that is, dressing in the clothing of the other sex. Transvestism is not the same as *transsexualism,* which is a persistent discomfort and a strong sense of inappropriateness about one's sexual identity. Also, contrary to popular thought, most transvestites are heterosexual, not homosexual, and the cross-dressing is really a kind of fetishism. Some clinicians today prefer the term *transvestic fetishism* since it emphasizes the act of cross-dressing for fetishistic purposes, not a preset sexual preference.

Voyeurism. Voyeurism, (from the French verb meaning ''to look''), also called ''peeping,'' is an atypical behavior in which the person becomes sexually aroused by looking at unsuspecting people, usually strangers, who are either naked, in the process of disrobing, or engaging in sexual activity. The sole purpose of looking is to achieve sexual arousal; the person does not usually seek direct sexual activity with the person or people he is watching. The voyeur may masturbate to orgasm while watching others or later on, as he recalls the scene.

Further Reading. American Psychiatric Association. (1994). *Diagnostic and statistical manual of mental disorders* (4th Ed.). Washington, DC: Author; Money, John. (1984). Paraphilias: Phenomenology and classification. *American Journal of Psychotherapy, 38,* 164–178; Moser, Charles. (1988). Sadomasochism. In Dennis M. Dailey (Ed.), *The sexually unusual.* New York; Harrington Park Press; Sargent, Thomas O. (1988). Fetishism. In Dennis M. Dailey (Ed.), *The sexually unusual.* New York: Harrington Park Press.

SEXUAL DYSFUNCTION. A sexual dysfunction is broadly defined as a problem in sexual responding. The problem may occur at any phase of the sexual response cycle, and usually there is a disturbance in both a person's subjective sense of desire or pleasure and one's sexual performance. The actual diagnosis of a sexual dysfunction is made by a clinician, who must take into account such factors as how often the problem occurs, the subjective distress it triggers, and its effect on other areas of functioning. The persistence and recurrence of a sexual problem are important diagnostic considerations.

Sexual dysfunctions may be physical only, or physical and psychological. Sexual problems may have been experienced since the beginning of a person's sexual functioning, or they may appear suddenly after a period of normal sexual activity. They may occur in all situations, with all partners, or they may occur when an individual is with a particular person. Also, some people may exhibit more than one sexual dysfunction.

According to the American Psychiatric Association, the exact prevalence of sexual dysfunctions is not known. However, the majority of them are believed to be common, especially in milder forms. The statistics are gathered from people who seek help, and one should realize that many people do not go for help. Therefore, reported statistics may be underreported instances of those with sexual dysfunctions. It is estimated that 8 percent of young adult males have experienced an erectile disorder. About 20 percent of the total population are believed to have experienced a sexual desire disorder, 30 percent of the female population have an inhibited orgasm disorder, and another 30 percent of the male population have experienced premature ejaculation.

Excessively high subjective standards of sexual performance, anxiety, and unusual sensitivity to real or imagined rejection by a sexual partner may predispose one to the development of acquired sexual dysfunctions. For example, the women's movement may have led some men to feel sexually inadequate as women have become more sexually aggressive. Men may develop "performance anxiety" if they believe that they are unable to please their female partners. However, women need to take responsibility for their own sexual satisfaction and teach men how they are to be pleasured. Any negative attitude toward sexuality due to internal conflicts, adherence to rigid cultural values, or particular experiences may also predispose one to sexual problems.

The years of early adulthood are the most common age for sexual dysfunctions, although premature ejaculation more commonly begins with the first sexual encounters. Typically, men seek help in their late 20s and early 30s, a few years after the formation of a sustained sexual relationship. But the initial onset of a dysfunction, especially male erectile disorder, may be later in adult life. The sex ratio varies for the particular dysfunction. For example, inhibited orgasm and hypoactive sexual desire disorder are more common in females. While dyspareunia can occur in males, it rarely does.

The course of development for sexual dysfunctions is variable. Some sexual dysfunctions may limit themselves to a single, short-lived episode; others represent a recurrent pattern of episodic dysfunction. The major complications consist of disrupted sexual relationships.

Often, no other signs of disturbance accompany sexual dysfunctions. This is especially true in inhibited sexual desire, since it does not necessarily entail impairment in sexual performance. In other instances, there may be a vague feeling or sense of not being able to live up to some vague concept of sexual normality. Or there may be an assortment of complaints, such as guilt, shame, frustration, depression, or somatic symptoms. For many, there is a fear of failure and the development of a type of self-monitoring behavior, with acute sensitivity to the reaction of one's sexual partner (see SELF-MONITORING BEHAVIOR). This kind of self-monitoring behavior (often called "spectatoring") results in a type of cognitive interference that occurs when individuals focus more on critically analyzing their sexual performance than on enjoying the moment. Spectatoring may further erode satisfaction and performance and lead to secondary avoidance of sexual activity and poor communication with one's sexual partner. (See SEXUAL DYSFUNCTIONS, CATEGORIES OF.)

Further Reading. American Psychiatric Association. (1994). *Diagnostic and statistical manual of mental disorders* (4th Ed.). Washington, DC: Author; Kaplan, Helen S. (1979). *Disorders of sexual desire and other new concepts and techniques in sex therapy.* New York: Brunner/Mazel; Leiblum, Sandra R., and Raymond C. Rosen. (Eds.). (1989). *Principles and practice of sex therapy.* New York: Guilford Press.

SEXUAL DYSFUNCTIONS, CATEGORIES OF. A number of different types of sexual dysfunctions exist. For the dual purpose of convenience and organization, they can be placed into broad categories: sexual desire, arousal, orgasm, and pain disorders. The following is a summary of each category.

Sexual desire disorders. Sexual desire disorders are characterized by a lack of sexual drive or motivation. Sexual desire disorders can be broken down into two specific types, a hypoactive sexual desire disorder and a sexual aversion disorder. *Hypoactive sexual desire* is characterized by recurrently deficient or absent sexual fantasies and desire for sexual activity. A person with a *sexual aversion disorder* persistently avoids all or almost all genital sexual contact with a sexual partner. Over the last decade, sexual desire disorders have become one of the most common sexual dysfunctions. They are found in young and old, in intact and broken marriages, among traditional and nontraditional couples, and among the healthy as well as the ill and the disabled.

Both women and men can experience sexual desire disorders, although research focusing on men is relatively recent. A person with such a disorder typically lacks erotic feelings and is unwilling to either initiate or participate in sexual activity. For those suffering from sexual aversion, the thought of sexual activity often becomes disgusting, and many feel anxiety and tension whenever sexual contact is initiated. Some individuals with an aversion to sex may even experience panic disorders. In some cases, sexual trauma, such as rape or incest, triggers the aversion.

It is believed that a number of factors contribute to sexual desire disorders, paramount among them fatigue and the boredom of routine. Other possible causes include fear of pregnancy, depression, hormonal imbalances, and medication side effects. Drugs such as antidepressants, sedatives, and antihistamines have been known to reduce sexual desire. Other causes may be lack of attraction to a partner, relationship conflict, and poor lovemaking skills.

Sexual arousal disorders. Sexual arousal disorders are characterized by a general lack of sexual arousal when there is adequate stimulation during sexual activity. There are two main types: female sexual arousal disorder and male erectile disorder.

In general, women with an arousal disorder do not exhibit the physical signs of sexual responsiveness such as vaginal lubrication and swelling. They also tend not to experience erotic feelings and sensations and may feel little or no arousal from sexual stimulation. However, arousal difficulties may originate because manual stimulation does not create an adequate sexual response. Or there may be insufficient awareness of stimulation to be able to respond sexually.

Many psychological causes for female sexual arousal disorder have been cited. For example, unpleasant childhood experiences, such as sexual abuse or emotional neglect, may trigger this condition. Other factors could include the quality of a woman's relationship with her partner; the presence of stress, fear, or anger; general fatigue; or even a fear of pregnancy. Arousal disorders can have physical causes, too. For example, lack of vaginal lubrication can originate from an estrogen deficiency, such as may occur during menopause. In other instances, arousal disorders can be linked to illness and certain drugs, such as tranquilizers or antihistamines.

Male erectile dysfunction, once referred to as *impotence,* refers to the inability to attain or maintain an erection until completion of sexual activity. Male erectile disorder can be caused by physical and psychological factors, although in a majority of cases, both types of factors are responsible. Male erectile dysfunction is quite common and is generally more easily treated in sex therapy. It has been estimated that almost one-half of the total adult male population may experience occasional episodes of this dysfunction, and this figure sharply escalates for men over age 50. Among the overall male population, an erectile disorder can occur at any time from adolescence to old age and in every culture, race, or socioeconomic status.

Physical factors that may cause an erectile dysfunction include alcohol, smoking, drug abuse, diabetes, barbiturates and amphetamines, cardiac and respiratory disorders, and neurological diseases, as well as surgical complications from cancer of the bladder, prostate, and rectum. Other noteworthy physical causes include pituitary-gland dysfunctions, chronic kidney failure, and spinal-cord injuries. Psychological factors include anxiety over performance and partner satisfaction, depression, tension and pressure, feelings of worthlessness, hostility, fear of rejection, frustration, self-pity, or even guilt over the sexual encounter. Lack of knowledge about how to sexually satisfy oneself and one's partner may also be a contributing factor.

Orgasm disorders. Orgasm disorders represent a category of sexual dysfunctions that can be experienced by both women and men. The orgasm disorders are subdivided into three basic types: female orgasmic disorder, male orgasmic disorder, and premature ejaculation.

Female orgasmic dysfunction refers to a persistent or recurrent delay in, or absence of, orgasm following adequate sexual arousal and stimulation. Today, it is a common sexual complaint of women. The causes of inhibited female orgasm disorders are varied, but mostly psychological in origin. Among the causes are depression, fear of losing control, performance anxiety, fear of being abandoned, or a reluctance to assert independence. Some women with this dysfunction experience guilt about their sexuality or have unresolved, unconscious conflicts and fears, such as those that might result from sexual abuse or rape. Physical causes might include degenerative diseases or tumors that destroy the spinal centers and nerves that mediate the orgasmic reflex, diabetes, and disorders of the endocrine system. Female orgasmic disorders may also be linked to alcohol as well as drugs such as psychotropic medication.

Male orgasmic disorder is defined as a persistent or recurrent delay in, or absence of, orgasm following normal sexual excitement. Men with this dysfunction are capable of becoming sexually aroused and having a full erection, but they do not experience an intravaginal climax. The primary causes of male orgasmic disorder are psychological, including guilt, fear of partner rejection, or even a fear of intimacy. Ambivalence or anger toward a partner may also be predisposing factors, as is compulsion to please a partner sexually. Certain medications can create male orgasmic disorder. For example, phenothiazines and certain antihypertensives may impair the ejaculatory reflex. Other possible factors include the use of alcohol, barbiturates, and methaqualone.

Premature ejaculation refers to persistent or recurrent ejaculation with minimal sexual stimulation or before, upon, or shortly after penetration and before the couple want it to happen. The causes of premature ejaculation are primarily physiological, although sometimes an overly sensitive penile glans may suggest a physical basis for this dysfunction. A much more frequent theme in the literature is that affected males have learned through early training experiences to reach orgasm as quickly as possible. Other possible explanations for premature ejaculation include the male's need for power or control over his partner. Or the presence of anxiety may have heightened sexual arousal processes and created the premature response.

Sexual pain disorders. Sexual pain disorders, characterized by genital pain associated with sexual intercourse, consist of two main types: dyspareunia and vaginismus. Dyspareunia can occur in either a male or female and includes such sensations as tearing, burning, aching, and pressure. Dyspareunia can have both physical and psychological causes. It can be caused by gynecological and urological disorders, including diseases of the urethra and bladder. The formation of fibrous plaques, adhesions, or lesions in the genital tract may also produce pain during intercourse. Psychological causes might be the presence of anxiety or tension, resentment toward one's sexual partner, or previously painful coital experiences such as might occur in the aftermath of rape or incest.

Vaginismus is characterized by recurrent or persistent involuntary constriction of the musculature surrounding the vaginal opening and the outer third of the vagina. In the most severe form of vaginismus, penetration of the vagina by any object, including a penis, may be impossible. In less severe cases, penetration may be possible, but painful. Most cases of vaginismus evolve from psychological causes, although endometriosis, pelvic tumors, and surgical injuries to the genitals are physical conditions that can create pain during intercourse. Psychological causes might include fear or guilt about intercourse, prior sexual trauma, unconscious conflicts, a learned phobia, or a strict religious orthodoxy.

Further Reading. American Psychiatric Association. (1994). *Diagnostic and statistical manual of mental disorders* (4th Ed.). Washington, DC: Author; Leiblum, Sandra R., and Raymond C. Rosen. (Eds.). (1989). *Principles and practice of sex therapy* (2nd Ed.). New York: Guilford Press; McConaghy, Nathaniel. (1993). *Sexual behavior: Problems and management.* New York: Plenum Press; Wincze, John P., and Michael P. Carey. (1991). *Sexual dysfunction: A guide for assessment and treatment.* New York: Guilford Press.

SEXUAL FANTASY. A sexual fantasy is a mental image or series of images centering around erotic thoughts and desires. Fantasies typically occur during daydreams, masturbation, foreplay, or other sexual activity. They often play a significant role in sexual arousal, and almost everybody has them, if only from time to time. Sometimes fantasies are enhanced by watching an erotic movie, reading an erotic book or magazine, or actually viewing an erotic encounter.

A glance at the literature reveals how widespread sexual fantasies are. For example, noted sex researcher Alfred Kinsey found that about 85 percent of the men queried and almost 70 percent of women reported having sexual fantasies at one time or another. Other researchers have uncovered equally high percentages, including among those who fantasize during intercourse. Sometimes when people are making love, one or both parties may fantasize about other people, including a friend, a roommate, a relative, a rock star, or some other celebrity.

Sexual fantasies serve a number of purposes. For example, fantasies provide sexual pleasure and fulfillment. For many, they provide a way to escape from boredom and routine. The use of sexual fantasy can bring variety into the life of the individual or couple or relief from a negative sexual situation. Sexual fantasies can bring the element of control into one's sex life; that is, a person can put fantasies into any imagined scenario. Fantasies also have the potential of heightening sexual arousal during masturbation and coitus. They may also serve as a rehearsal for a new sexual experience such as a novel lovemaking technique. Sexual fantasies may also elevate a person's self-worth, especially when the fantasies make a person more attractive and sexually irresistible.

There is great diversity in the sexual fantasies of men and women. They can take the form of repeated erotic thoughts, fleeting images, or memories of previous sexual encounters. Some people construct elaborate fantasies about making love in romantic settings, while others have fantasies related to masturbation, mate swapping, or same-sex sexual encounters. Some like to fantasize about watching others engaging in sex, while others envision being watched. Women, more so than men, fantasize about being forced to have sex, while more men than women fantasize about forcing someone to have sex. However, it is important to point out that fantasizing about forced sex does not mean that the person really wants to assault someone or be assaulted. Such fantasizing may instead reflect a person's need for control or power.

Most researchers feel that sexual fantasies are normal and not a symptom of relationship problems. Many researchers find a positive link between couples' sexual fantasies and a satisfying sex life. Additionally, many sex therapists recommend sexual fantasy as a technique to enhance sexual arousal. What appears to be important is being able to separate sexual fantasies from real life and removing the guilt that often accompanies them. The healthiest and most rewarding practice may be to cultivate a number of different fantasies, enjoy them all, and not feel guilty about fantasizing. In this fashion, sexual fantasies can become a help to us rather than a threat. They emerge as a mental bridge to add arousal and excitement to our sexual expressions.

Further Reading. McCarthy, Barry. (1988). *Male sexual awareness.* New York: Carroll and Graf; Nass, Gilbert D., and Mary Pat Fisher. (1988). *Sexuality today.* Boston: Jones and Bartlett; Stanway, Andrew. (1989). *The art of sensual loving.* New York: Carroll and Graf.

SEXUAL HARASSMENT. See WOMEN, SEXUAL HARASSMENT AND.

SEXUAL HEALTH AND WELL-BEING. See SEXUALLY TRANSMITTED DISEASES, SAFER SEX AND THE PREVENTION OF.

SEXUALITY EDUCATION. Sexuality education is intervention on the part of parents and teachers to provide children and adolescents with age-appropriate sex-related information. The combined forces of the home and the school setting will greatly influence a young person's sexual attitudes and behaviors. However, whether or not such attitudes and behaviors are healthy is greatly influenced by how such information is taught as well as how parental teachings and classroom strategies converge and complement one another.

Sexuality education is an important parental right and responsibility, and how such information is presented is vitally important. The home environment, including child-rearing practices and the quality of the parent-child relationships, exerts a significant influence in shaping a child's sexuality and future behavior. However, whether or not all parents are knowledgeable about the topic of sex and comfortable enough to discuss it properly is debatable.

Experts maintain that in homes where sexuality is discussed, the discussions tend to be infrequent and to restrict themselves to the biological aspects of reproduction. Several factors account for this limited communication. Because many parents lacked appropriate role models, they cannot draw on past experiences when attempting to approach their own children. Many parents also see themselves as being unable to provide adequate education because they feel that they are not knowledgeable enough or because they do not know how to explain what they do know. Uncomfortable with the topic, they tend to postpone discussions of sex or avoid them entirely. Some are torn between new and old values and are confused about what they believe and what they want to convey to their children. Others believe that if their children are interested, they will ask; and they are fearful that providing information prematurely will lead to sexual experimentation.

Experts also point out that too many modern parents have not conquered their inhibitions about sex and thus, in their desire to protect their children and safeguard their innocence, surround the subject of sex with silence. These adult anxieties do not protect children but rather expose them to danger and teach them about guilt. Misled by confused ideas about sex, parents assume that children cannot cope with sexual knowledge and that it will shock and disturb them. They therefore develop elaborate strategies of concealment. As children grow older, parents feel that they ought to let them in on the secret. Unfortunately, though, most parents do not know where to start. Hiding sex makes children's learning far harder and aggravates the pain and trials of adolescence. In addition, inequality is promoted when we bring up boys and girls to share different aims and different desires.

Despite these difficulties, most sources indicate that both parents and children think that parents should be responsible for their children's sexuality education. Moreover, research indicates that children want both mothers and fathers to share this responsibility. Additionally, both children and parents desire more open communication on the topic. Finally, most parents express a desire to acquire more sex-related information so that they can be more prepared to meet the needs of their children.

Many structured programs on sexuality education for parents have emerged in recent years. Such programs range from a few hours' duration to courses stretching over months. Programs are offered to parents of various ethnic groups and to parents with children ranging in age from infancy to 18 years of age. They are sponsored by federal agencies, private foundations, health clinics, social service organizations, and churches. Such programs usually help parents to become more comfortable with their own sexuality, teach communication skills, provide accurate sexual knowledge, explore attitudes and values, and address sexuality issues in the home.

Within the school, sexuality education represents specific intervention that provides information and self-assessment opportunities in an age-appropriate manner. Coupled with sexuality education taking place in the home, school programs seek to provide a unique opportunity for children and adolescents to have serious peer exchange of ideas, thoughts, and feelings under the guidance of a trained facilitator. Sexuality education in the school is also designed to help children be prepared for life changes—puberty, adolescence, and the stages of adulthood. It helps them know that the changes are normal. The education also helps young people learn to make decisions that take into account possible consequences and helps them understand, for themselves, the place of sexuality in human life and loving.

Unfortunately, comprehensive sexuality education in the school is not a widespread phenomenon. U.S. society tends to devote much time and energy to coping with unwanted pregnancy, sexually transmitted diseases, and related problems once they have occurred, but very little to helping people prevent them in the first place. Some experts believe that only a minority of young people in the United States receive adequate sex education in public schools. Most are exposed to scattered presentations on basic reproductive facts—the "plumbing," so to speak, of human sexuality. Since only a small number of parents educate their children about sex, the result is many sexually vulnerable citizens.

It is hard to understand why Americans fallen so short in this area since for years surveys have indicated that most Americans favor sex education in the public schools. Perhaps it is because there is so much disagreement about the content of sexuality education, how and by whom it should be taught, and whose values should be conveyed. Another reason is that the opponents of sexuality education tend to be well organized and determined. Some believe that knowledge is inevitably harmful ("If you tell kids about sex, they'll do it!"). Proponents of sex education acknowledge that kids are doing it, but without the benefit of knowledge.

Those in favor of sexuality education think differently, particularly about the notion that it leads to sexual experimentation. Proponents feel that adolescents participating in sexuality education programs at home and school are more likely to postpone sexual experimentation longer than their peers. Furthermore, when they do become sexually active, they are more likely to use contraceptives to prevent pregnancy. In short, if adolescents are provided with some information about their sexuality, they are apt to make decisions that are right for them based on fact, not peer pressure.

In spite of such controversy, concerned educators are continuing to develop and refine sexuality programs for both children and adolescents. The threat of AIDS and issues such as abortion, sexual abuse, and teenage pregnancy often motivate school boards to implement such programs. As a result, many new classroom approaches to meeting the needs of today's children are available.

Experts agree that one of the most important determinants of the success or failure of a sexuality education program is the teacher. In spite of a well-designed curriculum, a poor teacher can ruin the program. In fact, parents worry most that the teacher will convey personal values or inappropriate information to their children. However, once parents meet a well-trained and qualified teacher, they are usually reassured. It is essential that classroom teachers obtain training in all aspects of sexuality education. They need information, comfort with the topic, and comfort with their own values; they also need effective communication and group facilitation skills.

When properly implemented and taught, sexuality education becomes an integral part of the school curriculum. It thus becomes a gift for people of all ages, but especially for children and adolescents experiencing significant physical, emotional, social, and sexual changes. Sexuality education offers the opportunity to provide vital information, life skills, perspectives, and insights that can make important differences in how children and adolescents feel about themselves, relate to others, and approach day-to-day experiences and decisions. Sexuality education helps children develop into healthy, responsible, and informed adults. Such courses assist them in communicating comfortably about sex and help to answer the questions and concerns that arise at each stage of development.

Further Reading Alter, Judith. (1989). Sexual education for parents. In Carol Cassell and Pamela M. Wilson (Eds.), *Sexuality education: A resource book.* New York: Garland; Archer, Elayne, and Michele Cahill. (1991). *Building life options: School-community collaborations for pregnancy prevention in the middle grades.* Baltimore, MD: Academy for Educational Development; Sears, James T. (Ed.). (1992). *Sexuality and the curriculum: The politics and practices of sexuality education.* New York: Teachers College Press.

SEXUALLY TRANSMITTED DISEASES. Sexually transmitted diseases, sometimes called *venereal diseases,* are contagious infections that, for the most part, are passed on by intimate sexual contacts with others. The sexual contact can be through French (open-mouthed) kissing, coitus, oral-genital sex, or anal intercourse. Sometimes, infections can be transmitted without sexual contact, such as by sharing needles. Sexually transmitted diseases can be grouped according to bacterial, viral, and parasitic causes. (See SEXUALLY TRANSMITTED DISEASES, CATEGORIES OF.)

Sexually transmitted diseases are quite widespread in modern society and bear many consequences. Researchers estimate that between five million and eight million people in the United States are newly infected with a sexually transmitted disease each year. Furthermore, about one in four Americans between the ages of 15 and 55 will eventually acquire a sexually transmitted disease. It is estimated that approximately 200 million new cases of gonorrhea and 40 million new cases of syphilis occur annually in the world. Cases of genital herpes in the United States have increased tenfold in the last 20 years.

In relation to these statistics, it should be pointed out that the law requires the reporting of a number of sexually transmitted diseases, including AIDS, gonorrhea, syphilis, and hepatitis B. Many others, such as chlamydia and herpes, do not require reporting. Because of this, one can only make an educated guess at the number of cases of the nonreportable diseases. Complicating matters is that many physicians and clinics fail to make reports on a regular basis, perhaps because they are trying to protect a long-time patient or family friend from the embarrassment. Unfortunately, this prevents adequate follow-up of sexual partners and makes it difficult to break the chain of infection.

Certain population groups are at risk for contracting sexually transmitted diseases. These groups include individuals under the age of 25, minorities, the medically underserved, and gay men. For example, two-thirds of reported cases of gonorrhea occur in those 25 years of age or younger. Rates of syphilis, gonorrhea, and hospitalized pelvic inflammatory disease are highest in adolescents and decline with increasing age. (See ADOLESCENCE, SEXUALLY TRANSMITTED DISEASES DURING.)

African Americans are also two to three times more likely than whites to contract a sexually transmitted disease. An overlapping group, low-income persons in urban areas are also more vulnerable to STDs than individuals of higher socioeconomic status or those who live in suburban or rural areas. A number of reasons can be cited to explain why these population groups are more vulnerable: inadequate medical services, higher rates of other diseases, unsanitary conditions, overcrowding, and lack of knowledge regarding STDs as a whole. Other groups—such as migrants and immigrants—may also be medically underserved or difficult to reach through traditional health channels. Such groups may have language and cultural barriers to treatment and may carry resistant strains of sexually transmitted diseases. (See AIDS, AFRICAN AMERICANS AND.)

Sexually transmitted diseases embody a kind of biological sexism. The signs and symptoms of most STDs are more easily noticed in males, and women with STDs frequently have no complaints or clinical signs in the early phases of the disease (particularly gonorrhea and syphilis). Women also suffer more serious long-term consequences from all STDs. Women are also more likely than men to contract a sexually transmitted disease from any single sexual encounter. As an illustration, the risk of acquiring gonorrhea from a single coital encounter (where one partner is infectious) is about 25 percent for men and 50 percent for women. Finally, the death rate for women with AIDS has quadrupled over the last ten years. Worldwide, more than one-third of HIV-infected adults are women, and it is projected that the annual number of AIDS cases in women will begin to equal that of men by the year 2000.

Further Reading. Crooks, Robert, and Karla Baur. (1993). *Our sexuality* (5th Ed.). Redwood City, CA: Benjamin/Cummings; Hatcher, Robert A., James Trussel, Felicia Stewart, and Gary K. Stewart. (1994). *Contraceptive technology* (16th Ed.). New York: Irvington Publishers; King, Bruce M., Cameron J. Camp, and Ann M. Downey. (1991). *Human sexuality today.* Englewood Cliffs, NJ: Prentice Hall.

SEXUALLY TRANSMITTED DISEASES, CATEGORIES OF.

There are many different types of sexually transmitted diseases and several ways to categorize them. One approach is to classify them according to their symptoms, such as skin lesions. Another way is to classify them according to their prevalence. The approach of this volume, though, is to categorize them according to their etiology, or causes. Even though some STDs are not caused by any one agent in particular, we can nonetheless distinguish between three categories: viral, bacterial, and parasitic diseases. The following discussion highlights these three categories and some of the more common sexually transmitted diseases that fall into each.

Viral Diseases

Viruses have no metabolism of their own; consequently, they borrow what they need for growth and reproduction from the cells they invade. Viruses direct cells to produce more virus instead of more cells. Viral sexually transmitted diseases include genital herpes, genital warts, and viral hepatitis. The acquired immunodeficiency syndrome, or AIDS, is also a viral disease and is fully described elsewhere (see AIDS; AIDS, AFRICAN AMERICANS AND; AIDS, CHILDREN AND; AIDS, DIAGNOSTIC TESTS FOR; AIDS, PREVENTION OF; AIDS, WORLDWIDE RATES OF INFECTION).

Genital herpes. Genital herpes is caused by the herpes simplex virus, which exists in two forms: herpes simplex I (HSV-I), which causes cold sores and fever blisters above the waist, and herpes simplex II (HSV-II), which causes lesions and infections below the waist on the genitals, anus, buttocks, or thighs. However, the two forms often mix, and either virus type can infect skin or mucous membranes anywhere on the body. Thus genital herpes represents an infection of the genital area by either herpes simplex I or herpes simplex II.

Genital herpes is spread primarily through intimate sexual contact. Those who began having sex at early ages and have multiple partners are at risk for developing the disease. Genital herpes can lead to such complications as meningitis, a narrowing of the urethra, and even blindness. Moreover, a pregnant woman infected with genital herpes can transmit the disease to her child if she delivers vaginally during an active disease stage. Consequences to the child include skin infection, nervous system damage, and even death. Finally, there may be a link between genital herpes and cervical cancer in women.

The herpes virus does not travel from one location to another; instead, it tends to recur at the site of the original lesion. The herpes virus lodges in the center of a specific sensory nerve cell. These viruses become inactive, or latent, when they reach the nerve cell center. However, herpes will "flare up" in a recurrence, and the virus becomes reactivated. It is thought that the virus follows the same nerve and multiplies on the skin at or near the site of the original sore. Sexual contact is not necessary for a recurrence.

Tingling or burning in the infected area typically accompanies the primary outbreak of genital herpes. Usually, a rash of red patches with white blisterlike sores appears, often in clusters. The infection usually appears on or around the penis in men and the vagina in women. Internal sores can also occur in the mouth, vagina, cervix, or anus—actually, anywhere the virus first enters the body. Beyond the rash, one or all of the following may be present: pain and discomfort in the area of the infection, fever, headache, and general feeling of ill health. Also common is pain or burning when urinating. Glands in the groin area may become swollen. Women may notice a vaginal discharge.

Herpes sores are present for quite variable amounts of time, some healing in a matter of days, while others may take a month or more. Once the sores are healed, the infection seems to have left the body, but this is not the case. Even though the sores disappear, the virus remains in the nerve tissue in the body and possibly in the skin. The redevelopment of initial herpes symptoms is related to the virus's recurring cycles of infectious activity and inactivity. Each time the infection recurs, the person is contagious again (the risk of infection during asymptomatic periods is much lower). Many stimuli can trigger an eruption, including emotional stress, sun overexposure, colds, fever, menstruation, or physical activity. Generally, the symptoms of the first outbreak are more serious than those of recurrent infections.

There is no cure for genital herpes. However, acute outbreaks can now be treated either with the antiviral drug acyclovir (Zovirax) or with laser therapy, both of which heal blisters, reduce pain, and most important, kill large numbers of the herpes virus. For many, acyclovir can reduce the reproduction of the virus in initial outbreaks, thus possibly lessening the number of subsequent outbreaks. For laser therapy to be effective, however, it must be started immediately after the first sores appear. Other recommended treatments include the use of aspirin or other pain relievers, as well as the application of ice packs to the affected area.

Genital warts. Genital warts originate from the human papilloma virus (HPV) and are transmitted almost exclusively by sexual contact. There are many different strains of genital warts, and they are usually found on the penis or vulva or in the vagina or rectum. In rare instances, they appear on the mouth, lips, nipple, and umbilicus. Genital warts are a widespread viral condition and tend to afflict those men and women who begin sexual activities early in life and who have multiple sexual partners.

Genital warts may occur as single or multiple growths. When they develop in clusters, lesions take on a cauliflower appearance. Some are flat or appear deep within the vagina or on the cervix. In recent years, genital warts have been linked to growing numbers of cervical cancer cases. Moreover, research tells us that the human papilloma virus (HPV) looms as one of the major causes of cancers in the lower abdominal organs. Because of this, any woman with a history of genital warts should have an annual Pap smear.

There are several different modes of treatment for genital warts. A popular approach is the local application of podophyllin, a cytotoxic agent that removes genital warts in two to four days. Other approaches include cryotherapy (freezing the warts with liquid nitrogen) and electrocautery (the use of an electric current to burn away the warts). Still other techniques involve burning the warts away by means of laser therapy or by the local application of such substances as idoxuridine, 5-Fluorouracil, and trichloracetic acid.

Viral hepatitis. Viral hepatitis is an infectious disease that attacks a person's liver and causes inflammation. The disease is caused by several viruses, the most common strains being hepatitis A, hepatitis B, and non-A, non-B hepatitis. Hepatitis A is caused by a virus that is typically excreted in the feces and can be passed by direct contact with fecal matter or through oral-anal contact or anal intercourse. Hepatitis B is found in the body fluids of the infected person and can be transmitted sexually or from the transfusion of contaminated blood or from contaminated needles, syringes, or other instruments. Non-A, non-B hepatitis is a more obscure viral strain and is transmitted primarily by blood transfusion from an infected donor. However, it can also be passed through other means, including sexual contact.

The early symptoms of viral hepatitis include general fatigue, joint and muscle ache, loss of appetite, fever, and headaches. Because of the similarity to flu symptoms, hepatitis often goes untreated and the virus is allowed to spread. As the disease develops, the liver enlarges and becomes tender. Usually there are weight loss, chills, and a distaste for cigarettes, coffee, and tea. In time, other symptoms unique to hepatitis develop. These include darkening of urine color, lightening of stool color, increased liver sensitivity, and jaundice (a yellowing of the skin and whites of the eyes, caused by an accumulation of yellow pigment in the blood).

There is no specific treatment for viral hepatitis. Usually, the body's immune system subdues the disease, although for more severe cases this can take several months. The best treatment is avoidance of all strenuous activity, increased fluid intake, and a light, healthy diet. Alcoholic beverages should be avoided since they further strain the liver and can cause serious injury. Sexual contact with others must also be avoided until a blood test indicates that the virus has left the body. In acute cases of viral hepatitis, strict bed rest is usually advised. Also, serious cases may require an exchange blood transfusion to aid recovery if the body cannot overcome contamination by itself.

Viral hepatitis can be prevented or minimized with an injection of antibodies obtained from a donor pool. One such serum is gamma globulin, particularly effective against hepatitis A and offering some protection against hepatitis B. Another serum named hepatitis B immune globulin (HBIG) is effective against the hepatitis B viral strain. In recent years, a vaccine against hepatitis B has also been developed. When introduced into the body, the vaccine stimulates the production of antibodies to fight the viral infection. In its present state, the vaccine is effective at preventing the infection, but does not help those who have already become ill.

Bacterial Diseases

Bacterial diseases enter the body primarily through sexual contact and cause infection in the genitals as well as other parts of the body. Unlike viruses bacteria are able to multiply on their own outside a living cell. Among the more common bacterial diseases are gonorrhea, syphilis, and chlamydia.

Gonorrhea. Gonorrhea is a highly contagious sexually transmitted disease caused by a bacterium that can live on any mucous membrane. The bacterium is spread for the most part by direct sexual contact with an infected person. Gonorrhea is a disease that usually affects the penis in men, the vagina in women, and the throat and anus in both sexes. Gonorrhea is more common in males than in females.

Left untreated in both women and men, gonorrhea can lead to a generalized blood infection, sterility, arthritis, and heart trouble. In men, it can spread throughout the prostate gland and the male duct system, causing painful inflammation. In women, untreated gonorrhea can lead to pelvic inflammatory disease, tightening of the urethral passage, and infertility. Gonorrhea can also lead to other types of infections if the bacteria come in contact with the eyes. This can happen, for example, if the person rubs the eyes after having contact with the infected genital organs. Also, during the birth process, a baby can contract this disease when it passes through the mother's infected birth canal. Left untreated, this infection can cause blindness. Today, most states require that a few drops of silver nitrate or penicillin be placed in the eyes of all newborns to prevent gonococcal infection.

For males, symptoms of gonorrhea include a thick, creamy yellow discharge from the penis. Painful and burning urination is also commonly reported. For females, gonorrhea may exist in the early stages without any observable symptoms. It is estimated that as many as one-half of women infected with gonorrhea fall into this category. However, in time gonorrhea is often marked by a discharge from the vagina and urethra; frequent, painful urination; cloudy urine; vomiting; and diarrhea. Gonorrhea of the throat may have no noticeable symptoms or may reveal itself only by a scratchy, sore throat. As with other infections, gonorrhea is often accompanied by a fever and swollen glands.

Uncomplicated gonorrhea can usually be controlled by antibiotics such as penicillin or tetracycline. While under treatment, the patient should abstain from sexual activity until further tests have confirmed that gonorrhea is no longer present. Such tests are usually done one week after treatment begins and sometimes again two weeks later. The treatment of gonorrhea, as of all forms of sexually transmitted diseases, requires that every sexual partner of the infected person be examined and, if necessary, treated.

Syphilis. Syphilis is caused by a spirochete, a thin corkscrewlike bacterial organism. The spirochete thrives in warm, moist environments and is highly infectious. It enters the body through any tiny break in the mucous membranes and then burrows through into the bloodstream. Left untreated, syphilis can affect all parts of the body, including the brain, bones, spinal cord, heart, and reproductive organs. Blindness, brain damage, heart disease, and even death can result. Syphilis can also be transmitted from a mother to her unborn baby, causing congenital syphilis in the child. This may eventually result in blindness and deafness, among other serious consequences.

As a progressive disorder, syphilis passes through four stages: primary, secondary, latent, and late. *Primary syphilis* is marked by a painless, open sore called a *chancre*. This appears at the site where the spirochete entered the body, and it is usually the size of a dime or smaller. The chancre typically appears between 10 and 90 days after exposure to the disease and, with or without treatment, disappears in three to six weeks. However, although the chancre has disappeared, the disease is still active within the body and will enter the second stage if left unchecked.

Within six weeks to six months after contact with the disease, *secondary syphilis* appears. The symptoms of secondary syphilis include a skin rash, whitish patches on the mucous membranes of the mouth, temporary baldness, low-grade fever, headache, swollen glands, and large, moist sores around the mouth or genitals. These symptoms typically last from three to six weeks without treatment, and the disease then progresses to the third stage.

During the *latent stage of syphilis,* all symptoms disappear and the patient appears healthy. However, the spirochetes are still in the bloodstream and at this point are burrowing into the central nervous system and skeletal structure. This stage is a precursor to the highly destructive late stage.

During the stage of *late syphilis,* which may appear up to 15 or 20 years after the initial exposure, the symptoms are quite lethal. About 10 percent of patients develop *neurosyphilis,* or syphilis of the central nervous system. Neurosyphilis may manifest itself in delusions and hallucinations, seizures, paralysis, and coma that leads to death. In some cases, neurosyphilis can cause destruction of nerve cells in the brain, meningitis, and vertigo. In the late stage, syphilis can also cause damage to the heart, skin, and bones.

Despite its damaging effects, syphilis is fairly easily treated. Like gonorrhea, syphilis can be controlled with antibiotics. Penicillin, tetracycline, and erythromycin are usually the drugs of choice. Babies born with congenital syphilis are usually treated with penicillin. Those persons suffering from late forms of syphilis usually need more aggressive treatment. Often, the required dosage of antibiotics is four times that prescribed for early syphilis.

Chlamydia. Chlamydia tends to be one of the lesser-known sexually transmitted diseases, but it is the most widespread. Chlamydial infections occur in the urethra, cervix, or rectum and can produce serious complications. In recent years, chlamydial infections have reached epidemic proportions, affecting three to five million persons annually. Chlamydia is particularly common among college-aged persons.

Besides infecting sexually active adults, chlamydia can be transmitted from mother to newborn during delivery. Babies can acquire this infection while passing through the birth canal, often developing an eye infection called chlamydial conjunctivitis, as well as pneumonia. Pregnant women with chlamydial infections also risk spontaneous abortion, stillbirth, and postpartum fever.

Chlamydial infections are caused by the organism *Chlamydia trachomatis,* which has both bacterial and viral characteristics. Chlamydia is an insidious disease; that is, signs and symptoms of infection may not appear until complications set in. For women, chlamydial infections often lead to pelvic inflammatory disease (an infection of the pelvic organs, particularly the upper genital tract) and cervicitis (inflammation of the cervix). Chlamydial infections in men often develop into nongonococcal urethritis (an infection of the urethra not caused by gonorrhea), epididymitis (an inflammation of the epididymis, causing pain and swelling of the testicle), and proctitis (an inflammation of the mucous membranes of the rectum).

Parasitic Diseases

Parasites live on, in, or at the expense of another viable organism, known as a host. Parasitic diseases can be spread by sexual contact or infected objects such as clothes, bed linens, and towels. Scabies and pubic lice are examples of parasitic diseases.

Scabies. Scabies is a highly contagious parasitic disease caused by an organism called a mite. The mite lives, burrows, and lays eggs in the outer layers of the skin. Sexual activity plays a major role in the transmission of scabies. However, scabies can be transmitted from person to person by other forms of contact, such as shaking hands. Scabies can also be transmitted via infected clothing, bedding, and other inanimate objects. The disease is more common in men than in women.

Raised, reddish tracks develop along the burrowing site. Itching is also a common symptom, usually becoming very intense at night. Intense scratching of the infected area often causes scabies to spread and usually aggravates the lesions, resulting in further infection.

Scabies is typically treated with lindane (Kwell) lotion or cream. A thin layer of it is applied to the entire body from the neck down and left on for eight hours. It is then washed off. Usually one treatment of lindane is sufficient, but some doctors recommend a second application one week later to ensure that all mite eggs have been killed. Alternative treatment for scabies includes the use of crotamiton (Eurax) and sulfur ointments. Finally, recent sexual partners and close personal contacts should also be examined and treated. Clothing and bedding should be washed in hot water and machine dried (hot cycle), or dry-cleaned.

Pubic lice. Pubic lice or "crabs" feed on human blood and are transmitted primarily by sexual contact. Pubic lice infest the pubic, genital, groin, and anal areas. However, they do not usually infest the scalp because their mating habits require hairs that are relatively far apart from one another. For this reason, they usually prefer pubic hair, hair on the upper legs and abdomen, underarm hair, and chest hair. Sometimes, eyebrows, eyelashes, mustaches, and beards are affected.

Once a person is infested, the female louse begins to deposit eggs at the base of hair shafts. These eggs, called nits, are attached to the hair shafts with a cementlike substance. Within ten days or so, young lice begin to emerge from the eggs. Seeking nourishment, the young lice feed themselves by piercing the skin and sucking blood from the human host. Within two to three weeks, they reach maturity and are ready to repeat the reproduction cycle. The average life cycle is about one month.

Sometimes, infestation produces no symptoms and people are surprised to learn that they have pubic lice. Often, though, intense itching and a rash accompany infestation. Intense scratching of the infected area may produce secondary bacterial infections. Other symptoms might include a mild fever, swollen lymph glands, and muscle aches.

Like scabies, an infestation with pubic lice is usually treated with lindane. Available in shampoo form, lindane should be worked into the infected area for five minutes, then rinsed thoroughly. A fine-toothed comb should be used to remove nits from the hair shafts. Other types of medication include malathion (Prioderm) and pyrethrins (A-200 Pyrinate). All sexual and close personal contacts of the infected person should also be treated. Moreover, clothing and bedding should be washed in hot water and machine dried (hot cycle), or dry-cleaned.

Further Reading. Core-Gebhart, Pennie, Susan J. Hart, and Michael Young. (1991). *Living smart: Understanding sexuality into adulthood.* Fayetteville: University of Arkansas Press; Gordon, Sol, and Craig W. Snyder. (1989). *Personal issues in human sexuality: A guidebook for better sexual health* (2nd Ed.). Boston, MA: Allyn and Bacon; Nevid, Jeffrey. (1993). *A guide to AIDS and other sexually transmitted diseases.* Boston, MA: Allyn and Bacon; Yarber, William L. (1993). *STDs and HIV.* Reston, VA: American Alliance for Health, Physical Education, Recreation, and Dance.

SEXUALLY TRANSMITTED DISEASES, SAFER SEX AND THE PREVENTION OF. Safer sex refers to actions and behaviors that minimize sexual risk taking and reduce the chances of infection from a sexually transmitted disease. While the concept of safer sex also applies to reducing unwanted pregnancy, today it is applied more to the realm of sexually transmitted diseases. In these modern times, safer sex looms particularly important as national attention remains riveted on the prevention of the human immunodeficiency virus (HIV) as well as a wide range of other potentially harmful sexually transmitted diseases (see AIDS, PREVENTION OF; SEXUALLY TRANSMITTED DISEASES; SEXUALLY TRANSMITTED DISEASES, CATEGORIES OF).

Health experts point out that the promiscuity and sexual freedom that have become widespread today have also prompted the need for protection. Even casual sexual relationships have resulted in an increased number of infections. While contraception is important in avoiding unwanted pregnancies and allowing for sexual pleasure, protecting oneself and one's partner from the ever-growing threat of STDs is equally important.

In regard to STDs, a number of safer sex practices and guidelines have been suggested. For example, it is recommended that individuals refrain from sexual intercourse at early ages and limit the number of sexual partners. Sexual partners who have had many partners in the past should be avoided. Clear and open communication with one's partner is necessary, including the mutual exchange of sexual histories. Individuals need to share information about previous partners and infections once it is clear that a new relationship might become sexual. (See COMMUNICATION, SEXUAL.)

Other safer sex recommendations are targeted at specific sexual practices. For instance, the following sexual activities are regarded as high-risk for STD transmission unless a person is absolutely certain that neither partner has any infections: vaginal intercourse without a latex condom, fellatio, cunnilingus, a partner's semen or urine touching a mucous membrane (vagina, rectum, urethra, mouth, or eye), oral-anal contact, blood contact (including menstrual blood or blood transferred by sharing injection needles), or sharing sex toys that have contact with body fluids without washing them between partners. The highest risk of all is receptive anal intercourse without a latex condom.

Many experts believe that safer sex also entails maintaining sexual health and well-being. This means being knowledgeable about those factors that create optimum sexual functioning. The maintenance of sexual health and well-being is not automatic. Rather, responsibility becomes an individual matter and reflects intelligent decision making. The concept of sound sexual health rests on building a foundation of knowledge and applying that information on a regular basis. Moreover, prevention is the best way to minimize the risks of the sexually transmitted diseases and other disorders. In short, sexual health and well-being mean taking responsibility for one's own health.

Sexually healthy adults observe their sexual health on a daily basis and carefully monitor their sexual lifestyles. They are aware of the importance of cleanliness, sexual self-examination, and regular physicals. They know that a gynecologist can be consulted for women's reproductive health issues or a urologist for men's reproductive health problems. Sexually healthy individuals help their bodies defend against disease by keeping themselves well: exercising, eating a balanced diet, maintaining proper weight, and getting enough sleep so that the body can replenish itself and produce immune-related cells.

Further Reading. Allgeier, Elizabeth Rice, and Albert Richard Allgeier. (1995). *Sexual interactions* (4th Ed.). Lexington, MA: D. C. Heath; Crooks, Robert, and Karla Baur. (1993). *Our sexuality* (5th Ed.). Redwood City, CA: Benjamin/Cummings; Turner, Jeffrey S., and Laurna Rubinson. (1993). *Contemporary human sexuality*. Englewood Cliffs, NJ: Prentice Hall.

SEXUAL MASOCHISM. See SEXUAL BEHAVIORS, ATYPICAL.

SEXUAL ORIENTATION. Sexual orientation is the direction of our preferences for partners, including sexual as well as affectional attractions. Some people are attracted to individuals of the other sex, some are attracted to members of their own sex, and some are attracted to members of both sexes. How these sexual preferences develop has long been a puzzle to human sexuality researchers, and many efforts over the years have sought to unravel the mysteries attached to this aspect of human behavior (see SEXUAL ORIENTATION, THE-ORIES OF).

One's sexual orientation can be heterosexual, homosexual or bisexual. While *heterosexuality* involves sexual attraction and emotional attachment to members of the other sex, *homosexuality* is sexual attraction and emotional attachment to persons of the same gender. Today, there is movement away from using the term homosexual because of the tendency to think of it in sexually exclusive ways. While sexual interaction is shared by many partners, it is not the primary focus of all relationships. The terms *gay* and *lesbian* are preferred because they seek to take into account nonsexual aspects of a person's life. The word *gay* is a general term that is often applied to both men and women. Finally, *bisexuality* is sexual attraction and emotional attachment to both females and males.

It is difficult to assess the prevalence of heterosexuality, bisexuality, and ho-mosexuality. According to noted sex researcher Alfred Kinsey, a precise dis-tinction between the three sexual orientations is not possible. Rather, heterosexuality and homosexuality represent extreme poles on a continuum, and in between we find many individuals whose experiences and behaviors combine both components. In his own classification attempts, Kinsey devised a hetero-sexual-homosexual rating scale to illustrate the continuum of sexual orientations. The scale ranged from 0 to 6, with 0 representing an exclusively heterosexual orientation and 6 representing an exclusively homosexual orientation. A person whose overt experience and psychological reactions were more or less equally heterosexual and homosexual would be rated a 3 on this scale.

Using this classification, Kinsey found that about 75 to 85 percent of men and 80 to 90 percent of women were exclusively heterosexual, 4 percent of men and 2 percent of women were exclusively homosexual, and 10 to 15 percent of men and 8 to 10 percent of women had bisexual preferences. About 37 percent of males and 13 percent of females reported at least one overt homosexual experience to the point of orgasm sometime between adolescence and late adult-hood. Overall, Kinsey found that homosexual responses had occurred in about one-half as many females as males, and contacts that had proceeded to orgasm had occurred in about one-third as many females as males. Moreover, compared with males, there were only about one-half to one-third as many of the females who were, in any age period, primarily or exclusively homosexual.

If we compare Kinsey's data with the findings of other researchers, we see similar patterns of prevalence. For example, some researchers have found that in both Europe and the United States, the figure for exclusive homosexuality is about 4 percent of men and 1 percent of women. Others have found between 2 and 5 percent of the adults queried to be exclusively homosexual. Research such as this shows that the numbers of gays and lesbians in our society has remained fairly constant since the time of Kinsey's investigations.

However, in relation to all of these statistics, percentages may vary depending upon locale of the study, age of the respondents, and the possibility of con-cealment when respondents report sexual behavior. Conformity to social pressure may prompt respondents who are homosexual or bisexual to shield their sexual orientation. Thus there is no way of knowing exactly how many people are heterosexual, homosexual, or bisexual. (See BISEXUALITY; GAY AND LESBIAN RELATIONSHIPS; KINSEY, ALFRED C.)

Further Reading. Diamant, Louis, and Richard D. McAnulty. (1995). *The psychology of sexual orientation, behavior, and identity.* Westport, CT: Greenwood Press; Hunt, Morton. (1987). *Gay.* New York: Michael di Capua Books; Laumann, Edward, Robert T. Michael, Stuart Michaels, and John Gagnon. (1994). *The social organization of sexuality.* Chicago: University of Chicago Press.

SEXUAL ORIENTATION, THEORIES OF. Over the years, a number of theories have been developed regarding the origins of sexual orientation. These theories can be grouped according to biological, psychological, and interactionist properties. While these theories have enhanced our understanding, it needs to be pointed out that a precise and conclusive explanation about the origins of sexual orientation has yet to emerge. At best, it appears that a number of forces blend together to create sexual orientation.

Biological Theories

Biological theories emphasize biology as the primary determinant of sexual orientation. Two of the more important biological perspectives are the genetic and hormonal imbalance theories.

Genetic theories. Genetic theories propose that the predisposition to sexual orientation is inherited. To discover whether such an explanation is correct, some researchers have studied identical twins who were separated early in life and raised in contrasting environments. In so doing, the relative importance of heredity and environment (nature and nurture) in determining sexual orientation is analyzed. Because identical twins share the same genetic makeup, it is reasoned that any differences in their sexual orientation must be due to environmental influences (in contrast, it is suggested that differences in sexual orientation between fraternal twins are due to either hereditary or environmental influences). On the other hand, the extent to which they exhibit similarity in sexual orientation, despite being raised in different environments, underscores the importance of a genetic explanation. In utilizing studies of twins reference is often made to a concordance rate, the percentage of cases in which a particular characteristic (e.g., sexual orientation) is present for both twins if it is present for one member. In this case, we would expect a high concordance rate for sexual orientation among identical twins and a low concordance rate for fraternal twins.

In a study of twins conducted in 1952 by Franz Kallman, a 100 percent concordance rate for homosexuality was reported, compared with 12 percent for fraternal twins. However, there were important research flaws in this study, including the fact that all of the identical twins were raised together (environmental factors might thus explain the observed similarities in sexual orientation). The twins were also recruited from prisons or psychiatric institutions, thus raising the issue of how representative the subjects were. Other studies of twins have been conducted, but the concordance rate in these was much less than was reported by Kallman.

However, in 1991, a resurgence of interest in the potential role that genetics plays in sexual orientation took place. Michael Bailey and Richard Pillard studied concordance rates of homosexuality in 56 identical twins, 54 fraternal twins, and 57 adopted brothers of gay men. They discovered that 52 percent of the identical twin brothers of gay men were also gay, compared with 22 percent of the fraternal twins and 11 percent of the genetically unrelated brothers. The researchers estimated that the degree of the genetic contribution to homosexuality could range from 30 percent to 70 percent, depending on varying estimates of the prevalence of homosexuality in the United States and how representative the sample was of twins in the general population. In addition to a genetic link, the researchers also acknowledged environmental forces in shaping sexual orientation.

Another important study conducted in 1991 by neurobiologist Simon LeVay also showed that sexual orientation may have biological origins. In this investigation, autopsied brain tissue from a portion of the hypothalamus in 19 gay men, 16 heterosexual men, and 6 heterosexual women was examined (the hypothalamus is part of the limbic system and plays a role in sexual functioning). It was discovered that in gay men, a small segment of the anterior hypothalamus was only one-quarter to one-half the size of this area in heterosexual men and closer to the size of this area in heterosexual women. This segment was almost undetectable in gay men, but about the size of a large grain of sand in heterosexual men.

It was speculated that the hypothalamic variation arises during fetal development, but whether it is the result of genetics or hormonal interactions during pregnancy that affect fetal brain development is unclear. LeVay also did not rule out the possibility that sexual orientation could somehow influence neural pathways later in life. This study has important implications for future research. Indeed, given the spark created by this investigation, follow-up studies on brain structure may shed new light on biological aspects of sexual orientation. While LeVay acknowledged that sexual orientation is likely due to a combination of inborn factors and environmental influences, the finding may also affect attitudes toward gays. If sexual orientation is viewed as being shaped by some definitive, innate foundation rather than a willfully chosen lifestyle, gays may be more easily accepted by mainstream society. Research suggests that those who believe that sexual orientation is uncontrollable hold fewer negative attitudes toward gays.

Hormonal imbalance theories. Another theoretical approach suggests that hormonal imbalances are largely responsible for the development of sexual orientation. Some researchers maintain that compared to heterosexuals, homosexual males have lower testosterone levels. However, other investigators have failed to support such findings. Relatedly, higher rates of homosexuality have not been found among males with hypogonadism, a condition characterized by a deficiency of sex-hormone production in the body. Also, medical treatment with sex hormones to change endocrine imbalance has not been shown to affect the direction of sexual behavior. Finally, persons may shift from a homosexual to a heterosexual sexual orientation without a change in hormone balance.

Some researchers have also focused on the impact of prenatal hormonal imbalances on later sexual orientation. During prenatal life, hormones serve to either masculinize or feminize the brain. It has been proposed that males who receive too little testosterone may be predisposed to homosexuality during later life, while females exposed to too much testosterone may be predisposed toward lesbianism. These are intriguing propositions, and some support for them has emerged in studies with animals.

One line of research proposes that a critical period of brain development occurs between the second and the fifth months of prenatal life. Exposure to the hormone levels typically experienced by females may predispose the individual (female or male) to become attracted to males. However, conclusive research may be a long way down the road; no systematic data connecting prenatal hormone functioning and subsequent sexual orientation in adulthood have yet emerged. This fact makes many skeptical of hormonal imbalance theories.

Psychological Theories

Generally, the psychological perspective examines how interactions between parents and child as well as the overall psychological dynamics of the person affect sexual orientation. One of the earliest contributors to this field of study was Sigmund Freud, who proposed a psychoanalytic interpretation of sexual orientation. His writings provided interesting food for thought and served as an impetus for many researchers to explore the area of family dynamics.

Psychoanalytic theories. In his stage theory of psychosexual development, Sigmund Freud proposed that the third, or phallic, stage was crucial in shaping sexual orientation (see PSYCHOSEXUAL DEVELOPMENT). More specifically, Freud proposed that between the ages of four and six a boy develops a close bond with his father. The boy's strong but unconscious romantic feelings for his mother lead him to fear that his father—with whom he is now in competition—will castrate him. This castration anxiety can be resolved only if the boy keeps his desires for his mother under wraps and instead focuses on identifying with his father. According to Freud, the foregoing is normal behavior through which all boys go.

Some boys, however, become unnaturally preoccupied with the possibility of being castrated, and to counteract this fear, Freud said, they block out any awareness of female genitalia—their mothers' or anyone else's. Freud also suggested that some boys may see the female genitalia as capable of tearing off the penis. Either line of thinking could lead to the avoidance of women and, perhaps by default, to an interest in other men.

Freud attempted to adapt the psychoanalytic dynamics of the phallic stage to the lives of females, but even he was forced to admit that his efforts were far from satisfactory. During the initial phases of this stage, a girl realizes that she and her mother do not have a penis, which she feels symbolizes a lack of power (Freud referred to a female's unconscious disappointment over not having a penis as "penis envy"). She blames the lack of a penis on her mother and turns away from her, in the process becoming romantically attached to her father. However, rejection by the strongly loved father causes a girl to transfer her romantic attachment back to her mother, who then becomes the object for sexual identification. According to Freud, homosexuality results when a girl realizes that she cannot have sexual exclusivity with her mother and chooses not to transfer her affections to her father. Instead, she directs her affections and attachments to other women, or "mother figures."

Freud's early work spurred considerable research activity into the area of family dynamics and sexual orientation. For example, psychoanalyst Irving Bieber studied the family backgrounds of 106 homosexual and 100 heterosexual men and their early interactions with parents. Bieber reported that homosexuality was influenced by the presence of a dominating and overprotective mother and a detached, hostile father. Often, the mother dominated the father and prevented the son from pursuing masculine interests. Many mothers, unhappy with the marital relationship, also directed frustrated romantic and seductive wishes to their sons. Meanwhile, the detached and often absent father served as a poor sex-role model. In the midst of such family dynamics, many boys developed an aversion to females and a renunciation of heterosexuality.

Other researchers have also uncovered a link between troubled family relationships and homosexuality. Some have found that among populations of male homosexuals, many had overpossessive mothers and stormy relationships with their fathers. Certain research shows that compared to heterosexual women, many lesbians had rejecting, indifferent mothers and distant fathers. Other researchers, though, have failed to find a connection between troubled parent-child relationships and homosexuality.

In conclusion, we really do not know whether troubled family relationships are a cause of homosexuality. While human sexuality researchers agree that negative family dynamics are important factors to examine, there is no firm agreement that rocky parent-child interactions are the primary cause. Although researchers feel that more study of family dynamics may bear fruit, there is at present no solid evidence that troubled parent-child interactions cause homosexuality. Furthermore, there appears to be little evidence that gays are not well adjusted. Indeed, with the exception of their sexual preference, most lesbians and gays are remarkably similar to heterosexuals.

Environmental theories. Environmental, or behavioral, theories look at sexual orientation essentially as a product of conditioning and learning experiences. Behavioral researchers maintain that it is through interaction with the environment that individuals develop their sexual orientations. In this sense, individuals experiencing pleasant or rewarding heterosexual contacts might develop a heterosexual sexual orientation. On the other hand, homosexuality depends on contingencies that positively reinforce, or reward, homosexual behavior, punish heterosexual behavior, or both. According to this view, homosexual behavior would be established when it is followed by pleasurable events such as orgasm or when heterosexual exploration is accompanied by threats or punishment. In the latter case, parents could be seen as shaping a child's sexual orientation by punishing certain kinds of behavior.

Considerable controversy swirls around environmental explanations of sexual orientation. It has been pointed out, for example, that even if positive reinforcement accompanies a same-sex experience, society's scorn of homosexuals should serve to undermine homosexual leanings. But it does not seem to have this effect. Sexual orientation also does not appear to be determined by parental conditioning. For instance, research involving male homosexual children has shown that signs of sexual orientation are exhibited very early in childhood, at a time before their parents could have had an appreciable impact on their sexual preferences.

Interactionist Theories

It was earlier pointed out that no one theory adequately explains the origins of homosexuality. Many researchers today tend to lean toward an interactionist perspective of sexual orientation, one that acknowledges both biological and environmental forces. The interactionist perspective takes into account such factors as heredity, hormonal imbalances, parent-child relationships, and behavioral forces. No one factor overshadows the other; rather, each interacts and blends to create a person's sexual orientation.

Researcher Michael Storms reflected the interactionist perspective in his thinking. He posited that sexual orientation is a mixture of sexual maturation and social development during early adolescence. More specifically, hormonal activation initiates the sex drive during the teenage years (usually between the ages of 13 and 15), and the people with whom socialization occurs shape the direction of sexual orientation. An unusually early sex drive (at about age 12) may create homosexuality since the person's social contacts consist primarily of friends of the same sex. Storms felt that in the midst of homosocial groupings and before the development of heterosexual interests, erotic feelings become centered on members of the same sex and a homosexual orientation emerges. Should social conditions be reversed and the teenager encounter a primarily heterosexual environment, then a heterosexual orientation is likely.

Certain research supports Storms's theory of sexual orientation. For example, there appears to be a significant difference in the age at which adult gays and heterosexuals recall being aware of their own sexuality, including sexual arousal. Studies reveal that about 70 percent of gay males report having sexual drives before the age of 13. On the other hand, only 25 percent of heterosexual males report having sexual drives that early. A similar pattern of early sexual awareness and arousal seems evident for lesbians. However, it needs to be pointed out that studies such as these are based on retrospective analysis; that is, respondents are asked to recall past sexual feelings and experiences. Such recollections may be inaccurate or subject to distortion as time wears on.

In conclusion, while all of these theories are useful, the reader is reminded that a single, conclusive explanation concerning the origins of sexual orientation has yet to emerge. The theories covered suggest that unraveling the causes of a gay or lesbian orientation is just as complicated as searching for the sources of heterosexuality or bisexuality. While the determinants of sexual orientation are becoming less of a mystery, there is still limited evidence to suggest that one's sexual preference reflects a common biological predisposition, family history, or set of environmental influences. On the contrary, it seems that sexual orientation represents a convergence of all of these forces. In years to come, we can expect to see more research efforts aimed at solving this complex puzzle.

Further Reading. Birke, Lynda. (1981). Is homosexuality hormonally determined? *Journal of Homosexuality, 6,* 35–48; Freud, Sigmund. (1905). *Three essays on the theory of sexuality.* London: Hogarth Press; Kallman, Franz J. (1952). Comparative twin study on the genetic aspects of male homosexuality. *Journal of Nervous and Mental Disease, 115,* 283–298; LeVay, Simon. (1993). *The sexual brain.* Cambridge, MA: MIT Press; Storms, Michael D. (1981). A theory of erotic orientation development. *Psychological Review, 88,* 340–353.

SEXUAL RESPONSE CYCLE. The sexual response cycle is a predictable sequence of events marked by a cyclical pattern of physiological responding. Since the turn of the century, a number of researchers have constructed theoretical models of such a cycle, most notably William Masters and Virginia Johnson. Their four-stage model is considered the most detailed to date and reflects the findings of their extensive research at the Washington University School of Medicine in St. Louis. The population they studied—382 women and 312 men—consisted of both married and unmarried subjects and ranged in age from 18 to 89, though most subjects were between 18 and 40.

In their work, Masters and Johnson recorded over 10,000 episodes of sexual activity. Although these researchers acknowledged that there is wide individual variation in the duration and intensity of physiological responses to sexual stimulation, the foundation of their research has been the concept of a typical sexual response cycle. They have proposed four phases of such a cycle: excitement, plateau, orgasm, and resolution. These phases are successive and exist along a continuum. Together, they provide a framework for describing the physiological variants in sexual reaction, some of which are frequently so transient in nature that they appear in only one phase of the total orgasmic cycle. The phases of the sexual response cycle are essentially the same for women and men, and both sexes often show similar patterns of sexual response within these phases. However, there are some very important differences in the sexual responding of men and women. The following is a description of the four stages of the sexual response cycle as theorized by Masters and Johnson.

Excitement phase. During the excitement phase, sexual arousal begins. It can originate from a wide range of stimuli—a look or touch, for example—and builds as attention is focused on the particular sexual activity. Sometimes partners are aroused simultaneously, but at other times one person becomes aroused first, and foreplay then becomes both a way of arousing the other person and a way of heightening both partners' excitement and tension. As sexual stimulation continues, the intensity of sexual response tends to escalate. The excitement phase and the resolution phase consume most of the time expended in the overall cycle of human sexual response.

Foreplay or activity in which partners arouse each other or intensify their arousal is the substantive portion of this phase. Kissing on the mouth, kissing other parts of the body, and stroking and caressing any body part are all part of foreplay. The duration of foreplay is a very individual matter, and it may also vary with each sexual encounter. Some of the more prominent female physiological responses during this phase include vaginal lubrication as well as an expansion and contraction of the vaginal walls. Men will experience penile erection, scrotal tension, an increase in testicular size, and an upward movement of the testes toward the perineum. For both sexes, there is an increase in blood pressure and heart rate, heightened muscular tension in the arms and legs, and nipple erection.

Plateau phase. During the plateau phase of the sexual response cycle, there is both an increase and a leveling off of sexual tension. In essence, this phase represents a continuation of the excitement phase and moves the person toward possible orgasm. The length of this phase depends on whether sexual stimulation is maintained; if it slows or stops, orgasmic release will not be achieved. Females will experience vaginal and uterine swelling, as well as an increase in breast size. For many men, preejaculatory fluid is released and testicular size further increases. For both men and women, muscle tension continues to increase throughout the body, and people may experience involuntary muscle contractions of the arms and legs. Not uncommonly, both men and women may look as if they are in pain or distress, as their facial muscles contract involuntarily in apparent frowns or grimaces. Late in the plateau phase and during the orgasm phase, breathing becomes faster, and both blood pressure and heart rate continue to rise.

Orgasm phase. The orgasm phase is the shortest phase of the sexual response cycle, lasting only a few seconds. This involuntary climax and release of sexual tension is reached at whatever point represents maximum tension for the particular sexual experience and for the individuals themselves. Although the total involvement of the body can be defined in physiological terms, the experience of orgasm can only be described subjectively, on the basis of individual reaction patterns.

The primary component of the female orgasm is a series of rhythmic, rapidly occurring contractions of the orgasmic platform, the outer third of the vagina and the engorged tissues surrounding it. A mild orgasm may be accompanied by three to five contractions, intense orgasm by as many as twelve. The intervals between contractions lengthen in duration after the first few, and their intensity diminishes progressively. The intensity and the duration of contractions vary from woman to woman and within the same individual from one orgasmic experience to another. For males, the orgasm results in ejaculation, the process by which semen is expelled from the body through the penis. For both sexes, there are usually involuntary muscle spasms throughout the body. Excessive rates of respiration (hyperventilation) are considered normal at this time, as are elevated heart rates and blood-pressure readings.

Resolution phase. During the resolution phase, the last stage of the sexual response cycle, the person returns to an unstimulated state. Women have the potential of returning to the plateau phase and of having additional orgasmic experiences from any point in the resolution phase if they are stimulated sufficiently. For men, however, immediately following orgasm, a *refractory period* ensues during which they are unresponsive to sexual stimulation. The duration of the refractory period is highly variable; it may last for a few minutes or for several hours or longer. Generally, the refractory period lengthens as a man grows older. Effective restimulation to higher levels of sexual tension is possible only after termination of this refractory period.

Following orgasm, a woman's vagina and uterus return to their unstimulated state. The breasts also reduce in size and the nipples become less erect. For men, the penis diminishes in size as it returns to its unstimulated state. The scrotum and testes also decrease in size and descend to their original position. If a man's nipples have become erect, they will slowly relax. Muscle tension, heart rate, blood pressure, and respiration rate all return to normal during the resolution phase.

To date, the sexual response cycle as proposed by Masters and Johnson's research is the most detailed ever developed. Of particular value has been their analysis of the internal genital responses that accompany female sexual arousal. Before their findings were made public, little was known about these events, partly at least because of their hidden nature. Perhaps most important has been Masters and Johnson's proposal that both men and women not only progress through four phases of a sexual response cycle but share similar responses. This notion has added to the groundbreaking nature of their findings.

At the same time, the manner in which Masters and Johnson gathered their research data has sparked considerable controversy over the years. Critics have maintained that their research procedures created a sterile, artificial setting. Many feel that the two researchers mechanized and dehumanized sex, deemphasizing its emotional qualities. Other critics question their four-phase model of sexual arousal and response, suggesting that it oversimplifies sexual response processes. Some, however, find little or no distinction between the excitement and plateau phases proposed by the two researchers. Some critics maintain that the effort to equate male and female sexual responses overlooks possible sex differences. (See MASTERS, WILLIAM H., AND JOHNSON, VIRGINIA E.)

Further Reading. Masters, William H., and Virginia Johnson. (1966). *Human sexual response.* Boston: Little, Brown; Masters, William H., and Virginia Johnson. (1970). *Human sexual inadequacy.* Boston: Little, Brown. Masters, William H., Virginia Johnson, and Robert C. Kolodny. (1988). *Sex and human loving.* Boston: Little, Brown.

SEXUAL REVOLUTION. The sexual revolution refers to changes in thinking about human sexuality that occurred during the 1960s and 1970s and focused on gender roles as well as other aspects of sexual behavior. Historians point out that the sexual revolution ushered in changes that shaped society's present attitudes and behaviors. Among these were a shift in relations between men and women, the continuing and escalating commercialization of sex, changes in the ways sexual behavior is regulated, the emergence of new social antagonisms, and the appearance of new political movements.

Researchers studying the sexual revolution have generated conflicting interpretations of it. Some suggest that the sexual revolution brought about more relaxed and tolerant attitudes and a more flexible morality. Some hold that it has brought about greater equality, both general and sexual, between men and women. Others argue, however, that the only freedom women gained was to be more sexually active and responsive to the desires of men. As far as equality of the sexes in other aspects of life is concerned, some researchers hold that the liberation of women as defined by the sexual revolution is largely a myth. Although many women today hold managerial and leadership positions, most remain trapped in low-paying jobs, have few career opportunities, and, in addition, still shoulder the burden of child care.

From a historical standpoint, the conservatism of the 1950s appears to have been a springboard for the many changes that occurred during the latter half of the twentieth century. Vivid eruptions of sexual display characterized the sexual revolution. For example, many movie and rock stars began to present themselves in highly erotic fashion through their appearance, dress, and movements on stage and in the lyrics of their songs.

In major cities, commercialized sex—for example, prostitution and the sale of pornographic materials—grew rapidly. There is some evidence that attitudes toward birth control, divorce, abortion, premarital and extramarital sex, cohabitation, and homosexuality relaxed somewhat. The 1960s also saw a great change in the openness with which sexual matters are discussed. Today sex is spoken about, written about, and visually represented in ways society could never have imagined 30 years ago.

The media played a significant role in the movement away from traditional morality. Bans on books such as *Lady Chatterly's Lover* were removed, and Hollywood movies contained more sexually suggestive themes. A number of Supreme Court decisions of the 1960s and 1970s were influential in promoting more liberal sexual attitudes. For example, the Court ruled that graphic discussion and depiction of sexual acts were protected by the constitutional right of free speech. Although standards of enforcement varied from state to state, sexually explicit books, magazines, and films became widely available. Complete frontal nudity of both men and women was no longer restricted to hard-core pornography but began to appear in such over-the-counter magazines as *Playboy* and *Cosmopolitan.* Sex manuals such as *The Joy of Gay Sex, The Joy of Lesbian Sex,* and *The Sensual Couple* also found their way onto bookstore shelves, offering readers an assortment of sexual pleasuring techniques. In the world of advertising, sex was used in more direct ways to promote a diversity of products, from bluejeans to sports cars.

Gender-role attitudes and behaviors also began to change. During the 1960s, the women's liberation movement worked for the enforcement of laws and regulations promoting the equality of women in the workplace and in other areas of life, as well as greater rights for many other groups. Although this movement was prominent in North American society from the 1840s until the granting of women's suffrage in 1920, public interest in it declined until the 1960s. Then, spurred on by such publications as Betty Friedan's *Feminine Mystique* and Kate Millett's *Sexual Politics,* the women's movement began again to protest the second-class-citizen treatment given to females. The National Organization for Women (NOW), founded in 1966 by Friedan and others, is the largest formal organization in the women's movement and has been especially active in implementing reform in the educational and vocational arenas. NOW, for example, was instrumental in framing the Women's Equal Rights Amendment to the constitution, which states in essence that gender has no effect on equality of rights under the law. The ERA passed both houses of Congress in 1972. The fact that by the extended ratification deadline of June 1982, only 35 of the 38 states required to ratify the amendment had done so, and that since then no house of Congress has passed the amendment a second time, is an indication of how painfully slow progress in this area has been.

Because of the work of NOW and other similar organizations, and because of growing levels of social consciousness as a whole, however, the belief in male superiority has dimmed a little. Some relationships have moved from a patriarchal to an egalitarian structure, and a considerable number are characterized by changing activities within the household. Some couples share domestic chores and choose to deemphasize traditional gender-role stereotyping, a concept known as androgyny (see ANDROGYNY). As a result, relationship dynamics are based on mutuality and reciprocity. We also find more dual-earner households; that is, both husbands and wives are working outside the home.

Changes in sexual values have not altered the popularity of marriage. Indeed, marriage continues to be the chosen lifestyle for a significant portion of the population. About 90 percent will opt to get married at one point or another in their lifetimes. However, growing numbers are choosing to delay marriage. There are many reasons for marriage postponement, including the fact that many men and women are placing their careers ahead of marriage, and more people are enrolling in colleges and in graduate and professional schools. (See MARRIAGE, TRENDS IN.)

Other lifestyles besides marriage are being chosen by growing numbers of persons. Cohabitation, for example, became more common in the 1990s and has gained in public acceptance. *Cohabitation,* the sharing of a residence by an unmarried man and woman, became popular during the 1960s when college administrators began to relax campus residence rules against opposite-sex visitors. Students, who had pressed for more liberal regulations, began to take advantage of new options to rent off-campus apartments. Meanwhile, young adults began to liberalize their sexual attitudes and behaviors, making premarital sex more openly acceptable. In the 1990s, cohabitation continues to be a popular lifestyle among college students, but it also appeals to older adults. For most, cohabitation is generally seen as an additional stage of courtship, not a permanent alternative to marriage. (See COHABITATION.)

Singlehood has also become a viable alternative for some people. Although being single was once considered evidence that a person could not attract a mate, it is now thought of as an acceptable lifestyle. Many single people believe that they can lead happy, productive lives and do not need to be part of a "couple." Today, single people often choose to adopt and raise children without help from a partner. Some single women choose to give birth to their own children. (See SINGLEHOOD.)

Although marital disharmony and collapse did occur in the past, divorce was not widespread until this century. Since the late 1950s, the proportion of first marriages ending in divorce has risen sharply. The granting of approximately one million divorces in 1974 marked the first time in American history that more marriages ended by divorce than by death. Between 1970 and 1980, the number of divorces increased almost 70 percent. In 1994, over 1,100,000 divorces were granted involving nearly two and one-half million adults and over one million children. The United States has the distinction of having a higher divorce rate than any other Western nation. (See DIVORCE.)

Why in the past did so many couples remain together, even in the wake of disharmony? Many—perhaps most—stayed together for economic reasons. The family produced and consumed as a unit, and a divorce would cripple the household's overall operation and finances. It did not make economic sense to divorce. Many other couples stayed together "for the sake of the children." They believed that offering their children the advantages of a two-parent home was more important than seeking personal fulfillment. People also remained married out of a concern for their standing in the community or because divorce was expensive and obtaining one was tedious and time-consuming.

Although a few of these reasons still hold for some couples, others do not. Most households no longer produce as a total working unit, and growing numbers of women are no longer economically dependent on their husbands. Divorces have become easier to obtain, and although divorced people do experience role readjustment, their sheer numbers have lessened negative community reaction. Certain societal values have also changed as divorce rates have increased. Many people have begun to place an increasingly high premium on individual choice and personal fulfillment, and divorce for many may reflect this attitude. Thus divorce is often viewed not as personal disorganization but as a way to improve one's life.

A greater tolerance toward sexual experimentation and alternative sexual lifestyles such as homosexuality and bisexuality has also become apparent. Although a few organizations, such as the Mattachine Society and the Daughters of Bilitis, had provided support to gay men and lesbians for some years, it was only in 1969 when the patrons of a New York City gay bar fought off a police raid that the gay rights movement was begun. The Stonewall incident (the Stonewall Inn was the name of the bar) was the catalyst for the formation of the National Gay and Lesbian Task Force, established to reduce discrimination and ensure the civil rights of gay men and lesbian women. There are now a host of regional and state organizations dealing with gay and lesbian issues and an annual celebration of Gay Pride Week. Lesbian and gay couples living together openly have also become part of the sociocultural scene in the 1990s; public attitudes have become somewhat more tolerant of living arrangements that were once taboo. (See GAY AND LESBIAN RELATIONSHIPS, HISTORICAL AND LEGAL PERSPECTIVES.)

In sum, greater sexual freedom and some positive lifestyle options and changes have been brought about by the sexual revolution of the 1960s and 1970s. But these changes have created a new set of problems. Sexual freedom, for example, often pushes young people into relationships that they are unprepared to handle. Moreover, medical research has not yet been able to eliminate venereal diseases; rather, our relaxed sexual behavior has contributed to sharp increases in such sexually transmitted diseases as gonorrhea and syphilis. Worse, and most disturbing of all, the acquired immunodeficiency syndrome (AIDS) remains without a medical cure. (See AIDS.)

Further Reading. D'Emilio, John, and Estelle B. Freedman. (1988). *Intimate matters: A history of sexuality in America.* New York: Harper and Row; Friedan, Betty. (1964). *The feminine mystique.* New York: Dell; Weeks, Jeffrey. (1981). *Sex, politics, and society: The regulation of sexuality since 1800.* London: Longman.

SEXUAL SADISM. See SEXUAL BEHAVIORS, ATYPICAL.

SEXUAL VALUES, IMPACT OF ON INTIMATE RELATION-SHIPS. Sexual values are important integrating forces of one's sexuality and are influential in shaping the course of intimate relationships. Broadly defined, a sexual value is a conceptual structure of a prescriptive nature. Sexual values represent a person's beliefs about what is appropriate or inappropriate, desirable or undesirable, and so forth. An important category of sexual values is moral values, ethical standards of right and wrong that guide sexual decision making and overall standards of conduct. Combined, such beliefs represent a sexual value system, a framework that enables individuals to appraise, explain, and integrate sex-related situations. In a broad sense, a sexual value system represents a frame of reference, a set of assumptions that shapes a person's sexual life.

The selection of values to guide one's sexual life is a multifaceted process, one that follows a sequential pattern. Initially, a person may be confronted with an issue that stimulates her or him to form an opinion as to what is good or bad, right or wrong. Some such issues are the acceptability or unacceptability of premarital intercourse, the notion of shared contraceptive responsibility, the "fairness" of traditional gender-role behaviors, or the desirability of same-sex relationships. When a person confronts such an issue, he or she usually recognizes the need to establish some type of sexual value. Beyond consulting one's existing sexual value system (which consists of values that have already been taught), individuals may solicit input from family, friends, teachers, or other socialization sources. The values gathered are then compared and contrasted, and one is ultimately chosen.

Values may be extrinsic or intrinsic. *Extrinsic values* are derived from society's standards of right or wrong and are usually grounded in intellectual conviction. Because extrinsic values typically represent a conception of the ideal (such as values related to morality), they sometimes are limited in their practical application. *Intrinsic values,* on the other hand, are internalized from personal experience and represent those beliefs that govern everyday behavior. Because there may be a gap between extrinsic and intrinsic values, it is important to examine what a person says and how, in fact, he or she actually behaves. As examples, the husband who extols agape love outside of the family but batters his wife, or the woman who promotes the value of self-disclosure to others but always keeps her problems to herself, reflect discrepancies between conceived and operative values.

A number of social agents shape the formation of sexual values, including parents, siblings, peers, schools, religion, and the media. It is from such socialization agents that sexual value orientations or ideologies emerge, sets of assumptions about the purpose(s) of sexual activity and its place in human life. Such orientations represent the basis for norms that specify what types of activity are appropriate or inappropriate, and what types of persons are appropriate partners for sexual activity. The following are some of the more common sexual value orientations or ideologies that may offer guidelines for people making decisions about their sexuality:

Ascetic orientation. The roots of the ascetic orientation can be traced back to early Christianity and the teachings of St. Paul and St. Augustine. Essentially, the ascetic orientation, also known as *celibacy,* advocates sexual self-denial, the avoidance of all sexual activity, and the implementation of spiritual self-discipline. Emphasis is placed on developing the romantic and spiritual facets of a relationship rather than on sexual involvement.

Procreational orientation. The procreational orientation is another Christian ideology and emphasizes that coital activity is acceptable only within marriage for the purpose of having children. This orientation also views any behavior other than vaginal intercourse as undesirable. Most religions in the United States espouse a procreational, somewhat ascetic, sexual value orientation.

Relational orientation. The relational orientation, also called "person-centered" sexuality or "permissiveness with affection," views sexual activity as a natural extension of intimate relationships. While coital activity within casual relationships is considered wrong, sexual intercourse is acceptable if accompanied by love and emotional attachment between partners. Indeed, sexual intimacy within a committed relationship is perceived as enhancing emotional attachment.

Situational orientation. The situational orientation suggests that sexual decision making should take place in the context of the particular situation and those involved. Rather than making decisions about sexual matters solely on the basis of rules, this case-by-case orientation carefully examines motivations and consequences. Thus the acceptability or unacceptability of a sexual act depends on what it is intended to accomplish and its foreseeable consequences.

Hedonistic orientation. The hedonistic orientation, sometimes called the recreational sexual standard, emphasizes the importance of sexual pleasure and satisfaction rather than moral constraint. Sexual desire is seen as a legitimate and appropriate appetite to be satisfied with maximum gratification and enjoyment. Unlike the relational standard, which views coital activity as acceptable provided there is attachment between partners, the hedonistic orientation views intercourse by itself (without emotional commitment) as acceptable. Adherents thus see sexual gratification as an end in itself. While the hedonistic orientation received considerable attention in the 1960s, it is likely that only a small number of men and women cling to this standard. Fear of contracting HIV and other sexually transmitted diseases has created a shift toward more conservative sexual value orientations.

It is obvious from the foregoing that our complex and changing society offers divergent sexual value orientations, from celibacy to casual sex. Moreover, individuals are usually exposed to several different orientations throughout the course of their lives, making value choices even more difficult. It should be pointed out, though, that these orientations are not entirely separate entities; rather, it is possible that many individuals incorporate portions of all these sexual orientations into their sexual value systems.

The task of selecting suitable sexual values involves examining extrinsic values, such as those just discussed, and adopting those that have intrinsic worth and validity. This is no easy chore since individuals must strike some kind of balance between what values they have been taught growing up and those that have become personally meaningful. Most experts agree that the development of a sound value system does not happen overnight; on the contrary, it is a process that takes time, dedication, and considerable deliberation. One needs to avoid making snap judgments or gravitating toward values just because they seem popular or trendy.

Once values have been examined and weighed, a person needs to have faith and confidence in those selected. The overall system should be consistent with one's personality and everyday behavior; thus there should not be a gap between what a person says and what that person does. Individuals with sound value systems also hold accurate assumptions about reality. They tend to be fully informed and to keep their knowledge about human sexuality up-to-date. Those with healthy value systems also often recheck their values, testing them against their own subsequent feelings or life experiences. They also are tolerant of the value systems of others, being nonjudgmental and open to new ideas and suggestions. To illustrate, they are usually able to accept the sexual orientations and activities of others without feeling personally threatened or without moralizing or judging the other person. Sound and healthy values are also flexible ones, remaining fluid enough to allow for adjustment or correction. Finally, those with healthy value systems derive satisfaction from living by their chosen values because those values provide meaning to one's sexuality and a sense of purpose to one's life overall.

Further Reading. McCammon, Susan L., David Knox, and Caroline Schacht. (1993). *Choices in sexuality.* St. Paul, MN: West; Strong, Bryan, and Christine DeVault. (1994). *Human sexuality.* Mountain View, CA: Mayfield; Turner, Jeffrey S., and Laurna Rubinson. (1993). *Contemporary human sexuality.* Englewood Cliffs, NJ: Prentice Hall.

SIBLING RELATIONS. Sibling relations are the interactions that occur between brothers, sisters, or both. Sibling relations represent an intimate connection, one that teaches the importance of reciprocity and mutuality as well as the sharing of privileges and affection. The advantages of having siblings outweigh the disadvantages, and throughout the course of the life cycle, we can see the support and assistance that siblings bring to one another.

Initially, siblings usually discover that they must share possessions and compete for what the home has to offer. This has a tendency to create anxiety for many firstborns, especially if they are of preschool age. Unsettled feelings may give rise to *sibling rivalry,* a form of competition between children of the same family for the attention of the parents. If the former only child is old enough to perceive that the newcomer will be sharing the parent, there may be a considerable amount of jealousy exhibited during the early years.

Sibling rivalry is most likely to develop if parents exercise inconsistent discipline or if household disharmony exists. Along these lines, it has been found that sibling conflict and aggression are related to such factors as high levels of conflict between parents and children, overindulgence and favoritism toward a particular child, and insecure bonds of attachment. Secure and affectionate relations between parent and child, on the other hand, tend to be associated with harmonious modes of sibling interaction.

Although jealousy toward a new arrival is a completely normal emotion for the child, parents can take definite steps to help make the adjustment period smoother. Making the child aware of the baby's arrival beforehand and attempting to tell him or her of the personal significance involved (having a new brother or sister) may prove particularly helpful. Allowing children to become involved with the infant's homecoming preparations can indicate to them that they are active and important in the family's activities. Later on, the proper attitude demonstrated by the parents can help to keep sibling rivalries at a minimum. As indicated, parents should avoid showing any kind of favoritism or unfairly comparing one child with another.

It is not uncommon for sibling rivalries to persist for years, however. In fact, competition between siblings may be the norm rather than the exception. While it is recognized that the most intense sibling rivalry is between sisters, this may be due to the fact that females are more willing than males to express their feelings openly.

The degree and nature of sibling interaction vary greatly, not only from one set of siblings to another but within the same pair at different points in their lives. For example, some siblings become close, sometimes perceiving themselves as being more like one another than do their parents. As they watch out for one another, they loom as important sources of trust, security, and support, particularly within the social arena.

Other siblings detest each other and avoid as much contact as possible. Adolescence has the potential of being a particularly stormy time for sibling relations. In some instances, love and hate may exist side by side in an uneasy equilibrium. It might be added, too, that *sibling abuse* is more than a remote possibility in families today. Researchers maintain that sibling abuse is five times more prevalent than child abuse and may include such aggressive behaviors as hitting, slapping, pushing, or the like. Reasons for sibling abuse range from jealousy and aggression to acting out socially learned forms of behavior. As in other forms of domestic violence, many sibling abusers have been abused themselves. Researchers acknowledge that children who abuse their siblings are often at risk for extending their violent behavior toward peers and ultimately toward their spouses and children.

Siblings appear to have the most interaction and greatest influence on one another when they are close together in age. Significant age differences alone are enough to create physical and psychological distance between siblings. If they are similar in age, siblings may experience positive patterns of interaction, such as shared activities and interests, as well as negative patterns, including intense competition and a continuous struggle for separate identities. All of this is particularly true for twins, most notably during their early years of development.

Younger siblings often try to imitate older siblings. They are far more likely to be followers of their older siblings, the latter often assuming the role of model and initiator. In most families, the oldest sibling is usually expected to assume some degree of responsibility for younger siblings. The fact that this expectation exists may help to explain why firstborns are generally more adult oriented and responsible than laterborns. Interestingly, an older sibling may serve as a potential buffer or support system in the wake of family disharmony, such as divorce or separation. In support of this, research has shown that adolescents with no older siblings from divorced families exhibit more behavioral problems than do those with older siblings.

While the study of sibling relations has not received as much past attention as have other aspects of family life, researchers today acknowledge its importance. Sibling relations have come to be recognized as a unique facet of the child's life. Furthermore, the attachment between siblings often transforms itself into a special bond that endures as time goes on, even after brothers and sisters have gone their separate ways in the world.

Further Reading. Bank, Stephen P., and Michael D. Kahn. (1982). *The sibling bond.* New York: Basic Books; Dunn, Judy, and Shirley McGuire. (1992). Sibling and peer relationships in childhood. *Journal of Child Psychology and Psychiatry and Allied Disciplines, 33,* 67–105; Newman, Joan. (1991). College students' relationships with siblings. *Journal of Youth and Adolescence, 20,* 629–644.

SIGNIFICANT OTHERS. See MEAD, GEORGE H.

SINGLEHOOD. Singlehood is a lifestyle in which persons choose not to marry. There are currently over 20 million never-married single adults 18 years of age and older. Moreover, this figure has been steadily rising. Since 1960, the number of singles living apart from relatives has increased over 100 percent.

These statistics do not include the numbers of divorced and widowed persons also single, populations that are increasing as well. One out of every three married persons will be single within the next five years, and the figure will inflate to about one in every two by the end of the 1990s. They will join the ranks of the 67 million single adults in America, a group comprised of divorced and widowed individuals as well as those who have chosen to postpone marriage or never marry at all.

There are many reasons why singlehood is so popular today. One important motive is the fact that there are growing career and education opportunities for women. Pursuing a career or a degree rather than marrying at an early age is today attractive to many. Both single men and women are able to devote more time and energy to their careers. Another reason for the increase in singlehood is that there are more women than men of marriageable age, thus creating a surplus of singles. Yet another reason is that more individuals desire freedom and autonomy. Many who choose this lifestyle are also aware of today's gloomy divorce statistics.

Singlehood is a lifestyle that offers considerable potential for happiness, productivity, and self-actualization. Among the positive features of single life are its unfettered opportunities for development and change. The years following high school and college are typically a time for men and women to clarify career goals, lifestyle preferences, and political and sexual identities; by remaining single, an individual enjoys that much more freedom to reflect, experiment, and make significant changes in beliefs and values should he or she so desire. The single person has an enormous opportunity to construct new identities—or, of course, perhaps to be confused by finding too many new identities. Yet the friends and other support networks that singles can develop may help to redress some of these conflicts.

Singlehood has had various images and misconceptions attached to its lifestyle. For some, singlehood was viewed with suspicion. Singles were regarded by many as being different or lonely losers. Other societal images paint the swinging-single picture: a jet-set lifestyle characterized by fast-paced excitement and exclusive forms of entertainment and recreation. These types of myths and stereotypes are not representative of the singlehood lifestyle. The latter, for example, is characteristic of only a select few, contrary to the images generated in the media.

Finally, the literature indicates that singles are not as lonely as society paints them to be. To be single does not necessarily mean to be alone. This is particularly true in regard to living arrangements. For example, many single adults live with their parents, share apartments with friends, or cohabit.

Single people usually want to meet other people for dating and for companionship. Where do single people meet? Singles bars were very popular in the 1980s, but seem to have lost their appeal in the 1990s. Women, especially, do not like the ''meat market'' feeling, and some men did not appreciate having to take on the role of the ''aggressor.'' Presently, fitness clubs, ads in newspapers and magazines, and dating services have become popular among single adults. Introductions to other available people by friends and engaging in sports or hobbies are other ways to meet people.

Further Reading. Knox, David, and Caroline Schacht. (1994). *Choices in relationships* (4th Ed.). St. Paul, MN: West; Stein, Peter J. (Ed.). (1981). *Single life: Unmarried adults in social context.* New York: St. Martin's; Turner, Jeffrey S., and Donald B. Helms. (1994). *Contemporary adulthood* (5th Ed.). Fort Worth, TX: Harcourt Brace.

SINGLE PARENTHOOD. Single parenthood is a type of family composition in which one parent assumes the responsibility for raising biological or adopted children. The single-parent household is the fastest-growing family form in the United States today. The proportion of single-parent households almost tripled from 9 percent in 1960 to almost 25 percent in 1994. Nearly one in eight families was headed by a single parent in 1994, with women five times more likely than men to be raising a family alone.

While the single-parent household often consists of a divorced mother and her children, divorce does not represent the only reason for this domestic arrangement. Rather, single parents may also be widowed, separated, or never-married men or women. Others may have had their children naturally, through adoption, or through artificial means.

African Americans are almost three times more likely than whites to be single parents. Single-parent families represent one in five white families with children, one in three Hispanic-American families with children, and six in ten African-

American families with children. It is projected that a significant majority of all African-American children will experience a single-parent household and will spend a majority of their childhood in such a living arrangement.

Single parents face numerous problems; paramount among them is financial hardship. Many single-parent families are poor, especially if a female is head of the household. Such economic difficulty reflects the problems associated with conflicts between employment and home responsibilities, job discrimination against women, and a reluctance by ex-husbands to assist the female head of household. In regard to the latter, court-ordered child support is not large and is frequently not paid. Moreover, it is time-consuming and expensive for mothers to collect unpaid child support from their former husbands, and few are successful.

The supervision and care of the children become an additional financial problem, not to mention the quest for reliable and affordable day care. This is difficult for couples and even more so for single parents, particularly if one considers the costs, transportation, teacher conferences, and the like. Role alignment, loneliness, and stigmatization are other commonly reported adjustment problems. Furthermore, both parent and child have to adapt to a changed family structure.

Today, we have a better understanding of the needs of single parents and their children. Most experts stress the importance of minimizing guilt and ambivalence toward single parenthood and generating positive acceptance about this new social role. Many emphasize the positive features of rearing children this way, from the establishment of a single and consistent standard of discipline within the home to the encouragement of more self-reliance within one's offspring. While single parenting is a draining and often thankless task, it is not without its reward.

Further Reading. Campbell, Marian L., and Phyllis Moen. (1992). Job-family role strain among employed single mothers of preschoolers. *Family Relations, 41,* 205–211; Kissman, Kris, and Jo Ann Allen. (1993). *Single-parent families.* Newbury Park, CA: Sage; Stewart, Dana G. (1991). Single custodial females and their families: Housing and coping strategies after divorce. *International Journal of Law and the Family, 5,* 296–317.

SITUATIONAL CRISIS. See FAMILY CRISIS.

SKINNER, B. F. B. F. Skinner (1904–1990) brought great advances to the theory of behaviorism, one of psychology's major schools of thought. He was born in Susquehanna, Pennsylvania, and received a Ph.D. in experimental psychology from Harvard in 1931. Skinner held teaching positions at the University of Minnesota, Indiana University, and Harvard University. At Harvard, he was appointed Edgar Pierce Professor of Psychology in 1958.

Skinner maintained that psychology needed to restrict itself to the study of observable and measurable behavior. Influenced by the writings of John Watson, the founder of behaviorism, Skinner sought to explain behavior in terms of stimulus-response mechanisms and environmental conditioning. He stressed the importance of positive reinforcement: that is, consequences that are rewarding increase the likelihood of a behavior being repeated. However, he believed that reinforcement can be either positive or negative. Whereas positive reinforcement involves the occurrence of something desirable, negative reinforcement involves the withdrawal of something undesirable or aversive. Both positive and negative reinforcement increase the likelihood of the response they follow.

Throughout his professional career, Skinner was a prolific writer. He also was the recipient of many teaching and research awards and honors. Among them were an honorary doctor of science degree from Hamilton College in 1951, the Howard Crosby Warren Medal in 1942, and the American Psychological Association Distinguished Scientific Contribution Award in 1958. (See BEHAVIORISM; WATSON, JOHN B.)

Further Reading. Skinner, B. F. (1953). *Science and human behavior.* New York: Macmillan; Skinner, B. F. (1957). *Verbal behavior.* New York: Appleton-Century-Crofts; Skinner, B. F. (1974). *About behaviorism.* New York: Knopf; Thomas, R. Murray. (1992). *Comparing theories of child development* (3rd Ed.). Belmont, CA: Wadsworth.

SOCIAL COGNITION. Social cognition is the mental awareness of how individuals perceive themselves and others, including other persons' thoughts and feelings. Put another way, social cognition involves thinking about people and utilizing information about one's social world. Social cognition embraces many areas, including the sense we make of our social existence, the social judgments we make about others, and the interpretations we make of social rules, regulations, and roles.

Social cognition requires the use of mental faculties to understand oneself and the general fabric of social relationships. Thus social cognition tends to mirror developmental advances made in cognition (see COGNITIVE-DEVELOPMENTAL THEORY). As cognition matures, individuals are able to gain more insight into themselves and the manner in which their behavior impacts on others. Advancements in thinking herald the way for more accurate social perceptions, including the understanding of social inferences, empathy, and the establishment and maintenance of more meaningful social relationships.

Further Reading. Baron, Robert A., and Donn Byrne. (1994). *Social psychology* (7th Ed.). Boston, MA: Allyn and Bacon; Ross, Lee, and Richard E. Nisbett. (1991). *The person and the situation: Perspectives of social psychology.* New York: McGraw-Hill.

SOCIAL EXCHANGE THEORY. Social exchange theory is a major school of thought in human development, sociology, and family studies and is widely used in the study of close relationships. It proposes that our interactions are largely governed by self-interest. Individuals desire the maximum positive outcomes or rewards in relationships along with the least amount of costs or trade-offs. Within the social exchange context, a type of bargaining situation exists; that is, individuals weigh the rewards gained against the costs incurred. This bartering of rewards and costs determines the flow of our relationships with others. At the heart of social exchange theory is the notion that individuals will involve themselves in rewarding relationships and avoid those that are too costly.

Social exchange theory emphasizes how constraints interact with satisfactions and impact on persons of all ages. Thus this theory might prove useful in analyzing the perceived costs and rewards of such topics as friendships, prosocial behavior, dating relationships, or caring for an aging parent. Consider as another example how social exchange theorists would approach the topic of parenthood. It might be argued that most couples enter into parenthood with the hope that it will be a mutually gratifying endeavor, and that children are desired because of the perceived rewards and gratifications that they offer. However, many couples experience a system of deficient reward exchange; that is, the costs and sacrifices of parenthood may outweigh the benefits. Social exchange theorists would emphasize the concepts of equity and fairness when examining the scope of parenthood and would note that tension and stress often develop when reciprocity between parents is lacking. The key to establishing and maintaining parental satisfaction is the negotiation of expectation.

Further Reading. Nye, F. I. (Ed.). (1982). *Family relationships: Rewards and costs.* Beverly Hills, CA: Sage; Sabatelli, Ronald M. (1988). Exploring relationship satisfaction: A social exchange perspective on the interdependence between theory, research, and practice. *Family Relations, 37,* 217–222.

SOCIALIZATION. Socialization is the process of learning how to behave in a socially approved manner. Socialization begins early in life and includes the acquisition of knowledge, skills, and values a given culture deems important. When socialization occurs, cultural traditions are passed on from one generation to the next.

Further Reading. Landis, Judson R. (1995). *Sociology: Concepts and characteristics* (9th Ed.). Belmont, CA: Wadsworth; Levin, William C. (1994). *Sociological ideas: Concepts and applications* (4th Ed.). Belmont, CA: Wadsworth.

SOCIALIZATION AGENT. A socialization agent is a parent, sibling, friend, teacher, or other important person or group involved in the socialization of a person. A socialization agent is instrumental in shaping a person's lifelong personality and social development, as well as the roles, norms, and values needed to participate in society.

Further Reading. Bryjak, George J., and Michael P. Soroka. (1994). *Sociology: Cultural diversity in a changing world* (2nd Ed.). Boston, MA: Allyn and Bacon; Ferrante, Joan. (1995). *Sociology: A global perspective* (2nd Ed.). Belmont, CA: Wadsworth.

SOCIAL LEARNING THEORY. Social learning theory is a major school of thought in psychology and is widely used in the field of lifespan development. Social learning theory suggests that behavior is influenced by observing and copying others. Social learning investigators devote their time not to laboratory research but to direct observation of human behavior in both structured and unstructured situations. Researchers such as Albert Bandura emphasize that *observational learning* accounts for much of human behavior. By watching the behavior of others in our environment and then emulating what is seen and/or heard, unique patterns of learning unfold.

Some researchers within this theoretical framework choose to emphasize environmental components as well as cognitive dimensions of social learning. This has led to a theoretical variation known as *social cognitive theory*. Adherents to this framework emphasize that cognitive expectations and perceptions affect what we do, and our awareness of the consequences of a given behavior influences our choice of behavior. Thus, while observation is important, our cognitive abilities enable us to engage in self-regulation and the evaluation of our behavior. It is in this way that environmental learning and cognitive development converge to shape the course of human behavior. (See BANDURA, ALBERT.)

Further Reading. Bandura, Albert. (1971). *Social learning theory.* New York: General Learning Press; Bandura, Albert. (1973). *Aggression: A social learning analysis.* Englewood Cliffs, NJ: Prentice-Hall; Thomas, R. Murray. (1992). *Comparing theories of child development* (3rd Ed.). Belmont, CA: Wadsworth.

SOCIAL REFERENCING. Social referencing occurs when a person is in an uncertain or ambiguous situation and another person's emotional expression is used to determine a course of action. Social referencing is particularly prominent among infants and young children. Researchers have found that young children often watch the facial expressions of their parents to clarify situations. Positive emotional expressions on the part of the parent, such as happiness or joy, promote childhood trust and inquisitiveness, even in the midst of unfamiliar or strange surroundings, Parental fear and mistrust, on the other hand, often serve to discourage exploration and instead create more reserved and withdrawn reactions. Psychologists thus argue that the facial expressions and behaviors of significant others serve to regulate our own behavior, particularly in uncertain or novel situations.

Further Reading. Dickstein, Susan, and Ross D. Parke. (1988). Social referencing in infancy: A glance at fathers and marriage. *Child Development, 59,* 506–511; Ross, Lee, and Richard E. Nisbett. (1991). *The person and the situation: Perspectives of social psychology.* New York: McGraw-Hill.

SOCIAL SELF. See MEAD, GEORGE H.

SOCIAL SUPPORT, ELDERLY. Social support for the elderly represents a process of transactions that assist older persons in meeting psychological, social, and physical needs. Social support is extremely important during all phases of adult life, most notably during the later years. Social support is instrumental to the experience of aging well, including adjusting to the many challenges characterizing late adulthood. Indeed, informal and formal social support systems play a crucial role in providing assistance and services to aged persons.

In meeting the needs of the elderly, social support entails many activities and services. These include aid (instrumental support such as transportation, household repairs, lending money); affect or emotional support (making the elderly person feel liked or loved); or affirmation (sharing another person's perspective, attitudes, or values). Combined, such assistance is influential in the care, continued health, and sustained independent living of older persons.

A support system can be *informal* (e.g., family, friends), *quasi-formal* (e.g., churches, fraternal organizations), or *formal* (e.g., social service agencies). Depending on the needs of the elderly, these three levels or layers are capable of offering a unique combination of social support and are often used in conjunction with one another. Researchers have found that these social support layers provide different levels of closeness to the elderly person. That is, those within the inner layer are people (family, friends) with whom the focal person feels very close; they transcend role requirements and represent stable relationships over the lifespan. Movement away from the informal circle is accompanied by a gradual reduction in emotional closeness with those involved and an increase in role-prescribed behavior among the supporters.

Social support enhances the ability of older persons to retain their integrity and remain independent and autonomous in the community for as long as possible. It is important for elderly persons to experience satisfaction and pride with their lives, not sadness and sorrow. An effective social support network, particularly its more formal aspects, needs to acknowledge and accommodate the strengths and needs of the individual. Researchers maintain that dehumanizing older adults by providing impersonal and mechanical services is an insult to aging, patronizing, and a threat to psychological well-being. Such depersonalization is one of the psychological risks when institutional care of the elderly is needed (see INSTITUTIONAL CARE, ELDERLY).

It is important to point out that the size of a social support network does not dictate quality of care (e.g., there can be too much support and not enough distance). One must also recognize that not all of a person's social ties are organized into a single, broadly based resource or "system"; on the contrary, social support is often transmitted in variable, often ambiguous ways. Relatedly, it needs to be recognized that individuals often participate in several social networks in different spheres of their lives. Contrary to what many think, social ties are not always supportive or positive. Indeed, several forms of nonsupportive relationships can be noted: ineffective help, excessive help, and unwanted or unpleasant interactions.

When they function smoothly, social support networks not only provide care and assistance when needed, but also enhance the psychological well-being of older adults. For example, research consistently shows that greater integration in a supportive network is associated with fewer mental and physical health problems, less incidence of hospitalization and psychiatric admissions, and more positive outcomes when coping with stressor events. Also, support systems may positively promote health-related behavior (such as exercise or the use of medical services), serve as an important source of support in times of crisis, and provide feedback essential to normal behavioral functioning.

Positive social relations and a support network are influential in maintaining positive self-regard and heightened levels of self-esteem. Elderly persons with a lifetime of positive social relations have typically come to realize, because of their interactions with others, that they are able to cope with life's experiences, including the many challenges and transitions associated with aging. Supportive relationships provide individuals with an enhanced sense of personal control and integrity. Supportive others also develop or reinforce a person's self-worth and social competence.

It is important to recognize how the different levels of social support operate to achieve such positive outcomes. Consider first the informal level of social support. At this level, one's spouse represents an important source of companionship and assistance. Siblings, too, represent integral elements of the informal network and have the potential of supplying additional support and assistance. Intergenerational relationships represent other components of the informal social support network and are also instrumental in providing care. As far as kinship is concerned, most of the aged are geographically near at least one of their children, shattering the myth that the elderly are alienated or isolated from their families. Adult children supply elderly parents with important levels of attention, comfort, and help. (See AGING PARENTS, CARING FOR.)

Friendships are another facet of the informal social support level and shape an elderly person's adjustment and adaptation to life. Friendships are important at any age, but this appears to be especially true during late adulthood. Although there is a predominance of family in the networks of aged persons, there is often a preference for friends as support providers. When family members are not available, friends may step in and provide heightened levels of social support. Thus friendships represent a key ingredient of the informal social support network, offering participants such important benefits as loyalty, trust, intimacy, honesty, and reciprocity (see ADULTHOOD, FRIENDSHIPS DURING).

Beyond the informal layer of assistance offered by family and friends is support made available by the quasi-formal and formal social support levels. The quasi-social support network might include churches or fraternal organizations. For the focal person, such social structures are personally meaningful and provide a sense of belonging and identification. The church in particular offers an important connection between formal and informal services in addition to respite for informal caregivers. As far as more formal social support is concerned, government and other formal organizations provide basic social, economic, and health-care services to elderly persons in need. Examples of formal social support might include home health agencies, Meals-on-Wheels, or an Area Agency on Aging. Such assistance usually represents specialized services the informal or quasi-formal social support networks are not equipped or qualified to undertake or provide.

A few practical examples will illustrate how the levels of informal, quasi-formal, and formal social support combine to offer care and assistance. Consider, for instance, the experience of widowhood. At the informal support level, family and friends usually provide comfort, strength, and consolidation to the widowed person. At the quasi-formal support level, the church often looms as an influential source of emotional sustenance and may provide the widow or widower with a needed sense of belonging. At the formal support level, more specialized assistance is available if needed, such as therapeutic or medical intervention.

Retirement offers another example of the integrative nature of the various social support levels. For instance, when the retirement transition occurs, informal support (e.g., family, friends) might be sought for psychological or emotional encouragement, and some retirees might seek assistance from a work-related fraternal organization at the quasi-formal support level. The formal support level comes into play when retired persons request or require assistance from the Veterans Administration, Social Security, or other large-scale bureaucratic organizations.

It is in this way that the informal, quasi-formal, and formal social support systems provide a wide range of services and functions. In so doing, these social support systems become quite influential in buffering the impact of late adulthood's transitions and challenges and sustaining an individual's overall psychological well-being. Indeed, support systems are crucial to the concept of successful aging. Such supportive input from others serves to protect older persons by minimizing distress originating from age-related problems. Researchers maintain that social support facilitates adjustment by promoting a clearer understanding of stressful transitions, and that feedback from others helps the aged individual develop, implement, and evaluate a sensible plan of action for dealing with life's challenges. In so doing, effective social support usually reinforces a person's sense of integrity and autonomy and assures her/him that although a difficult transition or challenge may be troublesome, it can be tolerated and that successful outcomes usually follow her or his actions.

Further Reading. Armstrong, M. Jocelyn. (1991). Friends as a source of informal support for older women with physical disabilities. *Journal of Women and Aging, 3* (2), 63–83; Bury, Michael, and Anthea Holme. (1990). Quality of life and social support in the very old. *Journal of Aging Studies, 4,* 345–357; Trippet, Susan E. (1991). Being aware: The relationship between health and social support among older women. *Journal of Women and Aging, 3,* (3), 69–80; Wenger, G. Clare. (1991). A social network typology: From theory to practice. *Journal of Aging Studies, 5,* 147–162.

SOCIOBIOLOGY. Sociobiology is a conceptual framework that applies evolutionary theory to the study of social behavior. In so doing, it offers a unique combination of biological and sociological components. Adherents to this theory claim that any human behavior has a genetic component that serves an adaptive function. That is, characteristics are selected and inherited because they serve a function. Sociobiologists carefully detail how such evolutionary factors shape the nature and course of our social interactions. Behaviors such as male dominance and basic needs such as the sex drive are inherited and serve to help preserve the nuclear family, the building block of nearly all human species. However, not all agree with the sociobiological perspective. Holding that there are fundamental differences between men and women that serve the purpose of survival, sociobiologists have incurred the wrath of feminists and others, who argue that this view of social relationships not only perpetuates the notion of male superiority but denies the possibility of sexual and loving relationships between people of the same sex.

Further Reading. Bleier, Ruth. (1984). *Science and gender: A critique of biology and its theories on women.* Elmsworth, NY: Pergamon Press; Wilson, E. O. (1975). *Sociobiology: The new synthesis.* Cambridge, MA: Belknap Press of Harvard University Press.

SOCIOGRAM. A sociogram is a schematic diagram showing patterns of group organization and interaction. It is used by sociologists and other social science researchers to visualize relationship patterns, including those related to leadership, popularity, and group cohesion. A sociogram can be developed by observation or by asking group members specific questions. In the latter case, each person might be asked to designate those group members they would most prefer as an associate for various group activities. The answers are collected, tabulated, and schematically displayed as a "map." Members are usually drawn as circles or square, with lines and arrows indicating popular choices, social isolates, and friendship clusters.

Further Reading. Forsyth, Donelson R. (1983). *An introduction to group dynamics.* Monterey, CA: Brooks/Cole; McGrath, Joseph E. (1984). *Groups: Interaction and performance.* Englewood Cliffs, NJ: Prentice-Hall.

SOVIET UNION (FORMER), LIFESPAN RELATIONSHIPS IN THE. The Soviet Union, once consisting of 15 separate republics, experienced sweeping political changes in the 1990s. In 1991, Soviet president Mikhail Gorbachev announced his resignation, paving the way for the newly formed Commonwealth of Independent States under the leadership of Boris Yeltsin. The breakup of the Soviet Union was further hastened by a growing spirit of nationalism, a political ideology that emphasized the importance of independence and self-governance within the different Soviet republics. Three former republics—Latvia, Lithuania, and Estonia—have gained independence. Additionally, the Ukrainians have declared their independence, the Armenians have voted theirs, and independence movements have taken place in several other Soviet republics.

The people of the Soviet republics are quite diverse and represent over 100 officially recognized ethnic groups. While many refer to the Soviet republics as

"Russia," only one-half of the people are ethnically Russian; that is, they speak Russian or have family roots in Russia. The other one-half consists of a wide range of population groups, from the European, mostly Christian Estonians to the central Asian, Islamic Uzbeks. While Russians have settled in every location of the country, different nationalities form the majority in all of the national republics that now constitute the Soviet republics. The primary religion of the Soviet republics is Orthodox Christian, while Islam is the second-largest religious group.

The Soviet republics have a high marriage rate, a reflection of the emphasis placed on family life. Paradoxically, such high marriage rates exist in a country where women outnumber men, more so than in any other developed nation. Unlike the delayed marriage trends in most European nations, Soviet couples tend to marry at early ages. According to some researchers, this may reflect the shortage of available men and a parental desire to have daughters marry early. Regarding living arrangements, it is not uncommon for newlyweds to live with one of the couple's parents in order to save for their own residence. In such domestic arrangements, grandparents often assist with children, which serves to ease child-care costs.

Divorce is becoming widespread in the Soviet republics. Currently, approximately one out of every three marriages ends in divorce, a figure affecting almost 750,000 children. This upswing of divorce has created a large number of single-parent households headed by mothers. Single mothers face a number of problems, particularly economic difficulties. Soviet law requires that fathers pay monthly alimony, but this is not large and is generally insufficient to raise a child. Given the fact that most mothers work to make ends meet, the supervision and care of the children become an additional hardship. In addition to divorce, the number of childless marriages in the Soviet republics has increased, as has the number of children born out of wedlock.

Marriages in the Soviet republics tend to be patriarchal in structure. Husbands are usually the principal breadwinners and control major household decision making. Because of financial need, most Soviet wives work, including about 70 percent of those with children. However, Soviet women are traditionally confined in low-paying jobs with few opportunities for advancement. Despite guaranteed equal rights, both at home and in the workplace, Soviet women earn lower wages than men and must juggle their employment demands with the brunt of household responsibilities. Thus, as is the case for their female counterparts throughout the world, the burden of trying to balance work and parenthood falls on the shoulders of Soviet women.

As far as family planning is concerned, the average woman in the Soviet republics gives birth to about 2.5 children. Like many European nations, the Soviet republics experienced a drop in fertility between 1975 and 1985, but have since experienced a gradual increase. This fertility increase can be explained, at least in part, by such pronatalist policies as partially paid maternity leave for women, some provision of housing for married couples having children, small lump-sum payments upon birth, and other government incentives. The Soviet republics, along with Ireland, Malta, and Poland, are now the only European nations that have fertility levels high enough to keep births and deaths in balance and thus maintain population stability. It should be noted that fertility rates vary among the Soviet republics' ethnic groups. To illustrate, the average Tadzhik woman gives birth to 5.1 children over the course of her lifetime, while the corresponding number for Georgian women is 2.1.

Children are highly valued in the Soviet republics, and family life represents the foundation for socialization experiences. Since most mothers work outside the home, Soviet children are typically exposed to a day-care experience. Recognizing the importance of its female labor force, the Soviet Union developed a multitude of such educational settings over the years, often at minimal or no cost to families. Common curriculum components are physical and cognitive stimulation as well as group socialization experiences. Day care provides the first step in the education lives of Soviet children, who are expected to complete at least 11 years of school and are encouraged to enroll in some form of post-secondary education, such as college or technical training.

As in other nations, the chances of surviving to older ages have increased in the Soviet republics: for women, life expectancy is about 73 years, while for men it is approximately 66 years. Soviet families place great stress on family honor and respect for elderly family members. Consequently, family members are instrumental providers of support and assistance to the elderly. Given the Soviet republics' current political upheaval, gerontologists maintain that such familial assistance is critical today. The breakup of the Soviet republics has created considerable social and economic turbulence, in the process creating a decline in the social support services available to many of the republics' elderly.
Further Reading. Kalish, Susan. (1991). Nationalities in the USSR: Nations in embryo? *Population Today, 19,* 3–4; Novosti Press Agency. (1987). *Yearbook USSR, 1987.* Moscow: Author; Takooshian, Harold. (1991). Soviet women. In Leonore L. Adler (Ed.), *Women in cross-cultural perspective.* Westport, CT: Praeger; Zhernova, Lena. (1991). Women in the USSR. In Leonore L. Adler (Ed.), *Women in cross-cultural perspective.* Westport, CT: Praeger.

STABILITY-CHANGE ISSUE. The stability-change issue is a philosophical issue debated among developmental psychologists. Essentially, this issue concerns itself with whether behavior remains consistent over time, changes, or reflects a mixture of both stability and change. The issue of stability and change is an important one to examine, particularly as it relates to such important topics as personality dynamics or intellectual functioning. If behavior does remain stable, researchers want to discover if it is consistent and reflects a long developmental plateau. If change is apparent, attention is focused on whatever age-related modifications take place. Many researchers acknowledge that both stability and change characterize the life cycle and create a blending of these two forces, thus mirroring endurance as well as alteration. Also, it is acknowledged that both environmental and genetic forces converge to determine stability and change throughout the lifespan. (See CONTINUITY-DISCONTINUITY IS-SUE.)

Further Reading. Baltes, Paul B. (1987). Theoretical propositions of lifespan developmental psychology: On the dynamics between growth and decline. *Developmental Psychology, 23,* 611–626; Lerner, Richard M. (1986). *Concepts and theories of human development* (2nd Ed.). New York: McGraw-Hill.

STATUS, DEFINITION AND DIMENSIONS OF. A status represents a rank or position in society and embodies a set of rights and responsibilities. A status is a set of privileges and duties and entails subscribing to a role, a pattern of behavior consisting of societal expectations and attitudes. The words ''professor'' and ''student'' are examples of statuses; the expectations of behavior that go along with being a professor and a student are roles. In this way, status and role involve each other and reflect a constant interplay. For most individuals, this interplay becomes complex because more than one status is usually occupied at the same time. The various statuses of an individual are referred to as a *status set.* A status set would be evident in the case of a professor who is also a husband and father.

Status can be either ascribed or achieved. *Ascribed status* is one into which a person is born and that rarely can be changed over the course of the lifespan. Examples of ascribed status include sex, race, and age. *Achieved status* is one that is chosen or earned. Usually, achieved statuses are secured through ability or performance, although good or ill fortunes sometimes exert an influence. Examples of achieved status include becoming a college graduate, a doctor, or a home owner. Getting married, having children, or becoming grandparents are examples of achieved statuses that occur throughout the family life cycle. (See ROLES, DEFINITION AND DIMENSIONS OF.)

Further Reading. Landis, Judson R. (1995). *Sociology: Concepts and characteristics* (9th Ed.). Belmont, CA: Wadsworth; Levin, William C. (1994). *Sociological ideas: Concepts and applications* (4th Ed.). Belmont, CA: Wadsworth.

STERNBERG, ROBERT. See LOVE, CONCEPTUAL MODELS OF.

SUB-SAHARAN AFRICA, LIFESPAN RELATIONSHIPS IN. Sub-Saharan Africa consists of 42 nations located south of the Sahara. This land region occupies approximately 20 percent of the earth's land surface and contains approximately 10 percent of the world's population, estimated to be at 550 million. Over 60 percent of the population lives in the countries of Nigeria, Ghana, Sudan, Uganda, Zaire, and Zambia. The people of Nigeria alone represent 20 percent of the population, estimated to be 110 million. Throughout sub-Saharan Africa, the people tend to live in rural areas, and most are farmers.

The population of sub-Saharan Africa is young, the result of high birthrates and, to a lesser extent, recent declines in infant and child mortality. It is estimated that at least 45 percent of the population is under age 15 in most African countries. Sub-Saharan Africa also has considerable population diversity. There are approximately 800 ethnic groups speaking over 1,000 different languages or dialects. While millions of Africans are of mixed origins, the population includes five major physical types: Negroid, Pygmoid, Bushmanoid, Caucasoid, and Mongoloid. Many African religions are tribal religions; however, Islam is becoming increasingly popular. Sub-Saharan Africa has also experienced an increase in various Christian churches.

Marriage is widespread in sub-Saharan Africa, and rates of remarriage are high. Marriage is often seen as a contract between families, with reproductive rights belonging to the husband and his family. Most Africans marry at young ages. To illustrate, the mean age at first marriage in Nigeria and northern regions of Sudan is 16 years. Polygyny is not uncommon in some sub-Saharan countries; for example, about 45 percent of married women in Mali and 38 percent in Liberia live in such arrangements. However, polygyny is an expensive venture, and few men have the finances to support several wives and even more children. As far as marital structure is concerned, most sub-Saharan marriages are patriarchal. Both husband and wife tend to agricultural chores, while the wife handles domestic chores and child-rearing responsibilities.

As far as family planning is concerned, sub-Saharan Africa has the highest population growth rate of any region on earth, almost 3 percent annually. Demographers predict that nearly a billion persons will be added to this region between 1980 and 2025. Overall, the fertility rate, or the average number of children that a woman in sub-Saharan Africa will have over the course of her lifetime, is 6.6. It should be recognized, though, that fertility rates vary within the various countries of sub-Saharan Africa. For example, the average Rwandan woman will give birth to 8.3 children over the course of her lifetime, while the corresponding figure for women in Nigeria is 7.1. The fertility rate is lower in Lesotho and South Africa, 5.8 and 4.5, respectively. A number of factors account for such large families: limited knowledge of family planning, poverty, early marriage, and the economic value that children have, to name but a few.

As far as parent-child relationships are concerned, children are viewed with considerable pride and psychological satisfaction. Indeed, becoming a mother is considered a great achievement for most sub-Saharan women. Because most households are extended in structure, children are cared for by grandparents and other relatives as well as parents. This practice tends to promote consistency in child care as well as harmonious intergenerational relationships. When children are old enough to contribute to the household, they perform an assortment of tasks, such as fetching water, collecting firewood, tending to the livestock, and various cooking and housekeeping chores. Since women traditionally do not own assets or inherit the use of land, male children, especially, represent economic security for the mother should she become widowed.

Depending on the country consulted, life expectancy in sub-Saharan Africa is low; for most it hovers between 50 and 55 years. Such shortened lifespans are caused by many factors, including infectious diseases, malnutrition, poor sanitation, and limited health-care services. Invariably, whatever medical intervention is available is directed toward the young and not the old. In sub-Saharan countries, most health professionals, virtually all hospitals, and the majority of other health facilities are located in urban centers. However, as earlier indicated, most of the population resides in rural areas. Thus a majority of elderly Africans have little or no access to modern health care.

However, the foregoing does not mean that Africa's elderly are without supportive assistance. On the contrary, the extended family emerges as a valuable source of aid and service. The elderly are highly regarded family members, and their continued well-being is a primary concern. Adult children and grandchildren see to it that the elderly enjoy personal autonomy and control over day-to-day living. Moreover, should supportive care be needed, the elderly are not made to feel that they are a burden on younger generations. Such care is performed willingly, largely because children have been taught to contribute to their parents' health, safety, and well-being, especially during their later years. The failure to provide such intergenerational care represents a form of family dishonor and can bring exclusion from the affairs of the extended family.

No discussion of relationships in sub-Saharan Africa would be complete without some mention of the AIDS epidemic. AIDS is widespread in all of Africa, but especially so in urban areas south of the Sahara. As many as two or three million Africans are thought to be infected with HIV, and because the deadly virus is spread primarily through heterosexual activity, the number of women infected roughly equals the number of men. Because many of the infected women are in their childbearing years, HIV transmission from mother to baby is an increasing problem. The adult populations of some entire villages in sub-Saharan Africa have already been destroyed by the disease, and in many areas, AIDS is the leading cause of death among young adults. Despite massive AIDS educational campaigns launched by the African governments, misconceptions about the disease continue to exist, and preventive measures such as latex condom usage are not universally practiced.

Further Reading. Goliber, Thomas J. (1989). *Africa's expanding population: Old problems, new policies.* Washington, DC: Population Reference Bureau; Okafor, Nmutaka A. O. (1991). Some traditional aspects of Nigerian women. In Leonore L. Adler (Ed.), *Women in cross-cultural perspective.* Westport, CT: Praeger; Radloff, Scott R., Barbara H. Seligman, Judith R. Seltzer, and Richard M. Cornelius. (1989). Reproductive risks and intentions in six countries in sub-Saharan Africa. *Family Planning Perspectives, 21,* 136–143.

SURVEY. A survey is a research technique employed in the fields of lifespan development and family studies, as well as in other branches of psychology and sociology. A survey is a method of gathering information from people and usually takes the form of a *questionnaire* or an *interview.* A survey is directed toward a *sample,* a group of people representative of a larger population.

If a questionnaire is used, those within the sample mark their own answers. Background information is often gathered (e.g., age, education of the respondent), but respondents remain anonymous. The latter is particularly important because subjects often do not want to be identified with their answers on sensitive topics. Researchers are drawn to surveys because they are easy to administer and inexpensive. Results are immediately available, and the procedure does not involve the training of interviewers.

However, researchers must take care in the wording of instructions as well as the actual items appearing on questionnaires. Wording must be concise so that respondents do not get frustrated or confused. Frustrated or confused respondents often give inaccurate information or, in some instances, give up completely. Surveys can supply researchers with valuable data on how people think and act, but only if this assessment device is properly designed and worded.

Interviews, on the other hand, require a face-to-face encounter. In the standard procedure, a trained interviewer asks questions and then records the responses. Although the interview technique is more expensive than questionnaires, it is generally more flexible and yields more accurate data. An added advantage is that interviewers can listen to the responses as well as observe the respondent. This enables interviewers to better "read" the respondent and the quality of information given. The interview is especially valuable for collecting sensitive data. Once trust has been established by skilled researchers, respondents tend to disclose such information.

It is important to recognize, though, that interviews have their drawbacks. For example, while items on questionnaires are uniform and consistent, a staff of interviewers can ask the same question in different ways. Such a mixture of interviewing styles can contaminate a research design. Additionally, interviewers may not record clear and concise responses. For that matter, some interviewers may be uncertain as to which responses to record, and as pointed out earlier, the interview technique is more expensive to operate than the questionnaire format. Finally, a drawback for both questionnaires and interviews is the "words versus deeds" issue. A gap might exist between what respondents *say* and what they in fact *do*. Thus respondents might give answers that they think are compatible with the expectations of the researcher or consistent with peer standards. **Further Reading.** Breakwell, Glynis, Sean Hammond, and Chris Fife-Schaw. (1995). *Research methods in psychology.* Thousand Oaks, CA: Sage; Creswell, John W. (1994). *Research design: Qualitative and quantitative approaches.* Thousand Oaks, CA: Sage; Heiman, Gary W. (1995). *Research methods in psychology.* Boston: Houghton Mifflin.

SWEDEN, LIFESPAN RELATIONSHIPS IN. Sweden, also known as the Kingdom of Sweden, is one of the Scandinavian countries of northern Europe. It occupies the eastern half of the Scandinavian peninsula and is bordered by Norway and Finland. Sweden is the fourth-largest country in Europe, a bit larger in size than the state of California. However, Sweden is thinly populated and has one of the world's lowest population growth rates. Its population is about 8.5 million, most of which is concentrated in urban areas, particularly in southern regions of the nation.

Most of Sweden's people are ethnically and culturally homogeneous, although there are small minorities of Lapps and Finns in the north. Swedes are closely related to the Danes and Norwegians. The universal language is Swedish, a Germanic tongue that resembles Danish and Norwegian. The dominant religion is Lutheranism; other religious groups include the Missionary Union, the Pentecostal Movement, Baptists, Roman Catholics, and Jews.

Changes in lifestyle and demographic shifts have altered the course of close relationships in Sweden and have prompted many scholars to question the stability and future of Swedish marriage and family life. To begin with, marriage rates are quite low and have been declining in Sweden since 1970. Today, Swedish couples are less likely to marry than couples from any other industrialized nation. Swedes who do marry are also more likely to delay their union. The mean age of first marriage is about 27 for women and 30 for men. Should these trends persist, it is predicted that only 60 percent of Swedish men and women will ever marry. Interestingly, the mean age of Swedish women at first marriage is now higher than the mean age of Swedish women at first birth. Because of this, it is not uncommon for children to be present at their parents' first wedding ceremony.

Sweden has also experienced an increase in cohabitation, a lifestyle that has become a way of life for many of the country's young adults. Sweden was among the first countries to accept and adopt this lifestyle, which was uncommon until the end of the 1960s. Unlike the United States, cohabitation in Sweden is usually not a prelude to marriage. Rather, it has become a lifestyle in and of itself. Instead of being a trial marriage, it is regarded by many Swedish couples as a distinct alternative to marriage. In addition to being a popular alternative lifestyle for adults, cohabitation has also affected Sweden's fertility picture: about one-half of all births in Sweden are to unmarried parents.

In addition to low marriage rates and an increase in cohabitation, Sweden also has a high divorce rate (one can only speculate how many nonmarital cohabitation relationships dissolve). This has resulted in a large number of single-parent households, mostly headed by women. Divorced Swedes also demonstrate a general reluctance to remarry. While the number of second marriages has increased, many divorced or widowed men and women are now opting to remain single rather than entering another marriage. In many cases, this decision is influenced by financial concerns, such as the prospective loss of benefits or pensions derived from the former marriage. But a more basic reason may be the waning of marriage as an institution in Sweden. With the widespread acceptance of cohabitation, not marrying or remarrying has become a legitimate lifestyle option. For that matter, divorce is much easier to consider than it was generations ago in Sweden and other nations.

The foregoing lifestyle trends have resulted in a small family size. Women give birth to an average of 1.7 children, a fertility rate that places Sweden below the level of replacement (about 2.1 lifetime births per woman are needed to keep a nation's births and deaths in balance). The Swedish government provides parents and children with considerable support, including extensive medical coverage, child-care payments, and housing subsidies. Also, the Swedish government supplies parental-leave packages for both mothers and fathers. These policies provide for up to nine months of maternity or paternity leave (at 90 percent of full pay) with a guaranteed job upon returning to work, as well as a guarantee that a parent can receive full-time pay for working six-hour days until the child's eighth birthday. Such benefits are particularly important to family life as well as the vocational lives of women. With regard to the latter, Sweden has the lowest percentage of full-time homemakers and the highest percentage of females in the labor force in the Western world.

Many Swedish children are raised in households that reflect egalitarianism. That is, many mothers and fathers share the burden of child care as well as other domestic responsibilities. Because of the dual-earner nature of most Swedish homes, children are often exposed to early childhood education settings at young ages. In an effort to protect the vocational interests of women, Sweden has established an extensive network of government-supported day-care centers. A leader in educational programming at all levels, Sweden acknowledges the importance and value of early childhood education, whether or not mothers are working, for socialization and educational reasons as well as for responsible child care when parents are at work.

With 18 percent of its population 65 years of age and older, Sweden has the largest share of elderly of any major country. Swedish society captures the elderly in a positive light. They are respected and admired and neither rejected nor ignored. In times of need, family members loom as the primary caregivers for the elderly, although the aforementioned lifestyle changes may reduce the pool of available assistance. Recognizing the need for additional support services, the Swedish government has established various types of programming for its aged population. Among the services available are housing and medical assistance, expanded institutional facilities, and caregiver support packages. The latter are designed to assist caregiving families and caregiver relatives by providing economic assistance as well as more focused service support. Sweden also has a care leave policy that entitles employed persons to take time off from work and be paid an insurance allowance for up to 30 days to care for an elderly family member.

Further Reading. Haas, Linda. (1992). *Equal parenthood and social policy: A study of parental leave in Sweden.* Albany: State University of New York Press; Moen, Phyllis. (1989). *Working parents: Transformations in gender roles and public policies in Sweden.* Madison: University of Wisconsin Press; Popenoe, David. (1987). Beyond the nuclear family: A statistical portrait of the changing family in Sweden. *Journal of Marriage and the Family, 49,* 173–183; Van de Kaa, Dirk. J. (1987). *Europe's second demographic transition.* Washington, DC: Population Reference Bureau.

SWINGING. Swinging, also called *mate swapping,* is a relationship involving two or more married couples who decide to switch sexual partners or to engage in group sex. Swingers are usually liberal, upper-middle-class individuals who are employed in professional and white-collar occupations. Swinging is not a widespread sexual activity, and it is considered rare for persons under age 30.

Swingers often locate partners from a variety of sources, including newspaper ads, swinging bars, and socials sponsored by swinging magazines. Swinging can take several different forms. For example, several couples may arrange to meet, swap partners, and then pair off in separate rooms for sexual pleasuring. Other sets of couples may swap partners and engage in sex in the same room. Some swinging sessions are carefully planned affairs, while others reflect spontaneity. Most experts agree that a wide variety of sexual activities are usually accepted among swingers.

Many couples turn to swinging in the hope that it will strengthen an otherwise strained or bored relationship. Some regard it as a sexual adventure, a way to act out their inner fantasies and create excitement in their lives. Some swingers are curious, while others enjoy the sexual satisfaction that it brings. While swinging is not a widespread sexual activity, it is even less popular today than it once was. The threat of AIDS and other sexually transmitted diseases gives pause to many males and females who otherwise might feel more free to participate.

Further Reading. Strong, Bryan, and Christine DeVault. (1994). *Human sexuality.* Mountain View, CA: Mayfield; Turner, Jeffrey S., and Laurna Rubinson. (1993). *Contemporary human sexuality.* Englewood Cliffs, NJ: Prentice Hall.

SYMBOLIC INTERACTIONISM. Symbolic interactionism is a major school of thought in human development, sociology, and family studies and is widely used in the study of close relationships. Symbolic interactionism emphasizes the association between symbols (i.e., shared meanings) and interactions (i.e., verbal and nonverbal actions and communications). Essentially, this approach seeks to understand how humans, in concert with one another, create symbolic worlds and how these worlds, in turn, shape human behavior. Within the study of relationships across the lifespan, symbolic interactionists are particularly interested in how persons nurture a concept of self and of their identities through social interaction, thus enabling them to independently assign value to and assess value in their lives.

Symbolic interactionism, then, carefully analyzes the actions of individuals, since covert activity is deemed crucial in understanding the impact of society on development. Thus the dynamics of lifespan development are best understood when they are examined in the context of the social setting in which they take place. Relatedly, patterns of interaction, such as those taking place during peer-group or sibling interactions, parent-child relations, or caring for an aging family member, are best understood when their shared meanings are fathomed.

This theory is especially useful in analyzing how individuals adjust to various roles as they develop. As an example, consider how a person adjusts to the role of a marriage partner. Symbolic interactionists would view the spousal role as a process rather than a set of rigidly defined expectations or rules. Individuals develop their roles through cooperative patterns of interaction, processes that usually involve role taking (learning about the spousal role, including its expectations). For couples, one adjusts and modifies the spousal role based on what he/she perceives the other is going to do. Symbolic interactionists are particularly interested in the active role of couples as they negotiate and modify their way throughout the marriage experience. Satisfaction with the spousal role hinges on congruent expectations between wife and husband. Given this logic, symbolic interactionists would probably argue that incongruent expectations account for any stress, tension, and conflict experienced throughout the course of married life.

Further Reading. Boss, Pauline G., William Doherty, Ralph LaRossa, Walter R. Schumm, and Suzanne K. Steinmetz. (1993). *Sourcebook of family theories and methods: A contextual approach.* New York: Plenum Press; Stryker, Sheldon. (1972). Symbolic interaction theory: A review and some suggestions for comparative family research. *Journal of Comparative Family Studies, 3,* 17–32; Turner, Jonathan H. (1986). *The structure of sociological theory* (4th Ed.). Chicago, IL: Dorsey Press.

SYMMETRICAL STYLES OF INTERACTION. See INTERACTION, STYLES OF WITHIN RELATIONSHIPS.

T

TABULA RASA, CONCEPT OF. See LOCKE, JOHN. DOCTRINE ON CHILDREN AND CHILD-REARING.

TEMPER TANTRUMS, CHILD. See CHILDHOOD, OPPOSITIONAL BEHAVIOR DURING.

THEORY. A theory is a conceptual framework that provides a foundation as well as a guide for the particular topic being investigated. A theory organizes and gives meanings to facts, and it serves as a foundation for further research. A theoretical framework also helps to guide researchers with questions related to research settings and designs. For example, it helps to address such issues as what aspects of behavior to measure, how observations should be conducted, and where such observations should take place.

In psychology, a theory is a way to view behavior. A lifespan developmental theory attempts not only to describe and explain changes in behavior as aging occurs but also to show individual differences in these changes, for example, differences between males and females, African Americans and Hispanic Americans, urban and rural dwellers, and so on. An effective theory should be able to describe and explain the course of development generally as well as specifically, such as with these variations.

There are a wide variety of theories in the social sciences, many of them no more than speculative. The most speculative or weakest theories need considerably more research to support them. They are sometimes based on preconceptions. That a theoretical preconception sounds right or makes sense is no guarantee that it is correct. In the field of lifespan development, as well as in other disciplines, reliable data are needed. This is as true for research undertaken in the laboratory as it is for general theories related to life.

The better theories are generally those that have stood up to additional research and empirical (scientific) evidence. The best theories in lifespan development as well as any other discipline are those that evolve and in the process become more logically and empirically sound. Such theories are also internally consistent, with no statements that contradict each other. Moreover, good theories always come to serve a heuristic purpose: a conceptual framework to guide other perspectives and generate new observations and insight.

Further Reading. Lerner, Richard M. (1986). *Concepts and theories of human development* (2nd Ed.). New York: McGraw-Hill; Salkind, Neil J. (1985). *Theories of human development.* New York: Wiley; Thomas, R. Murray. (1992). *Comparing theories of child development* (3rd Ed.). Belmont, CA: Wadsworth.

THERAPEUTIC RELATIONSHIP, FOR ATYPICAL SEXUAL BEHAVIORS. Therapy for atypical sexuality focuses on changing those behaviors society deems abnormal and unacceptable. The treatment of such behaviors poses at least two problems. First, those who suffer with these disorders usually do not seek help for their condition, unless of course they have broken the law and are forced to do so or have been discovered by family members or loved ones. Second, current methods of treatment are less than satisfactory. To date, no one approach or technique has proven superior to others or boasts a high recovery rate. Of the modes of treatment available, the most notable are behavioral, psychoanalytic, and biological approaches.

Behavioral approaches. Behavioral therapists maintain that atypical disorders are learned forms of behavior (see BEHAVIORISM). Just as normal behavior is acquired through the process of conditioning, so too is the sexually atypical. The thrust of behavioral therapy is to replace undesirable behaviors with more appropriate ones by employing conditioning techniques.

A number of different therapeutic techniques are used by behaviorists, including aversion therapy and systematic desensitization. *Aversion therapy* seeks to reduce or extinguish inappropriate behavior by pairing it with an unpleasant stimulus. Initially, electric shocks and things like actual pictures of the person were used to try to uncondition undesirable behaviors. For example, a person with a fetishism might be given a series of small but nonetheless irritating electrical shocks while viewing pictures of himself in female clothing. Or the shocks might be administered at random intervals while the person was putting on his favorite female attire. Contemporary aversion therapy procedures, however, rely on techniques called *covert sensitization* and *assisted covert sensitization.* In covert sensitization, a person imagines himself engaging in the sexual behaviors in question. In assisted covert sensitization, a foul odor such as valeric acid is presented to the client along with the imagined behaviors in an effort to heighten the effect of the conditioning procedure.

Systematic desensitization entails the elimination of an undesirable sexual response. In this procedure, structured experiences are used to teach the person how to relax and reduce the stresses that may have precipitated the atypical behavior. For instance, suppose that an exhibitionist feels a need to expose himself whenever he experiences anxiety or is forced to submit to someone's authority. In the process of systematic desensitization, the person might be asked to imagine anxious moments in the presence of authority. At the same time, he might be desensitized by inducing relaxation responses and assertiveness rather than submissive behavior. In this fashion, strengthening the relaxation response is used to weaken his learned response and the anxiety surrounding it.

Psychoanalytic approaches. Psychoanalytic approaches emphasize the importance of past learning and how it affects present-day behavior. Influenced by the psychoanalytic writings of Sigmund Freud, such approaches suggest that repressed experiences from childhood are largely responsible for atypical sexual behaviors. For instance, there may be a preoccupation or excessive psychological investment, or perhaps a disturbance at some level of psychosexual development (e.g., castration anxiety or an attachment of the child to the parent of the opposite sex). Therapists utilizing a psychoanalytic approach believe that such sexual turbulence remains active but away from the individual's level of awareness.

The therapeutic challenge in a psychoanalytic approach is to uncover repressed experiences, bring them to a level of conscious awareness, and place them into a proper perspective. This is often attempted with what is called *free association,* in which the client is asked to verbalize all thoughts, dreams, and fantasies. Or hypnosis may be used to uncover similar material. With both approaches, an effort is made to make conscious what is unconscious and, with the help of the therapist, to interpret sexual conflicts and turmoil. When this approach is effective, the person gains conscious insight into the irrationality of his sexual behavior and may then be able to redirect his energies into more socially acceptable channels. However, the psychoanalytic treatment approach often lasts for years, and overall results have been mixed.

Biological approaches. Biological approaches in the form of antiandrogens have also been used, often in combination with the behavioral and psychoanalytic forms of treatment. *Antiandrogens* are drugs designed to reduce testosterone levels on a temporary basis, thus moderating sexual aggressiveness. An example of an antiandrogenic drug is medroxyprogesterone acetate, sold under the trade name of Depo-Provera. This drug has been used, for example, with pedophiles and other paraphiliacs, and although it is experimental, it does offer promise as a treatment option. (See SEXUAL BEHAVIORS, ATYPICAL.)

Further Reading. Dailey, Dennis M. (Ed.). (1988). *The sexually unusual.* New York: Harrington Park Press; O'Connell, Michael A., Erik Leberg, and Craig R. Donaldson. (1990). *Working with sex offenders.* Newbury Park, CA: Sage; Travin, Sheldon, and Barry

Protter. (1993). *Sexual perversion: Integrative treatment approaches for the clinician.* New York: Plenum Press.

THERAPEUTIC RELATIONSHIP, FOR MARRIAGE AND FAMILY PROBLEMS.

Marriage and family therapy is designed to assist the conflict-resolution skills of couples and to restore equilibrium to the family unit. Prolonged exposure to a stress or crisis may herald the depletion of internal resources and the family's inability to perform basic functions. Such a state usually means that therapeutic intervention is needed so that the stressors creating the crisis can be effectively managed. For some families, help is sought only for the principally affected individual. For others, the entire family unit or segments of it are the focus of therapeutic intervention.

Much as in other therapeutic relationships, marriage and family therapists use a range of theoretical orientations. For example, *behavior therapy* proposes that family adjustment and maladjustment are learned forms of behavior, and that change can be shaped and conditioned. *Cognitive therapy* seeks to replace irrational thinking of family members with more logical and sensible strategies. *Psychoanalytic therapy* places its emphasis on the resolution of unconscious conflicts that possibly are creating individual and family problems. *Adlerian therapy* regards marriage and family turbulence as a consequence of power struggles between family members. *Strategic family therapy* offers a brief, pragmatic, method-oriented approach to problems. Finally, *family systems therapy* believes that the behavior of the family is best understood as a product of its organizational characteristics.

Couples turn to marriage and family therapists for a variety of issues, which can vary considerably in magnitude, duration, and frequency. Examples of such issues include communication difficulties; sexual problems; child-oriented concerns such as discipline, misbehavior of children, or child care; financial concerns; problems with in-laws; religious topics; or problems related to alcohol or other drugs. It is not uncommon for marital partners to experience recurrent conflicts with these issues. Moreover, more than one issue may be experienced at the same time.

Experts in the field point out that success in marital therapy hinges on certain factors, such as how long the stress or crisis has occurred, the severity of the situation, and the motivation of the partners. Ideally, marital therapy represents an opportunity for growth and change, intervention designed to promote conflict-resolution skills and restore the adaptation abilities of the family. Therapists seek to identify and define the stress or crisis situation and then utilize the family's coping skills to deal with the situation. Specific tasks are often assigned to each family member in an effort to resolve the problem. An important feature of marital and family therapy is its emphasis on the prevention of future crises.

In recent years, prevention and enrichment programs have become a part of marriage and family therapy. Prevention and enrichment programs are aimed at dealing with problems before they occur, such as communication difficulties, issues facing dual-earner couples, drug abuse, or situations involving remarried families. Prevention and enrichment programs are designed so that they are applicable to a large number of persons; thus they offer considerable community appeal. Regardless of the audience or topic, prevention and enrichment programs seek to strengthen the family as a system and improve the psychological, emotional, and social well-being of each family member.

Further Reading. Goldenberg, Herbert, and Irene Goldenberg. (1994). *Counseling today's families* (2nd Ed.). Pacific Grove, CA: Brooks/Cole; Piercy, Fred P., and Douglas H. Sprenkle. (1991). Marriage and family therapy: A decade review. In Alan Booth (Ed.), *Contemporary families: Looking forward, looking back.* Minneapolis, MN: National Council on Family Relations; Worden, Mark. (1994). *Family therapy basics.* Pacific Grove, CA: Brooks/Cole.

THERAPEUTIC RELATIONSHIP, FOR SEXUAL DYSFUNC-TION.

Therapeutic intervention for sexual dysfunction is directed toward the resolution of sexual conflicts or other factors that have created a barrier to normal sexual functioning. Important advances have been made in the treatment of sexual dysfunctions. Today, not only are there more choices of therapy models, but new knowledge and clinical sophistication have been brought to bear on effective interventions in the treatment of sexual dysfunctions. Among the approaches available to treat sexual dysfunction are the Masters and Johnson, Kaplan, behavioral, cognitive, and group models. The following is a brief overview of each of these approaches.

The Masters and Johnson model. This approach to sex therapy evolved from the clinical work of William Masters and Virginia Johnson. This model emphasizes that in any relationship in which there is some form of sexual inadequacy, both partners must be involved in the treatment of the problem. The Masters and Johnson model also uses male and female cotherapists. This way, each partner has an advocate as well as an interpreter in the therapeutic setting. Following history taking and physical examinations, an extensive discussion among therapists and patients focuses on the sexual activity of the couple as well as the sexual dysfunction being evaluated. Throughout the program, which lasts two weeks, couples are given exercises that are designed to heighten their awareness of each other's sexual needs and enhance sexual pleasure and enjoyment. In each specific sexual dysfunction, various other techniques may be added in order to accomplish particular goals. (See MASTERS, WILLIAM H., AND JOHNSON, VIRGINIA E.; SEXUAL RESPONSE CYCLE.)

The Kaplan model. Sex therapist Helen Singer Kaplan expanded the Masters and Johnson model of sex therapy and combined it with parts of the psychoanalytic school of thought. The Kaplan model of sex therapy seeks to explore both immediate and more deeply rooted and hidden causes of sexual dysfunctions. While some couples are treated by a male and female cotherapy team, most are seen by one sex therapist of either gender. Kaplan emphasized that many dysfunctions are the product of unconscious motivation and conflict. Such turbulence must be brought to a conscious level of awareness and put into a proper perspective to restore sexual harmony and stability. Because Kaplan believed that the past has created present-day sexual problems, her plan for therapy leans heavily on a ''here-and-now'' approach.

The Behavioral model. The behavioral model of sex therapy is based on the notion that sexual dysfunctions are conditioned forms of behavior. Just as normal sexual behavior is learned, so too are sexual disorders. According to behavioral therapists, most sexual dysfunctions are the result of conditioned anxiety responses. Thus the therapeutic goal of this model is to eliminate or extinguish undesirable sexual behaviors and replace them with more appropriate ones. Behavioral sex therapists employ a diversity of techniques and approaches. One such technique is *systematic desensitization,* which serves to counteract the anxiety aroused by a sexual situation by interposing and associating a relaxation response with that situation. Variations of *operant conditioning* are also used, a process by which individuals learn to repeat those sexual behaviors that yield positive outcomes or avoid those with negative outcomes.

The Cognitive model. The cognitive model of sex therapy proposes that thinking processes are the driving force behind how individuals feel and what they do. Cognitive theorists maintain that when thinking is logical and sensible, behavior is stable and harmonious. If thinking is contaminated by irrational thought processes, maladjustment is likely to occur. Sexual disorders, then, are the result of faulty or distorted styles of thought. To correct dysfunctional behavior, individuals must change unrealistic and irrational perceptions and conditions. This is done through systematic analysis and manipulation of the client's thinking and reasoning. The therapist plays an active role by pointing out illogical thinking and suggesting more realistic ways of handling problems. Attention is focused on disputing irrational sex beliefs, attacking myths, and providing accurate sex information and partner education.

The Group model. The group model of sex therapy is a form of sex therapy that involves a group of people (usually six to eight) meeting at planned times with a qualified therapist to focus on a particular sexual problem. This therapeutic approach has been used successfully with both individuals and couples and has been directed to a wide range of sexual problems. The group model has several advantages. For one, some individuals may feel more comfortable in a group setting than in individual therapy. It is reassuring for many to receive group support and to recognize that they are not alone with their sexual problem. Groups also afford individuals the opportunity to observe how their behavior affects others and to benefit from group feedback. The group approach also helps avoid the problem of not having enough skilled therapists available to meet everyone's needs. It is also economical in terms of the therapist's time. Finally, many sex therapy groups are less expensive than individual therapy. (See SEXUAL DYSFUNCTION; SEXUAL DYSFUNCTIONS, CATEGORIES OF.)

Further Reading. Leiblum, Sandra R., and Raymond C. Rosen. (Eds.). (1989). *Principles and practice of sex therapy* (2nd Ed.). New York: Guilford Press; Roller, Bill, and

Vivian Nelson. (1991). *The art of co-therapy: How therapists work together.* New York: Guilford Press; Wincze, John P., and Michael P. Carey. (1991). *Sexual dysfunction: A guide for assessment and treatment.* New York: Guilford Press.

THERAPEUTIC RELATIONSHIP, FOR SURVIVORS OF CHILD SEXUAL ABUSE AND INCEST. In recent years, a number of therapeutic strategies have been developed for use with survivors of intrafamilial and extra-familial sexual abuse. The age and developmental status of the survivor usually determine the mode of therapeutic intervention. Play therapy is often regarded as the treatment of choice for the very young child. School-age children often respond effectively to a mixture of activities, including therapeutic games and exercises, art therapy, and playacting. Of the treatment modes available for older children and adolescents, conventional individual or group therapy (or both) are usually prescribed. Individual therapy allows privacy during the initial period of shock and may be needed for more intensive care and closer monitoring of conditions such as fear, withdrawal, or depression.

Group therapy, which assists victims in feeling less different and alone, has become a popular treatment approach today and is recommended by many. Groups tend to reduce isolation and facilitate peer relationships in a manner not possible in individual therapy. The support that groups offer may also prove useful in helping to reduce the stigmatization, shame, guilt, and feelings of worthlessness, as well as other intense emotions often felt by incest and sexual abuse victims. Because anxieties, uncertainties, and sexual inhibitions may endure for years, group intervention and individual modes of therapy are often productive during the adolescent and adult years.

Intervention with parents is an important part of therapy for survivors of child sexual abuse and incest. Parents need to be educated about the effects of sexual victimization and how to best support the child. They also need to know what steps to take if their child has been sexually assaulted. Many parents desire help with their own reactions to sexual victimization as well as other possible disruptions to their lives that may be directly or indirectly associated with the sexual abuse. Individual, family, or group therapy or participating in support groups are therefore recognized as important adjuncts to child-focused treatment.

Another component of therapy for parents and children is education about the prevention of sexual offenses. Most researchers believe that an important aspect of coping with an abuse experience is reducing the sense of vulnerability to subsequent abuse. Indeed, there is some evidence that victims are at an increased risk for future victimization. Some investigators feel that such vulnerability represents a manifestation of the powerlessness often experienced by victims.

When properly executed, prevention programs reduce the numbers of children sexually victimized. More specifically, they provide important information about child sexual abuse and incest, including the recognition of inappropriate behavior on the part of the offender and how to respond should sexual coercion occur. A pivotal feature of such prevention programming is teaching children realistic ways of saying no and being assertive. Other prevention efforts may include workshops geared toward teachers, day-care providers, and other professionals who work with children. (See CHILDHOOD, SEXUAL ABUSE DURING.)

Further Reading. Nelson, Mardell. (1991). Empowerment of incest survivors: Speaking out. *Families in Society, 72,* 618–624; Patton, Michael Q. (Ed.). (1991). *Family sexual abuse: Frontline research and evaluation.* Newbury Park, CA: Sage; Paxton, Cynthia. (1991). A bridge to healing: Responding to disclosures of childhood sexual abuse. *Health Values, 15,* 49–56.

THERAPEUTIC RELATIONSHIP, FOR SURVIVORS OF RAPE AND SEXUAL ASSAULT. Therapeutic intervention for survivors of rape focuses on the physical, psychological, social, and/or sexual disruption brought about by the assault. The *rape trauma syndrome* has many sides to it and does not disappear suddenly (see RAPE, EFFECTS OF). Some elements of it may never disappear completely. For example, fear is a persistent problem for survivors of sexual assault, as are depression, difficulty in achieving satisfaction in sexual interactions, and maintaining stability and harmony in social relationships.

In order to overcome these and other adjustment problems, experts emphasize the importance of resolution and coping skills. Survivors need to accept the fact that rape has occurred and that the crime cannot be undone. In order to put their lives back in order, survivors need to evaluate their resources, choose the coping strategies with which they are most comfortable, and begin the process of resolution. While this can be done alone, rape counseling and other forms of therapeutic intervention tend to facilitate the overall adjustment process.

Issues unique to the crisis need to be resolved and integrated, or the victim will fail to return to a precrisis level of functioning. *Rape work* refers to the issues specific to rape that need to be addressed. The aim of rape work is to regain a sense of safety and a valued sense of self and to reestablish sharing, altruistic, mutually satisfying partner relationships in a world where rape remains a threat. The type and severity of a rape survivor's responses, particularly the more long-term ones, are related to such factors as a person's general coping abilities, age, preexisting state of mental health, presence of supportive significant others, and the particular circumstances under which the assault occurred.

It is generally recognized that four models of therapeutic intervention exist. The *medical model* includes determining the extent of physical damage as a result of the rape, making a medical diagnosis and prognosis, seeking criminal evidence, preventing disease, and providing appropriate follow-up. The *social network model* focuses on using the survivor's social network to strengthen her or his self-esteem and to facilitate return to normal daily routines. The *behavioral model* of counseling focuses on helping the survivor "unlearn" maladaptive behaviors, such as unwarranted fears and stresses, and helping her or him learn self-confidence by dealing assertively with daily tasks and expectations. The *psychological model* seeks to help survivors come to psychological terms with the assault, including the impact of the rape on overall personality functioning.

It is important to include a survivor's partner in therapy. Male partners of female rape victims usually benefit particularly from therapeutic intervention since it helps to reduce anger, anxiety, and guilt. Therapists may help couples by encouraging the significant other to express these and other feelings about the incident, helping the partner understand the meaning of the incident to the survivor, educating the partner about the violence and the victimization syndrome, and offering individual counseling, if needed.

In addition to therapeutic intervention, survivors of sexual assault need the support of family and friends. More specifically, survivors need assistance in gaining control of their lives. Because it is difficult for survivors to be alone, they need to feel safe and accepted by others. Family and friends can offer immeasurable support by being available and listening. Also, letting a survivor know that she or he is not to blame is an important step toward recovery. A survivor needs to be reassured that the rapist is to blame, not the victim. (See RAPE; RAPE, ACQUAINTANCE; RAPE, EFFECTS OF; RAPE, MALE; RAPE, MARITAL.)

Further Reading. Frazier, Patricia A. (1990). Victim attributions and post-rape trauma. *Journal of Personality and Social Psychology, 59,* 298–304; Kramer, Teresa L., and Bonnie L. Green. (1991). Posttraumatic stress disorder as an early response to sexual assault. *Journal of Interpersonal Violence, 6,* 160–173; Weinstein, Estelle, and Efrem Rosen. (1988). Counseling victims of sexual assault. In Estelle Weinstein and Efrem Rosen (Eds.), *Sexuality counseling: Issues and implications.* Monterey, CA: Brooks/Cole.

THERAPEUTIC RELATIONSHIP, FOR SURVIVORS OF VIOLENCE AND ABUSE.

Therapy aimed at survivors of violent relationships is designed to break the cycle of abuse and to deal with whatever effects have occurred. Violence and abuse usually refer to the intentional use of physical force by an individual directed at hurting a partner. However, other forms of abuse exist in relationships. For example, verbal abuse has been known to cause serious emotional, mental, and psychological distress. Also, violence and abuse can occur in many different forms, such as within dating and marriage relationships, within parent-child relationships, between siblings, and when adult children care for elderly parents.

Therapeutic interventions as well as prevention efforts designed to stop abuse face a formidable challenge. While numerous and commendable attempts have been made, experts are quick to point out that continued research and more innovative approaches are needed. Most contend that while dealing with the aftermath of violence and abuse is critical, the causes of relationship violence and abuse must be the focal point of future efforts. Many believe that we have placed too much emphasis on remedial attention and not enough on stopping the problem before it occurs.

A number of therapeutic approaches are available. Individual approaches or family therapy are among the most popular approaches. Therapeutic strategies typically focus on the resolution of conflicts in nonviolent ways and on establishing more effective communication techniques among family members. Although progress has been reported with such approaches, obstacles can develop in therapy. Individuals may continually deny the use of violence or the existence of personal problems, hostility is typically present, and frequently there is little guilt expressed over violent and abusive behavior.

Self-help groups such as *Parents Anonymous* as well as other community organizations have also proven to be effective modes of intervention. The basic underlying theme of these programs is group support. Abused parties usually meet in small groups under the guidance of trained counselors and offer understanding and empathy to one another. Such therapeutic self-help systems not only come to the assistance of abused parties, but they also place the family in a more meaningful social context. Therapists point out that the family should be treated not as an independent social unit, but as embedded in a broader social network of informal and formal community-based support systems.

Unfortunately, many individuals and families fail to seek psychotherapy or assistance from self-help groups. To illustrate, many battered women remain in the home that promotes violence rather than seek help. Some are ashamed of their situation and feel that they are the only abused person in the community. Many refuse to get help because they fear retaliation from the abuser. Many also experience a sense of helplessness because they feel that little will come of their efforts to improve their situation.

The provision of support and services for all abused parties needs to be continually stressed. For example, emergency shelters for abused family members are considered critical in overall intervention efforts. Transportation, food, and emergency money are frequently provided by these temporary facilities. Some even help survivors of violence and abuse to find new jobs and homes. Most experts agree that these are indispensable services when a family member is seeking refuge from violence. Telephone hotlines available 24 hours a day are also valuable therapeutic tools. In addition, trained counselors who assist the abused in obtaining legal assistance on such matters as filing formal complaints and advice on child custody and legal rights in general provide important services, as do those who conduct self-defense training sessions for women.

Surprisingly, there are many people in society who refuse to acknowledge the severity of violence and abuse in relationships. Psychologists, sociologists, and other professionals feel that educating the public about the magnitude of this social problem may be one of the highest priorities in combating this problem. Training workshops for those who deal with abuse, such as police officers, social workers, lawyers, and counselors, are needed. The shroud of secrecy that surrounds all forms of violence and abuse has to be removed. To effectively implement all of these strategies, more federal, state, and local funding is needed. Financial aid is needed to establish more shelter homes, to provide more efficient types of legal assistance, and to provide support for those researchers exploring the causes and cures of violence and abuse in relationships. (See ABUSIVE FAMILY RELATIONSHIPS, CHILDREN AND ADOLESCENTS WITHIN;

ABUSIVE FAMILY RELATIONSHIPS, ELDERLY WITHIN; ABUSIVE FAMILY RELATIONSHIPS, SPOUSES WITHIN.)
Further Reading. Busby, Dean M. (1991). Violence in the family. In Stephen J. Bahr (Ed.), *Family research: A sixty-year review, 1930–1990.* Lexington, MA: Lexington Books; Jean-Gilles, Michele, and Patricia M. Crittenden. (1990). Maltreating families: A look at siblings. *Family Relations, 39,* 323–329; Wolfe, David A. (1991). *Preventing physical and emotional abuse of children.* New York: Guilford Press.

TOUGHLOVE. Toughlove is a controversial style of parental discipline used with teenage offspring. Toughlove is designed for parents who are having extreme problems with their adolescents. The approach entails a self-help organization that asks parents first to admit that they have a problem they can no longer handle on their own—that they cannot control their children's behavior. Parents turn to toughlove for a variety of teenage problems, including drug abuse and delinquency.

An important feature of toughlove is the view that parents often cannot be effective in a permissive, child-centered culture. Meeting regularly in parent support groups and maintaining contact between sessions with other group members, toughlove parents are encouraged to take firmer positions with their children and to set a ''bottom line'' on acceptable behavior in their household. When this standard is violated, the parents, with the support of other group members, are expected to follow through with the consequences that they have established. Suppose that a teenager has a drinking problem and nothing that the family has done to help works. Should the teenager be arrested for drunk driving, a toughlove approach would be to let the adolescent stay in jail for three days. In other instances, the parents might withdraw material resources as the bottom line on unacceptable behavior.

The ultimate sanction is making the teenager move to some other living arrangement—often to the homes of other toughlove parents. These parents are called ''advocates,'' and they help the teenager and his or her parents negotiate a contract setting out the conditions for returning home. Other concerned adults in the community, such as teachers, social workers, and therapists, may also serve as part of the toughlove network.
Further Reading. York, Phyllis, David York, and Ted Wachtel. (1982). Toughlove. *Family Therapy Networker, 6,* 35–37; York, Phyllis, and David York. (1982). *Toughlove.* New York: Doubleday.

TRANSACTIONAL-ANALYSIS APPROACH. See PARENTHOOD, CHILD-REARING OPTIONS AND STRATEGIES.

TRANSFORMATIONS, FAMILY. See FAMILY SYSTEMS, EXTERNAL BOUNDARY STRATEGIES.

TRANSVESTISM. See SEXUAL BEHAVIORS, ATYPICAL.

TRIAD. A triad is a three-person group. Compared to a dyad, a triad represents the beginning of more complex social interaction patterns and the development of an identifiable group structure. Whereas in a dyad both members must participate or the group ceases to exist, in a triad one person may leave, but the group structure remains intact. The addition of a newcomer to the dyad qualitatively alters the previous direct bond that may have existed between the original pair. For example, the addition of the firstborn baby dramatically alters the relationship of a couple, including levels of marital satisfaction and happiness. By changing the husband-wife dyad to a father-mother-child triad, new demands and potential conflicts have been introduced. The same holds true when two best friends are socially joined by a third person. Often, one of the parties begins to feel like the proverbial third wheel, experiencing a distinct change in the previous relationship. Obviously, the transition from dyad to triad requires special adjustment and flexibility. (See DYAD.)

Further Reading. Bryjak, George J., and Michael P. Soroka. (1994). *Sociology: Cultural diversity in a changing world* (2nd Ed.). Boston: Allyn and Bacon; Landis, Judson R. (1995). *Sociology: Concepts and characteristics* (9th Ed.). Belmont, CA: Wadsworth.

UNITED KINGDOM, LIFESPAN RELATIONSHIPS IN THE. The United Kingdom, known officially as the United Kingdom of Great Britain and Northern Ireland, is a union of four countries: England, Scotland, Wales, and Northern Ireland. Commonly referred to as Great Britian or Britain, the United Kingdom encompasses most of the British Isles, which are located off the northwest coast of continental Europe. The combined population of the United Kingdom is about 57 million, with most of this total (47 million) living in England. Of the remaining nations, Scotland has a population of about 5 million, Wales about 3 million, and Northern Ireland about 2 million. The United Kingdom is thickly populated, but has experienced a slow rate of growth in recent years.

Most Britons are descendants of Celtic, French, Germanic, and Scandinavian peoples. Among the few minority groups are people from the West Indies and Asia. English is the universal language, although Welsh is spoken in Wales and Gaelic is spoken in some northern regions. The United Kingdom has two national churches: the Church of England, which is Episcopal, and the Church of Scotland, which is Presbyterian. Other important religions are Roman Catholicism and various Protestant denominations, such as Baptist and Methodist.

Marriage and family life in the United Kingdom reflect traditional and conventional ways of life. Marriage is considered important, a fact evidenced by one of the highest marriage rates in northern Europe. Dating and courtship are marked by freedom of choice, and most Britons choose partners within relatively close residential proximity. Traditional gender roles greatly shape the course of dating: the male takes the initiative to ask the female out, provides whatever transportation is needed, and absorbs the expenses. Should marriage be in the picture, Britons tend to exchange wedding vows earlier than their northern European neighbors, at ages of about 24 years for women and 26 years for men. While rates of cohabitation and singlehood have increased, most notably in England, they have not nearly reached the levels of popularity demonstrated in such countries as Sweden or Denmark. As far as divorce is concerned, England and Wales have witnessed an increase in marital dissolution. Currently, about one in three marriages in these countries now ends in divorce.

Marital structure throughout the United Kingdom is largely patriarchal. The husband is recognized as the head of the household and the principal breadwinner. While growing numbers of households are dual-earner, many husbands take great pride in being able to financially support their wives and children. The focus of women's lives, on the other hand, tends to be on the home and the family. Should women work outside of the home, they are likely to be employed in low-paying jobs that offer few, if any, opportunities for advancement. For those who join the labor force, employment obligations are combined with domestic work. While some British husbands assist with housework, such responsibilities are considered the female's domain.

Since the 1970s, Britons have been having fewer children. Currently, the average woman in the United Kingdom gives birth to 1.8 children over the course of her reproductive years. This is a total below the level of replacement, or the number of births needed to keep births and deaths in balance and ensure population stability. A number of reasons can be cited for such a fertility decline, including financial considerations, more efficient contraceptives, relaxation of abortion laws in the late 1960s, and educational and vocational commitments. As far as family-planning methods in the United Kingdom are concerned, women traditionally assume the responsibility for birth control. Oral contraceptive use tends to be widespread among younger women, while tubal ligation (sterilization) has risen in popularity among older women.

As far as parent-child relationships go, mothers and fathers operate as a team in rearing their children. As primary agents of socialization, they provide a secure environment, impose on the child their standards for proper behavior, and serve as role models. As earlier indicated, mothers represent the primary caregiving figures, but in recent years, more fathers have become involved in child care, particularly in dual-earner homes. Not unlike child-rearing goals in other countries, an emphasis is placed on self-control, cooperation with others, respect for authority, and family loyalty. As might be expected, traditional gender roles, particularly parental expectations, shape the course of childhood. Traditional parents are apt to perceive their children in gender-related ways (e.g., boys should be aggressive and confident, while girls should be emotional and affectionate) and encourage gender-appropriate activities (e.g., boys should play with trucks, while girls should play with dolls). For most, such traditional gender-role expectations will persist outside of the home, for example, among peers and in the school setting.

Because of low fertility levels and a high life expectancy (about 74 years), the United Kingdom is experiencing a significant increase of its aged population. In times of need, such as in periods of declining health or difficulties with daily living, the family usually provides support. However, the growing number of elderly in relation to a continually smaller working population will likely erode the number of family caregivers available. As far as formal support beyond the family is concerned, there is increased governmental recognition that more elderly programming and services are needed. While there have been improvements in various forms of elderly support, such as home care and community-based services, officials agree that the United Kingdom needs an expanded and coordinated network of programs so that the well-being of its aged population can be assured.

Further Reading. Lowenstein, Ludwig F., and Kathleen Lowenstein. (1991). Women in Great Britain. In Leonore L. Adler (Ed.), *Women in cross-cultural perspective.* Westport, CT: Praeger; Marquette, C. M. (1987). Spotlight: United Kingdom. *Population Today, 15,* 11; Sturges, Phyllis J. (1992). Comparing case management practice of the elderly in the United States and the United Kingdom. *Ageing International, 19,* 15–18; Van de Kaa, Dirk J. (1987). *Europe's second demographic transition.* Washington, DC: Population Reference Bureau.

VENEREAL DISEASES. See SEXUALLY TRANSMITTED DISEASES.

VICTORIAN ERA, LIFESPAN RELATIONSHIPS DURING THE.
The Victorian era was a period in British history named for Queen Victoria, who ascended the throne in 1837. At a time when people neither liked nor respected those in power, Victoria proved to be a leader of considerable virtue and diligence, and under her rule Great Britain's territorial and economic powers soared.

By being above reproach herself, Queen Victoria raised the throne to a position of respect and veneration. Her strong moral character and lack of self-indulgence soon became standards of conduct for many influential English citizens. Many began to lead more austere lives in which high-mindedness, modesty, and self-righteousness were considered prime virtues.

The Victorian era, then, was a time of heightened morality, a morality that included, among the middle classes, a very repressive attitude that affected many aspects of close relationships. The gender roles assigned to Victorian men and women reflected the prudery of the times. Men were taught to be assertive, dominant, and in control. Men were expected to postpone marriage until they had established themselves in the vocational world. Commitment to the latter probably helped to sublimate the sexual drive. Women, on the other hand, were brought up to be subservient, dependent, and fragile. They were taught to be sexually submissive to their husbands, but not to enjoy sex. A woman was not to have sexual feelings of any kind, and her modest clothing reflected her asexual image.

Male dominance and assertion greatly influenced how households were run. Clearly, the male was the authority in terms of decision making, and he owned whatever property and possessions the couple had. While the male controlled financial matters, the female saw to the day-to-day operation of the home, including child-rearing chores and responsibilities. Care for elderly parents was seen as both dutiful and honorable, and wives and daughters were given the role of supportive caregivers. As in other historical eras, children at early ages were taught to respect their parents and to exhibit subservience to their wishes. As might be expected, a high premium was placed on teaching children to be virtuous and righteous.

Beyond gender roles, Victorian morality had interesting implications for the expression of sexuality. Among the general population, the topic of sex became shrouded in silence, and many tried almost to pretend that sexual desire did not exist. This battle, underlain as it was by an intense preoccupation with sex, was doomed to fail eventually. In the meantime, anxiety, guilt, shame, and confusion compounded each other as Victorians struggled to achieve the high morality they envisioned.

Victorian sexual repression took many forms. For example, art was censored and often altered to suit the purist attitude. Fig leaves and other adornments were strategically placed over the genitals in museum sculptures. Any work of literature that contained sexual themes or language was attacked. Shakespeare was perceived as a corrupter of morals, as were many other English poets. Novels in general were condemned. Editors of the English *Evangelical Magazine* wrote during this time that "all novels, generally speaking, are instruments of abomination and ruin." Many publications went underground, and pornographic material flourished secretly.

Profanity became taboo. Even words used in the Bible, such as "fornication" and "whore," were forbidden. Anything sexual was often referred to in euphemisms. For instance, the word "pregnant" was replaced with the expression "with child," and the word "accouchement" was deemed much more acceptable than the phrase "delivering a child." Coyness and diminutives, not to mention ambiguity, surrounded most euphemisms. Sexual intercourse was referred to by some as a "four-legged frolic," "doing the naughty," or "giving the old man his supper." Even nonsexual words that seemed a bit crude were replaced. For example, the words "perspire" (for men) and "glow" (for women) replaced "sweat."

Most Victorians believed that masturbation was a pathological habit. They ascribed many dire consequences to it, including lowered intelligence, nocturnal hallucinations, and suicidal tendencies. Victorians invented special devices to prevent boys from masturbating or from having nocturnal emissions while they slept. For example, a cagelike shield could be fastened over the genital area to prevent self-stimulation, or a metal ring with spikes that protruded inward could be slipped on the flaccid penis. If the boy had an erection, the spikes caused him excruciating pain.

Prostitution, although viewed as immoral by the Victorians, was a thriving business. Many viewed it as a necessary sexual outlet and a lesser evil than adultery. By the late 1800s, there were over 120,000 prostitutes in the city of London alone, and they catered to all social classes of men. Three types of prostitutes were noted: the well-dressed ones of the brothels, those walking the streets, and the prostitutes of the slums, or "motts." The widespread nature of prostitution is evidence that behind Victorian self-righteousness and prudery was a strong interest in sex. Thus, although the official attitude toward sex was one of repression, realists knew that prostitution was an outlet for sexual desire.

Further Reading. Barber, Bernard. (1965). *European social class: Stability and change.* New York: Macmillan; Gooch, Brison Dowling. (1970). *Europe in the nineteenth century.* New York: Macmillan; Gregersen, Edgar. (1983). *Sexual practices.* New York: Franklin Watts; Ittmann, Karl. (1995). *Work, gender, and family in Victorian England.* New York: New York University Press.

VOYEURISM. See SEXUAL BEHAVIORS, ATYPICAL.

WATSON, JOHN B. John B. Watson (1878–1958) was an early influential proponent of behaviorism, one of psychology's major schools of thought. Born in Greenville, South Carolina, Watson received his Ph.D. from the University of Chicago in 1903. He held teaching positions at both the University of Chicago and Johns Hopkins University. Watson also served as president of the American Psychological Association in 1915.

Watson was initially trained in functionalism, a school of thought in psychology exploring conscious processes and experiences. However, he became dissatisfied with the subjective manner in which functionalists gathered data. Watson argued that psychology should concentrate on learned aspects of behavior and environmental influences. According to Watson, observable behavior was the only subject matter that psychologists could study in an objective and scientific manner.

Watson conducted a classic experiment in 1920 that showed how behavior was a product of environmental conditioning. More specifically, he demonstrated how fears may be learned. Albert, an 11-month-old child, was conditioned to fear the presence of a white rat. The rat initially produced no fear in the infant. However, the presence of the rat was accompanied by a loud, sudden noise, which produced a fearful response in the child. After a number of trials in which the white rat was paired with the loud noise, Albert reacted fearfully to the sight of the rat alone. Then Albert began to generalize his fear to stimuli similar to the rat. Albert would cry and tremble at the appearance of other white fuzzy objects, such as a rabbit or a man with a white beard. According to Watson, this experiment illustrated the concept of conditioning and how environmental interaction is responsible for various types of behaviors, including children's fears. (See BEHAVIORISM.)

Further Reading. Todd, James T., and Edward K. Morris. (Eds.). (1994). *Modern perspectives on John B. Watson and classical behaviorism.* Westport, CT: Greenwood Press; Watson, John B. (1913). Psychology as the behaviorist views it. *Psychological Review, 20,* 158–177; Watson, John B. (1930). *Behaviorism.* New York: Norton.

WIDOWHOOD. Widowhood is the loss of a marriage partner by death. In the United States, there are more *widows* (a woman who has lost her husband by death) than *widowers* (a man who has lost his wife by death). In fact, widowhood is the most common status among elderly women and more likely to be a permanent one for these women. This is because mortality rates are lower for women and because they tend to marry earlier than men, thus outliving their husbands.

Losing a spouse is a severe crisis at any time, but especially so during the retirement years. If institutionalization preceded death, it is likely that the remaining spouse has already faced an assortment of pressures and strains. The loss of a loved one can abruptly remove the major source of human companionship and love from one's life. Grieving has the potential of taking a serious toll on one's health and well-being. However, the physical and psychological health of the survivor greatly influences one's ability to cope with loss. How one handles the loss of a loved one is influenced by the way other major life stressors have been handled. In this respect, it is likely that those who experienced difficulty adapting to other crises will face adjustment problems when loss occurs.

When a loved one is lost, there are many different reactions. For example, grieving persons report many physical symptoms, such as loss of sleep and appetite, a lack of energy, or heightened anxiety. Many experience depression and preoccupation with thoughts of the deceased. Emotional reactions are multiple and diverse, such as guilt, anger, denial, or sorrow.

The very nature of widowhood itself usually creates significant turmoil. For example, the loss of a partner usually disrupts plans, hopes, and dreams for the future. Survivors must also adjust to new role realignments and new self-images. Related to the latter, surviving partners must reexamine their self-images, which have been embedded in long-term relationships, and move to selves based on "I" rather than "we." One also typically faces establishing a new social support network and concern for children's and other family members' grief. Perhaps most stressful, survivors must face the loss of emotional support and companionship.

Mourning the loss of a loved one varies in intensity and may take months or years. Regardless of its duration, grieving is a way of healing. When survivors allow themselves to express their innermost feelings, a loss is usually more clearly understood. Learning how to free oneself emotionally from the deceased, readjusting to a life of missing the dead person, and forming new relationships with other individuals are important tasks for the mourners.

Successfully adjusted widowed persons have developed ways to cope with the day-to-day problems of living alone and receive emotional support from various persons. Their support networks include family as well as friends. While there are still feelings of loneliness, successfully adjusted widowed persons have developed ways to cope with these problems. These survivors have established a new identity with the help of their support network. The path to recovery from bereavement may also include remarriage. Many widowed adults choose to remarry, although remarriage is more common for widowers than it is for widows. According to some researchers, widowed older adults who remarry have higher morale and a better self-image than those who choose not to remarry.

The establishment of independence plays a major role in how well widowed persons are able to develop emotionally. When recovery has been successful and independence has emerged, widowhood usually does little to damage an individual's self-regard. The widowed, like other bereaved people, move from the sadness of loss to a gradual sense of incorporating the loss and detaching from the deceased spouse. Some researchers feel that for many bereaved persons, such psychological processes promote new patterns of positive behavior and/or ways of thinking. Some who lose spouses, however, seem unable ever to fully resolve the pain of their loss. Dependency, ambivalence, and helplessness characterize many of those who struggle during bereavement. Those who cannot successfully cope with loss often report poorer perceived health, lower self-esteem, and reduced coping abilities.

The examination of recovery from bereavement reveals interesting gender differences. More specifically, it seems that men, more so than women, face difficulty in adjusting to their new roles as widowers. Researchers acknowledge that traditional men are less apt to express grief and tend to be more socially isolated than widows. Also hampering the recovery process is the fact that ties with the extended family are typically maintained by the woman. Often, the traditional male lacks the skills for maintaining or reestablishing such relationships. Men also report difficulty taking care of themselves during the recovery process, having previously left household responsibilities to their wives.

Many male and female survivors today turn to support groups and other service programs for assistance. Such support groups have been shown to provide a safe, nurturant, and mutually supportive environment that can facilitate a healthy grieving process. Perhaps the most widely known is the Widow-to-Widow Program. Volunteers who have been widowed maintain phone hotlines and make home visits to newly widowed persons. The phone hotlines serve to provide listeners to the lonely, to help widowed persons make new friends, and to provide some specific piece of information. The primary aim of the entire program is to help the widowed person progress through the developmental stages involved in the transition from married life to widowed life. Aides provide support and serve as role models of what it is to be widowed. In addition to the hotline and home visits, another program that provides social gatherings and community seminars has also been developed.

In short, successfully adjusted widowed persons have found new outlets for their energies. Moreover, they have sorted out their feelings surrounding the loss, a process that enables them to reflect on the past and recall both the pleasure and pain of a departed loved one. The successfully adjusted have come to terms with themselves and their future, which serves to create a renewal and reestablishment of their normal lifestyle. For many, this means the establishment of new friendships and intimate relationships. It may well be that experiencing widowhood promotes a stronger faith and more compassionate care and appreciation of the living. Those who have felt the pain of loss often learn to live their lives with more meaning—with appreciation of their finiteness and of the limits of their time here. (See BEREAVEMENT; GRIEF; GRIEF WORK.)

Further Reading. Lindemann, Erich. (1995). Symptomatology and management of acute grief. In John B. Williamson and Edwin S. Shneidman (Eds.), *Death: Current perspectives* (4th Ed.). Mountain View, CA: Mayfield; Rose, Xenia. (1990). *Widow's journey: A return to the loving self.* New York: Henry Holt; Stern, E. Mark. (Ed.). (1990). *Psychotherapy and the widowed patient.* New York: Haworth Press; Wortman, Camille B., and Roxane C. Silver. (1990). Successful mastery of bereavement and widowhood: A life-course perspective. In Paul B. Baltes and Margret M. Baltes (Eds.), *Successful aging: Perspectives from the behavioral sciences.* New York: Cambridge University Press.

WOMEN, EMPLOYED. Increasingly large numbers of women, single and married, are employed in the nation's labor force. Perhaps a few statistics will illustrate how widespread female labor-force participation is. Currently, women constitute about 45 percent of the total labor force. By the year 2050, the 67 million women projected to be working will constitute about 47 percent of the entire labor force, up from 40 percent in 1976 and 45 percent in 1990. Over 60 percent of all adult females will participate in the labor force by the year 2050. For every two men who enter the workplace today, three women join.

What factors account for such increases in female labor-force involvement? Obviously, economic necessity is one reason. A single income is no longer enough for many couples. Also, growing numbers of women are heading single-parent families. Higher divorce or separation rates require more women to live on their own incomes. Another motive is the need for achievement beyond the home and family, particularly among college-educated women.

The contemporary female worker is succeeding in removing traditional gender-role barriers, not only by the work she does, but also by the fact that she often operates from a set of carefully cultivated career goals. Such careful planning was virtually unheard of in previous generations because yesterday's females were not expected to have career goals. For many today, this is a societal expectation that still lingers. There are also those who feel that success in a career is something to fear, since they have been taught that being competitive and successful is unfeminine. The increase in women entering the labor force has helped to change these attitudes and, in turn, has encouraged more women to seek employment.

While there are still problems of inequality facing the working woman (see WOMEN, EMPLOYMENT DISCRIMINATION AGAINST), there are more career options available today than ever before in this nation's history. Women now represent more than one-half the work force in nearly a dozen industries, including the fast-growing health services, banking, legal services, insurance, and retail trade. Women also hold jobs previously held down only by men: firefighters, pilots and navigators, professional athletes, auto mechanics, and electricians, to name but a few. Many women have also moved into managerial and professional specialty occupations.

In recent years, many researchers have explored how female paid employment impacts on marriages. Most investigators acknowledge that a dual-earner marriage has the potential of promoting considerably higher levels of happiness, satisfaction, and accomplishment. Many dual-earner couples report stability in their marriages and contentment in their career pursuits. Indeed, some say that the involvement and sacrifices required in a vocation make marriage and domestic life more meaningful. Thus, two time-consuming, bustling vocations may bring considerable enrichment and contentment, not to mention elevated levels of finance.

However, there are two sides to every coin. Because of its demands, a two-paycheck marriage may also snap the patience of even the most dedicated couples. Such a domestic arrangement has the potential of bringing headaches and sacrifices, the pressures of which often overwhelm marriage partners. To illustrate, the household division of labor among dual-earner couples also poses problems. While many women are employed, most of the traditional gender roles attached to them are still in place. While egalitarian relationships are increasing in many homes, they are still overshadowed by traditional gender-role orientations to household chores. This means that in addition to vocational demands, working women still carry the brunt of household chores. This situation worsens during parenthood when child-care chores are added to the woman's domestic routines and responsibilities (see PARENTHOOD, THE ROLE OF THE MOTHER).

Another problem associated with dual-earner marriages is the pressure and competition they often create among traditional couples. The husband's psychological identity with his work is often the underpinning to this problem. When both partners work, some men feel threatened because traditional gender-typed boundaries have been crossed. Having a wife who works is contradictory to those who grew up in homes where only the husband worked. This becomes particularly evident in dual-earner households where wives are earning nearly as much as, or even more than, their partners. This is unsettling to many men because money translates into power, and men are unaccustomed to yielding power to women. Many take pleasure in a woman's success, but only as long as it does not challenge their own. Conflict is likely to increase unless men learn how to accept their partner's achievement without feeling threatened.

Researchers point out that when communication and interaction are marked by one-upmanship, bickering and bad feelings almost always follow. Because of this, working couples need to talk about their competitive feelings openly with one another. Comparisons between them are natural and expected. Angry competition and the unhappy feelings it arouses are not. Experts recommend that working couples should try not to view each other's professional gain as a personal loss. Being allies rather than adversaries will often turn a threat to a relationship into an opportunity for growth.

Further Reading. Denmark, Florence L., and Michele A. Paludi. (Eds.). (1993). *Psychology of women: A handbook of issues and theories.* Westport, CT: Greenwood Press; Googins, Bradley K. (1991). *Work/family conflicts: Private lives, public responses.* Westport, CT: Auburn House; Jacobs, Jerry. (1994). *Professional women at work.* Westport, CT: Bergin and Garvey; Kelly, Rita M. (1991). *The gendered economy: Work, careers, and success.* Newbury Park, CA: Sage.

WOMEN, EMPLOYMENT DISCRIMINATION AGAINST. Employment discrimination refers to the unfair and unequal treatment of a person on the basis of her or his sex. Women are the most frequent targets of employment discrimination. In 1964, Title VII of the Civil Rights Act prohibited discrimination in private employment on the basis of sex as well as of race, color, religion, and national origin. In 1971, the Supreme Court ruled that unequal treatment based on sex violates the Fourteenth Amendment to the U.S. Constitution, which mandates equal protection of all citizens.

Unfortunately, the most comprehensive statement of the equality of the sexes before the law, the Equal Rights Amendment (ERA), is still far from becoming a part of the Constitution. First introduced into Congress in 1923, this amendment was finally passed by both the Senate and the House of Representatives in 1972 and, with a seven-year deadline for ratification attached to it, was sent to the states for their action. As 1979 approached, an insufficient number of states had ratified the amendment, and an extension of time was granted in response to the lobbying efforts of women's groups. However, by the extended deadline of June 1982, only 35 of the required 38 states (three-fourths of all states must ratify a constitutional amendment) had ratified the ERA.

Thus we are back at square one. The ERA has been reintroduced into every session of Congress since 1982, but no body of Congress has passed it for a second time. When both the Senate and the House have again voted in favor of the amendment, each by the required two-thirds majority, it will again go the states for ratification. To date, the ERA has been mired in the legislative process for over 70 years.

Let us examine sex inequality and discrimination in the work force a bit more closely. A century and a half ago, women were excluded from all paying occupations of any significance. They could not vote or hold public office, and married women could not make contracts or hold property. Despite the fact that growing numbers of women are entering the labor force today, many are still confined to low-status occupations. Women continue to be a minority in professional and skilled careers, especially managerial positions. The majority of women who work in office settings today handle secretarial and clerical chores, while the more prestigious and better-paying executive positions are held mostly by men. This unequal treatment extends even to such areas as access to credit and obtaining insurance at reasonable rates.

Consider some occupational groupings. Most physicians, dentists, and lawyers are men, whereas most secretaries, nurses, schoolteachers, and librarians are women. Few women work in construction or engineering, although their representation in such nontraditional jobs has been increasing from the negligible levels of a decade ago. The number of women holding political office has also gone up in recent years, but remains disappointingly small. As experts point out, the greater a job's income and prestige, the more likely it is that that position will be male dominated.

Worse, even when they occupy the same jobs as men, women receive substantially lower salaries. The clustering of women in low-paying jobs is the largest factor accounting for this pay discrepancy, but even women with college degrees tend to earn less than men who have only high-school diplomas. To illustrate, a college-educated woman between the ages of 18 and 24 earns an average of 92 cents for every dollar earned by a man of the same age and education. Her earnings relative to those of men drop steadily with age, and by the time she is between ages 55 and 64, the average female worker is making about 54 cents for every dollar earned by a man. Retirement benefits are also far lower for women. In 1994, retired female workers averaged 78 cents for every dollar paid to retired male workers.

As earlier indicated, Title VII of the Civil Rights Act of 1964 prohibits sex discrimination in the workplace. This is the principal law that protects workers from sexual inequality because it prohibits discrimination in recruitment, testing, referrals, hiring, wages, promotion, and fringe benefits. The Equal Employment Opportunity Commission (EEOC), which has the primary responsibility for enforcing Title VII, has published guidelines on sex discrimination making it a violation of Title VII to refuse to hire any individual on the basis of stereotyped characteristics of the sexes. It is also a violation to base employment decisions on the preferences of coworkers, the employer, clients, or customers. An employer cannot label a job a "man's job" or a "woman's job" or indicate a preference or limitation based on sex in a help-wanted advertisement unless gender is a bona fide occupational qualification for the job (which it rarely is).

Further Reading. Haas, Linda. (1990). Gender equality and social policy. *Journal of Family Issues, 11,* 401–423; Kelly, Rita M. (1991). *The gendered economy: Work, careers, and success.* Newbury Park, CA: Sage; Mason, Mary A. (1991). Equal rights fails American mothers: The limitations of an equal rights strategy in family law and in the workplace. *International Journal of Law and the Family, 5,* 211–240.

WOMEN, SEXUAL HARASSMENT AND. Sexual harassment refers to any unwanted sexual advance, verbal or physical, that occurs in the workplace or in an academic setting. Sexual harassment is a sexually oriented practice that undermines job performance (including that of a student) and threatens one's economic livelihood. Women are the most frequent targets of sexual harassment. While sexual harassment can and does occur with men, research indicates that males are more tolerant of it. Anytime unwelcome sexual conduct creates an intimidating or hostile environment and an inappropriate use of power, sexual harassment has occurred. In extreme or coercive forms of harassment, a person is forced to comply sexually or else lose some occupational or academic benefit. Less obvious harassment takes the form of sexual innuendoes and comments and sometimes inappropriate touching. All forms of sexual harassment are exploitive and make the work or academic environment either uncomfortable or intolerable.

Sexual harassment is widespread in the workplace. Sexual harassment received national attention in 1991 when University of Oklahoma law professor Anita Hill leveled charges against then U.S. Supreme Court nominee Clarence Thomas during his confirmation hearings. Hill appeared before the Senate Judiciary Committee and maintained that she had been sexually harassed by Thomas when she worked for him a decade earlier at the Education Department and the Equal Employment Opportunity Commission. She claimed that Thomas made unwanted sexual advances to her, as well as obscene and lewd remarks. Thomas, who denied the allegations, was not formally charged with sexual harassment. He was later confirmed to the Supreme Court.

Also in 1991, a highly publicized case known as the Tailhook incident raised the public's awareness of sexual harassment. At a meeting of the Tailhook Association of Navy and Marine Corps aviators in Las Vegas, male officers sexually assaulted at least 26 women, including 14 of their fellow officers. The assault victims made their complaints public, leading to a period of intense military self-examination. Three admirals were eventually removed from office for failing to aggressively investigate the Tailhook incident. Further, the House Armed Services Committee reported that personnel must learn to recognize and cease harassing behavior, and the military must create a well-defined system for reporting incidents of harassment.

Until ten years ago, sexual harassment in the occupational world was defined narrowly by the courts. To win a case, the accuser had to prove that someone in a position to hire, fire, or promote asked for sexual favors as a condition of employment or promotion. It is now recognized, however, that sexual harassment can take many subtle forms and that even mild harassment can seriously jeopardize an employee's position in the workplace. By the early 1980s, the Equal Employment Opportunity Commission (EEOC) and some federal appellate courts began to recognize these subtler conditions as forms of harassment. In 1986, the U.S. Supreme Court ruled that "a hostile or abusive work environment violates the law,'' confirming for the first time that the very atmosphere in some offices may be abusive enough to violate people's civil rights.

There are many reactions to sexual harassment. Fending off unsolicited and offensive sexual advances on a regular basis often causes tension, anxiety, frustration, and anger. Most persons find that their job performance suffers as they are forced to take time and energy away from work to deal with sexual harassers. The anger they feel at this unjust treatment is often internalized as a deep sense of guilt. Society wrongly views sexual harassment as sexually motivated. Women, especially, are socialized to think that it is their responsibility to control sexual matters. When they are unable to do so, many believe that it is due to some shortcoming on their part.

Tension and anxiety can also accompany a person's refusal to comply with the harasser's demands. Many victims fear loss of job status and pay. Work-related reprisals create stressful states, such as those accompanying poor work assignments; sabotaging of projects; denial of raises, benefits, or promotion; and sometimes the loss of the job with only a poor reference to show for it. Anxiety originating from harassment can drive women out of a particular job or out of the workplace altogether.

If the latter is the case, women are not the only ones who suffer. Organizations do, too, because they lose the energy and creativity of capable female workers. Organizations may also be hampered in fulfilling their affirmative action programs. Women may be hired into traditionally male jobs, but unless the employer sees to it that they work in a harassment-free environment, they may leave at the first opportunity. Finally, it was indicated earlier that EEOC regulations make employers responsible for sexual harassment. Because of this, the number of cases is likely to rise dramatically. Thus there are both internal and external pressures on organizations today to be concerned with sexual harassment and to try to eliminate it.

Further Reading. Bingham, Shereen G. (Ed.). (1994). *Conceptualizing sexual harassment as discursive practice.* Westport, CT: Praeger; Cohen, Lloyd R. (1991). Sexual harassment and the law. *Society, 28,* 8–13; Connell, Dana S. (1991). Effective sexual harassment policies. *Employee Relations Law Journal, 17,* 191–206; Kaplan, Sally J. (1991). Consequences of sexual harassment in the workplace. *Affilia, 6,* 50–65.

WORK RELATIONSHIPS. See EARLY ADULTHOOD, WORK RELATIONSHIPS DURING; LATE ADULTHOOD, WORK RELATIONSHIPS DURING; MIDDLE ADULTHOOD, WORK RELATIONSHIPS DURING.

WORLD VIEWS OF LIFESPAN DEVELOPMENT. World views of lifespan development are philosophical assumptions about how people develop. In a broad sense, world views are beliefs about behavioral structure and functioning. They are important in the scientific study of lifespan development because they describe how a specific developmental process is thought to occur and how such a process is organized.

In this sense, world views supply the bedrock on which theories in lifespan development rest. While they cannot really be tested or evaluated in terms of whether they are correct, they are instrumental in shaping the theoretical viewpoints we use to interpret facts. The major world views are the mechanistic, organismic, and contextual models. The following is an overview of these three models.

The mechanistic model. The mechanistic model, rooted in the models of physics developed by Isaac Newton, regards humans as highly complex machines. Humans are composed of many separate parts, each of which is interrelated with the others. Consequently, the whole is equal to the sum of the parts. Going a step further, the machine is inherently at rest and inactive unless some force external to the machine is applied. Related to human development, individuals are thus viewed as being passive (or reactive), whereas the environment is considered relatively active. Moreover, change is quantitative rather than qualitative.

The organismic model. Compared to the mechanistic model, the organismic model views humans as dynamic and active participants in their surroundings, not passive observers. Also, the organism is not equal to the sum of its parts; instead, the whole is considered equal to more than the sum of the parts. Indeed, it is argued that the whole gives the parts unique meaning. The parts of the organism only have meaning when they are examined in the context of the system of which they are a part. Development is thus seen as a process emerging from self-initiated activities, and regularities in behavior are examined so that the wholeness or integrated nature of the organism can be understood.

The contextual model. The contextual model views the individual and the social environment as reciprocal and mutually influential, acting upon one another in dynamic interaction. More specifically, this model emphasizes the role of society, culture, and family, as well as the historical period in which the person develops. In this fashion, behavior only has meaning in a context, and development is seen as a continuing, adaptive, lifelong process. The contextual model reflects features of both the mechanistic and organismic models. It is mechanistic since it is concerned with the influence of the environment on the person, and it is organismic because it views development as a manifestation of organism-environmental interaction and searches for universal developmental principles. However, unlike mechanism and organicism, contextualism embraces a conception of reality that is open, dynamic, and teleological.

Further Reading. Baltes, Paul B. (1987). Theoretical propositions of lifespan developmental psychology: On the dynamics between growth and decline. *Developmental Psychology, 23,* 611–626; Birren, James E. (1988). A contribution to the theory of aging. In James E. Birren and Vern L. Bengtson (Eds.), *Emergent theories of aging.* New York: Springer; Lerner, Richard M. (1986). *Concepts and theories of human development* (2nd Ed.). New York: McGraw-Hill.

APPENDIX: SELECTED PROFESSIONAL JOURNALS AND ORGANIZATIONS

The following resource is designed for those readers seeking the names and addresses of professional research journals as well as those organizations supplying continuing sources of information. The over 100 journals and 65 organizations listed are drawn from a variety of disciplines, and their focus reflects many different aspects of relationships across the lifespan.

PROFESSIONAL JOURNALS

Adolescence
  Libra Publishers
  3089C Clairemont Drive, Suite 383
  San Diego, CA 92117

American Anthropologist
  4350 North Fairfax Drive, Suite 640
  Arlington, VA 22203

American Behavioral Scientist
  Sage Publications
  2455 Teller Rd.
  Thousand Oaks, CA 91320

*American Journal of Community
  Psychology*
  Plenum Publication Corporation
  233 Spring St.
  New York, NY 10013-1578

American Journal of Family Therapy
  19 Union Square West
  New York, NY 10003

Archives of Sexual Behavior
  Plenum Publication Corporation
  233 Spring St.
  New York, NY 10013-1578

*Australian and New Zealand Journal of
  Family Therapy*
  Family Therapists of Australia
  P. O. Box 633
  Lane Cove NSW, Australia 2066

*Australian Journal of Marriage and
  Family*
  P. O. Box 143
  Concord NSW, Australia 2137

Basic and Applied Social Psychology
Lawrence Erlbaum Associates
365 Broadway
Hillsdale, NJ 07642

Behavior Modification
Sage Publications
2455 Teller Rd.
Thousand Oaks, CA 91320

British Journal of Developmental Psychology
13A Church Lane
East Finchley, London N2 8DX
United Kingdom

British Journal of Social Psychology
13A Church Lane
East Finchley, London N2 8DX
United Kingdom

British Journal of Social Work
Cambridge University Press
Edinburgh Building
Shaftesbury Rd.
Cambridge CB2RU
United Kingdom

Canadian Journal of Sociology
Department of Sociology
University of Alberta
Edmonton, Alberta, Canada T6G 2H4

Child Abuse and Neglect
Pergamon Press
Maxwell House, Fairview Park
Elmsford, NY 10523

Child and Family Behavior Therapy
Haworth Press
10 Alice St.
Binghamton, NY 13904-1580

Child and Youth Care Forum
Child Welfare League of America
440 First St. NW #310
Washington, DC 20001

Child Development
University of Chicago Press
Journals Division / P.O. Box 37005
Chicago, IL 60637

Child Psychiatry and Human Development
Human Sciences Press
233 Spring St.
New York, NY 10013-1578

Child Welfare
Child Welfare League of America
440 First St. NW #310
Washington, DC 20001

Children and Youth Services Review
Pergamon Press
Maxwell House, Fairview Park
Elmsford, NY 10523

Clinical Gerontologist
Haworth Press
10 Alice St.
Binghamton, NY 13904-1580

Clinical Nursing Research
Sage Publications
2455 Teller Rd.
Thousand Oaks, CA 91320

Cognitive Development
Ablex Publishing Corporation
355 Chestnut St.
Norwood, NJ 07648

Communication Monographs
Speech Communication Association
5105 Blacklick Rd.
Annandale, VA 22003

Communication Research
Sage Publications
2455 Teller Rd.
Thousand Oaks, CA 91320

Community Alternatives
Human Service Associates
336 North Robert St., Suite 1520
St. Paul, MN 55101-1507

Contemporary Family Therapy
Human Sciences Press
233 Spring St.
New York, NY 10013-1578

Development and Psychopathology
    Cambridge University Press
    40 W. 20th St.
    New York, NY 10011

Developmental Psychobiology
    John Wiley and Sons
    605 Third Ave.
    New York, NY 10158

Developmental Psychology
    American Psychological Association
    1400 North Uhle St.
    Arlington, VA 22201

Developmental Review
    Academic Press
    1250 Sixth Ave.
    San Diego, CA 92101

Early Childhood Research Quarterly
    Ablex Publishing Corporation
    355 Chestnut St.
    Norwood, NJ 07648

Families in Society
    Family Services of America
    11700 West Lake Park Drive
    Milwaukee, WI 53224

Family and Conciliation Courts Review
    Sage Publications
    2455 Teller Rd.
    Thousand Oaks, CA 91320

Family Process
    29 Walter Hammond Place, Suite A
    Waldwick, NJ 07463

Family Relations
    National Council on Family
    Relations
    3989 Central Ave. NE, Suite 550
    Minneapolis, MN 55421

Feminism and Psychology
    Sage Publications
    6 Bonhill St.
    London EC2A 4PU
    United Kingdom

Gender and Society
    Sage Publications

2455 Teller Rd.
Thousand Oaks, CA 91320

Infant Behavior and Development
    Ablex Publishing Corporation
    355 Chestnut St.
    Norwood, NJ 07648

Infant-Child Intervention
    Singular Publishing Group
    4284 41st St.
    San Diego, CA 92105

Infant Mental Health Journal
    Clinical Psychology Publishing
    Company
    4 Conant Square
    Brandon, VT 05733

*International Journal of Behavioral
    Development*
    Lawrence Erlbaum Associates
    27 Palmeira Mansions Church Rd.
    Hove East Sussex BN3 2FA
    United Kingdom

*International Journal of Law and the
    Family*
    Oxford University Press
    Walton St.
    Oxford OX2 6DP
    United Kingdom

Journal for the Theory of Social Behavior
    Basil Blackwell
    Journals Department
    Box 1320 Murray Hill Station
    New York, NY 10156

Journal of Adolescent Research
    Sage Publications
    2455 Teller Rd.
    Thousand Oaks, CA 91320

Journal of Aging and Health
    Sage Publications
    2455 Teller Rd.
    Thousand Oaks, CA 91320

Journal of Aging and Social Policy
Haworth Press
10 Alice St.
Binghamton, NY 13904-1580

Journal of Aging Studies
55 Old Post Rd./#2 Box 1678
Greenwich, CT 06836-1678

Journal of Applied Gerontology
Sage Publications
2455 Teller Rd.
Thousand Oaks, CA 91320

Journal of Applied Social Psychology
V. H. Winston and Sons
7961 Eastern Ave.
Silver Spring, MD 20910

Journal of Child and Adolescent Group Therapy
Human Sciences Press
233 Spring St.
New York, NY 10013-1578

Journal of Child and Family Studies
Human Sciences Press
233 Spring St.
New York, NY 10013-1578

Journal of Child Language
32 East 57th St.
New York, NY 10022

Journal of Child Sexual Abuse
Haworth Press
10 Alice St.
Binghamton, NY 13904-1580

Journal of Clinical Child Psychology
Lawrence Erlbaum Associates
365 Broadway
Hillsdale, NJ 07642

Journal of Clinical Psychology
Clinical Psychology Publishing Company
4 Conant Square
Brandon, VT 05733

Journal of Cross-cultural Psychology
Sage Publications
2455 Teller Rd.
Thousand Oaks, CA 91320

Journal of Divorce and Remarriage
Haworth Press
10 Alice St.
Binghamton, NY 13904-1580

Journal of Early Adolescence
Sage Publications
2455 Teller Rd.
Thousand Oaks, CA 91320

Journal of Elder Abuse and Neglect
Haworth Press
10 Alice St.
Binghamton, NY 13904-1580

Journal of Experimental Social Psychology
Academic Press
1250 Sixth Ave.
San Diego, CA 92101

Journal of Family Issues
Sage Publications
2455 Teller Rd.
Thousand Oaks, CA 91320

Journal of Family Psychotherapy
Haworth Press
10 Alice St.
Binghamton, NY 13904-1580

Journal of Family Therapy
Academic Press
24-28 Oval Rd.
London NW1 7DX
United Kingdom

Journal of Family Violence
Plenum Publication Corporation
233 Spring St.
New York, NY 10013-1578

Journal of Feminist Family Therapy
Haworth Press
10 Alice St.
Binghamton, NY 13904

Journal of Gay and Lesbian Psychotherapy
Haworth Press
10 Alice St.
Binghamton, NY 13904-1580

*Journal of Gay and Lesbian Social
   Services*
   Haworth Press
   10 Alice St.
   Binghamton, NY 13904-1580

Journal of Gerontological Social Work
   Haworth Press
   10 Alice St.
   Binghamton, NY 13904-1580

Journal of Health and Social Policy
   Haworth Press
   10 Alice St.
   Binghamton, NY 13904-1580

Journal of Homosexuality
   Haworth Press
   10 Alice St.
   Binghamton, NY 13904-1580

Journal of Humanistic Psychology
   Sage Publications
   2455 Teller Rd.
   Thousand Oaks, CA 91320

Journal of Interpersonal Violence
   Sage Publications
   2455 Teller Rd.
   Thousand Oaks, CA 91320

Journal of Marital and Family Therapy
   American Association for Marriage
   and Family Therapy
   1100 Seventeenth St., NW
   Washington, DC 20036

Journal of Marriage and the Family
   National Council on Family
   Relations
   3989 Central Ave. NE, Suite 550
   Minneapolis, MN 55421

Journal of Men's Studies
   Men's Study Press
   P.O. Box 32
   Harriman, TN 37748-0032

Journal of Mental Health Counseling
   Sage Publications
   2455 Teller Rd.
   Thousand Oaks, CA 91320

Journal of Pediatric Psychology
   Plenum Publication Corporation
   233 Spring St.
   New York, NY 10013-1578

*Journal of Personality and Social
   Psychology*
   American Psychological Association
   1200 Seventeenth St. NW
   Washington, DC 20036

*Journal of Psychology and Human
   Sexuality*
   Haworth Press
   10 Alice St.
   Binghamton, NY 13904

Journal of Sex and Marital Therapy
   Brunner/Mazel Publishers
   19 Union Square
   New York, NY 10003

Journal of Sex Research
   Society for the Scientific Study of
   Sex
   P.O. Box 208
   Mount Vernon, IA 52314

*Journal of Social and Clinical
   Psychology*
   Guilford Publications
   72 Spring St.
   New York, NY 10012

*Journal of Social and Personal
   Relationships*
   Sage Publications
   6 Bonhill St.
   London EC2A 4PU
   United Kingdom

Journal of Social Issues
   Plenum Publication Corporation
   233 Spring St.
   New York, NY 10013-1578

Journal of Social Psychology
   Heldref Publications
   4000 Albemarle St. NW
   Washington, DC 20016

Journal of Women and Aging
Haworth Press
10 Alice St.
Binghamton, NY 13904-1580

Journal of Youth and Adolescence
Plenum Publication Corporation
233 Spring St.
New York, NY 10013-1578

Marriage and Family Review
Haworth Press
10 Alice St.
Binghamton, NY 13904-1580

Monographs of the Society for Research in Child Development
University of Chicago Press
Journals Division/P.O. Box 37005
Chicago, IL 60637

Personality and Social Psychology Bulletin
Sage Publications
2455 Teller Rd.
Thousand Oaks, CA 91320

Population and Development Review
Center for Policy Studies of the
Population Council
One Dag Hammarskjold Plaza
New York, NY 10017

Pre- and Perinatal Journal
Human Sciences Press
233 Spring St.
New York, NY 10013-1578

Psychology and Aging
American Psychological Association
1400 North Uhle St.
Arlington, VA 22201

Psychology of Women Quarterly
Cambridge University Press
40 W. 20th St.
New York, NY 10011

Research on Aging
Sage Publications
2455 Teller Rd.
Thousand Oaks, CA 91320

Research on Social Work Practice
Sage Publications
2455 Teller Rd.
Thousand Oaks, CA 91320

Sex Roles
Plenum Publication Corporation
233 Spring St.
New York, NY 10013-1578

Sexual and Marital Therapy
Carfax Publishing Company
Oxfordshire OX14 3UE
United Kingdom

Sexuality and Disability
Human Sciences Press
233 Spring St.
New York, NY 10013-1578

Social Cognition
Guilford Publications
72 Spring St.
New York, NY 10012

Social Forces
University of North Carolina Press
P.O. Box 2288
Chapel Hill, NC 27514

Social Problems
University of California Press
Journals Division
2120 South Berkeley Way
Berkeley, CA 94720

Studies in Family Planning
Population Council
One Dag Hammarskjold Plaza
New York, NY 10017

Work and Occupations
Sage Publications
2455 Teller Rd.
Thousand Oaks, CA 91320

Youth and Society
Sage Publications
2455 Teller Rd.
Thousand Oaks, CA 91320

PROFESSIONAL ORGANIZATIONS

Adulthood and Aging

Administration on Aging
  U.S. Department of Health and
  Human Services
  Washington, DC 20202

American Association of Retired Persons
  1909 K St. NW
  Washington, DC 20049

American Nursing Home Association
  1101 Seventeenth St. NW
  Washington, DC 20036

Gray Panthers
  3635 Chestnut St.
  Philadelphia, PA 19104

National Association of Area Agencies on
  Aging
  Suite 208 West
  600 Maryland Ave. SW
  Washington, DC 20024

National Council of Senior Citizens
  925 Fifteenth St. NW
  Washington, DC 20005

National Council on Aging
  West Wing 100
  600 Maryland Ave. SW
  Washington, DC 20024

National Institute on Aging
  Building 31, Room 5C35
  Bethesda, MD 20892

National Support Center for Families of
  the Aging
  P.O. Box 245
  Swarthmore, PA 19081

Older Women's League
  Lower Level B

1325 G St. NW
Washington, DC 20005

AIDS and Other STD Information

American Red Cross AIDS Education
  Office
  1750 K St. NW
  Washington, DC 20006

Division of Sexually Transmitted
  Diseases
  Centers for Disease Control
  Atlanta, GA 30333

Herpes Resource Center
  260 Sheridan Ave.
  Palo Alto, CA 94306

National AIDS Information Clearinghouse
  Education Database Distribution
  1600 Research Blvd.
  Rockville, MD 20850

National Association of People with
  AIDS
  1413 K St. NW, 7th Floor
  Washington, DC 20005

Caring for Aging Parents

Caring Children of Aging Parents
  4835 E. Anaheim St.
  Long Beach, CA 90804

Children of Aging Parents
  2761 Trenton St.
  Levittown, PA 19056

Family Services of America
  44 E. 23rd St.
  New York, NY 10010

National Support Center for Families of
  the Aging
  P.O. Box 245
  Swarthmore, PA 19081

Childhood and Adolescence

American Academy of Pediatrics
 1801 Hinman Ave.
 Evanston, IL 60204

American Psychological Association
 Division of Developmental
 Psychology
 1200 Seventeenth St. NW
 Washington, DC 20036-1426

Child Study Association of America
 50 Madison Ave.
 New York, NY 10010

Committee for Children
 P.O. Box 15190
 Seattle, WA 98115

National Institute of Child Health and
 Human Development
 U.S. Public Health Service
 9000 Rockville Pike
 Bethesda, MD 20014

Conception and Contraception

American Fertility Society
 1608 13th Ave. South, Suite 10
 Birmingham, AL 35205

American Society for Psychoprophylaxis
 in Obstetrics
 1523 L St. NW
 Washington, DC 20005

International Childbirth Education
 Association
 P.O. Box 20048
 Milwaukee, WI 55420

National Clearinghouse for Family
 Planning Information
 P.O. Box 2225
 Rockville, MD 20852

Planned Parenthood Federation of
 America
 810 Seventh Ave.
 New York, NY 10013

Divorce Mediation

Academy of Family Mediators
 111 4th Ave.
 New York, NY 10012

American Arbitration Association
 140 S. 51st St.
 New York, NY 10020

Family Mediation Association
 9308 Bull Run Parkway
 Bethesda, MD 20034

Domestic Abuse Prevention

Department of Health and Human
 Services
 Office of Domestic Violence
 P.O. Box 1182
 Washington, DC 20013

Family Violence Research Program
 Sociology Department
 University of New Hampshire
 Durham, NH 03824

National Coalition Against Domestic
 Violence
 1728 N Street NW
 Washington, DC 20036

National Committee for Prevention of
 Child Abuse
 332 S. Michigan Ave., Suite 1250
 Chicago, IL 60604-4357

Gay and Lesbian Relationships

National Gay and Lesbian Task Force
 1517 U St. NW
 Washington, DC 20009

National Lesbian and Gay Health
Foundation
P.O. Box 65472
Washington, DC 20035

Parents and Friends of Lesbians and Gays
P.O. Box 27605, Central Station
Washington, DC 20038

Parenting Issues

Parents Anonymous
22330 Hawthorne Blvd., Suite 208
Torrance, CA 90505

Parents without Partners
7910 Woodmont Ave.
Washington, DC 20014

Single Mothers by Choice
501 12th St.
Brooklyn, NY 11215

Stepfamily Association of America
28 Allegheny Ave., Suite 1307
Baltimore, MD 21204

Population Issues

Population Association of America
1429 Duke St.
Alexandria, VA 22314-3402

Population Council
One Dag Hammarskjold Plaza
New York, NY 10017

Population Reference Bureau
777 14th St. NW, Suite 800
Washington, DC 20005

Sexual Abuse and Coercion

Clearinghouse on Child Abuse and
Neglect Information
P.O. Box 1182
Washington, DC 20013

National Clearinghouse on Domestic
Violence
P.O. Box 2309
Rockville, MD 20852

National Rape Information Clearinghouse
5600 Fishers Lane
Rockville, MD 20857

Working Women's Institute
539 Park Ave.
New York, NY 10021

Sexuality Education

American Association of Sex Educators,
Counselors, and Therapists
435 N. Michigan Ave., Suite 1717
Chicago, IL 60611-4067

Sex Information and Education Council
of the United States
80 Fifth Ave., Suite 801
New York, NY 10011

Society for the Scientific Study of Sex
P.O. Box 208
Mount Vernon, IA 52314

Sources of Statistical Information

National Institute of Mental Health
5600 Fishers Lane
Rockville, MD 20857

Research Institute of America
589 Fifth Ave.
New York, NY 10017

U.S. Bureau of the Census
Superintendent of Documents
U.S. Government Printing Office
Washington, DC 20402

World Bank
1818 H St. NW
Washington, DC 20433

Therapeutic Intervention

American Association for Marriage and
  Family Therapy
  1717 K St. NW, Suite 407
  Washington, DC 20006

American Association of Marriage and
  Family Counselors
  255 Yale Ave.
  Claremont, CA 91711

American Association of Sex Educators,
  Counselors, and Therapists
  435 N. Michigan Ave., Suite 1717
  Chicago, IL 60611-4067

American Institute of Family Relations
  5287 Sunset Blvd.
  Los Angeles, CA 90027

American Psychiatric Association
  1400 K St. NW
  Washington, DC 20036

American Psychological Association
  1200 Seventeenth St. NW
  Washington, DC 20036

Association for Family Living
  33 West Randolph St., Suite 1818
  Chicago, IL 60601

Association of Gay and Lesbian
  Psychotherapists
  90 Chandler St.
  Boston, MA 02116

Association of Sexologists
  1523 Franklin St.
  San Francisco, CA 94109

Widowhood

Older Women's League
  1325 G St. NW
  Washington, DC 20005

Widow-to-Widow Program
  Department of Psychiatry
  Harvard University Medical
  Center
  Cambridge, MA 02138

Widowed Persons Service
  1909 K St. NW
  Washington, DC 20049

SELECTED BIBLIOGRAPHY

The following bibliography is designed to supplement the volume's existing references. The sources are drawn from a wide assortment of articles, research studies, and books and were chosen on the basis of subject matter as well as overall relevancy. It is hoped that the further investigation of these sources will provide the reader with even greater insight into and knowledge of relationships across the lifespan.

Acock, Alan C., and David H. Demo. (1994). *Family diversity and well-being.* Thousand Oaks, CA: Sage.

Adelmann, Pamela K., Toni C. Antonucci, and James S. Jackson. (1993). Retired or homemaker: How older women define their roles. *Journal of Women and Aging, 5,* 67–78.

Aiken, Lewis R. (1995). *Aging: An introduction to gerontology.* Thousand Oaks, CA: Sage.

Alexander, Renata. (1993). Wife-battering: An Australian perspective. *Journal of Family Violence, 8,* 229–251.

Alva, Sylvia Alatorre. (1993). Differential patterns of achievement among Asian-American adolescents. *Journal of Youth and Adolescence, 22,* 407–423.

Ambert, Anne-Marie. (1994). A qualitative study of peer abuse and its effects: Theoretical and empirical implications. *Journal of Marriage and the Family, 56,* 119–130.

Anderson, Elaine A., and Jane W. Spruill. (1993). The dual-career commuter family: A lifestyle on the move. *Marriage and Family Review, 19,* 131–147.

Andre, Thomas, and Lynda L. Lamport. (1993). AIDS knowledge and sexual responsibility. *Youth and Society, 25,* 38–61.

Angel, Ronald J., and Jacqueline L. Angel. (1993). *Painful inheritance: Health and the new generation of fatherless families.* Madison: University of Wisconsin Press.

Aponte, Robert. (1993). Hispanic families in poverty: Diversity, context, and interpreta-
    tion. *Families in Society, 74,* 527–537.
Archer, Sally L. (Ed.). (1994). *Interventions for adolescent identity development.* Thou-
    sand Oaks, CA: Sage.
Arcus, Margaret E., Jay D. Schvaneveldt, and J. Joel Moss. (Eds.). (1993). *Handbook of
    family life education.* Thousand Oaks, CA: Sage.
Atwood, Joan. (1993). AIDS in African American and Hispanic adolescents: A multi-
    systemic approach. *American Journal of Family Therapy, 21,* 333–351.
Bank, Barbara J. (1994). Effects of national, school, and gender cultures on friendships
    among adolescents in Australia and the United States. *Youth and Society, 25,* 435–
    456.
Bartlett, Jane. (1995). *Will you be mother? Women who choose to say no.* New York:
    New York University Press.
Beller, Andrea H., and John W. Graham. (1993). *Small change: The economics of child
    support.* New Haven, CT: Yale University Press.
Bertoia, Carl, and Janice Drakich. (1993). The fathers' rights movement: Contradictions
    in rhetoric and practice. *Journal of Family Issues, 14,* 592–615.
Biller, Henry B. (1993). *Fathers and families: Paternal factors in child development.*
    Westport, CT: Auburn House.
Boyd-Franklin, Nancy, Gloria L. Steiner, and Mary G. Boland. (1995). *Children, families,
    and HIV/AIDS.* New York: Guilford Press.
Boyes, Michael C., and Sandra G. Allen. (1993). Styles of parent-child interaction and
    moral reasoning in adolescence. *Merrill-Palmer Quarterly, 39,* 551–570.
Brewster, Karin L., John O. Billy, and William R. Grady. (1993). Social context and
    adolescent behavior: The impact of community on the transition to sexual activity.
    Social Forces, 71, 713–740.
Broman, Clifford L. (1993). Race differences in marital well-being. *Journal of Marriage
    and the Family, 55,* 724–732.
————. (1993). Parenting behavior and children's social, psychological, and academic
    adjustment in diverse family structures. *Family Relations, 42,* 268–276.
Burns, Ailsa, and Cath Scott. (1994). *Mother-headed families and why they have in-
    creased.* Hillsdale, NJ: Erlbaum.
Burr, Wesley R., and Shirley R. Klein. (1994). *Reexamining family stress: New theory
    and research.* Thousand Oaks, CA: Sage.
Card, Josefina J. (Ed.). (1993) *Handbook of adolescent sexuality and pregnancy: Re-
    search and evaluation instruments.* Newbury Park, CA: Sage.
Chow, Nelson. (1993). The changing responsibilities of the state and family towards
    elders in Hong Kong. *Journal of Aging and Social Policy, 5,* 111–126.
Christensen, Kathleen. (1993). Eliminating the journey to work: Home-based work across
    the life course of women in the United States. In Cindi Katz and Janice Monk
    (Eds.), *Full circles: Geographies of women over the life course.* New York: Rout-
    ledge.
Christopher, F. Scott, Diane C. Johnson, and Mark W. Roosa. (1993). Family, individual,
    and social correlates of early Hispanic adolescent sexual expression. *Journal of
    Sex Research, 30,* 54–61.
Cicirelli, Victor G. (1994). Sibling relationships in cross-cultural perspective. *Journal of
    Marriage and the Family, 56,* 7–20.

Clulow, Christopher. (1993). New families? Changes in societies and family relationships. *Sexual and Marital Therapy, 8,* 269–274.

Collins, Randall, and Scott Coltrane. (1995). *Sociology of marriage and the family* (4th Ed.). Chicago: Nelson-Hall.

Collins, W. Andrew, and Daniel J. Repinski. (1994). Relationships during adolescence: Continuity and change in interpersonal perspective. In Raymond Montemayor, Gerald R. Adams, and Thomas P. Gullotta (Eds.), *Personal relationships during adolescence.* Thousand Oaks, CA: Sage.

Colpin, Hilde. (1994). Parents and children of reproductive technology: Chances and risks for their well-being. *Community Alternatives, 6,* 49–71.

Conway-Turner, Katherine, and Rona Karasik. (1993). Adult daughters' anticipation of care-giving responsibilities. *Journal of Women and Aging, 5,* 99–114.

Cooper, Catherine R. (1994). Cultural perspectives on continuity and change in adolescents' relationships. In Raymond Montemayor, Gerald R. Adams, and Thomas P. Gullotta (Eds.), *Personal relationships during adolescence.* Thousand Oaks, CA: Sage.

Coupland, Nikolas, and Justine Coupland. (1993). Discourses of ageism and anti-ageism. *Journal of Aging Studies, 7,* 279–301.

Crouter, Ann C., Susan M. McHale, and W. Todd Bartko. (1993). Gender as an organizing feature in parent-child relationships. *Journal of Social Issues, 49,* 161–174.

Cummings, E. Mark, and Patrick Davies. (1994). *Children and marital conflict: The impact of family dispute and resolution.* New York: Guilford Press.

Cunningham, John D., and John K. Antill. (1994). Cohabitation and marriage: Retrospective and predictive comparisons. *Journal of Social and Personal Relationships, 11,* 77–93.

Daly, Kerry. (1993). Reshaping fatherhood: Finding the models. *Journal of Family Issues, 14,* 510–530.

Darling, Nancy, Stephen F. Hamilton, and Starr Niego. (1994). Adolescents' relations with adults outside the family. In Raymond Montemayor, Gerald R. Adams, and Thomas P. Gullotta (Eds.), *Personal relationships during adolescence.* Thousand Oaks, CA: Sage.

Davies, Jody Messler, and Mary Gail Frawley. (1994). *Treating the adult survivor of childhood sexual abuse: A psychoanalytic perspective.* New York: Basic Books.

Davis, Deborah, and Stevan Harrell. (Eds.). (1993). *Chinese families in the post-Mao era.* Berkeley: University of California Press.

DeKeseredy, Walter, and Katharine Kelly. (1993). The incidence and prevalence of woman abuse in Canadian university and college dating relationships. *Canadian Journal of Sociology, 18,* 137–159.

DeLoache, Judy S. (Ed.). (1994). *Current readings in child development* (2nd Ed.). Boston: Allyn and Bacon.

Demo, David H., and Alan C. Acock. (1993). Family diversity and the division of domestic labor: How much have things really changed? *Family Relations, 42,* 323–331.

Denzin, Norman K., and Yvonna S. Lincoln. (Eds.). (1994). *Handbook of qualitative research.* Thousand Oaks, CA: Sage.

Deutsch, Francine M., Julianne B. Lussier, and Laura J. Servis. (1993). Husbands at home: Predictors of paternal participation in childcare and housework. *Journal of Personality and Social Psychology, 65,* 1154–1166.

Diamond, Milton. (1993). Homosexuality and bisexuality in different populations. *Archives of Sexual Behavior, 22,* 291–310.

Dickerson, Bette J. (1995). *African American single mothers: Understanding their lives and families.* Thousand Oaks, CA: Sage.

DiClemente, Ralph J. (1993). Confronting the challenge of AIDS among adolescents: Directions for future research. *Journal of Adolescent Research, 8,* 156–166.

DiLeonardi, Joan W. (1993). Families in poverty and chronic neglect of children. *Families in Society, 74,* 557–562.

Donnelly, Denise A. (1993). Sexually inactive marriages. *Journal of Sex Research, 30,* 171–179.

Dorius, Guy L., Tim B. Heaton, and Patrick Steffen. (1993). Adolescent life events and their association with the onset of sexual intercourse. *Youth and Society, 25,* 3–23.

Dowrick, Stephanie. (1994). *Intimacy and solitude: Balancing closeness and independence.* New York: Norton.

DuBois, David L., Susan K. Eitel, and Robert D. Felner. (1994). Effects of family environment and parent-child relationships on school adjustment during the transition to early adolescence. *Journal of Marriage and the Family, 56,* 405–414.

Ducharme, Francine. (1994). Conjugal support, coping behaviors, and psychological well-being of the elderly spouse. *Research on Aging, 16,* 167–190.

Duck, Steve, and Julia T. Wood. (1995). *Confronting relationship challenges.* Thousand Oaks, CA: Sage.

Dunn, Judy. (1993). *Young children's close relationships.* Newbury Park, CA: Sage.

Elliott, Stephen N., and Frank M. Gresham. (1993). Social skills interventions for children. *Behavior Modification, 17,* 287–313.

Emery, Robert E. (1994). *Renegotiating family relationships.* New York: Guilford Press.

Fincher, Ruth. (1993). Women, the state, and the life course in urban Australia. In Cindi Katz and Janice Monk (Eds.), *Full circles: Geographies of women over the life course.* New York: Routledge.

Fitness, Julie, and Garth J. O. Fletcher. (1993). Love, hate, anger, and jealousy in close relationships: A prototype and cognitive appraisal analysis. *Journal of Personality and Social Psychology, 65,* 942–958.

Ford, Kathleen, and Anne E. Norris. (1993). Urban Hispanic adolescents and young adults: Relationship of acculturation to sexual behavior. *Journal of Sex Research, 30,* 316–323.

Forehand, Rex, and Britton McKinney. (1993). Historical overview of child discipline in the United States: Implications for mental health clinicians and researchers. *Journal of Child and Family Studies, 2,* 221–228.

Freeman, Ellen W., and Karl Rickels. (1993). *Early childbearing: Perspectives of black adolescents on pregnancy, abortion, and contraception.* Newbury Park, CA: Sage.

Fullerton, Carol S., and Robert J. Ursano. (1994). Preadolescent peer friendships: A critical contribution to adult social relatedness? *Journal of Youth and Adolescence, 23,* 43–63.

Furman, Wyndol, and Elizabeth A. Wehner. (1994). Romantic views: Toward a theory of adolescent romantic relationships. In Raymond Montemayor, Gerald R. Adams, and Thomas P. Gullotta (Eds.), *Personal relationships during adolescence.* Thousand Oaks, CA: Sage.

Ganong, Lawrence H., and Marilyn Coleman. (1993). An exploratory study of stepsibling subsystems. *Journal of Divorce and Remarriage, 19,* 125–141.

————.(1994). *Remarried family relationships.* Thousand Oaks, CA: Sage.

Gelles, Richard J., and Donileen R. Loseke. (Eds.). (1993). *Current controversies on family violence.* Newbury Park, CA: Sage.

Gerald, Lynn B. (1993). Paid family caregiving: A review of progress and policies. *Journal of Aging and Social Policy, 5,* 73–90.

Gilbert, Lucia A. (1993). *Two careers, one family.* Newbury Park, CA: Sage.

Glasgow, Nina. (1993). Poverty among rural elders: Trends, context, and directions for policy. *Journal of Applied Gerontology, 12,* 302–319.

Gold, Joshua M., Donald L. Bubenzer, and John D. West. (1993). The presence of children and blended family marital intimacy. *Journal of Divorce and Remarriage, 19,* 97–108.

Gonsiorek, John C., Walter H. Bera, and Donald LeTourneau. (1994). *Male sexual abuse.* Thousand Oaks, CA: Sage.

Goodman, Aviel. (1993). Diagnosis and treatment of sexual addiction. *Journal of Sex and Marital Therapy, 19,* 225–251.

Goonesekere, Savitri. (1994). The best interests of the child: A South Asian perspective. *International Journal of Law and the Family, 8,* 117–149.

Gordon, Tuula. (1994). *Single women: On the margins?* New York: New York University Press.

Grau, Lois, Jeanne Teresi, and Barbara Chandler. (1993). Demoralization among sons, daughters, spouses, and other relatives of nursing home residents. *Research on Aging, 15,* 324–345.

Griegg, Robin. (1995). *Pregnancy in a high-tech age: Paradoxes of choice.* New York: New York University Press.

Guttman, Joseph. (1993). *Divorce in psychosocial perspective: Theory and research.* Hillsdale, NJ: Erlbaum.

Habib, Jack, Gerdt Sundstrom, and Karen Windmiller. (1993). Understanding the pattern of support for the elderly: A comparison between Israel and Sweden. *Journal of Aging and Social Policy, 5,* 187–206.

Hall, Barry L. (1993). Elderly Vietnamese immigrants: Family and community connections. *Community Alternatives, 5,* 81–96.

Hall, Liz, and Siobhan Lloyd. (1993). *Surviving child sexual abuse: A handbook for helping women challenge their past* (2nd Ed.). Washington, DC: Falmer Press.

Hare, Jan. (1994). Concerns and issues faced by families headed by a lesbian couple. *Families in Society, 75,* 27–35.

Hecht, Michael L., Peter J. Marston, and Linda Kathryn Larkey. (1994). Love ways and relationship quality in heterosexual relationships. *Journal of Social and Personal Relationships, 11,* 25–43.

Hendrick, Susan S., and Clyde Hendrick. (1993). Lovers as friends. *Journal of Social and Personal Relationships, 10,* 459–466.

Hennessy, Michael. (1994). Adolescent syndromes of risk for HIV infection. *Evaluation Review, 18,* 312–341.

Henwood, Karen L. (1993). Women and later life: The discursive construction of identities within family relationships. *Journal of Aging Studies, 7,* 303–319.

Herold, Edward S., and Dawn-Marie K. Mewhinney. (1993). Gender differences in casual sex and AIDS prevention. *Journal of Sex Research, 30,* 36–42.

Hill, Robert Bernard. (1993). *Research on the African-American family: A holistic perspective.* Westport, CT: Auburn House.

Hood, Jane C. (Ed.). (1993). *Men, work, and family.* Newbury Park, CA: Sage.

Horowitz, Ruth. (1993). The power of ritual in a Chicano community: A young woman's status and expanding family ties. *Marriage and Family Review, 19,* 257–280.

Hubbard, Julie A., and John D. Coie. (1994). Emotional correlates of social competence in children's peer relationships. *Merrill-Palmer Quarterly, 40,* 120.

Hudson, Liam, and Bernadine Jacot. (1993). *The way men think: Intellect, intimacy, and the erotic imagination.* New Haven, CT: Yale University Press.

Hughes, Fergus P. (1995). *Children, play, and development* (2nd Ed.). Boston: Allyn and Bacon.

Hurl, Josef. (1993). Eldercare policy between the state and family: Austria. *Journal of Aging and Social Policy, 5,* 155–168.

Huston, Ted L., and Gilbert Geis. (1993). In what ways do gender-related attributes and beliefs affect marriage? *Journal of Social Issues, 49,* 87–106.

Hyde, Janet Shibley, Marilyn J. Essex, and Francine Horton. (1993). Fathers and parental leave: Attitudes and experiences. *Journal of Family Issues, 14,* 616–641.

Ickes, William. (1993). Traditional gender roles: Do they make, and then break, our relationships? *Journal of Social Issues, 49,* 71–86.

Ingoldsby, Bron B., and Suzanna Smith. (Eds.). (1995). *Families in multicultural perspective.* New York: Guilford Press.

Jacobs, Jerry A. (Ed.) (1995). *Gender inequality at work.* Thousand Oaks, CA: Sage.

Jendrek, Margaret P. (1993). Grandparents who parent their grandchildren: Effects on lifestyle. *Journal of Marriage and the Family, 55,* 609–621.

Kaffman, Mordecai. (1993). Kibbutz youth: Recent past and present. *Journal of Youth and Adolescence, 22,* 573–604.

Karpel, Mark A. (1994). *Evaluating couples: A handbook for practitioners.* New York: Norton.

Kaslow, Florence. (1993). Attractions and affairs: Fabulous and fatal. *Journal of Family Psychotherapy, 4,* 1–34.

Katz, Cindi, and Janice Monk (Eds.). (1993). *Full circles: Geographies of women over the life course.* New York: Routledge.

Kayser, Karen. (1993). *When love dies: The process of marital disaffection.* New York: Guilford Press.

Kibria, Nazli. (1993). *Family tightrope: The changing lives of Vietnamese Americans.* Princeton, NJ: Princeton University Press.

Kirkpatrick, Lee A., and Keith E. Davis. (1994). Attachment style, gender, and relationship stability: A longitudinal analysis. *Journal of Personality and Social Psychology, 66,* 502–512.

Kirschner, Sam, Diana Adile Kirschner, and Richard L. Rappaport. (1993). *Working with adult incest survivors: The healing journey.* New York: Brunner/Mazel.

Klerman, Lorraine V. (1993). The relationship between adolescent parenthood and inadequate parenting. *Children and Youth Services Review, 15,* 309–320.

Konek, Carol W., and Sally L. Kitch. (Eds.). (1994). *Women and careers: Issues and challenges.* Thousand Oaks, CA: Sage.

Kouri, Kristyan, and Marcia Lasswell. (1993). Black-white marriages: Social change and intergenerational mobility. *Marriage and Family Review, 19,* 241–256.

Krull, Catherine D. (1994). Level of education, sexual promiscuity, and AIDS. *Alberta Journal of Educational Research, 40,* 7–20.

Kuehl, Bruce P. (1994). Child and family therapy: A collaborative approach. *American Journal of Family Therapy, 21,* 260–266.

Kurdek, Lawrence A. (1993). The allocation of household labor in gay, lesbian, and heterosexual married couples. *Journal of Social Issues, 49,* 127–139.

L'Abate, Luciano. (1994). *Family evaluation: A psychological approach.* Thousand Oaks, CA: Sage.

Lauritsen, Janet L. (1994). Explaining race and gender differences in adolescent sexual behavior. *Social Forces, 72,* 859–884.

Laursen, Brett. (1993). The perceived impact of conflict on adolescent relationships. *Merrill-Palmer Quarterly, 39,* 535–550.

LeJeune, Chad, and Victoria Follette. (1994). Taking responsibility: Sex differences in reporting dating violence. *Journal of Interpersonal Violence, 9,* 133–140.

Lerner, Jacqueline V. (1994). *Working women and their families.* Thousand Oaks, CA: Sage.

Lichter, Daniel T., and David J. Eggebeen. (1993). Rich kids, poor kids: Changing income inequality among American children. *Social Forces, 71,* 761–780.

Liebig, Phoebe S. (1993). The effects of federalism on policies for care of the aged in Canada and the United States. *Journal of Aging and Social Policy, 5,* 13–38.

Luckey, Irene. (1994). African American elders: The support network of generational kin. *Families in Society, 75,* 82–89.

Major, Brenda. (1993). Gender, entitlement, and the distribution of family labor. *Journal of Social Issues, 49,* 141–159.

Manning, Wendy D. (1993). Marriage and cohabitation following premarital conception. *Journal of Marriage and the Family, 55,* 839–850.

Marion, Marian. (1995). *Guidance of young children* (4th Ed.). Columbus, OH: Merrill.

Markman, Howard J. (1993). Men and women dealing with conflict in heterosexual relationships. *Journal of Social Issues, 49,* 107–125.

Marsiglio, William. (1993). Contemporary scholarship on fatherhood: Culture, identity, and conduct. *Journal of Family Issues, 14,* 484–509.

McAdoo, Harriette P. (Ed.). (1993). *Family ethnicity: Strength in diversity.* Newbury Park, CA: Sage.

McCurdy, Karen, and Deborah Daro. (1994). Child maltreatment: A national survey of reports and fatalities. *Journal of Interpersonal Violence, 9,* 75–94.

McDougall, Graham J. (1993). Therapeutic issues with gay and lesbian elders. *Clinical Gerontologist, 14,* 45–57.

McKenry, Patrick C., and Sharon J. Price. (Eds.). (1994). *Families and change: Coping with stressful events.* Thousand Oaks, CA: Sage.

McWilliams, Susan, and Judith A. Howard. (1993). Solidarity and hierarchy in cross-sex friendships. *Journal of Social Issues, 49,* 191–202.

Mendel, Matthew P. (1995). *The male survivor: The impact of sexual abuse.* Thousand Oaks, CA: Sage.

Min, Pyong G. (Ed.) (1995). *Asian Americans: Contemporary trends and issues.* Thousand Oaks, CA: Sage.

Mir-Hosseini, Ziba. (1993). *Marriage on trial: A study of Islamic family law: Iran and Morocco compared.* New York: I. B. Tauris.

Momsen, Janet. (1993). Women, work, and the life course in the rural Caribbean. In

Cindi Katz and Janice Monk (Eds.), *Full circles: Geographies of women over the life course.* New York: Routledge.

Montemayor, Raymond, Gerald R. Adams, and Thomas P. Gullotta. (Eds.). (1994). *Personal relationships during adolescence.* Thousand Oaks, CA: Sage.

Morokoff, Patricia J., and Ruth Gillilland. (1993). Stress, sexual functioning, and marital satisfaction. *Journal of Sex Research, 30,* 43–53.

Nichols, Michael P. (1995). *The lost art of listening.* New York: Guilford Press.

Nichols, William, and Mary Anne Pace-Nichols. (1993). Developmental perspectives and family therapy: The marital life cycle. *Contemporary Family Therapy, 15,* 299–315.

Niles, Florence Sushila. (1994). Sex-role attitudes among northern Australians. *Australian Journal of Marriage and Family, 15,* 23–29.

Noller, Patricia. (1994). Relationships with parents in adolescence: Process and outcome. In Raymond Montemayor, Gerald R. Adams, and Thomas P. Gullotta (Eds.), *Personal relationships during adolescence.* Thousand Oaks, CA: Sage.

Ogawa, Naohiro, and Robert D. Retherford. (1993). Care of the elderly in Japan: Changing norms and expectations. *Journal of Marriage and the Family, 55,* 585–597.

Oggins, Jean, Douglas Leber, and Joseph Veroff. (1993). Race and gender differences in black and white newlyweds' perceptions of sexual and marital relations. *Journal of Sex Research, 30,* 152–160.

Olson, Philip. (1993). Caregiving and long-term health care in the People's Republic of China. *Journal of Aging and Social Policy, 5,* 91–110.

Oppenheimer, Kim, and Joseph Frey. (1993). Family transitions and developmental processes in panic-disordered patients. *Family Process, 32,* 341–352.

Orbuch, Terri L., Joseph Veroff, and Diane Holmberg. (1993). Becoming a married couple: The emergence of meaning in the first years of marriage. *Journal of Marriage and the Family, 55,* 815–826.

Papini, Dennis R., and Lori A. Roggman. (1993). Parental attachment to early adolescents and parents' emotional and marital adjustment: A longitudinal study. *Journal of Early Adolescence, 13,* 311–328.

Paulson, Sharon E. (1994). Relations of parenting style and parental involvement with ninth-grade students' achievement. *Journal of Early Adolescence, 14,* 250–267.

Phalet, Karen, and Willem Claeys. (1993). A comparative study of Turkish and Belgian youth. *Journal of Cross-Cultural Psychology, 24,* 319–343.

Pilkonis, Paul A. (1993). Studying the effects of treatment in victims of childhood sexual abuse. *Journal of Interpersonal Violence, 8,* 392–401.

Ragin, Charles C. (1994). *Constructing social research: The unity and diversity of method.* Thousand Oaks, CA: Pine Forge Press.

Ramanathan, Chathapuram S., and Pravina N. Ramanathan. (1994). Elder care among Asian Indian families: Attitudes and satisfactions. *Community Alternatives, 6,* 93–112.

Raphael, Dennis, and Ben Schlesinger. (1994). Women in the sandwich generation: Do adult children living at home help? *Journal of Women and Aging, 6,* 21–45.

Regan, Milton C. Jr. (1993). *Family law and the pursuit of intimacy.* New York: New York University Press.

Reiss, Ira L. (1993). The future of sex research and the meaning of science. *Journal of Sex Research, 30,* 3–11.

Reskin, Barbara, and Irene Padavic. (1994). *Women and men at work.* Thousand Oaks, CA: Pine Forge Press.

Rhode, Deborah L. (1993). Adolescent pregnancy and public policy. *Political Science Quarterly, 108,* 635–669.

Ribbens, Jane. (1995). *Mothers and their children.* Thousand Oaks, CA: Sage.

Richards, Leslie N., and Cynthia J. Schmiege. (1993). Problems and strengths of single-parent families: Implications for practice and policy. *Family Relations, 42,* 277–285.

Ridley, Jane. (1993). Gender and couples: Do men and women seek different kinds of intimacy? *Sexual and Marital Therapy, 8,* 243–254.

Robinson, C. Sean. (1994). Counseling gay males with AIDS: Psychosocial perspectives. *Journal of Gay and Lesbian Social Services, 1,* 15–32.

Ronnau, John P., and Christine R. Marlow. (1993). Family preservation, poverty, and the value of diversity. *Families in Society, 74,* 538–544.

Rose, Damaris. (1993). Local childcare strategies in Montreal, Quebec: The mediations of state policies, class, and ethnicity in the life courses of families with young children. In Cindi Katz and Janice Monk (Eds.), *Full circles: Geographies of women over the life course.* New York: Routledge.

Rose, Madeleine Kornfein, and Harriet H. Soares. (1993). Sexual adaptations of the frail elderly: A realistic approach. *Journal of Gerontological Social Work, 19,* 167–178.

Rothbart, Mary K., Stephen A. Ahadi, and Karen L. Hershey. (1994). Temperament and social behavior in childhood. *Merrill-Palmer Quarterly, 40,* 21–39.

Rowe, David C. (1994). *The limits of family influence: Genes, experience, and behavior.* New York: Guilford Press.

Rubin, Rose M., and Bobye J. Riney. (1994). *Working wives and dual-earner families.* Westport, CT, Praeger.

Rubinstein, Robert L., James E. Lubben, and Jacobo E. Mintzer. (1994). Social isolation and social support: An applied perspective. *Journal of Applied Gerontology, 13,* 58–72.

Rudavsky, T. M. (Ed.). (1995). *Gender and Judaism: The transformation of tradition.* New York: New York University Press.

Sabini, John. (1995). *Social psychology* (2nd Ed.). New York: Norton.

Scharlach, Andrew E., and Karen I. Fredriksen. (1993). Reactions to the death of a parent during midlife. *Omega, 27,* 307–319.

Schiavi, Raul C., John Mandeli, and Patricia Schreiner-Engel. (1994). Sexual satisfaction in healthy aging men. *Journal of Sex and Marital Therapy, 20,* 3–13.

Schwartz, Richard C. (1995). *Internal family systems therapy.* New York: Guilford Press.

Seifert, Kelvin L., and Robert Hoffnung. (1994). *Child and adolescent development* (3rd Ed.). Boston: Houghton Mifflin.

Seltzer, Judith A., and Yvonne Brandreth. (1994). What fathers say about involvement with children after separation. *Journal of Family Issues, 15,* 49–77.

Serra, Piera. (1993). Physical violence in the couple relationship: A contribution toward the analysis of the context. *Family Process, 32,* 21–33.

Settles, Barbara H. (1993). The illusion of stability in family life: The reality of change and mobility. *Marriage and Family Review, 19,* 5–29.

Shapiro, Ester R. (1994). *Grief as a family process.* New York: Guilford Press.

Sharabany, Ruth, and Hadas Wiseman. (1993). Close relationships in adolescence: The case of the kibbutz. *Journal of Youth and Adolescence, 22,* 671–695.

Shenk, Dena, and Kitter Christiansen. (1993). The evolution of the system of care for the aged in Denmark. *Journal of Aging and Social Policy, 5,* 169–186.

Sirkin, R. Mark. (1995). *Statistics for the social sciences.* Thousand Oaks, CA: Sage.

Small, Stephen A., and Tom Luster. (1994). Adolescent sexual activity: An ecological, risk-factor approach. *Journal of Marriage and the Family, 56,* 181–192.

Smith, Gregory C., Paul W. Power, Elizabeth A. Robertson-Tchabo, and Sheldon Tobin. (1995). *Strengthening aging families: Diversity in practice and policy.* Thousand Oaks, CA: Sage.

Somers, Marsha D. (1993). A comparison of voluntarily childfree adults and parents. *Journal of Marriage and the Family, 55,* 643–650.

Sprecher, Susan, and Kathleen McKinney. (1993). *Sexuality.* Newbury Park, CA: Sage.

Stafford, Laura, and Cherie L. Bayer. (1993). *Interaction between parents and children.* Thousand Oaks, CA: Sage.

Starrels, Marjorie E. (1994). Gender differences in parent-child relations. *Journal of Family Issues, 15,* 148–165.

Stets, Jan E. (1993). Control in dating relationships. *Journal of Marriage and the Family, 55,* 673–685.

Stith, Sandra M., and Sarah C. Farley. (1993). A predictive model of male spousal abuse. *Journal of Family Violence, 8,* 183–201.

Stolar, G. Elaine, Michael I. MacEntee, and Patricia Hill. (1993). The elderly: Their perceived supports and reciprocal behaviors. *Journal of Gerontological Social Work, 19,* 15–33.

Stoller, Eleanor P., and Rose Campbell Gibson. (1994). *Worlds of difference: Inequality in the aging experience.* Thousand Oaks, CA: Pine Forge Press.

Strong, Bryan, and Christine DeVault. (1995). *The marriage and family experience* (6th Ed.). St. Paul, MN: West.

Taylor, Robert Joseph, Linda M. Chatters, and James S. Jackson. (1993). A profile of familial relations among three-generation black families. *Family Relations, 42,* 332–341.

Teja, Sameera, and Arnold L. Stolberg. (1993). Peer support, divorce, and children's adjustment. *Journal of Divorce and Remarriage, 20,* 45–64.

Thurer, Shari L. (1994). *The myths of motherhood: How culture reinvents the good mother.* Boston: Houghton Mifflin.

Tu, Edward Jow-Ching, Vicki A. Freedman, and Douglas A. Wolf. (1993). Kinship and family support in Taiwan: A microsimulation approach. *Research on Aging, 15,* 465–486.

Tully, Carol T. (1994). To boldly go where no one has gone before: The legalization of lesbian and gay marriages. *Journal of Gay and Lesbian Services, 1,* 73–87.

Turner, Pauline H., and Tommie J. Hammer. (1994). *Child development and early education: Infancy through preschool.* Boston: Allyn and Bacon.

Udry, J. Richard. (1993). The politics of sex research. *Journal of Sex Research, 30,* 103–110.

Van Dyck, Jose. (1995). *Manufacturing babies and public consent: Debating the new reproductive technologies.* New York; New York University Press.

Vasta, Ross, Marshall M. Haith, and Scott A. Miller. (1995). *Child psychology: The modern science* (2nd Ed.). New York: Wiley.

Vaz, Kim M. (1995). *Black women in America.* Thousand Oaks, CA: Sage.

Vogt, W. Paul. (1993). *Dictionary of statistics and methodology: A nontechnical guide for the social sciences.* Newbury Park, CA: Sage.

Wachtel, Ellen F. (1994). *Treating troubled children and their families.* New York: Guilford Press.

Wadsby, Marie, and Carl Goran Svedin. (1993). Children's behavior and mental health following parental divorce. *Journal of Divorce and Remarriage, 20,* 111–138.

Walker, Alexis J. (1993). Teaching about race, gender, and class diversity in United States families. *Family Relations, 42,* 342–350.

Walsh, Froma. (Ed.). (1993). *Normal family processes* (2nd Ed.). New York: Guilford Press.

Wentzel, Kathryn R. (1994). Family functioning and academic achievement in middle school: A social-emotional perspective. *Journal of Early Adolescence, 14,* 268–291.

Whatley, Mark A. (1993). For better or worse: The case of marital rape. *Violence and Victims, 8,* 29–40.

Wile, Daniel B. (1993). *After the fight: A night in the life of a couple.* New York: Guilford Press.

Williams, Mary Beth. (1993). Assessing the traumatic impact of child sexual abuse: What makes it more severe? *Journal of Child Sexual Abuse, 2,* 41–59.

Wineberg, Howard. (1994). Marital reconciliation in the United States: Which couples are successful? *Journal of Marriage and the Family, 56,* 80–88.

Witt, Judith LaBorde. (1994). The gendered division of labor in parental caretaking: Biology or socialization? *Journal of Women and Aging, 6,* 65–89.

Wolcott, Ilene, and Ruth Weston. (1994). Keeping the peace: Resolving conflict between parents and adolescents. *Family and Conciliation Courts Review, 32,* 208–229.

Xie, Qing, and Francine Hultgren. (1994). Urban Chinese parents' perceptions of their strengths and needs in rearing "only" sons and daughters. *Home Economics Research Journal, 22,* 340–356.

Zsembik, Barbara A. (1993). Determinants of living alone among older Hispanics. *Research on Aging, 15,* 449–464.

INDEX

Page numbers in **bold** indicate main entries.

havior of, 20; adolescent sexually transmitted diseases, 21; adoption patterns of, 22; AIDS and, 45, 48–49; caring for aging parents, 43–44; children and divorce, 133; fertility patterns of, 173; intergenerational relations among, **34–35;** Life Expectancy of, **35;** Lifespan Relationships among, **30–34;** parenting experiences of, 319–321; patterns of divorce among, 131; as single parents, 412–413; as survivors of rape, 347

Age. *See* Adolescence; Early Adulthood; Early Childhood; Infancy and Toddlerhood; Late Adulthood; Middle Adulthood; Middle Childhood; Newborn

Aging: ageism and, 22–23; caregiving by adults for aging parents, 42–43; Changes in Sexual Functioning due to, **36–37;** Impact of on Sexual Intimacy, **37–38;** infertility and, 224; kin relations and, 41–42; Processes of, **38–39;** Successful, **39–41.** *See also* Late Adulthood; Middle Adulthood; *specific ethnic and racial groups and specific nations*

Ahrons, Constance, 138–139

AIDS: adolescents and, 16, 21–22; African Americans and, **45, 48–49;** Children and, **49–50;** Diagnostic Tests for, **50–51;** gays and, 45; heterosexuals and, 45; nature and scope of, 44–48; Prevention of, **51–52;** safer sex practices, 392–393; in Sub-Saharan Africa, 425; World-Wide Rates of Infection, **52**

Alimony, 134

Allport, Gordon, **52–53**

Anal stage, 342

Ancient Egypt, Lifespan Relationships in, **53–55**

Ancient Far East, Lifespan Relationships in, 55

Ancient Greece, Lifespan Relationships in, **56–57**

Ancient Hebrews, Lifespan Relationships among the, **57–58**

Ancient India, Lifespan Relationships in, **58–59**

Ancient Rome, Lifespan Relationships in, **59–60**

Androgyny, **60–61**

Annulment, 61

Antinatalism, 336

Artificial insemination, 226

Ascetic sexual value orientation, 407

Asian Americans, caregiving patterns among, 44; Lifespan Relationships among, **61–63**

Attachment: contact-comfort and, 202–203; defined, 63; separation anxiety and, 64; stranger anxiety and, 64; Theories of, **64–66**

Australia, Lifespan Relationships in, **66–68**

Authoritarian style of child discipline, 127

Authoritative style of child discipline, 127

Authority, Marital. *See* Marriage, Variations in Structure

Autonomy vs. doubt, 343

Bandura, Albert, **69**

Basic trust vs. basic mistrust, 343

Behavioral theory: of attachment, 65; of gender-role development, 194–195; therapeutic relationships and, 432–433, 434, 436, 438

Behaviorism, **69–70**

Behavior-Modification Theory. *See* Parenthood, Child-rearing Options and Strategies

Bereavement, **71**

Bilateral descent. *See* Marriage, Variations in Structure

Biological aging, 39

Birth control. *See* Contraception

Birth process. *See* Childbirth

Birthrate, **71**

Bisexuality, **71–72**

Blacks. *See* African Americans

Blended family. *See* Family Composition, Types of

About the Author

JEFFREY S. TURNER is a Professor of Psychology at Mitchell College in New London, Connecticut. Dr. Turner is the co-author of many college-level textbooks, among which are *Marriage and Family: Traditions and Transitions*, *Lifespan Development*, *Human Sexuality*, *Contemporary Adulthood*, and *Exploring Child Behavior*. He is also the author of numerous articles and studies, and has served as a book review critic for the magazine *Marriage and Family Living*.

ISBN 0-313-29576-X

EAN

9 780313 295768

HARDCOVER BAR CODE